Praise for *I've Known Rivers*

"A compelling and nuanced group portrait of black achievers who are haunted by, rather than dismissive of, their backgrounds."
—Maureen Corrighan, *New York Newsday*

"A refreshing and inspiring look into the lives of six successful African-Americans. Lawrence-Lightfoot presents people determined to remember where they—individually and as a people—came from, and she brings her formidable storytelling gifts to their lives."
—*Kirkus Reviews*

"In this deft and loving volume Sara Lawrence-Lightfoot puts us into conversation with men and women who, inspiring us to affection and respect, can shape our lives."
—Mary Catherine Bateson, author of *Composing a Life*

"Lawrence-Lightfoot and the men and women who trusted her to capture their voices and the complex realities of their journeys generously share with every reader their compelling and involving stories."
—Mary Carroll, *Booklist*

"It is not easy to invent a new genre but that is what Sara Lawrence-Lightfoot has done in her latest book."
—*Publishers Weekly*

"Fascinating . . . the stories read as passionately as if the accounts were straight from personal diaries. In the end, Lawrence-Lightfoot brings them together as one mighty river. She leaves it to the reader to see the connections and understand the universality of these experiences."
—*Detroit Free Press*

PENGUIN BOOKS

I'VE KNOWN RIVERS

Sara Lawrence-Lightfoot is the author of several books, including the highly acclaimed biography of her mother *Balm in Gilead: Journey of a Healer*, winner of the Christopher Award for "literary merit and humanitarian achievement." A sociologist, she is a Professor of Education at Harvard University and was a 1984 recipient of the prestigious MacArthur Prize Award. Professor Lawrence-Lightfoot has been a Fellow at the Bunting Institute at Radcliffe College and at the Center for Advanced Study in the Behavioral Sciences at Stanford University. In 1993, she won Harvard's George Ledlie Prize for research that "makes the most valuable contribution to science." She resides in Boston, Massachusetts with her family.

I've Known Rivers

Lives of Loss
and Liberation

SARA LAWRENCE-LIGHTFOOT

PENGUIN BOOKS

PENGUIN BOOKS
Published by the Penguin Group
Penguin Books USA Inc., 375 Hudson Street,
New York, New York 10014, U.S.A.
Penguin Books Ltd, 27 Wrights Lane, London W8 5TZ, England
Penguin Books Australia Ltd, Ringwood, Victoria, Australia
Penguin Books Canada Ltd, 10 Alcorn Avenue,
Toronto, Ontario, Canada M4V 3B2
Penguin Books (N.Z.) Ltd, 182–190 Wairau Road, Auckland 10, New Zealand

Penguin Books Ltd, Registered Offices: Harmondsworth, Middlesex, England

First published in the United States of America by
Addison-Wesley Publishing Company, Inc., 1994
Published in Penguin Books 1995

1   3   5   7   9   10   8   6   4   2

"The Negro Speaks of Rivers" from *Selected Poems* by Langston Hughes, copyright
1926 by Alfred A. Knopf, Inc., and renewed 1954 by Langston Hughes.
Reprinted by kind permission of the publisher.

THE LIBRARY OF CONGRESS HAS CATALOGUED THE HARDCOVER AS FOLLOWS:
Lightfoot, Sara Lawrence.
I've known rivers: lives of loss and liberation/Sara Lawrence-Lightfoot.
p.   cm.
"A Merloyd Lawrence book."
Includes index.
ISBN 0-201-58120-5 (hc.)
ISBN 0 14 02.4970 2 (pbk.)
1. Afro-Americans—Biography.   2. Afro-Americans—Interviews.   I. Title.
E185.96.L54   1994
920´.009296073—dc20
[B]   94–17422

Printed in the United States of America
Set in 12-point Goudy
Designed by Greta D. Sibley

For the Ancestors

Especially
Mary Elizabeth and Sandy Alonzo,
Letitia Burnett and Charles Radford

In deepest gratitude for their
wisdom, their resilience, and
their water music
calling us home

The Negro Speaks of Rivers

I've known rivers:
I've known rivers ancient as the world and older than the
    flow of human blood in human veins.

My soul has grown deep like the rivers.

I bathed in the Euphrates when dawns were young.
I built my hut near the Congo and it lulled me to sleep.

I looked upon the Nile and raised the pyramids above it.
I heard the singing of the Mississippi when Abe Lincoln
    went down to New Orleans, and I've seen its muddy
    bosom turn all golden in the sunset.

I've known rivers:
Ancient, dusky rivers.

My soul has grown deep like the rivers.

—Langston Hughes

Contents

Acknowledgments

For a portraitist to see her subject clearly, she must fall in love. This love has many dimensions; respect, advocacy, intimacy, and admiration, and the curiosity and skepticism required to penetrate layers of image toward the essence. This love allows for both connection and challenge, identification and scrutiny. In our long journey together, my feelings for each one of the storytellers in this volume moved through all of these dimensions. I was amazed by their courage, their endurance, and their honesty. I felt honored by their trust; inspired by their legacies and commitments; warmed by their laughter; pained by their trauma and tears. I am deeply thankful to them all—to Katie Cannon, Charles Ogletree, Toni Schiesler, Tony Earls, Cheryle Wills, and Orlando Bagwell.

Throughout this project I was nourished by my own family's embrace. Now old enough to understand (if not appreciate) what I do upstairs behind closed doors ("in Mom's tree house"), my children traced my progress; Martin David carefully measuring the growing inches of manuscript and Tolani capturing some of her favorite "book stories" in gorgeous, evocative drawings. My mother Margaret Morgan Lawrence—who braved her "second analysis" in *Balm in Gilead*—understands the power and difficulties of this work and believes in its authenticity. I drew strength from her unyielding support. As always, my brother and sister—Charles Radford Lawrence and Paula Lawrence Wehmiller—stood on either side, cheering me on, promising to catch me if I faltered. Their partners, Mari Matsuda and John Wehmiller, were with me as well—Mari with her metaphors and piercing analysis, and John with his geological language and lessons on the river. Lisa Valerian, energetic and gifted, helped support my work in the most important way possible, by nurturing my children.

xvi   *Acknowledgments*

I am thankful to the quartet whose creative spirits supported my improvisation. Irving Hamer brought penetrating eyes, probing questions, and big-hearted criticism to the research and writing, and circled me with love and wise witness. As the manuscript grew, my dear friend Jessica Davis read every line and savored every word, writing me powerful critiques, full of intelligence, wit, and challenge. Wendy Elisabeth Angus, my devoted assistant, transcribed hundreds of hours of interviews, typed numerous drafts, and enthusiastically participated in every phase of this project. I am always grateful for her loyal commitment and excellent work. Merloyd Lawrence, my gentle, strong, fearless editor, balanced insight and scrutiny with steady and generous support.

There were many friends and colleagues who were part of this great adventure, offering attentive listening, encouragement, and counsel. I want to thank Susan Berger, Lisbeth Schorr, Florence Ladd, Judy and Dan Katz, Janet Surrey, Linda Whitlock, Derrick Bell, Patricia Graham, Tom and Katie Cottle, Marti Wilson, John Wright, Sissela Bok, and Will Davis. Allison Hausman wrote thoughtful and discerning reviews of the literature.

Finally, I want to express my appreciation to the Spencer Foundation for their generous support of this work, for their understanding of the broad and deep contours of educational research.

I've Known Rivers

LISTENING

TO THE CURRENTS

In my family's house, the dining room table was the center of gravity. Everyone was drawn to the table and once you settled there, it was almost impossible to move away. Friends and neighbors who dropped by claimed that any time of day or night you could find the Lawrences sitting around the table. Long after we finished eating, we would still be there—my parents, my maternal grandparents, my brother, my sister, and I—three generations under one roof. Generational contrasts and regional differences were reflected at the table: my grandparents' traditional southern diet—fried catfish, cooked cabbage, corn bread, and yams—alternated with our northern dishes—broiled chicken, barely cooked asparagus, and corn on the cob from the local farm stand.

Around the table we would tell stories, relive the day's events, explore new ideas, and compete for airtime. It was here that we always brought our tales from school, sometimes tales of victory and sometimes miserable laments. Sometimes my brother Chuck, a star athlete, would keep us on the edge of our seats with a detailed play-by-play of an "unbelievable" touchdown scored at a football scrimmage, or a "gorgeous" jump shot made in the final seconds of basketball practice. (We were present and cheering at every single one of his games.) Or else my sister Paula might do devastating imitations of our hapless teachers, and I would follow with accounts of terminally boring lectures, our French teacher's excruciating pronunciation, or ridiculous rules regarding hall passes. One grievance would inspire another. If the accumulation of complaints became too heavy, my mother would step in. A child psychiatrist and psychoanalyst, she believed in the value of "catharsis" and always encouraged us to express our feelings. But after a lengthening parade of woes, she would deliver the familiar ultimatum: "If you can't say something good, don't say anything at all." There would be a precious moment of silence as someone—usually a parent—tried to turn to more positive and productive conversation.

Even though my father was vice president of the local school board, there was much that was taught in school that opposed my family's teachings, and there was much that was not taught that my parents considered central to our education. Through twelve years of school, I remember being asked to memorize the verse of only one black poet, Langston Hughes. Around our table at home we recited the poetry of James Weldon Johnson, Gwendolyn Brooks, Countée Cullen, W.E.B. Du Bois, Pauli Murray, Paul Laurence Dunbar, Margaret Walker, Arna Bontemps, and Jean Toomer, feasting on the rich language, rhythms, and imagery. We sang the Negro spirituals the way my parents had learned them growing up in black churches and schools in Mississippi. My father insisted that we not confuse spirituals with gospel music, that we honor the "dignity" and power of the simple verse. My parents knew that in our predominantly white school (often we were the only black students in our college preparatory classes) we would never learn about our African-American heritage. Their family curriculum was ritualized, consistent, and intentional.

In my eighth-grade citizenship education class, Miss Shopper— her pale face caked with powder, her eyebrows drawn on with black pencil, wisps of white hair escaping from underneath her red wig— taught us that Abraham Lincoln led the country in the War between the States and that the battle had nothing to do with slavery. Her eyes rested on me—the only Negro child in the class—daring me to challenge her interpretation of history. That evening my parents made the correction. It was "the Civil War," and the institution of slavery was at its very center. And I will never forget my father's rage at discovering the word "barbarian" used to describe the Mayan Indians of Central America in my social studies book. He could not resist lecturing us on the "extraordinary" Mayan civilization—its creativity, organization, and resilience—and then immediately sat down at his typewriter to bang out a restrained but angry letter to my teacher. So it was around our own dining room table that we children first heard the dissonance of values and beliefs between our family and our school, and learned that education was not limited to classrooms.

Before dinner, with the candles burning and our hands joined, we always sang grace. As we grew, the parts multiplied—my first soprano, Mom's second soprano, Sister Paula's alto, Dad's tenor, and Chuck's bass—and the harmonies became more intricate. The singing, the food, the conversation, the theater were nourishing to our bodies, our minds, and our spirits. So much love was wrapped up in the dinner ritual that many years later—as I struggled to lose extra pounds—I had to unlearn the habit of experiencing food as the embodiment of family love. And the one time when I was dismissed from the table for bad behavior, I still regard as the worst punishment I ever received from my folks. At sixteen years old, I was on the eve of my departure for a senior year abroad in Scandinavia. My mother and I had a brief, angry exchange (she wanted me to resist a second helping of food), and I erupted, "Boy, will I be glad to get out of here, away from you hassling me all the time. I'm sick of it... and sick of you." I could hear my siblings suck in their breath. I could feel their bodies tense up as they waited for the shocked response. My father's sharp voice cut through the silence. "Sara, leave the table." Banished from the warm center of our lives, I flew to my room, threw myself on the bed and sobbed.

The number of people at the table often expanded beyond the seven of us. The round shape would turn into a long oval with the addition of leaves as friends and extended family joined us. Early afternoon Sunday dinner—always big and festive—was a favorite time to have folks over for my parents' collaboratively cooked meals. Dressed in his long chef's apron, my father would stick the cloves of garlic into the leg of lamb and season the meat with an exotic mix of mustard and spices. With a big knife and swift strokes he would dice the fresh vegetables for a hearty salad or chop the collards for greens. My mother would work around Dad's exuberant movements, finding counter space to punch out the biscuits with a jelly jar or roll out the dough for pie crust. As they worked, they would entertain their guests. Only a counter separated the

kitchen from the dining room area, and we would all huddle around
the counter, munching on cheese and crackers and sipping what my
father always called our "preprandial" drinks.

On one of these Sundays, our guests included several of my
father's black male colleagues and their wives (all of whom had their
own careers). These brainy black brothers had known each other for
years. Like my father, who was a professor of sociology at Brooklyn
College, of the City University of New York, this handful of schol-
ars—who represented a substantial portion of our "black intelli-
gentsia"—had been reared in segregated schools, attended Negro
colleges, and received their Ph.D.'s from white universities, such as
Harvard, Columbia, and the University of Chicago. There was John
Hope Franklin, the historian; Kenneth Clark, the psychologist;
Hylan Lewis, the sociologist; and Hobart Jarret, in English literature. All of them were pioneers, lonely travelers whose intellects
and achievements were often judged through a discriminatory lens,
whose careers were checked by the heavy hand of prejudice. On this
particular Sunday we were enjoying one of my mother's favorite
dishes, a casserole that she called Tuna Surprise. As she took the
steaming pot out of the oven, Hylan Lewis recognized the familiar
fragrance. "Ah, Tuna Anticipation!" he grinned.

To my seventeen-year-old eyes, these men were "the brotherhood," with bonds that were deep, language that was fascinating,
laughter that was infectious, and conversation that I only half-under-
stood. I could feel how much they needed and loved one another in
their charged and fiery dialogues, in their siblinglike rivalries, in the
ways their ideas danced in and out of one another. Coming to our
table, they looked forward to a comfort and camaraderie that they
could never fully achieve in the university settings where each was
usually the token Negro and often the first of his race to set foot in
the place. Since it was my father's table, he began the conversation.
On that day he asked what his colleagues thought about E. Franklin
Frazier's new book, *Black Bourgeoisie*. He knew that this study of the
Negro middle class would be certain to engage this gathering of friends.

My mind lingered on the title *Black Bourgeoisie*. Out of the
opaque stream of grown-up table talk, the title stung my adolescent

ears and captured my attention. In the early '60s the word "black" still felt strange and abrasive. At a table where my grandparents insisted upon calling us "colored" (a label my parents didn't like and thought demeaning), and where my parents referred to us as "Negroes," the term "black" sounded harsh, aggressive. And "bourgeoisie" seemed an exotic companion. I was fascinated just by the contrariness carried in those two words.

Beyond the strange juxtaposition, I began to be captivated by the conversation clearly galvanized by Frazier's account. His description of us was apparently both true and false, honoring and devastating, intimate and distancing. At seventeen I didn't fully understand the substance of their analysis, but I did feel the rising emotion and knew that this book had tapped a raw nerve in these men.

Less than a decade later, when I was a graduate student in sociology and education at Harvard, "Black Power" was at its peak. "Black" no longer sounded strange or threatening. The rhetoric extolled the beauty of black and gave it a resonance both challenging and comforting. During my second year of graduate training, I took a course taught by a white social psychologist named Thomas Pettigrew, an early investigator of racial and cultural identity. His course, called Race Relations, gave me the opportunity to revisit *Black Bourgeoisie*. The echoes of that Sunday dinner discussion at my parents' table sounded through me as I read Frazier's book straight through, never stopping to eat, hardly taking a breath. I was again captured. Here was a book that talked about "us," the black middle class. Heretofore, the great bulk of the literature on black families and communities had focused on the pathologies and deficiencies of poor blacks. It was a harsh and condemning literature that "blamed the victims," citing their inadequacies, their passivity and weakness in the face of discriminatory institutions and policies. Preoccupied with studying the behavior of the poor, the literature masked the diversity within the black community and led the uninitiated reader to link poverty and blackness. As a graduate student raised on these "cultural deficiency" readings, I had begun to suspect the social scientists' penchant for studying "down" and their inclination to search for pathology. Poor blacks provided rich data, ripe for caricature and distortion.

Black Bourgeoisie was a welcome departure from these earlier studies. It revealed the diversity among us and documented the experiences of those of us who were not poor, who enjoyed a certain degree of abundance and privilege. I applauded the counterpoint in Frazier's work, the new features he had drawn on the landscape, the ways he resisted the leaden assumptions of earlier scholarship. Here was a black social scientist writing about his own people, with the promise of a rewarding symmetry between the investigator and his subjects.

My excitement was muted, however, by the character of the sketches Frazier painted and by their tone and that of his analysis—a searing, mocking tone, a tone that I began to suspect reflected evidence of self-deprecation. I came upon this passage and felt my rage rise.

> The black bourgeoisie has been uprooted from its "racial" tradition and as a consequence has no cultural roots in either the Negro or the white world. In seeking to conform to bourgeois ideals and standards of behavior, this class in the Negro community has sloughed off the genteel tradition of the small upper class which had its roots among the Negroes who were free before the Civil War. But more important still, the black bourgeoisie has rejected the folk culture of the Negro masses. The artistic creations of the leaders of the Negro Renaissance in the nineteen twenties, who turned to the black masses for inspiration, were regarded largely with indifference by the increasing number of Negroes who were acquiring a middle-class outlook on life. As a consequence of their isolation, the majority of the black bourgeoisie live in a cultural vacuum and their lives are devoted largely to fatuities.

I tried to cool the fires within me by using my newly learned tools of social science inquiry. I began to ask the skeptical questions about research design and methodological strategy that I had learned the semester before. Were Frazier's data reliable? Had he selected a random and representative sample? What about the

validity of his interpretations and the *generalizability* of his findings? This crude methodological critique offered me some distance
and perspective, but it was not successful in ridding me of an over-
powering feeling of protest. These feelings seemed to peak when I
reached this passage.

> Since the black bourgeoisie live largely in a world of
> make-believe, the masks which they wear to play their sorry
> roles conceal the feelings of inferiority and of insecurity and
> the frustrations that haunt their inner lives. Despite their
> attempt to escape from real identification with the masses of
> Negroes, they cannot escape the mark of oppression any
> more than their less favored kinsmen. In attempting to
> escape identification with the black masses, they have devel-
> oped a self-hatred that reveals itself in their deprecation of
> the physical and social characteristics of Negroes. Likewise,
> their feelings of inferiority and insecurity are revealed in their
> pathological struggle for status within the isolated Negro
> world and craving for recognition in the white world. Their
> escape into a world of make-believe with its sham "society"
> leaves them with a feeling of emptiness and futility which
> causes them to constantly seek an escape in new delusions.

My passionate response held a mixture of recognition and
estrangement. In Frazier's images, I could see glimpses of the middle-class lives I knew—of me, my family, and the people who sat
around my parents' table. I knew that part of the pain and anger I
felt was a response to Frazier's bold truth telling. But it seemed to
me that the portraits he drew also held lies, damaging distortions. I
struggled to untangle my troubled response. How much was a reaction to Frazier's disdain and denigration of middle-class blacks and
how much reflected my own defensiveness, my refusal to accept a
discerning and critical rendering of our lives? To what extent were
Frazier's conclusions based on a systematic scrutiny of data and to
what extent did they reveal his own deep ambivalence about himself and his origins?

With more study of Frazier's text, I began to recognize that the answer to these questions lay partly in his two-dimensional descriptions of black lives. The resulting caricatures masked the complexities of our lives and missed the nuances of our experience. These flat portraits did not capture the perspectives of the people I knew so well, did not recognize the ambivalence in our ambition, did not acknowledge our own insight into the losses embedded in our gains. In Frazier's account, we heard nothing about how the black bourgeoisie actually negotiated and interpreted their daily lives, how they managed the generational contrasts, how they bridged the distance between their origins and their destinations.

I put down Frazier's book, angry, frustrated, energized, feeling both affronted and affirmed. The book's message mixed with the tumultuous social and political context. It was the early '70s—the height of social activism on university campuses and the height of the Black Power movement—and I was young, impressionable, confused, struggling with issues of identity and purpose. In the black political cant, I heard the rejection of traditional white standards of beauty, status, and knowledge, and I tried to find my place in the adversarial conversation. Like many other privileged blacks, I often felt guilty about my situation, caught between the values, perspectives, and habits of the predominantly white, middle-class world in which I had been raised and the idiom, language, and ideology of the black community with whom I wanted to affiliate more closely. The yearning I felt at that time—for identification and connection with blacks, for a way to come to terms with my privilege, yet to use wisely the resources of my origins—did not fit with the image of materialistic bourgeois assimilationists drawn by Frazier. I felt a need for a portrait of middle-class black society in more dimensions, and for a more generous portrayal.

I've Known Rivers is my response to the adolescent curiosity I felt sitting around my family's table hearing the strange juxtaposition of words in Frazier's title. It is my response to the graduate student's passion and skepticism. The book also reflects more than two decades of research and writing about matters related to education, development, and identity in human experience; as well as a long interest in the dynamic intersection of class, race, culture, and gender. I've set out to explore the troubling dissonance I experienced when I first read Frazier and to challenge the now extensive studies about the black middle class, influenced by Frazier's imprint. In the six lives portrayed here, I search for an authentic and subtle rendering of African-Americans of privilege. This is a book that acknowledges loss and ambivalence, celebrates accomplishment, and examines the power of storytelling in shaping and interpreting the journey.

The six storytellers—three women and three men—speak about how they perceive and navigate the generational contrasts between their lives and those of their parents and grandparents, and about the ancestral legacies that have survived and those that have been discarded. They speak about their feelings of loss—loss of security, of community, of relationship, of rootedness, of family bonds, of heritage—when all the external signs point to gains in education, status, income, mobility, worldview, and effectiveness. They reveal the nostalgia, ambivalence, insecurity, and guilt that often accompany ascendancy; the seemingly inevitable trade-offs between the riches of relationship and rootedness and the riches of status and station. Actually, these stories reveal the very notion of trade-offs—of giving up one good for another—to be too simply construed, too black and white (if you'll excuse the expression). As the stories are told, we see simultaneous layers of feeling, often contradictory—feelings of security *and* discomfort, trauma *and* wholeness, movement *and* inertia. Many of us have known what it is to arrive where we hoped to land and to discover that we have found a perch for looking backward, for experiencing with increasing force the pull of nostalgia, the emptiness of loss.

I do not think these themes of yearning and loss are peculiar to middle-class blacks. (Part of my interest in writing this book reflects my wish to explore perhaps universal experiences of all kinds of people who choose to move "up and out" and away from what seemed familiar and certain in childhood.) However, I have found the experience of African-Americans intensified in this respect. Perhaps this is due, in part, to the ancestral journey of enslaved blacks, which was cruel and involuntary, which destroyed families and communities and detached us from our precious cultural roots. African-Americans have been compelled to invent a hybrid new cultural/familial form under extremely brutal and harsh conditions. Perhaps this ancestral legacy of dislocation and rootlessness still haunts the contemporary journeys black Americans make from their childhood homes to some newly composed existence.

In addition to these historical echoes in the black experience of today, I also think that the losses that accompany privilege are felt more fully by blacks because the predominantly white worlds we enter tend to be so unwelcoming. We strive to arrive at a secure place only to discover the quicksand of subtle exclusion. We work hard to amass the credentials and signs of status even as we recognize that our status will never assure a sense of belonging, or full membership in the white world. We feel ourselves moving toward the center of power even as we feel inextricably tied to the periphery; our outsider status becomes clearer as we work to claim an insider's place. For privileged African-Americans, these contradictory experiences of insider/outsider, power/impotence, security/uncertainty are felt, I think, with particular force.

But it would be inaccurate to characterize black ascendancy as defined only by a preoccupation with loss, with divided allegiances, and with profound ambivalence. These storytellers describe a journey that is also marked by hope, creativity, and purposeful design. They are resourceful, self-critical, and courageous in pursuing their dreams and in reconciling with their roots. As a matter of fact, their success is partly due to their ability to embrace and live with contradictions.

The six storytellers are all in their middle years—between their early forties and mid-fifties—a developmental place from which we tend naturally to look backward and forward. They can feel the imprint of their ancestry and rehearse the values taught by their parents even as they fashion a life for their children. They tell intergenerational stories that underscore the power of ancestry—the losses and traumas revisited by each generation—and they come to realize how difficult it is to reverse historic patterns. They also

tell equally potent stories of commitment and creativity, of deliberate and imaginative ways they have constructed their work and
their lives.

Not only do the middle years provide a wide-angle view of generational contrast, they are also a propitious moment for reflection
and reinterpretation of a life story. After years of single-minded
ambition, middle age can feel like a time to pause, a time for self-
reflection and stocktaking, a time to reenvision the future. For these
storytellers, I realized, it is also a time to take risks. Having hit
their stride, discovered their strengths, developed a craft and found
a voice, they become more daring.

This daring is reflected in the willingness of the six individuals
to participate in the intense, demanding process required by this
book. I spent close to a year in deep conversation with each one.
Our conversations were intense, exhausting, exhilarating, and often
painful. All six were willing to appear here under their own names.

∼

Katie Cannon, a "womanist" philosopher and theologian, professor at the Episcopal Divinity School in Cambridge, comes from
Kannapolis, North Carolina, a tiny segregated town where the Ku
Klux Klan still "ride at their whim and will," and where when you
refer to "field work," you mean back-breaking farm labor.

Charles Ogletree, a criminal defense lawyer, political activist, and
professor at the Harvard Law School, grew up in the sun-baked countryside outside of Merced, California. His mother and her five children often labored in the fruit orchards with other migrant workers.

M. Antoinette Schiesler, born in Chicago, the illegitimate child
of a rape victim, can barely remember the places she and her
mother lived as her mother desperately searched for ways to support
them. "Toni" found home and family in a Roman Catholic
parochial school and convent, where she became a nun, and studied to become a research chemist. She later left the order, married,
and became a candidate for the Episcopal priesthood.

Felton Earls, an epidemiologist and psychiatrist at Harvard's
School of Public Health, can still picture the large shade tree in

front of his house in New Orleans under which he and his friends played marbles; he can hear the soulful jazz of the funeral parades, taste the Cajun catfish and saffron rice, and feel the warm embrace of a large extended family. Earls, known as "Tony," revisits these comforting childhood images as he investigates the social and psychological roots of violence and crime.

Cheryle Wills, entrepreneur and owner of radio and television stations across the country, was born in Jefferson City, Missouri. The daughter of the first black Ph.D. from M.I.T., Cheryle grew up in relative affluence all over the country and finally landed in Cleveland where she became a prominent businesswoman, civic leader, and political activist.

Orlando Bagwell, a documentary filmmaker, grew up in a close-knit family of five children. The ambition, discipline, and educational pursuits of his very young parents pulled them out of poverty. Uprooted as a teenager from a lively black neighborhood in Baltimore to the foreign, white, harsh climate of New Hampshire, Orlando still yearns to "return to my Baltimore." His films merge artistic vision with a complex rendering of social and political history.

~

As I listen to these extraordinary women and men tell their life stories, I play many roles. I am a mirror that reflects back their pain, their fears, and their victories. I am also the inquirer who asks the sometimes difficult questions, who searches for evidence and patterns. I am the companion on the journey, bringing my own story to the encounter, making possible an interpretive collaboration. I am the audience who listens, laughs, weeps, and applauds. I am the spider woman spinning their tales. Occasionally, I am a therapist who offers catharsis, support, and challenge, and who keeps track of emotional minefields. Most absorbing to me is the role of the human archaeologist who uncovers the layers of mask and inhibition in search of a more authentic representation of life experience. Throughout, I must also play stage manager, coordinating the intersection of three plays—the storyteller's, the narrator's, and the reader's—and inviting you to add your voice to the drama.

As I listen to these stories, I hear deep and powerful currents. It is no longer possible to think of a single stream. There is both loss and new strength as these mingled waters carry ancestral wisdom to the next generation. Our stories are dynamic, unsettled. As I listen, I hear echoes of Jean Toomer's poem "Brown River, Smile," words we recited around my family's table.

> The Mississippi, sister of the Ganges,
> Main artery of earth in the western world,
> Is waiting to become
> In the spirit of America, a sacred river.
> Whoever lifts the Mississippi
> Lifts himself and all America;
> Whoever lifts himself
> Makes that great brown river smile.

KATIE CANNON

The Fruit
of My Labor

Beginnings

Katie Cannon is a large brown-skinned woman with penetrating eyes, big sweeping gestures, and a full, contagious laugh. We have a 1:00 P.M. lunch date and she arrives ten minutes early (having explained on the telephone that she always eats on "the dot of noon"), saying she has taken the edge off her hunger by eating a banana. Then with mischief in her eyes she jokes, "I *work* at being this fat. This doesn't just come naturally. It's not as easy as you think to stay this big." Katie then discovers she has lost the backing of one of her earrings and begins to remove both of them. I suggest she just wear one. "I'm not ready for that," she replies. "I can't do all those wild things... I tell my friends that even if I only preach three times a year, I need *access* to the pulpit. If I want access, I can't be wearing one earring... I can't be wearing dreadlocks or dressing crazy... I need to be very correct."

To my surprise the conversation then careens into a discussion of body massages. Katie mentions that in order to have *access* to the pulpit, she must keep her clothes on, which somehow leads her into thinking about her wish to keep her clothes on "even for massages." She tells the story of her *one* experience several years ago with a Japanese masseuse in New York who "believed in people keeping their clothes on." I am incredulous, exclaiming that to be covered up with clothes would seem to miss the whole point of the sensuous experience. But Katie remembers it as being "soothing and lovely," as feeling "so wonderful" even though she had every stitch of her clothes on. "Well, I took off my shoes (but I left on my socks), and I took off my gloves." Even though I know her only slightly, I already feel comfortable teasing: "Well, this minister status certainly offers a safe rationalization for whatever inhibitions you may have." She raises her eyebrows in mock disbelief, "I thought you were supposed to be a sociologist, an educator, *not* a psychotherapist."

Katie Cannon is an ordained Presbyterian minister, with a Ph.D. from Union Theological Seminary in New York. She is also an associate professor with tenure at the Episcopal Divinity School in Cambridge, Massachusetts, where she teaches liberation theology. She has a reputation as a "truth teller," an ardent feminist (referring to herself as a "womanist"), a committed and inspired teacher. She is forty-one years old but seems to me both older and younger. Older, in the sense that she sometimes seems to be old-fashioned in her style, idiom, and connection to her roots—like someone from our mother's generation. (Katie notices that her white women colleagues often say to her, "You sound just like my mother." And with the undergraduates she teaches at Wellesley College, she says, "I feel like their *grandmother*.") She appears younger than her years, however, in her eagerness, her idealism, her commitments, and her irreverence.

On the first day of her undergraduate course on liberation theology, Katie wanted to shatter the Wellesley "girls'" narrow image of "minister" and did it all in one swoop. She opened her first class by proclaiming, "I've already done in my life *everything* that I said I wouldn't do!" She makes a big whirling motion with her arms and spins her head around to show how "those children's minds were blown." She clearly enjoys her role as provocateur, relishes the chance to challenge the stereotype, to do the unexpected. In these moments of challenge and irreverence, she seems almost adolescent. Her eyes are mischievous, her face unlined, her body in motion.

∼

Katie Cannon grew up one of seven children in a town close to Charlotte, North Carolina, called Kannapolis. "Have you ever heard of Cannon Mills?" she asks me. "That's my family. We all live there… have worked for the mills for generations, first as slaves, then as indentured servants, now as employees. We dominate the place… there are thousands of us." Maybe not thousands, but the numbers are breathtaking. Cannon's mother was the nineteenth of twenty children, and each of her siblings had at least seven or eight children. Her father was one of thirteen or fourteen, all of whom reproduced bountifully. "And there are *lots* of kids out of wedlock... If a Cannon man impregnates a woman, if there is an ounce of Cannon blood in you, then you are one of us. You should see us at funerals—*all* of us are there." To give me a sense of the magnitude of her family, Katie says, "There are twenty black males from my family—nineteen cousins and one brother—who are in the Gulf. Can you imagine! None of them are back yet. At least I'm glad *they claim* the war is over."

Katie's siblings span the ages from twenty-eight to fifty-four years old; she has three brothers and three sisters. Except for the oldest (who is "our streetwise hustler"), all her brothers and sisters have at least a master's degree. The youngest is also a minister and has a church in Washington, D.C. Katie's mom calls him the "real minister," to distinguish him from Katie. When I ask why her youngest brother is any more *real* than she is, Cannon says matter-of-factly, "Well, I don't have a parish, I teach, I'm a woman, I'm not married, I don't have kids, I do not follow the absolutes... How could I be a real minister in my family's eyes?" It is not clear to me which one of these reasons is most important in denying her the lofty status of minister in her mother's eyes. But the list does convey to me that Katie is something of an oddball, an eccentric in her family. Also that, while she speaks about the members of her family with such honor and connection, at the same time she experiences the ways in which their lives have diverged.

Later, in telling me about a ranch outside of Santa Fe, New Mexico (Ghost Ranch, where Georgia O'Keefe lived and painted), where she has gone for rest and religious retreat for several summers, Katie announces, "I have decided when I die to have my ashes buried there." On the heels of this surprising statement, she says, "But I don't know how that will happen, because my family would *never* allow cremation... No one in my whole family has ever been cremated. There is no way that would ever fit into their theological conceptions. My mother always says, 'If you were cremated, how could you get up and strut around all over God's heaven?'" Katie connects these seemingly contrary notions together as if there is no dissonance. When I ask simply, "Then how are you going to do *that?*" Katie looks unworried—"I haven't figured that out yet." Her determination (and calm) amidst these irreconcilable forces (her own spiritual need versus her family's religious convictions) is impressive. She shows a reluctant recognition of the contrary themes but no apparent anxiety or impatience to resolve them.

Doris, who is thirteen months younger than Katie, is her closest sibling. The older sister became "the knee baby," and they were often mistaken for twins. Katie went through periods of both enjoying and resisting the closeness between them—sometimes feeling "crowded in… pushing her away… needing my own space," and sometimes relishing the company and intimacy. When they were seven and eight years old, their uncle asked Katie what she wanted for her birthday. "A horse" was her answer. Without skipping a beat, Doris shouted, "And for my birthday I want a barn to put Katie's horse in." As an adult, Katie feels none of the childhood ambivalence she experienced in her relationship with Doris. "We write to each other three or four times a week," she reports. When I respond in amazement, "I can't imagine that. Do you also call one another?" Katie says, "Oh, we *never* call. We'd hardly know what to say to each other on the phone. She only calls me when someone dies. But we write about anything, everything. I hear about her spats with her husband, her child's first words, stuffy noses, bowel movements… all the details."

Doris now has two children, five and seven years old, both of whom Katie cherishes. "I'm not like a second mother. I'm the *aunt,*" she says clearly when I inquire about the depth of the closeness. (Katie is the only one of her siblings who does not have children.) But later on she does reveal the seriousness she assigns to the role of aunt. "In Virginia, my sister has lots of close friends whom the kids call 'Aunt,' and when I hear that I feel *real* jealous and put out." In fact, these friend-aunts know the children better because they see them much more often "in a daily way," but "the children *do* recognize the power of my connection to my sister and they try to imitate that."

Last summer, Katie took Doris and the children to her sacred place, Ghost Ranch, a pilgrimage she hopes will become a family ritual. They rode the train across country "taking turns with the kids in half-hour segments." At the beginning of the journey, Katie had just started reading the book I wrote about my mother, *Balm in Gilead*, so she decided to include her niece and nephew (then six and four years) in her reading of the tale. "I would read on my own for half an hour while my sister would take care of the kids. Then it would be her turn to read, and I'd tell the kids the next install-ment of 'Dr. Margaret's life.' But *each* time, they'd make me go all the way back to the beginning of the story... they wouldn't just let me continue where we had left off. They *insisted* upon the repeti-tion... my niece just loved the beautiful wedding picture of Dr. Margaret, and my nephew felt very identified with Candy Man... felt very sad about his death." I am reminded of this image of the devoted Aunt Katie traveling across the country and reading to the children when she comments later on, "I feel a big responsibil-ity for shaping the values of this next generation."

Her responsibility for imparting values is central to Cannon's teaching as well. Not only does she seem to enjoy the theater and energy, the *performance* of teaching, and the intellectual discourse, but she also, perhaps primarily, sees her teaching as a vehicle for social justice and liberation. "I used to want to change the world, to get rid of racism and sexism through my teaching. Then when that didn't happen, I became frustrated and then cynical. Now I say to myself, if I can change *one* person's perspective so that they leave my course with a changed perspective and ready to be part of the struggle, then I'm satisfied."

Katie Cannon seems like a profoundly committed teacher, hard working and extraordinarily demanding of herself. "My colleagues say I give too much to my teaching. I do too much for my students." The undergraduate course she is teaching at Wellesley is a "sur-prising gift," a "great experience." She agreed to teach a seminar and was surprised and pleased when sixty women showed up for the class; fourteen of them were Wellesley professors and staff. "Even the chaplain is taking the course," she says proudly. The stu-dents are required to write short pieces every week, and despite the incredible workload, Katie reads all of the assignments because "that is how I know what is happening with them, whether I'm making an impact, where to go next with them." She's fascinated by the growth and transformations both in herself and in her students.

Home for Katie is North Carolina, and she has recently begun to recognize her powerful need to stay connected. She tells me about a colleague, a black male theologian at Union Theological Seminary in New York, who makes a distinction between his "nurturing community," which is roots and family, and his "sustaining community," which is where he works. More and more he feels the need to return to his nurturing community for solace and love. More and more he recognizes that this connection to home allows him to tolerate, survive in, and manage the alienation of his work world. Katie likes this distinction. When she heard her colleague talk about the contrasts in the depth of his affiliation, it struck a deep chord in her. "I hadn't gone home for a year and a half," she admits.

These days Katie is making a greater effort to go home more frequently, and when she goes, she experiences complicated feelings. "It's so *hard,*" she says with a sigh, even as she talks about the wonderful familiarity and comfort. The pilgrimage home always points to the sharp contrast between Katie's life and her family's reality. "They think everything I do is strange—like reading books and thinking thoughts. I need so much solitude and quiet, and my mother's house is like Grand Central Station—people constantly moving in and out, the television is on all the time… So I have a small pad of paper and I sit at the kitchen table doodling."

The Cannons are a proud family, and they value their honor and their privacy. Katie also claims to be a "very private person," but even she is sometimes astounded by the insularity of her family. When, a few years ago, she and her mother became subjects of a book written by a close, "trustworthy" white woman colleague (a book about white and black women of the region), her family was upset and appalled by what Katie revealed about them. "Did you forget the tape recorder was on?" her mother asked. Katie had spoken about the alcoholism in her family, particularly one aunt who used to get so drunk that she would ask Katie (then a young girl) to take her place doing housework in "the white woman's home."

She had also spoken openly about the tough hierarchies of skin color in her family, about the distancing and rejection by the light-skinned aunt who hated their blackness and didn't want to be seen as related to the dark-skinned members of the family.

The extended family responded to Katie's published revelations with horror. How dare she air dirty laundry in public? Since Katie was far away up north in Cambridge, "My mother took all the heat!" Katie uses this as a reason for why she has some feelings of reluctance about participating in the *I've Known Rivers* project. She does not want to cause her family further humiliation. She does not want to hear from her mother the dreaded words, "Katie, won't you ever write something that will make us feel proud?"

The other part of Katie's reluctance stems from the contradictions she feels within herself between self and persona. She describes to me how others see her: gracious, warm, giving, open, responsive—"projections of who they need me to be. People always think I'm much more open than I am, much more available to them than I feel... I think I am the only faculty person who lives on the EDS campus who does not invite students to my home. They'll call me at eleven at night and I'll tell them I'll meet them the next morning *in my office*." Katie's availability in the eyes of others jars with her clear sense of public/private boundaries and leads her to recognize the needs of others to make her bigger than life. "When people first started coming up to me asking for my autograph on their napkin, on their program, on their hand, I used to laugh. That's not ME, I thought... then I realized it was very unkind to laugh at them... but their view of me was so dissonant with my view of myself."

She tells the story of a huge gathering of Presbyterian women at Purdue University a few years ago. There were five thousand women there, including Katie's mom and aunt, and Katie was the celebrant for communion—a very important experience for her, one that *would* make her mother feel deeply proud. Just as she was about to begin the communion service, the ministers were notified that there was a bomb threat in the sports arena where the service was being held. One of Katie's fellow celebrants softly pleaded with Katie, "Whatever you ask them [the congregation] to do, they will do… You do something and they will follow." Inside Katie felt panicked, but outside she appeared cool. She looked over at her mother and aunt for help in making her crucial decision, but they just grinned back at her, reflecting all of their "bursting pride." All the congregation remained seated. "It was amazing… I think only one woman got up and went to the door and said, 'If something happens to me, tell my husband I love him.'" A sea of women stretched out in front of Katie, silent and waiting for her to make a move. Finally (it felt like forever but was probably less than a minute), Katie stepped forward, raised her arms in a wide arc and said, "I don't know why no one has left, but I hope it is that the Peace of the Lord that passes all understanding is with us." With that soothing, calm statement, she proceeded to celebrate the communion service.

Katie's memory of that extraordinary moment is one of surprise, panic, and awe; she remembers acting quickly, almost involuntarily. But since then people who were at the service have been coming up to her wanting to relive the exquisite moment of spiritual communion and celebrate Katie's "presence" and "grace" and "courage." The overblown, exaggerated memories surprise and disturb Katie, who works hard at not defining herself the way others perceive her, who recognizes the dissonance between her public persona and her self-image. Pushing her hands hard against the space surrounding her, Katie exclaims, "I have to push those public images away from me. They are so distorting… at the same time as I have to hold them, accept them as important to the people who see me that way." She worries out loud about whether joining in this project will enlarge this already unwieldy public persona.

Deciding whether to participate in these interviews was a tortured process for Katie Cannon. Like almost everything she does, she gave the decision her full attention. She wrestled with it, raged against it, tried to deflect it, reflected on it, and finally decided to say yes, with certainty *and* skepticism. In one of our talks she outlined the stages of her inner deliberations.

At the outset, she felt delighted and honored that I would ask her to participate in the project. She felt trusting of my identification as black woman, and of the pride and pleasure I took in that identity. However, she also began to experience a growing apprehension at the intrusiveness of this work. Although I assured her that she could always determine how much she was willing to reveal, she knew that once I began asking probing questions, she would start talking, let down her guard, and say things she would later regret. "It's like my mother said to me, 'Katie, did you forget the tape recorder was on?'"

Katie then began to think of other people who would be much better subjects for the book—more worthy, more interesting, more articulate. "I thought of Barbara Harris [recently appointed Suffragan Bishop of Massachusetts]... I'll make a list of excellent people for Sara. She'll love talking to *them*." Katie wanted to "get it away from me. Give it—this precious opportunity—to someone else."

This response, this wish to direct me to other, more compelling and interesting people, reminds Katie of her retreat from the ministry when the career prospect seemed both alluring and threatening to her. She would compare herself to her younger brother, who was also studying for the ministry, and say that *he* was the one who was gifted and talented in this work. "After all, I had the speech impediment." (Katie has a slight lisp and hesitation in her speech that I probably noticed the first time I met her. But it is not until she mentions her "speech impediment" that I realize it has become inaudible to me. I no longer hear it. I *do* hear rapidity and urgency in her speech. I see her mouth racing to keep up with the thoughts and images in her head. But her ability to communicate is so compelling that I have missed, totally missed, what to her must be a frustrating impediment to getting the words out.) How could she become a fine preacher with this speech problem? Her brother's language and style were so smooth. Now Katie knows what she was doing with this self-denigration, this self-denial that expressed itself in constant comparisons to her brother. She was refusing to accept the challenges and responsibilities of the path stretching out before her. She was denying her powers, retreating from the awesome task of defining her ministry. Remembering this earlier reluctance helps Katie resist this tendency in herself and shed her apprehensions.

Aunt/Mummy/Villain

Katie is seated in my office, her large body comfortably perched on my purple chair. After surveying the space and taking everything in, she remarks on how the place looks like me, and finally focuses on the pictures of my children. Her appreciation of them seems to combine admiration and yearning. This childless (child-free) woman clearly loves children and has collected many surrogate offspring to whom she is a devoted and generous aunt and godmother. When she asks about my children and my life, I describe in detail the three days I live each day: the first day that begins at 5:00 A.M. with an hour and a half of early-morning work on my writing or teaching before waking the children, helping them get dressed, making breakfast, helping in the race to do leftover homework, and offering a final send-off and kiss as they go out the door to the car pool. The second day—when I go to work, to my teaching, research, committee work, advising, and so on—is easier because I feel I have some measure of control. People sometimes listen to me; there is structure and order. Katie understands completely. "Is *anyone* listening?" she jokes. "Walls, do you hear me? Doorknob, do you hear me?" Then in my car, on the way to my third day, I try to "cool out" by putting on some soothing music—a Mozart piano concerto, the sweet sounds of the Modern Jazz Quartet. Then I'm home greeting my children, catching up on their days, making dinner, lighting the candles, singing grace, framing the peaceful interlude around the table before it all begins to unravel with our collective weariness. Then good-night songs, and our version of prayers. Katie listens intently to all this and exclaims, "That's four days, not three."

We continue talking about the details, the rhythms, the texture of our lives—a uniquely womanly encounter. "I wake up at five too," she says. "For the first half hour I lie in bed with my head-phones on and listen to Leontyne Price or Sweet Honey in the Rock—that's the way I locate the center of my peace. If I didn't do that, I would get up and hit the ground *working.*" Her work not only consumes every weekday hour from 5:00 A.M. to 10:00 P.M. ("when I turn off the telephone because I can no longer *receive* any more stimuli") but also seems to crowd into almost every weekend. "In the last three weekends I've been away: at Stanford, at Carol Gilligan's thing on the Cape, and at Princeton," she says, shaking her head in weariness.

Two of these three trips have caused her pain and disquiet and, she feels, have had an impact on her final decision to commit her-self to my project. The women's retreat on the Cape was particu-larly difficult. For several months five black women, five white women, and one Argentinian woman ("who flips back and forth in her identity as a woman of color or white") have been meeting to discuss the ways in which they can help young girls resist "the pow-erful message of patriarchy." Beginning with Gilligan's assertions that around age eleven girls stop speaking their minds, asserting their points of view, and go underground with their feelings and thoughts, this biracial women's group has gotten together to dis-cuss the ways to counter the submergence of voice and perspec-tive. The intent is to begin with assuming the validity of Gilligan's findings and move to a consideration of what to do as responsible, nurturing women who care deeply about the development of girls.

Actually, the agenda is not as well articulated as Katie would like. In response to my query about the focus of their discussions, she throws up her hands in a gesture of despair. "I really wish I knew why we are here… what the purpose of this whole thing is!" She is frustrated by the inefficiencies of the wandering, unstructured task and by the process's lacking a clear goal. She hates to waste her precious time. Even though she is ideologically committed to par-ticipating in the discourse, she does not see the value in navel gaz-ing or indulging in a stuck process. But it is not only these inefficiencies that made her impatient on the last retreat; it is also "the blindness" of the women that has left her feeling hurt and abandoned. Katie's eyes fill with tears as she tries to describe the group dynamics. The hurt still lingers in her uncharacteristic inarticulacy. She is a woman used to confrontation, used to being in the eye of the storm, used to *creating* controversy. Why did this gathering of eleven women feel so traumatic, cause her "to throw my head back and let the tears roll into my ears... in order to hide my pain."

The central trauma seemed to grow out of an extended conversation with the Argentinian woman who was offended by Katie's need to speak from her place as a black woman. "Why can't I just respond to you as an *individual?*" the woman had demanded of Katie. "Why do you insist upon putting up barriers to my communicating with you as a person?" Katie had explained—over and over—that a central part of her identity, through which all else is filtered, is her blackness... that it was not a matter of creating a barrier to communication; it was a matter of recognizing that her full identity had to be engaged in any real discourse. The exchange between Katie and the Argentinian woman had become heated and charged. Katie began to feel attacked as other women—white women—joined up on the other side, but none of the other women of color rose up in her defense. How could they not see that the analysis must include race/class/gender? Katie's face shows more than puzzlement. She is angered and pained by the isolation she experienced. "That evening after the session ended I went to Janice Ward's room. Why didn't you help me out?... Then she promised she would. But it was too late!"

The isolation in this group brings on familiar feelings of being unique in her history and experience. So much of the time, she does not see herself reflected in other women's perspectives or realities but finds herself "coming from a very different place." Sometimes this divergence and contrast seem to inspire in her a clear and aggressive stance; other times, much more rarely (like at this retreat), they cause her to feel alone and desperate. "This experience made me keep thinking about your book. If my experiences are so *unusual*, so different, maybe it would help other people if I would tell my story to someone I could count on to convey it sensitively and authentically."

The weekend following the Cape Cod retreat, though not as torturous for Katie, added to her feelings of isolation. She had been invited down to the Divinity School at Princeton University by a group of black students, "primarily middle-aged women returning to school in order to pursue a second career"—women being under-written by funds from the school, which is very well endowed; women who were "grateful" just to be admitted to this elite, presti-gious institution. Katie was stunned by their innocence, by their allegiance to "a patriarchal perspective," by their discomfort with her ideas ("I don't think they really had any idea who they were inviting"), by how they needed to guard their fragile status by mouthing institutional canons. For three days, these black women students resisted Katie's exhortations, refused to consider her provocative questions, and became angered and embarrassed by her irreverence. Again she experienced her apartness, as well as their disdain. "They seemed to be saying, 'How dare she claim a promi-nent place in the discourse. Who is she? Where did she come from? She didn't go to any of the fancy schools.'" This experience also encouraged Katie to tell her story to me… Perhaps in her narra-tive she could legitimize other black women's lonely quests. Perhaps in having a receptive, "perceptive" listener she could reduce her own feelings of isolation.

A central experience of her teaching at the Episcopal Divinity School (where she teaches adults, primarily white women) is her "black womanness." She is constantly challenging and battling the racist "projections" of her students—even those who consider them-selves politically correct feminists. "I often begin my courses saying that I know they can only see me in two guises: *mammy* and *villain*… and I reject the mammy image, so I'll be the villain." This warm and generous woman does not seem to speak these harsh and compelling words out of rage, but out of a profound determination that it is pos-sible to rid people of deep-seated prejudice. But the transformation process requires articulation, conflict, anger, and anguish. Her stu-dents are offended by her opening remarks. They want to reject Cannon's characterization of their racism; they hate what they feel is *her* rejection of them. "The white women get very angry; they get petulant and begin to throw tantrums. They *need* me as their black mammy." Cannon's provocative opening "produces response and feeling," and for those who can tolerate the discomfort, it becomes an experience to be worked on, wrestled with, and understood.

Blackness for Katie Cannon is connected to culture, roots, and ideology. It is also related to the blackness of her skin, the kinkiness and thickness of her hair. She describes herself as "dark-skinned" and sees color consciousness as a central part of her identity. She mentions an aunt who is "light-skinned," who would have nothing to do with her and her sisters when they were growing up because their darkness offended her. In the segregated schools in which she grew up, despite the fact that she was the smartest, she could never be a valedictorian or salutatorian because she was dark-skinned, and in college she had a lab partner, a light-skinned girl whom she "assumed must be smarter because she was light." Katie couldn't believe that this lab partner didn't know the answers and couldn't figure out the problems. For most of the year, she kept on assuming that this girl knew more than she did despite daily evidence to the contrary. Now, when Katie stands in front of her class refusing to be the "black mammy," she is casting off the ugly caricature inflicted by the white patriarchy and reflected in hateful black intraracial hierarchies. Despite the pain of these memories of denigration and exclusion, the absurdity of it all makes us laugh together. "They are so *offended* by dark skin," says Katie. *"It's as if it makes their teeth hurt."*

Katie again asks about my children. She asks about their summer plans, exploring possibilities for camp for her goddaughter from Atlanta who will be spending several weeks with her this summer. This goddaughter is also Katie's niece, and I ask whether this is the niece who traveled by train to Santa Fe with her. It turns out this is a different child, a ten-year-old, who is the daughter of another sister whom Katie later describes as my "younger sister-cousin." I am reminded of how large Katie's family is and how many children she seems to take on as her responsibility. She speaks about them with love and pride in her voice, a kind of *pure* and uncomplicated pride that mothers can rarely achieve. Her godmother/aunt status allows her a benign and whole view of her "children." This goddaughter to whom she now refers seems to have a very special place in her heart. Katie's voice thickens with yearning as she describes Etta Marie Katherine Moon, her godchild.

Etta's mother came to live with Katie's family when she was suddenly orphaned at three years old. After murdering her mother, Etta's father was never formally accused or convicted. "*Nothing* was done to him," recalls Katie. When the family came to the house following the murder, they asked the little girl to choose with whom she would like to live. The three-year-old responded immediately, "I want to live with Uncle SeeSaw." She was referring to her uncle and Katie's father whose name is "Esau" but whom the girl always called "Uncle SeeSaw." That very night the family delivered the child to the Cannons' house, stretching the number of children from six to seven. Etta was woven into the family as "sister" and lived with them until she went off to Spelman College in Atlanta ("the big city"). A smile spreads over Katie's face as she recalls the pride they all felt in her sister-cousin going off to the "fancy elite" private college. All the rest of them had gone to local black church-related schools, and here *she* was going to Spelman. Katie had worked very hard to help raise the funds, secure her sister a scholarship, and encourage her to take "the big leap" to Spelman. After a couple of years there, her sister got pregnant, a "big mistake" that Katie's mother held *Katie* responsible for. If Katie had not paved the way for her sister to go to Spelman, Etta never would have been corrupted by the "city folk"; she would never have gotten pregnant. Katie throws her head back with a deep throaty laugh. "I said, 'Mama, in my whole life, I have never gotten anyone pregnant.'"

This sister-cousin went on to have three children, the oldest being Etta Marie, whom Etta promised to give to Katie when she was born. But when the child arrived, her mother could not bear to part with her, so Katie lost the promised child. Katie skips over this loss quickly, her voice hardly pausing to let me absorb the disappointment. But her pain surfaces as she describes the naming of the child. Since this baby could not become Katie's child, the mother promised that she would get Katie's name. But one of

Katie's aunts, also named Katie, objected to a third Katie in the family. "It sounds too much like the KKK [the Ku Klux Klan]," she said. So it was decided that the baby would be named Etta (another family name) Marie Katherine ("which is not Katie, but close") Moon. Despite the broken promise, the bond between Katie and Etta grew strong. Katie's great fondness, her commitment, her maternal instincts show as she thinks about designing the summer weeks they will spend in each other's company.

The Great Escape

As usual, Katie has arrived at my office a few minutes early. She is full of anticipation as she gives me a warm hug, lets out a throaty laugh, and announces that she has been "full of anxiety." She has spent a sleepless night, tossing and turning, worrying about the "expectations," the "exposure," the performance. Now she has a rumbling in her belly like she has "before every one of her speeches," even though she has been giving them for fifteen years. Cannon is looking much brighter and more festive than usual in a teal, purple, and white handwoven Guatemalan tunic over black pants. In fact, we are matching in our teal and purple garments, the first visible signs of our developing synchrony and sympathy. I notice a big contrast in her dress. During our earlier visits, Katie's dark woolen skirts and large sweaters seemed purposely muted and understated. Today, her colors sing. Our appointment is scheduled for 11:00 A.M.–1:00 P.M. and I have told her that she should feel free to bring her lunch with her. But in anticipation of our interview, she has decided to have "brunch" earlier. "I didn't want to be munching and crunching on your tape," she says with a nervous smile.

With her arms wrapped around her middle, leaning forward slightly, looking directly at me with very large eyes, she is ready. Sensing the importance of her teaching, I ask her about her course at the Episcopal Divinity School, and she launches into a response with grateful gusto. Her first statement is simple and full of feeling: "Teaching is the love of my life." "Where I grew up in North Carolina," she recalls, "folks said that teachers were *born*, not made." In her county, "where the Klan marched at whim and will," black women had two choices: they could become domestics, or if they were educated (a tiny elite group), they could become teachers. "The most honorable thing you could do was be a teacher," says Cannon with reverence still heavy in her voice. From a very young age, Katie began practicing for a career in teaching. "I loved playing school as a child." She would gather her sisters and brothers together and become the teacher with a classroom full of children. When her siblings grew tired of the school games, she would beg them to continue. "I loved giving tests, determining whether they had learned the material. I loved creating plays... My sister Doris and I would do comedy routines." Theater and humor were "all part of teaching."

Katie has quickly become animated and focused. Her talk is rapid-fire; words sometimes get tangled together as they spill out. She makes sweeping gestures as she describes teaching as theater and replays the comedy that she and her younger sister invented. "For a while I had fantasies of becoming a comedian, a stand-up comic." This seems quite believable. Katie is so funny, so vital, so surprisingly irreverent, and carries a listener along in the wave of her infectious laughter.

"School was the place of my affirmation," a place of safety, productivity, and joy. "I liked the rules," says Katie remembering her very early attraction to the structure and clarity of the classroom. "Even as a child of three, I'd be lining up the other children." Her attraction to the rules is connected in her mind to her precocious and sure devotion to religion. "I was overendowed with Christianity," she says without defensiveness. "This was linked with education."

Katie started school at three years old at a school created by Lutherans, "the only place in the county where blacks could go to preschool." In this region, at this time (1953), it was not considered "natural" to send your children to preschool. "It was a very progressive thing to do... people worried that kids would be distorted" by this early education that took them away from their family. But Katie's mother—who believed in the power of education and was fiercely determined in her effort to send all of her children through school—resisted the local disapproval and sent Katie, and her older sister Sara, off to the Lutheran school. "It was a hardship [for the family] at fourteen dollars a month for each of us," says Katie appreciatively. At 6:00 A.M., the two girls would be dropped off by their mother or Cousin Waddell at one of their teacher's homes, Mrs. Skinner's or Miss Lindsay's. The teacher would just be rising when they arrived, and the little girls would have to occupy themselves quietly in the living room while the teacher washed up, dressed, and had her breakfast. Katie would sit and look at "the same book over and over again," or she would play with her miniature animals. Even though she and her sister had to be quiet and stay out of the way, Katie loved the feeling of being in the teacher's home, glimpsing the private life of an admired mentor, watching the sequence and order of her daily preparation.

When Mrs. Skinner or Miss Lindsay had finished breakfast, they would be on their way to Mount Calvary Lutheran School where they would arrive well before any of the other children. Katie relished this time of day. "Opening up the school. It was almost like you lived there. I felt ownership of the space." The quiet morning hours would be suddenly shattered by the arrival of the other small children, and Katie would energetically and enthusiastically join the activity. School was a place of excitement, accomplishment, and reward. "Education was always my life-giving source," she says simply. Katie would get so deeply involved in the school day that she would usually forget to go to the bathroom. By the time they reached the point in their daily schedule when the teachers and children bowed their heads to recite the Lord's Prayer, Katie would—as if on cue—proceed to wet her pants. "It was the first time in the day when I would pause long enough to realize I needed to go to the bathroom. My bladder was full, but I had been so involved in the action in the classroom that I wouldn't even notice. I'd wet my pants every time!" So Katie and her teacher worked out a system where she would ritualistically rise to go to the bathroom as soon as she heard the opening words, "Our Father, who art in heaven…" "I was the only one to get permission to go to the bathroom during the Lord's Prayer," remembers Katie proudly.

She still seems to appreciate the place of "special privilege" she had with the teachers, a privilege she worked hard for and earned. It was the perfect match: the teachers who wanted order, civility, quiet, and poise from their rural black children and Katie who loved rules, structure, engagement, attention, and control. She especially loved the "rote learning," which was the teacher's specialty, and she excelled, mightily memorizing all the grammatical rules, Bible verses, and poems. As a matter of fact, at a very tender age, she gained a big reputation for her recitations. At the beauty shop, at Sunday dinner, at a church supper, the grown-ups would ask her to stand and recite a verse. She would rise up and with a large voice and astonishing poise deliver the memorized lines perfectly. Applause and admiration would follow as Katie learned early the rewards of performance, the convergence of order and creativity, the connections between Christianity and education.

Katie leaps across the years, from the Mount Calvary Lutheran School to Barber-Scotia, where she went to college. She remembers both educational environments as powerful. Katie had longed to go to college at North Carolina A&T, "far away from home." She was desperate to leave the big family and the tiny town of Kannapolis, where she had grown to feel inhibited and stifled. She begged her mother to let her go to A&T. But her mother would hear none of it. She gave Katie a choice: she could stay home and work in the mills, or she could go to Scotia, seven miles down the road. Barber-Scotia, started in 1867 for freed slavewomen, was the local college, a stone's throw from home, a place many Cannon extended family members attended. Katie "hated" the idea of going to this place, which didn't permit dancing or card playing, or eating popcorn, or going to the movies. But mostly she hated the idea of being so close to home. She had thought of college as the great escape from the narrow parochialisms she had lived with for too long. But when her mother issued the nonnegotiable ultimatum— either the mills or Scotia—Katie knew there was no real choice, and she began to pack her trunk for Scotia. Even though the college was only seven miles away, she packed up her big black trunk with all her earthly possessions "like I was going way across the nation, thousands of miles away." Katie knew, at some level, that she would never return home. She would construct deep psychological boundaries that would make these few miles feel like a large liberating chasm.

When Katie arrived at the dormitory and met the other girls—also from poor, southern country families—she joined enthusiastically in the intentional, deliberate socialization the college had to offer. Most of the young women had "no sophistication, had not been exposed to anything worldly," were leaving their rural North Carolina towns for the very first time. Scotia prided itself on training these "diamonds in the rough." "They always said that they would teach us how to walk with the peasants and ride with the kings," recalls Katie in admiration of this core curriculum that was unambivalently and completely conveyed in every corner of college life. "You see," she explains to me, to give me a sense of the depth and breadth of the deliberate socialization, "we were first-generation collegegoers from poor families. Some of us had never slept in a bed by ourselves. Some of us had never slept on sheets. They believed in exposing us… and *everything* was mandatory." There was no choice, no thinking, no criticism, only obedience to the rigid standards the college set. "Our parents had taken us as far as they could in bringing us to Scotia. Now the college had to take over and prepare us for the world. Most of us came from homes where there were no books. When we were required to buy *Webster's Collegiate Dictionary* for ten dollars, it was a great hardship for many of us." One girl in Katie's dormitory was unique in her affluence. She brought a small window fan from home. "And all of us talked about her… she must be a real bourgeois to own a fan. It was just inconceivable to the rest of us."

Katie's family, in fact, was relatively sophisticated. They owned a set of encyclopedias, and her mother and grandmother were "avid readers." They would buy the ladies' magazines "that you see in the supermarkets— *Redbook, Ladies Home Journal*"—and read them from cover to cover. They often had their heads in "religious stuff" that they picked up from the church. But blacks in town were not allowed to go to the library. "It was against the law," says Cannon almost nonchalantly. "This was the mid-sixties, and you couldn't go to the library in my town… We couldn't go roller-skating, couldn't go to the pool… I still can't swim."

As I listen to Katie, I fasten on the extreme deprivation of not being able to use the *library*. She responds to the look of horror on my face by saying, "Well, there was a bookmobile that would come from time to time... but it had a black side and a white side, and the books were of different quality on either side. When the bookmobile would stop in the neighborhood and we'd borrow the books, my grandmother always insisted that we return the books in the same condition that we received them. This was her effort to *prove* to the white community that we were decent human beings." So even though they would only be allowed to take out the second-rate, lower quality, tattered books from the black shelves of the bookmobile, they had to return them in the shape in which they received them, to prove their worthiness, to prove their civility to the white folks. To this scholar and teacher who loves books, who describes education as "the life-giving source," the experience of not being able to use the local library, of being allowed to borrow only "low-quality" books, of having the treatment of the borrowed books be connected to proving the race worthy in the eyes of whites —all of this must have felt unbearably oppressive. It must have been part of the reason that Katie, even now, says with such urgency and passion, "I wanted *out* so bad... out of North Carolina.... I thought, There must be a place where I can just be ME." Katie traveled the seven miles to Scotia with that deep determination. "Education was going to be the ticket out. I thought, I've got to excel!" And excel she did, working diligently on her studies, consistently making the dean's list, rising to the top of her class, proving herself worthy.

Along with her serious commitment to education, and her determination that it would take her to a place where she could finally be herself, Cannon discovered that student life at Scotia focused on sex and sexuality. In the dormitory, sex was the omnipresent topic of conversation among the young women. For Katie, who was a confirmed prude, the talk was both alluring and threatening. "I think I was the only virgin on my floor," says Katie with dancing, mischievous eyes. Her friends were amazed and dismayed by her innocence and determined that they would introduce her to the pleasures and passions of sex. "Their sole purpose was to get me to have sex by the end of the year." They were graphic in their description of the ecstasy that sex would bring. There would be firecrackers, brilliant orgasmic explosions, fingers and toes curled up like paws, unleashed screaming. "They drilled me in the ecstasy of sex." Katie listened, "curious and bug-eyed," but she was not convinced by the hype. "I had no point of reference… I was disbelieving."

In 1956—after almost one hundred years as a women's college—Barber-Scotia turned coeducational, producing a gender ratio of nine women to one man. Once the men arrived, despite their minority status and poorer preparation, they began to assume prominent leadership roles in the college, always bolstered by the support of the women. Katie explains why the women "gave away some of their influence and power" to this minority of men. "You see, we already knew that we were responsible for protecting our black men because they could be lynched."

Katie then continues to describe the dormitory talk about sex, the extreme peer pressure she felt, and her rigid reluctance to give in to their urgings. Her language is plain and evocative. Then she steps back to reflect on the reasons for her resistance, and her words assume a distant, analytic tone. "Growing up, we were drilled that we had no worth beyond our virginity. If we got pregnant our lives were over… I viewed it like a body count." To lose your virginity was to lose your dignity, your worth, and to get pregnant was to end all possibilities of a useful or productive life. For Katie, to get pregnant was to risk her ticket out of North Carolina and be stuck at home, demeaned and diminished, for the rest of her life—a fate worse than death.

While her friends' insistent proddings made her feel conflicted, she held fast to her precious virginity. Her resistance was firmly bolstered by her Christianity. "The closeness of sex was *sinful*. There was nobody who worked on salvation the way I did… I was a super-Christian kid." But even this shield of religiosity could not save Katie from the anxiety of peer pressure and from her inner fear. "During my first semester at Scotia, I went from a size thirteen to a size twenty-two." The layers of fat might protect her from the assaults of eroticism or make her so unattractive that she would be spared the advances of men. "I was so desperate, so alone… there was no one there to help me process this thing.... Even though there were only five hundred people at Scotia, I felt like I was living in a foreign country of thirty thousand people." Sex was scary, dangerous, exciting, unknown. She longed for adult counsel and direction. There was none. She turned to eating, anything and everything in sight, as a way to relieve her anxiety and set up physical boundaries. "I would eat leftover cold grits!" says Katie incredulously.

But her girlfriends in the dorm would not let up. They continued to press the message of sex on Katie. They were merciless in their sex rantings. Along with the constant talk about sex, they mixed conversations about "voodoo, about LIFE, stuff from home, violence, knifings, sensationalist stuff... the stuff that Zora Neale Hurston writes about." The dormitory was always abuzz with these exciting, frightening, intoxicating exchanges; groups of girls gathered in tight knots spurring each other on in recounting the horrors and pleasures of their young lives, exaggerating and embellishing their tales, competing with each other for the most bizarre, titillating stories. "And I was wanting to talk about literature," recalls Katie with a sigh.

Katie traveled the seven miles from home to Scotia, with her black trunk filled with all her possessions, to escape the claustrophobia of her family and town, but most important, to escape the oppressive company of her sisters. I am still unclear about who is in Katie's family and where she is in the sequence of siblings, so I ask her to slow down and tell me their names and ages. Whenever I stop her for clarification or discrete facts, a look of dismay spreads over Katie's face. She seems surprised that I do not know all of these basic facts, and she is so caught up in the momentum of her tale, that my question causes her frustration. But she pauses and indulges my need to know who the family characters are: The oldest (thirteen years Katie's senior) was James Ernest. The next baby born was Esau Levon (named after Katie's father), who was born with a "hole in his heart" and died when he was six months old, causing their mother a grief and pain from which she never fully recovered, and causing her to unleash rage and impatience on some of the later siblings who managed to survive. When Sara Elizabeth arrived (twenty-three months before Katie), she was welcomed like "God's greatest gift" and became the favorite, most indulged offspring. Katie Geneva's birth, however, was neither wanted nor welcomed by her mother. From time to time, in cold candor, her mother used to tell Katie that she had wanted to abort her when she discovered her pregnancy. When Katie would respond in quiet horror and incredulity, her mother would protest, "Well, I didn't do it, did I?" as if her decision not to get an abortion could be a comfort to her fourth born. But the question remained—it still does—a haunting, deep assault to Katie's psyche. "People tell me that I delivered myself... When my mother was having me, she refused to scream out... she refused to admit I had come." And very early Katie got the message that she "mustn't be a bother" to her mother. "She would always declare that we [the children] wouldn't hold her back!" At forty-one, Katie is still working out this early rejection in her therapy, and still struggling with feeling unwanted and unloved. Katie's birth was followed thirteen months later by the arrival of Doris Corine, and then John Wesley, who was younger by four years. Sylvia Denise (seven years younger than Katie) was the three-year-old "sister-cousin" who arrived in the Cannon household after her mother was murdered. Suddenly and brutally orphaned, Sylvia chose to come and live with "Uncle SeeSaw" and was folded into the family forever. With Sylvia's arrival, there were six surviving Cannon children competing for meager resources, and for their mother's reluctant attention and love. Two years later, in 1962, Katie's "baby brother," Jerry Lytle Cannon, was born.

Katie's claustrophobia came mostly from being sandwiched between Sara and Doris. For different reasons, Katie felt that both sisters were more powerful than she: Sara because she was the most prized child, the golden gift from heaven who came after brother Esau died; and Doris because she arrived when Katie was thirteen months old and seemed to squeeze out all the meager nurturance that her mother, Corine, had left over. Katie also knew that she was the unwanted child, and she took seriously her mother's frequent admonitions that "We [the children] would not hold her back... we would not be a bother." Knowing that her birth felt to her mother "like a nail in her coffin," Katie's defense was to be as accommodating and unobtrusive as possible—not to make waves, to behave herself admirably, and to stay out of the way of her two sisters and their fireworks. "I got crowded out very early," recalls Katie. "I always felt, I don't want to be a *bother*... I was caught between two sisters who were very demanding. Anytime we got in the car, they would immediately each take a window, and I'd sit on the hump between them. I would always acquiesce to these two powerful sisters."

Scotia, only seven miles away, offered the great escape from this family claustrophobia. Going off to college, Katie felt she was in a "totally different world." She almost never traveled home, even on school vacations. "Sometimes I wouldn't even go home for Christmas." The only time she would travel back to Kannapolis was when the dorms were closed down at Scotia. But even then, as soon as they reopened the buildings, she would make herself available for "preparing the place before everyone came back to school." This image of Katie, the college student, readying the dormitories for her peers, helping the adults fix the environment for the others' return, reminds me of her role at Mount Calvary Lutheran School, when at three years of age, she would arrive very early with her teacher Mrs. Skinner or Miss Lindsay to set up the classroom before the children arrived in the morning. As a preschooler, she relished "the quiet," "the order," the purposeful rituals of preparation. She loved the feeling of "ownership." "It felt like we had slept there overnight."

Interestingly, despite the fact that Katie went to Barber-Scotia partly to escape her demanding sisters, both Sara and Doris attended Scotia as well. Sara had preceded Katie by two years, but after a couple of months she couldn't bear to be so far away from home, so she returned to Kannapolis, to the bosom of her family. Eventually, Sara completed Scotia by traveling the seven miles to her classes and returning home each evening. Doris followed Katie to Scotia two years later, and they managed to coexist there comfortably, enjoying the intimacy of sisterhood but allowing each other more space than they could ever achieve in the family.

When Katie thinks of "great escapes," she remembers the desperation to get out of Kannapolis she felt when she was thirteen years old. It was a desperation so fierce that she felt that if she were forced to spend another summer in the crowded Cannon household, she might suffocate to death. So at thirteen, she used "the only currency" she had with her mother. She announced to her: "If you don't let me go, I'll get pregnant." Katie knew that she was using the biggest threat in her arsenal, and she knew her mother would take her seriously. But she was also aware that she might not be able to carry out the threat if her mother didn't succumb to her demand. Katie's eyes twinkle with mischief—"I didn't have the *slightest* idea about how you get pregnant." So Corine sent her daughter off to live with her aunt Pearl, twenty-seven miles away in Gastonia, North Carolina. Even though it was less than an hour's drive away, it felt to Katie as though she had arrived on another planet. "It felt like New York City" in its range of pleasures and activities. "It had a swimming pool, a library, a recreational center, shopping."

Aunt Pearl was a "light-complected" woman of great poise and dignity. Her light skin gave her a "higher currency" in the family. She always seemed prominently poised between "two worlds," "both black and white." She was a "smart, dignified, proud" woman whom Katie admired and treasured. Her sophistication and style were so different from the country ways of Katie's big family in Kannapolis. Underneath Aunt Pearl's smooth exterior, there was a deep, probing wisdom; she could teach Katie important lessons about survival and achieving that Katie needed and wanted to learn. So for an entire summer, Katie watched and listened to Aunt Pearl carefully and received her instructions in the art of combining dignity and deference.

Aunt Pearl was the longtime housekeeper of a millionairess, but her duties extended well beyond cooking, washing, and cleaning. She was her employer's companion and confidante; she did everything for her. Without Aunt Pearl, this rich white woman would have been totally helpless. Each morning very early Katie would travel from Aunt Pearl's house on the colored side of town to the fancy estate across town, where she would assist her aunt in her duties. "My job was to clean up the dog shit every time I'd go into the house... I hated that dog!"

Liberation and Control

Katie and I greet each other with a big, long bear hug. "How are you doing?" I ask. "I don't know, Sara," she says mischievously, then ominously, "I have nothing more to say." She is resplendent in a deep purple tunic from West Africa, which covers a bright gold long-sleeve shirt. Long amber and brass earrings are dangling from her ears, catching the sunlight that is filtering through the window and brightening up her dark face. She is a vision of intense colors. I beam across at her face admiringly—"You are looking so vibrant with color! What a contrast from your winter costumes." To which she responds, "Oh, I'm going through my midlife crisis... I've taken off all the heavy covering... I'm out there!" She spreads her arms like an eagle in flight. "The way you see me now is the way I'll always be... from now on." Liberation rings in her voice as she throws her head back in a long hearty laugh.

I have now heard Cannon refer many times to her midlife crisis; to wanting to return home to visit her parents and talk about the pain, the distance, the closeness to them; to needing to visit her grandmother's grave and finally admit the enormous loss. In her references to midlife, she always links it to crisis and seems to welcome this tumultuous interlude with all of its risk and drama. Her mention of it brings laughter and teary eyes. She is both joking and dead serious.

I assure her that she has *lots* more to say; we've only just begun... and that I will find the questions to ask that will inspire her to talk. I am aware that she knows there is much more to her story but might be reluctant to say much more.

I immediately suspect that our last interview has left her feeling vulnerable and exposed, as if she has given away too much. She is feeling guarded, with a combination of reticence at the thought of more exposure and intrigue at the anticipation of deeper dialogue. My suspicions hold true. She left our last session feeling excited, "exhilarated," turned on by the discoveries, "high as a kite." But as soon as she got home, all of the electric energy suddenly fizzled and she felt exhausted and "completely wiped out." All afternoon she was overcome with weariness. She woke the next morning still hungover by exhaustion from the day before. "What did Sara do to me?" she said out loud to herself. She remembered my warning that an hour and a half of intense, probing dialogue would be enough for both of us, that this is a surprisingly intrusive and demanding process. She recalled feeling that I was being overly cautious, trying to protect her from wearing herself down. But as she sat in her house, shades pulled down, reviewing the incredible ground we had covered the day before, she completely understood my caution and was surprised at how much she had "given up."

As she relives the exhaustion and exhilaration following our last session, Katie focuses on the fragments of stories she has told me about Phifer, "the only man I ever loved." Although last time she had barely mentioned her relationship to Phifer, a friendship that lasted several years during high school and college, Katie's memory is that she talked "on and on" about him, that tales of Phifer dominated our conversation. Since last week, she hasn't been able to get him out of her mind. Resurrecting the memories of Phifer has been puzzling and unnerving.

Katie had gone home from our last session and immediately begun a search for their class rings from high school. For months Katie and Phifer each had saved up their money to buy a class ring at the end of their senior year. With the help of both parents they had bought their rings, and two weeks later, in a moment of generosity and affection, Phifer had given his to Katie. More than twenty years later, she still has it, or she thought she had it safely put away somewhere. After our last interview, she was "moved" to find it, hold it, think on it. She had looked everywhere and "turned the house upside down," but could not find it anywhere. The disappearance of the precious ring has caused her frustration, then a building anxiety. Finally she sat down, made herself get very still, and she prayed that the whereabouts of the ring would either be revealed to her or that she "would be able to live with the loss." It has now been several days and the ring has not appeared. Katie still looks disoriented. Perhaps her dismay is related less to the missing ring than to the feelings of dislocation that this "Phifer talk" has brought on.

Not only did our last interview cause her to search for the ring; it also made her want to write to Phifer. She had, in fact, written him a postcard, a short note with a big message. She had told him that she was engaged in the book project, that he had come up as a central character in her stories, that the next time she was home she wanted to ask him how much *he* would feel comfortable about *her* revealing. Katie had been haunted by the idea that she might expose her dear friend. She kept asking herself, "How much would Phifer want me to tell?" In agreeing to participate in this project, she was allowing herself to be vulnerable, but she had begun to worry about the exposure and visibility of people she would be "naming." She knew that she had some "responsibility to them," that they deserved her protection. In worrying out loud about her responsibility to her loved ones, Katie seems to be asking me to use my best judgment and care. She has trusted me with her story, and she beseeches me to guard that trust carefully and stretch it to include the people to whom she is deeply connected.

But before moving on, Katie has one final thought inspired by our last interview. I am relieved to hear her say, "I need to slow down," because the pace and intensity of her talk had left *me* feeling breathless and exhausted last time. But Katie is not only referring to the tempo of her talk last time; she is remembering its pitch, its urgency and energy. She wants to make a distinction between real life and melodrama, between nonfiction and fiction. Referring to a contrast she first heard made by Maya Angelou, Katie observes that fiction is a gentler form more bearable in its expression of pain. Nonfiction, which records people's real lives, can be too harsh, too traumatic for the reader to incorporate. The storyteller must be "careful" not to assault the listener with too much emotion, or else the story will not be heard and received. The listener will put up a shield to protect himself or herself from the barrage of intense feelings. Katie worries that in her last interview she might have been "too raw" and too intense in telling of her experiences, that maybe some of the feelings are "too painful to even name." She ponders about the need to "filter" some of her emotions, dilute some of the pain, and hold back some of the tears so that I will not feel assaulted or overwhelmed by her narrative. I see her look of concern; I hear her message of identification with the *listener*, and I am moved by her empathy. But, though I too was "wiped out" by our last interview, I feel fully able to withstand the "raw feelings" and strong enough to hear her "name to the pain." I say as much as clearly as I can. Katie smiles, looking thankful and relieved—"Yes, I have no doubt you're sturdy enough to hear this."

Having expressed her inhibitions, Katie feels released to speak openly. She launches into "the Easter story," a tantalizing tale about losing her virginity to Phifer. Like most of Katie's stories, she begins at the vortex of the drama and emotion. It was 1968, Katie's freshman year at Barber-Scotia, and she was anticipating going home to Kannapolis, and to Phifer, for Easter break. As the time approached, she was feeling increasingly desperate to travel the seven miles down the road home. She recorded her mounting anxiety in a "composition book full of letters to God." Her aching words and her tears fell on every page. She was haunted: "Where is the prophet?... I need help... I am on the cross being crucified, and there is no one there to save me, no one to run it by." After torturous, lonely conversations with God, Katie finally decided to "acquiesce" to Phifer. The decision, though certain and irreversible in her mind, caused her "so much gloom." The last week at school felt like she "was in a death march." If she gave up her virginity to Phifer, would she "ever have any worth?... Would she lose the *essence* of who she was?... Would she ever have a life again?" The questions were penetrating; their answers terrifying.

But at the same time as Katie hated the idea of "ruining her life" by giving away her virginity, other voices within her fought for Phifer. "I love Phifer enough... If I am causing him so much pain, let me lay down my life." While Katie was at Barber-Scotia, Phifer had remained in Kannapolis and was living with Patsy, the other woman in his life who had, all along, been giving him sexual pleasure. From Katie's point of view, this double life that Phifer led—with Katie for companionship and Patsy for sex—had worked reasonably well for all of them. Katie got the intimacy of relationship without the assault of sex; Patsy got good sex without the complications of relationship; and Phifer got it all. It may have been a reasonable relationship for the three of them, but it was totally unacceptable to Katie's parents, who forbade her to see Phifer. "He was living with Patsy... people knew it... and my parents were adamant in their objections."

So when Katie arrived home for Easter break, she let Phifer know that she was back, and he came by the house to pick her up "in his '63 Chevy Impala." They went to the drive-in movie to see Sidney Poitier in *To Sir with Love*. "I hate the movie to this day," howls Katie as she recalls the moment. "The sound track makes my teeth itch." Her story seems to speed up in the telling, the words blurring together as she paints the picture of their bodies finally connecting. "We begin kissing and petting. At the point at which I usually say no, I let him continue on... He seems surprised... flips me over onto the backseat of his Chevy, he's on me, in me... and it's over... all in a matter of maybe three minutes." As soon as it was over, Phifer fell asleep. Katie's voice is incredulous. "He's sleeping and snoring, and I'm sobbing." It felt like "forever" that she lay there, weeping and moaning, feeling ruined. When she could stand the loneliness no more, Katie woke him up out of his deep sleep. "What's wrong with you?" he asked when he saw her tears. "Phifer, am I pregnant?" she asked desperately. "You mean you didn't use anything?" he shot back. "What do you mean?" asked Katie revealing her total ignorance. "I was sobbing and sobbing, deep from the pit of my stomach. I was crying so hard I couldn't get any oxygen."

"You've got to marry me," Katie wailed over and over. Phifer kept trying to comfort her, kept trying to stop the flow of tears by talking gently to her. "Just relax," he repeated over and over. They pulled their clothes on. Katie could hear the movie sound track in the background. The love story on the big screen—Poitier professing his love for this white woman—seemed light years away from the eighteen- and nineteen-year-old black lovers in the backseat of the Chevy. Then they went to get hamburgers at a nearby joint, and the whole time Katie kept pleading, "You're going to marry me." She was not reassured by his vague response. "All I could feel was devastation, not ecstasy."

The Sunday following the lovemaking, Katie sat in church feeling alone and empty. "I felt the farthest away I've ever felt from God... God was nowhere to be found." So much of her self-image centered on being a "super-Christian kid... a Goody Two-shoes," and in one sweeping act she had decimated that shining image. She knew her life must be over if she felt this remote from God. But the devastation and emptiness was balanced against some feeling of relief. It felt good not to have to uphold this impossibly pure standard. "The pressure was off... I was relieved that I was not special." She could now join the other legions of adolescent girls who had lost their virginity, who lived ordinary teenage lives, who gossiped, danced, and went to the movies. "What's the big deal?" thought Katie to herself as she finally felt herself in the company of regular mortals.

When Katie returned to Barber-Scotia at the end of spring break, all of her friends in the dormitory were waiting to hear the news about whether she "had given it up to Phifer." They huddled in her room poised to hear the juicy stories of sexual ecstasy. But Katie disappointed them with a simple yes. Yes, she had had sex with Phifer. The young women whooped and hollered at the great news but must have noticed Katie's lack of enthusiasm and her unwillingness to fabricate exciting details. It was over. She had done it. "It was devastation, not ecstasy. Why do it again?"

Very early in her life Katie had begun to link Christianity with prudishness—with civility, correctness, and cleanliness. She also linked it with struggle and liberation. These connections to religion were vividly drawn by Katie's grandma Rosa, whom she describes as "the most formative person in my life." In her stories and her life Grandma Rosa modeled both the inhibitions and the freedom, the passivity and the militance, of Christianity. "My *rebel* spirit came from Grandma Rosa," says Katie simply. Born in 1882, Grandma Rosa used to talk to her granddaughter about the torture of slavery and the "brutality of white people." "She would mix the slave stories in with the Bible stories... It was a whole consistent story of liberation." Katie used to love to hear these powerful tales of struggle, and she loved how Grandma Rosa wove the dramas of liberation and spirituality into one colorful cloth. The fight for justice always included a lesson on civility and respect for all people no matter where they came from or what their backgrounds. In fighting for equality, you had to do it with dignity and grace. "Grandma Rosa used to always say, 'It's nice to be important, but it is more important to be nice.' She told us we always had to have dignity, respect for all people. We were *never* to laugh at others or consider ourselves better than anyone else."

As a child, Katie greatly admired Grandma Rosa's liberation message and her dignified decorum. These were a powerful combination, and Katie felt deeply identified with Grandma Rosa's style and her thinking. But she now recognizes some of the costs of her grandmother's unerring dignity. "I never ever saw Grandma Rosa get angry. She was so super-Christian... she held in all her feelings. She had rheumatoid arthritis, and now I think that is because she turned all of her rage inside." As an adult in her middle years, Katie does not intend to be crippled by anger that cannot find its expression "outward." She is "having to debunk" this repression of feelings in her Jungian therapy work. She wants to hold onto Rosa's rebel spirit and her respectful regard of all people no matter what their station in life. But when she is raging at the indignities she is suffering, she wants to learn to unleash the anger, not hold it inside. The expression of her rage may occasionally render her undignified or ungracious, but at least it will not fester inside of her and cause her internal damage.

Daily prayer was at the center of the Cannons' life at home. Every day the whole family, except for Pop Esau, would kneel down in front of the couch, heads bowed in prayer. (For some reason, Esau was excluded from the prayer session. He "would be laying up in the bed.") The prayers would usually be led by Corine and Grandma Rosa, and they would go on and on asking the Lord for safety, good health, and well-being. Katie, who considered herself a deeply religious person, found these prayer sessions difficult and humiliating. She couldn't wait for the long-winded soliloquies to be over. "I was embarrassed by all this prayer… *My shame was prayer.*" It was not the petitions to God that caused her to shudder; it was the public display of prayer that she hated. "I thought the Christian thing should be individual. Doing it corporately, collectively, brought on a *vulnerability*… To have to say it out loud, publicly, was horrible." At church, she always cringed at the exposure that came with having to pray out loud in front of other people. She worried about "letting go," about "where the spirit might take" her if she lost control in prayer.

She remembers that those feelings of vulnerability came flooding back during her first year in seminary when she was asked to offer up a prayer in the service. Sudden panic, a shivering fear shot through her as she resisted the request. "I don't pray," she said militantly. "I'm a *revolutionary.*" But despite her protestations, they all just sat there in stony silence ("You know how black folks do!") and waited for her to lead them in prayer. They just waited and waited, their faces impassive. "No one was exempt from praying." Katie's heart raced. "All that silence… I was out there all by myself… SHIT!" Finally, the waiting wore her down, and she struggled to bring up the feelings, convert them into words, and make a public prayer. She was determined to pray carefully and cautiously. She was determined not to lose control.

Control seems to be deeply linked with religiosity, with doing the Lord's work, and Katie wanted to be in perfect control from a very tender age. When she thinks about her early years in school, the first thing she mentions is her role as rule keeper and controller of her classmates. At six years old, when Katie was in second grade, she remembers being the person the teacher always left in charge when she had to leave the classroom. Katie was the "name taker," recording all of the transgressions of her peers and reporting them to the teacher upon her return. "I always knew how to be the teacher's pet. I always got good behavior marks. I scored lots of brownie points. The teacher always left me in charge of taking people's names down. I took it upon myself to help save their souls."

Katie's role as surrogate teacher is the first thing she mentions when she recalls her initiation into public school in the second grade. Her teacher, Mrs. Gwendolyn Smith, was loved and respected by Katie. She was part of "the insular community" and "had been a friend of the family's for years." With Mrs. Smith, the connections among home, school, and community were deep and unbroken. "You always knew that what you did at school would be known at home" and vice versa. That was pretty much true for all the teachers who were part of the community and felt accountable to it. The sense of responsibility and connection to the community was part of what Katie proudly calls their "greatness." "They were black teachers who believed in black children. They believed that we were *somebody*.... They stood up and preached to us, 'The world is mean. It's a jungle out there. They will try to rip you off... But no one can take your thoughts away from you.' There was no subtlety in their message. The teachers felt a responsibility to save the race." It was a clear, consistent demand, boldly articulated each day, woven into the lessons and folded into the prayers. And it was a lesson required of *all* students. "Everyone learned. They insisted on it," says Katie whose voice is ringing in admiration and praise for these "great and devoted teachers."

All the children learned, but Katie stood out as an excellent and diligent student. It was not only her impeccable behavior that captured the teachers' attention, it was also Katie's inquiring mind. "I loved learning. I loved being challenged." The teachers would watch Katie's insatiable appetite for learning, her zest for knowledge, her determination to prove herself. She was a joy to teach. But Katie's energetic achievement would sometimes be dampened by the deep-seated prejudices that defined opportunity for black children in Kannapolis. She puts it starkly, "I was too dark to be top in my class. Dark-complected kids were always in the slow group." It was assumed that there was some inextricable link between color and intelligence.

Very early Katie learned to think of herself as dark, and, therefore, as ugly. "I grew up perceiving myself as the color of tar. My sister used to say to me, 'You are an old black dog,'... and I grew to think of myself as pitiful looking—black, ugly, and puny with big bulging eyes and a big head." For Katie, school became a place to prove herself worthy *despite* her despicable dark skin. If she could succeed and excel in school, then she might be able to overcome the shadows of darkness. "I thought that education was the way to gain respect—if I could get strokes and accolades for all my wonderful recitations, that would make my blackness less of a handicap." And for the most part, Katie's work in school was so unquestionably superior that her darkness and "ugliness" did not hold her back. "The teachers and I made good chemistry together. The color thing was still operative, but I was an enthusiastic and successful student." Soon her reputation as an excellent student was firmly in place and she was "expected to do well."

However, her superior achievement couldn't completely eradicate the damages of darkness. Katie remembers 1956, as "the year I became color conscious." It was December and the second grade was beginning rehearsals for the annual Christmas pageant. For months Katie had had her heart set on getting a major role. She knew the lines by heart. She could have recited them perfectly in her sleep. "More than anything I wanted to be the angel." But despite her reputation in town as the best reciter of Bible verses and despite her impeccable preparation after weeks of diligent practice, Katie did not get the part of the angel. As everyone expected, the part went to a light-skinned girl named Jackie Young. "She had long thick hair, gray eyes and a soft voice... so she got the part. I was too dark, my hair was nappy, my eyes were too big, my voice too heavy." The choice felt inevitable. Although she was deeply disappointed, Katie was not surprised by the teacher's decision to cast Jackie.

The hierarchies of color were everywhere: in the ability grouping of children for reading and math, in grading patterns, and in assumptions about intellectual abilities and achievement potential. This stratification was also evident in the images the black school tried to convey to the white community. Every time a white person came to visit the school, the teachers would parade out the light-skinned children, and the darker ones would be kept safely out of view. "Only the light-complected kids would be allowed in their presence... It was as if it would cause the white people too much pain if they cast their eyes on us... It might make their brains sneeze!"

At seven years old, Katie was already engaged in trying to figure out "the curse of blackness." Why was it that black people were being so brutally punished? What had we done that was so horrible, so wrong, to deserve this kind of abuse and suffering? It didn't take her long to examine the evidence and come up with the answer. Katie's face brightens in mock resolution of her queries. "I figured this whole thing out—the curse of blackness had to do with SEX." It was because blacks indulged in all of this promiscuous, dirty behavior that God was punishing us and making all of us suffer. "White people don't do this," reasoned Katie, "which is why they don't suffer. We drink, we party, we dance, we have children out of wedlock—all of this animalistic behavior—no wonder we are enslaved." Once Katie had "figured this out" at the tender age of seven, she decided to devote her life to the abolition of savagery among blacks. "The energy needed to be controlled. I decided I would become a missionary, a nun, I'd go to Africa... I'd save us!"

Katie lived with this view of the "curse of blackness" for several years until she discovered in her first year in high school that some white girls in the white school on the other side of town were having babies out of wedlock. This "animalistic behavior" was not limited to the black community; white people also partied, cursed, got drunk, and had extramarital affairs. "If white girls were having babies out of wedlock, there was no logic to all of this... there was no reason why blacks should suffer so brutally." This was a radicalizing moment for Katie. "That is when I became a militant."

Minefields

Katie arrives at my office with a story to tell. The story has weighed heavily on her mind and needs immediate expression. She now seems to have become thoroughly immersed in and committed to our interviews, which echo through her hours and days after each session. Last time she burst into my office with the news that she had nothing more to say, an expression of her sense of vulnerability and exposure. She needed to tell me about the raw feelings, her wish to slow down, to dilute the intense melodrama, to contain some of the pain. She still needed to be assured that I could be trusted; that I would not recoil from the drama or the pain; that her stories were heard, received, remembered. This time, she needs no such assurances. She wants to begin by backtracking to an important event that has left a deep imprint on her but has remained undisclosed since 1965, the year Katie was in the tenth grade.

"I need to tell you about the time I drew a knife on my teacher," says Katie theatrically. Her opening draws a loud exclamation from me, "Really! Wow!" I have begun to sense that her life is full of extraordinary, dramatic, powerful moments—some having happened to her fortuitously, circumstantially; some having been created by her. Regardless of their origin, all of them are made more vivid by Katie's dramatic interpretations. Simple facts become complex and significant from her perspective. A beautiful thing may be seen as ugly (or vice versa) because of the context in which she places it. Nothing in Katie's world is discrete or one-dimensional. It is not merely that her forty-one years have probably been more exciting and complicated than most lives, but it is her lively interpretation of those life experiences that captivates and amazes the listener. She is the actor and the creator of her stories, the subject and the author, and these dual roles bring life to all her stories.

Katie leans forward, her voice rapid and as intense as ever. She was the tenth-grade class president at the George Washington Carver High School, and together with a few classmates was planning the culminating event of the year, a class trip. They were sitting in a cluster in the classroom having an energetic, spirited conversation, "laughing, talking, planning." Miss Boulware came from across the hall and began to complain loudly about all the noise the group was making. With a shrill voice, she berated them, told them they were "acting like fools." Katie and her friends were surprised by her harsh tones and accusations. Although they had been enthusiastic and occasionally loud in their planning, they were not being disruptive or raucous. When their homeroom teacher, Mrs. Martin, came back, Miss Boulware reported the group's transgressions, and Mrs. Martin felt compelled to punish them. She "had thought she could trust them"; she had expected them to act responsibly and they had disappointed her. For their sins, they each received "five licks on our hands" (with a ruler) and her words of recrimination.

Katie was outraged, seething with anger at the injustice. Suddenly the fury inside her erupted like a volcano. She said to her friends angrily, brutally, "If I had a knife, I'd kill her." Her classmates were stunned by her statement. James Torrence decided to test her sincerity. He reached in his pocket and pulled out a pocketknife. "Here is the knife," he challenged. "I couldn't back down. I just couldn't reverse myself. I was just shaking with anger," recalls Katie, her voice still ringing with rage. She strode across the hall with the knife in her hand and said to the people gathered, "I'm looking for Miss Boulware." The answer came back, "She's not here." So Katie walked out, slowly. She left Miss Boulware's classroom, but she did not leave her anger behind. Now her voice is shaking—"She was not there to kill, but I would have staked my life on it... as long as there was any energy left in me, I was going to kill her. She had violated me... I was humiliated."

Katie walked back across the hall to the classroom where her expectant peers looked at her with new eyes of awe and apprehension. "My whole image among my colleagues had changed. No more

Goody Two-shoes." The anger did not subside. "I could feel the quaking, the shaking… I could feel how close I was to altering my life forever." During the next class period, in Mr. Thompson's Algebra II class, Miss Boulware strode in. "I understand Katie Cannon's been looking for me." To which the whole class chorused back, "Oooh." In silence, head bowed, Katie followed Miss Boulware out of the class. Standing outside against the concrete wall under the fire escape, the teacher confronted her. "Do you have something to say to me?" Katie "said the Lord's Prayer over and over again" to herself, trying not to unleash her anger and remaining steadfastly silent. For two years after, every time Katie would see Miss Boulware, she would stare at her in hateful, blunt silence. In the hall, on the lunch line, in the library, their eyes would lock in mutual enmity.

By day's end the grapevine had carried this story to every corner of the school. "Katie Cannon was looking for Miss Boulware with a knife. She was ready to stab the life right out of her. Everyone was buzzing about it. It was the hum of the school." And Sister Sara just couldn't wait to carry the news home to their mother. She couldn't wait to watch Katie receive their mother's wrath. As the time drew closer for Katie to go home, she felt a wave of panic more serious than any she had experienced the whole day. "All the fear of mother had come down on me." She knew her mother's outrage would be much worse than anyone else's, that she would have to endure terrible humiliation once she got home. And she was infuriated with Sara's obvious pleasure over the anticipated pain. "This was going to be worse than going to prison," thought Katie as she headed home on the school bus. As soon as they landed at the door, Sara told Corine Cannon the terrible tale and paused long enough to wait for the fireworks. But none came. No fireworks. No screaming. No humiliation. Only a simple and strange directive to Katie, quietly spoken: "I want you to go and clean the living room," said Mrs. Cannon.

Relief is written all over Katie's face as she relives this treacherous moment. "For the very first time in my life, my mother came through!" Katie still has no clue about why her mother responded as she did. It was completely, shockingly uncharacteristic of her mother, who was not shy about berating her children. She never spared them her anger. But here she was telling Katie to clean the living room, the one room in the house that never even got dirty. "We have a poor working-class living room. You know, one of those rooms with plastic all over everything, a room that is never used... nothing at all to clean!" Her mother's words felt like a blessed gift. "To me, it felt like *paradise*, that living room... Nothing to dust, nothing to do. I thought it was the most *beautiful* space, heavenly." Cannon stayed in her newfound asylum feeling deeply relieved and grateful to be spared her mother's wrath. But even more shocking than *not* getting punished was the way the event got buried forever. "It was never mentioned again." Not by anyone—her mother, her sisters, the kids at school, her teachers. It vanished, erased from the local lore. "It was very strange that there was no mention of it... That is probably the reason I forgot to tell you about it last time." For some reason it is still a forbidden tale in Katie's hometown.

The image of Katie stalking her teacher with a knife haunts me. It brings home to me the rage that she harbors, the anger that coexists with her laughter. Both her rage and her laughter are expressed with exuberance and intensity and often seem to explode at the same moment. Katie knows the knife was not just meant for Miss Boulware. "It was a *life rage*. I could feel all the anger, all the energy drain right out of me... I felt exhausted." It was the response to all the years of accumulated abuses: "all the violation, all the humiliation, all the Jim Crow!" Katie also knows that "the prisons are filled with fifteen-year-old black girls" who have suffered the same abuses—stoically, silently—and then in a moment of electric irrationality have committed a crime that will keep them incarcerated for the rest of their lives. "One moment they're talking to their friends on the phone or dancing, doing their teenage thing... and the next moment they're killers." They are ordinary girls who have endured extraordinary pain, who finally can't take it anymore, who suddenly go out of control, do violence to the nearest victim, and who are finally themselves victimized for life. Katie knows their reality. She has suffered like them. She, too, but for the grace of God, might have lived her life locked in a prison cell.

The echoes of violation, the identification with young African-American women in prison, the recognition of the adolescent understanding of injustice, reminds Katie of November 1963, when she was in the ninth grade and John F. Kennedy was murdered. "It was a *comical* day at Carver," recalls Katie. The ninth-grade civics class listened to the news of Kennedy being shot and waited for reports from the Dallas hospital emergency room about whether the doctors, with all their best efforts and fancy technology, would be able to revive the president. "Are these white people going to be able to do this resurrection thing on Kennedy? Are they going to be able to pump the life back into him?" The Carver students' questions were laced with bitter laughter and mixed with conversation about "the horrors that occurred in the colored wing of the hospital. We knew we were not first-class citizens... Our lives were worth nothing to these white people.... In ninth grade, we were already working on organically critiquing society. We knew the country was evil and violent. None of us really mourned Kennedy's death." No one except Katie's sister Sara, who was "the *only* one who cried." Everyone else experienced the injustice, the inequalities, the white privilege of this event—even in death, Kennedy's one life was worth more than hundreds of theirs. "But my sister Sara wept. I was so embarrassed!... How could she cry?" says Katie, remembering her incredulity.

Katie characterizes the class discussion, the bitterness and attitude of deep suspicion. I ask her about this suspicion, and she replies without skipping a beat. "It means that you know danger without having to be taught.... It is what June Jordan calls 'jungle posture'... what Ntozake Shange calls 'the combat stance'... It is like when Sojourner Truth said, 'Nobody lifts me into carriages or over mud puddles, but I am a woman.' You know where the minefields are... there is wisdom... You are in touch with the ancestors... and it is from the gut, not rationally figured out. Black women have to use this all the time, of course, the creativity is still there, but we are not fools... we call it the 'epistemological privileges of the oppressed.' How do you tap that wisdom—name it, mine it, pass it on to the next generation?"

I recognize that my eyes have widened in amazement and I'm sitting with my back straight as a rod, stretching to understand this gushing avalanche of words and feelings flowing out of Katie. She seems to be saying so many things and speaking on so many levels, all at once. There is the idea of the "organic" understanding African-American youngsters possess: they sense that they are second-class citizens in an unjust society, that their lives are not counted or treasured in the same ways as white lives. There is the idea that the development of this understanding is not rational—it comes from "the gut"; it is based on experience and intuition. There is the idea that this suspicion is passed down from the ancestors who teach the next generation the subtle dangers—through act and deed— who instruct their offspring in how to walk through treacherous minefields, who show them jungle posture. There is the idea that this suspicion is healthy, necessary for survival *and* that it can coexist with creativity—that even in creativity and expression one must always be watchful, clear-headed, not "act the fool." And finally, there is the idea that African-American women have this deep, instinctive suspicion down to a science. We use it subtly, deftly, wisely. If we didn't know how to use it, we would be destroyed. Some of us have begun to give it high status by labeling it a privilege, the epistemological privilege of the oppressed.

This is vintage Katie Cannon: the vivid ninth-grade story of Kennedy's assassination, the analysis of its meaning in historical and cultural context, the use of the story as a lens for revealing broader societal patterns, philosophical insights, the easy return to the threads of the original story. "So for all those reasons, it is even more horrifying that Sara cried. I couldn't believe it!"

"The comedy" of Kennedy's death contrasts sharply with the tragedy of the assassination of Martin Luther King, Jr. "It was April 4, 1968, my freshman year," begins Katie. "Martin Luther King died. *That* was a day!" She seems to relish the chance to tell the story—to rehearse the painful details, to relive the anguish, to reexperience the power that came out of the trauma. But before she launches into a memorial of the day, she provides the context, her own developmental context. "Barber-Scotia College... freshman year... I started school as a Negro and emerged as black! I had on my dashiki. I had my Black Power fist dangling from my neck... My mother said, 'Kate, you are *ultrablack.*'... If I went home and anyone dared to slip up and say 'Colored,' I would get up on my soap box. It was like a transfusion of blackness. I was high on it. I *loved* it." Katie also began sporting an Afro to go along with the rest of her Black Power uniform. Less than a year before, in the fall of 1967, she had seen her very first Afro on a young woman at Scotia named Mildred Dobbs. The sight of this "natural" was shocking, "awesome" to Katie. All she could do was laugh. "I laughed until I was in pain... Up until that point, I was wearing my hair *fried.*"

I look at the thick halo of hair framing Katie's face and I can't imagine her hair any other way. Long after the strident Black Power rhetoric has softened and grown more complicated, long after the ultrablack exaggerations, the Afro crowns her head and seems to match the woman in her "midlife crisis." I imagine that the Afro will be with her into old age, silver gray—that it has long since moved from being a faddish, ideological statement to being a part of her cultural, personal, and aesthetic identity.

But in 1968, the "'fro" was a statement of defiance and liberation for the "only Black Panther" in the county. When the news came to Scotia that King had been killed, the campus rose up, five hundred strong, in "collective rage." "Scotia came together in one voice... We'll burn this place down!... We were ready to march on this town of Concord, North Carolina." The adults at Scotia saw the fire in their students' eyes. They heard their voices cry out in rage and terror. They knew that if they didn't do something to harness the energy and dampen the fire, the students would get themselves killed. "They knew it would be suicidal for us to go up against the white establishment." So for several days running, they gathered all the students in the chapel and "they just kept talking to us... It felt like a lock-in... It was vent and talk, vent and talk, vent and talk." But it wasn't only outrage—it was also "grief," a deep, penetrating feeling of loss. "They've killed him. Who is going to step in his place?" They listened to the Mountaintop Sermon over and over again, until they had it almost memorized word for word, until they could mimic every inflection. They were astonished again by King's premonition of his own demise *and* by his fearlessness in the face of it. "We were all overchurched. We all understood the spiritual and political meanings there."

But out of this loss, out of this grief and rage came new perspectives and new commitments. Out of this collective spirit, a new sense of community grew. And out of the "organic analysis" of this event, new insights were discovered. "We were all *furious* with the government. In our daily lives we knew what the Civil Rights movement was about… We knew that one man didn't kill King. We knew it was a conspiracy. We knew that anyone they wanted to off, they would off. *Naivete has never been our privilege.*" Now Katie's face, all the red shining through the brown, is flushed with excitement as she experiences again the adolescent discoveries. "The assassination of King gave us voice. *We had this analysis in us!*"

The analysis went even further and joined with the teachings and preachings of Dr. King from the latter years of his life. The Scotia students not only saw the injustices related to race, the black-white inequalities as they got expressed in North Carolina; they also saw the mix of racism and classism that produced the human fodder for the Vietnam War. Most of the Scotia girls were engaged to soldiers fighting in Vietnam. Each day they would listen to the long list of casualties and hope that their loved ones were not named. And every several days another one of their men would come home in a wooden box. You could hear the haunting wails of the women grieving over their lost lovers. Death consumed this tiny college as the women twisted their glass/diamond engagement rings on their fingers, hoping their men would survive to marry them; or watched their bodies swell into pregnancies begun before their men departed. Death enraged them, as well, because they knew that their men were fighting for a country that did not value them, a country where their lives did not count for much. The rage over the war, the death of their men, *and* the rage over King, the death of *The Man*, combined to create a black rage hotter than any this county had ever known. "We became empowered students. We couldn't let the dream die. We would shout, 'It's nation time!'"

Katie's anger and action outstripped that of her newly empowered peers. She became a member of the Congress of African People, the president of Scotia's Black Heritage Club (which "probably had two members"), and "thought hard about getting a gun." She consumed the new militant black literature, poetry, essays, articles, and books. She became a devotee of Malcolm X. "The black stuff was *most* important" even as she maintained her lofty place on the dean's list. While diligently accomplishing her academic work, she immersed herself in the black literature, feeling the expansion of her head *and* her heart.

But even as her "public understanding was deepening" she was experiencing a personal emptiness. By her sophomore year, she had hit a serious state of depression. Phifer had left North Carolina and gone to New York to work and live with his sister. That was part of the emptiness. But the pain also seemed to be related to the striking juxtaposition of her powerful public experience and her personal isolation. Katie's voice is thick with emotion—"My heart was breaking wide open."

She actually had the *physical* sensation of her heart being shattered, so she went to the "heart doctor" to get an electrocardiogram. She knew something was very wrong, but this white male doctor could find "nothing wrong." So he put her on valium for her "nervous condition" and on diet pills to lose weight. Katie was functioning fine in her studies, being the affable, engaged student, but privately she was withering inside. "Academically I was getting A's, but I would go to my room after class and curl up like a monkey on the bed. There was no concern from anybody because I was doing well in my classes." Cannon became dependent on her pills. They brought her some relief from the pain. She never took more than the prescribed allotment, counting them out very carefully to make sure that she didn't run out of them. "All I knew was that I had a nervous condition and I needed the pills to keep me going." One day she asked her mother to fill the doctor's prescription at the pharmacy in Kannapolis. The pharmacist asked who the prescription was for, and Corine told him it was for her daughter Katie. "You know these things are addictive," said the pharmacist with alarm in his voice. Mrs. Cannon had not known and neither had Katie. When her mother passed on the pharmacist's warning, Katie resisted the news, denied that it was a problem, and continued to take the pills. She needed them badly. They helped to blunt the anguish, and she considered her mother's admonitions intrusive.

But even with the help of the pills, Katie knew she was in trouble, and she thought that part of the trouble was related to her desperate need to get away from home—to escape the Jim Crow, to escape the closed-in family, to escape the deadening parochialism. She searched for the way out. "I decided I've got to get out of Kannapolis." While poking around the library one day, Cannon found an ad in a Presbyterian periodical, a small announcement of jobs for college interns at Ghost Ranch in Sante Fe, New Mexico. She and her friends didn't even really know where New Mexico was geographically. They kept on getting it confused with Mexico, the place where people speak Spanish. But wherever it was, it was far away from Kannapolis, and Katie immediately sent off a letter of application. When she learned several weeks later that she had been accepted as an intern, she was "ecstatic. The sun started to shine. I was going to get out!" The anticipation of her summer in Santa Fe seemed to lift her out of depression and give her hope. It was as if she could already feel her broken heart beginning to heal. In a moment of clear and adamant resolve, Katie announced to her mother, "'When I get on the plane, I won't take any more medicine'... And I never did."

Without her stash of pills and with great anticipation and excitement, Katie left for Ghost Ranch in late May of 1969. It was the first time she had ever been on a plane, and the flight was treacherous. "I had never experienced this before. We hit a lot of turbulence, and it felt to me like an amusement park ride... I had no fear. I thought it was funny." The plane got "stranded somewhere in Texas," and the passengers had to stay at the airport overnight while they waited for a new plane. There was Katie, a small-town country girl from Kannapolis, unsophisticated and untraveled, stuck in a strange airport in Texas. As she stood in the airport, wondering what her next move would be, a young white woman approached her and they struck up a conversation. Soon they discovered they were both going to the same place to be college interns at Ghost Ranch. With lightning speed, Katie, the black girl from Scotia, and Ruth Beyers, the white aristocrat from Princeton, became fast friends. "She was like an *angel*... she saved me. Ruth and I were both nineteen years old and we were *bonded*." They braved the rest of the trip together, and by the time their plane finally touched down in Albuquerque, a day late, Katie was no longer alone in facing the great Southwest.

"This was truly the land of enchantment," says Katie with a dreamy gaze. "Ghost Ranch was twenty-three thousand acres of gorgeous land." It seemed to extend for miles. "For the first time, [she] became a physical person," hiking, climbing, feeling her body growing stronger. "I was seeing orchids growing wild, seeing eagles soaring in the sky." It was a comforting, magical place. The peacefulness seemed to fill her soul. It is a tranquility that feels connected with the land, the wide open sky, and makes Katie know that Ghost Ranch is where she wants her "ashes to be buried" when she dies. "The ranch is what gave me hope. I knew that I would be able to get out of Kannapolis. *It opened up the horizon and pushed it toward the sun.*"

In addition, the ranch brought exotic adventures for Katie. This was the first time in her life that she had known "real white people who were human beings," with whom she could "open up." And she discovered that these white folks—at least the ones at Ghost Ranch—were very strange creatures. "They were involved in a whole lot of touchy, feely stuff—encounter groups, back rubs, skinny dipping. I thought white folks were *weird!*" As Katie observed these friendly strangers, she also became the target of their intrigue and naivete. "These white folks had never met a black person before, and they had lots of stereotypes." For two weeks they begged Katie to sing a Negro spiritual—Katie who "can't carry a tune to save myself." And for two weeks she "let them beg," making them wait, whetting their appetites. Finally, with much fanfare, she sang them a spiritual. "Then they begged me to stop." Katie is holding her belly and laughing at the memory of their intense anticipation, and the disappointed looks on their faces when they heard her monotone squawking. All summer, Katie and her white friends were experiencing, observing, and experimenting with one another. "We were a living laboratory. It was strange and liberating!"

It also felt good for Katie to be in a place where the struggle between blacks and whites was not the central drama. In New Mexico, the conflicts and tensions were primarily among the Anglos, the Mexicans, and the Indians. For a moment, Katie could feel free from the harsh victimization. She could stand on the sidelines and observe someone else's battle for survival and dignity. "I was not the enemy. In New Mexico, I was not the butt of the hatred... The pressure cooker of reality was not there... For a moment, I could be an honorary white person, but at the same time I felt solidarity with the Mexican and Indian people." Katie began to feel complex changes within her as she experienced these new group dynamics—mixing it up with her "weird" and wonderful white friends, feeling their affection and their strangeness; not having to use all of her energies fighting Jim Crow and defending herself from the harsh assaults of racism; *and* having the new experience of identification and solidarity with other "people of color." When Katie returned home after this summer of *Hope, Horizon*, and *Solidarity*, she "went back to Scotia as the only black hippie!"

Swimming in Deep Water

Katie Cannon arrives with photographs and notes in her hand. She has gathered the photos from various albums at home. It is surprising to see the *real* faces of Corine, Esau, Sara, Doris. Over the months I have constructed my own images of them, which do not match their photographs. It is surprising to see Katie as a wisp of a girl. At four she is brown-skinned with big beautiful eyes, plump cheeks, skinny limbs. Her short hair is tied up neatly with a bow. A high school senior photo shows a fine-boned, slender young woman with smooth straightened hair and lively eyes and smile. At twenty-seven years old, in the minister's garb of a black suit and white collar, she is standing up and preaching, gesturing with her hands, a serious and intense look on her face, underneath an Afro halo of hair. A gorgeous picture, taken years later, shows Katie in Nigeria at a church conference. Her head wrapped regally in African cloth, she wears a long printed cloth skirt and looks gently imperious.

I look at these growing-up pictures, match them to the stories I have heard, and contrast them with the person sitting before me. Today Katie is wearing an African Kente cloth shirt, which is draped gracefully over her large frame. She is stouter than she looks in any of the photographs, her face smooth and unlined. Her cheeks are still round, and her eyes have the same intelligence and luminosity. Those eyes—which she learned to hate as a child because everyone saw them as "big and bulging"— are the most striking part of her face. They seem to pull you in as they look deeply into yours. They seem to miss nothing. I wonder as I gaze at the photographs whether Katie has revised her view of her eyes; whether she is now seeing them as the rest of us see them—as beautiful.

Then a surprising photograph of Phifer emerges among the pile of "family members." Katie digs it out and shows it to me proudly.

"Here is Phifer. *Got* to see him!" It is his senior photo from high school, and he is all dressed up in a coat and tie. His skin is dark, his lips very full, his nose broad, and his eyes are looking upward, almost crossed. He seems uncomfortable, maybe shy about looking directly at the camera, and Katie comments, "Grandma Rosa said, 'What in the world is wrong with that boy's eyes?'" We laugh. I am aware of Katie's deep connection to, and affection for, this man. As we look at his eighteen-year-old image, it is almost as if no time has passed and she is proudly displaying a picture of her sweetheart. We are two giggling adolescent girls.

Along with the photographs, Katie is clutching some notes, ruminations and stories that she has gathered since our last interview ten days ago. "It's been a *very* long time and I've had a lot of time to think. I was hit by a bolt of lightning," she says dramatically before launching into her agenda. I feel pleased by the way she works between our sessions; by the responsibility she takes for "shaping the discourse"; by her obvious engagement in this project. The experience feels symmetric, dynamic, like a real dialogue. We are cocreators of this narrative, and Katie seizes the moment to direct and shape the conversation.

Now she is ready to talk about her teaching. She has now given me enough of the history and experiences of her life to make a focus on her teaching meaningful, and to explain its riveting centrality in her life. I can begin to understand why there is nothing more important to her. She calls it simply "the fruit of my labor." It is the inevitable conclusion of her life of struggle, learning, inquiry, and action.

She wants to begin by drawing the connections between her teaching and her early life experiences, and she takes me back to "the mourning and grief" surrounding Martin Luther King's death. "If you've never lived Jim Crow, there's no way you can understand the enormity of the loss, the deep sadness." The Cannon family— along with Grandma Rosa and Aunt Emma (sister to Grandma Cora, Esau's mother)—had been sitting in their den watching Dr. King give his "I Have a Dream" speech at the big march on Washington. They were all silent, riveted to the television screen as the sermon rose to its climax, "Free at last. Free at last. Great God Almighty we're free at last!" At the sound of these words Aunt Emma rose up out of her seat, spread her arms toward the heavens, and exclaimed reverently, *"Children, you are free!"* Katie felt the seriousness, the magnitude, the depth of Aunt Emma's pronouncement. "It was a hot August day... A chill went right through me. Here was Aunt Emma announcing that we were free... we were in a spirit place." The "feeling of freedom" was "real and embodied in that room" on that sweltering summer day. "It was the moment when the radicality of my own energy came into being."

Then the images shift again as Katie's voice continues in one steady stream of words, which feel to me like the essence of "free association," or perhaps "freedom to associate, to narrate." In this next scene Katie was seven or eight years old and the family was in front of the television watching the evening news of the desegregation of Central High in Little Rock, Arkansas. The scene was threatening, volatile—the white crowd screaming racist assaults, the police dogs snarling, the hoses gushing, the beer cans being hurled, the stoic, dignified Negro students marching. Katie looked on in horror, feeling her whole body shaking with fear. "I couldn't stand the abuse... the spitting from the crowds." Right then and there Katie made her mother promise that she would never send her over to the white school as a sacrificial lamb. "Please, please don't punish me for being smart," she pleaded. To Katie this was slaughter, the worst kind of terror for a child. How could black parents and teachers, how could responsible adults make their children so vulnerable? How could they willingly send their offspring off to be slaughtered? "It's like James Baldwin said, 'Some day black adults will have to reckon with sending their kids to the gestapo.'"

Another Jim Crow image takes over as Katie recalls how her family used to take water to the black chain gangs working on the roads in the brutal summer heat. "North Carolina always had the best roads and highways because they would just send out the black prisoners to repair them and keep them up." As the black men spread the gravel and smoothed the tar, backs bent over, feet scorched, bodies sweating, the white guards would be standing on their trucks with rifles in their hands ready to shoot. "Our job was to carry water out to the *men*," says Katie, knowing that the prisoners were always called "boys." "They were our family," she continues with passion in her voice. "We were not afraid. They were one of us." So throughout the hot day, the Cannon children would carry the buckets out to the men on the chain gang—feeling concerned, feeling identified, feeling like family with them. "It's like Zora Neale Hurston says, 'I've always been connected to the Negro farthest down.'" Katie pauses for a moment and shakes her head. "This is why I'm so committed to conscientization." (This is a Katie Cannon word, repeated like a litany throughout this interview. After hearing it several times, I begin to get a feel for its meaning. "Conscientization" seems to refer to the process of making values and experience that are most often repressed or hidden, conscious and visible to oneself and others. It has to do with courageously uncovering the pain, making it articulate, reckoning with it, and entering it into the public/private discourse. It is an uncomfortable, demanding process, requiring both thought and action.)

The final wrenching Jim Crow image leads directly into Katie's experience as a teacher. "It was the summer of 1967, the War on Poverty." Katie was seventeen years old and had been hired as an assistant teacher for the Head Start program. "My family had started getting the surplus food—big cans of peanut butter, flour, cornmeal, rice... something called 'wonder meat' because you wondered what it was. For the first time, I understood that we were poor. Our whole county was poor... Everybody was struggling, either working in the mill or as a domestic... Then there were twenty or so black teachers who did dignified work." When Katie was hired for the summer program of Head Start, she was the youngest black person on the staff and was the assistant for a white teacher. But the fact that she was black meant that the children and their parents saw her as *the* teacher, as responsible and accountable to the community.

Part of Katie's job was driving the children to and from school. Early in the morning she would begin her rounds in the Cannons' '64 Chevy Impala (Katie never forgets the year, style, or make of a car) collecting the black five-year-olds across the county. She loved gathering the kids, talking and joking with them, watching them play with one another. "You see, I was the teacher. I was accessible to them. I belonged to them." Her "favorite kid" was a little boy named Donnary Butler, a cute child with reddish skin, pale eyes, and light sandy hair. One day she went to fetch him for school and was told that he had drowned the day before in a nearby lake. "Some white boys called him into the lake... He couldn't swim, they knew it, and they let him drown... They thought it was fun. Nobody did a thing because black people knew that nothing would be done... It was white water only... You don't go near the water because white people will get upset. They don't want you in their pool. They don't want you fishing in their ponds. They don't want you swimming in their lakes... You just stay away from their water." So when Donnary, "cute as a button," drowned at age five, his death was quietly, painfully absorbed by the community. No one did a thing.

But Katie held onto the pain, held onto the tragedy and the symbolism. She has told this story to black audiences, to colleagues, and students, as a lesson about treachery, danger, and survival. She shakes her index finger at the rapt audience as she delivers her punch line: "Don't ever let anyone call you into the lake in water deeper than you can swim." She says to black women trying to learn the lessons of survival in a white male-dominated institution: "You can't let the white men dictate the conversation. You can't let them tell you the subject matter. You can't let them call you to swim in deep water... You take it where you can swim... if you don't, you'll be like Donnary, and they'll just laugh at you as you fight for your life." She shakes her head, remembering the death that taught her the lesson she now teaches to others. "Even at five, black children have to know good from evil." Her voice is now raging—"Even at five, Donnary should have known better."

These Jim Crow images haunted Katie's late adolescence. Over time, they accumulated and crowded into her psyche, causing her to become a raging, seething militant. By her second year of college, she had entered what her mother called her "ultrablack stage." "My focus was on the eradication of racism." She felt like screaming (and she sometimes did), "Get the fuck out of my face!... This is wrong... this is death dealing." The rage took so much energy. It was all-consuming. It turned back on itself. There was never any peace living with the ghosts of Jim Crow. By her mid- to late twenties, Katie began to recognize the costs of this anger, the debilitating effects of the fury. She thought that there must be another way to channel her energy so that it could be used more productively and so that it would not get turned back on her "insides." "This had been killing me... my channels were getting clogged in rage and fury. How many times do you have to say 'My face is on fire,' before someone listens?"

The question hangs in the silence as Cannon seems to turn her face in a new direction and examine the choices. "First of all," she says with hope in her voice, "I had to cut back on my expectations." She couldn't expect, or even hope for, the "eradication of racism." She had to work for the slow dismantling of its pathological origins. She couldn't expect revolution; she had to participate in evolution. "Do you know Nikki Giovanni's poem 'Like a Ripple on a Pond?'" she asks. "Truth is like a pebble in a pond." It is the same with the fight for justice. "If everyone would just take a pebble-size action every day of their lives, there would be ripples that spread out from them. If people try to scale mountains and leap tall buildings in a single bound, nothing gets done. People feel overwhelmed."

So "even as a graduate student" Katie began to recognize the need to find a more "creative way to confront the rage." She did not deny the rage or suppress the stories so central to her identity, but she did decide to use the rage productively. She decided to light small fires of insight in people's minds rather than feel tempted to torch buildings. She decided that "everyone was not mean-spirited"; that there were some white people of goodwill who could gradually learn to recognize their racism and its pernicious effects. "You see, part of the privilege of being white is that they don't have to see racism." She decided that she couldn't hope to be one hundred percent effective in teaching people about the origin and ravages of oppression. So she modulated her goal to make it more comfortable and more attainable. "If in every course I teach, *one* person will make a lifetime commitment to be a doer of justice, that's all I ask for."

Katie's "reduced expectations" sound bold and courageous to me. They do not sound like discarded remnants of a more vital life. Her voice rings with energy and determination still. The shift I hear is not in her level of energy or commitment to the struggle for justice; if anything, she has grown stronger in that determination. Rather the shift is one of strategy and perspective. It is also one of self-preservation. In fighting for justice she is not consumed by rage; she focuses and channels it outward. No longer shooting for the moon, she keeps her feet planted firmly on the ground. Instead of trying to beat the racism out of "bad people" (yelling "Stop it right now—shut up. Get the fuck out of my face!"), she seeks "a less threatening way, a creative way to help people become 'conscientized' about what they don't know and *do something about it*." Such a strategy requires vigilance, patience, dialogue, criticism, reflection, and action. It is a gently militant process that both recognizes the evil and searches for the good. It is work that is both public and private, both political and personal. When Katie says, "Teaching is my life," she means that all of her images, stories, experiences; all of her mind, soul, heart, and sexuality; all of her pain and rage; all of her struggle and reconciliation are woven into it. "Teaching is the fruit of my labor," she repeats with certainty.

Corine Cannon wonders why her daughter uses all of that passion, intelligence, and energy in the service of *white* people. She pleads with Katie to come "home" to the black community where she belongs, where she is needed, where she would be appreciated. Mrs. Cannon says bluntly, "We did not ordain you to teach white people." Katie has responded to her mother's begging, "Ma, give me five years. I've got to be at a place with resources, with libraries, with time to do my writing... a place where I can work on designing ways of thinking." Katie has taken her five years in the rarified environment of the Episcopal Divinity School (EDS), and now three more. "It has been eight years, and my mother is still demanding that I come home."

When she thinks of working in a black school, she understands the difficult ties and barriers she would inevitably face. She knows that the struggling historically black institutions with meager resources would not allow her the space and freedom she enjoys at EDS. She would be stifled in her teaching and thinking by the parochialisms and the strident need of faculty to "always prove themselves worthy." In the "white liberal space [of EDS] survival is not the daily fare." The abundance allows for thinking, risk-taking, reflection, and criticism. "I can *demand* abstraction," says Katie in her inimitable style. At EDS, a place she labels "a feminist environment," there is even "abundance for white women" that permits them to be "welcoming of our [African-American women's] reality."

In some sense, the abundance of this privileged white feminist environment allows Katie to devote herself fully to teaching, to "the center of my reality." In this place, she can be demanding, serious, and provocative. She says matter-of-factly, "I am the most demanding teacher in all of the Boston theological institutions—I'm after *transformation!*... I'm here for *conversion*. I teach at a very high pitch. I say to my students, 'The life you save may be your own.'"

Her demands were a tricky issue before she became tenured two years ago. As an assistant professor without tenure she had to be careful not to turn off the white students who might then turn on her. She says clearly, "Black women professors who flunk white students before they get tenure, do not get tenure." So before the tenure decision, her teaching was filled with a difficult tension, and her work was sometimes compromised by the competing goals of teaching as transformation and promotion into full membership in the institution. She could be demanding, but not too demanding. She could be improvisational, but not too bold in the risks she dared take. She could be critical of students, but not as penetrating in her criticism as she thought her teaching required. She couldn't engage fully in the pedagogy of "conversion." Now that she has tenure, a lot (but not all) of the constraints and inhibitions have been lifted. She need not be cautious or restrained in her demands. Her teaching has reached its "highest pitch." She can take full advantage of the white liberal abundance.

Close to Foreclosure

For the first time, Katie Cannon looks washed out, weary, distracted. She is wearing a deep purple Nigerian tunic, but her brown skin has a gray cast and her large eyes do not have their usual intensity. She has just returned from North Carolina, a few hours before, having taken a nonstop flight from Charlotte. I think to myself that she must be tired from her early-morning journey, but I don't understand her distraction and her empty eyes. She sits down, groans, moans, "I have nothing to say, Sara, nothing." Having heard this before, I remain optimistic and ask, "Haven't you just come back from the Cannon family reunion?" "Yes," she says, still in a low-spirited voice, "and I saw Phifer... I was with him yesterday from one to five in the afternoon. I was at the reunion for the picnic on Saturday, the church service on Sunday... then I called Phifer on Sunday and made the date to see him on Monday, the day before I left—I didn't want to have any time left... I planned to connect with Phifer, then leave the next morning."

As if to appease my appetite for news of the Cannon family reunion, Katie relates the experience briefly but lets me know that it was not "a big deal." "Talking with Phifer was much more important than the family reunion." The family gatherings always make Katie feel different and lonely. She is in the midst of all of these familiar blood relatives, feeling like an exotic stranger. Most of her "estrangement" she thinks derives from the minister "persona" they cast her in. "Once they introduce me as a minister, the only people who will talk to me are the children and the seniors... and it's too lonely," she complains. "A *woman* minister is such an enigma to them"—odd and maybe threatening. She contrasts this image of Katie as different and divergent with the family's comfortable, familiar image of her youngest brother, also a minister. Her brother arrives at the reunion looking large, prosperous, and correct in his minister's garb. Behind him trail his three children. His wife is at his side. He is gregarious, reaching out with handshakes and greetings to all the appreciative relatives. Katie does a perfect imitation of the southern black preacher "in his element," working the crowd, leaving blessings in his wake. She laughs, "And he's only twenty-seven!" When Katie arrives—a woman, unmarried, no children, an academic, from the white North—the extended family is made uncomfortable. "They stop their conversations in the middle… When they curse, they apologize." They put her up "on a pedestal. …They act as if I've just flown in from Jupiter or Saturn."

After the picnic on Saturday afternoon, the whole clan had gone to the Sunday morning service at the AME Zion Church, "filling up three-quarters of the place" with family members. Katie had delivered the benediction from her "pedestal," comfortable for the moment with her brief ministerial duty. The church service was followed by a big Sunday midday dinner at Katie's parents' home. Corine had cooked all the festive dishes—sweet potatoes, greens, rice and beans, ham, chicken, potato salad—and the huge family crowded around. The rising decibels of talk, banter, and laughter were disorienting to Katie who sat in the crammed space feeling the people pressing in on her and the space growing smaller. "There was too much chaos… too crowded… too much *devastation*." Under these claustrophobic circumstances Katie didn't even try to eat her mother's bountiful food. It would have been impossible to digest. "I wasn't even hungry until the next day." Instead she spent her time "feeding the children," making sure their plates were full and even spoon-feeding the little ones who needed extra encouragement. The chaos of her parents' home felt so dramatically different from the orderly home she has created in Cambridge, where "when you lay something down you can find it in the same place the next day." Now in her mother's house, Katie reexperiences the disorientation, claustrophobia, and exclusion of her childhood. She sits in the midst of the wall-to-wall people and yearns for solitude. "I'm used to *quiet*," Katie says with reverence. "I need peace and space."

Not only does Katie ache for the comforts of her orderly life when she returns to North Carolina, she also senses the irony of feeling so alone in the crowded family living room in Kannapolis. Corine, Katie's mother, adds to these feelings by her intrusive questions. This time she was rehearsing an old, tired tune: When was Katie planning on getting married? She was complaining that Katie had been unsuccessful in finding a husband because she was setting her sights too high, "looking too high up." Incredulous, Katie reports, "She was saying that she wanted me to look in *prisons!* That's an insult." But this time Katie had decided not to be provoked by her mother's invasiveness. Her response was somewhere between serious and frivolous. "'I'm an official old maid, Mom... I'm forty-one.' ...For the first time I could laugh it off."

After the lonely chaos of the family reunion, it was exciting to anticipate her visit with Phifer. "I knew I could be *real* with Phifer... no professional persona." Phifer had received her card a couple of months ago telling him that she was involved in working on this book project and saying that she hoped to talk to him about it when she came home to Kannapolis for the family reunion. She had signed her card "As always, Katie." Phifer's twelve-year-old daughter, Tiffany, had picked up the card, read the closing, and shown it to her mother. Phifer's wife had gotten "very threatened by the 'as always' part" and had confronted her husband—"Does that woman still love you?" So Katie's brief note to her old boyfriend had caused ripples in his household. Phifer assured his wife and daughter that his romance with Katie was in the distant past; that there was nothing, absolutely nothing, to worry about. Then he waited for Katie's return to North Carolina with great anticipation.

When Katie called him on Sunday evening after the family reunion, his voice sounded familiar and wonderful. Just hearing him brought back a flood of memories and feelings. She was surprised by how deeply she still cared for Phifer; how immediately they were able to reconnect. The last time she had seen Phifer was in 1987, and here they were four years later "teasing, joking, talking, and flirting" on the telephone. Phifer wanted to know what Katie wanted from him; how she was thinking of the anticipated encounter. "He asked me on the phone whether he should bring a condom," says Katie incredulously. "'No, no, no. I want to go some place and *talk*,'" responded Katie, still feeling the pleasure of his sexual interest but certain that she "really only wanted to talk... to look into his eyes."

They decided to meet for lunch at a local restaurant. When they sat down, Phifer felt uncomfortable, complaining about the air-conditioning not working properly. So they drove to another place, Denny's Restaurant, and found themselves sitting by two women from Katie's church. Katie's face looks panicked as she describes the shock of being seated "right next to these neighbors, these kinfolk, these people I've known since I was a child." Once the church ladies had seen her, it was too awkward and embarrassing to leave. So she introduced them to Phifer, trying to keep her voice even and calm, but feeling inside like an adolescent caught in the act of doing something illicit by her stern elders.

At first, Katie felt the inhibitions of the church women who, she was sure, were straining to hear every word of her conversation with Phifer. Then she became so engrossed in talking with Phifer that the neighbors slowly disappeared from her peripheral vision, and after a while they got up and left. Katie was sure that news of her private reunion with Phifer would soon become public in Kannapolis. The women would waste no time putting it on the grapevine. The lunch with Phifer stretched to four hours; it was a wonderful conversation that moved from being frivolous and teasing to serious and nostalgic. They had shared so much history, and although their lives had taken radically different paths, they still felt a primal and deep connection.

Katie gazed across the table at the only man she had ever loved and thought he looked beautiful. Age had brought out the traces of Indian ancestry in his face. "He looked very fit, just terrific!" and Katie kept telling him so. She also looked at him and remembered how deeply their adolescent lives had been entwined, and how miserable she had been when her parents prohibited her from seeing Phifer. She had loved him; she had begged her parents to let her see him. When they had denied her permission, for the first time in her life, Katie had defied them and snuck off to see her boyfriend. But eventually she had bowed under the pressure from her parents; Phifer was pulled into another woman's orbit, and Katie's relationship with him ended quietly and brutally. "My heart had been ripped out and torn off," says Katie, reliving the almost physical sensation of an old festering wound. Now, at forty-one years old, she recognizes how deeply pained she was by the loss of Phifer, and how she never let herself mourn the loss. "I never really grieved the end of the relationship... I hit the ground running. I've been on an accelerated course, so in a hurry, so ambitious, that there has been no time to grieve... but now in this midlife crisis I'm slowing down, and that lets me think about all of this... and I've wept lots of tears, heavy tears."

Katie's "slowing down" is a manifestation of her midlife crisis. She has paused long enough to hear her interior pain. "We talked about abundance last time," she recalls. "I now have abundance— space, time, resources—and I've been thinking about how I've been using this abundance lately." The afternoon with Phifer—the deep love still there between them, the happy companionship, the frivolous flirtation, the serious talk, the grieving over loss—was a sign of Katie's newly discovered abundance, and the personal courage that flows from it. The visit with Phifer reminds her of the other interior shifts brought on by this abundance. Katie begins to explore these emerging signs of change and growth.

"I'm trying very hard to reconnect to my black self. For fourteen years *white folks have been dead on my eyeball*... I have been spending my energy facing the white world. My colleague James Cone [a prominent black theologian at Union Theological Seminary and a mentor of Katie's] says that you must go home five times a year to stay connected. In the past, I haven't been able to go home... too much cognitive dissonance... I'd get sick. But now I'm feeling the need to learn how to journey home.

"I often ask myself," Katie continues reflectively, "what has been the price of my not going home and why is it so hard?... You know, part of going home is learning to accept my poverty, which I still feel deeply ashamed about. Another part of going home is learning how to tolerate the noise and the chaos—the people slamming the screen door and going in and out, the television constantly on. I'm used to quiet. When I go home, I always take a small pad and I sit up in the kitchen doodling. Nothing else to do. I remember growing up in my house you could never find the comb when you needed to do your hair. The brush was *always* lost, forget it!"

As Katie continues these rich ruminations, her tone becomes more mellow. "I went through a stage where I swore I wouldn't love my family until they got it right. I was hypercritical of all of them. I'd go home for a visit, plan to stay a week, and leave without notice after a couple of days... I specialized in *disappearing.* I'd figure it just meant one less mouth to feed. It's taken me a long time to know that I mattered. It's also taken me a long time to value what they've given me: my sense of humor, my sense of direction (I can drive anywhere and not get lost), and my storytelling. That's all from them."

Eventually Katie is drawn back to her reunion with Phifer. Some of the sadness that I saw as she arrived for our meeting seems to return to her face. "When I got together with Phifer, he asked me whether I wanted to have babies. I thought I'd made peace with this... but I guess I haven't fully. You know my mother had her last child when she was forty-two... she went through menopause at fifty. So the biological clock is still ticking. But you know, I've never wanted to have any other child but *his*. If Phifer and I had had a baby, I kept thinking, we would be sitting there with a twenty-one-year-old child... He and I could have had such a pretty baby. So I sit and ask myself whether I am satisfied with the alternatives I've chosen... the loss I've experienced."

Midlife, and its abundance, has unearthed all of these old questions for Katie. It is a time of reckoning with loss, reconnecting with ancestors, "scraping the whiteness off of her eyeballs," honoring the goodness in her imperfect family, getting in touch with feelings, slowing down. It is also a time of making "the translation" from her childhood home (poor, black, rural, chaotic) to her adult nest (abundant, predominantly white, urban, serene). "I come from a place," explains Katie, "where when people talk about *field work* they literally mean field work—work in the fields—not ethnographic research. I come from a place where there ain't but one kind of doctor, the person who takes care of you when you are sick.... I now live in a place where the assumption is that I know all about high culture—that I'm sophisticated about art, music, and food."

Katie refers to Carter Woodson's observation that there is a high rate of mental illness among black intellectuals, and she reasons that our craziness comes from trying to bring together such disparate worlds of childhood and adulthood. For Katie, the translation between worlds is negotiated in her Jungian therapy where she has begun to learn how to "catch the dreams and interpret them. Before midlife, I had no time to *feel*. I was only focused on *thinking*, on logic, on analysis, on rationality... but therapy has given me the space and the context to feel. You know my mother always says, 'Katie, if you had enough Jesus in you, you wouldn't need therapy,'... but therapy is essential for my survival. My therapy is *life giving*... it is absolutely consistent with my revolutionary stance... It is the translation of my worlds. Someone has to keep me in touch with my ancestors!"

The hard work of translation can sometimes become unbearable for Katie; the contrasts between her roots and her present can begin to feel too stark and divergent. She knows "you can never go home again." She knows that "once you've eaten from the tree of knowledge, you can't say you haven't eaten." She even knows there is "some truth to the statement that innocence is bliss." But it is painful to live a life so demanding in its dependence upon her facility and willingness to translate. She yearns for the "natural" company of more black folk for whom translation would be unnecessary. "I want pockets of my life where I'm not translating—where I'm just Katie... where I don't have to interpret... where I can just grunt, moan, cry, laugh loud... just BE, no interpretation."

The crisis part of her midlife grew out of the "loneliness" and pain of "endless and constant" translation and out of the temptation to give up and give in to the anguish. Katie's words reflect near-catastrophe, vulnerability, and opportunity. "My midlife crisis is scratching these cataracts off my eyeballs... getting the white man off my eyeballs. I was so close to foreclosure. I almost lost ME, almost lost my soul, and it scared the shit out of me."

Beyond Kannapolis

Katie Cannon is radiant and rested after an August of "real vacation." She is almost gleeful as she reports on her "amazing," "unbelievable" visit home to her parents in Kannapolis. It was so different from anything she had ever experienced. First of all, Katie stayed for a record number of days. "*Eleven* days, Sara, that is an *eternity*. I usually stay a couple of days and then get into my disappearing act and I'm out of there." Second, she stayed in her parents' home. "Usually, because all my siblings are married with kids, they get to stay in the house, and my mom tells me there is no room for me so I'll have to go to a hotel. Why should I come all the way to North Carolina to stay in a hotel?... This time, they gave me their bedroom. I stayed in my *parents' bedroom!*" Third, Katie's mother fed her. "Usually my mother is all busy with her church work, her Avon stuff... she's racing all over the place, and we *never* sit down for a meal. At most, we have a quick breakfast. This time, she was all solicitous and attentive. 'What would you like for lunch? Have you had enough to eat?'" Fourth, her mother seemed so much more relaxed, peaceful, and gentle. "Usually, she's on my case, in my face. This time my mom seemed so easy. Just as I was leaving—I was already in my car with my seat belt buckled, about to shove in my tape in the tape deck—she leaned in the window and asked me to pray for her. I asked her to pray for me, too... But I didn't have the nerve to ask her *why* she'd asked me to send up prayers for her. No, I just couldn't ask. I just got shivers all through me and roared off down Route 85." Cannon spreads her arms wide, leans back, and says again for emphasis, "It was *amazing*, Sara. I tell you, they treated me like the prodigal daughter."

Katie wonders out loud about the motivations behind this extraordinary transformation, and at first refuses to look at it closely. "I don't know... Maybe my mother and I are both about to die... or she is, or I am. Something is on the horizon." Then she remembers a dream she had had just before returning to Kannapolis. In the dream she is hearing or saying, "Katie, if you continue to lie to them, you will die." It was a potent, earth-shaking dream that haunted her for days, a dramatic warning. On the road to North Carolina she had decided "to tell the truth." She would answer any question they put to her honestly. She wouldn't "duck and dodge and hide." (Katie is in the chair making punching and ducking moves "like Muhammad Ali.") With that resolve, she was apprehensive, but clear and ready when she entered her parents' home. "Amazingly, they left me alone. They didn't ask me all these questions. They just *accepted* me. I kept on thinking to myself, Does the truth show on me so clearly? Do I just *look* like truth? No words passed between us about this."

The trip to her parents' home was strikingly different from all of Katie's earlier family encounters. It was warm, relaxed, nurturant, welcoming, and honest. She was enveloped, embraced, trusted, and loved. She is still beaming with the pleasure and newness of this experience. She is still incredulous about the dramatic changes. But her amazement seems mixed with a hint of caution and apprehension. "Is this a *real* change? Can I trust them to be this way when I return next time? Can I continue to tell the truth with them?"

Another summertime pleasure was seeing so much of her nieces and nephews. When she was in Kannapolis, she loved hanging out with the youngsters, especially ten-year-old Etta, who has always had a special place in her heart. Etta lives with her family in Atlanta, and Katie had picked her up there, along with another girl cousin, and driven them up to Kannapolis. She enjoys the playfulness of, *and* the responsibility for, these family children. Earlier in the summer, Etta had gone to camp for the first time (a treat that her Aunt Katie had paid for) and she had learned to swim. Katie's voice is filled with pride—"She is the first person in our family to learn how to swim. It is so exciting!... She loved camp, and now she has that to look forward to every summer. No matter how hard her life is during the year, she can anticipate camp in the summer... and *swimming!*"

I announce that this is our penultimate session, and Katie nods her head resignedly. There are a few clear gaps in Katie's chronicle, and I mention them. I ask her large, embracing questions as a means of getting into unexplored territory. Katie smiles, as though wanting to be caught up in the questions and to flee from them at the same time. There is a moment of quiet as she makes a quick decision about which part of her life story she wants to pursue, and then the words flow rapid-fire.

The place is the Johnson C. Smith Seminary of the Interdenominational Theological Center (ITC) in Atlanta, Georgia, where Katie went to study in the fall of 1971. But before she can even approach this part of her story, she needs "to back way up" to her senior year at Barber-Scotia and her Africa experience. In the fall of her senior year, Katie won the student election for Miss Barber-Scotia. She relates the happenings quickly, breathlessly. "I went to New York to get my gown for the ceremonies and returned immediately for the coronation ball... We called it, 'Young, Gifted and Black.'" Katie was statuesque and regal ("I was large and built, size sixteen, with big breasts and a big ass") in her Africa-inspired coronation gown, the most admired, respected, and loved student at her college; she was known for her mind and her heart, her politics and her humor, her serious commitment, and her fun-loving irreverence.

After the coronation, Katie settled into the fall semester of taking methods courses in teaching in preparation for the spring, when she would be doing her student teaching. Katie had not planned to become a teacher despite the fact that she had been diligently and enthusiastically practicing the role since she was a tiny girl. All of the women in her family—that is, the ones who had gone on to school—had become teachers, and everyone expected the same of Katie. But Katie's eighteen-year-old rebellious spirit had resisted the teacher role and fought against her mother's insistence that she become a teacher. Again, her mother had threatened her with the familiar ultimatum: "You either become a teacher or you come home to work in the mill." Katie struggled against the maternal pressure by changing her major every couple of months. "I was *everywhere*, all over the map." By the time she finally had to declare her major, she had such a chaotic, unfocused set of courses that the only choice that she was really eligible for was elementary education. The struggle and echoes had led her right back home. All that flailing around had brought her to the inevitable "natural" career.

After the fall methods courses (which were merely the superficial culmination of the training that she had pursued all of her growing-up life), Katie was on her way to Rochester, New York, for her senior student teaching. "Why all the way to Rochester?" I ask. Katie's response is brisk and incisive: "This was a student teaching program for young African-American women from the South whom they thought needed exposure to sophisticated northern teaching and schooling. *Actually* they were importing us for the black men who were training at Kodak, who needed dates and wives. No one *said* that was why we were there, but everyone *knew* that was the case."

Whether Katie was there to learn to teach or to be found by an eligible black male, her time in Rochester was wonderful. Her memories all center on the host family with whom she lived from January through May. It was a family life light years away from the one she had known. "It was the first time I was actually living in white people's homes. At Ghost Ranch I had been in a community of white folks, but here I was *living* with them. The father was an executive at Kodak. The mother was a full-time homemaker— the very first time I ever saw that. They had four children who were all healthy and nice. They had an automatic dishwasher. I had never seen a family that would go shopping once a week and pay a hundred dollars for a shopping cart full of groceries... My family would just go to the store for a loaf of Wonder Bread or a dozen eggs... They had dinner every night together around their dining room table, well-balanced meals, and conversations that were always stimulating and engaging." Katie goes on and on about the wonder and surprise of this privileged, educated northern white family life and says finally with frank admiration, "It was a *wonderful* experience... They were like a TV family, but they had a *consciousness*. They were good people."

The summer before her senior year in college, when Katie was in New York City working with the youth program of the Presbyterian Church, she had met James Robinson, a black man, a Presbyterian minister, and the founder and director of Operation Crossroads Africa. Crossroads, a work-study program for college students who want to travel and learn about Africa, was looking for more black participants, and James Robinson urged her to apply. Like so many people meeting twenty-year-old Katie, Robinson had been impressed with her keen intelligence, her exuberance, her energy, and her deep commitment to the Pan-African struggle. He knew right away that she would absorb a lot in Africa; that she would take in so much more than most young people of her age; that it would be a transformative experience for her. Katie was "blown away" by the idea of Africa. ("I couldn't believe I had made it as far as New York City, much less Africa!") But she took the leap of faith, applied to the program, and was accepted.

When she got the letter of acceptance, Katie could hardly contain her excitement. She was still shrieking when she picked up the telephone to tell her mother the great news. Then she couldn't believe the words she heard her mother say. "Mom said I couldn't go because Sara was getting married in June." She froze. She panicked. All she could think to do was call Ms. Porcher, her mentor at Barber-Scotia. "Ms. Porcher was the person who had given me all my clothes—hand-me-downs—when I was going off to Rochester and had no clothes to wear, nothing to pack in my suitcase. She had *saved* my life." And Ms. Porcher came through with flying colors. She said Katie *had* to go to Africa. She insisted that this was an important and critical experience for her. She declared, "You *must* go, absolutely."

But now with Ms. P.'s full support and encouragement she faced the next huge hurdle. How could she pay for the trip? The travel alone cost twelve hundred dollars, and Katie didn't have a penny to her name. Ms. Porcher reminded her of all the contacts she had made in New York City the summer before; all the people who had "genuinely and authentically" offered to help her in any way they could. All she had to do was ask. So without hesitation or embarrassment, Katie wrote a heartfelt letter to one of the people she had gotten to know the summer before ("a rich white man who lived in Larchmont, New York, and had thick carpets on his floor, the thickest I'd ever seen") asking him for his help. And without hesitation, he wrote her back and enclosed a check for twelve hundred dollars.

Almost as soon as she had received the check from her generous benefactor in New York, Cannon got another mailing from Crossroads with a list of all the supplies that she would need for her Africa trip. The twelve hundred dollars she already had was enough to pay for her travel. Now she needed to come up with more money to cover the cost of all the items on the list. She was momentarily discouraged by the unexpected challenge of finding more funds. She had never dreamed of spending so much money in such a short time. She had never imagined that the trip would be so costly and extravagant. But by now nothing could stop her. This time she wrote to Jim Hall, the director of Ghost Ranch in Santa Fe, asking him whether he knew of some people who might contribute funds for her Africa trip. Again the response was generous and immediate. Hall did not have the funds himself, but he was willing to contact four of his friends who each contributed two hundred fifty dollars. With the thousand dollars, Katie had enough money to cover all the expenses beyond the airfare, and she could hardly wait to leave.

When Hall's four friends came up with their two-hundred-fifty-dollar contribution, they made it clear that they were *loaning* the money to Katie (not giving it to her), and that they expected her to pay it back whenever she "got financially secure." "I still have a piece of paper with those names on it," says Katie gratefully. I am struck by Cannon's early ability to make her needs known and ask for others' money and support seemingly without embarrassment and without worrying about the risks of rejection. So I inquire, "Was it ever hard for you to ask for the money? Did it ever feel like begging?" Katie's face shows no recognition of those feelings. There seems to have been no caution or humiliation in making her requests. "You see, these people had *drilled* into me that they wanted to help me, and I completely believed them. I *needed* the money. I had no money, and I knew I would make good use of theirs. It is much more difficult for me to ask these days. But when I was young it felt comfortable and natural."

As Katie speaks about the various times in her young life when she saw something she wanted or needed and was determined to get it, I am amazed by her focused resourcefulness, her steady ambition, and her deft assertiveness. Whether she was breaking away from the seven-mile radius of Kannapolis and Barber-Scotia and crossing the country to Santa Fe, or developing her Pan-African ideology and politics in the Presbyterian Church in the Big Apple, or striking out across the ocean to another continent intent upon discovering her roots and her identity, Katie seemed determined to find herself in her adventures. The borders of North Carolina were barriers that needed to be crossed if she was ever to discover "the real Katie, the real ME." As long as she stayed in Kannapolis, she would have to wear an uncomfortable mask of decorum and religiosity; she would have to endure the controlling, invasive behavior of her mother; she would have to submerge her irreverent impulses, quiet her political activism, and stop asking questions. As long as she lived in Kannapolis, she had to stare at the impossible choice her mother always presented to her when she thought Katie was being overly ambitious or demanding: "You can go to Barber-Scotia or you can stay home and work at the mill... You can become a teacher or work at the mill."

The journey to Africa was a journey to the motherland. Katie hoped that the continent would feel like home—that it would be a place where she would discover her roots and identity, a place where she could be liberated and spiritually free. When she joined the group of Crossroads students for the orientation session before the trip, she was thrilled to discover that the group was half black. "We were the largest group of African-Americans they had ever had. Crossroads usually attracted liberal middle-class white kids, and James Robinson had made a big effort to recruit blacks." Most of the African-American students shared Katie's irrepressible hopes for self-discovery in Africa. They could hardly hear the warnings of the program leaders who told them that "all the people in Africa would not be wearing Afros and that many would not embrace or welcome African-Americans into their midst." Katie and her fellow travelers resisted the warnings and held fast to their dreams.

When James Robinson, the director of Crossroads, walked into the room where they were all assembled on the first day of their orientation, "people thought he was the janitor." Many of the students—even the African-Americans—had no idea he was black, and his quiet, modest style as he approached the stage did not give away his status. "Here we were going to Africa to discover our greatness, and here was a great black man in our midst who many folks took to be the janitor." But when Robinson stood up on the stage, when he opened his mouth to talk "and quoted Shakespeare," everyone was awestruck by his subtle intelligence and his power. "It was like *music!*" exclaims Katie. "Very impressive, very exciting." You couldn't listen to him without feeling inspired and proud, and without experiencing the importance and rightness of the Crossroads agenda. By the time Robinson left the stage, the new recruits thought they were ready to meet every challenge the continent offered.

When their plane touched down on African soil for the first time, in Dakar, Senegal, there were screams, cheers, and hollering. "We're HOME!" they chanted and then broke into exuberant singing. "It was *thrilling.*" From Dakar they traveled to Accra, Ghana, where Katie's group broke off from the others and flew to Liberia. For six weeks the students lived with Liberian families and worked on building a library. It was a demanding and difficult experience for Katie. "I just couldn't deal. It was so hard... the only meat we could get was goat... We could drink only boiled water. Mangy dogs would walk right through the house.... When I was there a woman had a baby in the house, and her screams terrified me. You know they had told us that we must be gracious, but one day I looked down in my soup and saw an eyeball staring up at me. I couldn't deal... I can't suck on anybody's eyeball!" Some of what Katie describes—the lack of resources, the limited diet, the crowded household—sound very much like the existence she knew in

Kannapolis, and I wonder out loud why she found life in Liberia so excruciatingly hard. "Didn't some of it feel familiar?" "Oh yes," responds Katie. "It reminded me too much of home—too much poverty and too much subsistence in *both* places."

On Sundays, their day off, the Crossroads students would go down to the beach. Katie loved those lazy days of escape from the labor and hardness of daily life. She would walk along the beach collecting sand dollars. Later on "sand dollars became my signature… my African connection… I would look at them and recall the beauty of Africa. I wore a silver sand dollar around my neck the way a lot of people wear a cross." When she recalls the "beauty of Africa," Katie thinks about the authenticity of the people, the way that the slow pace of life forced people to be "more real with one another." "I remember how they slowed us down. It was wonderful… They taught me that people were more important than things. When people died, they really knew how to grieve. There was screeching and wailing and beating of breasts. They were saying, 'This *hurts*. I'm in deep pain'—none of this Jackie Kennedy heroism stuff."

The Africa trip—difficult and beautiful—was very different from a journey Katie took the following summer of 1972 to Israel. Again, she discovered a way to design an experience that would push her far beyond the boundaries of Kannapolis. With the help of additional supporters who were willing to loan her money, she signed up to go on an archaeological dig. "I was majoring in Hebrew studies at seminary, and I always *loved* the Old Testament." But all of her hopes in going to the land of religious history and symbolism were ruined by the virulent racism that greeted her there. "I had never been called a nigger to my face until I got to Israel." She recalls angrily, "Most of the Jewish kids from stateside *iced* me… If you weren't pro-Zion, they wouldn't talk to you. I was so lonely… I had many meals alone. It was a wilderness experience… you know, you give up your slave experience and depend upon God."

The loneliness and despair of the wilderness experience, however, vanished when Katie traveled the short distance to Jordan. The change was dramatic and wonderful as soon as she arrived in

Amman. Unlike the Israelis with their scathing racism and name-calling, the Arabs saw her and said, "Welcome home. You are one of us." For the first time Katie was told repeatedly that she was beautiful. Men admired and desired her. "It was the first time that I had seen white women who were disregarded, seen as irrelevant, and black women revered. They thought black women were far more beautiful than white women... and all I did was cross the Jordan River." It was a brief, beautiful interlude in Jordan, but it could not erase the disappointment and sadness Katie had felt in Israel. She returned to North Carolina feeling needy. "I had had no physical contact, no one touching me." Then with mischief in her eyes she asks me, "So guess who I called as soon as I got home?" We both fall out laughing. Phifer is home base. Phifer is familiar. Phifer is comfort and nurturance. Now Katie's face is serious. "I said to Phifer, 'I don't want to have sex. I just want you to hold me.'"

The previous fall Cannon had entered the Johnson C. Smith Seminary in Atlanta. She had been drawn into theological studies by Dr. James Costen, the president of Johnson C. Smith and a Presbyterian minister. While she was in her junior year of college, Doc, as Katie calls him, had recruited her into a program that was designed to get intelligent, ambitious young people interested in the ministry. Costen had become very concerned with the "brain drain" away from the black church as more and more opportunities—in business, law, and medicine—were opening up for young African-Americans. For two weeks this program, designed by Costen and sponsored by the Presbyterian Church, exposed twenty-five talented black college students to "every aspect of the ministry." They traveled North and got a "panoramic view of rural ministries, city parishes, university chaplaincies, urban shelters." It was eye-opening and exciting to Katie who had never known women preachers and never imagined herself in that role, who harbored a stereotype (shared by her peers) of uneducated "jackleg black preachers who rip off the black community." This was an experience that helped her to recognize that the ministry could be "challenging for the mind" as well as a vehicle for social and political action. Through the ministry she could combine intellectual pursuits and "a commitment to the people." By the end of the two-week program, Katie felt "challenged in my identity as a black person," inspired by the rigor and eclecticism of the work, and newly able to begin to envision herself as a minister.

Doc was a very important figure in her life. She trusted him and was challenged and inspired by him. She also knew that he admired and respected her. "Jim Costen was the first positive, strong, *literate* black male in my life. My father was a strong, positive figure, but he is illiterate. Our *hearts* connect, but since the written word is so important to me, it *matters* that I can't connect with my father in this way. My father is an intelligent man, but he comes from a family of sharecroppers. The white people only let him go through the third grade of school." So in Doc Katie found a literate father surrogate with whom she could connect through language and intellect.

It was wonderful to see Doc again ("actually, I call him Doc, the original Black Panther") when she arrived at the seminary in the fall following her Africa trip. Actually, she landed in Atlanta "dead tired," after returning from Africa only twenty-four hours before, and she went into a deep, healing sleep. There were four women in Cannon's class at the Interdenominational Theological Center (ITC), a first for the seminary. The seminary didn't know quite what to do with them or how to treat them. For the first few weeks they housed the women in the "guest rooms" in the men's dorms. "Can you imagine what it felt like to be in the 'guest room'?" exclaims Katie. "We kept wondering, Are we citizens of this place?" Soon the women were moved into trailers behind the married-student apartments—temporary dwellings that seemed to symbolize the ambivalence of the institution with regard to their female presence. Beyond this handful of single women (all in their early twenties), the student body was made up "one-third of men who had been in Vietnam, one-third of those who were in seminary so they wouldn't be sent there, and one-third of men who had been training to be preachers all of their lives."

The first big surprise Cannon experienced in the seminary was the wonderful realization that the place was inhabited by "human beings." "Before arriving I worried that the seminary was one stop on the way to heaven." But instead of finding sanctimonious, self-righteous classmates, Katie enjoyed their irreverence and their mischief. "We were *real* people... I didn't have to give up partying. We called ourselves the 'Mood Squad,' and we partied hard and through the night." She also didn't have to relinquish her intellectual vigor or her political activism. "I knew right away that there would be a looping back and forth between the community and the seminary, that my mind would be challenged. I was an *agnostic*... I was searching, I was questioning, and none of the professors dismissed my questioning." She relished the aggressive dialogue and the chance to test her skepticism. "I *loved* my classes. Sometimes I'd ask so many questions that my classmates would wonder how I got into seminary." But Katie's agnosticism did more than challenge the prevailing canon; it also fueled a difficult and important dialogue between the searchers and the believers, or, as Katie puts it, "the thinkers and the preachers." For the men who had been preparing all of their lives to be preachers, Katie's skepticism was complex and disturbing. "We opened up the *injury* for these men... I watched people hurt for whom this was the center of their life." But along with the "hurt" there was growth for the people on both sides of the discourse. "We needed a little of their faith. They needed our facts... I helped to make the dichotomy real!"

Katie's Canon

For our last session, Katie has flown up to Boston from Philadelphia, where she is spending her sabbatical year at the University of Pennsylvania. There she is writing her "big masterpiece," her life's work (which her students have suggested she call "Katie's *Canon*"). Although we both feel sad about the finality of this meeting, Katie looks rested and bright-eyed. She is relishing the chance to give full attention to her writing; to pull together the threads of her intellectual life and trace the continuities and changes in her work. The book is the perfect exercise for this time in her life—a courageous stocktaking. She has the opportunity to look over all the work she has done, the vast territory she has covered in her forty-one years. The adventures and transformations are balanced by insistent, steady themes. Certain of her roots remain steadfastly grounded, no matter how far she travels in geography, mind, or spirit. It seems that she will *always* experience the haunts of poverty—the neediness, the embarrassment, the awkwardness. She will always be engaged in the process of self-definition. She will always want to escape (or be protected by) the "ugliness" of her body. She will always be struggling with the dualities that society seems to insist that she construct—the dualities of whiteness and blackness, of feminism and African-Americanism, of southern and northern, of thinker and preacher, of beautiful and ugly, of literate and illiterate, of cosmopolitan and provincial. She will always feel compromised (and exposed) by the choices she feels she must make. She will always feel torn.

By now I recognize both this discomfort *and* the pleasure Katie derives from it. I recognize, as well, that, in part, her creativity grows out of embracing, naming, and even exaggerating all these dualisms. In them lies her wellspring of strength as well as her greatest vulnerabilities. By marking and intensifying the dualities (in her life, her teaching, and her writings) she becomes better able to transcend the boundaries between them, but she also risks feeling endlessly torn, fractionated, uncentered.

Katie's sabbatical year in Philadelphia promises to be a time of reckoning (not for the first or the last time, but certainly an important one). She will strive to weave together the themes of her own brand of womanist theology—a *black* womanist theology, a *southern* black womanist theology, a southern *"working poor"* black womanist theology. More and more she sees the connections between her roots (in culture, race, class, region, gender) and her theology. This year—at midlife—she has been given the gift of privacy, solitude, and time to integrate her growing body of work. She is still young enough to feel its vitality and possibility and yet old enough to see the accumulated experience, the recurrent themes, the preoccupations, and the underlying legacy. Writing "Katie's Canon" is an act of courage and maturity. She is saying, "This is my imprint, my shadow, my mark."

The year in Philadelphia will also be a time of personal as well as intellectual reckoning. When Cannon arrived for our meeting in September, she had just had the extraordinary experience of traveling home to Kannapolis and being welcomed as a "prodigal daughter." The trip that left her feeling both warmed and shaken; enveloped by the expressions of welcome and generosity, and cautious about believing it was for real.

As Katie reported the extraordinary tale of familial acceptance, she told me that her determination to "tell the truth" was related to her involvement in this book project. Through our months of difficult, exhilarating dialogue, she had gained a new courage and self-acceptance. She had also felt a new yearning to see more of her "nurturant community"—to confront her roots, talk with her near-ancestors, make the long journey home. Just a few days before our present meeting, Katie had written the first letter she had ever written to her illiterate father. Esau Cannon, who had not yet learned to read when "the white folks made him leave to work their fields," had never been able to communicate with his daughter, the acade-

mic and writer, through the written word. Katie had tried to avoid
drawing attention to this stark contrast in their lives by never writing. She had often wanted to write and she had wanted her father
to be able to read her writings, but she had always resisted putting
words to paper, pushing back the pain of distance and yearning.
"But something about all of this work we've been doing together"
let her dare to write two lines, "even though I had no idea who
he'd get to read it to him."

When she was last home, she had borrowed money from her
father at a mutually agreed upon two hundred percent interest rate.
("I knew that if I promised to pay two hundred percent interest I
would pay him back soon.") Her father had lent her the money willingly but had not resisted the idea of the inflated interest. So when
Katie was ready to return the money, rather than just stick the
check in an envelope, she took a big leap of faith and wrote the
earthshaking two lines:

Dear Pop,

Here is a repayment of the loan.
Please do not deposit it before October 11.

Love,

Kate

Katie says the words slowly and proudly. So much living and
pain is loaded into this little note. So much yearning. Her voice is
heavy when she admits, "The fact that he can't read it doesn't mean
I shouldn't write it." Her words of explanation speak so clearly
about her need for connection; her determination to bridge some of
the dualities; her recognition of her father's ability to give to her (in
the form of the loan) and receive from her (by accepting communication in her own terms). The letter stands as a tiny/huge statement, a large leap for Katie who wants to wipe away some of the
caution and alienation that have marred her relationship with "the
first strong man I ever loved."

Philadelphia seems to be a halfway point between Cambridge and Kannapolis, a more comfortable place to test out some of these newly emerging connections to home. Katie has lots of relatives in Philadelphia on both her mother's and father's side, folks she barely knows but to whom she feels deeply connected. Since she arrived in their city they have found pleasure in treating her "like family" and "like a famous, important person" depending on the context and their needs. She has loved the feeling of their warm family embrace and the pleasure of the pride they have taken in her accomplishments. Katie feels comfortable with both being a family member at their table and being elevated by them in order that they might feel stronger or greater. Mostly, she has relished the long, lazy days of going to Sunday church services, attending funeral wakes, eating hearty midday meals, sitting up in their living rooms. There is a family rapport that she never experienced in Kannapolis, where she always felt excluded, resented, crowded out. In Philadelphia, at age forty-one, she is learning how to feel comfortable and included in the family circle. She is "practicing" this feeling in a less charged and passionate setting—not with her powerful and intrusive nuclear family, but with her more benign and distant extended family. Katie smiles with relief as she tells me this.

Not only does Philadelphia provide her with a host of extended family; it is also a black city compared to Cambridge and Boston, which are predominantly white. When Katie joined the health club in Cambridge, she always used to feel huge and awkward with her big bosoms, wide bottom, and thick thighs. All the white women working out on the exercise machines were lean and lithe, with shapes like adolescent boys. The contrast between her bigness and their smallness, her darkness and their lightness, her sweatiness and their cool glistening made her feel like a coarse stranger. But in Philadelphia when she goes to the health club to work out, she sees women who look just like she does—dark, ample, buxom, strong. She sits side by side with her black sisters on the Exercycle and feels harmony and delight in the mirror images shining back at her.

Katie experiences the same relief and familiarity when she goes into the drug stores, or even the supermarkets, in Philadelphia and finds all the stuff she needs—all the hair potions for her thick kinky hair; all the lotions for her dry skin. In Cambridge, you had to search far and wide for black cosmetics and sometimes make a special trip over to Roxbury to find the brand you wanted. And the churches in Philadelphia, the black churches, feel so familiar, so right. She can close her eyes and be transported back in time to Kannapolis, to the cadence and rhythm of the minister's sermon; the moaning and exclaiming in response; the harmonies and sway of the music; the dark suits of the deacon board; the elaborate, colorful hats on top of the pressed heads; the secretly mischievous and publicly well-behaved children. This feels like home. It will be hard to leave the blackness and warmth of Philadelphia to return to the whiteness and alienation of Cambridge. Although we are both mourning the end of our dialogue, I can see a restfulness in Katie's eyes, maybe even hear a slightly slower speech.

I am therefore surprised when she balks at my first question, about the Clarence Thomas hearings. It is an issue on *every* black person's mind; one that we are all wrestling with, horrified by, and about which we experience a collective distaste and humiliation. We are all—especially black women and most especially *professional* black women—implicated in the embattled saga of Clarence Thomas and Anita Hill. But Katie Cannon, who always seems to combine an intuitive gut reaction and a piercing analysis of the social-political scene, seems a little surprised when I bring this up, and much less articulate than usual in her response to it. She admits to experiencing "a big-time ball of confusion," and her discussion darts in contradictory directions.

Katie couldn't bear to watch the Thomas-Hill proceedings. It was too painful, too wrenching. She felt a great identification with Anita Hill, with her abuse and her victimization. "My blood pressure kept going up... my heart ached... I could feel the throb in my head." She was totally believing of Hill's story. "*All* of us have experienced harassment. I never doubted that she was sexually harassed." But the certainty of Thomas's guilt did not necessarily lead Katie to feel full sympathy for Hill. She wondered about Hill's naivete. Didn't she know how to protect herself? Didn't she feel badly about publicly violating a black man? "After all, I learned early that our fathers can't protect us... We have to protect ourselves." So the identification with Hill made Katie both rage for her and against her. She felt angry at the violence black women experience in subtle and explicit ways, *and* angry at Hill for her naivete and unpreparedness in dealing with it. Katie also hated the public spectacle of this event—the black gladiators providing entertainment for the white audience. The oversexed black stud out of control, looking powerful and threatening but feeling impotent as he faced "the twelve white men." Why had *Hill* staged this event, which provided the grotesque show for all the world to watch?

I listen to Katie's torrent of mixed feelings, spilling out in no particular order. The target of her rage keeps changing: the powerful white men who build the bankrupt institutions and call all the shots; who criticize and demean all black folks, men, women, and children. Clarence Thomas who abuses a sister, who takes his anger out on the black woman whose life and beauty nobody values. Then Anita Hill, who should know better than to leave herself unprotected and vulnerable (without a jungle posture) and who should not have participated with the white men in publicly victimizing her brother and creating the gladiator scene. I try to follow Katie's moving target, a little surprised that she is not firm and consistent in her support of Professor Hill. But then I remember that she was raised to believe that the black woman's job was to "protect the black men from getting lynched"; the Ku Klux Klan still rides in her home county in North Carolina. Lynchings do not feel to her like historical symbols.

One side of Katie wishes that Anita Hill had remained silent. Katie feels identified with the "older women" in the black community who are saying, "I endured it, so Anita should be quiet and endure it." But then a troubled look spreads across her face and she quotes the radical black lesbian feminist Audre Lorde, who said, "Our silence will not save us." Unless we speak out and name the violence, we will continue to be oppressed. Then Katie paraphrases another black feminist heroine, Barbara Smith, who points out that black women are not seen as legitimate members of their racial or gender categories. "All the women are white, all the blacks are men... when people talk about women they mean white women; when they talk about blacks they mean black men." So when Thomas claimed that he was the victim of a "high-tech lynching," thus engaging the most violent symbol of our collective history of oppression, he was excluding Hill from the picture—"like he was the only black person being lynched." From Audre Lorde to Barbara Smith, Katie Cannon seems to want to anchor her commentary in her black womanist stance. There is a war going on inside her as she switches from the feminist critique back to the images and feelings of a black girl growing up in rural North Carolina.

She calls on the support of a third sister, May Henderson, who wrote an essay called "Remembering the Body," based on Toni Morrison's *Beloved*. Katie paraphrases Henderson: "If you want to understand white male patriarchy, read black women's bodies as text for the violence perpetrated against the black community... all the forced sterilizations, all the weight black women carry." May Henderson's observation seems to strike the deepest chord with Katie. It is where her history and her ideology seem to converge. Suddenly, her ancient and powerful feelings about her body flood the conversation. "Since I turned adolescent, my body has been my enemy... I don't like my body."

On Katie's twelfth birthday, January 3, 1962, she started her period, a horrible birthday present. "I went to bed flat-chested and woke up 36D the next day." She knew immediately, intuitively that she would have to make her body unattractive, or at least neutral, if she was going to be taken seriously. "If I was going to think, I couldn't be in a female body. So when my breasts appeared, it's like, 'No, body, shit, you're doing wrong! You're wrong!'"

This memory leads her into the most painful period in her life, the years starting in the fall of 1974 when she began her Ph.D. studies at Union Theological Seminary in New York. She remembers this as the time when she felt the "pain of being poor" more deeply than she ever had before. Until she arrived at the "totally elitist" environment of Union, she had to some extent been protected from feeling the anguish of her poverty by the early forceful training of her grandmother. "My grandmother taught me that I have self-worth whether I have material things or not... and when I moved into the world, her words of encouragement were strong enough to go up against whatever I had to go up against. At Union, it was devastating for the first time to be ashamed, completely devastating."

Katie remembers, for example, the introductions of her fellow students sitting around the seminar table—their impressive experiences, their serious commitments; their elite schooling, their family lineage, their career goals. "The first week at orientation we were going around in a circle, and we talked about where we wanted to be ten years from now, and people were heaping one hype upon another hype—'I'm going to write this set of books, develop this philosophical treatise,' and so on." When they got around to Katie, she was feeling awkward and out of place, wondering how she could mask her pain and her deficiencies. She found herself blurting out in a big voice, "Ten years from now, I want to be partying on the West Coast." No one laughed. People squirmed. Katie's face echoes the old humiliation. "Wrong answer! Wrong answer! All I was trying to do was cut through the bullshit. I'd come from all-black schools, and whenever anybody was talking this highfalutin kind of stuff, people would say, 'Come on, let's be real. Get real!'" But Katie's efforts to cut through the "fancy talk" and diminish her discomfort only seemed to backfire, only made her feel loud, frivolous, and foolish.

This initiation rite was the beginning of Cannon's deep feelings of estrangement and exclusion. She was the stranger, the outcast, not knowing what to say, how to act, where to find things, what was valued and important. Her eyes are burning into me as she exclaims, "Sara, I had no understanding of white culture or educational culture. None. None. None. Students from Bangladesh were more acculturated than I was... Everyone was more ready than I was... That was part of the intensity of the pain. Here I was, born in the U.S., and I have no understanding of what it is to be in a white world... I laugh at the wrong time, talk at the wrong time... I'd go to these receptions and be like the only black person."

Katie had arrived at Union intending to study the Old Testament. Since the time when she was a tiny girl of three memorizing and reciting Bible stories, Katie had loved the Old Testament. While her upper-middle-class white peers at Union were "growing up on *Winnie the Pooh,*" Katie was learning the Bible stories at her grand-mother's knee. "I knew the Bible stories like I knew my name... I was shocked and continue to be shocked by white seminarians who don't know the stories... From the time I was three and memorized all the stuff by rote... I loved the Bible stories in the Old Testament." Her early fascination with these stories; her rehearsal of the talks in Sunday school and church; her examination and analysis of their content at the seminary in Atlanta; her trip to Israel for the archaeological dig, her study of the Hebrew language had all pre-pared Katie for what felt like a natural and inevitable choice: advanced study of the Old Testament. She had no idea, however, that her choice might ruffle the feathers of some of the academy's standard setters. She had no idea that there was an intellectual "hierarchy" at Union at the top of which perched the elite province of the Hebrew Bible. "I was the first black woman in the history of the world to try and get a Ph.D. in the Old Testament... and I did not know that brain power alone would not produce a Ph.D.... I did not know that it was seventy-five percent political—someone had to take you on as a mentor." So there she was in this all-white elite seminary feeling as if she had landed on Mars, not knowing the first thing about how to cope with this strange environment, having chosen the most ambitious, rarified, *and* closed field of study.

Union Theological Seminary felt not only rich and strange but also hostile. In Atlanta, at ITC, Katie had been in the middle of everything. She had loved the energetic intellectual climate, enjoyed the partying and raucous social life, thrived on the social and politi-cal activism. She had been admired by her peers for her courage, her vision, and her insights; and by her professors for her seriousness and inquiring mind. She had felt at home at ITC, comfortable in her place among "real people." But at Union she was out of it and didn't have a clue about how to get in. She tried, for example, to join a study group and was told by each group that she approached that there was no room for another member. Closed doors. "I was locked out... I got real depressed. Here I was not able to get into any of the study groups... At ITC, I had *controlled* them. I dominated... I mean,

I decided who was going to get in." With each rejection Katie grew more despondent. She could feel the accumulating assaults chipping away at her already fragile self-image. "More and more," she says sadly, "I was losing the will to live."

Katie felt excluded not just by the small student cliques but also by the character and quality of the classroom teaching, which felt stifling. At Union, the talk in the classroom always seemed to Katie to be designed to impress; it was arid, erudite, detached from the real world. Katie felt that the classroom experience was more about a kind of socialization into an elite club than it was about educational engagement. "I didn't know about learning how to be a colleague, how to be in the guild and name-dropping... and how to engage in argumentation that was irrelevant just so you can engage." This elaborate intellectual charade seemed so different from the real talk, the vigorous debate at ITC. When they had argued over theology, or politics, or ideas, they had engaged each other on issues in which they had a high stake. There was passion, confrontation, rage, laughter. "I loved being able to get my argumentation together to go and argue with the professor in front of the deans and get shot down even. But it was like, watch out, I'm coming back. We'd laugh, we'd joke about who got shot down... we counted on them to find loopholes in our analysis... we counted on them to push us." But at Union, the "cultural norm" was so different, and Katie found herself increasingly alienated. "It's only by grace that I didn't crack... I mean, suddenly the ground was opening up and I was falling down into the descent into Hell."

Part of Katie's anguish came from the stark contrasts between her interior feelings of dislocation and pain and the physically comfortable life she was living. After all, she was going to school for free, supported by generous scholarships that paid her more than both her parents made in two years of working, and more than her sister Doris's annual salary as a public school teacher. People at home were saying, "Kate, you're on top of the world up there!"

How could she write home to complain about her lonely and depressed life at Union when, by any objective measures anyone could name, Katie was leading a relatively privileged existence? When she would occasionally break down and reveal her frustration and anguish to her mother, Corine would respond with the inevitable litany: "Katie, if you're unhappy, you can always come home and work in the mill." By now, Corine must have known that the choice was no longer a real alternative for her daughter. It was merely used as a reminder that Katie should not indulge in self-pity when most of her family and her people had far, far less. And the choice had also probably become a metaphor for home, for the life that Katie had decided to leave behind. In leaving Kannapolis, she had gained status, education, adventure, but she had taken herself away from the bosom of the people who were like her, who understood her, who cared for her. Corine, like her strong-willed daughter, must have known that Katie would never return to Kannapolis; she used the mill as symbol and metaphor for all that was lost and gained by Katie's decision to leave.

At Union, Katie was also haunted by Ms. Porcher's insistent voice. Ms. P., her mentor at Barber-Scotia, had been so strong in her belief in Katie and in her support for adventuring. When Katie needed clothes for her student teaching, Ms. Porcher had provided her with the warm hand-me-downs. When Katie had been selected for Operation Crossroads Africa, it was Ms. P. who directed her to possible sources of funding. So when Katie was struggling with the elitism and rejection of Union Theological Seminary, it was Ms. Porcher who told her that she could do it. She had no choice; she *must* do it. Her litany was now as familiar, and as powerful, as Corine's: "You must do it for all of us."

So Katie lived with the stark contradictions of public recognition and private agony. She was the first black woman ordained in the Presbyterian Church, the first black woman to pursue a Ph.D. in the Hebrew Bible; she was a promising student on full scholarship. Everyone admired her and expected great things from her. Yet she was in such deep pain, feeling foreign, isolated, and lonely. The public/private juxtaposition brought echoes of her terrible terrors at Barber-Scotia when she was brilliant in her studies, revered as a political leader, when she was the life of the party at social events, in the bright spotlight. But in her room, where the applause and acclaim were inaudible, she would be crouched in her bed "like a monkey." When she speaks of her sadness at Union, she uses an equally devastating image for her private misery: "I wanted to throw myself in front of a subway... I wanted it to be over."

What she now recognizes as a deep and dangerous depression felt then like a chronic weariness. "I was just so tired all the time... I don't want to get up. Just let me lay here for a while." One of Katie's roommates, a black woman, kept hearing her tired lament, day after day and week after week, and soon recognized that her complaints were not merely signs of weariness. She, herself, was in therapy and used her own experience to urge Katie to give it a try. Katie was desperate, her resistance was low, and the crying spells would not cease. She picked up the telephone and called Betsy, a therapist whom her friend recommended, "way over on the East side, Eighty-third Street and Third Avenue... and I couldn't figure out how to get there." On the day of her first therapy session, she lost her way, almost turned back several times, but finally arrived thirty minutes late.

I ask Katie, who has been telling stories about "the white trauma" of Union Theological Seminary, whether the therapist was a black woman. "No," she retorts almost impatiently, "I've *never* had a black therapist." Then later she explains, "Betsy is the one who designated this white trauma. I would say, 'All white people,' and she would say, 'Well, wait a minute, Katie. Not *all* white people.' Our work together helped me start to make sense out of this big ball of whiteness that was scaring the hell out of me, so she started to make the white world more liveable... teaching me how to take one person at a time rather than all white people."

Katie admits that this therapeutic process of learning how to differentiate the shades of whiteness, the good and the evil, was a powerful and subtle socialization that drew her away from her black roots. "It meant I got farther and farther away from my Afrocentricity." This does not sound like progress to me. I feel suspicious of any therapy that moves people away from their cultural and familial center. I reveal my bias by exclaiming, "Are you calling that development?" And Katie responds with a big laugh—one of those hearty roars that expresses the convergence of irony, pain, and survival. "Malcolm X would call it the 'rape of the mind'... Carter

Woodson would call it 'the miseducation of Katie Cannon!'" Then her voice grows serious as she appraises the difficult compromises and tensions of her divided soul. "I couldn't have done it without Betsy. I couldn't be sitting here right now with the knowledge I have if I had not forsaken that which I knew as my identity and moved into this honorary white kind of position, because it was too traumatizing to hold my blackness in that world."

So Katie turned to Betsy, a therapist, a white woman, to help her "translate" the strange and baffling world she was living in, to help her unravel "this great big ball of whiteness." The "white feminist norm" that Betsy represented saved Katie and supported her through an intensely difficult period. But Katie now recognizes the costs. "It made sense to me… but it was a big investment. It was a big mortgage." Katie uses the words "close to foreclosure;" the white world was foreclosing on her mortgage, threatening to take over her whole life. Part of Katie's "crisis" in midlife is reclaiming the "Afrocentrism," the "nurturant" community that she relinquished when she became an "honorary white person," when she began "to learn by imitation" how to translate the white world.

The contrast between her public persona and her private self was not the only chasm of contradiction that Katie lived with at Union. There was also the gap between the white feminist world (which offered support, solace, criticism, and interpretation of the white male hierarchies) and the African-American community (which felt exclusionary in its northern bourgeois male orientation). The African-American students were so different from Katie's friends and colleagues at ITC. They did not value Katie's strength, intelligence, humor, and politics the way the southern seminarians had. They didn't treat her like "an honorary male," deal with her mind, or take her seriously. Mostly from northern middle-class families and elite schools, this group of African-Americans seemed to be threatened by Katie's persona and style. They even challenged her presence at Union. "I went to the Black Caucus meeting, and one of the brothers said to me, 'Katie Cannon, we want you to justify how in the hell you think God has called a woman to the ministry.' I was devastated. I didn't know an answer to that. I didn't know how to justify myself as a woman… I mean, coming from ITC where there were like six women out of three hundred men, and the *men* would say, 'More power to you... do it! The harvest is plentiful, but the laborers are few.'"

For the first time Katie felt torn by the allegiances of gender and race. Her "brothers" were diminishing her, questioning her right to be there, denying her access to the inner circle, and "it hurt like crazy." So she turned her back on them. "I went back to the Women's Caucus, where we were talking about how you defend yourself for being born female. I had been trained all my life to deal with race and white supremacy... but nobody had conscientized me in terms of what it meant to be born a female, a black female." The brothers' questioning at the Black Caucus meeting was Katie's "first incident of feminist conscientization." At that moment, "my whole world was being shattered. Everything that was known was now unknown; everything that was familiar was now very strange.... I was in a chasm."

The depth of the trauma rings out in Cannon's use of the word "chasm," indicating the great separations in her life that need to be bridged and reconciled in her middle years. Now, at forty-one, she must find a way to see the contradictions, name them, reckon with them, and pull them into a whole. The divisions between public persona and private self, between privilege and poverty, between African American roots and feminism, between the white paternalistic canon and Katie's Canon have begun to feel cataclysmic. Katie knows that reconciliation will not come through denying the contradictions or masking the pain. If reconciliation is to emerge, she knows that it will always be a fragile one fraught with small and large compromises. She knows, as well, that she will always live with the contradictions. Wholeness will not come out of erasing them, or even easing them. It will come out of embracing them *and* learning to move between (and among) them with purposefulness, grace, and humor (one of Katie's chief survival strategies). And just to show that she always has the latter in ample supply, she skewers the exclusionary attitudes of the Black Caucus at Union. "You see, they were afraid that if I came to their potlucks I might bring quiche or yogurt or tofu." A large grin spreads over Katie's face and we laugh together about the ancient and present pains.

CHARLES OGLETREE

Blow, Jazzman, Blow

Beginnings

When I enter his office, Charles Ogletree is on the telephone, his voice deep and resonant, his eyes shining. I sense that he is repressing the urge to shout the news, but his demeanor remains calm and deliberate. "Yes, we won... and we won big... Nine–zip... I don't know. I haven't seen the decision... they are going to FAX it to me... but I know it's thirteen pages.... I hope it's not too narrow a construction.... Yes, it was remanded *and* reversed... Souter wrote the decision. It was his maiden voyage." Sitting in his office, I can hear (but not decipher) the shrieks of joy coming from the person on the other end of the receiver.

Charles Ogletree has just won the first case he ever argued before the Supreme Court. The case, *Ford v. Georgia*, involved a black man convicted of murdering an "innocent white woman." The appeal to the Supreme Court did not involve the guilt or innocence of the alleged murderer but the selection of jurors who heard the case. The prosecutor had systematically excluded *all* potential black jurors, claiming that they would be biased and prejudicial in judging the black man's guilt or innocence. The man had been convicted of murder by an all-white Georgia jury (*whites* were assumed to be capable of being unbiased and impartial) and sentenced to death. The case had been appealed to the Georgia Supreme Court, who turned it back to the lower court, and finally up to the Supreme Court. Charles, the old public defender, the civil rights activist, the enthusiastic and skilled trial lawyer, could not resist taking the case when his colleagues on the Southern Prisoners Defense Committee, whose board of directors he chairs, asked him to get involved.

As he puts down the receiver, Charles greets me warmly and says simply, happily, "It's a case about a brother convicted of murder, facing death... He'll have to have a new trial. We won... big." His use of the term "brother" is what I hear. It sounds like a connection deeply felt and cherished. (Later, Charles tells me that he feels privileged to be doing the kind of work where he can "make a difference," "be of service," do something about the fires burning inside. "I couldn't be here [at the Harvard Law School] if I didn't also have the chance to practice law, to save people from death... I'd be racked with *guilt.*") As he goes out to the reception area (where the secretaries for several professors have their desks, and students sit to wait for their conferences), there are cheers, congratulations, and amazement. "When was the last time there was a 9–0 decision?" asks a teaching assistant.

While he is out of the office, I take in the large and cluttered space in which he works. High ceilings and a wall of windows make it feel spacious despite the heavy row of black file cabinets, the huge desk, the shelves of books, and the piles of paper stacked on every surface. Many details announce (even proclaim) Charles's African-American roots and identification. On the wall above photographs of his children (a son in high school and a daughter in the seventh grade) at various growing-up ages hangs the famous Douglas Turner print (*The Banjo Player*) of a gentle old black man and a young boy leaning into each other, wrapped in a warm light. Right next to it is a beautiful color photograph of Rosa Parks ("looking like all of our grandmothers"). And on the top of the file cabinets is a compelling, disturbing picture of a group of black men (it seems to be from the 1930s or 1940s) dressed in work clothes. They could be miners, I think to myself, or railroad workers. I can't place them in time or setting, but they look deeply familiar. Resignation, weariness, and struggle are written all over their faces. They huddle together, somehow expressing both resilience and vulnerability. (The graying black-and-white photograph turns out to be the Scottsboro boys, a group of young black men falsely charged with raping a white woman and facing the death penalty in Alabama in the 1930s.) I imagine that Charles is in daily communication with these men. Perhaps they remind him of his privilege and his responsibility.

A 1990–91 photograph of the Harvard Law School faculty, unframed, leans up against the huddle of black working men in the

Scottsboro boys photograph and creates a striking, jarring contrast. I am impressed with what seems to be an amazing number of black faces. In fact, there are six African-American men in a sea of about eighty to ninety white males, with a sprinkling of white women. There is one lone black woman dressed in a conservative suit with her hair pulled back, looking purposeful and serious. She is a visiting professor at the law school this year who has arrived after a year (1989–90) of strife and controversy over the nonappointment of a tenured woman of color. Derrick Bell, the major protagonist of the political activity, "the outspoken radical troublemaker" who at the time was taking an unpaid leave in protest (until the law school tenured a woman of color) is looking all of his sixty years as he stands in the middle of the back row of the photograph. I wonder to myself why Professor Bell chose to appear for the picture since he is in the midst of protesting his connection to this exclusive club. Why would he want to look like he belongs and put himself in the same frame?

All of the black folks are "dressed," looking clean and dignified for their school photo even though several of their white male colleagues are in shirtsleeves. The famous constitutional lawyer Lawrence Tribe doesn't even have a tie on; Garry Bellow, a clinical professor of law, has a broad mischievous smile and his belly is pushing against the buttons of his snug shirt. I am not surprised that the blacks are looking so correct in their lawyer uniforms, but I am surprised that I feel relieved that there are so many of them. Then I realize my reference point. In my mind's eye I can see the photograph of the law school faculty taken in 1978–79 when my brother Chuck was a "visitor" there. Derrick Bell was on leave that year, and Chuck was the only black face in the picture. I remember studying that late seventies photograph and feeling my brother's isolation and differentness. I was proud he was there—to my sisterly eyes he was definitely the most gorgeous man in the picture of any race, creed or color—but his lonely presence, the stark tokenism made me angry. So now, twelve years later, I am gazing at the new official photograph and being amazed at the color on the page. "It almost looks integrated!" I exclaim to Charles who returns a knowing smile. "That's an *illusion*," he says.

Charles has to make just one more call, to the law firm where he used to be a partner in Washington, D.C. It is clear that he is talking to a friend and colleague as he talks with growing excitement about the call from the Supreme Court clerk just minutes before. In fact, Charles had used his old colleagues to help him prepare for presenting his argument. Nine of them sat (in moot court) for a dress rehearsal, playing the parts of the Justices, voicing their legal positions, mimicking their styles, and firing tough questions at Charles. "It was much more difficult than the real thing," he recalls. "It was great in helping me prepare for the follow-up questions. I knew what to anticipate and how I wanted to handle it."

Although Charles is obviously pleased (even joyful), there does not seem to be an ounce of boastfulness or preening. When I ask him to describe what it felt like to appear before the highest court in the land, he describes the surprising feeling of "being three feet away from the Justices... so close to the bench. They are higher up, but they are very close... and that was kind of disconcerting. You know, when you see pictures of them they always seem so distant." The first thing he remembers is not the grandeur of the Court but the astonishing human scale; the austere and removed robed Justices who turn into almost ordinary people. Ogletree had only thirty minutes to argue his case; his argument was constantly interrupted by the Justices' questions. The old public defender, however, seems to relish the combat, the theater and improvisation of the court scene. He had an outline in front of him and lots of experience and practice behind him. He was prepared for the unexpected. "You get too wedded to a script and you can't be responsive."

I am moved to refer to Charles Ogletree as "an old public defender," but he is not old. He is not yet forty. His movements are vigorous, his face is open and unlined, his stocky, muscular frame looks strong, his energy seems vast, yet his countenance and his self-confidence seem old. I am startled when he says that he was an undergraduate at Stanford in the early 1970s (1971–75) and begins to identify his place in the post-1960s activism. As a student leader, he had organized a "black theme" house in one of the Stanford dormitories. Although the black students were in the

numerical minority, "we dominated the place." Twenty-eight percent of the students were African-American, but the place had a
distinctly black ambience. "We drank wine; they drank beer.... At
parties, we played *our* music, not theirs." We both grin at the way
it takes only "a few of us" to seem like a crowd.

A visiting professor, a Chicano, who is occupying the office
next door, was a student at Stanford during the same era. "He
always misinterprets the history," smiles Charles. "He says that the
black brothers even chased the *Chicanos* out of the dorm!" The
college memories and pranks—a vivid retrospective—recall a rare
experience of "black power" in the midst of institutional whiteness. Even if the power was seemingly limited to the trivia of wine
and music, it symbolized so much more about the contrasting
appetites of whites and blacks... and it reflected the political struggle that was still alive at Stanford. Twenty years later, Charles can
name all of the black professors who were there at the time, can
recall the optimism they all experienced after the civil rights gains
("meager though they were") of a few years earlier, and knows the
disappointment of hopes unrealized. "It's much worse now... the
numbers are worse... Some of the determination is gone."

From his desk, Charles can look at another large black-and-
white photograph hanging high on the wall and feel the "blasts
from the past" of his student activist days at Stanford. Seated
behind a long rectangular table are twelve young black men dressed
in dashikis. Huge Afros crown their hard, serious faces; dark glasses
hide some of their eyes. The photograph is an icon of Black Power
symbols, and Charles—looking young, round-faced, and threatening—is in the very center of the lineup. This photo stands as a powerful reminder of their "rage and the mask"—of a time when their
youth, anger, and idealism mixed with the political and cultural ferment to produce a fiery combustion. These themes of commitment
and activism are echoed in the several plaques, hanging just below
the college photo, that honor Charles's recent work: a personal
achievement award from the NAACP of Merced, California; an
appreciation from the Black Law Students' Association; the Public
Defender Service Association Award of Merit; the Nelson Mandela

Service Award; and a plaque from La Alianza for Charles's "extra-ordinary commitment to the Latino community at the Harvard Law School."

Charles had come to Stanford from a "small poor town" called Merced in central California. His family was destitute, ambitious, and generous. His father had completed the fifth grade and his mother the tenth, but they were both determined that their children would finish school. Charles attended the public schools in Merced—a lethargic, mediocre school system, "on another planet" from the snazzy abundance of Stanford. When he speaks about his origins, particularly his mother and father, Charles's voice is full of affection. "My father is deceased, but I want to make life good for my mother. I feel that as a deep responsibility... lots of people ask about my kids, providing the best in the world for them... but they are going to be okay. In the normal course of their lives they meet professors, lawyers, doctors. Before I got to college I had never met any of these kinds of people.... No, my impulse is look *backward*, not forward... to give back something to the people I came from, to make my *mother's* life comfortable. My wife feels the same way about her folks."

Charles's parents were divorced when he was young but "remained close friends" in this small town where everyone knew everybody else. His father was actively involved in his upbringing. Charles speaks lovingly about the deep affection he had for his father despite the meager conversation and the awkwardness and anguish caused by the vast generational distance. In 1983, when Charles was being sworn in as a public defender before the Supreme Court in Washington, D.C., he invited his parents to come from California for the big occasion. "I made a big deal about it in order to get them to come, as if it was the greatest occasion," explains Charles. "Actually, it wasn't a big deal for me... Actually, the big deal was that my folks *come*, not the swearing in." Both of his parents were reluctant to make the big trip, and Charles had to "work on them real hard." "They felt embarrassed, scared, and worried they wouldn't know what to do or say." To his great relief, they finally agreed to come, and Charles sent them their airplane tickets, bought his father a brand new suit, and awaited their arrival with anticipation and worry. How could he make them comfortable? How would the meeting with his father go? The occasion had another generational layer; Charles had also invited his father's older brother who, like Charles's father, grew up in Birmingham, Alabama, but had been living in Buffalo, New York, and had not seen Charles's dad for forty years. So Charles was not only anticipating his own reunion with his father—the successful, aggressive, public defender from the city and the simple, silent working man from the country—he was also excited about witnessing the long-awaited, much-resisted meeting of his male elders. Cameras recorded the airport embraces, the tears, the halting conversations. "It was just amazing, extraordinary!" beams Charles as he relishes the memory of the powerful moment of generational connection.

At the last minute, his father had almost not made it to D.C. The day before he was due to fly East from California, Charles called him to make sure all the plans were in place and to offer his parents final words of assurance and support. His father's voice on the telephone sounded disappointed and shaky as he told his son that he would not be able to come to his swearing in. Charles's mind raced. What could have happened in the last couple of days to change his father's mind? He thought he had covered all the bases, answered all their concerns, communicated how much he needed them there. All he could say into the receiver was, "Why?" The response from his dad was simple but charged, "Junior, I don't have a hat." At this moment in his Harvard Law School office, Charles's voice and expression seem just like the old man, and he knows completely why his father could not step on that plane without a hat. The hat would bring him protection, dignity, style, correctness; all of which he needed as he entered this distant, alien world of Washington society. So Charles hustled and schemed to get him a hat. He called a department store in Merced, asked his mother to go to the store to choose the appropriate hat, and arranged to have the hat charged to his credit card ("which wasn't so easy to do in those days"). Then he crossed his fingers and hoped with all his heart that his father would not invent another excuse not to come to

Washington. Their reunion was a powerful blend of anticipation, curiosity, resistance, apprehension, and love. "I'll never forget it. I'm so happy we got to do it before my dad died," says Charles, his eyes growing moist.

~

Charles Ogletree's response to my invitation to tell his life story is immediate and generous. He is delighted, eager, and "honored" to participate, and I am relieved and thrilled by his reaction. By this time, I have had several conversations with prospective participants who have struggled mightily with my invitation, but ultimately— with anguish, guilt, and relief—have decided not to tell their stories. The clarity and simplicity of Charles's response surprises me; there is no ambivalence. By now I have learned that this book project will be attractive to people to the extent that I can clearly convey my own deep interest in this work, my conviction that "we" must begin to construct a more authentic and complicated narrative about "our" lives—one that challenges the distorted, narrow caricatures of "successful" blacks. With Charles I feel much more fluid and practiced in these expressions of commitment, and he is with me all the way, nodding his head in agreement, reflecting back my excitement. We set up a date to begin ("What kind of time do you need... a half a day, a couple of hours?") after Charles returns from a few weeks of heavy travel. This man, whom others describe as "unbelievably busy," is eager to carve out the time for this exploration. He seems confident of the personal gain he expects in navigating this journey, and he seems convinced that our stories deserve telling as part of the reconstruction of our place on the American landscape.

The Art of Advocacy

In order to find quiet and privacy, we have to search for an empty seminar room on the second floor. Charles recognizes that there is no way that we can carve out two hours of uninterrupted time in his office, where the telephone rings constantly, colleagues stop by to chat, students stick their heads in with requests, and his assistant often can't shield him from the intrusions. As soon as we land in the empty conference room—with our coffee cups, tape recorder, and note pads—Charles is focused and eager. I suggest that we begin with the present, with his work. He leans into the table, folds his hands in front of him, looks at me intently, and seizes the first question with energy and precision.

Although there are many parts to Charles's vocational life, he begins with his teaching, describing an innovative course called Trial Practice that has his signature written all over it. Each fall and winter one hundred fifty second- and third-year law students take the three-week course that meets for nine hours each day (noon to nine at night). The complicated course structure includes large lectures, seminars, small working groups, clinical practice, mentoring, and structured criticism. The faculty include lawyers and judges from around the country and the Boston area who are eager to keep their hand in the academic arena, work with Harvard students, and reflect on their own practice. Just as this group of legal practitioners evaluate and critique the students' ideas and activities, so Charles judges and scrutinizes the work of his faculty. The curriculum incorporates an eclectic array of educational approaches including role-playing, videotaping, and simulation, and it is designed to move students from "theory to action to reflection to self-criticism… looping back to action."

The curricular structure and content reflect Charles's goals for the course, which he is able to articulate with ease. "I want the students to understand the difficult task of lawyering... to recognize the incredible amount of discretionary power lawyers have... to see the social and political factors that influence their work... to be aware of the ethical conflicts... and the often arbitrary, capricious, and inconsistent practices of the judges." Most importantly, Charles wants to convey the aesthetic insight that good advocacy requires. As he designs a series of structured exercises, as he underscores the exacting work of gathering and displaying evidence, eliciting information and marshaling facts, he wants his students to recognize the values and "the art" that shape the process. There is a "certain tension" between "the control" the lawyer works to achieve in the cross-examination of witnesses and the unexpected events that require spontaneous and resourceful response. Says Charles finally, "I want my students to see that the law is *not* a science... It is value laden, not pure, not objective."

This course—which makes the "connections between theory and practice"—is one of a handful of courses at the Harvard Law School that focus on clinical training—that see relationships as a critical dimension of legal practice; that scrutinize the action (rather than the ideas) of students. In this elite law school where theory and analysis shape discourse and where most of the graduates will never practice trial law, Trial Practice is not required nor considered central to the curriculum. But since its inception a few years ago, the course has grown in stature, prominence, and numbers. Now each time Charles teaches it, the course is oversubscribed and he must turn away students.

Often, as they begin the course, students are skeptical, even arrogant in their approach to the course, but as soon as they see how difficult, complex, and intelligent good practice is; how much must be kept in mind simultaneously; how quick responses must be; how adaptive a trial lawyer must be to the context, to relationships, and to the unspoken dynamics—the course gains their respect and admiration. They are amazed and challenged by the teaching model that blends thinking, analysis, and action, and that is designed to explore the values and temperament that get expressed in advocacy work. At first the students are surprised, then humbled, by the ambitious requirements and intensity of the course. But within days, says Charles, they are totally won over and involved. The course structure and design almost prohibit noninvolvement. Over time, many students even move to the opposite extreme of over-identification; they begin to try to mimic their mentors. The imitations rarely work. They are a first stage in learning. "A young twenty-two-year-old woman shouldn't necessarily adopt the style of her forty-two-year-old white male mentor—with a booming, strong voice, a strident gait, a very aggressive way." Her style may need to be very different—suited to her temperament, physique, and insights—in order for her to be effective. In fact, while offering a model of action, analysis, and self-criticism, Charles is also helping students to discover the connections between their character, their style, and their courtroom strategy.

Since this difficult process involves public criticism, I ask him how he manages this with his students and his faculty of practicing lawyers and judges. How does he manage not to offend them? How does he avoid injuring their egos? Charles admits that teaching can be treacherous. "Here I am standing before you. I'm vulnerable." He is conscious of working to create an environment of "safety and positive reinforcement." He offers lots of opportunities for practice, visible criteria for achievement, and honest and fair evaluations. As I sit with him in this conference room, I sense not only his watchful intellect, but also his acceptance, his warmth, and I imagine that his students must feel both challenged and safe in his presence.

Charles traces the connections between his teaching style and his years of experience as a successful public defender. "Despite the fact that people are supposed to be innocent until they are proven guilty, there is *always* the presumption of *guilt* whenever anyone is accused of a crime." He describes the cool, patient process he goes through in trying a case. The coolness is part temperament and part posture, a stance he learned as a child as he watched both his parents and his maternal grandparents' "cool" in the face of the crises that filled their lives. Charles masks his anxiety and the impatience raging inside. No matter what emotions are fired up in the courtroom, he tries always to be "courteous, attentive, deferential." He is intent upon being a "firm but fair advocate… sympathetic but not naive… open but focused."

Charles sees his work as convincing the jury—"these ordinary people" sitting in front of him—that they have the capacity to make wise and informed judgments based on the accumulated evidence. He wants to appeal to the best, smartest instincts in them. He sees himself as "teaching" the jurors, empowering them to make a judicious decision. "I try to question them *personally* during jury selection to get a sense of their character and reasoning. I try to let the client introduce himself (even though I rarely put him on the stand) so everyone can hear his voice, often tentative and scared. It humanizes the person for them even if he just says his name and address… I ask questions designed to reveal to jurors what is being left out of the story… I say, 'If you don't like me, don't hold that against my client. If I have to vigorously interrogate a rape victim, disagree with a judge, argue vociferously with the prosecutor—that may be behavior you don't like, but don't hold it against my client.'"

Charles works especially hard for clients who "appear to be guilty" because they are "black and poor." "People who are poor should have the same excellent representation. I make the maximum effort in cases that are the most difficult," he says. If the chances are fifty-fifty when he walks into the courtroom, he will prevail. "If it's even steven, I win," he claims without an ounce of boastfulness in his voice. I hear his calm, clear self-assurance and wonder when he began to recognize that he was a gifted trial lawyer. He smiles at the memory of his early wins and the way he at first interpreted his victories. "I would always claim that I won because of some external circumstances: the jury was unusually sympathetic to my case, the prosecutor was unprepared, I got a lucky break… It was only after I kept on winning and began to gain a strong reputation among my peers—other lawyers, judges, police—that I began to admit to myself that I had a special talent for this work."

In the beginning, winning cases was "incredibly important" to Charles. It wasn't "everything," but it was a major motivating force. Winning was attached to his feelings of self-esteem and self-confidence, and everything seemed to ride on his determination to be victorious. But after a while, winning lost some of its luster. As he became more experienced and more successful, Charles took on harder cases, murder and rape, not just burglary and breaking and entering. As the challenges became more difficult, as the successes continued, Charles found himself focusing less on the win and more on the process. His determination and ambition never flagged, but his efforts centered on the nuance and subtlety of the unfolding case, and on the extraordinary responsibilities of advocacy.

In his teaching, Charles challenges the competitive culture of the law school and tries to get his students to see how legal advocacy can be compromised by a preoccupation with winning. "Students get the message that they must do everything to win— that winning is the ultimate reward... that winning is everything." This focus on victory—at any cost—can blind them to the important moral questions that are woven into every legal case. Charles's voice is adamant, his eyes are intense. "When the competitive urge gets so great, it is very difficult to embrace a code of ethics... The moral dilemmas begin to be seen as a barrier—rather than a guide—to effective lawyering." His fist is punching the air for emphasis as he concludes, "I try to convey to my students that it is more important to be a respected lawyer than it is to be a financially successful one... Your reputation is the most important thing."

Charles's "cool" masks a great deal of anxiety and stress. Every time he goes to court, he loses his appetite and he stops sleeping. In his ten years working as a public defender in Washington, Charles would always stop eating when he was in the midst of a trial. He would become very "superstitious," believing that if he ate before making his argument he might lose the case, and since it seemed to work (that is, not eating *and* winning) he did not dare stop the superstitious ritual. During trials he would become weakened with fatigue, fueled only by the adrenaline of anxiety and determination. "There is nothing more agonizing than trying a case... It is excruciating to control external expression and repress feeling," says Charles. "I don't feel the pain until after the trial." All of this punishment to his body expressed itself in a mean, ulcerous condition from which it has taken him several years of careful diet consciousness to recover. This high anxiety, this superstition, seems so at odds with Charles's amazingly calm, unruffled exterior. Is it the cost of this calm that makes this young, energetic man seem like an old public defender?

Later on Charles describes "the dilemma that tears at him constantly," the tension he always feels between teaching and legal advocacy; between teaching lawyers and using himself "more directly" as a lawyer. Again, I am struck by the passion and feeling that he internalizes and absorbs, which never gets revealed in what looks like his comfortable existence at Harvard. These divided commitments are propelled by the same values. In both the university and the courts, he sees himself as "working for social justice." Charles continues to question seriously whether he should give so much energy to the academy. "This remains an open question," he says as he faces the ambivalence squarely. He seems haunted by his self-imposed role. "Is it enough to produce great lawyers who have social commitments and ethical values?... Is it enough to be the conscience of the institution?"

Big Daddy's Patience

As we begin our session I tell Charles that the reason I have chosen to use ninety-minute cassettes to tape our conversations is so that I will not be tempted to overstay my welcome and overtax him. I explain that I think of this as an intense, emotional process, and I do not want to wear him down or leave him exhausted. I want Charles to know this because at the end of our previous sessions, I felt I was stopping him before he was ready, in midsentence or midthought. Just as I said that our time was up, his thinking and language seemed to be soaring, and he looked at me with amazement and disappointment in his eyes. As I explain this now and express my worry about overtaxing him, Charles says exuberantly, "No, quite the contrary, I find it *liberating*."

We revisit some of the themes of our last session: his patient temperament, his changing views on winning, the mask he wears to hide strong emotions, his need to serve as an institutional conscience, and so on. Charles is immediately ready—eager, undefended, reflective. Today his ruminations move easily back and forth through time: from being a small child picking figs in the fruit orchards around Merced, California, to his years as an aggressive public defender in Washington, D.C.; from his freshman year at Stanford where he experienced "having a room of my own" for the first time, to returning to Merced for his twentieth high school reunion this spring; from watching his grandfather fish with a bamboo pole, weighed down by fresh wheat dough for bait, to using fishing to ease the intense anxiety brought on by his criminal defense work. The stories flow easily, disregarding time markers, following the path of experience and feeling rather than the strict chronology of years. This undulating movement, which feels almost like free association, strikes me as extraordinary for a man who is so skilled

in rational thinking and systematic analysis. I feel the same surprise when a story he tells from his early childhood—about learning
how to make his grandmother's rice pudding—gracefully lands in
the closing argument of one of his toughest criminal trials.

I am eager to know more about the origins of Charles's patience,
his view of "taking the long journey": not needing to win his cases
in the first five minutes, or even the first five days, but always looking for the long arc of emerging evidence. He immediately takes me
back to his roots, to his childhood in the country, to the way his
grandmother (Big Mama) and grandfather (Big Daddy) raised him.
Even as a child he could see the patience in the way Big Daddy
hunted and fished—waiting, watching, listening, always poised for
the moment. Big Daddy would sit for hours on the water's edge with
his handmade bamboo pole poised in his rough hands, absolutely
relaxed and still, never saying much. Young Charles would sit beside
him feeling his grandfather's peacefulness, trying to see what Big
Daddy saw in the still water. Charles would grow increasingly impatient as the pole would begin bobbing up and down, and he would
urge the old man to move quickly. But Big Daddy would not move a
muscle when he spotted the first ripples in the water. His practiced
eye and long years of experience made him able to distinguish the
serious interest of a big fish; all of his moves were methodical, strategic, and productive. Almost every time he would manage to haul in a
big ten- to twelve-pound fish, usually a huge carp, the fish that "only
poor people ate." "You would never find carp in the fish markets."

When Charles was about eight or nine years old he got his own
fishing pole (the modern, store-bought variety) and joined his elders
(his mother, grandmother, and uncles also fished) by the side of the
water. For years he had watched Big Daddy and tried to learn the
details and subtleties of his extraordinary success as a fisherman. "I
had the science down, the physics figured out. I held my chin the way
he did, leaned my body back... *but I didn't have the patience*... and I
would miss every single time. Big Daddy would just crack up!"

His grandfather's patience seemed to have both temperamental and experiential roots. Big Daddy's friends called him Snuff.
"White folks would probably call him derelict. It was not that he

was slow or lazy... it was just that he took his time." Even his dress seemed to express a solidity, a determination to live by his own rhythms. Every day, whether it was forty degrees in the winter or ninety-five in the summer, Big Daddy always dressed in two layers of shirts and pants. He never seemed to be too cold or too hot; even in the penetrating sun of central California, he was always the same comfortable, unruffled temperature.

As Charles sat next to this strong, silent fisherman, he often would wonder what he must be thinking. Thirty years later his face grows mournful as he recalls the missed opportunities. "I *never* asked him what he was thinking... I suspect he must have been recalling his painful experiences." Charles's grandfather had traveled from Arkansas to California, where he hoped to find work and freedom but instead discovered more racism and more poverty. As a child watching Big Daddy's impassive face, Charles never felt the masked disappointment and anguish. He could feel only his grandfather's calm, patient determination. As an adult, Charles suspects that a mask covered great sadness and unexpressed rage. Fishing was not sport; it was survival.

I suspect that in the midst of a trial Charles resembles Big Daddy—patient, discerning, strategic, and fully in control. Though no white folks would ever call him "derelict," and he doesn't wear two layers of clothing and dip snuff, Charles is a sophisticated, educated version of his grandfather. He also wears a mask, hiding his determination, anxiety, and wrenching ambivalence. Behind his courtroom calm, his air of control and poise, is high anxiety.

In his early to mid-thirties, Charles "discovered" fishing. After several years of trial work—when the stress seemed too much—he took up fishing, seriously and ritualistically. With a good friend and fishing partner, Charles would go out on a boat nearly every weekend. (I imagine their fishing gear and clothing looked very different from Big Daddy's simple double-layered uniform and bamboo pole.) These excursions became Charles's great escape. Out on the Potomac, three thousand miles from the muddy rivers where he watched Big Daddy pull in carp, he could feel the safety and calm of those early years. Charles also used the time and tranquility of "the fishing routine" to "refine" his trial work; to think through "the logic and themes" of his courtroom argument. Fishing offered rest and recuperation from the high-wire act of "courtroom combat," but it also became a time for developing the plans, strategy, and script of the courtroom action.

While Big Daddy deserves at least half the credit for teaching his grandson to be patient, enduring, and strategic, Big Mama—who taught him how to make "the best rice pudding in the whole world with raisins and coconut"—deserves the other half of the credit. One day when she was still a young woman, Charles's grandmother had suffered a heat stroke while she was picking cotton in the fields. The stroke left her paralyzed on her left side. From that time on, Big Mama moved slowly and walked with a cane, but she managed to do everything around the house that needed to be done. As the oldest grandchild, Charles was leaned on pretty heavily. "I was the model, and the rest of my brothers and sisters followed after me," he says without resentment. He would help Big Mama get dressed, rub her down with alcohol to soothe her aching joints, and fetch things for her while she cooked in the kitchen. She insisted that Charles learn how to make her famous rice pudding. From the time he was barely walking, Big Mama would make Charles fetch the ingredients. By the time he was nine or ten, she was already "testing my knowledge." Big Mama's teaching was always firm, patient, methodical. Her cooking instructions were life lessons. "She was teaching me how to be self-sufficient... teaching me accountability, responsibility... a set of values."

Many years later, in the closing argument of a tough criminal trial, Charles used the story of his grandmother's rice pudding—the way she showed him how to make it; the way she tested his knowledge and capabilities; how he memorized the ingredients and mastered the process but never managed to make a batch of rice pudding as gloriously delicious as Big Mama's. His cooking lessons became a powerful metaphor: if you amass and display all the pieces of evidence, if you enumerate and synthesize all of the facts in the case, you will not necessarily produce the same results. The story was very effective in the courtroom drama. It had the key ingredients of engagement and persuasion—a reference to "family, a sense of discovery, a recognition that things are not the way they appear... the opportunity for perspective taking."

The jurors were totally seduced by Charles's family story, by the way he told the tale and unraveled the moral lessons. "I try to massage the jurors," says Charles about the patience and subtlety required to pull this off. But the rice pudding story was even more effective with the prosecutor, who "froze," unable to respond effectively—or even at all—to the engaging family drama. Immobilized, he fell mute, unable to challenge the persuasive metaphor. Charles grins at the memory. "He must have thought, 'As a threshold issue I can't touch this.'" He admits that metaphors can be extremely effective in the courtroom, but they are "a two-edged sword—they can make you or destroy you." This analogy to Big Mama's rice pudding stopped the prosecutor cold, but he could have come back with a winning line like, "You're talking about the dessert—rice pudding—but we've got a full-course meal here... Let's begin with the appetizers, and so on."

The talk about this "winning metaphor" pulls us back into a discussion of the combat that is part of the courtroom drama. I ask Charles where he was trained in this competition. "Everything in my life stressed the importance of winning," he replies, "from the kickball games we played at recess in elementary school to arguing before the Supreme Court." Most of the time, however, he felt as if he was competing with himself, trying to best his own record or skill. He recalls his mother taking all six children with her out into the fields where they joined other itinerant seasonal workers picking peaches, almonds, and figs. They would get paid by the box, and each day they would try to work faster and more efficiently to fill more boxes. They would work against the goal set the day before. "If we made twenty dollars on Saturday, we'd try to make twenty-two on Sunday... We did this for economic benefit, to help the family."

Besting yesterday's record became linked with family survival, but Charles also began associating winning with the pursuit of knowledge. He recalls his favorite haunt, the public library on J Street in Merced. At the entrance to the library there was a display with a list of children's names, along with a star for each book they read. Between third and sixth grades, Charles's long list of stars

far outshone any other child's. He became an avid, enthusiastic
reader, devouring scores of books and amassing an impressive array
of brightly colored stars. "I really liked the stars," remembers
Charles gleefully. But beyond his galaxy of stars, Charles loved the
world that reading opened up to him. He could sit right there in
this little branch library and journey to faraway places, discover
new planets, pursue extravagant dreams.

Winning and survival, winning and knowledge, winning as
essential: these connections fueled Charles's success and shaped
his perspective on trial work. "There are two different ways people
practice law," explains Charles. "Some want to win in order to
avoid losing; others want to win because it is the right thing to do.
The first is a very defensive kind of practice... the second is my
approach. It is offensive." But Charles assumes his offense on behalf
of his clients—poor and disenfranchised—who "are in jail because
of their poverty... If they had the resources they would not be out
there robbing. I want to give them the best defense possible!" He
is winning for *their* survival, "to vindicate the rights of the unrep-
resented, to insure fairness, to rectify the judicial process, to balance
the ability of prosecutors to prosecute."

Charles admits that all of these high-minded purposes may be
elaborate "rationalizations for wanting to win." It may also be that
these morally upright offensives echo childhood battles where not
winning would have meant losing everything. Charles sometimes
feels the old fears and doesn't welcome their reappearance. He now
recognizes the origins and limitations of this primal instinct and
ponders it sadly: "After a while you have to worry about becoming
cynical... Winning is no longer very satisfying or effective... You
find you need something else." This is particularly true as he lives
with the growing realization that the victims and the criminals "so
closely resemble each other." They are both black and poor. They
both come from the same depressed, hopeless conditions; the difference lies in who managed to strike the blow first. "When victims
become indistinguishable from clients, I become very introspective
about what I am doing in the process, very self-critical about the role
lawyers play." Winning loses its meaning and passion.

Introduction to Trial Advocacy: The Defense Perspective

A few months later, Charles invites me to visit one of his classes. He is eager to show me how he helps students bridge theory and practice, how he urges the convergence of analysis and action. In his work with law students, he wants to "teach them how to think *and* what to think" in an effort to "balance the other messages out there that claim that the law is value free." He hopes that his teaching will allow students to see the law as "an instrument for social and political change... a tool to empower the dispossessed and disenfranchised... and a means to make the privileged more respectful of differences." I want to see how Charles tries to carry out these controversial, majestic goals; how he links evidence and intuition, control and chaos, and science and art in his teaching. On a breezy, warm afternoon in April, I visit Professor Ogletree's 4:00 P.M. class, The Defense Perspective.

~

The corridors of Pound Hall, the main classroom building at the Harvard Law School, are filled with casually dressed students—in jeans, shorts, tee shirts, warm-up suits—with only an occasional conservative suit. The classroom in which Charles teaches this third-year course is like all the others in its tiered, horseshoe shape, although it is smaller than most, with only thirty gray swivel seats and two rows of tables. In front of the seats there is a large square table below a long blackboard. One wall of the classroom is all glass, looking out on a partly cloudy day and Massachusetts Avenue traffic. In the low ceilings recessed lights shine down in a grid pattern between the gray acoustic tiles. The classroom feels functional, spare. The students seem slow and lethargic as they wander in to take their seats. Some sit alone daydreaming or reading; others are

gathered in small clumps talking about their other courses or their
court work in Roxbury, the "clinical" site for this course. These
third-year students are apprentice attorneys learning the real-life
activities of criminal defense lawyers. They are being tutored by
practicing lawyers, their supervisors in the field, and they are receiving the counsel and guidance of their professor, but they are doing
the work of real attorneys. This is not a class on abstract legal theory or a rehearsal of hypothetical cases. These students are defending real clients, a fact that contrasts sharply with their casual
conversations before class. A very Cambridge-looking young
woman dressed in light gray stretch pants, a magenta tee shirt, and
running shoes, calls across the classroom to a classmate, "Are you
driving over to Roxbury tomorrow morning?... Oh, you're taking
the bus... What time are you leaving?"

The students seem so young to me, so cavalier, not mature
enough to be doing the serious work of public defenders. Maybe I am
projecting my own cynicism, but my first response in hearing their
before-class chatter is to doubt their sincerity. I am, however, suspicious of my own doubts. After all, these students are much younger
than most of my graduate students and do not seem to possess the
seriousness and humility that often grow out of experience. For three
years they have survived the elite, competitive, combative environment of the law school, and their easy arrogance (if it was not there
before they arrived) is now firmly in place. I try to hold back on
these immediate, harsh judgments. After all, these are the twenty-
five third-year students who *chose* to take Charles's course. Their
choice must signal some inclination on their part to learn about
(and maybe practice) the relatively low-status, low-paying, high-
demand work of defending poor folks. I perch myself in the second
arc of seats, take out my pen and notepad, and work over these competing ruminations as the students saunter into the classroom.

Charles Ogletree arrives on the dot of 4:15 P.M., dressed in a
dark blue suit, light blue shirt, and wide blue, yellow, and white
flowered tie. He seems weary and a bit distracted as he places his
pile of papers on the square table in front, takes off his jacket, grabs
a piece of chalk, and with his left hand prints the day's theme on

the board: "Witness preparation defense." A few students approach him to chat, and he responds politely. But I sense a slight impatience in him, a push to move forward with the day's agenda. A low buzz fills the room as the students continue to talk with one another. The same woman calls out her request, louder this time and to no one in particular, "Is anyone going to Roxbury?" She gets no response. Finally, I hear Charles's deep, resonant voice say casually, "Any reports from the camp?"

An immediate response comes from a young white man sitting close to me. "I had a victory of sorts." He quickly summarizes the action taken by his lawyer colleagues and the "most favorable response" of the judge. His description is facile, unemotional. Charles stands at the front table, riffling through his notes, not looking at the student, but clearly listening. "Good," he says without much energy. "Anyone else?" In what sounds to me like modest one-upmanship, another man across the room pipes up, "I have had an unqualified success." His summary of the case is even quicker and blander than the prior one, concluding with a statement from the judge that brings brief laughter among his classmates: "I have no interest in warehousing this woman, but I also don't want to be suckered into this."

A third voice offers much more enthusiasm. This young man is clearly very excited, animated, and turned on as he relishes the details of his activities in court. "I got a dismissal on two counts,..." Now Charles is fully attending, leaning back against the blackboard and listening to the hyper-talk of the student. After the speaker— tall and angular, with awkward, quick gestures—has recounted the basic facts of the story, he admits that the judge had admonished him, "Counselor, *please* calm down." The judge's plea brings laughter from his fellow class members, who have obviously grown used to the high-energy talk of their classmate. The laughter subsides, and Charles responds, "Terrific. So it's over."

Much more deliberately Charles repeats the outlines of this last case. Clara Nelson is a forty-two-year-old black lesbian who was accused of assaulting a sixty-seven-year-old white guard and trespassing at the YWCA. Then he says admiringly, "This was the best establishment of an attorney-client relationship that I've seen this semester," and asks the student to describe his first encounter with his client.

Again the rapid-fire, loud voice. "Well, when she met me, she said, 'I'm black, I'm a woman, I'm gay. None of these charges would have been brought against me if I weren't all of these things…' So I said, 'Well, I'm white, I'm a man, I'm heterosexual. Are we going to have a problem communicating here?'" The "candid" greeting apparently led the way to a "mutually respectful relationship" that left the young counselor with a satisfied grin on his face.

Having heard the news from the camp, Charles gives the assignment for next week. He wants his students to prepare opening statements for a trial, based on the cases they have been working on in the Roxbury courts. In their preparation of the opening statement, he asks them to consider three objectives: (1) To what extent have you established a coherent theme? (2) Have you made a conscious effort to humanize the process? (3) Have you anticipated the prosecutor's response? All of these sound familiar to me. I have heard him refer to these goals in talking about his own work as a public defender. In every case, he searches for a theme—a line of argument, a compelling metaphor, a thread that will weave its way through the entire trial. In every case, he works to make his client be seen as human—vulnerable, responsive, anxious—and to call on the most empathetic responses from the jurors. And in every case, he tries to anticipate the prosecutor's next moves.

With these three simple declarations to the class, Charles reflects hundreds of hours of courtroom experience. The casual response of the third-year students—many do not even jot down the assignment in their notebooks—makes me wonder whether they understand the depth, complexity, and richness of experience that infuses their teacher's curriculum. Do they realize that his teaching grows out of a long history of practice, reflection, and self-criticism? Do they appreciate the competing tensions within their professor as he works to humanize the courtroom process while engaging in tough combat to win; as he struggles with the recognition that winning may not mean a victory for justice; as he maintains the mask of calm control even though inside he is burning with rage and anxiety? As I sit there and watch these students on this lazy spring afternoon, I suspect that there is no way for them to recognize fully their professor's commitment, his discipline, or his anger. I suspect that their young, ambitious eyes see only his deft courtroom strategy and his experienced technique.

The very next question from the floor—though claiming to be centered on the dynamics of the attorney-client relationship—seems to be focused on strategy. A male student sitting in the front row, dressed in a tee shirt, khaki shorts, and sneakers with no socks, says in a deep voice, "We want to discuss something with the class." Ready to move on with the day's agenda, Charles pauses, without irritation or hesitation, and gives the student the floor. The student describes a conflict with his client over how to present his case and a dispute over how he will plead. A white male activist who heads a needle distribution program for drug users in Roxbury wants his Harvard student attorneys to make "a big political point" in fighting his case. The activist is less interested in winning than he is in making the controversy visible, and he is willing to go up against some of the community's most powerful black leaders to make his point. Over the course of the semester, the young lawyers (a small group of students from the class have been involved in this case) have struggled with their client over goals and strategies. Says the first student, "We could move to suppress the evidence, but our client, at a minimum, wants 'not guilty' on the same substantive grounds." A second follows—"It gets a little *thicker* than that... I talked to our client yesterday, and he wants to go up against Reverend Stevens, a very articulate, convincing black minister of long-standing in Roxbury. Our client could be killed by the power of this man's convictions... by his standing in the black community." Charles listens to the students' description of their dilemma. His face is impassive; his eyelids are drooping over a weary but steady gaze. He reminds them that these client-attorney disputes were reflected in their early journal accounts. Charles had scribbled notes in the margins of their journal entries. "This is a classic case of where the *client* wants to make the choice... There are many clients who want to pursue a political cause."

The students seem resistant to conceiving of this case as political. They want to win, and they worry that their client's determination to make a political statement will compromise a court victory. Charles seems to be impatient with the students' need to control the case and make the choices for their client. Maybe he sees arrogance, born from inexperience or prejudice, in their refusal to hear, and act on, their client's wishes. More than once he says, "You may have to withdraw from the case... you have to question when you have lost rapport with your client... maybe he deserves to have a more zealous advocate." The student attorneys seem to be only half attending; frustration is written all over their faces. From the back, a white woman student speaks up. Her voice is raging. "I'm a political activist, and there is nothing we like less than having an attorney decide what is in our best interest." She is challenging her colleagues' perceptions of what it means to work "in the best interest of the client"; she is impatient with their "blind spots." "Your client *wants* to get himself arrested."

After a long and torturous discussion, one of the two practicing attorneys who serve as mentors and supervisors in this course speaks up. She wants to challenge the distinction being drawn by Charles and his students between cases described as political and criminal, "as if they are separate genres." She believes the boundaries are blurred; the purposes are often multiple and mingled. She says forcefully, "I don't like the thinking that political acts always come out of premeditation and choice, and criminal acts don't." To make her point, she uses the example of the Brinks robbery and murder several years ago in Nyack, New York, staged by an underground radical group called the Weathermen, in which criminality and politics were impossible to disentangle. "These cases are extremely *rich*. They raise all kinds of knotty questions about the lawyer's role."

Her comments—which seem to cut through the fog of student frustration—lead nicely into Charles's more formal presentation. He underscores the "richness" of the cases by pointing to three dimensions of courtroom argument: theory, operational issues, and tactical strategy. Then he constructs a complicated decision tree on the blackboard that describes some of the intricate choices and "extraordinary discretion" that lawyers have at their disposal. For each choice or decision path, Charles offers an explanatory anecdote, often derived from the cases on which the students are working. "What kind of theory do you have?... Do you maintain this throughout?... When I put this witness on the stand, what is my goal in pushing the theory?... You must have a basic foundation." A student asks, "Do you ever try working with two theories at the same time?" "*Absolutely*," responds Charles. "You are frequently working with more than one theory." A lawyer often works with competing theories until he/she is able to decide how the evidence is shaking out, how the courtroom dynamics are evolving, and what the prosecutor's line of argument will be. Attorneys must recognize that the theory of the case may take time to form and it must be open to reevaluation and modification.

Determined to move the discussion along, Charles says, "I want to take you beyond the obvious," and spends the next forty minutes describing the intricate dimensions of a theory. He draws a diagram on the blackboard.

Theory of case

identification

justification

- necessity—choice of lesser evils, balancing two different forces
- self defense

excuse

- insanity (must have some sense of moral culpability)
- entrapment

nullification

- minor drug cases
- social condition of defendant
- character

general denial

As Charles provides the examples and the reasoning, his voice and inflections echo the courtroom dramas he has heard over the years. At other times, he asks the students to provide the rationale. "Why might you ask a nonleading question?... What is the reason to follow that rule?"

"It is one way to establish witness credibility."

"To avoid objections."

"In order not to let the witness tell the whole story and give the sense that the lawyer doesn't know the case."

"And what are the reasons to break the rule and ask leading questions?" queries Charles.

"To jog the witness's memory."

"If you're dealing with a hostile witness or a child."

"To anticipate the cross."

"To establish preliminary facts."

Summing up the rationale for deciding whether "to follow the rules of nonleading questions" or not, Charles says, "All of this is about *control*... you are trying to control the testimony and the outcome. How do you control the use of information? How do you control the dissemination of facts?" As he moves through the discussion, he combines specific directives about do's and don'ts and general lessons on the conceptualization of the case. On theory, he is urging a consideration of control, credibility, argumentation, validity. On strategy, he sounds like someone who is offering the recipe for baking a cake or the design for putting the puzzle together, both metaphors used often by Charles. The essential ingredients of courtroom practice are specific, didactic, like the ingredients in Big Mama's rice pudding.

- Tell your client never to guess.... She gets into trouble if she says, "I guess so." The most important words are, "I don't recall. I don't remember." Don't allow your client to get locked into a particular story... You can say, "Let me help you recollect what happened."

- You want to help your client avoid being overly conclusive—saying it absolutely happened that way. It's better to say, "The best I can recall, the traffic light was not working that morning."

- You have to stay away from certain words like "To tell you the truth," which forces people to think, "Well, what have you been telling me all along?" It implies something that was said earlier or later isn't true, or is less compelling, less persuasive.

- The pacing of the testimony is very important... If you rush over critical information, it becomes obvious what you are trying not to reveal. You need to develop a story that is credible, believable, has pace and theme.

As I listen to the classroom discourse and watch Charles in action, I hear echoes of our earlier conversations. Charles wants to teach his students to become effective and committed advocates for the indigent. The poor must receive the best possible defense—a free defense as strong and as persuasive as that which can be bought by the rich. He also knows that many of these Harvard students—out of naivete, inexperience, and racism—may wrongly believe that their clients are guilty. Such an unconscious presumption might lead them to undermine or compromise their advocacy for their clients. He points out the progress the students have made during the semester. "Remember nine weeks ago how convinced you were of your client's guilt? Now you begin to recognize the institutional constraints... Conduct is a gray area... You begin to see the need to think in the long term. This might mean that along the way it will be necessary to forgo an immediate tactical victory." Charles is trying to persuade his students that winning is a very complicated, ambiguous notion; that strategy is immediate and concrete, but justice is elusive; that anticipation and patience are essential ingredients of success. It is not at all clear that these impatient third-year students—impatient for success, winning, getting out of law school and beginning their careers—hear his wise and steady admonitions. But Charles Ogletree, at least for the time being, has placed himself at the Harvard Law School and is committed to speaking his conscience.

Eugene

Charles Ogletree is forty minutes late. Having gone to lunch with his research assistants and several of his students, he has packed his day too full. He has left word with his assistant that she should let me know that he is further behind schedule than an earlier call to my office had predicted. While I wait for him, I study his office door, which is plastered with signs, letters, cartoons, and drawings. There is a big blowup of a cartoon showing a criminal defense lawyer being attacked by a gunman; a pretend correspondence between Charles and the newly appointed Harvard President Neil Rudenstine regarding affirmative action policies at the university; and a newspaper article on men's fashions with a handwritten caption about Charles's decorative ties.

One of these door decorations has captured my interest since my first visit. It is a drawing and poem by Charles's eleven-year-old daughter, Rashida. The crayon drawing shows a brown-skinned man looking dapper in a jacket, tie, and top hat. He is standing on a bridge above the water, playing the saxophone. The poem below the drawing reads:

There he goes again
Just blowing out the jazz blues
The water is shining in the light
So calm and smooth.

This nighttime jazz man,
The center of attention
Has already vibrated
His soothing tension
Blow, jazz man, blow.

The drawing looks done by a child's hand; the poetry seems more sophisticated; both are expressive character sketches of her father. In his top hat, Charles wears the dignity passed down through the generations; the dignity his father needed to travel from tiny Merced to the Supreme Court to see his son's swearing-in ceremony. The words in Rashida's verse speak about Charles's love of jazz; the "calm and smooth" mask covering his inner turbulence; his grace at "the center of attention," the performance that "vibrates" with power and "soothes" his "tension." I am astonished by this insight and the subtleties. Does this child know her father this well? Or am I making too much of this, reading too much into it? By the time I get to the last line, "Blow, jazz man, blow," I have convinced myself that Rashida, in her eleven-year-old precocity, knows her father and his father inside and out.

When Charles returns from lunch he is moving with characteristic high energy, seeming to carry around many agendas in his head. He reaches for his messages, checks with his assistant, begins to make an important telephone call, responds to a third-year student's invitation for an end of the year party, and welcomes me. I now anticipate this dizzying pace and wait calmly at the edges of the gentle cyclone until he is ready to settle into one agenda. In order to do this, he needs to make one more telephone call to New York (where he is due for an appointment later in the afternoon) to reschedule a meeting for the next day. Since he has arrived late for our session, he is carving out new time for us by pushing his New York trip forward. Even though every minute seems to count, his voice on the telephone is warm and calm. In two minutes the trip is rearranged and he gives me his full attention. I look over at him in his light gray suit and white shirt, and I spot his tie—a colorful, bold splash of purple and sea green against a black background. Blow, jazz man, blow!

I remind Charles that in the last two sessions he has ended with the same blues—a litany of ambivalence about his decision, for the time being, to teach at the Harvard Law School. He is constantly asking himself whether this work is a wise and productive use of his energies; whether he is using himself well to further the cause of social justice; whether his role in this elite university will help to reshape the institutional culture; whether the Harvard students—black and white—need him most. These questions weave themselves in and out of his days; they disturb his sleep; they cause him disquiet. I am interested in knowing how the present ambivalence might be related to what appears to have been an early and firm decision to become a lawyer. When and how did he decide?

Almost before the question is fully out of my mouth, Charles is shaking his head in understanding and launching enthusiastically into a coherent, well-organized reply. Although his responses are always immediate and fully developed, I never experience them as facile or canned. It is not that he seems to have said this all before, but that his mind works incredibly rapidly to retrieve and organize experience and his language accommodates with equally impressive precision and speed.

He has three stories to tell about why lawyering became an attractive career choice. The first reaches back to his ten-year-old boyhood in Merced; the second and third to his late adolescence in high school and college. All three seem to be potent, transforming experiences that bring tears to his eyes as he relives the feelings. Yet he frames his memories with a puzzling remark: "Harvard Law School is far away from the career path in law I imagined when I was very young."

Charles's early attraction to the law did not include an image of academic life. It was a far more gritty, active picture of lawyering that young Charles had in his mind when he experienced his first encounter with the police at a department store on the north side of Merced. Merced is a town divided into north and south by the railroad tracks. When Charles was growing up, all the blacks lived on the south side and the white folks, the schools, the stores, the businesses were all north of the tracks. One day, ten-year-old Charles and his friend Willie Phillips, who was three or four years older, decided to go to a department store on the north side to make a little mischief. Charles was caught in the act of shoplifting "one of those metal rattlers" that you whirl at New Year's Eve parties. His friend Willie went for something a bit more substantial. When the department store detective collared Charles, he ordered him to stick out both of his hands. The rattler went crashing to the floor, making a deafening noise. "Sounded like the loudest crash I'd ever heard," says Charles shivering with the memory. When the police came, they did not handcuff him as they marched him out to their cruiser.

At that moment, the *only* thing Charles could think of was the horrible punishment that would be awaiting him at home, a punishment far more brutal than the police could ever invent. "I was *terrified* what would happen when I got home!" He decided, right then and there, that he would "not let the police take me home. I would have to jump out of the car while it was moving. That was my plan." But when he got into the backseat of the cruiser, Charles discovered that the car doors had no handles on the inside. He was stuck! There would be no escaping his mother's wrath.

When the cruiser pulled up in front of his family's place, Charles was relieved to discover that his mother was not at home. Uncle Jabb, the husband of his mother's younger sister, was taking care of the children, and he received the report from the police with a sober, expressionless face. Charles worked quickly trying to get Uncle Jabb to be sympathetic. "I pleaded my case with him… said we could forget about this whole thing. I brought him his slippers, fixed him tea, made him comfortable." But Uncle Jabb was "noncommittal"; he refused to let his desperate nephew off the hook. When Charles's mother arrived home, the two adults had a few words in the kitchen, and his mother's voice rang out her fury. She acted in just the way her son had dreaded. "She sent me out to the yard to select my own weapon of punishment. She used to call it 'my persuader'—a branch from the tree that would be stripped of its leaves and used as a whip." Charles always considered it double punishment—suffering the fierce beating *and* selecting the weapon that would be used against him. This time when Charles returned from the yard with the switch, his mother was not satisfied with his choice. "Go get me a *real* switch," she shouted. "Get me a tree limb!" The punishment lived up to his worst expectations. It was the most terrible beating he ever got.

This brush with the law, though minor in contrast with his mother's wrath, made Charles feel impotent and defenseless. He was beginning to understand that even a very minor infraction—particularly an offense by a mischievous black boy who traveled to the wrong side of the tracks—could blow up into a major incident. He felt very vulnerable, like all of his south side neighbors, the boys and the men especially. Several times he had witnessed the painful spectacle of his father being picked up by the police at their home after a domestic dispute between his parents. Charles would watch his father's desperate resignation, his head hung low, his body slumped, as the police led him away, and Charles would feel "so hurt and embarrassed." His father would "look so defenseless." "It was so dehumanizing. It was as if the man was no longer a man… It is horrible to see your father with handcuffs on him." Thirty years later, Ogletree sits in his Harvard office, leaning his body back in his high swivel chair, swaying his head back and forth slowly with an expression on his face of quiet terror. "He would just disappear," he says very softly. Now, as an adult, he suspects that his father was living with fierce demons, "pressures that were so great that he found it necessary to hurt my mother." He does not condone his father's abusive acts, but he does understand his desperation and his feelings of impotence, an impotence that made him unleash his rage on his wife. But as a child, Charles would watch his father "disappear" and feel rage at the police for taking him away. "If I could become a lawyer, I'd have the power to control the police!"

Charles held onto these innocent ideals, held fast to his determination to become a lawyer and protect his people from the powerful, arbitrary police. The determination was heightened by "the most powerful and tragic" event of his life, an event that still haunts him daily. His very good friend Eugene Allen was a year behind Charles at Merced High School. He had faced terrible tragedy in his short life. His father had murdered his mother and had been incarcerated for life. Gene was being raised by his Aunt Maggie, a strong, loving woman, a very strict disciplinarian. Under Aunt Maggie's guidance and with his own sturdy fortitude, Gene was a clean liver. "He played football, ran track, did not drink or smoke." Gene and Charles were part of a group of about ten boys who were all great friends. They were a tight, loving group; their "strong bonding relationships" grew out of their collective determination to be "straight." Everyone was in school; everyone was an athlete; nobody used drugs; nobody had a record... "and Gene was the straightest of the group."

In 1970, Gene's sophomore year in high school, he "got himself involved with a young white lady," the daughter of a prominent judge in town. This relationship produced gossip and waves in the tiny town of Merced and was received with disapproval and anger by the girl's parents. At about the same time (in an incident that may or may not have been related to Gene's romance with the white girl), Gene started feuding with the high school football coach; he thought he wasn't getting enough playing time in the games. The coach was offended by Gene's impudence, and the two "had words."

A few days later, the coach's house caught fire, and Gene was accused of throwing a torch. No one was hurt, but there was a lot of fire damage to the property. Convicted of arson, Gene was sent away to a "youth camp," a prison for young offenders. This well-mannered, straight-arrow boy, this fine athlete, this good student, this wonderful friend suddenly was stripped of his promising future, and Charles watched helplessly as he "just disappeared." The boys in the group felt terrible. They mourned the loss of their beloved buddy, their standard-bearer, but they also felt guilt for not being able to protect Gene from this punishment, which they saw as ruthless and undeserved. And they all felt the burden of responsibility — a burden that Charles felt most keenly, a burden that weighs heavily on him today.

A little while after Gene Allen arrived at the youth camp, race riots broke out following a dispute between a black and a white inmate. In the midst of the violent fracas, a white inmate was stabbed to death, and Gene was charged with the killing. He was immediately transferred to San Quentin, one of California's maximum security prisons. By the time Gene was behind bars at San Quentin, Charles was a freshman at Stanford University. Every five or six weeks he would leave campus and travel north to visit his "homeboy" in prison. These visits would cause Charles so much pain—"I became increasingly guilt-ridden... I felt responsible and accountable to him." He kept wanting to trade places with Gene—to offer him the freedom and opportunity he felt Gene so justly deserved; to bring back the time when Gene seemed "the most promising, straightest brother in our group." "*He* should be at Stanford," Charles would think every time he saw his friend at San Quentin.

Then something even more terrible happened. While at San Quentin, Gene and a fellow inmate were accused of murdering a prison guard. Convicted of the charge, they landed on death row. Charles was horrified by the murder conviction and frightened by the specter of death row. His visits to San Quentin became more frequent; his efforts to help his friend, through political and legal channels, intensified. Charles and Gene would sit on either side of the bulletproof glass, unable to touch one another or find privacy. Gene was shackled with chains on his wrists and ankles. When Gene would lift up the phone to speak to his friend, the heavy chains would hang from his strong arms. Charles shakes his head, remembering the impotence and the humiliation. "Gene was *transformed*... He was still in a child's body, but he had become a man. I was sickened to see him."

Gene claimed he was innocent, and Charles never doubted his word. But Gene steadfastly refused to "snitch" on the man whom he knew had killed the guard. Finally, after months and years of legal effort, it was clear that there was not enough evidence to sustain the murder conviction. The case was reversed, and in a new trial Gene was acquitted and taken off death row. But he was still left with the 1971 charge of stabbing and murdering the white inmate during the race riots at the youth camp. Twenty years later, Gene Allen is still in prison, and Charles is still working on his behalf. Although the authorities will not admit to it, his long incarceration is almost certainly related to the charge of murdering a prison guard, a charge on which he has already been acquitted. Now Charles's voice is almost a whisper. "The image of Eugene is always with me... It is related to the reason I'm so conflicted about being at Harvard. I visit that question constantly."

Brothers and Sisters Back Home

"The Angela Davis trial was the crowning event in my introduction to the criminal justice system," says Charles. After his brush with the police as a small boy in Merced and his anguish over Gene's incarceration, the movement to free Angela Davis became his third reason for deciding to become a lawyer. His voice is rhapsodic as he describes Angela Davis: "I had never met anyone as powerful—her mind, her spirit, and her emotional voice, her confidence and conviction. I wanted to understand her... I wanted to know how she could risk so much. I guess I had met women like her with her kind of power, women from Merced... But I hadn't appreciated them fully... They were not that way in public... Angela Davis made her points known."

It was 1971, Charles's freshman year at Stanford. He became deeply enmeshed in the political demonstrations, rallies, protests, silent vigils, and fund-raisers in support of Angela Davis. It was a consuming, energizing, "mind blowing" experience for the small-town boy from Merced. After her arrest in New York, Davis was being detained at the Women's Detention Center in Palo Alto, just a few minutes' drive from the Stanford campus. The black students on campus, and their white liberal allies, felt the excitement and responsibility of their heroine's proximity and threw themselves into working on her behalf. They organized the Stanford Students for the Defense of Angela Davis and Other Political Prisoners to raise consciousness and money for the cause. On campus they built replicas of Davis's prison cell and distributed their propaganda through the prison bars. At football games they sold homemade soul food prepared by Big Daddy McCollum, a black chef who had worked at the Stanford Faculty Club and donated his services free of charge. And though Charles had no prior journalistic experience, he became the "self-appointed editor" of *The Real News* ("Actually the paper was originally called *The Real News, Motherfucker*, but we changed it"), a Black Panther rag, and "attacked everyone I could" in his "aggressive" support of Davis.

As often as he could—dressed in his cap, his black leather jacket, and sporting his Free Angela Davis button—Charles attended Davis's trial. At the doors to the courthouse, he would endure a "humiliating search" and then have to remove his button and hat. But he was totally captivated by the courtroom drama. He found that his attention was rarely focused on Angela; he trained his eyes on the lawyers, the jurors, and the judge, watched the interplay, anticipated the testimony and questions. "Even though a lot of it was boring—the registration of guns, the medical evidence—the process and strategies were fascinating," remembers Charles. "I sat there wondering how they were going to tie this all together."

The not guilty verdict came as a big surprise. Throughout the trial Charles had been overwhelmed by Davis's ability to play lawyer for herself, by her powerful analysis and arguments. But never once did he anticipate that "this reasonable group of twelve people on the jury would do the right thing. I didn't expect the jury to acquit her," recalls Charles. "I didn't trust the system to treat her fairly." When the trial was over and the victory was announced, Charles had a double-edged response. The first surprised him. "I heard the news and felt a sense of emptiness." His second reaction was comforting, hopeful. "I was reassured that lawyers can play an important role, not only in procedural matters but also in the fight for justice."

About a dozen Stanford students were actively involved in the political demonstrations surrounding the Angela Davis trial, but Charles was "thrust" into the fiery center of it. Charles often refers to the experience of being thrust into leadership roles almost as if he had nothing to do with creating the conditions for his elevation to positions of influence and responsibility, or as if somehow the positions were generously bestowed upon him. But time and time again—as student body president of Merced High School, as president of the Black Student Union at Stanford—Charles emerged as the leader, the one with the vision, strategies, energy, commitments, style, and character that made people want to follow him. Charles's description of his leadership is modest. He focuses on his diligence, his organizational talent, his ability to keep track of a lot of details. "I never wore the mantle of leadership... but I was never overwhelmed by it either. I thought of myself as doing just a few things... simple ideas... that over time made big things happen." The leadership question interests him, and he searches further into his past. "I've always thought of myself as shy and reserved. I never thought of myself as a leader... In many ways I've been oblivious to it. As a kid, you know, I was a crybaby... I was a thumb-sucker through the fifth grade.... I had no big brother around, no earlier generation to show me the way."

As I listen to Charles, I suspect that his leadership is less a reflection of organizational talents or charisma, and more a reflection of his profound commitments, and a hard-won self-assurance mastered over many years. He is someone who inspires trust and respect. People seem to recognize that Charles's work never seems to be about self-promotion or self-aggrandizement. He is always fighting for something larger than himself; laboring for the collective good, for "my brothers and sisters back home." His responsibilities are to his "home folks."

Charles sees the faces of his family and his childhood friends when he teaches criminal defense to his law students at Harvard and challenges the biases and perspectives that grow out of their privilege. Every day he thinks of his friend Eugene, who is a haunting reminder of how recklessly and unjustly the cards of life can be dealt. Charles is both burdened and inspired by these ghosts from his past, which direct his present commitments and give them purpose and meaning. He carries the burdens modestly and seriously. He is energized but not consumed by the guilt of becoming successful and leaving his buddies behind. He will never feel successful until all of his people have the chance to "play on a level playing field." There is little pleasure or pride for Charles in visibility or tokenism. He wants to be there arm in arm with the others, in the company of his "brothers and sisters" who are "just as deserving."

Charles vividly recalls his unbridled "innocence" and enthusiasm as he anticipated the visit of several of his buddies from Merced during his freshman year at Stanford. "Merced was light years away from my experience at Stanford," he recalls. In 1971, the Civil Rights clamor on college campuses was at its peak, and the black students at Stanford were determined and aggressive in their insistence that the university respond to their demands for a larger African-American presence—in the faculty, student body, and curriculum. Charles and his activist friends had pushed for a recruitment effort that would involve inviting black high school students to Stanford for a weekend conference; the purpose being to expose them to university life, and with luck, to get some of them to apply. Charles was at the center of the plans for the weekend. His excitement grew as he visualized the guys whom he would invite up from his own high school. He could hardly wait for the arrival of the ten students from Merced. He could hardly wait to make the connections, answer their questions, welcome them into his new world, and reduce some of the light years of psychological distance between Stanford and Merced.

Bobby Seale was scheduled to give the keynote speech at the conference, and Charles was both elated that they had managed to get a political leader of such stature and vision and a little worried that his "brothers" might find Seale's message overwhelming or incomprehensible. But what he had not prepared himself for was his "homeboys'" reaction to the *place*—the bigness, fanciness, abundance, and whiteness of the Stanford campus, the sheer scale of it all. "They were overwhelmed by the whole experience, overwhelmed by the environment, really—by my having my own room, by the black posters up on the walls, by people studying medicine and law... by Bobby Seale, *in person*." As Charles showed the prospective recruits around, as he tried to make them feel welcome and comfortable, he could feel them pulling away. He could see their faces closing down and their eyes glazing over as the experience "got to be too much" for them. The environment did not overwhelm all of them; a few students were turned on and inspired by the possibility of coming to Stanford and applied enthusiastically.

But all of Charles's friends got on the bus at the end of the weekend and traveled the one hundred miles south to Merced, back to the little rural town that seemed light years away. None of them sent in applications despite Charles's repeated urgings.

This experience, which Charles had helped push for and design, felt like a poignant disappointment for him. He was forced to let go of some of his idealism, to relinquish his wish that the distance between Merced and Stanford was just a matter of miles. He had to begin to confront the separations between his two worlds, the uniqueness of his place in the university, the ways in which the elite white world—even when it rolled out the carpet of welcome— seemed to send off signals of exclusion. Perhaps there was no way that the black kids from Merced could have been made to feel comfortable. He began to see the distance between home and school as a great, threatening abyss, impossible to span with the civility and pleasantries of a weekend.

Although the psychological distance was profound, Charles himself remained committed to bridging it, leaping over the ever-widening chasm and remaining in touch with his home folks. During his freshman year, he traveled to Merced frequently, partly because he had a girlfriend back home, but mostly because he missed the familiarity of the place. "My withdrawal to Stanford was gradual... I was not a stranger in Merced. I certainly felt the distance and the difference of being a *college student*, but I wasn't a stranger." Stanford felt abundant and alien, even though he had thrown himself into the middle of the fray of political action; even though he was doing very well in his courses; even though he had made some very good friends.

The summer between his freshman and sophomore years, Charles took a job back home as "a way to get back into the community." He could feel it slipping away. He was hired to manage the public pool and park on the south side—the black side—of Merced. The first thing he did was hire an all-black staff—guys who had been his friends in high school, athletes of distinction, good (if unorthodox) swimmers, but none of them lifeguards. This was the first time Merced had ever seen black lifeguards, even at the southside pool. Black guards, of course, would *never* have been hired for the white public pool. Charles promised his employers that all of his staff would earn their Red Cross lifeguard certificates before the opening of the summer season. So these black basketball and football players immersed themselves in an intense training course taught by a white instructor who had worked at the pool in previous summers. And each one of them, in turn, became full-fledged lifeguards and entered into an ambitious summer of special programs for the black folks on the south side.

For the first time, the lifeguards instituted adult night from 7:00 to 10:00 P.M. on Wednesday evenings, because with all the kids in the pool, the grown-ups never could find space to swim. Charles grins at the memory of Imogene Shephard, a large woman of over three hundred pounds, who used to come to swim every Wednesday night. As she approached the water, the lifeguards would hold their breath. Slowly, methodically, ritualistically she would lower her large body into the pool until she sank underwater. "It was a ceremony when she got in the water... She'd go in and our hearts would stop... God, bring her up, *please*." And each time, despite their trepidations, Imogene Shephard's body would come back up, and she would emerge with a broad smile. "Each time God would be generous and bring her back up," recalls Charles with relief. As he tells the story of his summer managing the black pool, Charles relives the pleasures of the camaraderie with his homeboys on the staff, the male bonding. But mostly he recalls how important it was for him to maintain the connections to home. "It was a way to get back into the community.... I felt the difference but I was not a stranger."

No Rain Without Thunder

For the first time I see Charles Ogletree looking casual. He is dressed in faded jeans, sneakers, a striped tee shirt, and a lightweight cotton jacket, and his athleticism is apparent: his dense muscular body, the slightly pigeon-toed stance of a runner. These "play clothes" contrast sharply with the dark blue or brown suits he wears as a uniform during the academic year, and they make him appear both younger and less encumbered. Charles has just returned from California, where he attended his first board of trustees meeting at Stanford University. His election to the board was a "big deal" for him. He is honored and pleased to be serving his alma mater, even though he knows that there is trouble on the campus that everyone calls "the Farm."

A few months ago, a distinguished female surgeon at the medical school resigned amid charges of sexual harassment. Weeks later an assistant professor was busted for drugs. Meanwhile, the federal government is accusing several administrators and faculty of misusing research grant funds. Charles shakes his head and says with a smile, "I sometimes wonder whether they chose me because I am a criminal defense lawyer and they thought they might need my services."

Actually, the Stanford people had been secretly checking him out for several months, making calls to people in California, Washington, and Cambridge, "a more thorough search than an FBI file." He is one of a few African-Americans on the thirty-five-person board and rare among these in having been appointed directly by the board, rather than elected through the alumni body. Charles is quietly proud of this new appointment. He is drawn by old connections and new controversy. His temperament, talent, and training seem a perfect counteractant for the institutional disruption.

After the board meeting, Charles went to visit his mother in

Merced. He describes his visits home as "bittersweet" and begins by describing the sweet part. The chance to fish (his "great vice") is at the top of his list of pleasures; he *always* manages to go fishing when he is at home. It gives him the chance to see old friends and establish an easy, familiar camaraderie; it allows him the time to "cool out" and test his well-developed skills; it brings back all the echoes from childhood of fishing with his grandfather, grandmother, mother, and uncles; and it takes him to the farmlands and woods around Merced, which he used to explore as a boy. Fishing is a sweet connection to his past in this town, a connection to the land, the rivers, and the people. Also, when he is home he spends a lot of his time just driving around town seeing as many of the folks as he can. "Everyone wants to do something special for me, and I'm always saying, 'I just want to drop by and hang out for a while.'"

Blacks make up only twelve percent of Merced's population, and most of them were born and raised right there in the San Joaquin Valley. As he visits old neighbors and friends, he begins to taste the bitter part of his experience at home. Everyone reports stories of human tragedy and defeat—the people who have been murdered or imprisoned, the old folks who have died, the children who have had babies or gotten hooked on drugs. There are, of course, a few tales of victory and achievement, but these are never as plentiful, or as dramatic, as the tragedies and defeats. So when Charles goes home, he experiences a dual sensation. People welcome him with open arms and sing his praises, but they also inspire the feelings of sadness and guilt that come with witnessing the injustices and wanting desperately to find a way to give back to his community.

One modest way he has decided to give back is through the creation of a scholarship fund for black students graduating from Merced High. He riffles through his briefcase and finds a Polaroid photograph of the two young women who were awarded the scholarships this year; both are tall, lean, dark-skinned, smiling, and proud as they hold up their shiny plaques. The scholarship is indeed modest at five hundred dollars, but it is meant to be an incentive, a public recognition of their diligence and motivation. Charles reviews the student applications (this year there were twelve applications, none of them from boys) and he decides, as a committee of one, who should get the awards. His decision is based largely on need; he does not necessarily give the scholarships to the highest achievers or the smartest students. He figures that the top students will be more likely to get funds from the colleges that they will attend. Instead, Charles identifies the candidates who come from backgrounds of poverty and who have shown an enormous determination "to work hard and move forward." They may not be honor roll students, but he wants to reward their character and drive. "This is something small and concrete I can do. I hope to encourage first-generation college goers—kids and their parents who are overcoming adversity."

This year's winners, looking fancy in their dark blue dresses and elegant corn-rowed hair, will be the first in their families to go to college. One is the daughter of a high school custodian and a food service worker; the other is the child of a single parent who "has worked hard every day to keep the family off of public assistance." Both girls are the daughters of people who were in high school with Charles. As he shows me the girls' applications, his voice fills with emotion, an emotion born out of deep identification with these students and of knowing the possibilities and casualties that lie ahead for them.

The two scholarships are given in the name of Charles's parents and his sister, Barbara, a law enforcement officer who was murdered in 1982. Mention of Barbara's murder almost gets lost in the description of the scholarship program, but it stops me cold. "How was she killed?" I whisper. Charles's voice is flat as he rehearses the tragedy. The oldest daughter in the Ogletree family, Barbara was an excellent student in high school, very involved in student government and school clubs, very active in the church and in the community. "Everyone expected her to have a vital and productive life... She was just as prominent as I was in high school, but in a different kind of way." She decided not to go on to college, choosing instead to get married and follow her lifelong dream of entering law enforcement. Barbara became the first black woman police officer on the county force, and she distinguished herself as a diligent and skilled professional and a dedicated community citizen. After her baby Alex was born, Barbara's marriage began to falter. Her husband seemed to have trouble with her ambitions and her assertiveness. "They went down separate paths," says Charles sadly. Her husband wanted her "to stay at home and be the traditional wife," so their marriage ended in acrimony.

Following the separation, one night someone entered her house and stabbed her one time in the heart, killing her instantly. The entry was not forced; there was no evidence of burglary. It was a simple, cold-blooded murder. When the police came to the house, they found three-year-old Alex curled up under a blanket, huddled next to his mother's body on the living room floor. Immediately the police arrested Barbara's husband as the prime suspect, but he was later released when the detectives claimed that they did not have enough evidence to hold him. "She was twenty-five years old, so vital, so committed... What a loss. She had stayed home while the rest of us had left... She was giving back to the community." Charles's face is impassive; his eyes are dry and tired. This is a story he has been over hundreds of times, and he seems unwilling to invest his emotions fully in this retelling. The scholarship in her name is designed to "keep the focus on Barbara's contribution to the community, *and* to keep everyone alert to the fact that the case is still unsolved." Every time Charles returns home, he talks to his friends on the police force—"guys I went to high school with"—and urges them to continue the search. But by now, almost ten years after the murder, most of the critical evidence has been lost or destroyed, and the investigation process has ground to a standstill, leaving everyone in a "lingering state of ambivalence."

~

Charles finished Stanford in three years, graduating with an excellent academic record and a Phi Beta Kappa key. But his college years had been filled with much more than academic work, student government, and political activism. Stanford University opened doors to the world, and Charles seized every opportunity to push against the boundaries of experience. Soon after arriving on campus, Charles sought out Dr. Sinclair Drake, a distinguished scholar in the African-American Studies Department and a special mentor and advocate for black students. Dr. Drake quickly recognized Charles's intelligence, his ambition, and his extraordinary commitment. The professor and student soon discovered they shared interests and values. With Drake's encouragement, Charles read Karl Marx, Frantz Fanon, Mao Tse-tung, W.E.B. Du Bois, and Frederick Douglass. He took courses in political theory, African liberation, and Third World development.

The rich academic experience was enhanced by international travel. By the end of his sophomore year, Charles was on his way to Cuba, as the only black member of a delegation of activist student leaders. The group traveled to Mexico and boarded a Soviet plane with a Cuban crew ("with beautiful black stewardesses decorated in lots of makeup"). Before the flight, Charles harbored "an image of Cuba as a place where everyone dressed in fatigues and carried machine guns." But when he arrived, he saw ordinary folks trying out brave new ideas. The delegation traveled to each province and met with student leaders, factory workers, teachers, and farmers working in the sugarcane fields. "My skeptical eye was always alert to racial differences," remembers Charles. He was inspired by the racial mixtures and the unity of spirit. "'We are Cubans,' they kept telling us. 'We are one.'"

Two years later, during his senior year, Charles was on his way to the Sixth Pan-Africanist Conference in East Africa—a Congress held every ten years on the "motherland." When Professor Drake couldn't attend, he asked Charles to represent him and to deliver his paper. Traveling to Nairobi with a group of two hundred African-Americans—then on to the University of Dar es Salaam in Tanzania—Charles felt his world expanding. He loved the diversity—of ideas, dress, ideology—that enlivened the student discussions. He loved this introduction to a broad array of African traditions and cultures. He felt compelled to learn more about African politics, and when he finished his undergraduate training, he decided to spend a year doing graduate study in international relations at Stanford.

At the end of the year, Charles collected his M.A., but he knew that the life of a scholar was too abstract for him, too removed from the action. He yearned for a profession in which he could be more directly engaged in social and political action. Working on the

Angela Davis trial, Charles had been fascinated by the legal process, by its concepts, strategies, and the theater of the courtroom. He had carefully watched the human drama, the boring rule-bound questioning, the turning points, the attorneys' strategies, the education of the jury, and the surprising verdict. He had emerged with a more complex and realistic picture of the legal process, and with a determination to use it as a weapon for fighting injustice.

But Charles had also watched helplessly as his friend Eugene got caught in the relentless workings of legal machinery; he saw how it seemed impossible to penetrate the system once a person—especially a poor black man-child—got locked inside of it. The legal process seemed both liberating and imprisoning, both surprising and inevitable, both impartial and prejudicial, both theater and nightmare. Perhaps Charles was inspired by the apparent contradictions and by the chance that he might be able to tip the scales toward the more benign uses of the law. Most certainly he felt drawn to the law as a way to use his heart and his head; as a way to think about and fight for justice; as a way to take advantage of his complex temperament of cool confidence and energetic aggression.

His decision to apply to Harvard Law School came at the urging of his fianceé Pam, a fellow student at Stanford, who had grown up in Compton, California. She saw her future husband's talents and knew his passions. She had witnessed his leadership on campus, his involvement in the civil rights struggle, his dedication to his academic work. She had watched him use his energies, seen him combine activism with academics, idealism with pragmatism. She was sure that he would be accepted at any law school to which he applied and sure that he would thrive and succeed wherever he decided to go. So Pam prodded, urged, and schemed as she tried to get Charles to apply to Harvard. She enlisted the help of good friends who also worked to convince him that he should at least "hold it open as an option."

To the young man from Merced, Harvard seemed too far away from home: too distant from the familiarity and comfort of California, too cold and gray. But at the urgings of his friends and professors, Charles finally agreed to apply to Harvard and to a few other law schools in California, including Berkeley and the University of

Southern California. He chose not to apply to Stanford Law School. "Four years was enough time on the Farm." When the acceptance from Harvard arrived, the first one he received, he did not tell anyone about it for several days. Finally hearing the news, Pam "pressed a lot, pushing and challenging" him in a way that she hoped he would not be able to refuse: "Do you want to get a good legal education that will help you fulfill your mission? Do you want to be most effective in helping communities of color? Are you afraid of the challenge, afraid you can't do the work and remain true to yourself?" Charles yielded under the pressure, but he remained "very ambivalent."

Some of Charles's ambivalence had to do with his image of Harvard's coldness and elitism. Some of it had to do with his worries about how he and Pam would weather the dislocation together. Pam had just graduated from Stanford; they were to be married that summer in Los Angeles and then head East to Cambridge. It made Charles uncomfortable that Pam did not have a plan. "What was *Pam* going to do there?... She had not yet decided whether she wanted to pursue education, business, or law." The entire move centered on Charles's career plans, and that made him uncomfortable.

All of Charles's reticence seemed well founded when the Ogletrees, newly married, arrived in Boston in the fall of 1975. It was a shock to all of his senses. "I found Boston and Harvard to be hostile places... The weather, the people, the city, the law school—all of it was harsh and difficult." It was particularly hard in contrast to the more "gentle" life at Stanford. "We called Stanford the Farm. It was genteel and bucolic... By contrast, Harvard Law School called itself The Law School, and it reflected arrogance, elitism, power. At Stanford, in classes I had experienced a range of compelling issues, a concern with democracy and the political process, a commitment to developing countries and international relations... By contrast, at Harvard they seemed to be narrowly focused on particular, insignificant cases that had little connection to the important social and political issues. At Stanford, the classes were more spontaneously run with the expectation of student participation but without pressure... By contrast, at Harvard the pressure was on, participation was mandatory, there was always a lot of competition and tension in the air.

At Stanford, there was not much concern about status and hierarchies or about the social standing of one's family... By contrast, at Harvard the wealth and origins of colleagues was terribly important, and there was a necessity to talk about it. I found this all *shocking!*" Charles draws the contrasts vividly. They still seem to be jarring in their uncomfortable opposition.

But it wasn't merely the coldness and elitism of the law school that offended the new transplant from the West Coast; it was also the larger context of Boston that felt cruel and cold. "We arrived in the middle of the busing crisis. It was shocking and ugly." As Charles dealt with the snobbishness of Harvard's elites, he watched the horrible battles over desegregation in Boston's schools, more than twenty years after the *Brown* v. *Board of Education* decision. He cringed at the racist harangues of Louise Day Hicks, the insulting slurs of the local politicians, the dangerous threats of the South Boston Irish, the fear and rage of the black community. In many ways, this crisis seemed worse in its smoldering hatred than the earlier civil rights battles in the South. The resistance seemed so deeply woven into the fabric of ethnic and racial territoriality. And the contradictions between the subtle pseudoliberalism of the Harvard elites on one side of the Charles River and the crude rage of the ethnic working class on the other side—in South Boston and elsewhere—were the most shocking of all. For the first time, I hear Charles use the language of extremes—"shocking, ugly, terrifying, harsh"—to describe the scene in parts of Boston and Cambridge in 1975. For a moment he relinquishes his normally moderate, carefully crafted sentences to spew back some of the venom that was unleashed on him a decade and a half ago.

Charles and some of his black male colleagues bonded together and sought refuge in sports. Ten first-year students organized "a rough touch" football team that they called the Black Plague. With black tee shirts and bold red letters spelling out "Black Plague," they became the winningest intramural team in the history of the Harvard Law School. They practiced hard, played with all their heart and soul, reclaimed all of their athleticism, harnessed their rage, and emerged exhausted and victorious. In their first year, the Black Plague was undefeated until the last game, in which they were beat by one point. "It was a heart breaker," recalls Charles, leaning back and clasping his heart, reliving the moment as if it were yesterday.

But the Black Plague was much more than a rough touch football team. It is the first thing Ogletree recalls when he thinks about his survival at the law school. "There was a strong sense of kinship. It was a source of identity... an inner circle of strength." It reminded Charles of hanging out with his "homeboys" back in Merced—the easy, fluid talk, the humor, the camaraderie. The warm blackness buffered him against the cold white climate of Harvard. Alone, each of the young men were vulnerable, exposed; together—in their Black Plague armor—they were invincible.

There was a political cast to the Black Plague as well, which was thrilling to Charles. The guys on the team were mostly left-leaning and "progressive." They did not share career goals but they held consonant values. "None of us were interested in the same law— there was a range—but we had very similar political views... There were no conservative black views on the team. Maybe only three or four of us were politically active, but we all believed in the struggle." Reggie Thomas, the man the team referred to as its "spiritual leader," was the president of Harvard's Black Law Students Association (BLSA) at the same time as Charles was the president of the national BLSA. So the Black Plague had more than its share of prominent black political leaders. Charles contrasts the Black Plague with the other intramural black team, the Mean Machine, which was made up of second- and third-year students who were thought to be both more conservative in their politics and more energetic in their social life. "They were in the fast lane," says Charles without a hint of accusation. "La Raza," the Latino team, provided a haven for its Hispanic members. As if to underscore the importance of the Black Plague, Charles says again, "It was a version of black male bonding... It provided an identity for us outside of the classroom." Fifteen years later, after scores of intramural teams have come and gone, the Black Plague, its name and identity intact, still survives. When Charles is in town, he often goes to their games—rooting for their victory as athletes and cheering for their identity as black men committed to the struggle.

In the classroom, off the playing field, Charles struggled with the methods, the curriculum, and the perspectives presented by his white male professors at the law school. He had never been "in such huge classes with so little student participation." He had never experienced such fierce competition among his classmates. But mostly, he struggled against the legalistic perspective that insisted upon objectivity and neutrality. "I found the first year very difficult, absolutely nerve-racking... It went against every instinct in my body." He had come to law school, after all, to prepare himself with the tools to fight for the causes he believed in. He could not see the value in trying to be dispassionate or neutral. "I came to law school convinced of the correctness of my stance, whether it was affirmative action or divestment in South Africa. I *resisted* the idea that there was another side to these commitments. I resisted the idea of the validity of opposing views... Being neutral was incredibly troublesome." So as he sat through his classes, Charles felt the impersonality of the large lecture courses, he chafed at the confrontational pedagogy that inhibited real dialogue and inquiry, and he mightily "resisted" the notion of cool neutrality. He kept saying to himself, "I have a mission here. I am here for an instrumental reason. I want to make critical choices."

Outside of class, Charles approached some of his professors, choosing the ones who might be open to his perspective and expressing his ambivalence. He tried to convey his dismay, his impatience, his deep frustration with what he was learning, and he seriously considered leaving. "I talked to my professors about whether I should even be there." His resistance was revealed in his grades. For the first time, his academic work was not stellar. "I was an average student, constantly disappointing myself and my professors. I kept on being distracted. I wanted to break away from the limited, narrow perspective. I was hopelessly bored. I came close to completely shutting down. I needed to be doing something NOW... I needed so badly to demonstrate a constant commitment to change, challenge, and reform."

As Charles recalls the frustration and disappointments of his law student days, I can almost hear echoes of "the conflicting agendas" in the dilemmas and ambivalence he faces as a professor. The echoes get played out in his determination to design a "convergence of his academic and political work." The echoes get played out in the way he deliberately joins conceptual and clinical work and seeks to create an atmosphere of inquiry, reflection, and dialogue in the classroom. The echoes get played out in his clear and constant support of black students who are feeling alienated by Harvard's aloofness and elitism or who are searching for ways to participate in the fight for equality and justice. When Charles recalls his student days—"my restlessness was great"—I hear the same restless urges in the professor today, causing him to question his purpose, his motivations, and the impact of his teaching at the law school. "It is still an open question, always haunting me."

One of the ways Charles tries to conquer his restlessness is to design a work life in which he is doing "three times as much as any other faculty person." This is the first time I've heard him admit how extraordinarily crowded his life is and the first time I've heard him take responsibility for having *chosen* to work so hard. Why, I ask, does he drive himself so hard? His voice is soft, reflective. "I need a lot of *encouragement* to spend my critical legal years at Harvard... I'm deeply ambivalent. The students are fantastic, my colleagues are thoughtful, there is tremendous opportunity here... But it seems so far removed from my mission in life, I want to use my talents and skills to improve the lot of oppressed people... I ask myself, 'Is there a direct benefit to anyone in my community?'"

Charles wrestles with his ambivalence by creating work for himself that will allow him to feel productive and accountable to his home folks; that will allow him to see the imprint of his labors on the institution and on his students, not just in law journals. So in addition to a heavy load of teaching—courses in criminal law, criminal procedure, criminal justice administration, and trial advocacy—Charles recently started a Criminal Justice Institute at Harvard. The institute, whose programs embrace teaching, research, policy, and social service, reaches its tentacles out into the community—working with gangs, health-care initiatives, Big Brother groups, and tutoring programs—and tries to change the nature of dialogue and theory within the academic legal community. Still in its infancy, the

Institute offers programs that are ambitious, eclectic, and activist in orientation. Charles is the visionary leader and the manager of a staff of three full-time clinical instructors, several part-time lawyers who work in a supervisory capacity, and scores of eager students.

Around the Harvard Law School, however, Charles is probably best known for Saturday School, a course he started three years ago, "designed to empower black students." The idea for Saturday School has autobiographical roots. "When I was a student here, there was a total absence of contact with black professionals: We never had any role models... We never saw law as an interdisciplinary topic, embedded in culture, politics, the economy." When Charles returned to Harvard to teach, he remembered his feelings of loneliness and isolation as a student; he recalled his unsuccessful search for mentors. Saturday School, a noncredit course, was his answer to these painful memories.

On seven Saturdays each semester, seventy to one hundred fifty students come to hear a rich mix of speakers, usually black, always prominent, always provocative, often controversial. The majority of students who come regularly are black. But the "nonminority" presence has increased as white students have heard the enthusiastic reports from their black peers and watched the parade of illustrious speakers. Everyone is welcome, but Charles's focus remains on the black students—on "building their self-confidence, increasing their academic strengths, challenging them to interact in discussions... so they will not be silenced." Saturday School is not part of the official law school curriculum, but when Charles petitioned Derek Bok for funds, the former president of Harvard endowed Saturday School for three years. "I regard this as a constructive—rather than a cynical—effort," says Charles about a program that offers him the "privilege" of "giving something back."

In fact, Charles's resistance during his student days at the law school seems to have had lasting educational value. "You see, I had to come up with an argument to articulate my resistance." The process of finding the language to articulate the contrary perspective was itself enabling and instructive. But the "real value" of his legal education—the socialization *and* the resistance—did not emerge until years later when Charles found himself able to call on the discipline, clarity, and rigor of his Harvard training. As a public defender he found he was able to join his passion with the logic, the strategy with the theory. "Afterward, while practicing law, I was amazed at how powerful a tool the law was. I had absorbed an enormous amount in law school... I had others marveling at my skills and my perspective." Using his law school training did not mean relinquishing his values or his commitments. It did not even mean inhibiting his passions. "The challenge was to maintain my vigor... to see that counterarguments did not mean I had to lose my perspective. It *did* mean I had to *refine* my views on justice and equality... refine my unrefined principles."

The training in law school also helped Charles develop the role he would so effectively play in courtroom drama. "It is not that law school *gave* me anything... It forced me to bring out some things that were already within me—scrutiny, mastery, and criticism." Within himself he found the qualities that allowed him to "withstand criticism and humiliation, including a strong *internal* constitution that supported his *external* appearance of confidence, clarity, and comfort in the courtroom. If law school had been easier and more fluid, if there had been a more perfect match between Charles's strong commitments and Harvard's insistent socialization, maybe the education would not have been as transformative. For Charles, there was (and is) power in the resistance and energy in the disharmony that caused him to clarify and articulate what he believed and caused him to develop a "convergence" of the opposing perspectives.

For months I have been noticing the Frederick Douglass quotation that is perched on the shelf behind Charles's desk. The handmade neon orange poster with the strong black calligraphy shouts the message of struggle. Today as I listen to Charles's soliloquy on the power of resistance, I hear Douglass's voice:

> If there is no struggle, there is no progress. Those of us who profess to favor freedom yet depreciate agitation are men who want the crops without plowing up the ground.

They want rain without the thunder and the lightning. They want the ocean without the awful roar of its many waters.

This struggle may be a moral one or a physical one, but it must be a struggle. Power concedes to nothing without demand. It never has and it never will. Show me the exact amount of wrong and injustices that are visited upon a people and I will show you the exact amount of words endured by these people. These wrongs and injustices must be fought with words or with blows or both. The limits of tyrants are prescribed by the endurance of those whom they oppress.

—Frederick Douglass

On Their Shoulders

It has been four weeks since I've seen Charles Ogletree. He has just returned, the night before, from a vacation-work trip to Hawaii with his family. ("Pam and the kids vacationed the whole time, and I was able to play seventy-five to eighty percent of the time. It was great!") He has gotten off the plane, come directly to his office, tackled six huge piles of already sorted mail, and gone home to sleep. He has one day in Cambridge—with two more big stacks of correspondence to pore through, scores of telephone calls to return, travel arrangements to make, and editing to do on works in progress—before heading back out to the West Coast the next day, where he will combine lecturing and his twentieth high school reunion in Merced, California.

When I arrive he is sitting behind his desk sorting through mail and talking with his assistant, who is bent over his calendar. His assistant reflects the pressures of his busy life. She looks overwhelmed and disgruntled as she squeezes another commitment onto the already crowded calendar; as he asks her to arrange another car rental; as he gives her the words to write a memo to incoming students about Saturday School; as he instructs her about which disk needs to be printed out. But Charles himself exhibits none of the stress as he fills his twenty-four hours between trips with forty-eight hours' worth of activity. He is the eye of the storm he has generated. He rises from his calm perch behind his chaotic desk, comes forward, gives me a big hug and exclaims, "It has been *ages!*" It does seem as if we have not seen each other for a very long time. Much has happened in Charles's life since we met a month ago.

Charles reaches for a flat folder on his desk. "Want to see what mischief I've been up to since I last saw you?... You know, of course, I've gotten in the middle of this Clarence Thomas thing."

One of Charles's old friends who works as counsel for the NAACP had called him in a panic a few weeks ago. "These Negroes are about to support the nomination of Clarence Thomas. They're saying that they can't publicly oppose the nomination because he's black—any black is better than no black at all." His friend had begged him to help change the tide of sentiment at the NAACP by preparing a professional legal assessment of Thomas's judicial experience, decisions, and perspective, a working paper offering evidence for opposing his nomination. Charles responded to his friend's plea for help and prepared a document ("The NAACP's Preliminary Assessment of Judge Clarence Thomas' Judicial Opinions and Legal Writings") in several days' time while he was "on planes, in airports, between all the other stuff" he had to do. The thirty-page document—full of case citations and careful arguments—became the basis for "ninety-five percent" of the statement of opposition (on the basis of Thomas's legal qualifications) that the NAACP adopted a couple of weeks later. Charles's quick work had provided the basis for the NAACP's surprising shift in position. With his persuasive legal brief, the NAACP senior staff felt that they could defend the anti-Thomas position that they knew would be unpopular in many circles.

As Charles tells me about his quick immersion in this project, this opportunity to use legal scholarship as the basis for political rhetoric and positioning, his movement across the boundaries of the academy into the real world—his voice is full of energy. He shakes his head at the near "catastrophe" of the NAACP supporting Thomas's nomination and says that somehow "our generation of black professionals" needs to assume a greater responsibility for the civil rights organizations—such as the NAACP, the Southern Christian Leadership Conference (SCLC), the Urban League—whose leadership has grown old and weary. "We need to find a way to reengage in the work of these organizations... We need to become recommitted, reenergized."

In many ways this document that Charles has prepared for the NAACP reflects the way he likes to work. He likes to work quickly, pragmatically, strategically toward a focused goal. He likes to respond to his old friends' pleas for help and resources. He likes to serve as interpreter between the worlds of scholarship, policy making, and activism. He likes to see the effects of his work. He likes to work behind the scenes, assembling the pieces that will produce visible change. He likes to move between the black community and the elite white spheres of knowledge and power, using his access to the latter to nurture the former. This is quintessential Ogletree: quick, productive, strategic, selfless, determined, and, through it all, calm.

~

After bringing me up to date, Charles seizes this moment to look backward and trace his family's ancestry. He begins with his mother's side of the family. Born in Little Rock, Arkansas, in 1933, Charles's mother, Willie Mae Reed, was the firstborn child of Essie D. (the middle initial "D" did not stand for a name; it was put there by Essie's parents "the way a lot of black folks did to give their names the ring of respect") and Willie. Willie Mae had three siblings: Edna (always called Etna "for some unknown reason"), Charlie, and Nadine. Nadine, the youngest, had had an identical twin, Madine, who had died when she was a baby. In the early 1940s the Reeds had migrated from Arkansas to Richmond, California. Willie Reed had heard about the great opportunities for work in the West and had dragged his family across the country with promise and hope in his heart.

Like so many other black men of his generation who wanted to believe that there was some place in this large country where racism would not be so virulent and oppressive, Willie discovered that California was not the land of opportunity. He got to Richmond, hoping for steady, respectable employment, and found himself once again at the bottom of the heap. Between the backbreaking work of migrant farming and infrequent employment repairing train tracks for the railroad, Willie managed to scrape together barely enough to feed his family. After a few years in Richmond, Willie heard news that there was steady work in the San Joaquin Valley, and he moved his family south to a little rural town outside of Merced called Chowchilla. In the hot sun, Willie and Essie and their four children worked the fields—hauling hay, chopping cotton, picking fruit and vegetables, and receiving an hourly wage. "It was really the 1940s version of indentured servitude," says Charles. They had to spend most of their wages on renting a room from their boss, a barely livable space with no running water or toilets and a corner for cooking.

It was at one of these migrant labor camps that Charles's father, Charles Ogletree, Sr., arrived in the early 1950s and began to court Willie Mae. She was eighteen and he was forty-two, and at first Willie Mae's parents did not look approvingly on this romance. "They knew my father as an older man and had questions about his amorous interest in my mother," says Charles using the old-fashioned language of his parents' generation. Despite the protests of Willie Mae's parents, the two were married in Chowchilla ("really just a rural post office box") in 1951, and their first child, Charles Jr., was born on December 31, 1952. The nurses at the local hospital in Merced kept on urging Willie Mae to try to hold out in her labor long enough for the baby to be the firstborn child in 1953. "But my mother would have none of that. She had carried me for nine months and that was enough." Charles was born at 12:35 P.M. on New Year's Eve, 1952.

After a stint in the military, Charles Sr. had migrated to California from Aniston, Alabama, a small town close to Birmingham. He was born in 1908 and was the third of four siblings. Clifford, the oldest, and Mary, the only daughter, had remained in Alabama, while Charles Sr. and another brother, Robert, had left the South to seek their fortunes in the West and Northeast. Charles Sr. had gone as far as the fifth grade in a public school for "coloreds" in Birmingham. He was not a diligent student, did not like school, and "tried to avoid it at all costs."

"My father would never have considered himself bright," says Charles as a way of contrasting his father's disinterest and lackluster performance in school with his mother's diligence and aptitude. Willie Mae sailed through the Oakland, California, public school system, always tracked at the top, enjoying her classes. "My mother was exceptionally bright, a very good student, a top performing student... I continue to urge her to go back and finish school. She is now working as a community aide in a school in Merced, but she could do so much more... even now." In tenth grade Willie Mae got pregnant and had to quit school. Charles's step-brother, Curtis Reed (he was given his mother's maiden name) was born nine months later, so at sixteen Willie Mae became a single parent.

When Willie Mae met Charles Sr. a year later, she was the mother of a small baby; he had been briefly married and divorced several years earlier. After Charles Jr. was born, they moved to their own one-room tenement at the farm where her parents were already working. A few years later, Willie Mae's father managed to buy a small piece of land and build a house, a modest three-room place with no bathroom on Vassar Avenue, "really a dirt road." The house was never finished; there was never enough money to do anything more than put the walls up ("just plain unfinished wood") and cover the rooms with a roof. Willie (Big Daddy), Essie D. (Big Mama), and their children and Willie Mae, Charles Sr., and the two boys all crowded into this tiny house, and "every couple of years there was another child." Robert was born in 1953, Barbara in 1955, Richard in 1957, and Rose in 1960. Five children in all; six counting step-brother Curtis. Willie Mae was still in her mid-twenties.

It was a life of "abject poverty," stretching meager resources until they could stretch no more. Big Daddy, "who was really the patriarch of the family, tried to find food from the land." He would get into his "long, big, dark car" and go out to the fishing holes to catch carp ("poor people's fish that tastes like mud") and catfish ("a real treat"). He would usually take the children along. "It was such a huge car, I remember I couldn't see out the back window," says Charles as he recalls his "grandfather much more vividly than my father." Big Daddy would hunt jackrabbit for his family's table and gather wild greens growing in the countryside, which Big Mama would cook up with some neck bones. They had a couple of hogs on their place, which they would slaughter and then fully devour. "My grandfather found a way to eat *every* part of the hog, from top to bottom, head to tail, inside out. It always amazed me... We'd eat the snout, the tail, the intestines, the feet—every single bit of it was used for our sustenance."

After Big Mama's stroke, she could no longer work the fields, but she continued to manage and run the household, cooking, cleaning, washing the clothes. Her infirmity slowed her down some but it didn't dampen her spirits or cause her to feel sorry for herself. "She had all of her mental faculties." She was a great pragmatist and had a wonderful sense of humor. "I was charmed and entertained by her," says Charles, grinning at the memory. "She never complained about her condition or her plight in life."

By the time all five Ogletree children had arrived, the three-room house on Vassar Avenue, packed with three generations, was definitely feeling overcrowded, so Charles Jr., his siblings, and his parents moved to a place a few blocks away. "I'm sure it happened like this," smiles Charles. "My grandfather told my grandmother that it was time for us to leave. My grandmother told my mother, and my mother told my father." Charles Jr. entered kindergarten at Weaver Elementary School, the "country school for farm kids nearby." Weaver was integrated by race and class. Black and white children who came from the families of the farm owners and their migrant tenants were mixed together in classes. Charles remembers two experiences from his kindergarten year. The first has to do with his teacher's determination to change Charles's habit from writing with his left hand to writing with his right. By his own admission, Charles's writing was "atrocious... and still is," and the teacher thought that his penmanship might improve if he switched to writing with his right hand. She also seemed to think that left-handedness was "bad," that it might interfere with his intellectual development. "So for the first months of kindergarten she worked to pressure me into being right-handed, and I steadfastly resisted." (Charles's mother, Willie Mae, was completely ambidextrous and could not understand why her son couldn't manage to use *both* of his hands to do whatever he needed to do.)

The second experience was a puzzling and embarrassing encounter. One morning he arrived at school, and his teacher immediately sent him from the classroom with a note that he was instructed not to look at. Soon he was being told "by some adult" to take his clothes off, and instructed to take a shower. At the end of his shower, he was supplied with another set of used, laundered clothes and returned bright and clean to his classroom. Even though he was singled out from his class for this treatment, Charles does not recall being chastised or publicly humiliated. It happened only once, and it was kept completely private. Now he shakes his head, still wondering whether this was a benign or a paternalistic gesture, and whether other children—particularly the poor kids who, like him, had no bathtubs or showers in their houses—might have also been led to the shower. His smile looks sad to me. "I am certain I had those same clothes on for several days."

The lingering sadness of the shower incident does not prevent him from remembering the mischief he and his cousin George invented in kindergarten. Cousin George, Aunt Edna's son, was the same age as Charles and even at age five took school far less seriously than his cousin. "George taught me to steal," recalls Charles, his face brightening. At recess when the other children would go to play outside, George and Charles would go through their lunch boxes scavenging for delicious, sweet goodies. They would manage to collect quite a haul, "cookies, candies, chips." But the petty delinquency was short-lived. Soon the other children began to complain to the teacher about their favorite treats disappearing from their lunch boxes, and George and Charles abruptly ceased their thievery, fearing that the teacher was hot on their trail and would soon expose them in front of their classmates.

After the children had attended Weaver Elementary School for two years, the Ogletrees moved from the country into the city of Merced. From the second through the fifth grade, Charles attended a city school, Galen Clark, a predominantly black and Hispanic school. The principal of Galen Clark was a Native American man named Gaither B. Haynes, "a tall, thin, light-complected, black-haired man who dressed in wonderful ceremonial costumes for special occasions." He was a powerful presence in the school: a visible symbol of diversity and an outspoken advocate of multiculturalism. He urged the students—through rhetoric, action, and ritual—to feel proud about their racial and ethnic origins. "This was the first time," recalls Charles, "that I had ever heard anyone talk about these things."

On his very first day of school at Galen Clark, however, Charles received a whipping from this "wonderful" principal. On his way home at lunch time, he had lost his way and returned to school late. "We had only about thirty-five minutes for lunch... and you know I was from the country and I was used to *strolling.*" His teacher sent him to Mr. Haynes, who would hear none of his protestations about this being his first day at school, and losing his way in the city, and being only seven years old, and promising it would never happen again. The principal went over to his desk and took out his wooden paddle, which he called the board of education, and he whipped young Charles's behind. Charles remembers feeling that the punishment was very unfair, but he also recalls that he was never late to school, for any reason, ever again and that this experience with the board of education was his first and last spanking in school.

Even after this inauspicious beginning, Charles loved his three years at Galen Clark. He was a motivated, determined, inquiring student. His voice is rhapsodic as he describes "the thrill of the place." "I *loved* school... this was my little piece of the world. I set the agenda. I had *control* over school... I felt as if every one of my wishes and commands were granted... I felt empowered, accomplished there. I could do my work and ask for more. I was a very good reader, very good at math." School was a place of constancy, safety, reward, and achievement compared to Charles's family life. "The abject poverty of my family, the devastating despair *disappeared* when I entered school... I felt aggressively academic and comfortable there." Even when Charles brought home straight A's and glowing reports from his teachers, his parents did not reward him with praise or special notice. Mostly they worried about the reports of misbehavior that the teachers might send home about their children. "You knew they were thinking, 'Don't bring me no bad news.' My brother Robert occasionally had disciplinary problems, and my mother would have to go up to the school to speak to his teachers. But it didn't seem to matter much to my folks that I did very well in school. As far as I can remember, they never appreciated a report card."

Charles's most memorable year at Galen Clark was fourth grade because he had Mr. Lee, a black teacher. "You know how unusual and special that was, first of all, to have a male teacher in elementary school and then a black male teacher." Charles remembers Mr. Lee's devotion and attention when he tells the tale of his teacher sending him down to the black barber at Robert's Barber Shop one day with a note. "My hair must have looked nappy and unkempt, and very much in need of some attention... and Mr. Lee just quietly took it upon himself to have my hair cut. It was a very caring thing." After the haircut, Charles returned to his fourth-grade class looking neat and shorn. Mr. Lee grew very attached to young Charles; he saw such promise in him. He loved Charles's quickness, his questioning, his motivation, his diligence. He used to say that Charles's sad, droopy eyes masked the most brilliant mind. Charles looked placid, but behind his calm, laconic aspect he was perceptive and inquiring about everything.

More than thirty years later, Mr. Lee, now a dean at a community college in southern California, saw those "sad, droopy eyes" again. He was reading the *Los Angeles Times* on May 23, 1990, when he saw those eyes and felt a surge of recognition and familiarity. They looked just like the eyes of the little boy he had taught in the fourth grade three decades ago. He scanned the article underneath the photograph and saw Charles Ogletree's name. The *Times* piece was reporting on a panel on ethical dilemmas sponsored by the Los Angeles County Bar Association Barristers that Charles had moderated. It identified Charles as a Harvard Law professor.

Mr. Lee wasted no time phoning Charles. Charles's voice is full of emotion as he describes the surprise call from Mr. Lee. There is nothing he likes better than to rediscover his roots. Home is Merced, California. The home folks are precious to him, precious reminders of his responsibility, precious links to his origins and his strength. He says with force, "I have great contacts with home people. *It is the way I survive*. There is no way I could be as successful as I am without close and constant contact with people in Merced. *I'm on their shoulders*. I shiver sometimes when I think of all the ways I might not have made it, when I think of all the equally talented people who have not been able to make it. How fortunate I am." Now his voice is soft and thick. "You know I have no fear in my life. I've already accomplished more than I ever could have expected. I feel as if there is not too far to fall. I'm a survivor. I'm ready for any kind of battle."

Charles's mother, Willie Mae, was also a survivor. By the time baby sister Rose was born, Charles Sr. and Willie Mae had separated, and she was a single mother with six children on public assistance. They had been through years of domestic battling; Charles Sr. would become physically abusive of his young wife. When Willie Mae could take no more, she would call the police and they would come and take him away. Again Charles recalls the pain, grief, and rage of witnessing his father brutalizing his mother, and the sadness and humiliation of seeing his father turn from attacker to victim as he was put in the backseat of the police cruiser. He watched in silent inner conflict as the police car drove off. They would take Charles Sr. to a road camp, a kind of jail for short-term offenders, and Willie Mae would often take all the children to visit him there. "*She* would take us to see him... I mean, she wouldn't send us with someone else... She'd be sitting there talking to him, and we'd be off on the grounds playing."

Charles thinks of the hard times, the poverty, the violence, the constant moving ("I feel as if my mother was moving us every year"), and he pictures his mother struggling alone to parent her large brood. "It was like the mother duck with all of her ducklings. If she had a doctor's appointment, we would all have to go, no dawdling. It was a quick pace, and we all had to keep up. We'd all be in a row; my mother followed by me, followed by Robert, followed by Barbara, followed by Richard, with Baby Rose bringing up the rear... and we were all moving fast." Now, when people walk with Charles across Harvard's campus and have trouble keeping up with his rapid gait, he is reminded of the Ogletree ducklings trailing after their young mother. "From that time on, I have walked very quickly."

Family Legacy

The usual swirl of activity that surrounds Charles Ogletree has reached a clamorous pitch today. He is sitting behind his big desk talking on the telephone. The Senate Judiciary Committee hearings are on the radio; the volume is low but the message comes through. Spread in front of him on his desk are about twenty-five pink slips, urgent messages demanding quick response. Charles's assistant comes in and says that if she is to get any work done, she will have to stop answering the phone; it is ringing off the hook. Charles, still on the phone, motions for me to come in, and greets me warmly before resuming his conversation. I offer to retreat; to reschedule our interview. Even for Charles, this seems like an impossibly frenetic scene. But he is unperturbed. "No, we can go ahead. The first few hours it is going to be the opening speeches of the senators... Thomas won't come on until later. I have to do a five- or ten-minute commentary for the local TV news, but I can just go out and come back." He is trying to decide whether he will go down to Washington, D.C., to appear before the Judiciary Committee—whether it would be a useless, empty ritual or whether it might make a difference. He says to a lawyer friend on the telephone, "I'll go down if Thomas continues to hide behind this up-from-poverty-pulling-himself-up-by-his-bootstraps *crap*... If he doesn't speak to any of the issues."

I listen to the surprising rage in a voice that is almost always moderated and restrained and think that Thomas's using his childhood of poverty as a smoke screen for his "reactionary and destructive" stance must strike a raw nerve. After all, Charles's family legacy is no less painful or destitute than Thomas's, but he has not turned his back on his people or indulged in projections of self-hate. With every statement, Thomas seems to want to get as far away from his poor black origins as possible. He speaks disparagingly about his sister who is on public welfare. He blames the black community for its own deterioration. Photographs show him beaming, sandwiched between his white wife and his former teacher and mentor, a white nun. This judicial nominee, who is about to take a seat on the highest court in the land, has become everything that Charles abhors; everything Charles fights to correct; everything Charles is not. The rage rising up in him, and his unusually furious words—"this bootstrap crap"—are startling. From Charles's lips, "crap" sounds like the most despicable, ugliest word in the world.

Perhaps because of the distractions of the Clarence Thomas case, which has consumed a lot of Charles's time and energy, his office looks more chaotic than usual. There are piles of library books, supplies and materials overflowing boxes, correspondence, memos, papers falling off of high places. His daughter Rashida's bicycle is sandwiched between the bookshelves and the visitors' chairs. He has been riding the bicycle to school every day for exercise because a knee injury has made him stop his usual regimen of running every other day. The knee was injured several years ago and acts up from time to time. If the "more conservative approach" of bicycle riding does not work, he will need to have arthroscopic surgery on his knee. He's aching to get back to his three-mile runs; the exercise is "critical to my well-being." Running helps him get rid of some of his aggression, keeps his body strong and fit, and keeps him connected to his athletic youth. He smiles, "Now when Pam and I go over to Fresh Pond in the morning, she runs and I ride my bike alongside of her... It looks kind of strange."

This is our last session, and Charles chooses to look at the contrasts between his life as a child and the life he has created for his children. He describes what it feels like to "live in poverty," to be "obligated to go to public schools, to be dependent on public welfare for our survival... It always troubled me." He remembers his mother waiting for the welfare check twice a month, on the fifteenth and the thirtieth. There was a monthly rhythm. When the checks came, there would be immediate abundance. "We'd eat a lot right away!" But after a day of splurging on store-bought food, they would return to their diet of government-issued food. "There were versions of Spam. The welfare Spam had more cartilage than store-bought Spam. It was more pink than red. There was rice and beans and powdered eggs... The other kids in the neighborhood would take eggs out of the refrigerator in shells. We would add water to the powder to make our eggs." It was not the "brown, government-issued bags" or the "cold gray steel cans" that bothered Charles so much (the food was not tasty, but it was tolerable); it was the humiliation of being laughed at by his friends. "They would come by the house and laugh at our food... I was embarrassed because people made certain assumptions about you based upon the food you ate and the clothes you wore."

"*Everyone* would laugh at our clothes," recalls Charles. The Ogletree children rarely had new clothes. "We had new versions of old clothes." Occasionally Big Mama, "the pragmatist," would take them shopping, and her choices always displeased her grand-children who yearned for something stylish, something that looked like what their friends were wearing. But she would always choose "clothes that last long rather than clothes that look good." In the fall, she would buy up the heavy flannel shirts that were on sale, and the children would have to wear them to school even though it was much too warm in the San Joaquin Valley for thick flannel. There was never money for "frivolity." "I don't ever remember going out to eat anywhere. We never went out to a restaurant. Maybe once or twice on special occasions we might have gone to the A&W drive-in or something."

But the old clothes, bleak food, even the taunting laughter of his friends did not make Charles feel inadequate or uninspired. "The poverty didn't dissuade me from pursuing activities," he says with a force that seems to indicate that it may have had the oppo-site effect—that is, the "abject poverty," with all its limitations and humiliations, may have provoked him into action, made him feel he had to *prove* something. Or he may have joined the various activities as a way of escaping the ravages of poverty. Whatever the impulse, very early Charles began a life of many involvements. Sports was always at the center. Football, basketball, baseball, swimming—they were all important to his survival. He loved the challenge, the competition, the strategy. But mostly he enjoyed the alliance and affiliation he felt with his teammates. Those guys with whom he played football at Merced High School are the men he still sees when he goes home for a visit. The connections are deep; the loyalty is unbroken.

While sports were an active, social escape, reading was solitary asylum. Charles always "had his head in a book." While he was still very young, he read his way through the local library. Sitting right there "on J Street" he could travel "from the real world to the next world. It was a way for the day to go by peacefully and productively." He joined the Boy Scouts, not so much because he was drawn to the organization or the rituals but because he wanted to master the skills they taught—camping, hiking, swimming, knot making. The skills were to prove useful "in terms of developing leadership, judgment, and self-confidence." So despite the meager resources of home and the embarrassments of poverty, Charles built a rich and varied life, and in each realm he applied himself with vigor: achieving in school, reading voraciously, hustling in sports, developing important friendships, and learning the skills of autonomy and survival.

Charles's determined pursuit in all of these realms must have been hard on his brother Robert, who followed him in the sibling line. From the beginning, Robert had trouble with discipline and truancy in school. "He was certainly smart enough," but he lived in the long shadow of his big brother whom everyone regarded as brilliant and diligent. People couldn't help using Charles as the standard for Robert. "Why can't you be more like your brother Charles?" folks would ask. Robert would stare back in silence and then resignedly act out the role of the naughty child. "Robert was at a great disadvantage because of the contrasts with me," says Charles sadly. "He chose to be a rebel." Willie Mae was always being called to the school because of Robert.

In frustration, the school counselor finally contacted a social worker from the welfare department, and "they" decided to put Robert in a foster home. I ask Charles whether his mother agreed to this plan, and he first responds, "She knew it was the best thing for

Robert." But then he thinks out loud, "I actually don't know how she felt about it. She was a young single mother with five kids, and I guess this was an offer she couldn't refuse... but I know I felt that the social workers were always trying to control our lives." Whatever Willie Mae's true feelings were about Robert's placement in a foster home, Charles thinks that "it was the best thing that could have happened to him." Robert went to stay with a "wonderful family" who lived on a farm outside of Merced. They had eight or nine foster children living with them. Robert was the only one whose parents were alive or whose whereabouts were known; the others were orphans. Most of Robert's younger years he spent living with this family and working on their farm. It was a disciplined, firm household, and he responded well to the structure and the responsibilities required of him.

On weekends, Charles would often go out to the farm and "provide comic relief" for everyone. His inexperience showed. "I didn't know the difference between a cow and a bull... I had trouble milking the cow, and I'd inevitably kick over the milk pail... Everyone would laugh at me." On the farm, Robert was the expert and Charles the humbler. The role reversal felt good to both of them. By the time Robert was in high school he had "straightened up," returned to the Ogletree household, and was in the grade right behind Charles. "His friends became my friends... Most of the brothers we hung out with were in Robert's grade." The brothers were reunited and many of the most difficult contrasts had melted away.

From a very young age, work was central to Charles's life. His very first job was a paper route that involved "[dealing] with a lot of adversities"—dogs chasing him, broken bicycles, stolen papers. But the biggest problem he faced was people who refused to pay for their newspapers. He explains, "At that time, you had to pay for the uncollected monies out of your own pocket. Say my expenses were eighty-five dollars per week and I had a potential revenue of a hundred thirty-five dollars if all my customers paid for their delivery. But if one of the households refused to pay, it would eat into my income, and my revenue would be reduced to a hundred twenty-five dollars." Many weeks, Charles could hardly cover his expenses because he would deliver the paper, but people wouldn't pay up at week's end. He felt angry and helpless as he'd ring their bells, bang on their doors, and wait forever for them to respond. "I could hear them inside talking, but there was nothing I could do... When people didn't pay, they didn't seem to care. It was a sad reality." After a couple of years of doing the paper route, Charles worked as a stock clerk in a mom-and-pop grocery store close to home, cut the neighbors' grass, and hustled other jobs—sweeping stoops, painting fences, raking leaves—around town. By the time he reached high school he was flipping hamburgers at McDonalds, working as a janitor at Castle Air Force Base, buffing floors and cleaning offices, and lifeguarding at the public pool in the summer. He says simply, "I have worked all my life... It was not optional. The family needed the money, and it was an extra means of survival."

Charles then leaps ahead to the next generation, the contrasting reality of his childrens' lives. "They have a *totally* different existence," he begins. "They have, for example, been around black professionals all of their lives. They've had close contact with lawyers, physicians, professors since they were four or five years old, been in their company... I didn't meet a black lawyer until my late teens, and then it was a very superficial meeting. They've lived in cities like Washington, D.C., and Boston, and visited New York, San Francisco, Los Angeles. They have vacationed in Hawaii, the Caribbean Islands... I grew up in the country and in a small town, on the black side of the tracks." He continues to describe the contrasts and then cuts through to what he thinks is the most important generational difference. "The key to our kids' success," he says forcefully, "is Pam's ambitious educational and cultural agenda for them." A devoted and creative mother, Pam began reading and singing to them "before they could say a word." And she wasn't just interested in their cognitive development. Very early, she worked on developing their motor skills: teaching them how to push the buttons through the tiny holes on their shirts, showing them how to tie their shoes.

When the children were nursery school age, Charles and Pam made a careful and deliberate choice to send them to a Montessori school in Washington, D.C., founded by "strong black women" and populated by black and brown children. It was a wonderful school that embraced the key values that the Ogletrees wanted to instill in their children. "There was a strong emphasis on freedom *and* responsibility. The kids had freedom of choice and movement. They were supported in their independence. But the teachers also insisted upon rigorous discipline. The teachers were pursuing the intellectual limits of the children and teaching them an Afrocentric curriculum. *They were melding two cultures* naturally and beautifully... And they insisted that parents get involved." Charles and Pam were staunch supporters of the school. Charles was on the board, and Pam participated actively in curriculum development— organizing school events, helping in the classroom, gathering books for the library. Both children, Mosi (born in 1976) and Rashida (born in 1979) entered the Montessori school when they were four and stayed for two years. Charles regards their early schooling as having been critical to their development as human beings, thinkers, and African-Americans.

But Mosi and Rashida's schooling was only a piece of their broader education, which the Ogletrees designed with intention and clarity. From the time they could walk, the children visited the Halls of Congress, the Smithsonian Museum, the Museum of Afro-American History. They explored and picnicked in the National Parks and attended an ecumenical assortment of cultural events around Washington. Charles smiles as he recalls the rich array of activities and says wistfully, "I sometimes felt jealous and deprived when I thought of all the resources at their disposal." His wistfulness seems to be a mixture of nostalgia and gratitude. Certainly he would have liked to taste some of these pleasures when he was a child. But, at the same time, he loves the fact that he has been able to offer his children this bountiful life. He loves the choices that his abundant life affords. And he loves raising these children with Pam. He gives Pam most of the credit for her inspired and devoted parenting. His voice is thick and proud when he says softly, "Pam always had a kind of *quiet activism*. She has pushed a *very aggressive* cultural agenda, as opposed to a political agenda...

Pam has *always, always* been involved with the children's teachers, with building the curriculum in their schools, making it more authentically multicultural. She has insisted on literature by and about African-Americans, has urged our kids to write about black cultural, intellectual, and political figures. My children have seen the commitment and the activism in *both* of their parents."

Charles and Pam have been joined in the struggle since they both arrived at Stanford for their freshman year in 1971. It was at the height of political and cultural ferment on the campus and both of them were drawn into the civil rights activities and demonstrations. They both participated in the Angela Davis trial, the South Africa antiapartheid movement, the tutoring program for black children in East Palo Alto, the efforts to get more black students and faculty at Stanford. "We were part of all of the incredible political activism and struggle... we were in it together. There was always something that kept us going."

Charles and Pam were comrades in the struggle, but their alliance went even deeper. "We had a natural chemistry," says Charles as a way of describing how their similarities in background and experience drew them together. Pam had come from "a working-class family" in Baltimore. Her mother had worked in a "white beauty parlor, not doing the hair but cleaning the brushes and mopping the floor." Her father had worked in the steel mill. When "things dried up" for him in Baltimore, the family had packed up and headed West, finally landing in Compton, just outside of Los Angeles. Pam had gone to the predominantly black public high school in Compton, where she had been a leader and an achiever. But her family life, like Charles's, was always precarious and difficult. The resources were meager; the struggle for survival was always part of daily life.

The parallels in their lives went beyond their backgrounds of poverty, and are extraordinary. "Both of us were from families with six children. Both of our mothers are named Willie Mae. Both of our mothers are the same age. Both of us attended public school. Both of us were intimidated by Stanford. Both of us chose to live in the black theme house. Both of us felt compelled to get involved in black political activities." No wonder there was a natural chemistry between them, one that neither of them resisted. Charles's description is spare and his voice loving and respectful. "Right from the beginning we spent a lot of time together. The relationship really started in the late fall of 1971... I was on my way to Gary, Indiana, to attend the National Black Political Convention. Just before I left, our *eyes caught*, and we both knew there was something between us... By the time I returned from Gary, we were an item."

Twenty years later, Charles's voice still resonates with admiration and respect for his partner in love and struggle. In the midst of all the calls and clamor surrounding the "Clarence Thomas stuff," he makes a date to have lunch with Pam. "We try to have lunch about twice a week. It's very nice. You should join us sometime." He relishes the morning runs with her around Fresh Pond. He cherishes her gifted parenting, her aggressive advocacy of their children, and their common views on politics and culture. He seems determined to sustain a family life for his children that will be very different from the one he knew. He is committed to being an active, engaged, loving, *present* father. He wants to be a good and loving partner to Pam and have his children witness their reciprocal relationship. He is haunted by the memories of his father's abusive treatment of his mother and the images of the police coming to take him away. He wants his children to feel the safety of their black family embrace—a safety that will allow them to face the challenges, treachery, and opportunities of growing up black in this society. The commitments to his family are connected to Charles's professional and political commitments, woven into one large liberation tapestry.

"My impulse is to look backward, not forward," says Charles Ogletree as he begins his story, "to give back something to the people I came from." In our final session he echoes the same theme, his voice thick with emotion. "There is no way I could be as successful as I am without close and constant contact with home people.... I'm on their shoulders.... *It is the way I survive.*" For Charles, home is anchor, home is identity, home is survival. Home is the poor, rural community in Merced, California, where he grew up. Home is fishing in the same rivers as his grandfather, returning to speak at the local churches or to attend a high school reunion. Home is both responsibility *and* liberation. Unless he continues to remain deeply connected with his community, Charles believes that his life will be without purpose or meaning. His personal liberation is tied up with the collective survival of his childhood community.

Part of Charles's interest in participating in this project had to do with creating an opportunity to journey home, revisit his roots, rehearse old family stories. Here was a chance to sit in his high-back leather swivel chair in his Harvard office and spin the tales of his childhood. In looking backward he could honor his elders, praise their courage and resilience, and be reminded of the ways in which their lives are echoed in his own. He spoke of the storytelling as "liberating": releasing the love and admiration he feels for his home folks, freeing his mind and heart to travel the three thousand miles from Cambridge to Merced, tracing each thread of coherence.

Charles's first journey away from home was to attend Stanford University, a foreign place that seemed "light years away from Merced." Just a few hours' bus ride north, the university felt like another world—white, abundant, cosmopolitan. But even at the adventurous age of seventeen, Charles seemed committed to keeping the connections to home. He struggled to bridge the psychological distance between his provincial, rural town and the worldly, urbane college; determined that his new status would not make him a stranger at home. When his attempts to get his homeboys interested in applying to Stanford failed, he increased his efforts to reduce the elitism of the university through vigorous political activism. He visited his folks frequently, relishing the comfort and familiarity of home, and using the university as a laboratory for learning the most effective ways to express connection to, and responsibility for, the people he had left behind. This early commitment survives in his life and work today.

For Charles, liberation arises from "responsibility to roots." Rather than involving an escape from one's origins, repressing the past, or facing toward the future, liberation for him means underscoring the connections to home, rehearsing the family history, and facing backward into the future. Charles's journeys home provide the fuel for his present pursuits and his future adventures. He experiences freedom—to be himself, to do his work, to sustain meaningful relationships—to the extent that he remains true to his origins and responsible to his "home folks." All his achievements are measured by that single standard.

As he lectures at Harvard, looking out at the mostly white, ambitious faces of his students, he sees the images of his black brothers back home. "Not a day goes by" when he doesn't think about Gene Allen, who remains incarcerated in San Quentin. Charles's friendship and his extraordinary legal prowess have not helped Gene break through the prison bars or the courts' bureaucracy. The ghosts of his "brothers" hover around Charles daily, a constant source of challenge, criticism, and energy; they burden his spirit and incite his talents. They also make him question his choices. "Is Harvard the place where I can make my greatest contribution? Is this the best way to use my training and experience, the best vehicle for fighting injustice, the best way to repay my debt to the home folks?" In almost every conversation we have, Charles expresses his certainty about journeying home and his ambivalence about his current choice. "Am

I doing right by my people working here at the university?" His eyes show pain and yearning. "This remains an open question."

Charles's journeys home during our sessions allow him to explore the rich resources that he draws from his childhood of poverty. He tells the story of going with his mother and siblings to pick figs and peaches in the hot California sun. They were paid by the box; the day's wages were the family livelihood. Each morning, loaded in the big truck with the other itinerant laborers, young Charles determined that he would pick more fruit than he had the day before. He traces his fierce competitive spirit to those days of laboring in the fields, trying to increase his yield. From this he draws his assurance that he will prevail in court if he is given an even chance. "If it is fifty-fifty, I will win."

In the same way, Charles traces the "mask of cool" he exhibits in the heat of a trial back to watching and waiting while his grandfather fished for hours at the river's edge. He carefully observed the way Big Daddy fastened the bait to the bamboo pole; the way he gazed into space, his face impassive; the way he held his body while he waited silently for the fish to nibble. His grandfather was the embodiment of strategic patience: the way he settled comfortably into the long, motionless hours, striking—with lightning speed—only when the time was ripe and the conditions were perfect. In court Charles imitates his grandfather's style, masking his inner anxiety as he slowly gathers and displays the evidence to the jury; as he calmly "teaches" the jurors and "massages" them into feeling identified with the defendant; as he looks beyond winning each battle, determined to win the war.

But it is not only the values socialized in early childhood and the temperament carved by early identification with family elders that have survived the journey from Merced to Cambridge; it is also the stories, the allegories he uses in the courtroom to dramatize a point. One of his favorites—the tale of his grandmother's instructing him in making her delicious rice pudding—offers the recipe for a convincing final argument. As the public defender, Charles journeys home, captures the perfect family story, uses it strategically, and wins for the defendant who is like all of his black brothers back in Merced.

Charles's frequent trips home to Merced are always bittersweet. It is a treat to "hang out" with old buddies, spend a lazy afternoon fishing in the rivers he knows by heart, to slow down and cool out. He feels the sweetness in the friendly gossip, the smell of the land, the hot sun hitting his face as he waits, like Big Daddy, for the fish to bite. But the bitter part is never far behind. The gossip and jive banter turns so easily into horrible tales of death and devastation that have befallen his home folks since his last visit. The news is both familiar and unbearable to hear. He listens with sadness and renewed determination.

The saddest tale of all—a still unfinished story—is the murder of his sister Barbara. Ten years after her death, he still returns home to the pain of lingering questions, and the terrible irony of her death. The one of his sisters and brothers who stayed home, who wanted to serve her own community, was brutally cut down. "She was so vital, so committed... She was giving back to the community...," and she was murdered. His voice sounds hollow. In honoring his sister's legacy—her decision to stay close to home and give daily, concretely to their community—Charles returns to the painful open question that continues to haunt him. He knows that his credentials and cosmopolitanism have increased the scope, influence, and visibility of his work and have thus allowed him to give more back. But he also sees the temptations of prominence, the seductions of privilege, the ways personal ambition can be confused with public commitment. Charles sees the brave clarity in Barbara's choice to stay rooted in Merced and build a career in law enforcement, making a simple and profound contribution at the local level. She gained deep respect from the home folks, but at great personal risk. Charles sees the potential casualties in both their choices. The college scholarships he gives, in Barbara's name, to Merced High School graduates join the memory of her local contributions with the advances gained from his national efforts.

～

In recent years, Katie Cannon has also begun to feel the need to reconnect to home. For most of her life she has been preoccupied with escaping the claustrophobia and chaos of her large family, the provincialism and bigotry of Kannapolis, the dangerous Jim Crow of rural North Carolina. At thirteen, she made her first "great escape" to Gastonia, North Carolina, twenty-seven miles away. She had begged her mother to let her visit her aunt Pearl for the summer. When her mother had resisted her pleas, she had used her most powerful threat: "If you don't let me go, I'll get pregnant." Gastonia felt big and free, like New York City, even though it was less than an hour away. When Katie's mom insisted that she attend Barber-Scotia College, only seven miles up the road from Kannapolis, the seventeen-year-old packed her trunk, pretended she was traveling "thousands of miles across the country," and returned home only when the college closed the dormitories. Later on, her escapes—to Ghost Ranch in Sante Fe, to New York City, to Liberia, and to Israel and Jordan—were all efforts to exaggerate the distance from home. She was seeking a place where she could find herself: discover her identity, express her talents. "I wanted out of North Carolina so *bad*," proclaims Katie. "I was searching for a place to be *ME!*"

Although these great escapes have brought adventure, exposure, and opportunity, they have not fully satisfied Katie's need to feel whole. With middle age, she has begun to recognize her desire to revisit, and reckon with, her roots. She is drawn to the wisdom of one of her mentors—a black male theologian—who distinguishes between the nurturant community (of family) and the sustaining community (of work). To negotiate the latter successfully, you need to be nourished by the former. He advises black professionals to make at least five pilgrimages home each year in order to stay sane and centered, in order to stay in touch with our identities.

Katie, who had avoided visiting Kannapolis for years, saw this book project as a way to rekindle these connections. In one of our later sessions, her voice was tentative: "I'm feeling the need to learn how to journey home." She was beginning to have the premonition that part of finding "ME" would involve a reconciliation with home, coming to terms with her origins, telling the truth about who she has become, seeing the good in her imperfect family, and learning how to forgive. Our dialogues helped her begin the journey.

Although Katie knew the power of home, her feelings about returning remained ambivalent. For most of her adult life she has felt unwelcome, awkward, and different when visiting her family. She has gone home planning to stay a week and "disappeared" after a couple of days without saying good-bye, feeling as if "they don't care," "they wouldn't miss me anyway." Some of the feelings of discomfort and exclusion are echoes of painful childhood experiences: learning that her mother did not want to have her, that her mother refused to acknowledge her birth by not even screaming out during her delivery; or being crowded between two demanding sisters whom Katie felt were much more favored by her mother. But some of the discomfort reflects the extraordinarily different path Katie's life has taken. She lives in a predominantly white, affluent, highly educated community, and her parents are from the families of sharecroppers whose field work is work in the fields.

For Katie, the journey home also has developmental reverberations. She links it to her middle-age passage, to what she proudly proclaims as "my midlife crisis." The middle years are generally a time of reckoning, fantasizing, and yearning. Katie's crisis is pregnant with promise, full of ferment, and potential catastrophe. For the first time in her life she slows down her ambitious pursuit, pauses for a moment, and "carves out a space to feel." The pause feels scary and threatening. It forces her to notice the velocity of her journey and what she has lost and left behind. Her mother's refrain about returning home to "the mill" reminds her how her climb out of Kannapolis has brought both freedom and loss: freedom from the parochialisms of the rural South ("where the Ku Klux Klan still rides"), and loss in her feelings of disconnection and alienation from her roots.

During our next-to-last interview, Katie walked in proudly proclaiming a successful return home, a promising reentry that "would have never been possible without these talks with you, Sara—very inspiring, very unsettling, real hard." The crisis of middle age helps Katie recognize the pain of the alienation, the price of the pursuit, and the need to make the "translations" between Kannapolis and Cambridge. She begins to see "the good" in her family, the sources within her that are mirrors of their strength and resilience. Her humor—exuberant, mischievous, intelligent—comes from the Cannon clan. Her sense of direction and her pragmatism can be traced back to her family roots. She begins to take small steps that feel like huge leaps of faith. She writes a three-line letter to her father even though he is illiterate and won't be able to read it. She returns home as the "prodigal daughter" and decides to tell the truth about her life. For the first time her parents greet her with open arms (Could they see the truth written all over her face?). Her mother feeds her; Katie sleeps in her parents' bed; she and her mother "really talk" to one another. It is so different from her usual visits to her parents' home that she doesn't know whether to trust her feelings. She is both wary and thrilled, skeptical and open-minded as she works to bridge the wide psychological and cultural chasm.

Katie's reconciliation with home also begins to be reflected in her work. The book she is writing—which her students have appropriately titled *Katie's Canon*—is both a retrospect and a declaration. In it she underscores the recurrent intellectual themes and displays the development of her thinking over the years. She is also discovering that her strongest and best work draws upon her southern-black-working poor—womanist origins. She is through with mimicking the "white male patriarchal" perspective. She no longer has time to fight their "oppressive and distorting" frameworks. She plans to use these middle years to carve out her own positions, to develop her own language and claim her own voice. And at the center of this reclamation is her discovery of the richness of her roots. She is searching for ways to create a dialogue between the abstractions of Cambridge and the experiences of Kannapolis. She knows that her scholarship will grow to the extent that she can find ways of "making the translation" between her "nurturant" and "sustaining" communities.

This is a difficult translation. Her fellowship at the University of Pennsylvania comes at a good time. Philadelphia—a much blacker city than Boston, a place plentiful with extended family—is a good setting to practice feeling at home. While pursuing her scholarship she can surround herself with family, enjoying both her celebrity and the ordinariness of being in their midst. She can indulge the "abundance" of her fellowship and at the same time relish the resonance of the black neighborhood Sunday church services. She can see reflections of her wholesome black beauty as she works out in the gym with her ample sisters or finds the lotions and potions for her kinky hair and dark skin in the local stores. Philadelphia "feels halfway home."

~

For these two storytellers, then, the journey home is key to their growth and creativity. For Charles, it is part of his daily survival. He is clear about his profound connection to his roots, his debt to his elders, and the inspiration and energy that flow from the home folks. Yet his certainty about his responsibilities to home causes a chronic ambivalence about his decision to teach at Harvard. This ambivalence permeates his experience of the abundance and elitism of Harvard and causes yearning in his heart—a yearning that incites guilt and inspires action; a yearning that always leads him home for sustenance and challenge.

Katie's journey home, though determined, is still fraught with anxiety. Only recently has she made the shift from searching for the "great escape" to searching for connection to her roots. The psychological distance from Cambridge to Kannapolis remains vast, and the translations are treacherous. She must stop thinking of her identity as defined by escape and begin to see it as partly shaped by reconciliation with home. Storytelling helps her blaze the trail home. She feels moved to reopen the channels of communication (to write to Phifer, to attend the family reunion, to visit her grandmother's grave, to write a letter to her father) and to celebrate some of the gifts of her upbringing. At midlife, she pauses and "takes the time to feel," to feel the pain of her distance from home, the anguish of being a stranger. She "scrapes the white off her eyeballs" so that she can see her way home.

TONI SCHIESLER

My Mother's Power
Was in Her Voice

Beginnings

Toni does not fit my fantasy of what a former nun would look like. She is exuberant in her style and carriage. Tall and lean, she is wearing purple from head to toe: purple stockings, a purple leather purse, a purple silk blouse, a large purple scarf over her white coat, and even purple eye shadow behind her large modern glasses. She is medium-brown-skinned with chiseled features, large expressive eyes, and a halo of white hair. It is very hard to tell her age; despite the white hair, her face is smooth and unlined, and her movements are strong and energetic. I am surprised when this striking woman announces that she is fifty-six years old.

At this first, exploratory meeting, she begins to tell me her story in quick vignettes, as if to let me know some of the variety, range, and change in her life. I pick up the pieces, not pursuing any in depth, satisfied that this is not our last conversation. (There is something about her that feels deeply familiar, pleasantly undefended, plainspoken and eager; something about her that seems poised, ready, accessible for this project.) I hear a little about her childhood in New Haven: she is the only daughter of a hard-working, determined domestic who decided very early that Toni was "a special child" whose gifts needed to be recognized, supported, and nurtured. Mother and daughter were poor, struggling and living in the projects, but Toni remembers an abundance of adventures—free concerts in the parks, trips to the library, touring on the public city bus, where Toni learned precociously to read by deciphering letters from the advertisements above the seats. "I remember learning to read on the bus, riding with my mother. I *loved* to read. I read everything I could get my hands on." Her memories are of a mother who "when she could manage it, gave her *all*."

These early loving images are diluted (or at least are brought into question) by her mother's frequent apology, "I'm sorry I wasn't a good mother," and by Toni's knowledge that her mother "didn't want children" and "didn't want to have her." Confusion mixed with sadness seems to sweep across Toni's face as she tells the story of visiting her mother the previous Sunday. ("I see her every Sunday. She is in a nursing home in Wilmington. She had a stroke.") Her mother at almost eighty-three years old has been diminished by a stroke; her speech is now labored and her thinking a bit confused. On Sunday her mother repeated the troubling words Toni had heard many times before: "You know I *never* liked children." This declaration feels so at odds with her daughter's experience. Toni wants to understand her mother's words, but at the same time she doesn't want to hear them. She quickly provides a response: "Why do you say that, Mom... because of the way *he* treated you?" "Yes," replies her mother in simple assent. I listen and try to understand this puzzling scenario: a mother who "gave her all"; who planned wonderful "free adventures"; who saw her only daughter as a gifted, special person; but who didn't like children and hadn't wanted Toni to come into the world. Nor was Toni the only child; she had a sister two years younger. "But we got separated when we were young, and she was adopted by another woman. Now that the other woman is deceased, we have rediscovered one another... and there is infrequent contact. So growing up I was really the only child." I see a sadness in her eyes as she races quickly through this story.

Other memories of her mother make Toni smile warmly, make her glow. Toni's mother was a singer with "a beautiful contralto voice" who had once sung with a big band (when the star performer got sick suddenly) and who sang on the radio (one of those programs where you called in requests). Toni remembers sitting on her grandmother's knees by the radio listening to her mother sing, loving the mellow, soothing voice. She aches in knowing that her mother had wonderful talents but was unable to make it as a musician "because of the circumstances." She reminds me of Alice Walker's essay "In Search of Our Mothers' Gardens" and, with tears in her eyes Toni says, "That moves me so much because it is my

mother's story of unfulfilled dreams... of the world not letting her
make it, not letting her realize her potential." The image of her
mother as singer seems to be the proudest childhood picture that
Toni has—one that expresses creativity and beauty; one that gives
her mother significance against the dark, poor landscape of New
Haven. She promises herself that she will pursue the history of her
mother's musical past. "I want to find out the name of the big band
leader she worked with, how she got the job at the radio station..."
Her voice trails off, as she holds onto these vestiges of pleasure and
expressiveness in her mother's impoverished life. "You see, we were
on and off welfare... my mother did day work in people's homes...
we were poor."

Today Toni is dean of academic affairs at Cabrini College, a
small, four-year liberal arts school on Philadelphia's affluent Main
Line. She has been there for three years and describes the life of an
administrator as hectic, demanding, and eclectic: "I do everything."
Recently, in the past year, she has begun to learn how to "be in control of my job" rather than "having the job control me." This shift
in power and responsibility ("after a very depressed period of several
months when I felt totally overwhelmed by the demands of the job")
has some "gains and some losses." "I no longer try to be perfect... I
can't give to everyone all the time." Later on Toni says to me, only
half-humorously, "When young women come to me for mentoring I
say to them, 'Before you decide to be an administrator, come and
see me first. And before you decide to marry a parish priest, come and
see me first.'" A grin spreads over her face. Over time, both of her
roles have required redefinition and renegotiation.

Toni is married to Robert Schiesler (Bob), a white man fourteen
years her junior, whom she describes as "perfect for me." Formerly
a Roman Catholic seminarian, he left the seminary and taught
school for a while, then decided to pursue training as an Episcopal
priest. Toni met him before he began his training and soon after she
had left the order, where she herself had spent twenty years of her
life as a nun ("a nun in a habit"). The only sign that I can see of
her former life is a gold cross on her purple silk blouse, blending
with other necklaces dangling around her neck.

Toni and Bob have been married for eighteen years; it is a marriage that Toni describes as satisfying and rewarding, a marriage that gives her room to be herself and pursue her interests. Toni seems to relish the space he allows her. "He is very understanding and supportive of anything I choose to do." She vigilantly avoids being a clergy spouse. "I had a real life and career *before* I became a clergy spouse," she explains. In addition, her work life and interests consume so much of her time and energy that, even if she wanted to, she would not be able to assume the traditional supportive duties of a priest's wife. "I am a radical feminist type," she says with a smile, "although many do not see me that way." She does not appear *radical*, though as I look at her stylish outfit I think she must feel she has made a "radical" transformation from the monotones and simplicity of her nun's habit.

The husband that Toni describes as "perfect for me" is the head priest at an Episcopal parish in Wilmington, about ten minutes from where they live—a distance that Toni describes as critical to their sanity. "When we were at the last church in Michigan, we lived right next door, and it was miserable, too close." Bob describes his ministry, in an inner-city parish with an aging congregation, as one of being a "change agent." He believes that part of his job and mission is to challenge the status quo. Toni seems proud of Bob's values and his courage in confronting the resistance that is inevitable from a complacent congregation. Bob is assisted by a woman priest who is middle-aged and feeling her way into her role and career after a life spent "not working." Toni describes this woman with a combination of identification and frustration. She feels the contrasts between her own life, which has always included work and career, and this woman's cautious, tentative moves into a vocational world she has never known; Toni feels some frustration with this woman's lack of certainty and assertiveness.

Toni herself has decided to train for the Episcopal priesthood. When she announced her plan to Bob, he gave her a surprising response. It was the first time in their marriage that Toni remembers him resisting her decision to do something. He immediately cited reasons why this was not a wise or well-thought-out plan on her part: At fifty-two, she was too old to begin a brand new career. She would have to take a major cut in her salary. Where would she go to divinity school? Would that require another move, long separations? His challenges were impatient and harsh and seemed immediately to Toni to mask an underlying, more authentic concern. After these immediate objections, "Bob walked out on the porch to smoke a cigar" and cool out. He seemed genuinely troubled.

Toni was surprised and baffled by his defensiveness but held firm in her determination to heed "the call from God." Weeks later, during a calm moment when they were driving somewhere in the car, Toni asked Bob about his initial response to her decision (she was not asking his permission or counsel) to enter the priesthood. Her tone was measured, her timing strategic, and he seemed ready to respond. He had obviously thought hard about his uncharacteristically "strong reaction" and now seemed prepared to explore the "real reason" that fueled his first response. He talked openly about his concern that Toni would invade his territory, become his competitor, be liked better than he by parishioners. It was a poignant declaration of his apprehension: both his competition with, and his admiration for, his wife. Toni slowly shakes her head as she recalls Bob's revelations: "I said to him, 'But Bob, we each have different skills, different talents. We do different things well. I would not be in your space. I would not draw attention from you.'" There was some relief in Bob's honesty and declaration, but not total resolution. Toni speaks of the issue as if it is *alive*, something to be negotiated and renegotiated over time, part of the process of conflict and growth that must accompany any intimate relationship.

Toni seems to welcome the chance our interviews give to relive and reinterpret her own life course. Part of the "great attraction" of the project is that it will give her the time and space to develop her introspective capacities, chart her growth, and gain new understanding of where she has come from and where she is headed. She says an enthusiastic and immediate YES to my request that she participate in the project, and then expresses her relief and pleasure: "When I thought about having lunch with you and thought about how much I'd *love* to work with you, I began to get *very* excited...

I said to myself, 'Gee whiz, I hope she finds me *interesting* enough!'" Toni's modesty contrasts with what I already know will be an extraordinary life story. I suspect, however, that she is expressing some shyness about being "the center of attention," and that she is hoping to make her life more "interesting" by practicing the skills of reflection and storytelling. She believes that to live her journey fully and wisely, she must be more "in touch with" the "early painful times" and develop her powers of self-analysis.

My Mother's Voice

At our first formal interview, I ask Toni where she would like to begin her story, and I tell her that wherever she decides to begin, there is no reason to try to be organized and orderly in her presentation. "It is my responsibility," I explain, "to worry about organization and sequence." She should feel free to move backward and forward in time, to take abrupt detours, to speak a mixture of fantasy and reality. I will follow her wherever she leads; I will keep track of the journey and the destination. There must be something in Toni's style and presence that makes me want to relieve her of the responsibility for orderliness; if she holds onto that responsibility, I fear it might inhibit her expressiveness. She beams at me in response, thanks me, but nevertheless proceeds to bring clarity and order to her story.

This time she is not wearing purple ("my favorite color for as long as I can remember") but a much more conservative black and white striped dress, white stockings, flat white shoes. She immediately describes this as her "dean's outfit." In her capacity as dean of academic affairs, she will be welcoming a class of incoming students at an orientation session later on in the afternoon, so she has chosen to look official. What *doesn't* look official are the very large black and silver earrings dangling from her ears with a Middle Eastern flair. Underneath her beautiful curly white halo of hair and against her brown skin, the earrings glisten in the sunshine. Her face is lively and mobile; her eyes are smiling behind the only evidence of purple found in the frames of her large glasses. This is a woman who seems to give a great deal of attention to her dress, a woman who likes clothes and jewelry.

Toni shows me around her house and points me to several closets full of her clothes (and the *one* closet that her husband's clothes inhabit). "Clothes are so important to me," she says emphatically. "I *love* clothes!" And later on, as she tells her story of poverty, inhibition, and self-denial, it becomes absolutely clear why this woman in her mid-fifties might want and need a house with big closets, all but one full of her clothes.

The house that Toni shares with her husband and her two beloved cats, Calico and Buffy, is in a quiet suburban section of Wilmington, Delaware. The houses in the subdivision, built thirty to forty years ago, are large and gracious though not distinctive. There is an attempt of variation among them, but they all strike me as very similar to one another. Behind manicured lawns, orderly gardens, pruned trees, and recently paved driveways, the houses stand stoically alone. I don't feel a sense of neighborhood, only a sense of separate families in separate dwellings. A zoning ordinance, Toni informs me, prohibits fences from being built to define the property lines between the houses. But it strikes me that no physical boundaries are necessary. The fences are in people's heads.

Recently, a black executive, his wife, and two young children moved into a house up the road from Toni's. They were transplants from Texas and they came with their dog. Not knowing about the zoning ordinance prohibiting the building of fences, they constructed a high fence behind their house to keep the dog from running loose in the neighborhood. They even planted trees in front of the fence to soften the lines of the barrier, to make it look almost the same as everyone else's property. Nevertheless, several of the neighbors were outraged by the Texans' fence, seeing it as a flagrant violation of the zoning code, and they insisted that the fence be dismantled. At least that is the *public* reason the neighbors gave for their unfriendly response to this young family. Six months later, the Texans moved out. The house is still empty, although the outside landscaping looks as if people still live there. A gardener is pruning hedges as I walk by. Did the fence or the family's blackness cause the neighbors to feel threatened? Were the neighbors fighting a violation of the zoning ordinance or a violation to their sensibilities? As I hear the Texans' tale, it is not the protest from the neighbors that disturbs me most, it is the silence that followed. It is the way the street remains unruffled and undisturbed, leaving no sign of upheaval, no record of pain.

Toni's house is the rectory of the Episcopal parish that Robert Schiesler heads in downtown Wilmington. Although the Schieslers do not own it, it is full of their furniture and Toni's taste in decoration. She has selected the curtains, rugs, and artwork and created a peaceful, orderly home. "It is a house in which I can pray in every room." On the first floor is a large sparsely furnished living room that looks as if it is rarely lived in. This room flows into the dining room, a simple rectangle with a large dark table and chairs. The kitchen is sunny and opens into a family room full of the activity of daily living. A large screened-in sun porch is Toni's idea of heaven with its view out into the peaceful green backyard. Between the trees hangs a hammock where Toni can look up through the umbrella of tree cover and "meditate." In a reverential spot there is a statue of Saint Francis of Assisi, who seems to be chosen as certain protection for Calico and Buffy. The final room downstairs is an office for Bob, dominated by a large half circle desk cleared of work and papers except for a couple of neatly stacked piles. Most of his work, Toni explains, takes place at his church office downtown. Upstairs is the master bedroom suite with Bob's bathroom, a guest room where Bob's parents often come for extended stays, a second bathroom that Toni proudly proclaims as her own, a bedroom used for storage, a bedroom used for Toni's projects where the sewing machine and computer sit side by side, and, finally, Toni's "favorite spot in the house," a cozy spacious room built over the garage where she thinks, plans, reads, prays, and enjoys her solitude. After this extended house tour Toni settles us here, taking her place in the large rolling chair in front of her big, heavy desk over which the sun is streaming. I sit facing her in a high-back, comfortable chair and place the tape recorder between us. Before we begin, Toni tells me how important it is to her that I have seen her home; clearly it is a place of solace, security, and pride. I sense that the house reflects who she is, what she values, and what she needs.

Toni begins at the beginning. Her birth, she announces, was "traumatic." Her eyes seem to blur with tears as she says simply, "I was the product of a rape." Born in Chicago, Illinois, on December 13, 1934, Toni was given the name Carole Virginia Rodez. She came into the world three months early, weighing only three pounds, five ounces, and spent three months in the hospital before being taken home. "It was amazing that I *survived*... that was 1934... I was tiny, but I was a healthy child."

Her mother, Gladyce, had traveled to Chicago from her home-town of New Haven, Connecticut, hoping to find work with big bands in the Windy City. She was twenty-six years old, but innocent to big-city ways. When a friend of a friend introduced her to a "Cuban man named Rodriguez," she accepted his invitation to go out to dinner. But before dinner, he claimed he needed to stop by his apartment to pick up something. Gladyce went up to the man's place and "he forced himself on her." She went through pregnancy all alone in a foreign city, scraping her resources together to keep a roof over her head, fearing the shame and wrath of her family should they discover she was having a baby out of wedlock. Gladyce did not want the child she was carrying—a fact she still reminds her daugh-ter of from her chair in the nursing home. She also felt enormous guilt for not wanting the child *and* a fierce determination not to reveal the name of her baby's father. "She was trying to protect the man who assaulted her," says Toni with a glimmer of amazement. Having been told that her name was Carole Virginia Rodez, when she was in her mid-thirties she discovered another last name on her birth certificate: something plain like Thomas or Cummings—Toni can't recall—was written in Gladyce's distinctive pen. So Toni's name, which is now Antoinette Rodez Schiesler, began as Carole Virginia Rodez. She was told her father was Rodriguez, a Cuban, but that was probably a pseudonym invented by her mother to protect her father, the rapist, whose real name may have been Thomas or Cummings. The complex of names confuses the listener and con-tinues to be a central and profound question for Toni: "It has been difficult trying to figure out who I am."

By the time Toni discovered a different last name on her birth certificate, not only did the news complicate her life; it caused her shame. By then, she was a nun and living in the convent. She approached her mother and asked why the last name on her birth certificate was different from the one she had been living with for over thirty years. It was then that her mother told her—for the first time—that Toni was the product of a rape and that the name change was designed to protect the man who had raped Gladyce. Toni's understated language does not capture what must have been the pain of that moment: "I had a difficult time with that." She returned to the convent and didn't tell a soul. "I kept it to myself," Toni says as she admits to still unresolved feelings that linger twenty-five years later.

When Gladyce brought her three-month-old daughter home from the hospital, she realized there was no way that she could take care of her in Chicago. So she headed back home to New Haven, where she was willing to trade being shamed and excluded from her family for the familiarity of the city. Those early years in New Haven are mostly "blank," washed out by pain and secrets. Toni says regretfully, hesitantly, "I don't remember a lot," and then offers the most vivid image from her early childhood. "I can recall sitting on my grandmother's lap listening to my mother sing on the radio." There is no memory of the house, the neighborhood, or even whom she was living with at the time. "My first memory is of listening to my mother's *voice*, rather than touching her or feeling her." Toni seems disappointed at not being able to retrieve the early memories and even apologizes to me for not being able to fill in her childhood story, but the underlying sorrow centers on the distance from her mother.

The fuzzy images of New Haven are filled with "the feeling" of dislocation, of being "put in lots of places by my mother," because "my mother could not take care of me." The places where Toni was deposited were not the homes of her relatives, who treated Gladyce like "sort of an outcast." Toni can't remember where she was left, but feels that she was living with strangers, "or maybe acquaintances." More importantly, she does not think she ever knew where to find her mother. "This is all blocked out," Toni says with frustration in her voice. "I have no recollection of where I lived; no recollection of the times I may have lived with my mother."

She does remember a woman named Aunt Rose, a person who was not her real relative but someone she knew in the neighborhood. "Maybe I was about three or four years old," says Toni trying to stretch her memory back. Toni was playing by herself on the side of the street, and Aunt Rose saw her, bent down, picked her up, and carried her home. "I was so alone and so dirty... she just picked me up, took me home, and gave me a bath. I think I began to live with her for a while." A smile crosses Toni's face as she remembers Aunt Rose's mercy, her firm warmth, and her cluttered, friendly house. She has no idea how long she stayed with Aunt Rose (a couple of days or a couple of months) or whether this rescue might have been something arranged by her mother. But she hangs onto this one warm image as if it represents her only glimpse through the dark veil that has shrouded her early childhood. And she tells the story, I think, both to convey the vulnerability and chaos of her beginnings and to show that at times of desperation and hopelessness people come forward to save you—God sends an angel to offer aid and solace. Aunt Rose was the angel who appeared to rescue the dark, dirty, helpless child on the New Haven streets.

Toni's voice is restrained and her eyes look distant. She is clearly struggling between the desire to forget the pain and feelings of abandonment and the wish that she could use this project to break through the "blank" spaces and recover more of her childhood. The memories become bolder when Toni recalls her life at seven years old, a year marked by her mother's decision to get married. Gladyce had been working as a live-in maid for a Jewish family: "So I couldn't live with her... I had to live in some other place." Her mother had met Lafayette, who was a cook and also worked as a chef on the railroad. They decided to get married in Florida where Lafayette's family lived, and Toni traveled down to the wedding. "I went to Florida on the train all by myself... and I remember I had a hat on." Toni is animated and moved by this picture of herself at seven, traveling the hundreds of miles, never taking her hat off. The journey took a couple of days, but she has no memory of how she passed the time, or who (if anyone) might have been charged with looking after her. Somehow the hat served as protection.

When she arrived in Florida, she was met at the train station by Lafayette's sister, Betty. They walked from the station to her car, to a brand new experience. "This was the first time I had ever been in a car in my whole life," says Toni with awe still in her voice. She climbed in the front beside Betty, and they headed off into the dark night. It had been raining earlier and there was still some slickness on the wet road. Toni remembers being suddenly consumed by fear as they approached what appeared to be a big gaping hole in the road. It looked like a wide chasm that they might drive into and disappear forever. She shrieked and screamed at Betty to stop as they drew closer to the huge black abyss. Betty slowed up but assured Toni that the dangerous blackness was only a huge puddle left over from the earlier storm. The child stopped shrieking and was finally reassured, but the image of "the big hole" is just as vivid as if it were yesterday.

When Toni arrived at Betty's house, she was overwhelmed by the lovely peacefulness of this simple place. "Betty had a pretty house with white sand," says Toni about the first beautiful home she can remember. When it was bedtime, Betty said that she would have to bathe and turn in. But Toni refused to take off her hat. She held it tightly on her head, perhaps fearing that all of her tenuous safety was wrapped up in this tiny covering. Betty gently and repeatedly assured her that she could relinquish the hat for the night, and finally convinced Toni to take it off.

After Gladyce and Lafayette's wedding, they had headed back North to resume their work as cook and housekeeper in the Jewish household, and they left seven-year-old Toni to live with Betty in Florida. Toni remembers two things about her time in Florida. She went to a one-room schoolhouse where she worked very hard and "accomplished a few years of school in one year," and she fell very sick with malaria and was bedridden for several weeks, or "maybe months." At the end of the school year, Toni returned to New Haven, moved into the projects ("where whites and blacks lived on separate sides") with her mother and Lafayette, and went to the neighborhood public school. She remembers "nothing" about the school, only that she came back from Florida far ahead of her peers

in New Haven, and the teachers wanted to skip her to fifth grade—
a request that her mother resisted because she did not want Toni
to be mixing with much older children.

One teacher from public school stands out, her English teacher,
a large white woman who was also on the New Haven police force.
For some reason this teacher figured prominently in a recurring
dream that haunted Toni for years after. In the dream, the police-
woman-teacher would be chasing her through the streets of the city.
When Toni could no longer escape her pursuit, she would take off
into the sky and fly over the buildings. Was the dream an expression
of danger, escape, or freedom? Did she like this teacher or fear her?
How come she can't remember anything about this woman in the
classroom? Toni shakes her head, unable to explain why this dream
stayed alive and still perplexed by its meaning.

Toni remembers knowing almost immediately that her mother
had married "the meanest man I'd ever known." Lafayette was cruel
and bitter. He was unkind to Gladyce and punishing to Toni. He
filled their lives with fear. When I ask Toni in what ways Lafayette
was cruel, she can recall only one instance. She and a girlfriend
were secretly looking through a pornographic magazine, shrieking
and giggling together as they gazed upon the outrageous, sexy pictures. Lafayette discovered them huddling over the magazine, sent
the friend home, and "punished me terribly." "What was the punishment?" I ask. Then her face looks questioning and fearful. "I
don't remember the specific punishment... but the fact that the
time with Lafayette is so blank in my mind must mean something."
Her voice trails off and then she almost whispers, "I don't know if
he abused me or not." Toni does recall that Lafayette insisted that
she come directly home from school each day. She was required to
do all the housework and not permitted to go outside even when all
her chores and homework were done.

Finally, Gladyce got tired of Lafayette's brutality and meanness.
She may have even suspected that he was abusing her daughter. And
she sent him away. "My mother said to Lafayette, 'If you cannot treat
my child nicely, you'll have to leave,'... and she put him out. He was
coming and begging her to be taken back... but she refused, so my

mother was alone again." Her mother's decision to save her from this horrible man rings out like a victory sign; perhaps this was the first time that Toni felt her mother's loyalty and protection. Even Lafayette's pleading to come back, even his facile and insincere apologies to Gladyce, did not change her mother's mind. She was steadfast in her decision to throw him out even if this meant that she would be alone again. Gladyce and Toni, alone against the world.

Curiously, Toni also remembers Lafayette for one saving gesture, one bright act of humanity. He once rescued Toni from her *mother's* violence. Several times during the interviews, Toni has reminded me that her mother had a "terrible temper," that she lived in fear of her mother's explosions. Gladyce was a "tiny woman" (five feet one inch tall and one hundred and ten pounds), but she was able to find enormous physical strength when she got angry. Her little body would fill up with fierce energy. One day when Toni was probably about eight or nine years old (and almost as tall as her mother), Gladyce got furious at her "for some reason. She picked me up, held me up above her head [Toni stands up and demonstrates the threatening stance], and was about to throw me on the hard marble floor... This little person about to heave me on the floor... Lafayette saved me. He wouldn't let her throw me down. He pulled me out of her arms. That was the only good thing he ever did." I feel the treachery of Toni's young life. "The meanest man" she'd ever known, the man whom her mother got rid of because she thought he was abusing her child, had rescued her from her *mother's* rage. "I could have been killed if I had landed on that marble floor."

Toni remembers another incident when her mother exhibited her "terrible, terrible temper." A couple of years after Lafayette left, another man who "was crippled in some way" came to visit. Gladyce, Toni, and the visitor were sitting around talking, and Toni said "something that made her mad." With lightning speed, Gladyce picked up the heavy cover of her sewing machine and heaved it across the room at Toni. But the cover hit the crippled man instead, which made Gladyce even angrier. The memory stops right there, but the apprehension remains. "These glimpses of her anger always made me afraid."

By the time Toni reached the seventh grade, she and her mother were living apart again. Gladyce was on her way to Aberdeen, Maryland, to work for her brother, George, and Toni was deposited with George's wife, Josephine, and her two sons in New Haven. Toni hated this time with Aunt Jo and the boy cousins. She felt unwanted and excluded. "I was not happy at all. I was always blamed for everything."

Worried about providing a structured environment for her almost adolescent daughter, Gladyce began searching for a boarding school where Toni would get a "good education" and be safe from the dangers and distractions of big-city life. Gladyce believed strongly in schooling and was fiercely determined that her daughter would be well educated. She herself had gone to two years of college at City College in New York before heading out to Chicago to pursue her singing career. "Education was very important to her and to her mother, too." So when Gladyce stumbled upon an advertisement for St. Frances Academy, a Catholic boarding school for "colored girls" in the *Afro-American Newspaper*, she immediately began to make inquiries.

St. Frances Academy seemed the perfect solution: a colored environment run by strict Roman Catholic nuns; a place of discipline, safety, and educational excellence. Toni did not see it her mother's way. She was "terrified" of being taken to a convent, terrified of the isolation, the mystery, the shroud of secrecy. "I had been raised an Episcopalian... I had never seen a nun up close... I just thought that my mother wanted to get rid of me." Despite Toni's fears and mild protestations—they were only half-hearted; she knew that there was no chance of changing her mother's mind—Gladyce prevailed, and the following September Toni was on her way to eighth grade at St. Frances Academy in Baltimore.

The whole way there in the car, Uncle George teased her, "You're going to be all alone there in the convent!" As they approached the wrought iron gate of the academy, with "the forbidding brick walls" and the deafening silence, Uncle George's taunts resounded in her head. Her heart pounded hard against her chest. She had never been so scared. "I went there in fear and trembling," she says with a visible shudder. Sister Liberata, the principal, greeted them at the door. A tall, imposing woman, "very fair and looking like white," the sister's piercing eyes seemed to penetrate right to her insides. Twelve-year-old Toni felt naked and exposed. Gladyce signed some papers, said a quick and unemotional farewell, and took off in the car with Uncle George. "It was my conviction that she was trying to get rid of me. I felt horrible inside as I watched them drive off. But I was determined not to cry."

The tears came in great heaving sobs after Toni was led into the tiny cubicle where she would sleep. She pulled the curtain closed and wept for the rest of the night.

Such a Good Girl

A bell rang at 6:00 the next morning. Toni's tears had dried, and she faced the day, and her new future, with a combination of apprehension and determination. Mass was at 6:30, and the girls, dressed in their school uniforms, lined up in pairs outside the chapel. With each step toward the chapel, Toni's anxiety rose. She could not enter this Roman Catholic place of worship, she thought, "I am not Catholic!" So at the door, Toni stopped dead in her tracks. Her partner, another eighth grader, leaned over and, in a hushed whisper, asked her what was wrong. "I can't go in," Toni explained. "I am an Episcopalian." Her partner could not dissuade her, so she nervously pushed herself forward, leaving Toni to struggle with her own resistance by herself. "I got out of line... This was my first day, but I was a determined little girl." Seeing Toni on the sidelines, one of the sisters approached her and gently inquired about why she had dropped out of line. Their conversation was brief and soothing. The sister assured Toni that she would not be relinquishing her status as an Episcopalian nor would she be insulting the Catholic Church if she joined in the worship, and the sister guided her into the chapel. What Toni remembers most is not the sister's explanation, not her momentary resistance at the chapel door, but the way in which the sister sought her out and welcomed her into the fold.

That was the last time Toni recalls resisting anything at St. Frances Academy. She took to the place like a duck to water. "I ended up loving the place," she says enthusiastically. In contrast to public school in New Haven where she has almost no memory of her teachers, Toni's memories of the sisters at St. Frances are detailed and vivid. She remembers how they looked, how they behaved, who they liked, the way they wore their habits, the timbre of their voices, and the nature of their characters. I am struck by how well she knew these women hidden under their habits. The first person Toni describes, with loving reverence, is Sister Boniface (Sister of Good Works), "her favorite" sister, her eighth-grade teacher. "Sister Boniface," she swoons, "was so completely beautiful... There was peacefulness in that face... Her skin was *perfect*. She was a little lighter than you are. She had gorgeous big brown eyes, a large nose. She was very light-skinned, a Creole from New Orleans." Toni gets up, retrieves a photograph album from the book shelf, and turns directly to Sister Boniface's picture. "You see," she says passing the picture to me, "there is such beauty in that face." I see before me a woman of transcendent beauty. It is almost as if the habit, which covers everything but her face, forces you to focus on the convergence of her physical and spiritual loveliness. I can imagine an impressionable twelve-year-old yearning to be the object of Sister Boniface's benign and queenly gaze. Toni, in fact, worked very hard to establish a special relationship with the sister. "She was so kind, so loving, so caring to this kid who was not a Roman Catholic. I sopped it all up... I studied and worked very hard and I got all A's in eighth grade. Soon I was the teacher's pet, and the other girls began to be jealous of me."

Toni's voice is full of emotion as she relives the passionate feelings she had for this icon of beauty and grace. The memories are over forty years old, but they enliven her face and blur her eyes over with tears. She tries to explain why these relationships were so potent. "You see, there was a strange culture at St. Frances. There were no boys to lavish our affection on, so we directed it all on the nuns." Toni's love for and curiosity about Sister Boniface consumed her thoughts and caused her to scheme about the ways she might get to know her better. One day she sneaked into the chapel, found Sister Boniface's prayer book, searched through it for some evidence of her secrets, and discovered a lock of her hair. "It was gorgeous brown hair," and it confirmed, again, that the sister's beauty was both earthly and spiritual.

Within months, Toni had decided that she wanted to be "just like" Sister Boniface, and she wrote her a note saying she wanted to become a nun. This did not feel like a frivolous decision. It seemed almost an inevitable extension of her devotion to Sister Boniface. But she wrote the note with apprehension. What if sister wasn't enthusiastic? What if she didn't take her seriously? What if she rejected her? Toni awaited her mentor's reply, and within days she received a written response. "Dear Carole, I'm so happy to hear that you have decided that you want to be a nun... Do you realize that before you become a sister, you must be a Catholic?" Toni was warmed all over by Sister Boniface's reply. "She was positive, so graceful, so encouraging." Right then and there, at twelve, Toni decided to become Roman Catholic.

St. Frances Academy felt so safe and orderly, so full of beautiful ritual and ceremony, so harmonious. It was so different from the life Toni had known before coming, a life filled with dislocation, disharmony, and struggle. It was hard to leave the asylum of St. Frances during the summer vacation after her first year. By every measure that mattered to Toni, her eighth-grade year had been a success. She had cheerfully settled into the rule-bound culture, relishing the discipline, relishing the righteousness. She had a stellar academic record and had become the eighth-grade salutatorian. At the eighth-grade graduation, where the girls had worn "blue two-piece cotton dresses and blue hats with flowers," Toni had been singled out for her excellent work. And she had carved a special place in the heart of Sister Boniface. The "freedom" of summer at home felt like some kind of chaotic incarceration.

"Mother had lost her job with Uncle George, and she was floating around somewhere in Philadelphia. I didn't want to go home. The convent felt safe." I ask Toni, "Where did you settle with your mother?" "I don't know, don't remember... all over the place... West Philadelphia, South Philadelphia. My mother was being a maid." The summer of her thirteenth year was an unhappy blur, defined by one major event: "It was the summer I got my period." The bleeding "came out of nowhere... I was completely naive." Toni approached her mother with apprehension. "I'm real upset," she stuttered to her mother. "I'm bleeding for some reason." Her mother offered no explanation of *why* she was bleeding, but she did reassure her that "nothing was wrong" with her and that this was something "all women go through." Despite her mother's assurances that this was "ordinary" and "natural" in the lives of women, Gladyce's constant references to menstruation as "a woman's *curse*" made it seem like a punishing omen on the horizon of adolescence. Toni did not welcome its appearance or take kindly to the paraphernalia of belts and napkins that were heavy and uncomfortable in the summer's heat.

But the belts and napkins were nothing compared to the inconvenience and humiliation of menstruation in the convent. "At the convent, we wore *diapers* during menstruation… We had to bring *baby* diapers. Every month when we got our period, we would scrub the blood out, soak the diapers in a bucket of cold water under our beds, boil them in water, and hang them out to dry." Toni looks over at my incredulous face and tries to soften the tale. "It was an ancient custom with historical roots… but it didn't change until the mid-seventies, when we were allowed to wear belts and napkins, but *never* Tampax. Of course, some of us snuck the Tampax anyway."

Toni seems to anticipate my surprise and my horror, but she herself shows no sign of anger or pain as she describes the monthly ritual, only mild bemusement. Later on, however, when she is speaking about a very difficult experience teaching at a parochial school, where her principal-superior relished bullying her, Toni mentions the ultimate punishment: "She would check my diaper pail every day of my period to make sure it was clean."

St. Frances Academy had been founded in Baltimore in 1828 by the Oblate Sisters of Providence, who were free black Roman Catholic nuns, primarily of Haitian descent. At the time "black children were not allowed to be taught" in Baltimore, and St. Frances Academy became the first school for black children in the city. When Toni arrived at St. Frances, it had been a school for black girls, eighth grade through twelfth grade, for more than a century, and it was still being run by the Oblate Sisters, disciplined, proud, impeccable black nuns. "I remember those teachers… *all* of them. I *see* those people. It is so different from elementary school where I can't remember anything!" Toni offers profiles of several of the sisters, still vivid in her mind.

> Sister Immaculate was my Latin teacher (now she has gone back to her given name, Naomi). She was short, dark-brown-skinned with no lines on her face. You know underneath their habit, you could never tell how old nuns were. They didn't age for a very long time. Their regular life of order and routines keeps them the same age forever. Then when they do age it is sudden, immediate, and they look very old. Sister Immaculate was one of these ageless ones. She was a scary person—not a friend but a *teacher*. She didn't laugh a lot and carried great authority. I respected her and *loved* Latin.
>
> Sister Edwina was my history teacher. She was a beautiful woman from Mississippi. Tall, very fair with a thin face. She had penetrating eyes. A *holy* woman... You could tell by the way she talked and prayed, always kneeling with a straight back. She spent a lot of time alone, a quiet person with a quiet voice. She almost seemed to *float* down the hall when she moved.... Today I would call her a mystic. Sister Edwina always told us we must be *perfect*... She would say "perfect" in this long, pure way... She meant perfect as far as God was concerned, not vanity. Her handwriting was lovely. We used to crochet together. She taught me how to crochet, but I would help her read and follow the directions... She wasn't good at making the translation from the directions to the stitching. One of my favorite, most peaceful memories is sitting in Sister Edwina's aura, silently together, crocheting.
>
> Sister Laurentia was another holy woman. She was an artist, a painter, with a very sensitive soul. She didn't have the authority the other sisters had. She couldn't control the class. We would often misbehave, and sometimes she'd get so frustrated, she'd cry. Underneath she was a peaceful, lovely person. She had a reputation among us as an "easy"

person. Sister Laurentia was your color, short, pretty, wrinkled, and older… maybe in her fifties. I think part of her vulnerability had to do with her being older.

Sister Frances was my chemistry teacher. She was medium height, thin, and very fair. You couldn't tell whether she was white or black. And she was *brilliant* and *loved* chemistry. She should have gone on for her Ph.D. She had a mole on the side of her face and spoke in a high-pitched, absolutely flat, monotone voice. [Toni mimics her voice.] She taught me to love science. Her enthusiasm was contagious. She left me in charge of her lab. I loved mixing and making things happen… I was in my element. But I was not the teacher's pet. She treated me like everyone else.

Sister Incarnata was my typing teacher. She had graduated from an excellent secretarial school, and she was very well trained. She was my role model. I wanted to follow in her footsteps and become an excellent secretary. Sister Incarnata was young, thin, and very fair. But she was not nice to me at all… By that, I mean that I wasn't her pet even though I wanted to be very much. She didn't treat me specially. In her eyes, I was just like everyone else.

As I listen to Toni's detailed memories of these powerful women who dominated her life as an adolescent, I sense that their importance was exaggerated by her determined search for a "good mother": a mother who would be stable, caring, safe, and loving; a mother whom she could "feel and touch." It was not enough to be one of many students liked by the nuns. She wanted to be cherished and loved specially by each of them. She worked to be the teacher's pet. She was even willing to tolerate the wrath of peers in exchange for special status with the sisters. When Sister Incarnata, the typing teacher, treated her "like everyone else," Toni felt that "she was not nice to me at all." Her most "peaceful" memory of St. Frances Academy is sitting in Sister Edwina's "aura," just the two of them "silently together" crocheting. Sister Edwina came close to being the "perfect" mother with her quiet voice, her straight-backed kneeling, her impeccable dress, her lovely handwriting, and the way she floated down the halls. For the child whose *real* mother was in Philadelphia "floating around someplace" looking for work, St. Frances, with so many motherly holy women, must have felt like heaven. Toni seized the opportunity to be mothered and worked diligently and earnestly to be the perfect child.

In Toni's characterizations of the Oblate Sisters, I am struck that their beauty is often linked with their fairness. Many of the sisters, she explains, were Creole, from New Orleans. They were "very fair and looking like white." Toni's focus on their nearly white beauty, and the grace and holiness that seems to flow from this, makes me ask her how she viewed herself during high school. Her response is immediate. "Rather negatively," she says matter of factly. "I was *not* attractive. I thought of myself as an ugly duckling. I was tall and skinny. My uncle used to call me a string bean. I had a friend Betty. Now *she* was really pretty. She was light-brown-skinned with long braids. I had thick hair... braids, too, but they were *thick* braids." One day, Toni approached her mother with a burning question. "I asked her, 'Am I pretty?'" Her mother's response was blunt and unapologetic. "You're not *pretty,* but you're *smart.*"

Compared to her friend Betty, who had "good hair" and "fair skin," compared to the beautiful Oblate Sisters, Toni felt diminished, "not attractive." This negative image was reinforced by her poverty. Being poor made her feel even uglier, even darker. Being poor among the predominantly middle-class girls at St. Frances was a source of humiliation. Mostly the offspring of the "black bourgeoisie" in Baltimore and Philadelphia, these girls had been raised to see themselves as gracious and attractive, or so Toni thought. Being poor, skinny, thick-haired, and brown-skinned made Toni feel like a homely outcast. But it is the mention of her poverty amidst their plenty that brings tears to Toni's eyes forty years later. "We wore uniforms during the week, but I hardly had any clothes to wear on the weekends... All the clothes I wore were handmade by my mother, and that embarrassed me a lot." Underneath the jumper of their school uniforms the girls wore white blouses. "Most of them had at least six or seven blouses," explains Toni. "They'd change them each day. I had only three or four that my mother made, and I'd have to turn them inside out... You could hardly tell that they were inside out because of the jumper on top of them. But *I* knew, and I hated it." Toni's voice chokes up as she describes the humiliation of poverty. She looks at me squarely. "These are tears you see coming down my face, Sara." Tears that water the scars that remain after four decades.

By the time the summer rolled around after Toni's ninth-grade year at St. Frances, Gladyce had been fired from her job as a housekeeper in Ocean City, New Jersey. Mother and daughter were, once again, homeless and destitute. "I remember walking the streets of Philadelphia with no place to go, no place to live, no job for my mother." They spent their first night in the Thirtieth Street Station ("All I can remember is eating frozen custard") and then resumed their search the next day. As they pounded the pavement and made brave inquiries, Toni's anxiety and desperation grew. This begging, this pleading, these dashed hopes seemed a world apart from her life at St. Frances. The chaos, filth, and danger of the big city streets seemed so far from the pristine orderliness of her boarding school. Finally, someone directed Gladyce and Toni to the Father Divine Hotel, where for a dollar a night and fifty cents a day they could share a clean room and eat a big meal. Father Divine, a powerful and mysterious religious figure, had a domineering presence among his followers who all, in total obedience to him, took on the last name Love. The followers who worked in his hotels and staffed his other properties acquiesced to his every whim and wish. It was a strange community of idol worshipers who, out of devotion to Father Divine, gave of themselves completely and accomplished good works in the black community. The hotel was one such place where the down and out could find a clean room, ample board, and safety from the rough streets. Toni and her mother stayed there for several months while Gladyce searched for a job.

At the end of the summer, Toni was "devastated" when her mother informed her that she would not be able to return to St. Frances Academy; there was no way they could afford it. All summer Toni had been aching to get back to school. She had survived the grueling summer only by keeping the serene picture of St. Frances firmly in her head. Now she would have to go to the huge public high school in West Philadelphia and live with her mother, whose temper and rage shook the walls of their hotel room; whose pain carved long silences between them. Toni wrote to the sisters at St. Frances, expressing her grief at not being able to return there. When school opened, she went solemnly off, walking the twenty blocks from the Father Divine Hotel at Thirty-eighth Street to school at Fifty-eighth Street because she did not have enough money to take the bus. At the high school she was tracked into the honors classes, the only black student in all her courses. She was miserable in this big, impersonal place and found it hard to make friends or develop real connections with her teachers.

After she had attended the West Philadelphia School for six weeks, a letter arrived from the sisters at St. Frances Academy bringing joyous news. They told Gladyce that Toni could return to St. Frances. She was such an excellent student, such a good girl, and the whole community missed her. They would give her a scholarship, and she would have to work two jobs to earn her keep, but they were eager to have her back. Gladyce was relieved and Toni was thrilled. If she had had wings, she would have flown down to Baltimore. Instead, within twenty-four hours, she was on the bus heading south to St. Frances.

"Tenth grade. That was the year I became a Catholic," recalls Toni with enthusiasm. The date of her baptism—December 7, 1950—is clear in her mind. "I had come to *love* this religion... I was floating on air... I thought, I'm a saint now, for sure." Toni was baptized in a beautiful white dress made by her mother, and she "floated" through the mass celebrating a decision that she knew she would never regret. Her love for Catholicism translated into a disciplined, exacting devotion. "I became a very *scrupulous* Catholic... I spent a great deal of time, for example, trying to distinguish between a venial sin and mortal sin." When she notices my puzzled look, Toni explains, "A venial sin is not very serious. A mortal sin has three ingredients: one, it is a grievous matter; two, you have given it sufficient reflection; three, you have given full consent of the will." She quotes the catechism. But these abstractions were never specific enough to offer moral guidance to the real-life decisions of a tenth grader. So Toni struggled each day with trying to judge the seriousness of her sinning. "I believed that God was up there writing down all the bad things Carole did." She knew, for example, that missing mass on Sunday was a mortal sin. So was letting a boy touch you. But what about looking at a magazine with dirty pictures? Was that a venial or a mortal sin? "It was so hard to figure out. I was *always* worrying about it." Toni "hated confession," but she went dutifully every single week because she knew that she couldn't take communion unless she went to confession, and she "loved" communion.

As a scholarship student, Toni continued to prove her excellence as a student, her worthiness as a good girl, and her devotion as a Catholic. No one was surprised when she graduated from high school first in her class; no one was surprised when Carole Rodez decided to become a nun. It seemed the natural and inevitable extension of the life she had so carefully shaped at St. Frances. But when Toni put in her application to the convent, she hedged her bets by also applying to the air force. She had to be cautious, she thought, because she knew that the convent would never accept "an illegitimate child." She was seventeen years old and had begun having premonitions that she might be illegitimate. She would not lie on the application. That would be a mortal sin, and God would punish her. "I just *knew* that I was illegitimate. I *felt* it in my bones. No one had ever told me so." Toni decided to ask her mother directly. When her mother assured her that she was *not* illegitimate, Toni decided to believe her even though she suspected her mother was not speaking the truth. Feeling she had made the appropriate inquiries, she submitted her application, and the convent accepted her even before she heard back from the air force. "I went gladly, enthusiastically." On September 8, 1952, when Carole Rodez was seventeen, she entered the Convent of the Immaculate Conception.

Bride of Christ

Several weeks before Toni entered the convent, she began packing her trunk. She could hardly contain her excitement. She counted the days and hours, arranging and rearranging the clothes in her trunk. "Everything was *white* and brand new. From time to time I would just open the trunk and feel the things, run my hands over the soft, clean piles. I felt I was going off on a new adventure! I believed I was dedicating my life to God." Carole Rodez was seventeen years old when she arrived at the Convent of the Immaculate Conception in Baltimore, and became a "postulant," the first stage in training to be a nun. "We were the children of the convent," remembers Toni. "We were wild and giddy and full of worldliness. They had to get the worldliness out of us."

Even the costumes worn by the postulants signaled their status as "the children of the convent." "We wore a special habit—'cute' is the only word for it. We had a little bonnet on our head, a black thin veil, a white Peter Pan collar on our long black dress, a black cape over the dress, black shoes, black stockings, and white underwear." All of Toni's descriptions of clothes are full and detailed. The nun's costumes are remembered with clarity and fondness. The whiteness of the underwear and the blackness of the dress, cape, and bonnet seem to have appealed to Toni's early sense of right and wrong, evil and purity, good and bad. From the very beginning she loved taking care of her habits, the washing and ironing and pleating and folding. She loved achieving perfection in preparing her costumes—as a sign of her religious commitment, her aesthetic taste, and her personal attitude.

One of the ways that the nuns in the convent "got the worldliness" out of their "children" was to insist upon a very rigid daily schedule full of hard manual work, hours of prayer, and imposed silence. For six months, the postulants followed this daily pattern, a structure that Toni easily recalls almost forty years later.

- 5:30 A.M.: Awakened by a bell. "We lived in cubicles... We would get dressed in fifteen minutes... We didn't have to comb our hair because it was covered... but we would do all of our dressing without a mirror... We'd be competing to see who could get to the chapel first."
- 6:00 A.M.: Morning prayer in the chapel, "where we chanted the office—one note intoning—said the Christian prayers and the liturgy of the hours. Followed by meditation."
- 6:30 A.M.: Mass with communion every day.
- Return to cubicle to make beds (in silence).
- Breakfast (in silence). "Every morning they would read us aloud a chapter from *Imitation of Christ*... usually the reading aloud was done by a senior novice dressed in a white veil."
- One half-hour for talking.
- Bell would ring signaling the time for more silence.
- Work, including washing clothes, scrubbing floors, working in the kitchen, cleaning and polishing religious artifacts, crocheting for benefactors.
- Classes "to learn about discipline, prayer, preparing and wearing our habits... studying the rule book."
- Prayers and chanting the office.
- Lunch (in silence). "Each day they would read us a chapter from the *Lives of the Saints*."

The afternoon would be as tightly scheduled as the morning with hard labor, prayer, the chanting of offices, classes, and silence. It took almost no time for Toni to feel acclimated to the rigorous schedule. She relished the routine, the structure. "The regularity was wonderful. It gave me the security I always craved." She even liked poring over the rule book ("As a postulant, we did not *own* the rule book, but we did learn to use it") and studying the details: "The dimensions of the habit, the number of pleats and how to press them to make it look perfect, the length of the veil." Toni's voice is a mixture of pride and incredulity when she recalls, "I was a very good postulant. I obeyed all the rules... I was a docile, obedient child." She does remember getting punished once, although she can't recall the transgression that led to the punishment. But she was not alone in whatever mild mischief she got caught in. A group of the postulants was caught and forced to kneel for hours on the hard stone floor of the front hallway in public view. This humiliation cured Toni of any further rule breaking. She was a diligent and dutiful child not only because she wanted to avoid punishment, but also because she loved the rules and the rewards of unquestioned obedience.

For many of the seventeen- and eighteen-year-olds, the imposed silences, for most of the day, were the most difficult discipline. Every meal was eaten in silence; work was usually done in silence; grooming, dressing, bed making were done in silence. And at the conclusion of each day, at 9:30 P.M., a bell would sound to mark the beginning of "The Great Silence—the most serious silence of all." Once the night was shrouded in the Great Silence, the postulants were not supposed to utter a sound, or "make a sound bodily," until the next morning. As they undressed in their cubicles, they had to move slowly and with great caution, tiptoeing in stocking feet and making sure they didn't drop anything. Even the slightest noise during the Great Silence was cause for severe punishment. For Toni, even the silences were not considered onerous or particularly difficult. "I *loved* the silences," recalls Toni. "I was an only child. I had grown up mainly *alone*. I had always been an avid reader... my mind was always filled with fantasies. The imposed silences came naturally to me."

By the end of the six-month testing period, Toni was more assured than ever that she wanted to be a nun. Everything she experienced fit her image of a life of perfection, order, and obedience, and left her with no doubts. "I never questioned for a minute whether I was supposed to be there. I felt I was getting holier and holier." Toni spent much of her time fantasizing about what it would be like to be a novice. She couldn't wait for the day when she would "put on her bridal gown and become a bride of Christ." She loved to picture the beauty of it all: the gorgeous white lace bridal costumes, the flowing veils, the ornate rituals, the passionate vows of devotion and love. "It was so romantic, so beautiful," Toni swoons playfully. "Of course, it was all the superficial stuff, but it is so unbelievably meaningful when you are an adolescent."

The great day came on March 9, 1953, "the special day, the bridal ceremony" when Carole Rodez became a novice. "I can still hear the hymn," says Toni standing up reverentially and breaking into song, "Come Thou Virgin Happy Bride." Her voice is a clear contralto, strong and filled with feeling. Tears spring to her eyes. "It was a very emotional thing." The postulants awoke with the bell at 5:30 A.M. and put on their "cute" habits for the last time. They participated in an early mass before putting on their fancy bridal gowns for the ceremony. Even though most of the other girls had gowns carefully chosen and generously bought by their mothers, on this wedding day Toni did not experience the familiar humiliations of poverty. Her mother could not afford to buy a bridal gown for her, so Toni used an ornate hand-me-down left over from another year. By now she had "internalized the vow of poverty" taught so adamantly and religiously at the convent. She knew that it was not good to covet worldly goods, and practiced her vow as she saw her sisters in their own new gowns. In any case, nothing could spoil the "holiness" and rapture of this wedding day. She felt so sure, so deeply committed in her decision to become a nun, so determined to become the bride of Christ.

The white procession of postulants flowed down the aisle of the "big beautiful chapel at the Mother House at St. Frances." As each one approached the altar, she received her novice habit, and for the first time, heard the *name* that she had been given. Weeks before, the postulants had submitted three choices of names to Sister Philomena, the novice mistress, but they had no idea which name they would be given. At the altar, each of them was handed a card with her new name on it. (Toni still has hers.) Toni looked down at her card and saw the careful calligraphy: Mary Antoinette. All of the sisters in the Oblate order "had to have some form of Mary" in their names. At this sparkling ceremonial moment, Carole Rodez became Mary Antoinette, Bride of Christ, and for the first time felt certain of her name. Joining her "new family," she gave herself over to "a life that was totally contained." She turned away from the chaos and confusion of her origins, the questions about her "real father," the haunting suspicions about her birth, the wounds of poverty, and turned toward safety, order, cleanliness, and clarity about her identity.

After collecting their new habits and new names at the altar, the postulants recessed back down the long aisle for the dressing ceremony. Toni suddenly realizes that she has forgotten a detail, an important symbol of her new identity, and says matter-of-factly, "Oh yes, at the altar, along with getting our names and our habits, they cut our hair... to signify getting rid of our vanity." I am struck by how quickly she dismisses what I perceive to be a major event. In our few hours together I have heard her refer several times to hair: the lovely lock of Sister Boniface's hair that she found in the sister's prayer book, confirming her true beauty; the "good hair and long braids" of her childhood friend Betty; her own sense of herself as "not pretty" because she had "thick hair." Like so many black women of her generation, she had inherited the damaging legacy of measuring her beauty by the texture of her hair and the color of her skin. Although I suspect that Toni, now in her mid-fifties, sitting down before me with a magnificent crown of white hair, has liberated herself somewhat from the self-denigration attached to "kinky hair," she is not completely free of the pejorative imprints. Listening to her almost forget the cutting of her hair at the bridal ceremony, I do not know whether having her hair cut and her head covered by a habit were liberating or traumatizing events for her: whether she was relieved to be free of worrying about her thick hair; whether cutting it off symbolized a new, more beautiful identity; or whether the haircut was the ultimate expression of a human, womanly hurt.

Each postulant got to choose her favorite sister to help her get dressed in the new novice habit. "I, of course, chose Sister Boniface," says Toni as if she is still relishing the "special privilege" of that moment of intimacy. Carefully, Sister Boniface helped her remove the wedding gown and then layer by layer, piece by piece, helped Mary Antoinette assemble her costume. Toni is now standing up demonstrating the complicated process: putting on the face piece, the starched head band, the gimp (a kind of bib), the veil, inserting a big veil pin to make the correct dip in the cloth. She explains all this in detail, even to the number of inches and folds, as though reliving the caring attentions of Sister Boniface. Finally, for full effect, she shows me a photo of herself in full novice dress. When everyone was put together perfectly, the junior novices returned to the chapel with their arms hidden underneath their habits and paraded solemnly toward their new resolve and commitments.

Toni makes it clear that these commitments came in the form of "promises," not "vows." As junior novices, a status they held for one year, they "lived in preparation for their vows," promising to be "poor, chaste, and obedient." Their life was completely cloistered. "We couldn't visit anyone, and we couldn't be visited by anyone… We were not permitted to receive any mail except on Christmas and Easter, when the already read mail that they had collected over the months would be given to us." Toni responded enthusiastically to the discipline of a cloistered life. "Cloistering didn't bother me. After all, I only had my mother from whom I was separated, and that didn't cause me pain… and I was so enthusiastic about becoming a nun." She threw herself into the community, declaring with each achievement of rectitude and self-sacrifice that she was worthy of her place in Christ's family. "I was determined to give it my all… My philosophy of life was that it was all or nothing at all… I tried to be in touch with how I felt *spiritually*. I did a lot of praying… always striving for perfection." Nothing less would do.

Her personal determination was enhanced by the rituals of the convent. Every first Friday of the month the junior novices would gather in the dining room, kneel down on the hard floor, and with straight backs and clear voices "confess their faults and receive public penance." The "chapter of faults" could include confessions about "serious stuff": running on the stairs, not wearing an apron to meals, breaking the silence, or staying in bed after the bell. Some of the novices would admit to only the most minor, trivial faults as a way of masking the more serious stuff. Others would say their penance only half-heartedly. But Toni saw this ritual as an important, if uncomfortable, part of her full immersion in the convent and worked extra hard to identify and disclose her misdeeds. "I don't think I held back, ever… I was always ready to please, always wanting to be a very good sister." She remembers the all-important words and delivers them with feeling, *"I accuse myself of the following faults."*

Lonely Mission

Mystery and silence shroud Toni's family origins. Her own coming into the world, confusion over her real name, her determination to remake her identity are all cloudy, yet troubling memories. In our meetings, she searches for the tiniest shreds of evidence, the most meager stories, to place herself in time and space. But at the same time, she seems to repress the urge to know the truth, perhaps feeling that the truth would be even more painful than the fantasies she has woven.

Toni mentions the discovery, when she was in her twenties, of a younger sister. It turns out that Toni had first learned that she had a sister years earlier when she was a small child. When Toni and her mother were living in New Haven, she used to search her mother's old purses looking for change. "I seemed to always be looking for money... I didn't have any, never had any, and rarely found any." One day when she was rummaging through a purse in her mother's closet, Toni unearthed some documents, neatly folded and official looking. "They had this child's name—Arvella—on them. They were adoption papers. And this child was born December 13, 1936." Toni's mind began to race; her heart started thumping as she tried to figure out who Arvella was. Was she herself Arvella? Was Arvella another child? "I've always been mixed up about when I was born because of this," says Toni with some sadness in her voice. "The logical thing was to think I'm that child... But I knew I was born in 1934. But I never said anything. I just wondered." Her voice trails off.

Her confusion was magnified. Arvella's birthdate was given as December 13, and Toni knew she had the same birthday. But she could see as she read the document over and over that these were adoption papers. "I knew they were adoption papers, but I didn't

231

know for whom. I didn't know whether I was adopted or whether this was another child named Arvella." All of these questions remained locked up inside Toni until one day when she was in her early twenties and getting ready to take her final vows. Just before her mother visited her at the convent, Toni had a dream about Aunt Rose, the woman who had picked her up off the streets of New Haven when she was a tiny child, brought her home, cleaned her up, and had taken care of her. This dream was about the one powerful, loving memory from Toni's childhood. Toni described it to Gladyce with a question in her voice. Her mother, who may have been waiting for the chance and the courage to reveal this news to her daughter, said quietly, "You know that may be a sign," and then moved immediately into a short, unembellished explanation. "I have to tell you something I've never told you before," she admitted to her twenty-year-old daughter. "You have a sister."

It turned out that Arvella had been born two years (to the day) after Toni, and that Gladyce had "put her up for adoption because she felt she couldn't take care of two children." "This was another child out of wedlock," explains Toni, "but I don't *think* this was a rape situation." Her voice is still heavy with the "rape question," however. As soon as Toni's mother revealed the existence of this second child, Toni began to recall the visits they used to make down to New York City where Arvella was living with her adoptive family, visits that stopped abruptly when Arvella's adoptive mother "became concerned that this child was getting very attached to her original family." Two decades later, Gladyce's explanation to her firstborn was very spare, and she only felt free to make it because of the recent death of Arvella's adoptive mother. Toni tells this story without visible emotion as if she wants to dispose of it quickly. Yet many questions still remain. "I don't think that Arvella was the result of a rape situation," she says again.

I ask Toni why she kept this big question about the adoption papers to herself for so long; and why, when the truth was revealed many years later, she got so little of the story from her mother. I am painfully aware that her mother, Gladyce, her mind, body, and speech weakened by a stroke, is no longer able to recall or tell the story and that many questions will remain unanswered forever. The half-told stories have receded into cloudy reverie, but the pain and disappointment remain strong. When Toni makes her weekly Sunday afternoon visits to the nursing home, Gladyce frequently returns to her deepest pain—that "she was not a good mother." She also probably remembers, but doesn't speak about, the rage that used to consume her and spill out on her helpless daughter. So when I ask Toni why she never asked the huge haunting questions or pressed for more details, she reminds me of her mother's "temper," a scary power that Toni never dared to push too far, that kept her silenced.

"It was traumatic," says Toni in her most demonstrative statement. Her constant apprehension—When would her mother explode? How could she avoid her rage?—was compounded by oppressive silence, and deep loneliness. "You see, I was alone a great deal of the time, very much alone, not communicating with anyone. I did a lot of reading… a lot of fantasizing. I made up a lot of fairy tales and dreamed a lot… and I became very shy and reclusive, very introverted and insecure." The saddest part about the silence was that her mother always seemed so distant. "I never really got to know my mother," she says simply

This loneliness also left her with a "shyness" and a "fear of rejection" that Toni still has difficulty conquering. She recalls how hard it was for her to reach out to her peers in school, how she kept herself apart from them because of a constant worry that they would exclude or humiliate her. "You know, peers can be so cruel." One of the reasons she worked to develop such close alliances with the nuns was that she feared the hostility of her schoolmates. "It was much safer to have relationships with the sisters… It was not only that I was looking for my good mother in the sisters—I was also looking for loyal friends."

One way she attempted to overcome her shyness was to learn to play the guitar. She eagerly taught herself the instrument, practiced diligently, and learned the basic chords. Accompanying her lovely contralto voice, Toni found "something to offer the group." Once she had the guitar in her hands, some of the fear would fade away and she could get wrapped up in the performance. The guitar was an "icebreaker," and Toni is still amazed that she knew as a young girl that she needed "a strategy" to overcome her fear of rejection.

As Toni recalls the few peers that became her friends at St. Frances, she recognizes that they were also "outcasts" from poor families. The two girls who became her friends were classmates for whom she felt sorry because they were being treated badly by "the girls from middle-class families." Barbarita, "an Asian-American kid," was the source of lots of peer hostility, and Toni reached out to her. "Nobody liked Barbarita... I don't know whether it was prejudice (I didn't identify it as that at the time), or whether it was just that she was different from the rest of us. She wasn't black. She was something else... There were Cuban girls at St. Frances, but they looked like we did. But Barbarita was definitely Asian." Toni's other good friend was Carolyn, who was also excluded by the "middle-class young women" who found her "boyish" and crude. "Carolyn was very much a tomboy," recalls Toni with a smile; she did not have the manners or grace that the "young women" required, and she did not seem to care very much about adapting to the social niceties. Carolyn was also a poor student who struggled with her studies. Toni, an excellent student, enjoyed the role of being Carolyn's informal tutor. Toni seems almost surprised to discover that "the real link" with her two best friends, Barbarita and Carolyn, might have been that all three of them were poor. In this setting dominated by young women from proper families, Barbarita, Carolyn, and Toni were the outcasts whose poverty shaped how they were perceived and how they felt. In response to the exclusion, they formed a tight knot of survival and support.

Toni still finds it very difficult to reach out to people, to enter a room where she will have to introduce herself, or suddenly to be the center of attention. This handsome, tall woman with the halo of white hair, this graceful figure dressed in bold purple colors still finds it hard to "make myself known" and still "fears rejection." This is not something anyone would know from looking at her. "I'm slowly getting better at this," admits Toni cautiously. "But I still cannot walk into a room and go up to people and say, 'Hi, I'm Antoinette Schiesler, the academic dean here...' I've done it just once! And every year I think, now this year maybe I'll do it twice... next year three times." Toni's voice reveals the pain and frustration. "It's scary... I mean, my rational mind says, 'Toni, you're not going to be rejected. I mean, *you're* the academic dean.' I keep telling myself, 'This is ridiculous. You've got to overcome this,' but I just don't feel comfortable."

As an example of the "excruciating shyness" that still overwhelms her, Toni tells me how, on the very morning we are meeting, she had gone for her usual walk in her quiet suburban development with the thought of stopping briefly to welcome a new family who had just moved in a few doors down. "I took my walk across the way to the home of a new priest and his wife who have just moved in, and their door was open... I've met him. I haven't met her... Because I know how lonely it is to move into these places and you don't know anyone... But still I'm saying to myself, 'No, I can't do it. I'll do it on my way back.' So on my way back, I went up to the house. I went to the front door and knocked *very* softly... and, of course, nobody's going to hear that. Then I walk around to the back, making no sounds... I don't see anybody so I leave. I've worked on it, but it is still too hard to do."

In her work at Cabrini College, Toni feels deeply identified with those girls who come from poor families, who experience the humiliation and exclusion of being in a relatively abundant environment. She sees these "poor kids, especially African-American students [who] don't have money to take a taxi to the shopping center or to buy pizza," and she relives her own childhood experiences. Even when an environment *appears* to be benign and welcoming, the subtle experiences of exclusion can leave deep scars. "At St. Frances, there were some girls who were very good to me, but I always felt inferior because I always felt poor." As dean at Cabrini College, Toni keeps her eyes on the students who may be suffering these quiet, but deeply felt, exclusions. She reaches out to them personally and also tries gently to educate the institution about ways of becoming more inclusive.

Toni recalls that her own shyness and lack of self-confidence made her draw back from the opportunity for teacher training offered at the convent. With her elevation to senior novice status, Toni was permitted to go to "real school... what was actually a normal school." The community had its own teacher-training school called the Oblate Institute, where the "smart sisters" were sent to learn to become teachers. Toni did not want to attend the institute. "I never wanted to be a teacher because I had no clear idea of who I was and what I could do... I had very low self-esteem... A teacher needs confidence and self-knowledge." Then, with stridency in her voice, Toni announces, "I came to the convent to be a *saint*, not a teacher!" She laughs. "That was *really* my ambition."

Despite her years of superior achievement in school, Toni had her heart set on becoming a secretary. She cannot recall why this was her chosen career. Being a secretary for one of the superiors in the convent might well have felt like the safest and most secure choice. It would allow her to remain within the boundaries of the convent and draw her even closer to the bosom of the community. But her superiors would not give in to her wish to be a secretary. "There were people in the community who realized that I was capable, so they insisted, 'You will go to school.' And, of course, once you were told what to do, who was to argue with them?"

Toni's memories of her two years of teacher training are not very clear. However, she vividly recalls the details of her religious life during that time, her experience as a senior novice and her great anticipation of becoming professed. She remembers the date—March 9, 1955, the Feast of St. Frances—when she was given a black veil to replace her white veil and when she received the simple wooden crucifix that would decorate her own "homemade habit." She remembers no courses in method or classroom management, although she thinks they must have studied something about curriculum and "various philosophies of education." The courses neither inspired her nor interested her very much, even though she continued to get the highest grades.

One course, children's literature, Toni remembers clearly, not because it captured her interest but because, in the end, it caused her embarrassment and disappointment. It was being taught by Sister Laurentia, the art teacher, and it was a course for which Toni went to class each day feeling fully prepared and confident. At the end of the semester, Sister Laurentia left the students alone as they worked on the final exam. "We were on our honor to do this exam." Everything was going along fine for Toni until she reached the last page of the exam and drew a blank on one of the questions. She had diligently studied all the material; she knew all the answers, but suddenly one vanished from her mind. Almost involuntarily she heard herself say out loud, "I can't remember the answer to the last question." She said it out of keen frustration. She never intended to cheat on the exam. One of the other students shot back the answer, "Oh, it's so-and-so," and Toni jotted the answer down. It all happened so quickly and automatically. At the time, it all seemed natural and fine. But as soon as she turned her examination in, she began to be haunted by what she had done. She had not intended to cheat. Her heart was pure, but she had committed a fault, a major fault, and she would have to confess it. "It worried me so much," recalls Toni. "It began to pain me so much that I went to Sister Laurentia and said, 'I have to tell you what I did.'" Toni may have hoped for understanding and forgiveness, but she was not surprised by Sister Laurentia's tough response. "She chastised me and said, 'For your punishment I'm going to disregard the entire last page of the exam '"

The punishment hurt. It was not merely the pain and embarrassment that came from her teacher's chastisement as well as her own self-inflicted obsession that caused the hurt; she was pained by the blemish that this fault caused on her otherwise perfect academic record. In all of her other courses, Toni had received an A, and up until the final exam, she had earned an A in children's literature. But with the last page of her exam being discounted, she got a B instead of an A in the course. This experience from her teacher training is the only one that remains unforgettable—the devastation of receiving a B.

The following September Toni was on her way to her first mission, St. Augustine School in Washington, D.C., where she was to teach a class of sixty fifth graders. She was nineteen years old, thoroughly inexperienced, very reticent, and "totally unprepared" for the challenges of her first year of teaching. She knew immediately why she had wanted to remain at St. Frances serving as a secretary, safe from the chaos and demands of the "real world." The children were impossible for Toni to control. She had no idea how to capture their attention, harness their energy, or discipline them effectively. She had no idea what to expect from them developmentally, socially, or academically. She focused all of her energy on just trying to keep them quiet. Having been schooled in an entirely disciplined environment where no student ever questioned the authority of the sisters, she was amazed by the fifth graders' lack of respect and self-discipline. She could not believe that they didn't fear her; that all of her yelling and screaming wouldn't silence them. Sometimes she would be pushed beyond her limit, and feeling overwhelmed and out of control herself, she would whip one of the children with a ruler. The offender would feel hurt and look sheepish. The onlookers would briefly quiet down, but the lesson would be short-lived. The noise and chaos would begin to build again almost immediately. For most of the year Toni felt very unsuccessful as a disciplinarian and a teacher.

Her struggles with teaching were magnified by the unsupportive environment in which she was working. She had no mentors, no close allies, no peer supervision. But the worst part, by far, was the hostility she received from the mother superior, Sister Consolata, a light-skinned woman from New Orleans. From the moment Toni set foot in St. Augustine's, the superior singled her out for harsh treatment. Toni puts it simply, "She disliked me very much... No, she hated me with a passion." In every way, the superior tried to make life difficult for her new fifth-grade teacher. Although all the other teachers were permitted to continue their schooling by attending classes at Catholic University on Saturdays, the superior refused Toni permission. When the sisters ventured outside of the walls of the mission, the mother superior insisted that Toni be under her strict supervision. "Every place I went I had to go with her." But by far the most humiliating and excruciating punishment was the superior's inspection of her diaper pail. Every time Toni had her period, she had to alert Sister Consolata and had to endure the daily checks of her pail. "We used to soak the diapers under the beds until we took [the diapers] downstairs to clean them. So it meant changing the water every day, and that was not pleasant. [Sister Consolata] would inspect the bucket under my bed and chastise me if it was not clean... It was a miserable experience." The struggles and failures in her teaching and the daily harassment of her superior began to wear on Toni. For the first time since her early childhood she began to have severe nosebleeds. The bleeding would come anytime, in great surges, a bodily expression of how vulnerable she felt at St. Augustine's.

When I ask Toni why she thinks that she alone became the target of the mother superior's harsh abuse, she still seems puzzled. She points to the superior's general prejudice against "the girls from St. Frances." It seems that Sister Consolata had a reputation for picking on St. Frances girls. She thought that they were coddled and spoiled, and that they felt entitled to special treatment. "She made it her business to humiliate us sufficiently so we wouldn't feel special," says Toni with traces of bitterness still in her voice. There were two other St. Frances girls at St. Augustine's, Sister Dolorosa and Sister Celeste, who were both already professed and had been at the school a few years longer than Toni. But they had never suffered the superior's hostility in the way Toni did. "They realized that she hated me, everyone could see it, and nobody could understand why she was doing it."

The antagonism of the superior must have felt particularly difficult for Toni who was used to being admired and loved by her mentors at St. Frances. At St. Frances she had worked hard to be a superior student, a perfect novice, an obedient and dedicated nun. She had succeeded in being seen as "special" in their eyes; the affection and loyalty had been bountiful and reciprocal. At St. Augustine's, her first mission, her first foray beyond the walls of the family convent, she experienced all the opposite feelings. There seemed to be no way to win the favor of the mother superior. From the moment Toni arrived she had been distrusted, undermined, and demeaned.

Toni admits that there was one incident that occurred soon after she arrived that "was probably my undoing." There was a community room at St. Augustine's where the sisters would all gather to talk, read, or write their lesson plans. It was a big room with a long table, chairs, and a metal cabinet where they each had a shelf labeled with their name. The mother superior had typed the labels and pasted them on the shelves. One of the older sisters, a Cuban, who served as the cook and the housekeeper at the school, was named Sister Sacred Heart. Toni remembers her as "very sweet and very saintly"; in disposition and demeanor she matched her name. But when the mother superior typed "Sister Sacred Heart" for the shelf label, she "accidently transposed two letters." One day Toni walked into the community room, noticed the label and squealed with glee, "Oh look, Sister Scared Heart!" Everyone laughed, but Sister Consolata's face grew grim. "She was very angry... That was probably the beginning of the end for me at St. Augustine's."

The nosebleeds continued, the teaching failures multiplied, the bloody diaper pails required constant surveillance, and the stress brought on severe headaches. Finally, Toni could stand it no longer, so she wrote a letter of petition to Mother Theresa, the superior at St. Frances, asking to be released from her mission at St. Augustine's. In the letter she described her troubles at the mission, being careful not to whine, or rage, or criticize. "You know this was a very big deal, because we were not allowed to be critical," explains Toni. The letter was strong, but it didn't begin to reflect the desperation Toni was feeling. Even as she carefully composed her petition, Toni knew deep within that Mother Theresa would not rescue her. She knew that the mother superior at St. Frances would not defy the authority of the mother superior at St. Augustine's, nor would she want to appear to show favoritism to Toni. But Toni felt desperate enough to risk speaking out even though she expected no real response. Mother Theresa read the petition from one of her most special and successful novices and dispatched Sister Angela, the director of education at St. Frances, to Washington, D.C., to calm the waters. Sister Angela, "a kind and caring woman," came to St. Augustine's with one agenda: to convince Toni of her religious commitments and responsibilities. She came to remind Toni that a "good sister" must learn to adapt to even the most hostile and uncomfortable conditions; that a good sister is forgiving, obedient, and resilient; that a good sister does not criticize or challenge her superior. These admonitions were delivered clearly and firmly. "All the big platitudes," says Toni shaking her head.

Particular Friendships

It is an unseasonably warm mid-February day, and the air is heavy and damp. Several months have gone by since I last saw Toni, and I am eager to see her and pick up the threads of her story. She bursts out of her front door, again dressed in bright purple from top to bottom. Her sweater is purple, the stretch slacks are purple, the leather walking shoes are purple. She smiles broadly and opens her long arms in a big warm hug. We are like two squealing long-lost friends. The halo of curly white hair looks longer, bigger, wilder than I remember, and it is a grand contrast to the vivid declaration of purple. But then I notice that her eyes do not mirror the vitality of her bold outfit. They are weary, swollen, and red. Her brown face has a gray cast. After the initial excitement of our greeting, her voice reveals the weariness as well. She speaks in low, measured tones as if there is no fuel left.

When we land in our chairs in her quiet study a few minutes later, she immediately picks up a book that she is in the midst of reading. "This is me. This is my condition," Toni says as she shows me Ellen Sue Stern's popular book, *Running on Empty: Meditations for Indispensable Women*. "This has been a difficult time for me... too much to do, pulled in too many directions... I'm exhausted." I am unpacking my tape recorder, my notes, and my paper, worrying whether our session will be another heavy burden on Toni or whether it might provide her with some measure of relief, and perhaps some insight into her weariness. Almost immediately I sense with relief that she has been looking forward to our time together as an oasis of quiet and self-reflection. So much of her life is responding to others' needs. She is hungry for the time and space to focus on herself. "I'm feeling change coming on, major changes," Toni explains to me. "And it scares me, exhausts me. You've come along at exactly the right time... to help me figure this out."

Her fears and her sadness ("It was really depression") recently led her to "a pastoral counselor for help... He's a minister, but he is also a trained therapist." Not only did she feel the need for support and understanding, but she was also seeking a legitimate place to "focus on *me*." "You see," Toni exclaims, "I'm feeling very selfish, so self-involved... My counselor says don't call that 'selfish.' Why not get rid of the negative connotation and call it 'self-focused.'" From time to time, the therapist has explained, people have a need, and a right, to be self-focused. This is particularly true during periods of change.

Toni has been soothed and reassured by his words but still feels a haunting guilt. Narcissism and self-centeredness, after all, are sins in a nun's lexicon of beliefs. Though it has been almost two decades since Toni left the convent, the ancient admonitions have not completely disappeared. She *knows* that, like everyone else, she needs to be nurtured, that she should be able to ask for what she needs, but she *feels* the old rules are deeply rooted. So she comes to counseling with a mixture of defiant entitlement ("I deserve to do this for myself... I'm running on empty!") and reticence born of guilt ("This seems so self-indulgent"). She comes with vivid "technicolor dreams" to recount and "amazing dreams" that are very "sexual," expressing both the inhibitions that she feels and the chance to release them.

Our project together "has come along at the right time," she says again. Telling the ancient stories may help her navigate through this "major life transition" and give her fuel to continue. Though our sessions are exhausting, for her it is an exhaustion born out of the strenuousness and excitement of self-discovery, not the sadness and depletion of being "an indispensable woman." As I turn on the tape recorder and prepare to take notes, Toni's tired face becomes animated with expectation. The weary eyes brighten as she looks backward into her future.

St. Joseph's School in Alexandria, Virginia, was Toni's second mission. She was twenty years old when she arrived to teach sixty third- and fourth-grade students. The four years she spent at St. Joseph's were so much more rewarding than the excruciating year at St. Augustine's, but they were still difficult. Toni's fragile confidence

had been thoroughly undermined by her sense of personal and professional failure at St. Augustine's, so she came to Alexandria with
a great deal of self-doubt, as well as minimal skills. "I continued to
be very shy and still had a hard time getting up in front of people."
The theater of teaching scared her. She couldn't stand the limelight
and public exposure. But Toni also felt inadequate in the craft of
teaching; she had developed no repertoire of methods and
approaches. And she did not feel she had a clue about child development, about what to expect and demand from third and fourth
graders. There seemed to be so much to put together in teaching, so
many insights and techniques to master and integrate before you
could begin to be good and comfortable in the classroom.

At St. Joseph's the teaching was made more difficult not only
because of the huge size of the class but also because half the students
were third graders and half were fourth graders. "The third graders
seemed so young. I couldn't find any way to relate to them." With
their lightning-bolt attention spans, their rowdy lack of self-discipline, their immature language, the third graders were a source of
mystery and frustration for Toni. The fourth graders seemed somewhat "less foreign."

As the months passed during that first year, Toni gradually
began to enjoy herself; she grew to feel "somewhat more relaxed
among the children." At first, it had been hard for her to feel comfortable in the children's presence. As a young girl in school she had
been trained to view the sisters as distant authority figures whom
you did not question, criticize, or know. The lines of authority and
deference were rigidly drawn. As a young teacher, Toni adopted the
same stern and punishing pose that she had experienced in her
growing-up years. "The children were not to know anything about
me... nothing about the person under the habit," recalls Toni. But
she soon discovered that if the teacher does not reveal "some of
her person," it is harder to capture the children's attention. "If the
person is not permitted to shine through," both teaching and learning will be impoverished. So Toni worked against some of the rigid
images and socialization she had known as a child to find a more
open approach to her third and fourth graders. "I was still very

stern," Toni admits, "but I did try to learn how to be a little bit more relaxed. I wanted them to see me as a human being." As a slightly more playful teacher, Toni could let go of some of the earlier inhibitions that seemed to invite disciplinary problems and limit the kinds of relationships she could create with her students.

As Toni began to relax a bit with her young charges, she also began to "grow up in my teaching." Through trial and error, through reflection and self-criticism, she began to develop her own most effective approaches. Through daily observation and closer interaction, she began to understand her students and draw the connections between her curricular demands and their developmental capacities. She also began to express her artistic side, filling her classroom with color and design. She enjoyed decorating the school's bulletin boards and corridors with a mixture of her own creations and the children's art, and as her reputation grew, other teachers would come to her for help in organizing and embellishing their classrooms. It was in this visual realm that Toni felt the most confident and expressive as a teacher. She shakes her head as she remembers these early joys. "Part of the problem with my life now is that I've lost touch with the creative dimension... and I'm suffering."

When Toni needed help and support in her teaching, she would walk across the hall and seek the experienced advice of Sister Esther, who taught the first and second grades. "She was the best they had in the community," says Toni about Sister Esther. She often sought out this inspired and knowledgeable teacher as a mentor. This was particularly true when Toni felt baffled or frustrated with her third graders. "Those little wiggly third graders didn't seem to know anything... I'd get stuck, so I used to go to Sister Esther and say, 'What do I do now?'... I remember in particular one lesson I learned. I was teaching English to the third grade, teaching them about putting periods at the end of sentences. They had their own books, so I asked them to open their books to page such and such and do the assignment—write the sentences and put the period at the end of every sentence. They just sat there and stared at me blankly. Some of them tried it and it didn't work." Puzzled and confused by her students' inadequacies or resistance, Toni found Sister Esther and asked her, "What's wrong? Why can't they do what I've asked them to do?" Sister Esther's response was immediate and clear. Toni was asking them to do something they had barely learned how to do the year before ("copy from a printed book"), in addition to something they had *never* done before ("put the printed words into cursive writing"), and asking them to hold all these steps in their heads at once. The students' blank response was not resistance to her teaching, it was utter confusion about what she was asking them to do.

There were many such moments of struggle and frustration in Toni's teaching during her first couple of years at St. Joseph's, and Sister Esther, ten years her senior, was always there for her, offering advice, support, and helpful criticism. In exchange, Toni brought her artistic talents into Sister Esther's classroom. There was a satisfying and comforting mutuality.

This warm reciprocal support turned into a "good friendship," and eventually into a "particular friendship." In the rules of the convent the former is permissible, and the latter is not. As close colleagues, Sister Antoinette and Sister Esther found themselves spending more and more time together. They not only helped each other with their teaching and schoolwork; they also became each other's favorite companion and confidante. The trust and respect turned into a deepening love, a love that often got expressed physically. Toni's voice is soft and measured as she explains the dimensions and depth of their affection. "In a way, it was a sexual relationship. There was a lot of touching... I mean there was not... what you see in the porno movies between women... but there was a lot of kissing involved and stroking and touching... and it felt good and comforting. This relationship with Sister Esther got very close... the word 'lesbian' wasn't in my vocabulary at the time, but later on I wondered what I was..." Toni's voice trails off as she recalls both the pleasure and the guilt associated with this relationship. She says simply, forcefully, *"Here was someone who loved me,"* and then remembers how that pure feeling got compromised and diluted by the strict prohibitions against "particular relationships." "I knew I was wrong. Sometimes I felt terrible and guilty."

Sister Margaretta, the mother superior at St. Joseph's, watched the developing relationship between Sister Antoinette and Sister Esther. As she watched their relationship move from a good friendship to a particular friendship, she admonished Toni. "She was always warning me about the particular friendship that was forming between us. She was absolutely right, but I was denying it." Unlike the cruel Sister Consolata at St. Augustine's, Sister Margaretta "truly cared" about Toni and did not want her to be seduced into the shadowy world of sexuality. She wanted Toni to remain pure, dedicated, and loyal to God's work, and she saw it as her responsibility to protect and restrain her young charge. "Sister Margaretta was a short woman with a high squeaky voice. She genuinely loved me... She was always after me because she wanted me to be a 'good sister'... Every time I'd walk by her office, she'd call me in and lecture me. She worried so much about the relationship forming with Sister Esther... and in this high squeaky voice she'd chastise me, 'Grow up, grow up.' I'd hate to pass by her office because she'd always call me in to tell me to grow up... But she was a good soul. She always tried to do everything for my own good."

As I listen to Toni thirty-five years later, I hear the deep appreciation she still holds for the "comforting and exciting" relationship she had with Sister Esther, but at the same time I also hear her fondness for the mother superior who cared enough about her to continue offering loving and scolding admonitions. The guilt and remorse seem gone from Toni's voice now; what remains is only the tenderness of recalling youthful passion and sweet comfort. Her voice is almost a whisper when she says again of Sister Esther, "Here was someone who loved me."

This distinction between good friendships (which were smiled upon) and particular friendships (which were considered bad) causes me to search for a definition of the latter. Toni takes me back to the "crushes" of the young adolescent girls at St. Frances. "In high school, you had a *crush* on special sisters... At St. Frances, I had a very strong attraction to Sister Boniface, my eighth-grade teacher, and Sister Frances, my chemistry teacher." When I ask whether she also had a "crush" on Sister Edwina—the sister Toni had described earlier as peaceful and saintly, who was "perfect in every way," whose aura she felt like a light in her soul—Toni laughs, "No, I *loved* Sister Edwina. You didn't have a crush on Sister Edwina… Never. Never." I press for more explanation. "You see, if you had a crush on a sister, you wanted to be with her as much as possible… you wanted to know *everything* about her—her age, her hair texture. Other girls would know about the crush and tease you about it. You were in competition with other girls who had a crush on the same sister. It was a very intense thing, but it had an adolescent flavor."

"When you move from high school to the convent and carry the crushes with you, they take on a different meaning," Toni goes on to explain. When the intense and consuming crush of adolescence turned into a particular friendship in young adulthood, it was no longer sweet and acceptable; it was wrong and illegitimate. In particular friendships, sisters "saw too much of one another, sent messages to one another via carriers, [and] were very physical, bordering on lesbian love affairs." Despite the official regulations against particular friendships and the harsh admonitions from superiors, there was a lively underground of these illicit love affairs, and everyone knew of their existence. The friendships brought joy and comfort as well as surreptitiousness and guilt. "Even when it felt good," recalls Toni, "I knew in the back of my head that it was not good or healthy."

The relationship with Sister Esther was Toni's first particular friendship. It was a relationship that grew out of a supportive and mutually satisfying colleagueship. But it was also a relationship sparked by physical attraction. "She was a beautiful woman," recalls Toni. "She was light-skinned." Sister Esther suffered from a chronic disease called lupus, and Toni thinks that part of her attraction might have been her vulnerability. "It was a relationship built on sympathy… she needed taking care of."

A few years after leaving St. Joseph's, Toni developed another particular friendship with Sister Catherine, "who was notorious for having relationships." Toni's face brightens as she describes the vitality and charisma of Sister Catherine. This was not a relationship "built on sympathy"; it had a charged electricity. I ask Toni whether Sister Catherine was beautiful, and she immediately responds, "No, she was not beautiful." Then she catches herself: "Well, yes, she was absolutely beautiful, but not in the classical way, not in the light-skinned way... She was dark-brown-skinned. She had a charisma that just attracted you to her." Then Toni's final words surprise her—"Sister Catherine had a *holiness* about her... I've never thought or said that before." Twenty-five-year-old Toni was captivated by this powerful, dark, seductive woman. Like so many others before her, she was drawn to Sister Catherine's sexuality and her sainthood, a combination that was impossible to resist. As if to blunt the potent memory, Toni spins her chair around, lets out a gleeful, adolescent squeal, and abruptly changes the subject. "After a while I began to get crushes on *priests*. Now I was becoming normal." She roars with laughter. "The crushes were mainly unrequited... at least at that point," she says mischievously.

During her four years at St. Joseph's Toni began to become a more confident teacher. She was becoming a woman, growing in self-esteem, as well as becoming a more skilled teacher. Her classroom was becoming much more orderly and disciplined as she "relaxed" more into "letting the kids know me." But from time to time, the frustration would mount and she would resort to punishing a child physically ("something that was done all the time in Catholic schools back then").

There was one particular child who used "to test my nerves." He was naughty, undisciplined, and very difficult to control. One day, after several episodes of misbehavior, Toni took out the heavy metal ruler from her desk and smacked him across his arm. The edge of the ruler caused an abrasion on his hand, evidence of corporal punishment that he displayed to his mother that afternoon when he arrived home from school. "At that time," recalls Toni, "most mothers of these kids would have given their child a second punishment. They would have said, 'You deserve what you got from the sister and I'm going to beat you again. You must listen to every word sister says and behave.'" For most parents, the authority of the nun was unquestioned. But in this case, Toni was in for a surprise. The mother of the naughty boy marched into school the next morning and complained loudly to the mother superior about Toni's abusive treatment of her child. Sister Margaretta called Toni into her office to meet with the irate mother. Toni listened with great relief as her superior defended her completely. "This mother was screaming. She was livid. She fussed and fussed. I give Sister Margaretta a lot of credit for this... She took my side in front of that woman... but as soon as that woman left her office, she laid my soul to rest... she blessed me out." Toni shakes her head at the vivid memory of the protection followed by the harsh reprimand. "I learned a couple of lessons. First of all, I shouldn't be hitting those kids. And second, I saw how Sister Margaretta stood up for me in front of that mother but reprimanded me in private." The second lesson may have had two parts. Toni learned about the fierce loyalty and mutual protection among the sisters, but she also may have learned a subliminal message about the pain of public humiliation. After all, her mother superior had saved her from public humiliation. Toni could have spared the boy the same grief. Maybe the pain that the naughty boy suffered was less from his bruised hand and more from the bruised spirits resulting from his public punishment in front of his classmates. "I never spanked anyone after that."

While teaching at St. Joseph's, Toni made a lifelong friend and at the same time became more aware of the color hierarchies within the convent. She gets up from her chair and fetches a photograph of Johnnella Butler. "I was just looking at the picture of her today and thinking she looks just like you, Sara—the same almond eyes, the same skin... She's so beautiful." Her voice is affectionate and admiring. "Johnnella was at Smith, and now she is at the University of Washington in Seattle, where she combines Afro-American Studies and Women's Studies. She was my maid of honor at my wedding." When Toni met Johnnella, she was a bright-eyed, ambitious, fifth-grade student at St. Joseph's. Johnnella's fifth- and sixth-grade teacher was Sister Madalen, "a very dark-brown-skinned woman... a wonderfully talented pianist" who had over the years become embittered by the barriers that prohibited her from expressing her full talents as a musician.

It turns out that Toni's story about Johnnella is really a tale about the insidious hierarchies of color within the convent. Sister Madalen was the victim of color discrimination: because of her blackness, she was barred from training and opportunity, from realizing her rich potential. Because her student Johnnella was beautiful, talented, and light-brown-skinned, she became the target of Sister Madalen's rage. The teacher could see in Johnnella the bright future that she herself had been denied because of her darkness. And because Toni befriended Johnnella, because she was drawn to the girl's intelligence, vitality, and beauty, Sister Madalen (by extension) began to resent Toni. Johnnella became a source of embittered competition between Sister Madalen and Sister Antoinette. "Because Sister Madalen was so dark and not very attractive, she was never given the opportunity to do anything with her music. She was not sent to school, and I think she resented this very much because there were other sisters going to school who were fairer than she was and didn't have anywhere near the talent that she had... so she took a whole lot of this resentment out on students. Johnnella was the object of her rage. Johnnella was pretty. She had nice long hair. Her hair was like yours... and she was smart and very talented too."

Sister Madalen's experience was not atypical. Although Toni admits to being slow in her awareness of the color stratifications within the convent ("I'm not sure when I became aware of it"), she now sees it very clearly, and she sees the suffering and the intragroup hostilities it engendered. Toni can think of only one exception to the rule that "the very fair-skinned sisters were given the most opportunity." Mother Theresa, the mother superior at St. Frances, was the big exception. "She was dark-brown-skinned, *real* dark-brown-skinned... but all the other higher-ups were fair, and many of them could pass for white." I ask Toni how she saw herself on the color chart, and she responds undefensively, "I saw myself as in the *middle*. Not too fair and not too dark." But she admits that even her "middle" darkness might have prohibited her from gaining access to certain educational opportunities if she had not been such a stunningly successful student. She is not being immodest as she describes the "cold reality": "*I* got the opportunity because

I was so bright that they couldn't deny it... plus I was a St. Frances girl. We were considered the best high school... we were given privileged status. And I was the best of the best... I was the eighth-grade salutatorian and the valedictorian of my senior class."

Toni's brainy brightness had outweighed her "middle" darkness and opened up avenues of status and opportunity as she progressed from Catholic student to nun. She was even "elected May Queen" at St. Frances, a prestigious position usually "reserved for lighter girls." I wonder what other criteria besides fair skin might have been important to the selection of May Queens, and I ask who participated in the election. "You had to have a certain amount of *piety*," explains Toni. "I think the sisters had a lot to do with the choice... My peers would probably not have chosen me as May Queen."

~

After four years of teaching third and fourth grades at St. Joseph's, Toni returned to the Mother House for a year of hard labor and prayerfulness in preparation for her final vows. She was twenty-six years old and thrilled to be returning "home." She so loved the convent—its peacefulness, its structure, its pure piety. She loved the rituals, the rules, the order, the safety, and she was so relieved not to be teaching. Although Toni had "grown into her teaching," she still found it fiercely demanding, potentially chaotic, and very strenuous. The grueling physical labor of the convent felt light in comparison to the demands of the students. "It was always a joy to go back to my house. And it was so peaceful," recalls Toni dreamily. On August 15, 1960, in a simple, quiet ceremony, Toni made her final vows and became "final professed." Kneeling at the altar, her tall back straight as a rod, she spoke her vows with profound, unalterable certainty. A plain silver ring was put on the ring finger of her right hand. Inside, it was engraved with four letters "JMJF" standing for "Jesus Mary Joseph Frances." "We were full-fledged members of the community... we were no longer children. I was there for life... or so I thought."

Modified Habits

When Toni was sent to her third mission, Saint Cecilia's in Baltimore, she was horrified to discover that her mother superior would be Sister Consolata. She could not understand the insensitivity of her superiors at the Mother House who made the assignment knowing that Toni had been victimized by Sister Consolata. Why would they send her back into such a painful situation? When she gently inquired of them, they told her that it was her duty as a "good sister" to enter this mission unburdened by old animosities, and that she needed to go to the place where she could be of the greatest service. Saint Cecilia's was such a place. In the Rosedale section of Baltimore, Saint Cecilia's served a poor black community. The priest wanted to staff his school with the best teachers, "so he asked for Oblates." The Oblates rose to the challenge. "They sent Sister Jacinta to teach the first and second grades. She was a wonderful, skilled teacher. They sent me to teach grades six and seven. They sent Sister Evelyn to teach the fourth and fifth. God knows why they sent her." Sister Evelyn was very strange. She would walk around for days without saying one word to anyone. "This was not a disciplined silence like we lived at the convent. Sister Evelyn had her moods. She was very troubled... She had a sister who had committed suicide, and she suffered from depressive spells, too."

But it was Sister Consolata, once again, who made life miserable for Toni. "She already had me in her craw, so before I even arrived, she told the other sisters that they were not to associate with Sister Antoinette." She kept close tabs on all of her charges, watching their every move like a hawk, ready to pounce on any mistake or indiscretion. She would not let the sisters associate with any of the parishioners at Saint Cecilia's. On Sundays they were all required to go as a group to mass, and right after the service Sister Consolata would lead them away from the church "like a mother hen with her chicks parading behind her."

Despite Sister Consolata's warnings that no one should associate with Toni, Sister Jacinta—the first- and second-grade teacher—struck up a deep friendship with her. The two were friends, colleagues, and confidantes. Their relationship made living under Sister Consolata's oppressive leadership almost bearable. "We had a good friendship, not a particular friendship," Toni assures me. "It was an important, healthy relationship." Besides the protection of this "good friendship," Toni also felt less vulnerable than she had before with Sister Consolata because she was now "professed." "There was nothing major that she could really do to me. She could try to hurt my feelings, but she couldn't do anything to me." This did not stop the mother superior from trying, however. Sister Consolata continued her harsh badgering and assaults. One day Toni had had enough. She could take no more.

The sisters were preparing for a special service in the chapel, and Sister Antoinette was supposed to change the garments on the Infant of Prague, a statue of Jesus as a young boy child. The Infant of Prague was dressed in fancy costumes made by the nuns, silks and satins with ornate beaded designs. Every season his costumes were changed. Sister Consolata inspected the new garments Toni had put on the statue, and she was not satisfied. She wrote a nasty note to Toni telling her to do it over again. When Toni found the mother superior's note in her box (she was constantly getting disapproving letters from her), the rage rose up inside her. Without hesitation she sat down and scribbled a response: "If you want it done differently, do it yourself." It was a clear, decisive act, an act of finality. Toni felt no guilt or fear, only cold clarity. "I never received another note from her," says Toni with resignation (not victory) in her voice.

Despite the fact that Sister Consolata tried to make her life miserable, Toni enjoyed her teaching at Saint Cecilia's. In one breath she says, "Saint Cecilia's was memorable because it was such a horrible experience, [but] as a teacher at Saint Cecilia's I had lots of fun. I was in my glory teaching science and math... I had the older kids, and they *loved* it. I could see that I was having an impact on their lives." Toni was thriving because finally she was able to teach the subject she loved so deeply, and she was able to pass that passion on to her students.

When Toni speaks about the attractions of science—particularly chemistry—her face grows intense and lively. She is in her element. She recalls her childhood fascination with the inner workings of things. "I was always a curious child," she exclaims. "I loved taking things apart... I took apart clocks... I took apart my mother's sewing machine. She wasn't too thrilled about that." When most little girls were cuddling their dolls, changing their outfits, and building fantasies about their lives, Toni was taking her dolls apart, unpacking the soft stuffing, inspecting the voice box, and moving the inner levers that worked their limbs. Her most memorable birthday present was a chemistry set that she had prayed and pleaded for from her mother. When she received it, she was "in heaven." The first concoction she whipped up was purple ink. "I loved that. It was the biggest thrill. *The curiosity was always there!*"

Her curiosity was reinforced and solidified in high school. As a senior, in the college preparatory classes at St. Frances, Toni was required to take chemistry, and it was everything she dreamed it would be. First of all, she loved her teacher. "A gentle soul and an excellent scientist," Sister Frances saw herself reflected in Toni's eyes. She could see that her student had a special fascination with chemistry and a wonderful aptitude for scientific inquiry. She would give Toni extrachallenging assignments and push her harder than the other students. Soon Toni was running the labs and teaching the classes when Sister Frances was absent. "I was the best in the class," says Toni matter-of-factly. Besides the special, mutually admiring relationship she had with Sister Frances (one of the sisters whom Toni had a "crush" on), Toni also loved the "structure and discipline" of chemistry. It was a discipline that joined "creativity and discovery." "I mostly loved how in chemistry everything fit together so beautifully. The formulas and equations were so satisfying to me, so exacting, so manipulable... You could calculate and figure out the *concentration* of a substance and then test it out."

The discipline of chemistry appealed to Toni's nature and the quality of her mind. But it also appealed to her stage in life. She explains, "I was looking for answers as an adolescent, and chemistry provided them. I was extremely scrupulous." As a matter of fact, her search for definitive and sure answers was part of a scientific *and* religious quest. The impulse was the same in the empirical and spiritual spheres. "As an adolescent I wanted to know exactly what constituted sodium chloride, and I wanted to know exactly what constituted a mortal sin." These were both solvable puzzles if you asked the right questions, gathered the right data, and used the right methods of interpretation and analysis. Toni was an enthusiastic puzzle solver. She would spend hours over crossword puzzles and feel such satisfaction when all the boxes were filled in. "In our yearbook the seniors all left things in their wills for the school... and I willed my crossword puzzles. I was totally taken up with finding answers and fitting things into boxes." As she hears her own self-description, Toni shakes her head at the adolescent tightness and rigidity. "I've become a bit more experiential... a bit more speculative."

I am intrigued by Toni's joining of the two disciplines—science and religion—so early in her life. I ask her how she sees the connections between them, how she manages the coexistence of these two spheres: one based on observable, testable data; the other based on beliefs that have no concrete or tangible evidence. How could she search for scientific evidence yet trust the canons of faith? Although Toni is not surprised by my questions, she would never frame them in the same way. In her mind and heart, science and faith are not in conflict. They reinforce and strengthen one another. "The beauty of chemistry and astronomy say so much to me about the beauty and wonder of God.... How could you take a chemistry course and not believe in God?... The order, the fitting together... all God's work. Chemistry is the microworld, disciplined and ordered, and astronomy is the macroworld, harmonious and ordered."

Toni rises from her chair and finds a recently published volume on her bookshelf entitled *Belonging to the Universe: Explorations on the Frontiers of Science and Religion,* written by a physicist and a Benedictine monk. It is a "fascinating dialogue" that Toni has just begun to read. It examines the connections between science and faith through the discourse of a skeptic and a believer. In their conversation, the authors discover there are many more similarities than differences between them. Their convergent visions do not surprise Toni. She is heartened, however, by the recent advances in science: "Many more scientists today are coming to the conclusion that there are many things that can't be explained.... I remember a paper I wrote about chemical evolution when I was getting my doctorate. The course was taught by a famous chemist, an East Indian man, and he strongly disagreed with my position. I'll never forget how I began the paper: 'There are some things that will never be explained because God wants it that way.'" The professor totally disagreed with Toni's premise, but he must have liked the clarity of her reasoning (and maybe even the depth of her faith) because he gave her "an excellent grade." Twenty-five years later Toni still holds both her beliefs and her faith. "We'll never be able to say how the earth began," she says forcefully. "That's God's stuff, not our stuff."

During the dozen years that Toni was teaching in parochial schools, she was also studying for her undergraduate degree in chemistry at the College of Notre Dame of Maryland. After a strenuous, demanding week of working with children and performing her duties as a nun, Toni would spend Saturdays attending her college classes. Each summer, as soon as school was over, she would enroll full-time. It was a grueling, exhausting schedule. Toni always yearned for the life of a full-time student. "I wanted to immerse myself in my work... I could never be as focused on my studies as I wanted to be," she says with lingering resentment. "It [going to school part-time] was slow and very difficult." The one "saving grace" was Sister Louis, her advisor and mentor at Notre Dame, who saw Toni's abilities and ambition and encouraged her scientific pursuits. She was a wonderful source of support, challenging Toni to complete her B.A. and urging her to do graduate training.

It was Sister Louis who suggested that Toni apply to a program for junior-college teachers of math and science sponsored by the National Labs in Oak Ridge, Tennessee (built by the Atomic Energy Commission). Even though Toni was an elementary schoolteacher and had just completed her bachelor's degree, Sister Louis thought she was ready for the stimulation and challenge of the Oak Ridge program, which included an intense year of scientific immersion followed by a summer of thesis writing at the University of Tennessee, culminating in a master of science degree. Admitting only twenty students, it was a highly selective program.

Sister Louis, who had for years advocated Toni's release from some of the demands of the convent so that she might focus more of her energies on her studies, now pushed even harder for the Oak Ridge program. But it was Toni who sent away for the application and secretly applied. After a decade of going to school on Saturdays and during summers, Toni longed for the continuity of full-time focused study. She longed to test her intellect in a tough educational setting. She knew that it would be difficult, if not impossible, to get permission from her mother superior at St. Frances to leave the convent for a year of study in Tennessee, so she proceeded quietly, cautiously, and with a determination that felt "surprising." "Without consulting anyone or asking anyone's permission, I sent in the application," she recalls.

When the acceptance letter came a few months later, she was stunned and excited. Twenty students had been accepted into the program—including two women, a Puerto Rican man, and Toni—the only African-American. It felt like the clearest sign she had ever received that she was "really smart." She was not just a "good sister," pious, compassionate, and caring. She was also a thinker. She had a fine mind. It was a moment of extraordinary transformation. But the exhilaration faded as she began to anticipate her encounter with the mother superior. How was she going to break the news? How was she going to rationalize her secretive behavior during the application process? How was she going to convince the mother superior that this independent quest would benefit their community and the people they served? She did not want to appear self-serving or personally ambitious, but she had never wanted anything more in her life than she wanted this chance to study science in Oak Ridge. She mustn't let her enthusiasm and her huge appetite show too much.

Sister Antoinette approached the mother superior with enormous trepidation. Sister William was "a light-skinned woman, very elegant," and her face grew hard as she listened to Toni's surprising petition. She could see through Toni's restraint. She could hear that there was passion and ambition behind Toni's carefully chosen neutral language. As she listened, the mother superior worried that if she released Toni from the convent, she might never return. She might be seduced away by the science or attracted to secular life, and that would be a great loss to the community. Her question to Toni was simple, "Are you sure you will come back?" Toni was shocked. She had never thought about leaving the convent. How could Sister William even imagine that this might be a first step to leaving? "I was *mortified!*" recalls Toni, "that she would ask that question. I couldn't believe the words that came out of her mouth." Trying to keep her voice steady, Toni assured her superior that she had every intention of returning, and that when she returned she would have more to offer the community. Toni's response did not soften the skepticism in Sister William's eyes. The answer was an unequivocal no. "She clearly did not want me to go," Toni says with understatement. Fortunately, Sister Angela, the director of education, intervened. For years she had watched Toni's growth, her academic perseverance, and her intellectual development. She saw rare talent in the emerging scientist, and she trusted Toni's depth of commitment to religious life. Somehow Sister Angela managed to convince the mother superior "that this was a good thing," and Sister Antoinette was on her way to Oak Ridge, on her way to "the best year, the happiest year of my life."

By 1967, Toni was no longer wearing the full nun's habit. "Things had loosened up" and the Oblates were dressing in "modified habits": a simple black skirt, a white blouse, and a veil. When she first arrived in Oak Ridge —"a black nun, a total oddity"—Toni lived in a convent of Dominican sisters. Sister William had insisted that Toni live in a religious community while she studied, hoping that the daily contact with the convent would sustain her attachment to the sisterhood. But almost immediately it became clear that living the double life of nun and student was too burdensome. Toni felt constantly torn by her responsibilities to the convent and her scholarly activities. "You see, I felt obliged to help in the convent, to go to mass, eat my meals, and pray with the community… It was impossible to combine all this with my studies." Again, she petitioned Mother William for permission to leave the convent and move into her own apartment. (She had earned a scholarship, which included a stipend for housing.) Toni was surprised and relieved by the mother superior's immediate and affirmative response.

She moved into a simple apartment and relished the solitary life that allowed her to devote her full energies to her work. She continued to go to 6:30 mass every morning, but the rest of the day and evening was reserved for her studies. And she worked harder and more enthusiastically than she ever had before, taking nuclear physics, chemistry, and astronomy. "It was so strenuous… real hard," Toni exclaims with pleasure. The group of twenty would have breakfast together, take most of their morning classes in the same room, and go off to the various laboratories in the afternoon. The camaraderie among them was collegial and supportive, and Toni loved being in the midst of "smart people."

Toni had to work especially hard because she had never studied some of the prerequisite course material. For instance, the Oak Ridge curriculum required nuclear physics, but she had never taken a physics course before. "So I had to learn the introductory physics course all on my own while I was doing nuclear physics." Toni shakes her head—"That seems to be the story of my life… having to teach myself things." In addition, Toni's "greatest challenge"—math—presented itself to her in the guise of a statistics course that turned out to be heavily mathematical. She struggled with all her might to master the math. She fought against the old anxieties. She sought help from other students. Every night she would stay up for hours doing all the problems and then go over them again in the morning. Despite all of her extraordinary efforts, she got a C in statistics. In order to balance the C, she needed to get an A in nuclear physics, the course in which she had had no preparatory instruction. "So I got an A in physics," says Toni simply, masking all of the sweat and apprehension that must have gone into achieving the top grade.

The grueling hard work was made bearable because "the science was so much fun." Toni pictures one of her teachers who was a physicist and an Episcopal priest (although she did not know of his religious connections at the time). He used to enter the classroom and begin an elaborate ritual: He would take out his pipe, fill it with tobacco, stuff the tobacco down, and light up. Finally, he would look up at the students and ask, "What would you like to hear?" Toni heard this as a powerful question pregnant with possibility. It appealed to the curiosity and adventurousness that she brought to science, and she admired the courage of a teacher who could risk having his students ask a question for which he might not know the answer. "If we responded to his opening question by saying we wanted to hear about black holes, he would begin to think out loud in front of us. He was a brilliant man." For the first time, Toni began to enjoy the part of science that was speculative and experiential, that wasn't wholly dependent on definitive answers.

Oak Ridge was the place where Toni finally began to feel self-confident as a student, a thinker, and an intellectual. Despite the fact that she had excelled in school and was always considered the brightest among her peers, she had never felt certain about her talents and her capabilities. "I had these huge insecurities... I always thought I'm not as good as, not as holy as, not as smart as... not as attractive as." A smile spreads over her face. "But Oak Ridge changed that... I said to myself, 'I've got to be *smart* if they chose me to do this.'"

Toni also enjoyed the "making of science," its craft. She always felt so at home in the lab, designing and fixing equipment. One of the high points of her year in Oak Ridge was building her own Geiger counter and telescope. Her voice is excited—"It was like shop. We made a refractor. I felt so productive—my head and my hands." For emphasis, she repeats herself, "It was the most exciting and rewarding year I'd ever spent in my life."

As she talks, I picture Sister Antoinette, twenty-five years ago, on the verge of discovering new capacities and new freedoms. Freed of the heavy, long habit, her gait was lighter. For the first time in her life, she was living alone, working in the midst of dedicated students, drinking in the teaching of experienced scientists, and tasting the excitement of scientific inquiry. These new freedoms were energized by the burning curiosity that has always been part of Toni's nature. In this cohort of serious students at Oak Ridge, Toni was the most disciplined, the most studious. And there was probably no one in her group who experienced as deeply the exhilaration and liberation that flow from studious pursuits. For Toni, freedom and discipline were joined.

While the classes and the labs at Oak Ridge were all she had hoped for, the relationship with her advisor was a great disappointment. She describes him bluntly: "He was an alcoholic, so he was useless to me." It took several months for her to admit to herself how "hopeless" he was. Then she had to scramble quickly to find a new advisor and another thesis topic. One of the faculty members, a biochemist, agreed to take her on but only under two conditions: first, that Toni work on a piece of his research; and second, that she not be demanding of his time and energy. He was not interested in becoming an active or engaged mentor. He would do her the favor of formally sponsoring her work, signing the necessary bureaucratic forms, allowing her to use his lab, and work on his research project. The research topic that her advisor selected—the effect of radioactivity on enzymes—was totally foreign to Toni and required that she learn "everything from the very beginning." Again, she was forced to teach herself the material. "This was a biochemistry topic, and I knew nothing about biochemistry... and I knew nothing about enzymes, but it was the topic my new advisor was interested in, so I learned it. I worked all alone, completely alone." Even with the pressure of having to absorb so much new material in such a short time, even with the loneliness of no guidance or collegial support, Toni managed to enjoy the substance of what she was doing. She became intrigued by the project. "I gained a healthy respect for radioactivity," she recalls, "substances with half-lives of thousands of years... It was awe-inspiring." For Toni, the mysteries of radioactivity became another reason to "believe in God's power."

Her master's thesis, entitled "The Inactivation of Pancreatic Lipase by Gamma Radiation" was completed during the summer of

1969 at the University of Tennessee, Knoxville. Toni lived on campus ("Again I was a real oddity. Everyone just gawked at me... this black nun working in the science labs") and traveled back and forth to Oak Ridge, where she was finishing up her lab work. By summer's end, Toni was typing her highly technical thesis—full of equations, charts, and graphs—on a new Sears Electric typewriter that she bought with the remainder of the monies from her stipend. She was proud of the work, proud of the science, and proud of the extraordinary effort that she had put forth. When she marched in the graduation exercises at the end of August, she was pleased to look up and see two of her best friends from St. Frances, Sister Paul and Sister Brenda, cheering her on. "They had defied authority in order to come down," says Toni appreciatively. "The mother superior had forbade them to come, but they had gotten on the train anyway... They were my friends, and they felt they should be there."

Oak Ridge was the first time Toni had taken her mind seriously. She now knew that she had academic strengths and that she could teach herself anything. But Oak Ridge also marked the beginning of her departure from the convent. She did not know it at the time, but Sister William's premonition that the adventures of Oak Ridge might draw her away from religious life forever, began to come true. She returned to the convent, but the cloistered life never felt the same again.

The Oblate Institute had relocated to a suburban campus outside of Baltimore and had been renamed Mount Providence Junior College. (The college and community included the Mother House, a large, elegant stone structure at the top of the hill; a building housing both the students and the infirmary for the elderly nuns; and the convent, all of which was part of the same small cloistered campus.) In its first year, Mount Providence was a tiny school with only fifty students. The young women at Mount Providence were students "who could not go anyplace else"—either because they had inferior academic training and were lacking a high school diploma, or because they "couldn't afford to go anyplace else." "It served a critical purpose for those girls," says Toni. "They got lots of individual attention, a great deal of care and guidance."

When Toni returned to Mount Providence and the Oblate Community she was assigned several roles. She was to teach math and physical science and be the college's registrar. "I was *very* disappointed not to be teaching chemistry," she recalls. "I had been so deeply involved in chemistry at Oak Ridge. I had prepared myself to teach it... and at the last minute they told me I wouldn't be teaching chemistry, but instead I'd teach math." Reluctantly she consented to the change in assignments for the first year, but the second year Toni "rebelled" and refused to teach math. She had felt like a fraud trying to teach calculus, and she knew her talents were not being used wisely. So during her second year at Mount Providence she was released from teaching math but given two additional roles. She became the academic dean, the registrar, the housemother, and the physical science teacher.

These multiple demands were exhausting. Toni never had a moment to herself. The campus had not originally been designed to be a college facility, so the housing arrangements were inadequate. The students, for example, lived on the third floor of a large rambling building, on the second floor of which was the infirmary. The young students, who were in Toni's charge as housemother, would make their typical adolescent racket, disturbing the elderly and infirm sisters who were resting below them. Toni would receive constant irate calls from the infirmary complaining about the clamor above, "reporting on every single footstep they heard below." As academic dean and registrar, Toni was also the recipient of all the telephone calls having to do with curriculum, teaching, credits, course work, and transcripts. Toni shakes her head—"Everyone called to complain to me—total harassment, a totally thankless position... To this day I hate the telephone!"

The demands of these multiple roles would have felt burdensome to any "good sister," but the burdens were magnified for Toni because her responsibilities were so much heavier compared to the freedoms of her relatively autonomous life in Oak Ridge. After the pleasure of independence, "a freedom I had never known in my whole life," it was shocking to return to a communal life crowded with chores, rituals, and enormous responsibility. "I found the reentry from Oak Ridge extremely difficult," recalls Toni. "At Mount Providence I had to wake before dawn, say the office, do my meditation, go to mass, have breakfast with the community, go to teach, do my administrative chores, and so on. The routine and the structure felt very inhibiting… claustrophobic." The very rules and rituals that used to provide a welcome asylum for Toni now felt stifling to her. The relentless demands of students, many of whom were ill-prepared academically, made her long for the intellectually stimulating environment of Oak Ridge. The walls of the convent began to close in.

Sister Antoinette was not alone in her restlessness and interior turbulence. It was the late '60s, and there was a palpable wave of change and resistance within the Catholic Church. Large numbers of priests and nuns were beginning to question the religious life. "People were beginning to leave right and left." Every week Toni heard another story through the grapevine about a nun who had decided to leave the convent. These tales of escape intrigued and terrified Toni. She had never imagined relinquishing the life she had known for twenty years, a life that had offered her structure, safety, and dignity.

At first she did not allow herself to think about leaving the convent. She just began to search for legitimate reasons for taking short sojourns away from the community. "I began to take my guitar on the road and perform at folk masses… I played at religious retreats and services… I joined a group of very liberal priests and nuns who were involved in creating a more relevant liturgy, and I was there making music." Toni seized every opportunity to join her friends in questioning, dialogue, and celebration. She loved getting away from the overwhelming duties and hierarchy of Mount Providence *and* she loved the spirited companionship of these religious activists.

One of Toni's escape routes was Saint Cecilia's (the parish that was connected to the parochial school where Toni had taught sixth and seventh graders) and its pastor. "In his mid-thirties, white, and very handsome," Father Joseph Walker, a Josephite priest, was an "extremely dedicated" pastor who devoted himself completely to the nurturance and development of his parish and the surrounding community. When Toni was teaching at Saint Cecilia's, she admired Father Walker from afar; she was intrigued by the man and his commitments. "He had a streak in him that was strange... maybe a martyr streak. He felt he couldn't live better than the people he served, so he cut out all the extras and many of the essentials... He carried this to an extreme of self-denial." When Toni returned to Mount Providence, Father Walker sought out Toni's help and support. He enjoyed her vitality, her intelligence, and her emerging skepticism of church hierarchy. Soon Toni became a frequent visitor. She would bring groups of students from Mount Providence over to sing and work, and increasingly she would visit alone to be in Father Walker's company.

The collegial relationship grew into a friendship, then developed into a "love relationship. I was in love with this guy... and he was in love with me... but from the beginning, he was clear and emphatic that he was going to be a priest forever... that he would never leave religious life." The relationship "lasted several years" off and on, sustained by their mutual attraction and affection, and by the boundaries necessitated by his absolute religious conviction. They would "sneak off" to go and visit Toni's mother in Philadelphia. "The mother superior knew that I was going to see my infirm mother, who had been weakened and crippled by a stroke, but she didn't know I was going with him. He was feeling very guilty. I was enjoying myself... He was a devoted, simple soul... intelligent, not pretentious. I liked his company."

Though she had admired priests "from a distance" for many years, Father Walker was Sister Antoinette's first male "crush" that "did not go unrequited." Yet her relationship with this handsome white man with the wavy brown hair does not sound as charged or as passionate as her adolescent crushes on Sister Boniface and Sister Frances, or later on, her particular friendship with Sister Esther at St. Joseph's School. The "love" for Father Walker that Toni describes seemed to be a "simpler," less intense feeling. He offered conversation and companionship. He represented commitment to values that she admired. He provided escape and adventure away from the convent. He allowed her to feel "normal" in her affections.

It was with relief and gratitude that the Oblate Sister fell in love with the Josephite Father; it was this relationship that supported her fledgling moves away from the sisterhood.

Like a Divorce

Life in the convent became increasingly difficult for Toni. Her frustrations and resentments turned inward and made her feel lethargic and sad. "I was desperately unhappy," says Toni with a heavy sigh. "I felt overwhelmed, unsupported, unrewarded... I couldn't get up in the morning. I was depressed." Toni spent two years struggling with "the difficulties of reentry" after her year in Oak Ridge, but instead of becoming comfortable, she felt more stifled than ever.

On one of her frequent escapes from the convent, Toni met Hugh Tornabene, a Jesuit who had recently left the priesthood. "Another man in my life," Toni smiles. An Englishman and a physicist, Hugh seemed elegant and brilliant to Toni. They enjoyed the companionship they found in science. Hugh was teaching physics at Bowie State Teachers College, a predominantly black school, and he invited Toni to co-teach with him. "I was running away," Toni reminds me. "Here was my chance." The science, the man, the context all appealed to her desperate need for change.

In a gesture that felt superficial and meaningless, Sister Antoinette sought permission to teach the course from Sister Mary of Good Counsel who had become her mother superior at Mount Providence. She was neither surprised nor discouraged when her superior said no. Toni's response was immediate: "I told her I was going to do it anyway. I had grown real bold, real clear." The affair with Hugh had the excitement, the passion, and the guilt that she had never before experienced with a man. Hugh was free, unencumbered, and he expressed his liberation with exuberance and style. "This was an exciting existence," Toni exclaims. "I was feeling guilty and enjoying myself immensely... He'd cook for me. He introduced me to all kinds of foods... We'd go to parties with ex-priests and ex-nuns... I was captured."

The passion for Hugh, the tantalizing taste of liberated life, were the feelings that finally allowed Toni to make the break. She makes it clear: "I loved Hugh, but he wasn't the reason I left the convent. This had been building for some time." But the love for Hugh was a critical new piece of Toni's emerging sense of self. Toni looks at me intently. "There was passion in this relationship, Sara. I learned that I can love someone *sexually* and that *someone can love me for me*... not because I'm a child of God, but because he loves *me*." The converse was equally powerful. "And I could love *him*. This was not part of a universal love for everyone. It was focused on him."

Before approaching the mother superior with her decision, Toni had consulted with a clinical psychologist. They had had several tortured sessions as Toni struggled to understand "the source of her depression" and to untangle the ambivalence. Finally, the therapist strongly advised, "What is most important is for you to make a decision... whether you decide to go or stay, you must decide now." He could see that her indecision was causing her the most pain, that delaying in making a decision was unproductive. These words were a final push before Toni's bold leap of faith.

Sister Antoinette decided to deliver the news in writing. When Sister Mary of Good Counsel was off on a trip to St. Louis, Toni wrote her a letter. By that time, Toni was absolutely certain that she had to leave the convent, but the words came hard. She struggled to find a way to express the complex of feelings. Finally she settled on a simple, clear message. "I said something about needing to leave in order to grow," recalls Toni. When the mother superior returned from her trip, she told Toni that before she had even opened her letter, "she knew what was inside." She was deeply disappointed by Toni's decision but not at all surprised. Even though the mother superior lectured Toni, admonished her, and asked her hard questions, she knew it was a lost cause. She had seen this coming for a long time—the restlessness, the frustration, the independence, the questioning of authority. She had seen it coming even before Sister Antoinette had gone off to study science in Oak Ridge. It was for that reason that Sister William had asked the question that Toni had found so "devastating": "Are you sure that you will return to the convent?" Toni had, in fact, returned to the fold, but this mother superior had known that Toni's days in the convent were numbered.

Now, as Toni sat before her in the Mother House, Sister Mary of Good Counsel went through the ritualistic "chastisements," but she knew this was a futile final gesture. Her voice was steady, muting the frustration and rage she felt at losing one of their very best. "You've been in the community for nineteen years," she charged. "You have a life, a vocation, a calling… How can you leave?… Why is it that the most intelligent of you are leaving the community?" Toni sat there stoically, quietly enduring a scene that she could have scripted herself. She knew all the questions, all the warnings, all the arguments. She knew the expression of weariness and betrayal that would appear on the face of her interrogator. She even knew the range of emotions she herself would experience but never reveal—the sadness, the guilt, the fear, the anger, the blessed relief. Her face was a mask of composure as she kept repeating, in various forms, her need to leave. She was thirty-seven years old and she had to find a new life that would allow her to grow, in which she could be of greater service.

Even though Toni stood firm and did not equivocate about her decision when she was challenged by the superior, she had lived through months of painful ambivalence. After all, she had been cloistered for more than half her life. The convent had provided a safe haven, an orderly and secure existence, a close family with a host of surrogate mothers, a livelihood. "The thought of leaving was very frightening," recalls Toni. "I was leaving the security of always having a job, three meals, friends, companionship… everything I needed. This had been my family." Her voice is now heavy with emotion. "It was like a divorce."

Like many women who go through divorce, Toni worried most about whether she would be "respected" outside of her role, without her habit. Without the protection of her nun's status, would she have any worth in society? "You see, when you're a nun, people are deferential, respectful. When people see you in your habit, they give you things, you get special privileges, you're treated differently." She had grown to depend upon the habit—as uniform, buffer, and status symbol—and she knew that without it she would feel exposed and vulnerable.

Once Toni announced her departure, the sisters turned their backs on her. "They didn't want me around… They couldn't even say good-bye." Toni will never forget the day in December when she drove up to Mount Providence in her newly purchased secondhand yellow Toyota Corolla. She was all alone. No one offered to help her pack. No one was there to wave farewell. The quiet felt like a raging winter wind. Toni loaded her meager belongings into the little yellow car and took one final long look at the big Mother House sitting handsomely on the top of the hill. The Mother source. She heard the determined words come out of her mouth and disappear into the cold air. "I've got to go. I must go," she said to herself, to God, to her sisters, to the mother superior, to everyone, and to no one in particular. With that declaration, she got in her car and drove away.

Her friend Johnnella had helped her find a small one-bedroom apartment. With the little bit of money she was earning teaching physics part-time at Bowie State, Toni collected pieces of secondhand furniture, pots and pans for her kitchen, and a few towels and sheets. She loved hunting for these, exercising her own independent taste, style, and judgment. The apartment was modest and the furnishings sparse, but Toni experienced the abundance and exhilaration of solitude. "All of this belongs to me." When she entered her new home for the first time after leaving the convent, a great wave of energy and relief shot through her. She could feel her whole body tremble. "God, I'm *free!* This is *mine!* I can do what I want to."

Letting in the Sunlight

This session with Toni will be our last. I am not looking forward to this encounter and feel a hard knot in my stomach. All the farewells in this project have been difficult. No matter how fully we anticipate the conclusion, we are never ready, never finished. No matter how long the conversation—in Toni's case one year—the finality makes it feel short. No matter how deeply we delve, the last words reveal the ground not covered, the realms unexplored. It always feels like a great loss. Today my trepidation is compounded because I know that this loss will be amplified for Toni by a much deeper pain. Two and a half weeks ago Toni's mother died.

It is an oppressively hot and humid day in Wilmington. Toni emerges from her house in purple shorts, a sleeveless white shirt, and sneakers. Her white hair is cut shorter than usual and less carefully coiffed. She is several pounds heavier than the last time I saw her—weight that her tall body carries well, but weight that seems to make her feel bad and move awkwardly. But it is in her face that I see the pain. Her brown skin has a dull look, and her eyes behind the purple glasses are puffy and red. We embrace, and as we pull away I see the tears streaking down her face.

Gladyce's death pushes everything else aside. This is the only conversation we can have. Before we sit down in Toni's study, she runs off to fetch "the only thing my mother left me," a photograph of Toni when she was three years old. It is a precious heirloom—the only picture of Toni as a young child, the only "possession" that survived Gladyce's nomadic life of poverty. "Everything else was lost," says Toni sadly. "But wherever she moved, my mother held onto this picture for dear life. She wouldn't let go of it... Several months ago, she allowed me to take it away long enough to find a new frame for it." In the eight-by-twelve-inch black-and-white photograph, little Toni ("actually Carole Virginia") is sitting on a low wooden bench, one leg dangling, the other pulled up under her. "Amazingly, I remember the dress!" exclaims Toni. "It was the first dress my mother ever made for me. The flowers were purple, and the cuffs and big buttons were yellow. They had a hard time making me laugh... you see I have a very tentative smile." Toni recalls the unusual extravagance of sitting for a photographer. "It was taken in New Haven by Loring, very famous and expensive photographers."

Whenever Toni used to visit her mother at the nursing home, she would see this beloved picture decorating the bureau. Gladyce "adored" the photograph and the little girl it portrayed. She would take it in her hands and gaze upon it, longing for the lost innocence and sweetness. "She wishes I had stayed just that way," smiles Toni. "Sometimes she would even speak about us as if we were two different people... the good little girl and the difficult older woman." Toni would remind her, "But Mom, that little girl is *me!*" and Gladyce would respond longingly, "But she was a good girl... she did everything I told her to do." And Toni would conclude the now-scripted exchange, "Yes, but she was only a tiny child and she was *stupid.*"

Toni's face explodes with laughter but her eyes fill with tears. "I cry about how little she left me." Her eyes search the room and land on a small green and yellow stuffed turtle that is holding a bouquet of purple flowers. "Oh yes, she left behind some stuffed animals that I, of course, gave her." Toni remembers a question that Gladyce recently asked her. "Did I ever give you stuffed animals when you were a little girl?" "Stuffed animals were not such a big deal back then," responded Toni, hearing her mother's familiar expression of inadequacy. "Besides, you probably couldn't afford it." Now the tears are flowing gently down Toni's cheeks, and she is making no effort to wipe them away. "As a child I always knew she couldn't give me stuff, so I didn't ask for anything." She picks up the turtle and holds it to her breast.

This fifty-seven-year-old woman, "now orphaned," lets her tears fall on the turtle and decides to tell about "the most painful revelation of all." It was a couple of weeks before Gladyce died. Her

weight had dropped to seventy-nine pounds. Her lungs were rav-
aged by emphysema, forcing her to be hooked up to oxygen. This
seemed to be the final phase of the stroke that had weakened her
body and slurred her speech twenty-five years earlier. "She was so
vulnerable... She was ready to die," reveals Toni. Gladyce struggled
to say the words her daughter knew so well and hated to hear. "I was
such a bad mother," she moaned. Toni heard a new finality in her
mother's familiar litany and dared to ask a question that had been
haunting her for as long as she could remember. "It doesn't matter
now," said Toni, "but why do you say that?" A long silence hung in
the air between them. Then Gladyce whispered, "I've blamed you
for everything." Toni is leaning back and holding her heart as if a
knife has pierced it. She is thankful for "the breakthrough," for her
mother's courage in the final days of her life. But she is wounded
by "the admission." "That has put a heaviness on me."

Toni needs no prompting. She goes right to the moment of
Gladyce's death. "She died on Friday, June 12 at four P.M." Toni had
been out of town taking a summer seminar at Virginia Theological
Seminary and was returning to Wilmington for the weekend. In
fact, she had arrived back in town at 4:00 P.M., but she had stopped
to do some shopping so she didn't get home until 5:00 P.M. Robert
had heard from the doctor the night before that Gladyce was having a great deal of difficulty breathing. The doctor had asked him
whether he should take any extraordinary measures to keep
Gladyce alive, and Robert had spoken for both of them when he
said no. Knowing that Toni was planning to return home for the
weekend, Robert had not called to alert her about the doctor's call.

In the hour between Gladyce's death and Toni's arrival, Bob had
begun "to take care of everything." "I had always told Robert," says
Toni appreciatively, "'When my mother dies, you'll have to do
everything'... and he did. I knew that I would not be able to function at all."

Before Toni could unfold herself from the car that evening, Bob
was by her side delivering the devastating news. They walked into
the house in silence, and Toni landed heavily on the couch in the
den. She felt nothing, only a blank numbness. The ringing of the

telephone pierced through the long silence. It was the nursing home calling to tell them that they would have to clear out Gladyce's belongings from her room before midnight. It all seemed so unreal to Toni. "Let's do it now," she said to Robert. "I had just gotten home. I was still totally stunned. But I wanted to get it over with." There was not much to clean out—only the photo of Toni, a Bible, rosaries, a few books and clothes. "She had very little," sighs Toni. "But that is probably the best way to die... not having a whole lot of clutter." Some of the nurse's aides who had cared for Gladyce came into the room to offer their condolences. They told Toni that they would miss her mother's wonderful laugh. Toni's face brightens— "We have the same big, hearty laugh." I remind her that the laugh is an inheritance that has survived her mother's death.

As Toni and Bob emerged from the nursing home they saw a familiar car rounding the corner. It was the bishop and his wife who just happened to be driving by. Toni speaks about their appearance as if it was a miraculous godsend. "They saw my face, knew something was wrong, stopped their car, and got out." She focused her eyes on the bishop. "He is a tall, big man. He came up to me and put one arm around me... *I was holding onto him for dear life.*" Toni felt protected and comforted leaning into this large man. She will always remember his words, words that sounded soothing to Toni but feel harsh to me as she repeats them. "Well, Toni," intoned the bishop, "now you're just like we are. You're an orphan." She realized immediately that losing Gladyce was like "losing a mother and a father all at once."

Even though Gladyce was a confirmed Catholic, Toni decided to have her mother's funeral at St. Andrews, Robert's parish, rather than at her mother's old church. "I took that decision upon myself... I wanted it to feel familiar." For as long as Toni could remember, her mother had asked to be cremated when she died. "Even as a child, she used to tell me this," recalls Toni. "I never really understood this request, and I never asked her why." She honored her mother's wishes even though it was "very difficult to think about." When the funeral director, a parishioner at St. Andrews, explained to her about the process of cremation, and the care they took to make sure that they actually "preserved *her* remains," Toni felt her first wave of uncontrollable grief. A long, hard life reduced to a mound of ashes. "I thought, My mother in that box!... The floodgates opened up and I couldn't stop crying." The tears flowed again when Toni walked into the church and saw the box on the table with a white cloth spread over it. "I lost it all over again."

There was only one other time in the service when Toni could not hold back the "floodgates." She had wanted to sing "Jesu, Joy of Man's Desiring," Gladyce's favorite song, at the funeral. But Toni feared she would "break down" if she tried to sing it, so she asked the organist to play it. She could hear the echoes of her mother's beautiful voice soaring through the long legato phrases, and for Toni, her mother's voice, more than anything else, carried intimacy and protection. Instead of singing, she decided that she could "make it through" a reading. "What was the reading?" I ask, and Toni's face looks blank. "I can't remember," says Toni as she rises to consult the funeral program and then finds the passage in the Bible—Revelation, chapter 7, verses 9–17. She *does* remember the words that caused her to weep, "a line that talked about the sun." As she reads the text, the tears come again. "They shall hunger no more, neither thirst any more; neither shall the sun light on them, nor any heat." Toni traces the wrenching connection: "Every time I went to visit my mother at the nursing home, she and I argued about the shades being drawn."

"Mom, why don't you open your shades and let the sun in?"
[Toni imitates her mother's gruff voice.] "No, it'll make me hot."
"But it'll make you *feel* so good, Mom."

As Toni read the passage from Revelation at the funeral, she relived their weekly confrontations. She recalled all the ways she struggled to bring light into her mother's dark existence and all the ways her mother drew the shades. "All I could think about were those shades, and I began weeping."

Robert planned the entire service, chose the scriptures and hymns, and gave the eulogy. Toni followed along. She felt comforted by the people who came to the service to offer their support. A few friends showed up, a collection of colleagues from Cabrini

College, some parishioners from St. Andrews, and to her great delight, four of her favorite sisters from St. Frances: Sister Alice, the superior general, Sister Marina, Sister Joetta, and her "very good friend" Sister Paul. Now older, but somehow ageless underneath their habits, the sisters brought solace from her old "family." When, over the years, Gladyce "wasn't able to be there" for Toni, the sisters had provided mother love and guidance. Their presence at the funeral was a precious reminder of the safe harbor they had provided. Toni watched in deep appreciation as her Catholic sisters joined in the Episcopal service officiated by her husband. When, at communion time, Robert announced "all baptized Christians can come to the table," Toni was overjoyed to see the nuns parade up to the communion rail to receive the wine and the bread. In that moment, her worlds seemed to come together. She felt forgiveness and coherence in this powerful ritual.

Two family members attended the service. Toni's cousin Herbie drove up from Maryland, and her sister, Arvella, arrived by train from New York. Seeing Arvella filled Toni with a complex of feelings— anger, detachment, sadness, and relief. She had not heard from Arvella since the previous October, had not seen her since "two Christmases ago," and knew that Arvella had not communicated directly with their mother in years. Every few weeks Gladyce would try to collect remnants of the lost relationship with her secondborn by asking Toni, "Have you heard anything from Arvella?" Toni hated to see her mother's pain. "She felt a lot of anguish related to my sister... This never got reconciled." It had been so long since their last contact that Toni didn't even have her sister's current home address and telephone number. She was forced to dial her at work to tell her about their mother's death. When Toni picked Arvella up at the train station the day of the funeral, she felt a strong sense of disconnection. It was hard to think of this woman as her sister and her mother's daughter.

The bishop's presence at the funeral was perhaps the most meaningful of all to Toni. She had not expected him to come. He had told her that he had a previous commitment and wouldn't be able to be there, so his surprise appearance brought her even more pleasure. His words to her after the funeral ring most loudly and offer her the most insight. The bishop had given her a long embrace and said, "There is so much unfinished business that we have to live with for the rest of our lives." Toni looks off into the distance—"It is the *unfinished* stuff I cry about... My mother won't be here any-more. I won't be able to talk to her. I think about her life and weep. I think about how unhappy and hard it was, about what great talent she had as a singer that she was never able to use... I think about all the years we spent apart... You know, I never really got to know her. We never really learned to talk with each other... It was actually a nonrelationship. I just rock in my hammock, think about all the unfinished business... and I cry."

At the end of the service, Robert picked up the box with Gladyce's ashes and led the small procession out of the church and into the garden where a hole had been dug to bury it in. As they walked out of the dark church into the sunshine, Toni saw a mother walking down the street pushing a baby stroller and holding her young son's hand. It was one of those shocking moments when you are suddenly brought back into the real world of ordinary events. Toni was startled as she heard the little boy ask loudly, "Did some-body die?" His mother tried to hush him, but he was insistent. Toni's response was calm and reassuring. She was also speaking to herself. "It's okay. It's perfectly okay. Yes, somebody died." Once the box was covered with soil, the group returned to the church for a small reception. Despite the "unfinished business," that Toni expects to struggle with for "a very long time," the funeral ritual provided some solace and closure. "The service helped me," says Toni. "Putting the box in the ground with the people surrounding me... I needed that wrapping around."

Toni's mother's death is magnified by another loss. After suc-cessfully completing her ordination examinations in March, Toni had expected to be ordained at a celebratory service on June 20. For months she had been preparing for this moment, a critical step toward priesthood. She had even hoped that her mother would be well enough to attend the ordination service. But the bishop had delivered a "terrible and unexpected blow." He had decided that she was not ready for ordination; that she would have to enroll in a year of formal seminary training before he would ordain her. It was crushing news. At first she was devastated and "silenced," unable to speak about the pain this caused her. Then she was consumed by frustration and unanswered questions. She couldn't understand the bishop's reasoning or his motivation. How could he do this to her when she thought she had successfully accomplished all of the requirements for ordination? For several days she lived with the disappointment, trying to discern what had gone wrong, hoping to find some relief in reflection and prayer. But the frustration turned to an anger that smoldered inside her. Finally, she voiced her questions and concerns in a carefully composed eight-page single-spaced letter. She struggled to find the appropriate tone and language that would be both strong and deferential. She worked to communicate her feelings clearly, but not offend the bishop.

Toni chose to respond to the bishop in a letter because she has always felt more comfortable confronting people in writing. "Writing is easier because there is a delay in the response. I know that the reaction will be tempered... I won't get the direct anger." Toni traces her anxiety about direct confrontation to her long history of living under the domination of her "superiors." "There have been so many people in my life who have had so much power over me. If the superiors in the convent didn't like what I said, they could put me out of the convent or not let me take final vows... I had to be so careful, so cautious, so nice. That is why I've spent most of my life trying not to offend people." I look at Toni, who seems crumbled, weary. Her hands are clasped tightly in her lap. "And, of course, my mother could get very angry. I was always living with the threat of her violence."

Toni finds the long letter to the bishop in her carefully ordered files, scans the paragraphs, and reads me some passages. Two major questions dominate: first, "Why can't I be ordained *before* I go to seminary?" and second, "Why are you requiring that I do a whole year of seminary?" As a prelude to these questions she describes in detail her progress over the last several months; notes her academic experience in courses, seminars, and tutorials; lists all of the books she has recently read; and mentions her personal development, including her work in therapy. The neutral voice of the progress report changes to more urgent pleas and questions. "I have no need to wear a cassock and a collar... that is not my motivation... All those years I was covered in a habit. I don't need it anymore. *Why can't you let the church publicly acknowledge my call?*" The final paragraphs speak directly about Toni's feelings of subordination and infantilization. "When I was a nun I was treated as a child. In the convent I did what I was told. Now I'm not a child. I'm fifty-seven years old. I'm your equal in age, if not in position and status." The letter closes on a powerful note, reaching out with balm. Toni found a "beautiful, healing poem" that fills the ninth page of the letter. She was moved to send it to the bishop, who had recently endured a bout of serious surgery. "I pray for him all the time," she says about the powerful man who has stopped her forward progress.

At first, Toni was surprised and thrilled to receive an uncharacteristically long reply of a page and a half from the bishop. She digs in her file drawer again and waves the letter in the air. "See, here it is, a response!" But the contents were disappointing. She had not really expected clarity or candor from the bishop, but she still felt frustrated by the masked emotion and paternalistic tone. "He responded to me without responding to me... which he does very well." Her voice is exasperated—"He never addressed my questions!" She reads his sentences, picks them apart, and argues with the language and the reasoning. He speaks of the "long-standing practice of the church," the history of the rules and regulations, and the need for Toni to follow normal procedures. Toni shakes her head and cuts through the bureaucratic rationale. "In a sense, he is saying, 'I am in charge.'"

For her it all boils down to a power struggle. In this journey toward priesthood Toni is working to "claim her voice," express her authority, emerge into full adulthood. She is struggling to develop relationships that are "equal," symmetrical, and reciprocal. She is resisting the rigid boundaries and bureaucratic responses of the church. She wants to establish a clear difference between being a nun in the convent and a priest in the world. Her urgency about all of this has forced a new and surprising outspokenness. She reports on a recent conversation she had with the bishop at a church gathering they were both attending. The exchange was initiated by Toni and just seemed to explode out of her. When she asked the bishop, "Why do you exert your power over me?... Why do you *do* that to me?" he responded, "Well, because you leave yourself open for that." Toni then pointed out, "But you don't have any power over me except the power I *give* you." "Yes," said the bishop, "but I have *authority*."

Toni's voice conveys the raw intensity of this interaction, its electric charge. It is a conversation about Toni's readiness for ordination, but it is also, for Toni, a bold effort to give voice to her feelings and resist subordination. As she struggles, she discovers her ambivalence. On the one hand, she wants to rebel against the infantilization created by the rigid roles and hierarchies of the church. On the other hand, she feels drawn to the bishop's power. She "holds onto him for dear life" when he comforts her after Gladyce's death. She finds his insights about unfinished business particularly compelling and insightful. And she even recognizes that her rebellious urges arise from a deep attachment to the bishop. She wouldn't have to fight so hard if their relationship didn't have such potency.

Toni is "torn" about how far to push the bishop. There is no doubt that she is deeply driven by the journey toward priesthood. Her eyes are fiery as she says, "Sara, I feel *urgently* called!... There is nothing more important to me than getting on with this work. I've been feeling *misplaced. I'm not where I'm supposed to be.*" She is clear about her mission, but "torn" about how to proceed strategically within the church hierarchy. At one moment, she wants to give in. "I'm tempted to say the hell with this. Just let him be in charge... Just play the game, Antoinette." At another moment, she imagines challenging the bishop's decision by appealing to church procedure. "According to the canons, I can be ordained a deacon right now. Suppose I just wrote him a letter demanding ordination?" But she always returns to the worry that she might "offend."

As Toni resists the domination of the bishop and the "male hierarchies" of the church, she becomes clearer about the focus and scope of her own ministry. She does not want to submit to or become a party to the inequalities of power, either as dominant or as subordinate. She imagines a circle rather than a pyramid as she thinks about her own ministry—one that is dynamic, participatory, and unencumbered by rigid roles. She wants to empower people, not silence them. She expects that during the week she will not wear a priest's collar but will put it on for officiating at Sunday services. She also hopes that her ministry will be primarily directed to women, to their special capacities and needs.

The women's spirituality group she created several months ago at Cabrini College is her first sustained effort to practice her "calling." Each Wednesday a group of eight or nine women, mostly staff, come together to "discover the spirit." Toni begins by "creating the atmosphere. We meet in an ordinary conference room... but I move the tables to the side, dim the lights, and put an oil lamp on a small table in the middle of the carpet... We create a circle... I take my portable CD player and we always have music, gentle music that helps us focus our attention and center ourselves. When it is over it is always difficult for us to leave the room because the atmosphere has been so calm and supportive and we feel nurtured... but it's also easier to go out into the world when we're feeling stronger."

Toni feels that "the atmosphere" is essential to the experience of spiritual nourishment. For her, it is difficult to separate the medium from the message. The aesthetic, spiritual, emotional, and intellectual dimensions flow together. "I use scripture, literature, music, prayer, images, metaphors, and storytelling," says Toni. "It is like weaving a tapestry. I want the women to wake up to who they are... discover our skills and our strengths... find our voices." As I listen to the goals of Toni's ministry, I am struck by how they converge with her own personal odyssey. She is working on the same issues— identity, discovery, and voice—that she is encouraging in these women. She is very much included in the circle that she is designing.

I ask Toni to speak about the contrasts between her experience of spiritual development in the convent and her experience in the women's group at Cabrini. Her response is immediate. "It's *totally* different. I wasn't *in charge* in the convent." I laugh at the notion, but Toni is dead serious. "Part of that religious community was doing what had been handed down for generations. In the convent, spirituality was *personal piety*... your relationship to God was expressed through devotional activities, pet prayers, going to chapel, stations of the cross... There were rigidly prescribed rules and offices. But in this women's group, spirituality is much broader... It includes taking care of yourself, growing up, understanding yourself, your talents and strengths... It includes being aware of how we deal with one another... determining the power we have and how we use it... It includes creating the time for prayer, exercise, meditation, reading."

As she describes the multidimensionality of this weekly spiritual encounter, Toni's voice grows softer and her face relaxes. She reaches over to pick up a large hand-carved wooden box, feels the texture of the smooth wood, turns it over and places it on her desk. It produces the most extraordinary sound. We sit and listen to the melodious chimes. Toni says, "This is called a rain machine," and opens the box to reveal the tiny metal balls falling on chimes. She recently saw it advertised in a music catalogue and sent away for it even though it was "unbelievably expensive." The rain machine has become part of her "created atmosphere," part of her effort to find quiet and peace. All of this seems far from the noisy, calculated ordination struggle.

I wonder out loud why ordination is even remotely important to the kind of ministry she is developing. "How would ordination change the quality and focus of your work at Cabrini?" Toni pauses for a long time, then says something vague about not wanting to mix her professional work at the college with her ministry. She is very clear, however, that if she were ordained it would "not make a bit of difference to the women" in her spirituality group. In a gesture of exasperation she throws up her hands—"Listen, Sara, ordination would be a stamp of approval for me." Then she murmurs, "There are vestiges of the old hierarchies still there in me, I guess."

The women's spirituality group is a creative interlude in a life phase that Toni describes as "the least creative time in my life." I suspect she is speaking about the anguish of losing her mother. But she claims that her mother's death doesn't account for the "stuck place" in which she finds herself. "I'm *bored* and *misplaced*," she says, weeping. Toni points to all the "artistic" things she used to do—sewing, knitting, crocheting, calligraphy—that she no longer has the time or energy to do. "My job takes so much out of me that I come home and don't feel like starting work on a project... and, you know, I'm fifty-seven. I don't have limitless energy like I did in my thirties when I would work hard all day and study all night." What seems to hurt most is not the reduced energy or the lack of artistic production; it is the fact that she feels no motivation, no impulse. "I don't have any *desire*, that is the worst part." She opens her journal and reads her one-line entry for the day: "Oh God, help me."

I want to reach out to Toni and comfort her. I want to tell her that she is being much too hard on herself. I want to point out all the ways in which she is being productive; all the ways she is bravely facing the "boredom"; all the ways she's resisting stasis. I see the "stuck place" as the turmoil that so often comes before forward movement, the suffering that comes before creativity. I witness her anguish, but I also anticipate movement toward a fuller, richer future. And I am totally in awe of how she bares her soul, how she allows herself to be so vulnerable. Just as she tried to do for her mother, I have the urge to raise the curtains and let the healing sunlight strike her face and penetrate her soul.

When Toni describes by contrast the "most creative period" in her life, her face brightens. "First, in Oak Ridge I *built* things. I built the telescope, the Geiger counter, with my own hands... I used the mechanical part of me. Second, I did so much by myself. I became an *individual*. I discovered I could live outside the Oblate Community... I could manage money, keep my apartment, and still do my sisterly duties. Third, I was *self-taught*. I taught myself so much new stuff... about enzymes and radioactivity. I felt very proud of myself." It was a time of extraordinary growth. Judged by this high standard, the present moment feels boring, lacking in "desire," unproductive. We are both able to smile at these "impossibly high expectations" that challenge her to greater heights and also hold her captive.

It is hard to know how to give shape to this final session, how to give words to the sadness we both feel. I am haunted by Toni's bereft feeling that her mother has left her so little. I remember that one of the most precious legacies left by her mother has been the memory of her wonderful voice. Toni has said repeatedly, *"My mother's power was in her voice."* She meant this in two ways, I think. First, she has always known her mother as outspoken, forceful in her candor, frightening in her honesty. Her mother possessed the voice of power, clarity, and confrontation. "My mother always said what she thought. She was *not* like me. She was not worried about other people's feelings." Perhaps Toni's struggle to "find her voice" is part of her determination to feel more identified with her mother, to draw on some of her mother's fight and power. But she is also thinking of her mother's beautiful singing, soothing, comforting—an expression of her artistry. Toni lives with both legacies. As we search for closure, I long to hear Toni's own voice. "Will you sing for me, Toni?" I ask. "In all this time, I've never heard you sing."

Toni needs no prodding. Moving swiftly and gracefully to a cross-legged position on the floor, she opens her guitar case, takes out an elegant and brand-new instrument, and searches for her purple pick. She pulls out a list of songs that she has titled Sacred Songs for My Ordination, which includes "The Lone Wild Bird," "Here I Am, Lord," "The Spirit of the Lord Is Upon Me." "I'm so tired of Bach, Beethoven and Brahms," she says. She chooses a song from her list, checks the tuning on her guitar, and tentatively strums a few chords. She apologizes for her fumbling. But there is no tentativeness or fumbling in her singing. Her voice is powerful and large and surprisingly sweet. Her singing seems free and totally unself-conscious. She is wrapped up in the music, in the poetry of the words, in the resonance of her voice. Sitting on the rug, leaning over her guitar, Toni's body looks relaxed. Her face is glowing, and all the weariness seems to be washed away. I know why she has spoken of "music as healing." I sit quietly on the rug, leaning my back up against the bookcase. I do not want to break the spell as she moves through a group of her favorite songs, so I don't comment or applaud. When she stops singing, she lets the silence linger and then muses, "My dream is to have a music group in a parish... to help people understand the possibilities for worship. Singing is not just performing, it is praying."

In a final parting gesture, Toni asks me the best last question. "Sara, have I told you what my goal in life is?" "No," I respond, surprised. "My goal in life is to be a *mystic*. By that I mean I want to always be in God's presence... so that people who meet me will feel that they are in God's presence, too." "Have you ever known a mystic?" I ask. "Yes, you remember Sister Edwina, the *perfect* nun, who seemed to float down the hall? I thought of her as a mystic. But I don't want to be otherworldly. I want to have my feet firmly planted on the ground." Toni rises and presses the button of her CD player. Haunting chants from a monastery in France fill the room. Toni explains that this is called Taize music, composed and sung by an ecumenical community of brothers. Every year thousands of people travel to a tiny village in Burgundy for a pilgrimage of prayer and reflection and to experience the brothers making the Taize music.

With the Taize chants, Toni has "created an atmosphere" for her meditation on becoming a mystic. The words and music converge. She continues very slowly, "It is kind of *presumptuous* to even *say* I want to be a mystic... You can't just *wish* it. I have no idea how I get from here to there... But I know it is about developing my relationship with God. That is why I spend a lot of time by myself... That is why I have a real *urgency* about carving out time for prayer and reflection." She falls silent. We are both swaying gently to the music. "Every day I struggle with centering myself *and* letting go. But the scientist part of me is always searching for the *perfect* formula... If I can once let go of that, then I could learn to pray. I must get more right-brained, try not to be so orderly and organized... try not to always require structure." Her face shows the tension, the contradictions she lives with. To reach her goal, to grow into a mystic, she must let go of her need for perfection, control, and certain answers. She must dismantle the personal and institutional structures that inhibit her "being in the presence of God." This feels light years away from the obedience and submission she lived with for twenty years in the convent, so far from the church hierarchies she must negotiate in order to become a priest. "Being a mystic," she says, "is the antithesis of organized religion." This former nun, this devoted scientist, this determined candidate for the priesthood ultimately wants to use herself in her work. This new "orphan" wants to return to her roots ("to who I am"), to an identity that has been forged out of "her own life experience." Toni's words come slowly. "As a mystic I would have knowledge of people's joy, pain, struggle... I'd find a way of relating to that through my own story... just being present with people... maybe not even talking."

TONY EARLS

Grounding with My Brothers

Beginnings

The Harvard School of Public Health, a gray hulking building, sits on Huntington Avenue, a wide street usually clogged with traffic traveling between downtown Boston and the suburbs—Brookline, Newton, Wellesley. Before Huntington Avenue turns into Route 9 and travels through the suburbs, it passes through what one of the students at the School of Public Health describes to me as "a very tough black neighborhood." He is trying to explain to me why "security is so tight" at the school; why only one major door is open for visitors to come through; and why I have been firmly and abruptly stopped at the door and asked to present my university I.D. card. The School of Public Health, appropriately enough, is situated on the boundary between the academy and the "real world." It is part of the more sedate medical school complex, and there are courtyards and stairs that connect it to the hospitals and laboratories of Harvard Medical School. But it also looks out on housing projects, noisy trolleys, grocery stores, banks, beauty parlors—the bustling sights and sounds of city life.

Inside the building at midday, students of all ages, dress, language, size, and color are jammed into a huge cafeteria, some in tight knots of serious conversation, others scanning notebooks or reading alone, others in raucous dialogue, laughing, gesticulating. The high ceilings do not absorb the sound, which ricochets off walls, floors, and tables. Trying to escape the noise and chaos, I find a chair slightly out of the action and close to the front door, and settle in to wait for Dr. Felton Earls.

He arrives a few minutes later looking very calm against this bustling backdrop. He greets me warmly and leads me through the crowded cafeteria to a small quiet room with a simple sign that reads A New Season. We enter into this soundproofed oasis where the

tables are covered with white cloths and decorated with vases of flowers. It is a tiny restaurant run by caterers who used to provide food
for special occasions and now have opened this noontime restaurant
in a corner space carved out of the larger cafeteria. There are five or
six entrees on the menu and one quiet, smiling waitress who serves all
the tables in the room. We settle in at a reserved table and hear about
the items on the menu that are no longer available (it is now 1:30
P.M. on Friday and we are the "last of the last diners" for the week).
We make our choices and almost immediately the food and the setting become totally secondary to our intense conversation.

Felton Earls, known as Tony, is a brown-skinned man with short
graying hair that is receding. He is relatively short (maybe five feet
seven or five feet eight) and slight in build, but his carriage and
peaceful determination make him seem bigger and taller. His features are not classically handsome; a large nose dominates his face.
His wide mouth with generous lips eases into a quiet smile. I am
riveted by his extraordinary eyes, both calm and penetrating. He is
a soft-spoken, articulate man who also listens with unusual intensity.

A couple of weeks ago, Tony turned fifty, a birthday he seems to
have welcomed with equanimity, if not enthusiasm. The celebratory
calls and cards from family and friends, reminding him of the great
significance of this half-century marker, seem to set the stage for
our interviews. When I remarked in an earlier telephone call that
Tony must feel satisfied with "all that he has accomplished in these
first fifty years," I was greeted by silence. At our lunch he revisits this
comment. "I let that go by. I just let it lay there… But mostly I was
feeling, What is she saying to me? There is so much to be done."
When he speaks those last words, his voice is full of emotion. I begin
to glimpse the standards by which he measures his life's work, as he
draws a distinction between his "career" and his "work." For Tony,
career is an institutionally defined notion. It is about status, position,
credentials—visible and tangible signs of success. By this set of standards and values, Tony has done a great deal in his first fifty years of
life. He is a distinguished researcher and tenured professor at the
Harvard School of Public Health. He is admired by colleagues for his
judgment, his contributions, and as a responsible and ethical citizen.

But after his fiftieth birthday, Tony is taking a different set of measurements, using standards that will not allow him to feel complacent, comfortable, or self-satisfied. He is thinking of his *work*, and of its impact on the world. Does his work matter to the lives of people, to their health, survival, and well-being? Is he making a contribution to the humanity and civility of society? Is his work saving lives? Protecting children from abuse and neglect? Helping medicine take a broader, more complicated view of trauma, pathology, and disease? Is he drawing productive connections between his research and public policy? In answer to these demanding questions Tony says again, "There is so much still left to do." The first fifty years feel like a training ground, an exercise for all the hard work ahead. He is now just beginning to be ready to use himself fully. His career may be developed and mature, but he feels that his work is in its infancy. He is both inspired and frustrated by all that needs doing, and does not want to waste precious time polishing his career.

Tony is not modest about his career or his accomplishments. He appreciates the benefits and rituals of his membership in the professional guild. That is why he "let it pass" when I commented on his illustrious accomplishments. But he wants me to know that he holds another, more important, set of criteria, which provide his energy and inspiration, which keep his feet to the fire. While his credentials, skills, and training make him a member of an elite circle of medical academics, his experience, values, and roots make him feel a personal responsibility to struggle against the injustice and pathology of society. Like the building in which we are sitting, Tony is poised on a boundary line, encompassing the two realities of career and work.

Tony has just returned from Dallas where he has been sitting for three days in a hotel conference room working with colleagues from around the country. The meeting was in Texas, but it could have taken place anywhere because the inside of these windowless, air-conditioned rooms all look the same. The last ten years of professional traveling have robbed Tony of his "nomadic spirit." He used to love to travel. He, his wife, Mary, and their two children have done a great deal of globe-trotting. But when they moved to St. Louis ten years ago, and Tony took on an administrative role in the medical school at Washington University, business travel began to dominate his work life. Rather than the pleasure and adventure he had known, traveling became redundant and boring; he'd arrive at another place across the country but see nothing new or different.

St. Louis was also a place where "careerism" in medicine seemed to be of ultimate importance, where colleagues approached the building of their careers with both caution and ambition. When I ask Tony to describe the differences between his experiences at Harvard and at Washington University, he begins by referring to this preoccupation with career. "St. Louis was a place where work was very compartmentalized... People would get very nervous and worried if you didn't fit into a particular compartment. I kept on wanting to create new compartments, and there was a great deal of resistance to that. My older colleagues kept on warning me to be careful: 'Just analyze this data set in a new way. Don't try to develop new paradigms.'" Tony's emerging interest in interdisciplinary inquiry; in making connections between research, practice, and policy; in taking on tough economic and social issues was seen by his colleagues as potentially compromising to his career at Washington University. "Within three months of arriving in St. Louis I was carrying an appointment book... for the first time in my life." In contrast, Tony feels that he has some colleagues at Harvard who share his values; who understand and appreciate the interdisciplinary dimensions of their work; and who feel the same sense of urgency and responsibility in making connections to the real world. At Harvard he feels freer to experiment and take risks in his work; he feels more support for his own breed of eclecticism; and he feels both more autonomy and more of a sense of community as he pursues his research.

At first, when Tony arrived in St. Louis it felt like a friendlier, more comfortable city than Boston. In his early years at Harvard, he had felt burdened by the institutional elitism and arrogance; Washington University seemed welcoming and inclusive in contrast. Rather than feeling peripheral and infantilized as he had at Harvard, Tony enjoyed full status and center stage. It was a time of growing into professional manhood; of attaining a status that, at that point in his career, Harvard would not have allowed him. He continued to feel productive and rewarded for the first four years of his stay there. But by his fifth year, Tony began to feel certain claustrophobic aspects of the place. Rather than supporting a continuing growth, the culture of Washington University seemed stuck at a developmental plateau. The traditions that had initially felt orderly and civilized now seemed rooted in a deadening conservatism. Although the Earls family ended up staying in St. Louis for seven years, Tony knew that he wanted to leave after four, and he knew that he wanted to head back East, "not necessarily to Harvard, maybe to Johns Hopkins in Baltimore or Howard in Washington."

"St. Louis is much more southern than it is midwestern," Tony says as a way of describing the heavy layer of racism just below the surface of demure civility. "All you need to do is barely scratch the surface, and there it is in all its ugliness." The racism "just below the surface" reminded Tony too much of his experience growing up in New Orleans, of the ghosts of oppression and prejudice that were always hovering around him as a child growing up in the South. It is not that he regards Boston as free of racism. Quite the contrary. But he has always felt that Boston's brand of racism was more open, palpable, clearer to recognize than the southern variety. ("At least that was true in the seventies. There was South Boston and Charlestown that you just stayed away from.") Tony's voice grows heavy, and I see a shiver in his body as he describes the familiar behavior of white folks in St. Louis that reminded him of New Orleans. The echoes were strong and inescapable; he knew it was time to leave.

One reason the Earlses stayed three years beyond the time when Tony was ready to leave was because Tanya, their younger daughter, who had suffered with the move to St. Louis, had finally begun to like it there. After a rocky and long transition to a new school, new home, new neighborhood, Tanya had found her niche and was flourishing there. Her parents didn't have the heart to uproot her so soon again. So they remained in St. Louis longer than Tony would have liked and found the last few years difficult and tedious.

As I describe to Tony Earls the work in which I am engaged and the nature of his possible participation, he listens intently and patiently, waiting for me to pull all the various threads together.

When I arrive at the question of whether he might have an interest in this project, his face shows a combination of surprise and
intrigue. He is quiet as he searches for the words that will express
the many feelings and thoughts converging in his head. "I'm flat-
tered," he says quietly. "I think this is important work... timely...
very, very ambitious." Then later on he says that he feels that it is
critical that we begin to develop descriptions of African-Americans
that are many dimensional and complicated, that express the
extraordinary variety among us. He dislikes the simplistic caricatures that are drawn by the media and by researchers, which are
often reflected in, and shaped by, the public consciousness. As a college student, he also had had a memorable and intense response to
E. Franklin Frazier's *Black Bourgeoisie*. It was 1959 and he was at
Howard University where Frazier was teaching. He read Frazier's
book and was not so much offended by the way Frazier characterized
middle-class black experience as he was by the study's lack of a
"scientific base." He could find no real data to support Frazier's
claims, no reliable empirical evidence. This caused Tony to question Frazier's science and to wonder whether this might be "what
people mean when they talk about political science," a scholar's
ideological perspective. In addition, he had witnessed Frazier's
behavior among his colleagues and with his students. Frazier
seemed to be perched high above everyone else, looking down with
an arrogant and elitist gaze. In his work, Frazier was describing the
materialism and vacuousness of the black bourgeoisie, the ways in
which they irresponsibly separated themselves from the black community. At the same time, he seemed to be mirroring the behavior
of the people he was describing and condemning. With a haughty
demeanor, he was declaring himself better than his people, sepa-
rating himself from his community. Tony's most powerful impression of Frazier, however, does not involve his arrogance or his elitism; he is struck by Frazier's faulty science—a science that seemed
absent of valid or reliable data; a science that seemed to confirm
(rather than question) bias.

The Right Place
at the Right Time

When I ask Tony Earls where he would like to begin his story, he leans forward in his chair, looks calmly but intently into my eyes, and leaps into the middle of an "internal struggle" he has been wrestling with since he read the morning paper. This struggle, both timely and age-old, is about institutional politics, personal identity, black-white relations, confrontation, and voice. It belongs both to the black law professor in the newspaper story and the black physician who is identifying with him and interpreting his story.

Derrick Bell, professor of law at Harvard, has come to town to speak at a student rally at the Harvard Law School. He has come to announce his intention to continue his boycott of the faculty there until his colleagues "appoint a tenured woman of color." Two years ago, he resigned from his full professorship in a protest that captured a great deal of press coverage and student sympathy, but only weak collegial support. Bell left in frustration, rage, and cynicism. He left feeling he had no other recourse. He had tried more "rational," conciliatory efforts to bring more diversity in color and gender to the Harvard Law faculty. He had tried to appeal to their sense of fairness, intellectual eclecticism, and ideological range. He had talked, prodded, pushed, threatened, and finally left.

Although Bell's gesture was bold, courageous, and visible, in career terms it was not a major risk. The law school dean had partly avoided the heat of the controversy by granting Bell a two-year leave. The first year, Bell had supported himself with a combination of speaking fees and book contract advances. He had traveled the country shouting his message of institutional racism and academic elitism to enthusiastic crowds, conveying his anger and pessimism through haunting parables like the ones he told in his book *And We*

Are Not Saved. The second year, Bell had joined the faculty of New York University Law School as a visiting professor while continuing his hectic schedule of speaking engagements. To many he had become an icon of courage and commitment. To others he was seen as a grandstander, an egotist who cared more about confrontation and visibility than about the cause for which he was fighting.

But now his two-year leave was coming to an end, and the Harvard Law faculty had still not hired a "tenured woman of color." This time his determination not to rejoin the Harvard Law faculty represented a considerable risk. In measured tones and bureaucratic language both the dean of the law school and the president of the university had said that they hoped Bell would return, that he was a valuable member of the faculty; that his protest would be more effective if it became part of the civilized discourse within the university; but that if he decided not to rejoin Harvard's ranks in the fall, he would risk dismissal from the faculty. They could not hold his faculty position open for more than two years.

This morning Tony Earls has read the *Boston Globe* article about Bell's latest confrontational act and he is feeling deeply identified and pained. He does not know Bell, but he has followed his story closely and has the urge to talk with him, question him directly, and lend him support. Bell's story causes Tony "enormous discomfort" and reminds him of all the ways he feels "uncomfortable" at the Harvard School of Public Health. Earls's commentary is raw and impatient. It sounds as if his reactions are so massive and complex that he almost doesn't know where to begin. "I have a strong need to talk to Derrick," he says urgently. "This has been on my mind for a very long time. The first time I met Neil Rudenstine, I asked him what position he had on Bell's protest... I said this to many other people I came in contact with at the School of Public Health and the Medical School... No one has given me a satisfactory response... The talk is always tainted with administrative and policy considerations, always avoiding the moral and ethical response. I think there is a great failure on the part of the people in the university to embrace the moral and ethical underpinnings of what Bell is doing." Tony's voice is soft but full of frustration.

Tony looks to Harvard for leadership, for a special sensitivity to the dilemmas of institutional racism. He sees Harvard as having a unique responsibility because of its elite status. "The minority issue is one that has deep moral implications for all of us. Harvard should be creating some leadership in this area. If it doesn't come from this place, where is it going to come from?" He seems to be casting around, talking to himself, as he searches for clues to some way out of this "depressing scene." "Maybe the church," he says halfheartedly. "But I don't have a strong allegiance to the church... I'm an atheist, not a believer... I'm not identified with the metaphors... I have used the church for political purposes. In St. Louis, I worked with a lot of the churches on antiapartheid stuff. So the university and the church are two spheres I've worked in... but both of them disappoint me—the church because of its metaphors, the university because of the way it insists upon administrative rhetoric and reasoning."

Tony's language sounds abstract to me, sweeping in its assertions. I want to know what he means by the church's "metaphors," "avoiding the moral and ethical responses," "administrative rhetoric and reasoning." But I choose not to probe. This is our first session, and I am listening for the cadence and style of his talk. I also feel that he has entered his story at the most vulnerable place—the place within him that is questioning how he is using himself in this world; whether he is being true to his values, his identity, his roots; whether he can be productive and worthy in a place that often feels resistant and alien. This vulnerability, I think, is expressed in the abstractness of his language, in the pain in his voice, in his choice of where he will begin his story.

I am relieved when he admits that his "reading of Derrick's story is total imposition." "I don't know Derrick... I'm imposing all this stuff... But what I see is this: He reached the point where his efforts to create dialogue with the university were impossible. He realized that it was impossible to have a person-to-person dialogue *from the heart.*" Tony's hand is on his heart and there is a long silence before he continues heavily. "It was intolerable for him in the sense that he wasn't getting through... He thought it was personally important that he not get trapped in this institution... in a kind of hopeless, mindless prison." Tony admires Bell's courage but is saddened by the meager impact of his protest. "This was a high-risk activity... Derrick hoped that he would be able to rally some support, ignite some protest movement, but he has not been able to generate real discussion."

Tony's voice trails off. He looks weary as he stares out the large floor-to-ceiling windows that look out on the concrete and stone medical school complex. It is a relatively mild early March day, but it is cold inside Tony's office. He leaves the heat off even in the winter and announces to me, "I like it to be cold in here... I'll turn the heat on if you like." I decline his offer but wonder out loud why a "New Orleans southern boy" would choose to have a freezing office. He smiles and shrugs his shoulders but does not offer an answer. I guess that the chilly temperatures are energizing, that he thinks better and more clearly in the brisk air. The office, in fact, has the spare simplicity fitting for someone who is focused on work. The large teak desk is mostly cleared off except for a few neat piles of memos, papers, and correspondence. There is a small square nook by the window where Tony's computer desk fits perfectly. The sitting area where we plant ourselves for the interview has two comfortable chairs and small tables over an Indian rug. The colors are soft browns, blues, and greens. On the wall behind Tony's chair is one of Romare Bearden's famous prints of jazz musicians, a splash of bold color in this subdued office. A large, very detailed map of Boston's metropolitan area is on the other wall, with pins marking locations that I suspect are part of Tony's research project. A huge print of Miles Davis, a closeup of his face, is leaning up against the wall, not yet hung. The trumpeter's brooding face keeps capturing my attention.

Bearden's jazz musicians and Miles Davis's gaze remind me of Tony's comment when we met a couple of weeks ago: "I think like a jazz musician... My roots are in New Orleans and the music there." He was describing his attitude toward giving speeches and talks. For Tony, speeches are never dull, never repetitive, never redundant, even when he is speaking about the same data or conceptual frameworks. Like the jazz music Tony listened to as a young boy, "the performances have a structure... but there is always opportunity for experimentation, revision, and improvisation." For Tony Earls, surrounded with cool jazz images, creativity flows from both structure and improvisation.

I ask Tony why he expected (and continues to expect) Harvard University to be responsive to "the moral and ethical" issues that Bell is raising in his protest. Why would he even anticipate that this patriarchal, elitist institution would "lead the way" in institutional enlightenment? I am frankly surprised by his expectation of Harvard's willingness or capacity to change, and his consequent despair at the university's bureaucratic inertia. Perhaps I am surprised by his lack of cynicism, by his stubborn determination not to give up hope. This hopefulness strikes me as admirable and promising even as it inevitably risks disenchantment.

My questions make Tony's eyes sparkle as he immediately revisits a twenty-year-old story. He is launched. "It was a freezing cold snowy day in January of 1971" when Tony arrived in Boston for his interview at Mass. General Hospital. He had come to Harvard Medical School to talk with Dr. Leon Eisenberg, "the best child psychiatrist" in the country. The memory of this winter day needs context, so Tony backs up several years to his graduation from Howard University's School of Medicine; he was the only one in his class of over one hundred graduates who did not go on to do an internship. Instead, he chose to do a postdoctoral fellowship at a neurophysiology laboratory at the University of Wisconsin. He had always loved science, had gone to medical school "for the science," and finally got the chance to work as a research scientist.

His commitment to science was more than cerebral. He was totally captivated by the scientific method, and even more by the connections between science and the real world. From as early as he can remember, Tony believed that science could change the world, that it had great transformative powers. This potential could be realized in brilliant discoveries and innovations—the work of Darwin, Pasteur, Einstein, Curie, Salk—or in the more modest insights and understandings that could flow from systematic, objective inquiry. The major, dramatic discoveries had clear, decisive effects. The quieter science had a less obvious impact on the "real world," and the relationship to change was nonlinear and complex, but influential nevertheless. From Tony's point of view, scientists are compassionate people whose work in the lab is linked to life in the world. "Those folks who describe scientists as not passionate are wrong," says Tony forcefully. "It enrages me when science is described as irrelevant to worldly experience and scientists are described as lacking in passion... I've always seen the emotional and intellectual connections."

So when Tony went to work in the research labs at the University of Wisconsin, he did not see this as an escape from the world. He saw it as the best way he could engage the world. But the death of Martin Luther King Jr. suddenly and dramatically challenged Tony's view of the purpose and ethics of his work. He puts it simply, "After Martin's assassination I wanted to be in the streets, not in the lab." Even with his perspectives on the usefulness of scientific investigation, Tony felt compelled to take to the streets and engage in direct action. He was young, impatient, angry. He took his rage and energy to Metropolitan Hospital, a throbbing city hospital in New York City's East Harlem. Metropolitan was located on First Avenue between 99th and 100th Streets, a block that was declared by Mayor Lindsay's task force on cities to be "the worst block in the country." It was an urban area with a concentrated intensity of poverty, crime, drugs, broken families, and deteriorated and vacant housing. In the late '60s the streets were battlegrounds between entrenched institutions and grassroots political groups, and between warring youth gangs. Metropolitan Hospital was the site of high drama. "There was a raging fire in the hospital and in the community... it was very unsettled, very confrontational, always on the edge of violence. ... There was antiwar stuff, antiracism stuff, women's stuff. The Young Lords and the Black Panthers were powerful forces... lots of standoffs between the administration and the community groups... lots of issues around housing...."

The scene was exactly what Tony wanted, exactly where he wanted to be just at that time. Amid the fires in East Harlem, Tony directed his own fiery energy toward learning pediatrics and saving babies. He remembers vividly the scores of "baby junkies" born on his unit, the offspring of heroin-addicted mothers. The detoxification of these babies was a complicated, treacherous procedure. "It was technically difficult and emotionally exhausting and strenuous," remembers Tony. "We would have to give these tiny newborns morphine, methadone, or high doses of valium to replace the heroin in their blood... It was very risky stuff. If you didn't calculate just right, you'd lose them... forever... and we were the interns... we did all the work." The political ferment, the rising confrontations, the angry rhetoric, and the helpless, dying babies were all fueling Tony's dedication. Death was all around him: in the baby junkies who didn't survive the risky transfer of body fluids; in the eyes of the angry adolescent boys in the street gangs; in the threatening language of the Black Panthers; in the slow erosion of hope in the community. Tony sighs, "Someone needed to take up the slack... Martin wasn't there anymore." So Tony fought back the death demons with grueling hard work and cold determination. "The whole time I was at the hospital I was sleep deprived, noise damaged, and always sick because the babies were always coughing on me. But I believed very strongly that I was at the right place at the right time. I considered myself very fortunate. This was very exciting."

But the smoldering fires and "the death experience" began to burn him out. After a while he began to feel that he "was just a part of the fire department" at Metropolitan. It was necessary, urgent work, but it wasn't sustainable. Tony always felt he was dealing with the surface burning and never with the fire's center. He needed to learn more about the source of the combustion. "I knew I needed to have a better education... I needed to learn how to build new structures to restore some order out of the chaos in these communities. I thought the solutions might be in mental health... After all, mental health was supposed to deal with fragmented minds."

Through the pediatric department at Metropolitan Hospital, Tony had been working closely with the Young Lords, a militant group of Puerto Ricans in East Harlem. He began to see that his help was coming too late in these adolescents' lives, that he would be more effective if he could intervene earlier. And he began to see that the intervention needed to be on mending the "fragmented minds" of young people so they could become strong and resilient human beings. "I began to think that what these kids really needed was mental health," remembers Tony. "I was interested in little kids, catching them early before they get to be rough and tough."

So he went about consulting his various mentors and colleagues about where he might get the best training. He received thoughtful counsel from a devoted teacher, Dr. Susan Gordon, who seemed to combine in her work a clinical commitment to excellent pediatric care and a social and political commitment to transforming the community. Gordon suggested that Tony speak to Stella Chess, a well-known developmentalist and psychiatrist, about her work. She offered to take him on as a short-term apprentice so that he could get a better feel for child psychiatry. He observed Dr. Chess, questioned her, worked with her for a month, and grew increasingly interested in the field of psychiatry. The counsel of both Drs. Gordon and Chess pointed Tony to Leon Eisenberg. From the fires of East Harlem to the bitter cold of Boston, the young black pediatrician journeyed to meet "the best child psychiatrist in the country" with "a thirst to learn more to better society."

Lost Brothers

Tony was immediately drawn to Leon Eisenberg. He liked his forthrightness and his worldliness. He admired the thoughtful way Eisenberg talked about his work. Eisenberg asked good questions and listened carefully. Tony described his work at Metropolitan Hospital and his sense of frustration and futility. He communicated his burning desire to learn more so that he might develop more effective ways of helping communities like East Harlem. He spoke about his love for science and his belief in the transformative power of scientific knowledge. And he articulated his values and his politics. It was a surprisingly comfortable and honest exchange between two men who had only just met.

Dr. Eisenberg must have been impressed with the young doctor who seemed to combine a devotion to scientific research with a commitment to social change. Eisenberg spoke from the heart when he told Tony, "We would love to have you here." But he immediately offered a caution: "You must realize that this is not Harlem." The patient population at Boston's Mass. General would be markedly different from the black and brown patients at Metropolitan Hospital. If Tony decided to come to train at Harvard, he would be working with patients from Charlestown, Revere, the North End—from "the white racist areas." Eisenberg stressed the strong academic program at Harvard but wanted Tony, who was "wanting to help pick up the slack after King's death," to realize that he would not be primarily serving the black community if he decided to come to Boston.

Tony was "somewhat disappointed" by the description of "the culture of Mass. General as being predominantly Italian and Irish." But he was drawn to the rigor and excellence of the training program at Harvard and deeply impressed by Eisenberg's candor. "Leon

was deeply sincere, extremely honest," Tony recalls. "He was so very
genuine... I was completely captivated." By the time he left
Eisenberg's office, he knew that he would accept his offer to come to
Mass. General. Tony tells this story as the first of three tales that
seem to reveal the promising potential of Harvard University as an
institution responsive to moral and ethical concerns. The Eisenberg
meeting—so welcoming of Tony's passions, skills, and politics; so
authentic in its description of the realities of the training program;
so revealing of institutional excellence—seemed to be the first sign
of Harvard's strength and potential. Tony felt challenged and
excited by what he heard and saw that day, and by what he read
between the lines. It is the first experience he turns to when I ask
him why he ever really expected that Harvard would respond to the
"moral implications" of Professor Bell's protest.

"Step two," Tony says as he moves into the second story that
raised his hopes about Harvard's potential for moral leadership.
When he arrived in Boston in 1972, there were two prominent
black psychiatrists at Harvard Medical School, Chester Pierce and
Alvin Poussaint, with whom he worked closely. Both faculty members were important to Tony's feelings of belonging and identification, but Dr. Pierce stood out as a mysterious and powerful mentor.
Tony watched Chester Pierce, tall, strong, and black; hidden
behind dark shades; aggressive and threatening in his silence and
spare in his talk. He admired Pierce's quiet courage, his visionary
perspective, his worldly experiences, and the way he "consistently
called it like it is." But there was one moment that Tony will never
forget; a moment that captured the quintessential "Chester"; a
moment that felt like "a rare gift" to Tony.

It was the end of his psychiatric training, and the third-year residents, "two black men, and about ten or twelve white residents,"
were participating in a concluding seminar on "cultural sensitivity."
The seminar, co-taught by Leon Eisenberg and Chester Pierce, was
run "like a T-group," with the residents learning about their own
cultural obsessions and defenses through interaction and introspection. With the reverberations of the Civil Rights movement
surrounding them, the T-group became a microcosm of the larger

societal struggles. "Week after week Chester would come with his sunglasses on," recalls Tony. "He was mysterious behind those shades. Leon would go on and on pontificating, and occasionally he would manage to draw Chester out." But mostly, the tall, dark senior psychiatrist remained quiet, hearing everything and revealing nothing; his smoldering silence was threatening. During the last session of the group, the final opportunity to extract Pierce's perspective, Mel Williams, the other black resident, questioned him directly. He had been listening hard to Pierce's description of "racism as all-pervasive... a mental health disease." According to Pierce, no white person growing up in our society could escape the malignancy of racism, and no black person could be totally free of the experience of oppression and victimization.

Throughout the seminar, Pierce's assertions had been blunt and all-encompassing. Williams's final question asked that Pierce be specific: "How many white folks do you know who you would not consider to be racist?" The question cut through the air and just hung there "for a very long time," while Chester slowly composed his answer and fueled the high drama. Everyone was visibly relieved when Pierce said that in his lifetime of knowing white folks, he could think of one nonracist. "Thank goodness Leon had made it under the wire," says Tony laughing. But the relief following Pierce's declaration lasted less than a minute before he whispered, "It's a woman in Texas." Eisenberg was not spared. He too was branded with the racist label. "Some white lady in Texas who had adopted a couple of black children" was remembered as a total anomaly; she was the only one free of the most virulent societal disease. "Everyone was stunned," recalls Tony.

Then Pierce did something even more amazing—he removed his shades, squinted his eyes, and directed his gaze on the two black residents. For the first time he came out from behind his dark glasses and let his black male students look directly into his eyes. His voice was dead serious. "I want to say something to Tony and Mel... A lot of black men burn themselves out by the time they are forty... You should have learned one thing here if you learned anything." He was both admonishing them and pleading with them: "You mustn't let yourself get burned out!" With those words, he put his dark glasses back on and fell silent. Tony's eyes are moist as he relives this extraordinary moment. "If someone ever gave me a pearl it was that. I will never, never forget it." He remains deeply thankful to Pierce for "the pearl" of wisdom; for modeling the self-sustaining behavior he was declaring as essential for black male survival; for directing his teaching to his young black colleagues. This was a special moment for Tony and Mel, a moment that would always be seared into their psyches.

"These were my early experiences, and they were very positive," says Tony as he collects the reasons why he was drawn to Harvard and why he continues to believe that it should be, and can be, an institution that deals with "the moral and ethical dilemmas" of our time. For "step three" in his storytelling, Tony skips across the years to 1978, when he returned to Harvard Medical School as a faculty member. He had finished his psychiatric residency, had completed further training in London, and by 1976 had rejoined the staff at Children's Hospital in Boston. He was the newest faculty member sitting on the admissions committee and he was involved in two unusual and controversial admissions decisions.

The first involved a twenty-six-year-old white male applicant who had been incarcerated in Utah after killing both of his parents. After numerous appeals by his lawyers, he had been pardoned by the governor because he had been a model prisoner and because he had been the victim of physical and emotional abuse by his parents. While in prison, he had taught himself premed science courses, becoming deeply knowledgeable about biology. He had completed the college equivalency examinations and had set up, designed, and staffed a first-aid clinic for fellow prisoners. "He was extraordinary," remembers Tony. "He took the MCAT exams and blew the top off the scores... but he also had impeccable integrity." The admissions committee agonized over his application. They talked about the fact that he "had been a victim, that he had been punished unfairly, that he had managed to rise above an abusive family and penal system." There were those, however, who worried about his criminal record—about the horror of killing one's parents whatever the provocation—and the potential embarrassment Harvard Medical School might suffer in admitting a former prisoner. The discussion within the committee was heated and vigorous, but the final decision was to admit him. As a new faculty member, Tony had appreciated the thoughtful, energetic debate among his colleagues and was relieved when they were able to reach a consensus to admit "this extraordinary man."

A few weeks later, however, the decision of the admissions committee somehow leaked out among the student body. "The first-year students found out and they protested vehemently," recalls Tony. "They did not want him among them… He was unacceptable." The students took their case to the dean, claiming that the admission of an ex-criminal would dishonor the entire student body. The dean, "in a most unusual act," decided to override the committee's vote and deny the applicant admission to the medical school. Tony shakes his head—"the man went on to another medical school… He's probably practicing medicine somewhere today."

This story is followed immediately by a similar one that had a different ending; it involved a black applicant from Watts. "This was the late seventies," says Tony, "and medical schools were trying to attract black students." The man from Watts, like the one from Utah, had a criminal record. In his youth, and late adolescence, he had been a heroin addict, and for years he had been very involved in the trafficking of drugs. At a point of despair and desperation, he was "picked up by the Black Muslims" and became a disciplined, hardworking member of their community. Returning to school, he graduated with honors from UCLA, "very well trained, excellently prepared in science." In his admissions statement, the young man was "forthcoming, very open about his drug history and the criminal activity that went with it." Once again, the committee deliberated for a long time. Everyone admired the applicant's courage and purposefulness, and everyone agreed that he was academically prepared and capable. But there was unease and dissension among the members about his early history and about whether he was completely free of his addiction. When the committee could reach no resolution, they decided that they needed more information, and they selected Tony to be their principal interviewer.

Tony describes their first meeting. "He came in the room dressed very conservatively in a suit and all choked up with a bow tie. He was very rigid, very stiff… and he made me sort of uncomfortable." Tony is sitting with his back straight, his legs held tightly together, his mouth drawn in a severe line, showing me the way his interviewee looked. During the interview, the former drug addict said that he wanted to become an anesthesiologist; this statement worried Tony. "I said to myself, 'Come on, man, tell me anything, but don't tell me you want to be an anesthesiologist. How can I take that back to the committee?… Tell me you want to be anything else, a dermatologist, maybe.' For a man who has had a drug problem, anesthesiology is not the wise choice!" After an hour of talking, Tony still felt he did not know this man. He distrusted his own discomfort, and he also knew that the applicant must have been feeling reticent about making open disclosures. He had no idea of what to recommend to the committee. So Tony suggested that they meet again. In fact, the two of them ended up having several meetings, trusting each other more and more each time and peeling back the layers of history and experience. "Ultimately," recalls Tony, "I grew to like him very much." He took a strong recommendation back to the committee, and they decided to admit the applicant. The following fall, the Black Muslim from Watts came to Harvard, and four years later he graduated with distinction.

Even though the second tale of the California man concludes with a happy ending, the first tale of the committee's deliberation about the Utah man and the reversal by the dean is also told as a sample of the "positive experiences" Tony has had at Harvard. In both cases, the discourse within the committee was spirited, controversial, "real." The members confronted "the moral dimensions" of these two life stories. They didn't hide behind bureaucratic reasoning and language. In the heated exchanges, they took off their administrative masks and revealed their fears and biases. It is this unmasking, this authenticity that Tony cites as "the positive side of being here."

But these positive experiences—the warm welcome by Eisenberg, the mentoring by Pierce, the genuine controversy within the admissions committee—have been counterbalanced by "negative experiences." As a matter of fact, the positive experiences are high-lighted against a backdrop of negative experiences. Tony puts it this way: "The negative stuff was continuing day to day... a chronic scratching away at the surface. The positive stuff was punctuated, episodic, but not sustainable." The everyday "microaggressions," as his mentor Pierce described them, were usually invisible, habitual, and cumulative in their impact. You had to ignore most of the sub-tle assaults and spend valuable energy deciding to which ones you would respond. Because the microaggressions were so minor, so much a part of the texture of daily life, they were harder to identify and capture in story form. Tony's face grows noticeably somber as he tries to describe the "chronic scratching away at the surface."

"When I returned from London in 1976 to join the faculty at Harvard, I did all the right things: I was getting big grants... I was setting up independent research projects... I was publishing papers in refereed journals... I was building a career. It would not have been inaccurate to call me a rising star." But all of these efforts required great determination and tenacity, and the medical school environment felt resistant and inhospitable. Tony offers an under-statement: "Nobody was making it easy for me." Most of the resis-tance seemed to take the form of bureaucratic inertia. For instance, when the money from a large grant came in and Tony was able to hire more research assistants, he would be denied additional office space. Even now Tony casts around for the reasons why his col-leagues and supervisors "kept on putting hurdles in my path." He wants to be fair in his assessment. "I never convinced myself that it was *primarily* racist... but racial discomfort was always there."

He knew, for example, that "in the culture of Harvard... beyond the issue of race... you were not supposed to rise from within." After your training you were supposed to leave Harvard, build a big career elsewhere, then return after you had proved yourself a star. Tony's almost immediate reentry into the Harvard orbit raised some eyebrows and caused discomfort. Tony also knew that "beyond the issue of race" within all faculties, there was likely to be per-sonal and professional competition and jealousies. He remembers one of his primary supervisors who grew increasingly competitive as

Tony became more and more successful. "As my reputation grew and I began to bring in more money, he became my big competitor." When one of Tony's early papers received a great deal of attention and the requests for reprints began to flood the collective mailbox that they shared, the supervisor winced in frustration. "He just lost it one day... he began screaming that he couldn't find his mail because of all the requests for this *flaky* paper I had written... He was furious. He said this to another colleague behind my back."

Tony surmises that there would be competition as well for a "rising star" who was white and male. He knows that the hierarchies of academic medicine, particularly at Harvard, reinforce the collegial conflicts. He does not have a trail of dramatic stories to tell that expose overt institutional and interpersonal racism. Nevertheless, he emphasizes "the chronic" and subtle "negative experiences" that wear down one's spirit. Finally, he gave in and decided to leave Harvard, a decision based more on frustration and weariness than on specific grievances. "Basically, I had to admit to myself that I found Harvard an insensitive place. I felt unsupported in my work. It was just a difficult place to function in. By 1980, I resolved that I had to leave Harvard."

Pierce's admonition to Tony not to let himself get burned out may have been part of Tony's calculation when he decided to leave Harvard. Rather than continue submitting himself to the microaggressions of an environment that was not explicitly racist but had "racial discomfort," he would move on to a place that would welcome him with open arms. Pierce's warnings also reminded Tony of all the talented young black men who burn out before they have the chance to grow up, who are victimized by explicit or subtle violence and oppression. His own memories of loss are bitter and personal.

He remembers Clarence Gamble, his classmate and "good buddy" as an undergraduate at Howard University in Washington, D.C. They were both lovers of science, both majored in chemistry, but Gamble was a more dedicated and serious student than Tony. Gamble studied science with an aggressive intensity. It was his life. Tony's approach was much more "diversified." He was eclectic in his interests. Both of them had a special aptitude and affinity for chemistry. (In eleventh grade, Tony had been anointed Mr. Chemistry at Booker T. Washington High School in Memphis, Tennessee; he had received a big science prize and had been written up in the local newspaper.) Tony's voice is excited as he remembers their differences and their deep bond. "He and I were the smartest dudes in chemistry. He was a much more intensely devoted student in science... but we were linked. We knew things others didn't know... We were close buddies because we were smart."

They had met during their freshman year in a huge first-year chemistry course taught by a Finnish taskmaster. Out of the three hundred students in the lecture class, Clarence and Tony were clearly the top students. When, at the end of the course, the professor had them take the national exam in chemistry, both of them scored in the ninety-eighth percentile. Gamble graduated with honors and was the first black person to be admitted to Johns Hopkins School of Medicine in 1963. "He was an extraordinary guy, and this was an extraordinary door he entered... admitted to the best medical school!" Gamble was so intense. From day one he knew he wanted to go to medical school. Tony speaks about the contrast with his own experience: "I had no real interest in going to medical school. I only went because my dad pressured me into going. I wanted to do graduate work in chemistry and be a researcher... I studied medicine for the *science*, not for the career. And I chose Howard Medical School because I thought I could continue doing all the things I wanted to do for the next four years... I thought if I went to medical school, I'd get my father off my back." His face is halfway between a smile and a frown. Then he laughs—"That's another story... but it didn't get him off my back, of course." Tony recognizes that he has followed a path that he doesn't want to pursue, at least for now, and he turns back to his story about his buddy Gamble. "He finished medical school successfully... with a great record. A couple of years later his wife killed him." I am shocked by the story's quick conclusion, and I let the stunning silence hang in the air. "Tragic, tragic," whispers Tony with a heavy sadness. "I'm talking about a talented, achieving, gifted, intense black man. I'm talking about tragedy."

Gamble's death reminds him of a story that is much more sketchy. He can barely recall the boy's first name and can't remember his last name, but his image is seared forever in Tony's memory. So is the promise and tragedy of his short life. When Tony was a high school student at Booker T. Washington, a boy named James came from "a tiny rural town in Mississippi" to Memphis so he could go to a decent school. He had been identified as a smart, disciplined student whose talents could be expanded by a more demanding education than he would have gotten in Mississippi. James excelled in high school, went on to college, and in 1968 was the first black to be admitted to the University of Mississippi Medical School. But in his first year there, he developed a very serious case of hypertension, "probably related to the enormous stress he was under... and he came close to dying." Tony shakes his head—"So he had to drop out... All that amazing work and talent, and he had to drop out."

Now Tony's eyes are filled with tears and his voice is husky as he pulls together the Clarence and James tragedies. "Sara, I'm talking about *loss*... They were my friends... There was talent connecting us... We were buddies through science." He seems to be missing them, longing for their "collegiality" and their shared passion for science. He is leaning forward in his chair with Bearden's jazz musicians playing behind him and Miles Davis's brooding eyes seeming to weep for the loss, the black brother loss. "Clarence, James, and I were like musicians who play together... who develop a bond, a communion."

New Orleans

Tony Earls was born in New Orleans on January 20, 1942, the firstborn child of Felton II and Ethelyn Earls. He smiles softly: "This year my fiftieth birthday coincided with [the celebration of] Martin Luther King's birthday... a wonderful gift for me." "By any standard you can think of, we were middle-class," begins Tony. Like many of the people in his extended family, his father had gone to Dillard University in New Orleans and gotten an M.A. at Atlanta University. After completing his graduate studies, his father had begun working for the post office and had risen rapidly through the ranks. Tony's mother stayed home ("You would call her a homemaker today") cooking, cleaning, and raising children. She had gone to high school, spent some time training in business school, but had never attended college.

The Earls family has deep roots in New Orleans and the surrounding countryside. The generations were close and passed down a genuine attachment to the culture, lore, and rituals of New Orleans. "One of the great fortunes of my early life," beams Tony, "is the presence of my grandparents on both sides." His paternal grandmother, Alberta Earls, lived right next door, and Tony visited her every day. His maternal grandparents, Clarence and Beatrice Lefebvre, lived in another neighborhood, but Tony could get on his bicycle and ride over there. Beatrice and Clarence were Creole and spoke patois. But when Tony would go over to see them, they would not allow him to speak their family tongue because they "thought it was a sign of poor education." The Earls and Lefebvre clans spread their branches and roots throughout the city, but most of them lived either downtown, around Second Street, or uptown close to Chestnut. There were lots of family gatherings and everyday contact with the extended family. For a young child growing up, this large family seemed like a big protective blanket, a source of security and rootedness.

But as Tony tries to reconstruct his childhood memories of his family, he is at first vague and then reticent. He knows that he is "inventing" much of the reconstruction. "This kind of retrospective assessment never feels completely authentic," he admits. "It is very difficult for me to generate comparative ideas about my childhood... It was just what I knew." The large, lively, imposing extended family, the grandparental closeness, the deep roots in the "parochial culture" of New Orleans all felt "ordinary" and natural when he was a child. As a matter of fact, when Tony tries to give me a picture of this "ordinary" childhood, his sentences underscore what it was *not* like. His words are measured, cautious as he reaches for authenticity (not drama or romanticism). "I didn't have a stressful childhood," he reports. "There were no catastrophic events that I can recall. I would characterize the environment of my childhood as safe, comfortable, and predictable."

"The big tree on the street in front of the house," with its gnarled spreading roots, its big green shade cover, was the neighborhood boys' haven and hangout. "I played marbles under that tree all my growing-up years... It was probably a three-foot square space where the neighborhood kids and I would gather... It was a very secure feeling." When Tony left the safety of home base, he would venture off around the city on his bicycle. From the time he was eight or nine, he owned a bicycle and would ride over to his grandparents' place, and by the time he was twelve, he would "ride around the whole city."

The Earlses' house was a "duplex," with his grandmother Alberta and her roomer living on the other side, which was "a mirror image" of their place. "In those days it was called a shotgun house. Every room was right behind the next one—living room, bedrooms, and the kitchen, like the caboose of a train." There were two bedrooms and a back porch, which was converted into a bedroom when the younger children arrived. From the back porch you could look out on a tiny backyard with flowers and trees. But in front the house rose right up on the street.

Tony remembers the mix of people who lived on his block. "It was an all-black community of mixed social classes." His father, for example, thought of himself as solidly and comfortably middle-class. "He was an administrator in the post office and had risen up through the ranks from mail handler to a very high government grade." There were other neighbors who were teachers. "But there were also families on my street who were barely making it. I don't even know if they had welfare back then, but these were families who would be eligible for welfare today… father out of work or alcoholic." The stability and decorum of the Earls family contrasted greatly with the vulnerability and chaos of some of the poor folks on the block, but Tony remembers that the social class differences were almost meaningless to the neighborhood kids. "For the kids, it didn't matter much. For us, two things mattered: first, how talented you were as a musician and second, what kind of ballplayer you were."

It was only when they moved to Memphis, Tennessee, when Tony was fourteen years old, that he began to recognize social class hierarchies. In "the informal environment" of New Orleans, class did not seem to be as divisive or as important to black folks' assessment of one another as it was in Memphis. The Earlses moved from their deep roots in New Orleans because of the lure of a big promotion in the postal ranks for Tony's father, and they moved into a fancier, more rigidly defined black society, "a bourgeois community." As a young adolescent, Tony noticed the contrasts between his new city and his "beloved" New Orleans, and he resented the formality and exclusivity of the Memphis community. With the family's move to Memphis, Tony began to recognize the special characteristics of the "ordinary life" he experienced in New Orleans. The contrasts between these two southern cities offered early and important lessons in the values and norms that define community.

Part of the comfort and safety of Tony's early childhood was a reflection of his mother's nourishing presence in the home. She seemed to be there all the time, keeping watch, offering help and guidance, cooking and cleaning. Even as a child, Tony noticed and appreciated the work his mother did around the house and viewed it as more demanding than his father's labors at the post office. "My mother put a great deal of effort into taking care of the household and a great deal of effort into caring for my father, who didn't do anything to assist her," recalls Tony. "There was a very sharp division of labor along gender lines... I didn't like that. It just didn't seem right to me that she should be doing all the work." I am impressed with this child's eye view of the inequalities between the work and rewards of his mother's and father's lives, and I ask Tony how he came to that consciousness. He shrugs his shoulders and is quiet for a moment, then says tentatively, "I always knew that she had aspirations that were unfulfilled. As a mother at home with an only child, she and I spent a lot of time together... and I seemed to develop an under-standing of and an identification with her predicament."

For the first eight years of Tony's life he was an only child. The memories are vague and disjointed, but Tony pieces together the time right after his birth when his father, who was enlisted in the army, "was sent to Asia, the Philippines, or somewhere over there. I must have lived alone with my mom for the first couple of years." His father stayed in Asia until the end of the war but remained in the army until 1946 or 1947. "My earliest memories are of going around to various army bases where my father was stationed." A few years after they had been settled back in New Orleans, the second child, Carol, arrived. "My father was going up the ladder at the post office... With a steady job and a comfortable life, my parents prob-ably thought that it was a good time to have more kids."

Having enjoyed his privileged status as an only child, and the undiluted intimacy of his mother's attention, Tony did not welcome his sister with an open heart. A grin spreads over his face—"I was at least ambivalent about her arrival. Of course, there are all kinds of stories of how I tried to do her in... pushing her carriage off the porch... and various other homicidal attacks." Two years later, brother Phillip arrived, and after a ten-year hiatus, the youngest daughter, Lynne (after her mother Ethelyn), was born. By the time Lynne arrived, Tony was already a sophomore in college. He recalls the shocking news that greeted him when he came home for the summer after his freshman year. "My mother sat me down and said with a very serious face, 'I have something to tell you... I'm pregnant.'" Tony's face still looks stunned, and we both laugh. "I never expected to hear that." Although he never inquired of his mother, Tony suspects that the pregnancy was "not intentional." There is some sadness in his voice as Tony admits to not ever getting the chance to know his youngest sibling because of the huge age gap.

By far the most important part of Tony's young life in New Orleans was music. He says forcefully, "I don't remember caring for much except this." When he was five or six, he started his musical training on the clarinet under the exacting tutelage of his uncle Oscar Hansberry. Hansberry, the brother of Tony's paternal grand-mother, was a very prominent musician and bandleader in New Orleans. Called "the Professor" by all the locals, he had a "big repu-tation" as a serious, classically trained musician. He had gotten his music degree at Fisk University, which at that time "had a very dis-tinguished department," and had returned to New Orleans with the goal of training youngsters to become skilled and disciplined musi-cians. His After School Music Program, which Tony attended every day, attracted fifty or sixty children, many of them from families too poor to buy them instruments or afford music lessons. Hansberry, whose passion was music but who made a living running a grocery store and dabbling in real estate, would provide instruments for the children who couldn't afford them and give them lessons for free.

The music school was Hansberry's love, his life, his calling. He saw musical training as much more than an aesthetic experience. It was, as well, training in discipline, punctuality, poise, and deco-rum. It was training in responsibility and citizenship, and Hansberry was the uncompromising, powerful autocrat. Tony's memories of his uncle are vivid. "My uncle was a dominant creature. He had strong and powerful ideas. There were a lot of kids who came from families where there was not a whole lot of parental guidance. They were sort of undisciplined, wild kids... and with all of us, my uncle was the autocrat. He required total obedience, total silence... If you dis-obeyed you were likely to get slapped... He had a *whip*." I shiver in response to Tony's picture of this "dominant creature" who whipped children into shape, but Tony's voice seems to express pure admiration and deep respect. As Tony gives an example of the intensity and threat that were part of his uncle's teaching, he seems to turn into the autocrat, pointing, gesticulating, yelling. "Say we were playing something like the 'Poet and Peasant Overtures'—We didn't play jazz. We played classical music, hymns, spirituals, band pieces. My uncle insisted that we learn the fundamentals… that it was important to get a strict training in the classical roots of music—he'd abruptly stop the playing, total silence, point to one kid, and scream, 'You go back to line so-and-so and play it by yourself'… He'd give the kid a couple of chances to get it right, but if in the playing the kid revealed he hadn't practiced, my uncle would get very angry and occasionally use the whip… It was real public humiliation." The stinging punishment was fairly evenly distributed, however, and it was always based on performance and achievement, not aptitude or social standing. Even within the atmosphere of threat, Tony always admired his uncle's evenhandedness. "He was really very democratic. He believed that *anybody* could play well. *Motivation* was most important, not talent." Tony lets out a big laugh—"And my uncle was the great motivator!"

But Hansberry's admonitions and punishments were not restricted to music. He infiltrated the entire life of "his boys," insinuating his values and his standards through a kind of invisible scrutiny. "He would also humiliate kids about things *not* having to do with music," recalls Tony. "In band practice he'd say, 'I saw you doing such and such on the corner the other day,' or 'Your mother told me that they caught you stealing a loaf of bread,' or 'Your teacher told me you are flunking your subjects.'" The Professor had eyes in the back of his head and antennae that reached across the community. He was everywhere. Tony sums him up: "He was kind, but he was also ferocious."

As his nephew, Tony felt a special sense of apprehension and responsibility. Every day after school he would hop on his bike and ride over to band practice. His uncle seemed larger than life, a demanding, consuming force. "I was definitely afraid of him… and I think as his nephew he treated me specially… in small, subtle ways… But I also practiced a lot, all the time. I felt a responsibility to act right so as not to disappoint him." Tony became very proficient on the clarinet, and "competent" on the flute, his second instrument, under his uncle's watchful and demanding instruction. Later on, he realized that his uncle's teachings required rigor but didn't necessarily encourage creativity. "I became a very good musician *technically*," Tony recognizes in retrospect. "But I discovered by the time I got to Memphis that I didn't *hear* music that well... As I got more involved in playing jazz, I realized that I could read music well, but I had a hard time keeping up with the transitions and changes in jazz." But music remained a powerful motivating force in his life. The chord structures, the improvisation, the freedom, the dance, the cultural connection continue to shape Tony's social and intellectual life. He repeats for emphasis, "As I look back on growing up, music was always the most important thing in my life. It was always much more intense than school. School did not have the same kind of intensity or centrality in my life."

Tony's memories of school do seem vague. "I don't have a lot of running memories of elementary school," he admits. There are snatches of recall, like when he was elected King of the School in third grade, a very prized honor based on popularity among his peers and good grades from his teachers. All across the city, the honor was being bestowed on one child from each public school as part of the celebration of Mardi Gras. Tony reminds me, "You know, in New Orleans, Mardi Gras is bigger than Christmas or New Year's. It's a huge deal." And he remembers a French teacher he had in fifth and sixth grades who "opened me up to new and exciting experiences." A man who had a certain mystery and savoir faire about him, "[the teacher] traveled a lot to faraway places. He was a Creole. He looked different from anyone I'd ever seen—light-skinned, very debonair and cultured. In dress and mannerisms, he was like a Frenchman, maybe from Martinique. I think he was the first man I ever saw who parted his hair—straight, silky hair—down the middle. He spoke with an accent, a musical cadence... His strangeness was captivating." The French teacher's exotic style, and his enthusiastic teaching, was thrilling to the ten-year-old. "I *loved* it." The man—his style, accent, dress—seemed inseparable from the language he taught.

Although the memories of elementary school are sparse, they are mostly benign. Tony recalls "enjoying school," "interesting teachers," and "superior" achievement. With discipline, but without too much effort, he was almost always at the top of his class. He was a voracious reader and was possessed with a "burning curiosity." "I always had a thirst for knowledge," says Tony. "I was a question asker… but the questions were inner directed—to myself, not others. I was interested in figuring out how things worked… But I always believed that *I* could figure it out." School was enjoyable, comfortable, but never as challenging as the interior intellectual life that Tony created for himself. "Academics were always easy," recalls Tony nonchalantly.

When Tony was eleven years old, he had to have his tonsils taken out. In those days, the surgery was a "much bigger deal than it is today," requiring a few days of hospitalization. His parents thought it would be nice to give him a present to honor his courage in going through with the surgery, and they asked him what he wanted. The extravagance of Tony's request surprised them, but not the substance. Tony smiles at the memory—"I said I wanted a set of encyclopedias, and they got them for me." It was a rare and wonderful gift. Tony savored every page. "I read the hell out of those books." Using the illustrations as a guide, he worked his way through the entire set of imposing volumes. "I'd see the pictures of pyramids and camels and read all the text about Egypt… or I'd notice the sketch of a stage set and read about the theater." He loved those books, the vast amount of facts and information they contained. He devoted endless hours to poring over the pages. Tony says proudly, "My folks still have that set of encyclopedias." When they bought them for Tony forty years ago, they were the only books the Earlses owned. "It was thought that you didn't have to have anything else if you had the encyclopedias," explains Tony. "My parents got me those books because they knew I'd use them… they could see I loved reading, questioning, knowledge." Very early it was clear that Tony was "an intellectual." No one in his family chose that path, but Tony clearly appreciates his folks' support of his interests and passions. "My father was definitely not an intellectual. He was an administrator, a bureaucrat... probably my uncle Oscar was the closest one in my family to being an intellectual because he had gotten his master's in music at Fisk and people called him Professor... but he was not an intellectual."

Tony's comfortable achievement in elementary school continued through the fifth grade. "Then there was sixth grade," he exclaims with great drama. "Sixth grade was extraordinary, momentous." He pauses theatrically, leans forward, and says in a stage whisper, "I discovered a *girl!*" Sara Nell Owens was her name, and she became Tony's total preoccupation. "All of what school stood for suddenly collapsed... I was madly in love with her." Tony thought about Sara constantly, gazed upon her longingly in class, and lingered outside her house for hours waiting for her to come out of her door and stand by the front fence for conversation. It was an innocent, loving relationship. Recalls Tony with a soft smile, "We didn't really need a lot of contact to satisfy. Both of us were nice kids, and neither of us wanted to push this. There was something kind of sweet about it."

Sara was Tony's passion, but she also represented safety and familiarity. Although she was a sixth-grade discovery, they had been classmates since the beginning of elementary school. "She lived right around the corner from us, which also made her feel comfortable and reachable." When I ask Tony why he chose Sara, his answer is immediate: "Well, she was beautiful." "How did she look?" I ask. "Well, she was lighter than I am, a little taller... we were all enjoying our puberty then...." But Sara's physical attractiveness does not seem to have been at the heart of his love for her. "She was kind, good, comfortable." Then Tony seems to warm to the real root of his passion. "We were both smart, both in the academic classes... She may have been an academic competitor... I do not remember distinctly, but there may have been a sense of rivalry that helped galvanize my interest." The memories are "sweet," poignant, and Tony's face glows as he sums up the year of "enjoying his puberty": "My memory of that time is primarily organized around Sara."

By the time Tony was fourteen he was facing what he now refers to as "the first traumatic event in my life." His parents decided they would move the family to Memphis, because they couldn't refuse the promotion his father had been offered by the post office. This promotion brought an attractive advance in salary and status and would make Felton II the "highest ranking federal officer in the city of Memphis," the site of the regional headquarters of the post office. When Tony heard the news of the impending move he was devastated, enraged. He couldn't believe his parents would inflict this kind of dislocation and suffering on him. He loved everything about New Orleans: the music, the food, the art, the informality, the familiarity. He couldn't imagine leaving his huge extended family, forsaking the loving embrace of grandparents, aunts, uncles, and cousins. "I was being ripped out by the roots," says Tony with a trace of bitterness left in his voice. "There is nothing that my parents have ever done that has made me angrier... and I still live with the disappointment. *This was my most profound, long-lasting loss.*"

It was not only excruciating to be torn away from his "beloved New Orleans"; it was also difficult for Tony to feel comfortable in Memphis. "I'd been pulled up by the roots... replanting in Memphis was not a good take." The atmosphere of Memphis seemed formal, traditional, and staid compared to the sensuous, jazzy style of New Orleans. Tony also felt that Memphis was a much more class-conscious city. Compared to the neighborhood in New Orleans that had a comfortable mixture of black folks from every social class, the neighborhood and social scene the Earlses entered in Memphis were almost exclusively upper-middle-class. Part of the bourgeois mantle reflected his father's elevated position in the post office. "His arrival in Memphis was celebrated... providing an easy entry into a set of professional and social activities," recalls Tony. His parents were almost immediately swept up into the social whirl of parties, sororities, clubs, and community work, and they took their children along in their wake. "I was a member of Jack and Jill... I was forced into all of that elitist stuff."

Tony never liked Memphis. On the outside, it appeared that he was successfully accommodating to the new scene, but on the inside he remained resistant and alien. He entered ninth grade at Booker T. Washington High School, one of the premiere public schools in the South, and was an achiever in every dimension. "Four years in what was considered the best high school... I was lead clarinetist in the school band, the best student in science, touted as Mr. Chemistry by the Memphis newspaper... good grades, at the top of my class, president of my senior class. But the sum of it is, I never did get used to Memphis. It was an okay place... *but it was not New Orleans.*" Tony shakes his head at the haunting power of his birthplace—"New Orleans is so deep inside of me."

The Roots of Improvisation

When Tony mourns his family's move to Memphis, he pictures the large, close extended family he left behind: the grandparents, aunts, uncles, and cousins whom he had seen almost every day. Most especially, he pictures his grandparents—both maternal and paternal—who were powerful and influential forces in his life. Clarence and Beatrice Lefebvre, Tony's maternal grandparents, lived on the other side of town from the Earlses in a "clean and organized" home with a beautiful garden in the backyard. Clarence devoted lots of energy and time to creating the luscious flower patches. Although Tony now recognizes that his grandfather's talents made a tiny plot seem grand and imposing, as a small child the backyard seemed to be "the size of a football field." The Lefebvres lived downtown on Second Street, about three miles, or half-an-hour's bike ride from the Earlses' house, uptown on Chestnut Street. Each day Tony would pass their house on his bicycle as he headed over to band practice at his uncle Oscar's house, which was right around the corner. At least once or twice a week, Tony would stop in at Clarence and Beatrice's for a visit.

Clarence Lefebvre, who died in 1975 when Tony was thirty-three, is remembered by Tony with appreciation and pride. Tony smiles as he describes his grandfather whose brown skin was "about my color," and who had "beautiful gray, silky, straight hair." "You can imagine," says Tony straightening himself up into an elegant pose, "what that combination of skin tone and hair texture and color looked like... extraordinarily handsome." Clarence was a civilian in the army, a quartermaster, a kind of supply clerk on a base close to the city. "It was a steady, stable government job with medical benefits and social security." His civilian work contrasted sharply with his young life in the army. Tony warms up to the colorful family lore, one of his favorite historic accounts. Clarence, a Creole, was a soldier in World War I, fighting with a brigade of French-speaking black men in France. The Negro troop was sent to the most dangerous region on the border between France and Germany, near Strasbourg, where they fought on the front lines. Their black lives were not considered as precious as those of the white American soldiers who were not sent into the raging region of Alsace. "Clarence was a brave soldier... He fought courageously and won a Medal of Legion from the French." Tony's voice turns from admiration to cynicism as he says, "Of course, all he got from the American army was the civilian job."

In 1978, when Tony, his wife, Mary, and their daughters were traveling in Europe, they visited Strasbourg hoping to trace the roots of this proud family legacy. They were strolling along the streets of Strasbourg when an old man passed them, "a man about the age of my grandfather, a white farmer-looking guy." The old man slowed up, then stopped and stared at Tony, a long, intense scrutiny. Tony felt the charged gaze. The old man seemed to be studying his face. "It was the eeriest, strangest feeling," recalls Tony. "He seemed to recognize something in me... he seemed to want to reach out." It was only a moment in time, but it was charged with feeling. The old man turned away slowly and sauntered down the street leaving Tony stunned. "Did the old farmer see my grandfather in me?" The Earlses then stopped in at a small café, where they sat down at a table and noticed the napkins. "It was amazing," says Tony. "The napkins had on them a picture of a black Sambo-like figure and the words, 'Bon Negro'—Good Negro. I looked at the picture and instead of getting furious at the negative caricature, like I usually would, I felt a connection, a sense of appreciation... In their own way they were trying to say that black people saved our lives... which is what my grandfather had always said."

Tony's maternal grandmother, Beatrice, had "very light skin... She could pass for white." Also of Creole origins, she was a large woman of poise and elegance. Although Tony never regarded her as domineering when he was a child, he sees her now as a woman with a "domineering pose" and thinks that she was probably "fairly overwhelming" to his grandfather, who was "shorter than she... calm and imperturbable." (I look over at brown-skinned Tony—centered, gentle, and clear-minded—and suspect that he must feel a strong identification with his mother's father, a connection born out of calm and courage.) To young Tony, Beatrice always seemed to be on the move—organizing things, planning meetings, leading groups. "She was a movement person, lots and lots of causes... worked hard for the Methodist Church." One of her favorite causes, to which she gave an enormous amount of time and energy, was the Eastern Stars, a Negro women's group steeped in ceremony and ritual. Clarence was a proud member of the Masons, the man's chapter of this "mysterious organization."

Although as a child Tony knew that the proud brothers in the Masons and the staunch sisters in the Eastern Stars were deeply involved in their organizations, he always wondered what all of the pageantry was about. The men wore large cylindrical hats with tassels, ribbons, and metals. The women wore starched white dresses with colorful Eastern Star banners, diagonally decorating their breasts. They had formal parades and elaborate gatherings. Tony shakes his head—"I spent a lot of time as a child trying to penetrate what it meant to be a Mason... There was great mystery and magic shrouding the whole thing. It was deeply symbolic... They seemed to talk in a different language." In their mystery and pageantry the Masons and the Eastern Stars seemed to melt right into the New Orleans cultural idiom. "You see, in New Orleans," explains Tony, "a lot of life is organized around funerals, and the Masons and Eastern Stars were enthusiastic participants. Funerals are more important and ritualized than weddings or births. They are real elaborate affairs going on for three or four days—first the wake, then the service, then the parade, then the house party—lots of music, wonderful food, extremely emotional." He throws his head back with a big laugh—"So if you have three or four funerals, then Christmas, New Year's, and Mardi Gras... the year is done!"

Clarence and Beatrice had two daughters, both born in New Orleans. Mildred was three years younger than Tony's mother, Ethelyn. Mildred had one son named Herbert, after his father, who was two years younger than Tony and became his close friend. When Herbert was three or four years old, his parents divorced and his father moved to California. When she became a single parent and sole breadwinner, Mildred returned to work, and Beatrice and Clarence took over most of the childcare duties for young Herbert. The boy cousins played several times a week at their grandparents' home. By the time Herbert was about nine, he was having a lot of behavior problems in school and becoming difficult for his mother to manage. Although Tony knows none of the details leading up to Herbert's moving in with Clarence and Beatrice, he vividly recalls the trouble his cousin was both having and causing, and his grandparents taking over the primary responsibility for him. "Herbert remained with them through high school," remembers Tony. "It was a real strain."

It is Herbert that Tony thinks of when I ask him to trace the origin of his two names (Felton, his given name; Tony, his nickname) that seem to bear no relationship to one another. When Herbert was a little boy, he could not say his big cousin's name. "Felton" was too hard, so Herbert came up with a name he could pronounce, "Tunny." Herbert's Tunny caught on with most of the family members and friends, although it was never used by his teachers and classmates in school. In addition, since Tony's father was also a Felton, it was hard to distinguish who was being referred to—Felton the Second, or Felton the Third. "So although Tunny was very childish, it served a dual purpose." Tony's parents, however, never used Tunny. At one point, in an effort to clarify things, Ethelyn began to refer to Tony as "Little Felton," a name her son "absolutely despised." "I hated that!" says Tony, recoiling at the sound. "You see, people said I looked just like my father... They would say, 'You're the spitting image of your dad'... I despised that, not because there was anything wrong about resembling him... it's just that I thought there must be more to life than being an absolute replica of my father."

When the Earlses moved to Memphis, Tony "put away the childish nickname" Tunny and became Felton to everyone he met during high school, college, and medical school. "I stopped that altogether... just didn't think about it," says Tony forcefully, as if the one appealing part of the transition to the new city is that it allowed him to get rid of the infantilizing nickname. In 1967, having graduated from Howard Medical School, he moved to Madison, Wisconsin, to do graduate work at the University of Wisconsin. There was an old professor there, one of his mentors, named Jerzy Rose ("He had a pretty wonderful name himself!") who said that they needed to find another name for him: Felton was too formal, too strange sounding, too difficult to remember. Tony's voice is surprisingly casual as he recalls his response to Jerzy Rose's playful request. "So I thought about my old childhood name Tunny and massaged it a little into Tony." Then, as if he regards his new nickname as reflecting only his adult identity, Tony concludes, "I don't think about it as connecting to my childhood especially." Now both names—Tony and Felton—seem to be used interchangeably by family, friends, and colleagues. In formal professional circles, on his speeches and articles, Felton is always used, and his mother still steadfastly calls him by his given name. But mostly people pick and choose what feels comfortable to them. Tony smiles—"My two sisters vacillate. They use Felton when we're talking seriously and Tony when we are just playing around. My brother Phillip always calls me Tony."

Alberta Hansberry Earls, Tony's paternal grandmother, was born and raised in a country town in Louisiana. She and her four siblings labored hard on the small family farm and moved to New Orleans as adults. They loved the city and never looked back. Tony recalls, "I don't know why they never talked about their life in the country. We never heard about it or saw the place... real nebulous. They must have been very enterprising people because they all worked hard and purposively... They all had a level of security." Alberta married Felton James Earls I, who died when Tony's father was a small boy. Felton II could barely remember his father, and his mother's silence did not fill in the empty pictures. "Alberta never talked about her husband much, and she never remarried," recalls Tony. Like her life on the farm, her husband disappeared into the past.

Alberta's life was "quiet." "She was to herself a lot... Over the years she had male roomers living in her house, but these were not romances or even friendships." Tony pauses. "Actually, I don't know about her life with other men, but I suspect she was alone. She never had many guests." Tony contrasts Alberta's solitary, quiet existence with the active, social life of Beatrice, who was "always moving, always going, always involved." Both grandmothers were deeply religious, but Alberta was a faithful Baptist who attended Sunday church services, prayed daily, but remained private in her spiritual devotion. For Beatrice, a Methodist, church was the hub of a great deal of social, religious, and political activity, much of which she organized and led. Alberta and Beatrice were also different physically: Beatrice was tall, imposing, and light-skinned; Alberta was shorter and darker. Tony's description of her focuses on her African roots. "Alberta was a little darker than I am... She was African-American... you know, some mixture of origins in the New World, but originally out of West Africa... She had the facial and hair characteristics of Africa."

Every day after school Tony would visit with Alberta. When she arrived home from her work as a housekeeper in the French Quarter, Tony would hear her weary footsteps mounting the stairs of their duplex. For years, Alberta worked for the old prizefighter, Peter Herman, cooking, cleaning, and organizing his life. At the height of his boxing career, Herman had been the featherweight champion of the world, and he was a local hero in New Orleans. His fighting days abruptly ended when he was hit so hard in the head that he was permanently blinded. "It was a real tragedy," says Tony, "and my grandmother took care of him for all the years I was growing up." Hard-working, loyal, and quietly observant, she was Peter Herman's eyes. When she returned home from work in the late afternoon, she would bring luscious pastries from the French Quarter. "The pastries were a great lure. I would come over after school and eat up those pastries."

The pastries may have been Alberta's "lure," but the visits were important to grandmother and grandson. "From the time I was about seven until I was about fourteen, I spent part of every afternoon with my grandmother." Tony recalls, "Most of her contact with our family was through me." They would sit together munching goodies and talking. Their conversations were slow and meandering with long quiet interludes. Frequently, Alberta would talk about her illnesses, her high blood pressure or her aching bunions. She'd report to Tony on her visits to the doctor. ("The doctor told her that salt was like poison for people with high blood pressure.") Then she'd ask Tony for his advice: "Do you really think he knows what he is talking about?" Tony would take her queries seriously; he'd "go read some books to find out," and report back to her what he had discovered. Tony's early interest in his grandmother's maladies, his careful listening to her descriptions of discomfort and pain, his pursuit of "scientific explanations" and medical diagnoses may have been related to his choice to pursue medicine later on. "It may have had something to do with my becoming a doctor," says Tony thoughtfully. "It certainly fascinated me."

Remembering his daily visits with Alberta makes Tony want to paint in the rest of his colorful childhood in his big New Orleans family. His voice is filled with nostalgia. "I've told you about my uncle Mack Hansberry's place, 'The Little Harlem,' haven't I?" Mack, Oscar and Alberta's brother, ran a famous "joint" where some of the best food in town was served and some of the hottest jazz was heard. Fats Domino played regularly at Mack's place. People would crowd into the place "and jam 'til morning." Tony is smiling at all the memories that come flooding back when he thinks of the place. Seminola, Mack's wife, was just as beautiful as her name, and she could really cook. From the tiny kitchen in the back she would serve up the most fantastic "catfish, oysters, crab, shrimps, and barbecued ribs." Tony is licking his lips. Mack and Seminola lived in an apartment right over The Little Harlem. Since they sold the place long ago, it has probably changed hands fifteen times, and the neighborhood around there has now become seedy and dangerous. Mack has long since "passed on," but Seminola—lovely in her aged beauty—still lives in the same apartment over the joint. And whenever Tony returns home, she is one of the people he enjoys seeing.

In addition to being the owner of The Little Harlem, Mack Hansberry was an avid and skilled fisherman. Over the years, he owned several boats and would sail down to the Gulf of Mexico to catch barracuda. "I wish I had spent more time fishing with him," says Tony a little sadly, "because he was a great fisherman... really knew the waters." Tony did go out with his uncle a few times and on one occasion came home injured. He lifts his shirtsleeve above his right elbow to reveal a large scar. "A big fish hook got lodged in my arm... real deep, lots of blood." He shakes his head, then leans forward and eyes me intently. "You see, Sara, why it was so hard to leave New Orleans. *I loved the place.* It was the greatest life for a kid." He seems to be feeling the moist gulf air, tasting the succulent catfish, hearing the hot jazz, riding the blue waves on a fishing boat, and traveling everywhere on his bicycle. As he tells me all this, he is devouring Alberta's sweet treats from the French Quarter, admiring Beatrice in her beautiful white dress, playing with his cousin Herbert, shooting marbles with the neighborhood kids under the safe shelter of the big tree, or marching with Uncle Oscar's band in a funeral parade and wailing on his clarinet. The images are so vivid, so potent, so present. Tony says again, "New Orleans is so deep in me." The bitter refrain follows. "The biggest problem I had with my parents was their decision to leave New Orleans... that was the beginning of my parting ways with them."

Tony has made connections before between his jazz origins in New Orleans and his current intellectual work, an analogy that intrigues me. On our first visit, he said that he often feels the structure and improvisation of jazz in the way he forms, communicates, and presents ideas. I ask him for examples. I sense that the "feeling" of connection is clear but that the explanation might be ephemeral and difficult to articulate. Tony makes several "false starts" as he tries to explore the music-mind transpositions, and then begins slowly. "I've always had trouble reading my papers in front of an audience. It always seemed strange and idiotic to get up there and *read*... So I've always separated out the task of writing and speaking. I always think of speaking as much more of a *performance*... my intention is to communicate with people. To insert a manuscript in there between me and the audience is troublesome to me." So "ninety-five percent of the time" Tony stands in front of the audience with an outline ("three or four major points"), the structure, and improvises the rest. The improvisation depends upon his mood, his purpose, the context, and the audience, but it is never chaotic. It returns frequently to the structure; it embellishes, it elaborates, it decorates the central theme. Since it is a "performance" in the New Orleans tradition, the purpose is to move the audience *and* inspire the performer. There is the sense of communication, even collaboration, between the performer and the audience, never the distancing and separation imposed by reading a static script.

Five percent of the time, Tony decides to read his papers. He chooses his moments carefully, strategically. "I decide to read a paper usually when I'm responding to some set of methodological issues... when I want to be very specific, discrete, very disciplined. I also will read a paper when I feel the need to disagree, criticize... when I really need to dissect someone's work." Tony uses an example from the day before. He has just returned from Washington, D.C., where he participated in a panel on which he was asked to respond to a colleague's paper. He had received the paper several days before, reviewed it, and disagreed with some of the analyses and interpretations. Since his response was supposed to be brief and focused and since he was highly critical of the paper's thesis, Tony decided to read his response. "I viewed it as an aggressive posture for me to read my piece." Tony's words were incisive, focused on the problems that he had uncovered, but he was not gratuitous in his criticism or overly harsh in his remarks. "A lot of people think of me as a nice, easygoing, gentle person... and that's true I guess. But I also know that I can lay into people... I think I'm principled about doing it, but I can be very, very tough.... Yesterday, the guy who wrote the paper was really angry with me." As I listen to Tony, I have no doubt that most people perceive him as "gentle"; I have no doubt that he can be very "tough" in a "principled way"; and I have no doubt that the combination of his calm, caring aspect and his incisive, aggressive words feels doubly wounding to the unsuspecting recipient. Reading a paper is an act of aggression. Improvising a talk is a performance, an act of communication.

Not yet satisfied with his explanation, Tony tries again to find his intellectual roots in jazz. He begins—"For the most part, jazz is ephemeral... you do it and it's gone... In a sense I translate this notion into my academic work." A long pause, then hesitantly he goes on, "Let me redefine that. If I am working on expressing an idea, something may come together, and I want to preserve it... but in getting there I experience a lot of false starts... it's transient." Tony is struggling to capture something fundamental to the way he approaches his work. He sees the movement, the change, the mistakes, the recoveries in his work. He sees the journey, the development, "the transience" as the most important. "A lot of my work is in process, germinating," he explains. "It is an effort to get someplace... along the way, I come up with half-baked ideas. At times I've written papers that represent only partially, minimally developed ideas... I produce them... they are over and done with." As intellectual or scientific work, Tony regards the pieces as "false starts," or even more self-critically, "as of no enduring value." But as points along the way, as experimental considerations, as improvisational exercises these pieces are critical to the "intellectual journey."

Recognizing the contrasts between the academy's standards for scholarship and his own perspective on "the ephemeral" properties of his work, Tony admits, "I may believe that very few things I've written have enduring value, but in the process I've created a large portfolio, which is clearly the most important thing to others evaluating me." He offers an example. "When I was being reviewed for my professorship at Harvard, they asked me to choose ten publications from a list of about one hundred." He shakes his head wearily. "I had a hard time choosing ten... Maybe there were five or six that I was really proud of, that have some enduring value,... but as far as the scientific literature is concerned, some of them really did not make a contribution." The judgment feels harsh to me, overly self-critical, but I discover Tony is referring to a "whole lot of the stuff in science," not just his work. And he reminds me that for him it is not the accumulated portfolio that matters most, but the ephemeral process of change, the improvisation, the transient efforts that expand the mind and the music.

Explorations

There was no spectacular New Orleans funeral for Tony's father. He died in 1989, at the age of seventy-five, and had a dignified but ordinary burial in Memphis. Felton II had been slowed by cardiovascular disease since 1982, when he began to suffer serious strokes. The first massive stroke had caused paralysis that he never recovered from. The memory of his father's slow deterioration is painful for Tony. His voice is husky as he describes the withering away of this strong man's body. "It was a slow death, a steady downhill course... He was bedridden for most of the time, in and out of the hospital... It was difficult to know when he had a stroke... He lost his voice... We watched his brain going away... He got so he couldn't control his emotions and would have these sudden shifts in mood, from uncontrollable weeping to outbursts of laughter. It was very bizarre and very difficult to explain to our kids, especially Tanya, who was so young."

Perhaps the most excruciating part of witnessing his father's decline was seeing the striking contrast between the way his father appeared on the outside and what was happening inside his body. "He looked so good, amazingly good," recalls Tony. "It was particularly difficult to see someone who looks so good but whose internal organs have all deteriorated." He is pensive, melancholy. He brightens a little remembering his mother's extraordinary devotion to her dying husband. "Once my father became ill, my mother became a full-time nurse... One reason he looked so good was because she took such good care of him. There were the daily rituals—brushing his hair, reading him the newspaper, washing him, feeding him." Ethelyn's caretaking and "altruism" were not surprising—"she had devoted all of her life to taking care of her family"—but it was still extraordinary to see how with her tender loving care, her "extremely sick" husband could appear to be almost healthy.

Tony describes his role during his father's long illness as largely "instrumental." As the physician in the family, he helped negotiate the hospital scene and translate the doctors' diagnoses. About twice a year, he would receive a panicked call and he would fly into Memphis immediately. Four or five times he was warned that Felton II was on his deathbed with just hours to live. He would race to his father's bedside and see no dramatic change in his father's condition, just the slow, painful fading away of his mind and body. "Mostly," remembers Tony, "my role was to keep the surgeons away from him. The surgeons would want to go in like a Roto-Rooter and clean out his arteries. I thought that he was too far gone for that kind of trauma." So Tony did what he could to help preserve his father's wholeness and dignity in the face of the humiliation of losing his mind, his voice, his robustness, his control. But Tony remembers his own helplessness mixed with grief. "It is extremely painful to see someone die so slowly."

Throughout the seven years of his father's illness, Tony and his siblings urged their parents to return "home" to New Orleans. Tony was the most outspoken in his insistence, but his brother and sisters shared his view that his father should reconnect with his origins at the end of his life. His voice is a mixture of passion and sentimentality—"I pressured them to go back to New Orleans... I thought it was where he should die... with old friends and family. I thought it would be an important sense of continuity for him, and I thought my mother would reconnect, get rejuvenated, and build a new life. I pushed her as much as I dared." Tony's voice trails off. "But she is still in Memphis... and my father died there... no New Orleans funeral."

The talk of funerals and death, the wish to have his father buried in the soil where his life took root, makes me ask Tony about his connection to religion and church. I remember his remark several weeks ago—made almost offhandedly—that he is "an atheist." I am frankly perplexed because I have experienced a deep spirituality in Tony. I have also heard him lovingly, reverentially describe the pageantry of New Orleans church rituals, especially funerals, so I wonder how his involvement in the rituals fits with his atheistic stance. My questions cause him to pause. Then he releases a long slow sigh. "I can't really remember being connected to church. It is hard to track down my atheism." His early memories are of going to church every Sunday. Most Sundays, "as a matter of convenience," he and his siblings would attend Sunday school at the nearby Methodist church in the neighborhood. But when his parents would occasionally decide to go to church, they would all travel across town to the Methodist church his maternal grandparents attended. Very occasionally, Tony would join his paternal grandmother, Alberta, for a special service at her Baptist church. At home, the family practiced no religious rituals except for the grace "of twenty words or less" that Felton II would perfunctorily recite before dinner each evening.

When the family moved to Memphis, Tony continued to attend Sunday school and church each week. His enthusiasm increased when church became a lively gathering place for the adolescents in the congregation. "Church was a major social event," Tony recalls. "I was always looking forward to meeting up with other kids, especially girls... It was a safe place to meet girls." Church in Memphis was also a place for exploration and learning. Tony remembers a Sunday school teacher who encouraged her class to bring in something interesting that they had read during the week for recitation and discussion. The reading did not need to be connected to religion in any way. "Once the norm got established" the students would arrive with an eclectic assortment of readings— from newspapers, novels, poetry volumes, horoscopes, science fiction—that would serve as the basis for discussion. "She created an interesting culture in the class," says Tony appreciatively. "We found ourselves telling about things in our lives and interests we had that we might not have talked about in school."

These Sunday school readings are one of the dimensions of church life to which he was drawn. He is still trying to track down the origins of his atheism and discovers, in the process, the sources of his attraction to religious practice. Tony leans forward thoughtfully—"Going to church was never a spiritual event for me... I had no interest in the metaphorical aspects of religion. I was intrigued by the poetic, aesthetic dimensions... by the beautiful things—the music, the people all dressed up, the candles, the stained-glass windows, the readings." Mention of the "beautiful things" takes him back to New Orleans and the church services that took full advantage of all the music and sensory pleasures of the region. Now Tony's eyes are sparkling. "Especially the funerals. Spectacular! Amazing events!... I remember my grandfather Clarence saying to me, 'You know why they call those things wakes? Because someone might just sit right up, wake up out of the coffin, and you have to make sure that you've done it just right'... The wakes were exotic, mysterious, suspenseful events."

When Tony was eight or nine years old, a little four-year-old boy who lived down the street died of meningitis. The tiny boy was given a grand funeral. As Tony stood over his open casket at the wake, he wished with all his heart that his grandfather's admonition would prove true. "I looked down at him and said if there would be one time to come alive—it is *now!*" The boy's body remained still and silent—stone dead—but the suspense and the mystery of wakes remained alive in Tony's bones, marking the part of religion that moves him "aesthetically."

Again, Tony is struggling to trace his "lack of connection to the spiritual dimensions" of church. "I was always skeptical about God... I always wondered about this guy who had all this power and wasn't using it better." As a child, these wonderings took the form of questioning the existence of a God who would fill "a life with disappointments." As Tony grew older, he wondered why this "powerful guy" would not correct the great injustices, inequalities, and suffering that Tony saw all around him. But Tony is searching for the more direct influences of his religious skepticism. "It must have filtered down from people around me... It is hard to trace out who would have encouraged a downplaying of religion." He takes the family inventory. His grandmothers, on both sides, and his mother he describes as "definitely committed to the spiritual, religious realm." His father was more of a puzzle. "He never talked about it much... Actually, I was sort of surprised at his involvement in the church. But then I began to see it as service—social, political service. He was a natural leader, and he used those talents in the church." He lands finally on his two uncles—Uncle Oscar and Uncle Mack—who were not regular churchgoers, and says with some relief, "Maybe it was *they* who taught me that it was all baloney."

Despite his early and persistent skepticism about God and religion, Tony attended church regularly all through high school and through most of college. In college, he was even briefly president of the Methodist Youth Club. At Howard the chapel was at the center of campus life, the setting for most of the political, cultural, and socially responsible activity at the university. Tony remembers hearing Martin Luther King Jr. preach several times from the pulpit at Howard's chapel; King's preaching was an "intoxicating blend" of religion, ideology, politics, and poetry. But by the time Tony was a junior in college, he was involved in a "trillion things— every manner of campus and community activity that you could possibly be in and still stay in school." Tony laughs heartily. "The church part of it got choked out and I never reconnected."

At present, a few times a year Tony and his family attend Quaker meetings, where they "identify strongly." The Quaker service has none of the grandeur and beauty of the New Orleans church services, none of the mystery and suspense of the elaborate funerals. "It is totally stripped down, totally opposite from my New Orleans roots," says Tony, reluctant to explore the vast differences. He just lets the observation hang unattended in the air. But in this "stripped down" setting, Tony seems to find solace, peace, maybe even spiritual resonance. He says with surprise in his voice, "In the Quaker service I find myself meditating… I don't remember ever meditating in church. Certainly, I don't remember praying in church… just kneeling and closing my eyes."

I ask Tony whether his belief in science, in the standards of empiricism, might have also shaped his religious skepticism; after all, if you are someone who requires hard evidence and exacting proof, you may never be satisfied with the ephemeral quality of faith. His response is immediate. "Yes, absolutely." Then he follows with a slightly different explanation. "Probably it was more my experience in medical school that ultimately moved me away from churchgoing. You know, medicine is like a culture, a way of life…

it took the place of a lot of things that were all disparate... it was an integrating experience, providing coherence." Science is the first, most obvious, ingredient of this "holistic experience" of medicine as Tony describes it. But the other two—social service/social action and philosophy—are equally important to Tony's cultural trilogy, and he claims them as "ancient" obsessions.

"You know," Tony says forcefully, "I've always been sincerely interested in the welfare of people." He proudly recalls his leadership of a food bank project during his junior and senior years at Booker T. Washington High School. Once a year, all the students and teachers would be asked to bring in food—cans, dried goods, nonperishables—to school. An enormous amount of food would arrive, and Tony and his crew would receive it, record it, and organize it for distribution. "The whole thing was a very big deal, but the hardest part was figuring out what neighborhood should be targeted for distribution. This meant understanding the demography of the city and identifying the neighborhood in greatest need."

Tony's involvement in this goodwill project coincided with his budding interest in philosophy. The activism and practicality of the former contrasted with the ruminations and abstractions of the latter. Both were part of Tony's character and commitment. By senior year, Tony was plowing his way through Will Durant's *Story of Philosophy* and even trying to decipher Kierkegaard and Schopenhauer. It was heavy stuff, and Tony loved its complexity and mystery. Amazed, I ask, "What did you mean by philosophy at sixteen and seventeen years of age?" Tony throws his head back in a big laugh— "It meant reading stuff I couldn't understand." Most of Tony's early forays into philosophy were private journeys, "interior, introspective stuff." But occasionally he would take an excerpt from one of his philosophical treatises into his Sunday school class and let some of his friends collectively puzzle over its meaning.

At the center of this cultural trilogy is science. "Always science," says Tony. He reaches back in time to the set of encyclopedias his parents gave him when he was nine to celebrate his bravery in facing surgery to remove his tonsils. Poring over those volumes by himself was a wonderful, adventurous experience. The following Christmas he got his first chemistry set ("a complete surprise"), and he quickly became hooked. He remembers lazy afternoons spent on the back porch quietly playing with his chemistry set. The introductory set was replaced the following year by a more complicated, sophisticated version. His parents could see that Tony was serious in his pursuit of chemistry, that his "play" was actually focused study and experimentation. "I spent a great deal of time working with these chemistry sets," recalls Tony. "I remember mixing compounds to produce a new color or a new substance. I was not interested in producing a product so much as I was intrigued by the *exploration*... what would happen in mixing. This was not product oriented." Tony's description of the heart of his childhood fascination—the *exploration*, the *process* of experimentation—sounds like the way Tony depicts his adult preoccupations in science. What he loves most about his research now is the "ephemeral" quality he spoke of earlier, the "improvisation," the "transcience," the "false starts" that lead to discovery.

The chemistry set was moved to Memphis and the "explorations" continued. Tony missed the back porch of their house in New Orleans where he used to spend hours mixing and experimenting. Their Memphis house was not as welcoming, as living space or as chemistry laboratory. "In Memphis we lived in a much less friendly house than in New Orleans," recalls Tony. "It was more formal. I'm sure my parents liked it more, but for a child it didn't feel well connected to the outdoors like the New Orleans house. I remember feeling I didn't have much space to operate in... to stretch out and do chemistry."

So he moved his base of scientific exploration to Booker T. Washington High School where he had access to the laboratories. Tony was "not too turned on" by his tenth-grade biology course. But when he took chemistry in the eleventh grade, he was totally in his element. He felt well prepared by his earlier self-taught, back-porch chemistry, knowledgeable about the materials and the procedures. But in addition to this "firm foundation" in chemistry, Tony always felt a particular "connection" to the subject. He points to his brain. "I always experienced a *creative* thing going on there with chemistry." Tony contrasts this strong attraction to chemistry with his lack of enthusiasm for twelfth-grade physics, a course he excelled in but for which he never felt a keen aptitude. "Chemistry seemed much more dynamic, real. Physics was more abstract, and the experiments were dull... Also, physics was much more mathematical. I've always felt average in math, so that posed a kind of limitation to my success in physics."

Tony is not able to remember his chemistry teacher's name, but he vividly remembers his talents and his commitment to teaching science. Almost immediately the teacher noticed Tony's extraordinary aptitude and enthusiasm for his subject. He became an active mentor and rewarded Tony's work. He would encourage Tony to stay after school and work in the laboratory. They would spend hours there together, often silently: Tony working alone at the lab tables—measuring, mixing, concocting, occasionally asking a question or seeking direction; his teacher working at his desk in the corner—grading papers, reading, sometimes getting up to stand quietly at his student's side. It was here that Tony learned to love the laboratory—a place where he could indulge his curiosity, raise burning questions, search for solutions; a place for quiet, focused thinking.

The chemistry teacher was one among several "excellent" teachers at Booker T. Washington, a school whose entire faculty and student body were black ("This was way before desegregation!"), a school that prided itself on being the best in the city. When Tony speaks about "excellence," he always refers to the teachers' "devotion" and "commitment." The best teachers were those who viewed teaching as a "calling." He also speaks about the good teachers in high school as being active and aggressive ("not a passive kind of pedagogy"), with a momentum born out of intellectual energy *and* the determination to communicate what they knew to students. One such teacher taught history and worked as a radio announcer and disc jockey at one of the black radio stations. Every Saturday he would do a current events contest on the radio. Students from rival high schools in the city would come down to the station and "compete with all their might." Tony participated in several of these contests, enjoying the mixture of aggressive competition, media hype, and his skill at retrieving the facts.

In high school Tony continued to be actively involved in music. Without effort he landed the first chair in the clarinet section of the band and was spoken of by his fellow musicians as "a phenomenal clarinetist"—a reputation partly derived from his skill and partly from his New Orleans roots. Although the Booker T. Washington band never had the color or glamour of Uncle Oscar's band, it was a "pretty good" group. As Tony begins to describe his experiences in the school band, he alters his view. "Actually, it was a *damn good* band." Mr. McNeil, the band leader and a "terrible philanderer," insisted upon devotion and discipline from his youngsters, and the band won several local competitions. One year they won a state competition and got to travel to Philadelphia to participate in the Elks Convention Parade. "It was a great trip," remembers Tony. "Really fun... thirty-five or forty kids on a bus to Philadelphia." He leans forward remembering the highlight of the trip. "We stayed at the hotel run by Father Divine!... I glimpsed him briefly once, then he disappeared. But the place was plastered with his pictures... powerful, mysterious man."

But there was more to high school than music and academics. Tony participated fully in the social scene, "right at the very center of the action." Booker T. Washington was known not only for its academic standing but also as a big football school. ("In my sophomore year, I went out for football, got tackled once, and that was it! I thought, These guys are *serious!*") Social life swirled around the football games in the fall, around basketball in the winter, and especially around track and field in the spring. There were elaborate proms and jumping dances. Tony smiles at the memory. "There was lots of it, and I was close to all of it."

In his junior and senior years, Tony was elected president of his class. It is a leadership role that still surprises him a little, and I ask him what qualities in him his peers might have been responding to when they voted for him. "I think people thought I was smart, and in this school there was a value put on that... They had a sense about my doing the right thing... And they saw me as not shy. I was a participant, in the center of it." Looking back, Tony's "centrality" in high school feels like an anomaly in his life, a position that "never translated beyond high school." He leans forward and looks away from me. "I never saw myself as a leader. I don't want to be in the thick of things."

Tony's voice is animated as he describes the educational and social scene at Booker T. Washington. His memories are vivid, unlike the meager memories he has difficulty retrieving from his elementary school days. I ask him about the contrast, and his reply is immediate. "High school was at the center of my life in Memphis. In New Orleans, music was my center, the focus of my intense attention. Maybe that had something to do with my age... the importance of peer contacts during adolescence." In Memphis, high school was an escape from the boring community into which the Earlses had moved. "We lived in a *dull, dull* neighborhood in Memphis. It was one of those new subdivisions on the outskirts of town, where they had chopped down all the trees in order to build the houses. Totally *barren*. Very painful to be living there... especially after the vitality of the New Orleans neighborhood." The Earlses' house was boxy, nondescript, "formal" ("It never felt like home"), and the streets were empty and colorless. Each morning Tony would catch a ride with his father who was going to work in downtown Memphis. Felton II would let him off several blocks from the school and Tony would walk the rest of the way. He would walk into the school building and feel drawn into his world. Tony puts his hand over his heart. "School really became the *living thing* for me."

Not an American...
a Black Man

It is five days after the Rodney King verdict. Los Angeles has gone up in flames. Twenty-seven years after Watts, the brutality, violence, and burning have erupted again in an even more virulent form. There is no way that black folks can meet without talking about this, obsessing about it, raging about it, weeping over it. So before I even take my coat off, I tell Tony I have been thinking about him and wondering how he managed the last few days. He does not need to ask to what I'm referring. He just nods slowly and sends out a heavy, aching sigh. His eyes look washed out, as if he has cried rivers of tears. I have been wondering about his response on at least two levels: his personal, feeling response as a black man, and his more distant, analytic response as a researcher, an epidemiologist who has spent the last decade studying societal violence.

He falls into his chair, pauses, and murmurs, "I'm overwhelmed, completely overwhelmed." Then he takes me back to Wednesday night at 11:30 p.m. when he heard the news; it was one of those moments—like when John F. Kennedy or Martin Luther King Jr. were shot—that will leave its imprint forever. Years from now people will ask, "Where were you when you heard the Rodney King verdict?" and you will be able to reconstruct the details of the moment, including the feelings and sensations. Tony had turned on the television to hear a few minutes of the Ted Koppel show ("a five-minute ritual I have every night of turning on the television for just long enough to create an interlude between my day and going to sleep"). He heard the headline—police in the Rodney King case found *not* guilty; riots have broken out in Los Angeles—and was stunned. "Whammo!" Tony shouts, holding his heart as if someone has gouged it with a knife. "I immediately felt *dumb*... that I didn't forecast it, didn't anticipate it... Then disappointed and very angry." The first response of "dumbness" seems to refer to his professional perspective; his trained eyes should have seen this coming. "I didn't believe… I just couldn't believe it was hurling at me with the speed of light." But his personal, affective response quickly takes over. He speaks of his "profound feeling of vulnerability and hurt," of how he "took it personally." Then his voice grows ominous. "It made me wonder about my survivorship as an American. I realized once again that I'm not an American, I'm a black man."

The morning following the verdict Tony traveled to New Haven where he was to meet with some colleagues at the Yale University School of Medicine. He was feeling raw, angry, vulnerable. He was struggling to put words to his feelings. And he was anticipating the questions his white colleagues would ask him, the demands they would put on him. They would be wanting to know his reactions and interpretations. They would be trying to read him like a complicated cultural text—watching for clues in his body language, hoping he would not unleash his anger at them. As he drove down to New Haven, Tony rehearsed the scene that he already knew so well. Once again, whites would be wanting him to explain how blacks were responding to racist assaults. But this time he felt totally resistant to his colleagues' need to hear his interpretations of the event. He would not gently guide them through the process of discovery and insight. "If they can't get this message," he said to himself, "they are not listening. They're deaf and totally insensitive…." He almost shouted, "What they are saying in L.A. is a message of despair, hopelessness, the feeling of 'We don't count'… The message couldn't be louder or clearer. It requires no interpretation." But the despair is not limited to Los Angeles. We all feel it. "This was a confirmation that black people really are marginal in this society." Tony worries about the spreading rage. "You know, it was Watts that kicked this thing off in the sixties… California is often a kind of barometer for what will follow in the rest of the country… All these powder kegs in New York, Chicago, Philadelphia, New Orleans, just ready to explode."

But Tony's "other major feeling" causes him some surprise. He is leaning forward intently, trying to describe that part of him that feels identified with the violence, that not only understands but applauds the retaliation. This response from "a pacifist" is unnerving to both of us, and Tony uses an old story to gain access to these new feelings. In January of 1967, Tony went to Montreal to do a six-week externship in neurosurgery at McGill University. He was in his senior year at medical school and "was planning on becoming a neurosurgeon." While he was at McGill, he roomed with a Japanese man, a resident in neurosurgery "who didn't know much about the United States" but was very curious about the history of our country. "One thing that puzzled him," recalls Tony, "was the response of black people to their oppression. He said that he understood the wars between the Indians and the white men who were trying to steal their homeland... but he never could understand why black people hadn't fought harder... why blacks hadn't waged real war." Tony remembers the many long evenings he spent trying to explain to his roommate the unique history of black-white relations—the ways in which blacks had struggled against oppression, fought discrimination, persevered against racism, nonviolently waged a moral war, and occasionally raged violently. But the Japanese resident "never got it." He continued to question why "black people did not fight back." Tony recalls, "He kept minimizing my claims of black struggle, saying that he could see no evidence of sustained and massive resistance." As Tony listened to his roommate's persistent questioning, he began to see his point of view and admit the partial truth in it. "I remember having to eat that finally... He wore me down. Something he was saying felt right and true."

As Tony watched the footage of the fires burning in Los Angeles and witnessed the eruptions of violence, he kept thinking of his conversations with his Japanese roommate twenty-five years earlier. The echoes reverberated in his head as he watched blacks strike back with violent rage. His usually gentle face looks hard and angry. "It has made me question the idea of aggression... to consider the extent to which we must check it, contain it, deny it... the way we often refuse to admit the pain. There is a certain *honor* in not letting others take advantage of you... Retaliation may be your last possible way to express your humanity." These words come slowly as if the idea of legitimate, appropriate, even "honorable" violence seems almost foreign to his code of ethics. It seems hard for Tony to admit that societal conditions have become so "hopeless" and "obscene" for blacks that the only way African-Americans can experience their "humanity" is to lash out violently. Until now, Tony has resisted this conclusion—through the deaths of Martin Luther King Jr. and Malcolm X, through the burning down of Watts, through the Civil Rights struggle in the '60s—but the Rodney King verdict and its aftermath have pushed him to a new place of questioning and desperation.

His voice is now seething; his eyes are rimmed with tears. "I'm still raging, still angry.... I haven't concocted a constructive agenda yet." He feels shaken, unsteady. The usual responses to race and racism do not seem workable. "Today I look at white people and try to place them. I desperately want to hold out a humane and reasonable perspective on all of this... I want not to be a racist and dismiss all white people... I want to find a way to discriminate among them. I've lost my bearings." Tony is shaking his finger, stabbing at the air. "I don't know what to use in figuring out who is on my side." He seems to be referring to the circles of people surrounding him— his friends, acquaintances, colleagues, employees, strangers on the street. "I'll tell you one thing, though, I would rather mistake a friend for an enemy than mistake an enemy for a friend. *I really want to know who my enemies are.*" He says this with such a raw force that I jump back startled, recover, and ask whether keeping an enemy inventory is new for him. "No, it has been *in* me all along," whispers Tony, "but it has all risen to the surface." He is holding his head with both hands, sensing the internal pressure. "It has exploded through my skull. It is deeply painful to know I feel this."

We both feel the need to move beyond this anguished conversation. Hurt and pain are consuming Tony—manifesting in his watery, red eyes, in his raging words, in his striking out gestures, in his moments of weary resignation. I sit there feeling deeply identified but helpless. I search my mind to find a bridge to another place, a way to move on that will not minimize or deny our anger and pain but will release us from dwelling on it. I recall that at the close of our last session Tony asked me to remind him to tell the story of Blair T. Hunt, the principal of Booker T. Washington High School. He didn't tell me why the story is important, but he conveyed the huge impact of this man on his life and the emotional violence the man inflicted. I sense that the tale of Blair T. Hunt—another time of pain—might be a productive next place to move our focus. I ask him about Dr. Hunt, and he looks like he has been hit with another huge blow. "Wow, what a bridge," Tony exclaims. "Yeah, I guess the stories of rage and hurt are related." He is silent for a long time and then launches into describing the context for "the most upsetting thing that ever happened to me." His tense posture, his heavy voice, and his charged tone convey the magnitude and depth of this experience.

For "thirty or forty" years Blair T. Hunt had worked at Booker T. Washington High School, first as a teacher and then as the principal. In June of 1959, he retired and celebrated his illustrious service and leadership at Tony's graduation ceremony. In Memphis Dr. Hunt was a revered educator, respected for his commitment to public education, his access to the white power brokers, and his high-class, bourgeois demeanor. In addition to his principalship at Booker T. Washington High, Dr. Hunt was the pastor of one of the largest Baptist churches in the city. The combination of these two lofty roles—preacher and educator—all wrapped up in one person, gave him enormous visibility and power in the city. "If you were to name the five most influential black people in Memphis at the time, Blair T. Hunt would have been among them," recalls Tony. "No one messed with Blair." With his "high yellow" skin, his "supercilious manner," and his "air of superiority," he seemed almost untouchable.

At the high school, Blair T. Hunt commanded total obedience and submissiveness from the students whom he took every opportunity to belittle and humiliate. "He had a very low opinion of black kids, and he constantly communicated that view. We'd have these school assemblies, and he'd stand up there in front of all of us and sneer... He'd be thinking, These niggers will be hard to control, and he would begin the morning by saying, 'You black hoodlums....'" His constant negativity and harassment were corrosive to the spirit and energy of the school, creating "a certain level of fear that was always present." Occasionally, some of the tougher boys would mumble a response under their breath, "You dumb motherfucker, if you mess with me I'll kick your ass." But the boys never spoke those words loud enough for Dr. Hunt to hear, and everyone knew that in reality, no one would ever dare to challenge their principal's power.

Tony admits that this malicious autocrat did some good things at Booker T. Washington. "He was supportive of his faculty," who responded by being completely submissive and fiercely loyal to him. "He attracted good teachers" who were well-educated and committed professionals. "And he seemed to be an effective manager"; the school ran smoothly and efficiently. Tony also admits that ten to fifteen percent of the students were troublemakers. There was always the potential for violence and disruption. "These boys had fighting on their minds all the time," recalls Tony. "They were very territorial—dangerous and threatening to everyone." So, to a certain extent, Blair Hunt's preoccupation with control was understandable. If this delinquent element was allowed to be aggressive in school, the whole place might have been thrown into violent chaos. But Dr. Hunt behaved as if *all* students had these delinquent inclinations, as if they were all "black hoodlums." "He lumped us all together. We were all ugly niggers, uncivilized savages, as far as he was concerned... He didn't discriminate among us. You know, many of us were diligent, hard-working students."

Having described Blair T. Hunt's role, personality, and style, Tony begins his story. At the end of Tony's eleventh-grade year, the students at Booker T. Washington High took the National Merit semifinalist exam. Their scores on the examination were returned at the beginning of the twelfth grade, and only two students in the entire grade were made finalists: Felton Earls and Clifford Shelby. In fact, it turned out that Tony and Clifford were the only two black finalists in all of Memphis. Although everyone was pleased with Tony's success, no one was surprised. He was an honors student with a consistent record of achievement, and everyone thought he was smart. But people were stunned by Clifford's examination scores because he was not known to be a disciplined student. "He did not care much about school, didn't have good grades... He was sort of half flunking." Both boys were celebrated with fanfare. The Memphis paper recorded their success, the school newspaper did a big story, and the two were given a prominent spread in the school yearbook. "I remember getting all dressed up in a suit and standing in front of the trophy case at school for the pictures," recalls Tony. As they enjoyed their new celebrity, they anticipated—with excitement and anxiety—taking the final exam in several weeks.

One day, after the pictures, the articles, and the celebration, Blair T. Hunt called the boys into his office. His voice always had that supercilious quality, but this time the message felt shocking and deeply humiliating. Tony could not believe the words that the principal uttered. "He said, 'In reality, you boys did *not* pass the exam... it was all a fabrication. We believed that it was time that black students excelled in this community, so Mrs. so-and-so (the English teacher who proctored the exam) and I monkeyed with the scores to make it appear that you two had passed." The boys sat there, stunned and disbelieving, trying to read Hunt's mask of a face to see whether this too was a cruel lie. In order to assure them that this was the "real truth," Hunt called in the English teacher who confirmed the story. Yes, it was true that they had "monkeyed with the scores" in order to give a couple of black kids visibility, honor, and a chance to succeed. But on afterthought, the principal and the teacher had determined that the hoax was unwise—that it might make the boys vulnerable or cause the school embarrassment. So they decided that since Tony and Clifford really didn't pass the eleventh-grade semifinal exam, they would not allow them to take the final examination.

Tony remembers the confusion and the excruciating pain. "This was totally crushing. I sat there and wept." After sleepwalking through the rest of the day, Tony told his father that evening about the deadly blow Dr. Hunt had dealt him, about his confusion and his anguish. His father listened, silent and angry, and wasted no time in seeking clarification and resolution. The next morning he marched into the principal's office and demanded an explanation. When he emerged from the office half an hour later, his message to Tony was simple and clear: "You're going to take the exam."

Later on he told his son the "real truth," "the obscene story." But even now Tony seems skeptical. He still doesn't fully trust the final version of the tale. "The story went something like this," he says sketchily. "We were the only black kids in Memphis who had passed this exam... The final exam was to be taken across town at a segregated white high school... The school board was nervous about black kids appearing at the white school, and they put pressure on Blair to make sure we didn't appear... He, of course, succumbed to the pressure and told us the lie."

The rage of thirty-five years ago is rising in Tony, mixing with the rage over the Los Angeles verdict. It is all one huge bubbling cauldron within him, about to "explode through his skull." The old feelings had long-lasting echoes. "I went on feeling crippled psychologically for a very long time," says Tony softly. "I didn't know what to believe—what was the truth, what was a lie... I believed that Blair T. Hunt was about as Uncle Tom as anyone could possibly be... and I knew that he had a very low opinion of black people. Even as a kid, I knew that he wouldn't even think twice about hurting me if it meant covering his own ass and getting over with white people." Tony's voice is biting and bitter—"You see, Sara, I knew he was a complete asshole... no doubt about it... but I also knew that as a big Baptist minister and prominent educator, he was highly respected in the community. These conflicting images of this man had a heavy, confusing effect on me."

The pain was magnified by the fact that Hunt's lie hit Tony at his most vulnerable spot. It was a lie about his intelligence. It undermined his sure sense of his capabilities as a student. "I was a *kid*," says Tony pointing to the horror of an adult manipulating a child in this way. "A kid who was very wrapped up in liking school and being good at it... I was clear I wasn't an athlete. I had gone out for football and practically got killed... and I was increasingly clear that I wasn't really a musician. When I had arrived from New Orleans in ninth grade, I could play circles around all those other kids in the band... But by senior year, they were catching up with me, right on my heels, and I was aware that some of the other kids could *hear* the music better than I could." Tony is intent on describing his ado-

lescent stocktaking, his growing understanding of his talents, interests, and capabilities. "So it was clear I had some limitations. *What
I was good at was being smart.*" Blair T. Hunt's lie hit at the heart of
that. It "shattered and confused" the one thing of which Tony felt
sure. As I listen to Tony's description of being crippled and disoriented by Hunt's "unbelievable" act, I remember his comments,
of an hour earlier, about how the King verdict and the Los Angeles
despair and violence have caused him to "lose my bearings." In both
cases—as an adolescent and as an adult—Tony felt not only anger,
vulnerability, and pain, but also an assault to his normal sense of balance and rightness. He felt "confused" about what is the truth and
what is a lie, about who is friend and who is enemy.

The drama of Blair T. Hunt has three acts. As Tony begins to
rehearse act 2, he pauses for a moment, realizing he has left me hanging in act 1. "Oh, by the way," he says casually, "I did very well on
the final and so did Clifford." I am delighted to hear that the two
boys were vindicated—the truth was in the second success—but I
know this success is not the heart of the story. Blair T. Hunt had
made sure that they would never experience the pure joy of victory.

Act 2 came during the winter of Tony's senior year when he was
applying to colleges. "I was thinking *big* about college," says Tony
dramatically. "What do you mean?" I ask. "Thinking big meant
thinking *beyond* Dillard!" responds Tony laughing. Everyone in
Tony's family, for generations, had gone to Dillard University in
New Orleans. Tony's decision not to attend Dillard—not even to
apply—was considered a radical, irreverent move. He was "stretching out" when he submitted applications to Morehouse College in
Atlanta and Howard University in Washington, D.C., both considered to be two of the most prestigious predominantly black institutions in the country. But Tony also had it in his head that he
wanted to "apply up North," and he fastened on the idea of Northwestern University. He had studied lots of college catalogues and
had discovered the fact that somewhere in its history, Northwestern
University had had some affiliation with the Methodist Church.
Also, he had heard of "some relatives who once lived in Chicago."
These thin and distant connections were enough to attract Tony

to Northwestern as his "definite first choice." "I remember vividly
that the application fee for Northwestern was fifty dollars, which I
had to pay for out of my hard-earned paper route money… So you
know I must have wanted it intensely if I was willing to fork over
fifty bucks!"

Tony worked diligently on all of his applications, meeting each
of the deadlines in good time and making sure that he completed the
various parts of the forms and essays. By late January, he had heard
back from all of the schools except Northwestern. Finally, he
received a letter from Northwestern saying his application was
incomplete and could not be processed. But Tony knew that he had
done everything he was supposed to. His suspicion immediately
turned to Blair T. Hunt. Had that man done something to sabotage
his dream? Had he, once again, destroyed Tony's chance for opportunity and success? Again, Tony turned to his father, who acted out
of the same "disbelief" and with the same "clarity and efficiency" as
he had before. "We were both very suspicious," recalls Tony.

This time Blair T. Hunt expressed no embarrassment and made
no apology. When Felton II pressed him about what might have
happened to Tony's Northwestern application, Hunt said that it was
his custom to screen all the college applications of the senior class,
and if he thought any of them was inappropriate, he would simply
not respond to the college's request for high school transcripts and
reports. In the case of Tony's application to Northwestern, he had
thought the choice too ambitious, so he had not forwarded the
school materials to the university. His air was sanctimonious, as if
this had been a lofty, olympian decision. "I thought about it long
and hard," Hunt told Tony's father, "and I decided not to send in his
records. I don't think the boy could have made it up there, so I did
him a favor." Felton II was furious. He couldn't believe that his
boy had once again been victimized by this spiteful man. "It was too
late to resurrect the situation at Northwestern," recalls Tony shaking his head. "On the heels of the other situation… the succession
of events was devastating. *I've never been so hurt.*"

The wounds from these two malicious assaults were still raw
when graduation rolled around in June. Tony's high school gradua-

tion coincided with Blair T. Hunt's retirement from Booker T. Washington, and there was a great deal of ceremonial fanfare. As senior class president, Tony was put in an "intensely awkward" position at graduation: "I found myself in a painful situation of having to say good things about this man and having to listen to him praise me and the senior class." The disgust shows on Tony's face. "There was all this platitudinous bullshit." "In the meantime," Tony announces as an aside, "I got scholarships at both Morehouse and Howard. I took the one at Howard." He comes back to the injury. "But the blow had been dealt... a very big blow."

Looking back on the painful events of his senior year, one image stands out for Tony. He sees his father, strong, clear, and protective. He feels deeply thankful for his father's staunch advocacy, for the way he responded immediately to Tony's cries for help, and for his courage in confronting Blair T. Hunt. Tony's voice is full of emotion. "I have great admiration for my father. I could not have survived without his intervention, and I knew my mother could not have done it. She surely would have been overwhelmed. Blair T. Hunt was domineering, overbearing, insulting to *everyone*. It took someone like my father to cut through that... He moved in, took care of things, cleaned it up." In expressing his gratitude for his father's forceful support, Tony thinks about his peers who were not fortunate enough to have the same kind of parental advocacy. "Even with my father's protection, I realize the damage Blair T. Hunt did to me... But think of all the damage he must have done to other kids who didn't have a parent who could move in and take care of business."

Tony feels privileged to have had his father's protection. He also sees the contrast between these extraordinary occasions of advocacy and his ordinary life with his father. In these moments of crisis, Tony always knew he could count on his father, even though Felton II was a difficult man for his son to know. Tony does not want to sound disloyal; he measures his words carefully. "You know, my relationship to my dad was very complicated... On a daily basis, it was not warm and wonderful. I always thought he was sort of overbearing, and I didn't like the way he treated my mother." His voice trails off. "But in this case, he protected me."

Act 3 of the Blair T. Hunt drama occurred a decade later, in 1969. In order to describe the complicated reentry of Hunt into the scene, Tony needs to back up a few years to the time of his graduation from Howard Medical School. As an undergraduate at Howard, Tony had been enrolled in ROTC, which was compulsory for all students "because the university received its major support from federal funds." During his time in ROTC, Tony played in the band and "never carried a rifle." When he graduated from Howard Medical School with a commission as lieutenant, the Vietnam War was being waged. He knew that if he went on to his planned internship in neurosurgery, he would certainly be drafted. So he decided to enroll in a postdoctoral program at the University of Wisconsin at Madison where he would do "laboratory research in neurophysiology with a neurosurgeon." His time at Wisconsin was short-lived. The laboratory training appealed to Tony's fascination with and commitment to scientific work, but as he has told me before, he felt removed from all the exciting "action in the streets." He felt he could no longer stand on the sidelines. "History wouldn't let me be shielded," declares Tony. "I decided I no longer wanted to be a neurosurgeon or a neurophysiologist."

"That is when I decided that I wanted to carry on the dream of Martin... That's when I went to work in Harlem... That's when I decided to work with children." Just after arriving at Metropolitan Hospital in East Harlem to do his pediatric residency, Tony received his draft papers sending him to Vietnam. His voice is ringing. "There was no way I was going to join the American army." He says "American army" with disdain, as though referring to some foreign enemy. I hear the same bitter tone I heard earlier when Tony said, "It made me wonder about my survivorship as an American. I realized once again that I'm not an American, I'm a black man." Tony sought advice from the New York chapter of the American Friends Service Committee, which had a very well organized program for counseling people who were considering declaring conscientious objector status. They listened to his anger at the American injustices, his earnest belief in nonviolence, and his determination not to participate in the war. Their counsel led Tony to a lawyer, one of

William Kunstler's associates, who helped him file the papers for C.O. status and represented him in court. The district court judge ruled in Tony's favor, and it "looked as though the situation was taken care of." Tony continued with his training in pediatrics, then went on to his residency in child psychiatry at Harvard.

But two years later in 1972, Tony received a letter that made his heart sink. The letter informed him that the army had appealed his case to the U.S. Court of Appeals, which had reversed the earlier decision. Now he would have to report for active duty in the army or go to jail. Tony's lawyer scrutinized the appeal and told him that the appeal was based on "some technicality," that if he reported for active duty he could promise Tony that he would only have to serve a very short time. So reluctantly Tony went off to San Antonio, Texas, where he reported for active duty. "I spent six miserable weeks there," recalls Tony. By then, he had attained the rank of major, but he felt totally alienated from and resistant to the army experience. His resistance took various forms as he struggled to "strike a balance" between letting them know he detested being there and "eroding the support" of the lawyers who were working on his behalf. So Tony refused to carry or use his gun, purposely wore his uniform incorrectly, and he "did everything not to be a role model" for the lower ranked soldiers. He smiles—"I was engaged in constant minor harassment and disobedience.... I remember once in class when a very militaristic instructor—perfect uniform, shoes all shined—was about to show us a movie and asked one of the men to 'kill the lights'... I jumped in and responded, 'I object to that!'" Through most of the six weeks Tony felt compromised and frustrated. But just as his lawyer promised, by the end of a month and a half, he was given an honorable discharge.

Tony returns to the original positive ruling for C.O. status in 1969. His lawyer had worked with him very closely to prepare documentation that would be unassailable. Tony had spent days poring over the C.O. application. Since he was by then a "committed atheist," he could not claim religious devotion as his reason for choosing "pacifism." "Writing that application was the most soul-searching experience I've ever had," recalls Tony. "I had to develop my own philosophy." In addition to his own carefully constructed statement, Tony's lawyer urged him to get letters of support from people who knew him as a child, who could claim that even at a very tender age Tony had pacifist inclinations.

As Tony and his lawyers reviewed the list of potential writers, they came up with Blair T. Hunt ("Dum-da-dum-dum!" intones Tony as he marks the reentry of the Memphis villain). Tony had not even heard from Hunt since 1959, and his old principal was now "somewhere in his eighties." Tony vigorously resisted his attorney's suggestion that he contact Hunt. He knew that this man was trouble. But his lawyer argued that Dr. Hunt, as a revered educator and prominent Baptist minister, was the perfect symbol of morality and religiosity, that a letter from him would greatly strengthen Tony's application. So Tony reluctantly agreed.

Blair T. Hunt's letter was swift in coming, and "what it said was worth gold." It said something like this:

To Whom It May Concern:

I remember Felton Earls III very well. He was a student of mine at Booker T. Washington High School. I remember him because there were many days when I saw him walking up and down the halls. *This boy was the image of Jesus Christ himself.*

Faithfully, the Reverend Blair T. Hunt

The letter, while startling, was priceless. Just the kind of testimony needed to complete Tony's file. Tony is smiling and shaking his head. I am sitting there stunned… too stunned to ask the next question, but my mind is racing. Was Hunt—in his old age—trying to assuage his guilt? Trying to make up for his earlier assaults on Tony? Was he a pathological liar, ready to lie whenever it fit his mood or fancy? Did he enjoy using his power capriciously, causing shock and surprise in those who begged for his help? Tony offers no explanation; the strange letter remains uninterpreted. He seems satisfied to live with the mystery. It is Tony who concludes our session with a litany that is now very familiar to me. It is the litany about his precious city of New Orleans. He is looking back at all the damage Blair T. Hunt caused, all the abuse. "I don't think that this terrible stuff could have happened in New Orleans. Blair T. Hunt was a Memphis phenomenon... part of that southern plantation, house nigger mentality... out of the rural cotton belt. New Orleans is more sophisticated. People have more pride. The kids would have refused to absorb that stuff in New Orleans."

From the Lab into the Streets

"I heard about Martin Luther King's assassination in a very provocative way," says Tony as a way of beginning a story about an event that transformed his life. Tony had a post-doctoral research position in neurophysiology at the University of Wisconsin at Madison. Working with Clinton Woolsey, an internationally recognized scientist on brain research, Tony was doing an experiment that required that he be in a soundproof laboratory for thirty-six hours straight. "I was in the process of doing an extremely tedious experiment on the area of the brain that receives sound," recalls Tony. "A cat is anesthetized. It is a terminal experiment—the animal is sacrificed. You fix the brain to correlate with the findings in order to confirm physiological evidence from the anatomy of the cat." He remembers the "absolute silence" of the laboratory and the meticulous and exacting procedures this experiment required.

After a day and a half, Tony emerged from solitary confinement to the deafening roars of the world outside. The campus was in an uproar; people were screaming out in rage or huddled together weeping. There were mass protests—banners, speeches, and chanting. Tony walked out into the blinding light and was stunned and disoriented by the noise and the chaos. He stood still trying to comprehend the scene. "I had no idea what was going on," says Tony quietly. "Then someone told me that Martin Luther King had been assassinated, and I felt absolutely terrible... There I had been ensconced in this soundproof room, and I didn't know anything about this." The more he heard about the killing, the more identified he felt. He could visualize the whole scene. "King was shot in my hometown. I knew right where the Lorraine Hotel was where they killed him."

The news was all the more shocking because of the way Tony heard it. There he was in the antiseptic, cloistered safety of his laboratory, doing exquisitely rarified work, cut off from the world by a sound barrier. Beyond the walls of the research laboratory all hell was breaking loose. His hero had been brutally shot, and he didn't even know it. People were out there expressing their grief and anger, writing their pain in graffiti on buildings, and Tony had to wipe the grogginess out of his eyes and inquire about all the commotion.

All through college, since 1959, King's life and work had been deeply affecting to Tony. As a member of the Du Bois Club at Howard, he had been actively involved in Civil Rights protests "whose philosophical base were King's passive resistance." On the weekends, the students would travel out to the Eastern Shore of Maryland ("a deeply racist area that felt like the most backward areas of Mississippi") and sit in at lunch counters that were refusing to serve "Negroes." When the cops would come and ask them to leave the premises, they would steadfastly and solemnly refuse, and they would be hauled down to the station and put in jail for a few hours. "We always told the police that we were from Howard, a federal institution, and if they arrested us they'd have to face federal investigation," recalls Tony. "But these dumb white cops never believed us. We'd tell them to call up and find out. They'd just growl and scowl at us."

The students in the Du Bois Club were constantly debating the ethics and the effectiveness of nonviolence. Some of them found the King philosophy of passive resistance deeply troubling, others were doubtful about the tactics, and a few wanted to retaliate with violence. But over time, they saw that King's strategy worked, so they continued to use it despite their widely diverse political views. Tony remembers, "I found the suppression of anger and retaliation very difficult in passive resistance... It was not as *temperamentally* difficult for me as it was *politically* difficult." But as he practiced passive resistance, as he participated in the weekly political rituals, Tony sensed the deepening impact of King's teachings. "I didn't even realize the extent to which I was being affected by it as it was going on." But by the time he graduated from medical school in 1967, Tony was "moving in the direction of becoming a pacifist," and he was "responding very positively to Malcolm and Martin's widening interest in the rest of the world."

Tony's first semester in medical school was dismal. Everything seemed pointless and trivial. Part of it was the materialistic culture. "It was a trade school," says Tony. "I couldn't wait to graduate so I could get into real science." Most of the students at Howard saw their medical training as a ladder ascending to money and status. "I was surrounded by a bunch of budding capitalists... They were always forecasting what kinds of cars they'd drive, the money they'd make, the houses they'd live in." When they were not anticipating their affluence, they were cramming for tests and grubbing for grades. "I heard almost no conversation about some idea capturing their imagination... no talk about the agony of being a doctor, of trying so hard to save someone and failing... nothing about wanting to help people and serve our community." Tony's voice is despairing. "It always seemed disturbing and alien to me." The science courses didn't even capture his interest. "I had already had most of the biochemistry, and the anatomy course was just rote memorization. Totally uninspiring." Then in November, John Kennedy was killed, and Tony's boredom was shadowed by grief and hopelessness. "All of this just didn't seem right," says Tony, still searching for the words to describe the confusion of feelings that made him abruptly leave campus.

Tony took the train up to New York City— a place about which he had always had fantasies—hoping to just "hang out" and soak up the scene. He had no plan, only the desperate need to get away from his "alien" existence at Howard. It was all very vague. Tony smiles at the memory of his youthful wanderings. "I thought I needed to be around poets, writers... or if I hung around the Village, I would be reborn in my music." The cultural experiment was short-lived. "After three days I spent up all my money... I came hobbling back to D.C. and reconciled myself to four years in medical school." There is resignation written all over Tony's face. "It was a failed attempt to keep my liberal imagination alive. I succumbed to trade school."

As Tony tries to piece together the lingering despondency that permeated his medical school years, he begins, "It was not a distinguishable period of my life... It was as if I was holding my breath all the way through." Along with his studies, he had a job working twenty hours a week at the Library of Congress, which consumed some of his energy and took him away from campus. He also remembers his one jazzy indulgence, "an MG sports car that I was working *for*. It was very fickle, always needed fixing, sucking up all my little bit of money… But it was *dazzling*, well worth pumping my money into… It was fun driving my MG around D.C.!"

But the dazzling distraction of his fast sports car didn't save Tony from what he now recognizes as the "loneliness" of his time in medical school. For the first time in his life he was not actively involved in school organizations or groups. "I didn't find many people I could get attached to." All through high school he had been at the center of school life, and he had emerged as a quiet, but forceful leader. The activism continued through college when he was "involved, immersed, and committed" to numerous causes and a variety of groups including the Chemistry Club, the Du Bois Club, ROTC Band, the Young Methodists, Alpha Phi Alpha fraternity, and the school magazine. In several of these organizations, he took prominent leadership roles. But despite the fact that he remained on the same campus at Howard, medical school was an entirely different experience. Tony felt the dramatic shift from being deeply involved to being on the periphery; from being intellectually engaged to being unchallenged and bored; from being politically active to having "no political energy or fervor." The lack of connection and attachment to the people and groups around him made him feel "lonely" and "alienated," made him feel like he "was holding his breath" until he could escape the emptiness.

He made two escapes during his fourth year of medical school. The first was a traveling fellowship to study neurosurgery at McGill University in Montreal for several weeks. The second was an externship at the Mayo Clinic in Rochester, Minnesota. Both were very cold places in the "dead of winter." Both were very white places, a dramatic contrast to the blackness of Howard. Tony recalls the remoteness. "Rochester was like being on a farm. It was very desolate." Despite the cold barrenness of the landscape, Rochester felt like an intellectual oasis, an invigorating scientific community. In retrospect, Tony sees his short time there as a major developmental moment. "There was some process underway encouraging me to make a transition from Howard Medical School to something else scientific and serious." But he sees another part of the transition: "In the process, I got unhooked from black society." We do not explore this. His words hang there heavy in the air. But I hear "serious and scientific" as connected to "whiteness," and I make a note to myself to pursue this idea when it feels less raw.

Tony returned to medical school and black life in March of his senior year, and he had a great many decisions to make in a very short time. The biggest among them was his decision not to do a medical internship and instead to pursue laboratory work in neurophysiology. He had heard about Woolsey's lab at Wisconsin and contacted him immediately. Fortunately, Woolsey had plans to come to D.C. in a couple of weeks, so he arranged a meeting with Tony that concluded with an invitation to do a postdoctoral fellowship under him. Tony was enthusiastic. He couldn't wait to join the disciplined life of serious scientific pursuit. But Tony's parents were "horrified." They could not understand their son's shocking decision. "The idea of leaving medicine was provocative... I was doing something inscrutable... something my parents couldn't understand or respect. It was as if I had wasted four years of medical school." "My graduation was soured by the conflict between us," recalls Tony. It was a disappointing conclusion to a disappointing four years.

Tony's choice to do research, as he pointed out earlier, was also part of a strategy to avoid being drafted. "This was at the peak of the war, the hottest years," says Tony. "I did not want to put myself in the position where I would have to face up to Vietnam." So the laboratory was a safe retreat, an asylum from the violence of racism and militarism, as well as an intellectual oasis for Tony. "I liked the lifestyle of being a scientist," says Tony enthusiastically. "In the lab, you start the day taking off from where you left off... There are no distractions. It may take months, years of ongoing sustained research to solve the problem. In science you can really *focus*."

Tony's decision to "leave medicine" and pursue laboratory work was not his only "inscrutable" decision as far as his parents were concerned. By the time he graduated in 1967, he was adamant in his antiwar stance. He was not yet calling himself "a pacifist," but he was clear in his opposition to the Vietnam War. His father, who had been "a prominent officer in World War II," thought being a veteran was a very important role of honor, dignity, and status. "He believed the army was the only institution in this country that was desegregated, and he was proud of that," says Tony. "But my father was also a Republican because Abraham Lincoln and Frederick Douglass were Republicans... He had all kinds of debts to pay that didn't make sense to me."

"Landing in Madison, Wisconsin, was like that movie *Brother from Another Planet*," says Tony with a big laugh. "The movie is about a guy who is dropped into a ghetto in the Bronx and has to learn how to survive." Madison was a clean, friendly midwestern town where Tony felt like an oddity and had to learn a new culture. "You know, there were not many black people in Madison," recalls Tony. "But it was a liberal place in the late sixties, and a black person was an instant curiosity, even an instant celebrity." Being a "brother from another planet" ("By the way, I discovered I look *exactly* like Joe Morton, the actor who played the brother in the movie," Tony remarks) did not feel alienating to Tony. After the loneliness of four years in medical school at Howard, Madison seemed like an easy place in which to feel "attached" and comfortable. "I found it easy to live there. People were friendly and kind. It was the first time I'd been absorbed into a white community, and I had to reformulate my views of white people."

The culture shock wore off amazingly quickly as Tony began to meet like-minded people who shared his political and moral commitments. His voice is alive with enthusiasm. "It was interesting to find people with whom I had a lot in common intellectually, philosophically, politically, and aesthetically... Within six months, I was socially and politically active again... Madison was similar to Berkeley's campus... I loved all the exciting and invigorating activity. Everyone was coming through there in a grand parade—Dick Gregory, when he was a presidential candidate, Jesse Jackson... My *man*, Sonny Rollins, came to give a concert." He is practically hooting with pleasure. "I became the resident expert on civil rights. On some occasions, I *was* a celebrity." He is only half joking.

For a time, this political activism and the cultural events were a wonderful counterpart to Tony's life in the laboratory. "I *loved* the lifestyle of being a scientist, the chance to really focus without distraction... but I could work the hours that I chose... and when it was time to attend to the big world with big activity, I loved becoming involved in that." After the barrenness of medical school, it was so good to feel the renewal of "energy, involvement, and commitment." "It was like getting back to the mind-set of college but in a very different environment."

Despite the progressive politics and liberal theater of Madison, Tony often felt the remoteness of Middle America. He felt far removed from the gritty activism of urban life that he had known in Washington, far from the intensity of southern race wars that he had known in Memphis. Also he sometimes felt suspicious of his token black status and the visibility and celebrity it caused. He yearned for the black activism he had known all of his life.

Now that Tony has sketched the scene, he is ready to focus on the central drama of Madison. His voice is theatrical. "It was in that rich, dynamic context that I met Mary." Also a postdoctoral student in the neurophysiology laboratory, Mary, who is white, had returned to Madison from Tulane University in New Orleans, where she had received her Ph.D. in experimental psychology. Tony and Mary shared an office, but they also shared stories about Tony's beloved New Orleans. While she was a graduate student at Tulane, Mary had lived in an apartment right above Preservation Hall in the French Quarter. She loved jazz and had gotten to know several of the musicians very well. Tony was immediately drawn to this woman who knew and appreciated the roots from which he came. "She was living as a student twelve blocks from where I grew up," says Tony in amazement. "I was very impressed with all we had in common." The New Orleans connection was not all that Tony and Mary shared; both were also devoted scientists and committed to the same social and political goals. "I think it was very important to me that Mary was very smart," recalls Tony. "I was drawn to her mind... But we also believed in the same values."

When Mary arrived in Madison she was pregnant and married

to a graduate student in physics. Since they shared an office and quickly discovered their common bonds, Mary and Tony found themselves spending a lot of time together. At first, when they were together they were mostly in the company of a tight group of colleagues working in the lab. But over time, they got "more and more selective" about spending time with one another. Mary's baby, Leigh, was born, and she would bring the tiny infant to the lab. Tony could feel his growing "attachment" to this mother and baby. "There was a kind of commonality of values, perspectives, and science... and now Leigh."

Tony tells this story slowly, reflectively, struggling to find the tone and the language that will both protect the privacy of their relationship and convey the poignancy of their deepening commitment. He seems to want to give the same seriousness and authenticity to the narration of this tale as he did to living through it. "After a while, I decided I really did like this woman," he says pensively. "It didn't seem right, but maybe I *loved* her. I was not obsessed by all of this, but I could feel something really *strong* here." One day he decided to take her out to lunch, "to put it on the line and see what happened." He talked to Mary about their important friendship, their common interests, and their growing bonds. But he also told her of a certain feeling of "awkwardness" he was experiencing with her and the surprising surge of "romantic" impulses. Finally, he disclosed that he had discovered that he *"loved"* her. Across the table, Mary was in shock. She had not expected to hear any of this from her close friend. "She occupied a certain settled place in life," says Tony. "She was married with a child, and I had shaken her up." Mary was too stunned to respond. She rose up from the table in silence and walked away.

Although they worked alongside one another in the lab, Mary and Tony didn't talk about their "shocking" encounter for a week. Tony felt relieved to have said his piece even though he had some apprehension about what was now stirring inside Mary. He wanted to give her the space she needed to think, *and* he was determined to have her make the next move. Several days after their lunch, Mary approached him wanting to talk. She confessed that her days had been filled with anguish as she struggled to make some sense of her feelings of connection to him. As she talked, as they looked deep into each other's eyes, it became clear. *"Then it happened,"* says Tony with a gesture of finality. "The love affair was on."

"This was strong, heady stuff that Mary and I were involved in," says Tony, and it combined with other stirrings in his heart and mind. "These were not ordinary times... Right across from our lab I had watched another science building blow up—all the animal cages exploded... monkeys and cats flying all over the place. It is very possible that the courage to have this encounter with Mary may have been an echo of the times we were living in. I was going for broke." As he was becoming involved with Mary, he was deciding that he could no longer "hide out in the laboratory." "It was too remote, too distant." After Martin Luther King's death, his part-time political activism in Madison no longer seemed sufficient. Tony felt compelled to "leave the lab and head to Harlem, to get back on track, to join with others in taking up this work."

As Tony revisits this time of passion and politics, he sees the converging forces that accelerated his departure from Madison. He felt compelled "to move from the lab into the streets." He needed to get some distance on this relationship with Mary. "I needed to get away... It didn't make sense to be having an affair with a married woman, a white woman... I kept on having images of the brutal lynching of Emmett Till." And he needed to give Mary some space to figure out how she felt. "The love affair and the decision to leave the lab propelled me to get in my car and explore the possibility of an instant internship."

Tony's destination was New York, a city that had begun to symbolize escape *and* commitment. He applied to three places for an internship in pediatrics—Bellevue, Harlem, and Metropolitan—all big-city hospitals serving poor communities with large brown and black populations. He chose Metropolitan Hospital in East Harlem because they responded to his application immediately and said he could "begin work tomorrow." Within the space of a few weeks, Tony had moved from a white midwestern university town full of culture, art, and intellectual politics to a black and brown city neighborhood raging with political action, poverty, and violence. He had moved from doing rarified research at a pristine laboratory to practicing frontline medicine treating newborn babies afflicted by their mothers' poisonous consumption of drugs. He had moved from a "wonderfully balanced" life of being both a scientist and an activist to an exhausting existence as an intern, always "sick and sleep deprived." And he had moved from a postdoctoral position that protected him from "having to face the Vietnam War" to a medical internship that made him immediately vulnerable to the draft.

Sure enough, six weeks after Tony arrived in East Harlem "the army pounced" on him. By that time, not only was he confirmed in his opposition to the Vietnam War, but he was also clear that— philosophically and ethically—he could not participate in *any* war. Although he had not yet developed a coherent and articulate philosophy, he had begun to think of himself as a pacifist. So when the army came after him, he knew that he would have to declare himself a conscientious objector. As Tony had explained earlier, he went to the American Friends Service Committee for guidance, resources, and networks. They pointed him to Stephen Hyman, a civil rights lawyer who questioned Tony about his reasons for seeking C.O. status. Tony's responses were earnest but vague. "I told him about my Civil Rights activities, the connections I saw between domestic and international struggles against oppression, and my strong sense that the war was wrong," recalls Tony. Hyman believed Tony's sincerity but knew that his argument was not strong enough to stand the test of legal scrutiny. "That's not good enough," Hyman said, and urged Tony to devote himself to developing a compelling and convincing statement of his philosophical position.

Tony took up the challenge and spent the next few months doing "a lot of reading, thinking, and soul searching." It was hard work but the kind of philosophical, mind-expanding exploration that Tony clearly loves. "I emerged with the Chinese painting orientation of my life," he says mysteriously. "Well, you know that Chinese paintings have big landscapes, massive mountains, rolling valleys, and *little* people. I've always been captured by the contrast with Western painting—where the person is huge, big head and prominent features, and the landscape is in the background... The Mona Lisa is a good example. My view of nature is like the Chinese landscape... People are rather small... Proper life is respecting this immense landscape." It was Chinese painting that Tony's mind saw as he worked on the development of his pacifist philosophy.

Tony's philosophical musings were "intellectually grounded" in the work of Spinoza and Darwin. He read Spinoza and "appreciated [his] movement away from Western thought, away from the idea of divine intervention." He was drawn to Spinoza's notion that a series of principles govern nature. The order and coherence to nature do not require a divine presence. But Charles Darwin, whom Tony regards "as the greatest of all scientists," provided the intellectual scaffold for Tony's emerging philosophy in his statements on natural law. Tony is reverential in paying tribute to Darwin. "He set forth a set of principles and ideas based on observational data. You don't need another text to do that. You need clear-sightedness." Spinoza and Darwin became "the intellectual component of a larger intuition" that was expressed in Tony's "antipathy toward war." He began to refer to himself as a "naturalist," and he developed his own naturalist philosophy: "War is wrong in minimizing or destroying nature, which includes people."

The months of reading and reflection were sifted and organized into a long essay with five chapters: the first on Spinoza, the second on Darwin, the third on the "naturalist philosophy growing out of that," the fourth on Tony as "an aspiring scientist," and the fifth, an integration of the scientific and philosophical themes. Tony's memory of the structure and argument of his C.O. statement is vivid, and his voice is proud as he recalls his lawyer's response to his "soul searching." Hyman was very impressed with the "hard intellectual work," but he knew that in order for the statement to be really convincing to the judge, it had to be more than cerebral argumentation. It had to touch an emotional chord. So Hyman told Tony once again, "This is not good enough," and directed his client to "return to his childhood" to gather "evidence" of his early pacifist inclinations. That is when, at the insistence of his lawyer, Tony appealed to his old nemesis, Blair T. Hunt, who responded with a letter "more precious than gold," a letter that likened Tony's spirit to that of Jesus Christ. Hunt's letter became a "huge factor" in Judge Morris Lasker's deliberations. The New York District Court judge decided in Tony's favor, "a tremendous victory that became the basis of a great deal of publicity."

Mary joined Tony in some of this soul searching. She spent long hours talking with him about his values and views, discussing his readings, and reviewing drafts of his essay. By the time Tony was preparing his C.O. statement, Mary had separated from her husband and moved with her daughter Leigh to Washington, D.C., where she was doing research at the National Institutes of Health. With Mary's move to Washington, the two of them could spend weekends together and see how it felt to renew their relationship outside of the hospitable embrace of Madison. Tony smiles: "In D.C. there were a few remnants of relationships with other women, all black. I had to ask myself, 'Do I really want to hang out with a white woman in New York and D.C.?'... Madison was a whole other thing." Tony recalls the hard questions he and Mary asked of one another. "We seriously considered what this might mean in relation to differences in race and culture... what the price would be for being an integrated couple...."

Even under the scrutiny of these questions, the relationship between them continued to "grow and mature." Tony became increasingly convinced that they had found a rare and enduring love, a "real companionship." "I realized I had found a friend with whom I shared experiences in so many ways, and so profoundly," says Tony softly. "We felt we were willing to pay the price for this love."

Adaptation and Advocacy

When Tony told his father that he was going to marry Mary, his father took in his breath very slowly, creased his heavy brow, and said, "Well, I hope she's Jewish." It was Felton II's last ray of hope that his son might have at least chosen a white woman who would "understand what prejudice is all about." Alas, Mary was not even Jewish. Tony's mother sat in stony silence. Her face did not seem angry or hostile, just quiet in her resignation. "She did not resist," recalls Tony in a minimalist statement. "By this time, you see, my parents had come to think I was very crazy." His decision to "waste his medical school training" and study neurophysiology, his decision to become a conscientious objector—these "inscrutable" choices seemed strange and wrong-headed to them, left them feeling disappointed and distant.

But it was the decision to become a C.O. that offended his parents the most—especially his father, the proud war veteran. About this choice, Felton II refused to remain silent. He worked hard to convince his son that his pacifism would "ruin his life," and he enlisted the help of his friends in trying to convince Tony how "crazy" it was. Tony remembers his father's desperate attempts to change his mind. "Each time I'd return to Memphis, he'd set a trap for me. I'd come in the door, drop my bags, and get a lecture from one of my father's important friends," smiles Tony. Felton II would arrange for the black men of status in Memphis—the judge, the sheriff, the deacon of the church—to come over and speak to his son. He hoped that their collective pressure and persuasiveness would knock some sense into Tony. Each one of the visitors spoke with determination and passion. "Boy, you're going to ruin your life with this C.O. stuff. They'll think you are a communist. Your professional life will be destroyed."

Not only did they worry about how Tony might be labeled and victimized by the C.O. status; they also believed in the honor and dignity of being a soldier and a veteran. They would preach to Tony, "Being a veteran will give you *leverage* in this society. If you are a veteran, you will never feel like a second-class citizen." Tony would sit and listen to the appeals of this parade of proud black veterans. He knew that he would not change his position no matter how deeply they believed or how persuasively they argued. He also knew that there was no use in his trying to convince them of his stance. But he greatly respected the ritual, the gesture of concern and advice giving from the community elders. For Tony, the ritual underscored their strong sense of connection and responsibility to the next generation *and* the break he was making with his family and community.

Felton II never respected or understood his boy's pacifist philosophy. He continued to believe the "C.O. stuff" was dead wrong. But he did warm up to his son's wife. Tony remembers his father visiting them one weekend in Washington, D.C., before they were married and the three of them going out to a jazz club. "When he was sick and dying he often referred to the wonderful time we three had together. He really grew to like Mary. Knowing her better made it seem as if I was not *entirely* crazy!"

Mary's daughter Leigh was four years old when Tony and Mary got married, but Tony had actually been "fathering" her for more than a year—"participating in decisions about her life, developing an important relationship, and deeply caring for her." The father-daughter bonds were already strong for both of them, making the marriage seem like a "nonevent" for the little girl. For the weeks leading up to the wedding ("You can't call it a wedding; it was an event") Mary was still negotiating the red tape of finalizing her divorce. She and Leigh had moved from Washington, D.C., to join Tony who was completing the first year of his psychiatric residency at Massachusetts General Hospital in Boston. As soon as the divorce was final, they decided to get married—without fanfare or ceremony, "even without music"—at City Hall in Boston. They didn't want a grand celebration that would force family and friends to attend. Tony's voice is poignant. "This was a deeply personal bond between us... We knew that there was nothing in our union that society or my family would celebrate... We were in a period of transition... We had not yet begun to really develop new friendships in Boston, and my old friends were not as conservative as my parents, but they found it hard to keep up with all the changes in my life." He repeats the list of "inscrutable" choices that over the years had baffled his friends, as well: "The C.O. thing, marrying a white woman, the change from laboratory research to clinical work—all these things made my friends feel as if they didn't know me."

So on the day of "the event" Mary and Tony fetched Leigh at her nursery school, which was right around the corner from City Hall. The three of them walked the few blocks up the hill and within moments were standing before "the magistrate." Although they were "fully prepared" in their serious commitment to one another, they had not given much thought to "the event." They regarded it as a "bureaucratic transaction." Tony was stunned when the magistrate leaned toward him and asked, "What do you have to give the bride?" He had brought "nothing" with him to present to Mary. "It had never occurred to me that I should have a ring!" says Tony with a big grin. He sees my look of incredulity and assures me, "It *really* hadn't, Sara." The magistrate told them that he could not "complete the transaction" without a symbolic offering from Tony. "We were silent for a while, then Mary came up with an idea." She remembered that months ago she had given Tony a gold chain necklace, which he was wearing that day. He could give the gold chain to her "and later on, she could return it to him." So that is what they did, and the event went forward without further delay.

At this point, Tony leaps at the chance to talk about his fathering. Parenting is a large and important part of his life, central to his identity, and he speaks about it with great passion. As a developmentalist and child psychiatrist, he has found that there are many ways in which his research, clinical work, and parenting inform one another. But it is clear that parenting is the most challenging and difficult work—that Tony's knowledge of child development theories do not necessarily make his fathering easier. He lets out a long sigh before beginning with a statement born out of his experience of parenting two daughters, not out of his reading of the literature. "Fathering is very much a business of adjusting to a child's temperament... It is a constant process of adaptation... accommodating to who the child is."

Tony learned this lesson of "adaptation" from Leigh, whose temperament, from the time she was a tiny baby, was very different from his own. The striking contrasts in their style and character were a constant source of dismay for Tony; Leigh was always testing his mettle and his patience, always "keeping me on my toes." As he speaks about the challenges of fathering Leigh, his voice is filled with love; his stories reflect the searching and vulnerability that characterize their relationship. "Leigh's development has been consistently marked by two characteristics: she is impulsive, and she is very, very smart. She is not a very reflective kid, not one to enlarge emotional issues... If she is going through something, she is not very introspective about it... Her impulsivity leads to anger... She has a hot temper. I have a lot of difficulty dealing with anger. I'm not impulsive... I think impulsivity is very dangerous." After drawing the first contrast he pauses and throws his head back as if it is heavy with the memory of hundreds of father-daughter struggles. I ask how he managed these big differences between them, and a large grin spreads over his face. (I think to myself that the passion of parenting seems to offer us two choices: we can either laugh or weep.) "I don't know, Sara," he says laughing. "It was off the cuff... trial and error. I tried to teach patience... whatever I did, it didn't work!"

Just as compelling as the emotional contrasts were the differences in the ways Tony's and Leigh's minds work, the character of their intelligence. "Leigh has a very quick, very literal intelligence... She reads something or listens to a set of facts and gets the picture real fast. There are these flashes going on all the time... flashes of brilliance and flashes of anger. This has been extremely challenging for me, many frustrating moments... I'm not that fast paced. I find myself not being able to adjust and respond quickly or strategically enough." As I listen, I am feeling deeply identified with Tony's parental perspective—with his recognition of the father-daughter differences and his admiration of Leigh's strengths; with his struggles to understand and negotiate with his daughter; with his frank admission of his own imperfections. I also hear in his description his recognition of the ways in which parenting instructs us in who we are and what we need. Tony speaks about fathering as deeply educational. He cannot always identify the contribution he has made to his daughter's development, but he knows it is there. "Over all, Leigh has succeeded... Whatever my contribution, it has been part of the success."

Tony's eyes brighten and his voice announces the "most frustrating" and hazardous era of parenting: "Aha! Then I made the most radical discovery of my life—what it means to raise an adolescent female." He begins with a statement that shows he recognizes that the hard and necessary work of adolescence—establishing autonomy—inevitably causes distance and creates conflict with parents. "Leigh—at fourteen—encountered the demands of being an adolescent. I found fathering during that period—from fourteen to eighteen—extremely difficult." The intense interactions that Mary and Leigh had always known were amplified during those years. "In order to protect her autonomy, Leigh became very demanding. She wanted to call her own shots... Mary worried about who she was going out with, whether she was drinking, and so on. The worry eroded Leigh's autonomy. They would have these huge clashes [he makes the sound of a cymbal]... going at each other... big, violent eruptions. Every day it was like this... two very strong, extremely stubborn women." Tony watched the fireworks, feeling "sidelined," powerless to do anything. "Before, I had always been part of the triangle, always had leverage. Suddenly I felt pushed out. I felt very weakened."

But the intense mother-daughter conflicts not only made Tony feel excluded and powerless (like he was a "referee"); they also scared him. "I'd worry about the conflicts getting out of control," he admits. "The conflicts would be very combative, very volatile... They'd get so angry... Then they'd walk away. Within ten minutes I'd find Leigh sitting at her desk studying or whistling... same thing with Mary. And I'd still be feeling devastated and involved!... Then they'd tell me *I* was overreacting." Watching the female warfare and feeling anxious about the dangers, Tony often wondered about the differences in the ways men and women, boys and girls, express anger and resolve conflict. Sitting on the "periphery," he remembers thinking, "If men were fighting this intensely, someone would be killed. How much of my response is male?... How much is my temperament?"

Tony keeps on returning to the most difficult part of fathering "an adolescent female"—the loss of "leverage," the loss of "control over this experience." "Fathering became a sideline activity." He recalls a passage from Bertrand Russell's autobiography that struck a deep chord in him when he read it several years ago. Russell had one daughter to whom he was deeply devoted. He was devastated when during early adolescence she abandoned him. Tony remembers Russell's anguished words—"I lost her"—and remembers feeling the same pain, "a sense of being disconnected." "I felt barren, barren, empty... You go through all of this deep involvement, and then suddenly there is nothing."

As Tony tells his story of Leigh's adolescence, I listen hungrily, trying to drink in all the wisdom as I anticipate the approach of my own daughter's adolescence in the next couple of years. I hear many sides to Tony's tale. All at once, it is a saga of the dynamics of one family's unique relationships, and it is also the universal developmental story of an adolescent's need to establish autonomy (what Tony refers to as "the demands of being an adolescent") and the inevitable clashes that erupt as parents and children struggle with new ways of relating to one another. And it is an unusual tale of a father's view: his sense of being "pushed out," "sidelined" from his central role as parent, and the pain this transition causes. Finally, I hear the intrigue of a developmentalist bringing his trained eyes to the scene, knowing in his head that this is the natural, healthy work of adolescence, but feeling in his heart the fear and barrenness.

I am so caught up in all of these stories that I heave a huge sigh of relief when Tony reports Leigh's emergence on the other side of this volcanic time—her "return to the person I knew"; his "amazement" that when she came home from her first semester at college, "she really enjoyed being with us." "She was launched, and we had *endured!*" Now as he watches the choices Leigh is making as a young adult, he admires her values, her ambition, her intellect, and he sees his and Mary's deep imprint. Her first two years after graduating from college she worked for Oxfam America in Boston, then she spent a year as a community worker connecting poor families to social services in Bedford Stuyvesant ("the only white person living in this all-black neighborhood"). Now she is in law school in Boston, focusing on public interest law. This summer she will be working for the Lawyer's Committee for Civil Rights. "She has been working and living for justice," says Tony proudly. Then reflecting back on their differences—in temperament and styles of intelligence—differences that have always made parenting "challenging," Tony says, "If I ever needed help in working out a puzzle or resolving a problem... if I needed an *activist*—someone real smart, real engaged, who could get it done—Leigh is the person I would call on."

When Leigh was seven, Tanya was born. The Earlses were spending the year in London, where Tony had a research fellowship to study epidemiology and Mary was enjoying the rare pleasure of not working. "It was a great year," remarks Tony, recalling the adventure and restfulness of this time when life slowed down enough so the family could "really prepare for" the new baby. Tony loved being the father of this beautiful newborn. "I enjoyed infancy. It was wonderful. I had missed this part with Leigh, and I had no idea it could be so amazing." I ask what the most amazing part was, and Tony's voice is soft and tender in response. "Attachment comes to mind—the fragility, dependency, purity of an infant... There is a straight, uncomplicated, direct interaction. The infant wants you, needs you." His voice brightens. "Tanya was an interested, spontaneous, effervescent baby, and we had a great relationship... She was the joy of my life."

At the end of their year in London, Tony, Mary, and Tanya stopped for a month in East Africa before returning home (Leigh remained in England). "It was a little daring traveling to Tanzania with a tiny baby, but we had a wonderful time." Tanya was the center of attention. "In East Africa babies are treated like princesses. Everywhere we went people would crowd around the baby." Mary and Tony thought briefly about living and working in Dar es Salaam, where he was being offered a job in the university's Department of Psychiatry. Exciting changes were happening in Tanzania under Julius Nyrere's inspired leadership. The Earlses felt drawn into the political and intellectual whirl of activity. They also loved traveling as a family, experiencing the rich differences in culture and terrain. Even though they decided to return to Boston ("We felt so vulnerable in terms of infectious diseases"), they knew that this was just the beginning of the international travel that would be a vital part of their family and work lives. As little baby Tanya grew, she would accompany her parents all over the globe—to China, to Australia and the South Pacific.

Fathering Tanya was another lesson in adaptation, a chance to adjust to his second child's special temperament. "Tanya was the opposite of Leigh, emotionally and temperamentally," says Tony. In contrast to Leigh, Tanya seemed "reclusive"; she didn't "[express] her feelings except through her poetry—in which she is very open about her feelings." In telling the story of Tanya's development, Tony focuses on the advocacy that is so central to parenting, on the ways he tried to protect, support, and guide her through difficult times. He remembers years of searching for rewarding educational settings that would nourish Tanya's intellect and soul, schools where teachers would be "empathic and caring"; environments where there would be a workable balance between structure and freedom. He remembers scores of parent-teacher conferences in which he and Mary would struggle to communicate their perspective and their concerns, their views of Tanya's strengths and vulnerabilities. He recalls Tanya's two "wonderful" years at a Montessori school in Boston (from nursery school through first grade), which were characterized by a consonance of values and ambitions between the school and the Earls family. And he recalls a "horrible" year at a school in St. Louis where Tanya was "losing skills and unlearning things... a chaotic scene where the class was out of control and three or four bully, monster kids were ruling the roost."

Tanya would come home with pieces of lead stuck in her arm, where the bullies had jabbed her with their pencils. Or he thinks about the years when Tanya's "self-confidence was in jeopardy" because the teachers couldn't see or reward her special gifts. And, of course, Tony remembers the shock of adolescence—the mood swings, the silences, the rage, and the breakthroughs. "Tanya's adolescence was even more dramatic than Leigh's."

All of these memories come flooding back—the dangers, the threats, the risks and the pleasures, the adventures, and the intimacy of parenting. There is a long silence before Tony offers a final stocktaking. "I think of myself as a caring, competent parent... very close to my children. I do not stand in their way... My role is to facilitate, to advocate... but not to lead or get in the way."

The Strategist

The year 1975 was "great" because that was the year Tanya arrived. But it was also a fruitful and exciting year in Tony's evolving work. The University of London was the place where Tony's professional identity was recast; from being a psychiatrist primarily interested in the emotional development of children Tony leaned toward using the tools of epidemiology to study the environments that shape human growth and experience. With three years of fellowship support from the Josiah Macy Foundation, Tony spent the first year at the London School of Hygiene and Tropical Medicine taking courses in biostatistics and epidemiology, and doing research at the Hospital for Sick Children.

The year before traveling to London, Tony had been doing his residency in general psychiatry at Massachusetts General Hospital, but he had been feeling increasingly frustrated by the individualistic focus of psychiatry. "I began to feel that the most powerful interventions would be *institutional*, not individual. I wanted to define a *science* in child psychiatry... to understand how *aggregate* populations of children manage to survive, thrive, or fall ill." There were not many who shared these interests or inclinations at Harvard, but there were colleagues at the University of London who were exploring the same ground—colleagues (like Michael Rutter, Philip Graham, and Naomi Richman) whose work combined child psychiatry and epidemiology. In London there was "an ethos that focused on solving big problems."

Tony could feel himself moving out into the world—away from the laboratory and into "natural living populations"; away from rarified empirical experiments into descriptive fieldwork. "Given my neurophysiology background," says Tony, "the natural thing for me to have done would be to do some sort of brain work... maybe psychopharmacology. But I didn't want to be in the laboratory locked away... I wanted to orient toward the community... I wanted to broaden my lens to include political, social, historical, and cultural work. London was a place where I could get excellent training in this relatively new and pioneering area."

Joining with his British colleagues, Tony participated in a large-scale survey research project looking at patterns of socialization and child development in immigrant families, mostly West Indian, Pakistani, and East Indian. "We were asking questions about how preschool children of immigrant families were doing compared to indigenous populations." They found that the behavioral adjustments of West Indian and Pakistani preschoolers were similar to those of their British counterparts, a finding that contrasted sharply with the low achievement and failure of immigrant children in school. "This was an important finding," recalls Tony, "because it indicated that the problems of immigrant children did not exist in their home life. This finding put pressure on the school system." Despite the careful design of the study and the systematic collection of data, these findings drew a skeptical response from the research and educational communities. "I had a lot of trouble publishing that paper," says Tony.

After a year of study and research in London, Tony returned to two more years of psychiatric training at Harvard, "calling myself an epidemiologist." I want to know how he defines the field and how he characterizes the work of epidemiology. Tony immediately corrects me. "Epidemiology is *not* a field. It is a methodology, a set of techniques... I am always saying I'm a *strategist*... armed with tools... trying to solve problems that are not easily encompassed by any single discipline. I might ask, How many people are ill? What kinds of illnesses do they have?... For those who are not ill, what protects them—their environment, development, constitution?... I might study aggression, violence, drug use, persistent poverty, poor achievement in school, low birth rates. I can't study all of these at once... That's why I need a whole lifetime!" Tony's face is intense, his voice animated as he describes the scope and eclecticism of his work.

His last line seems to hold lots of echoes: "Epidemiology is a ticket to go anywhere and study anything." As he almost sings these words, I can see eight-year-old Tony hopping on his bicycle and exploring the neighborhoods in New Orleans. I can see him driving across country, leaving the laboratory at the University of Wisconsin and heading for Metropolitan Hospital in East Harlem. I can hear the convergence of his scientific discipline and curiosity with his love for adventurous travel, his fascination with rich cultural variations. I can see him tracking the footsteps of his favorite scientist, Darwin.

The return to Harvard was not easy. In London, Tony had caught the research bug, and he was "itching to do more." His Harvard supervisors, many of whom were steeped in traditional interpretations of psychoanalysis, seemed to be speaking an alien language. Tony lets out a big laugh. "I saw psychoanalysis as being counterrevolutionary, if you will... I had an Antichrist mentality toward psychoanalysis... I had been with psychiatrists in London who were *resisting* psychoanalysis." Tony's quiet resistance was expressed in the way he structured his residency; he did very little clinical work. Instead, he focused on working with groups of patients—in clinics, on hospital units—and on continuing his research training. For example, he wanted to learn more about infant development, so he spent several months working on a research project with Dr. T. Berry Brazelton. But mostly, Tony anticipated the next step in his professional development—trying to figure out how he might continue his work in epidemiology.

When his three-year Macy fellowship ran out, Tony wrote a grant proposal to the National Institute of Mental Health. He was disappointed, but not surprised, when he did not receive an award. "I was turned down because they didn't understand or believe in epidemiology," recalls Tony. "I felt like a pioneer... I realized that I would have to *teach* the review committee about epidemiology in order to get funded." While he composed a new proposal, with a more didactic orientation, Tony worked at a community health center in Dorchester, running the mental health clinic; primarily he was supervising the care of chronic schizophrenic patients and others who had been released from state hospitals and were suddenly "out on the streets." Although he describes 1976–77 as a "tough year," Tony found his work in Dorchester challenging and eye-opening. Seeing hundreds of patients—mostly black and poor—he began asking himself questions about the convergence of poverty, race, temperament, and mental illness, questions that would inform his future research.

In 1977, Tony's second proposal to NIMH was successful, and he was able to begin a five-year epidemiological study of Martha's Vineyard. Using many of the methods he had learned in London, he chose the Vineyard as his research site because he thought of it as the "perfect microcosm": "close to ideal in terms of space, good medical care, good school system, enriching community, and responsive social networks." He thought of it as an "optimal laboratory" for examining the development of children in the first three years of life; for discovering the predictors—temperamental, familial, institutional—that lead to illness or vulnerability. Tony's voice is enthusiastic as he describes this "pioneering" work—the strategy, the discipline, the adventure, the learning. His years on the Vineyard were just as important to his development as a scientist ("I gained confidence as an epidemiologist") as they were to the amassing of research evidence. Although he learned a lot about how families raise their children and where they go for "institutional backup," Tony admits that he was not able to offer definitive answers on his "theory about [the Vineyard] being a microcosm." He is able to speak definitively, however, about how his craft and insights as an epidemiologist were strengthened and refined by the Vineyard study, about his growing independence and confidence as a researcher.

Tony used many of the same tools and techniques when, supported by a traveling fellowship, he and his family traveled to China for three months in 1981. For years Mary and Tony had been interested in China (Mary had been there for an extended visit in 1979), intrigued by the culture, the politics, the science, and the art. While in China, Tony hoped to examine the socioemotional development of Chinese children. He recalls, "I had heard so much about achievements under the Communist regime, particularly with regard to child health... I was interested in documenting how the society organized itself around children." From August to November, the Earlses were based in Shanghai, where Tony immersed himself in just the kind of work he loves. Although the three months only allowed him to collect preliminary data, he did emerge with strong impressions. "Chinese kids are remarkably healthy up through primary school... Repression occurs during adolescence (from twelve to eighteen years), when kids become much less spontaneous. A kind of rigidity sets in." More important, Tony emerged with a clear sense that this was the kind of work he wanted to do "forever." Epidemiology—his "ticket to travel"—combined all of his favorite things: his passion for science, his love of adventure, his curiosity about culture, his commitment to documentation, understanding, and social service/social action.

From the tiny microcosm of Martha's Vineyard, more than a decade ago, Tony has expanded his scope and his sights. Today he is in the midst of a massive study, funded by the National Institute of Justice and the MacArthur Foundation, trying to document the major sources of crime and violence in society. The big city of Chicago is the initial site where a large team of researchers from a variety of disciplines are spending six to eight million dollars a year investigating these critical questions of social pathology. "We are investigating the extent to which neighborhood, families, or individuals are major sources of crime or violence... looking at it as a complex system... asking where and when the interventions should optimally be made." Tony shakes his head wearily as if the magnitude of this huge effort is weighing heavily on him. Then he makes an initial prediction. "My hunch is that neighborhood-based or community-based interventions would make the greatest difference... rather than interventions at the level of family and individual."

But Tony's weariness not only reflects the large scope and ambition of the project; it also seems to mirror the controversial nature of the material. Doing this kind of science—the epidemiology of crime—inevitably puts Tony in the center of hot political and ethical disputes ("We are riding the crest of federal enthusiasm and incompetence")—dangerously close to the ancient and passionate arguments about heredity versus environment and uncomfortably close to the possibility of "blaming the victims." Doing this kind of science is about as far away from the secluded neurophysiology laboratory in Madison, Wisconsin, as Tony could possibly travel. Doing this kind of science is an act of courage and commitment for a black man who may have to say some things, based on his scientific judgments, that are unpopular or unsavory to the communities he serves: to his professional colleagues and to his community of origin. Doing this kind of science will require all the maturity, discipline, skill, and savvy Tony can muster.

Straight Up, No Chaser

Even though we have both anticipated this final session for several weeks, when I begin to speak about closing rituals, Tony spreads his arms and exclaims, "We've only just begun!" He is speaking for both of us. We are both feeling the sadness of concluding this rich conversation that has spread over several months. We are both amazed by how much ground we have covered and how deeply we have gone, and at the same time we feel as though we've just skimmed the surface of Tony's life. I make some feeble gesture to recognize the paradox and the sadness. "Research always feels like an oversimplification even when you try to capture the fullness and the complexity... and partings are so wrenching after you've shared so much." Tony makes a gesture of understanding. As both a researcher and a therapist, he has experienced these difficulties as well. So he helps me make a graceful exit by distinguishing between what he "knows" (which reflects a vivid understanding of an intimate and comprehensive research process) and what he "feels" (which is that I am leaving before he has told me the full story). "Life is like a river," he says. "It keeps flowing on and on... I think you have gotten most of it." We both fall back in our chairs and fall silent, feeling the moment of connection and separation and having given words to our complicated emotions.

I reach in my bag to pull out a small present, a ritualistic offering of thanks. I have searched my mind to come up with something that expresses the theme of our work together. I've chosen a small print of a Chinese landscape (to mark Tony's "Chinese landscape philosophy of life—big scenery and tiny people") and fancy cloisonne and ivory chopsticks for Tony and Mary. Tony looks at the print for a very long time and says softly, "Beautiful! Just right." Then he works the chopsticks. "You know, I used to carry around chopsticks in my briefcase all the time... and a small bottle of soy sauce so I'd always be ready. I'll have to start doing that again." He is grinning from ear to ear. "You know, we're going to Legal Seafood for dinner tonight, and I'll take along the chopsticks." His eyes light up. "This and the classical guitar." Now he has lost me. I get the scene of eating his fish dinner with his new chopsticks. But I don't get the guitar reference. He sees my puzzled look. "Well, I'm thinking this is the life... Legal Seafood, chopsticks... Now all that is missing is playing the classical guitar." He looks at me, laughing, and explains, "Didn't you know I studied the classical guitar... for almost ten years?" Here, in our last session together, Tony feels I know him well enough to conjure up the entire gestalt of all the "good things" (fish and chopsticks and music) that matter in his life. But, at the same time, he mentions an important experience—studying classical guitar—about which he has told me nothing.

Tony fills me in quickly. "I took lessons from the time I was about twenty-two years old. I learned it as an adult. It is such a beautiful instrument and so *hard* to play. Actually, I stopped taking lessons when my teacher, who was a wonderful lute player, left town... But I would love to return to it. It is a future goal." He goes on to say that the prospect is daunting because to move to the next level, to get really serious, he'd have to practice six or seven hours a day. Given the demands in his life, the time commitment would be impossible. But the fantasy of a life filled with the beauty, subtlety, and discipline of the classical guitar lingers and becomes part of a larger dream of a better, more fulfilling existence.

He tells the story of an extraordinary evening several years ago when he went to see Segovia play at Boston's Symphony Hall. Segovia was already in his eighties and suffering from Parkinson's disease. The hall was packed and quiet as Segovia walked through the stage door. Without assistance, he slowly made his way over to the chair that was center stage, weaving, bobbing, tottering from side to side as if he would never reach his destination. He managed to arrive safely and heave himself heavily into the chair. Even while seated, his body was in precarious motion. Tony kept worrying that he would fall too far forward, break his guitar, and bust his head wide open. It was a suspenseful moment as Segovia raised his trembling hands to the instrument. Just as his fingers reached the strings, they stopped shaking. The audience watched in awe and amazement as Segovia made the guitar sing eloquently. "It was magnificent!"

Music seems to offer Tony both beauty and nourishment. It is no surprise that he links it with chopsticks and seafood. It resonates from his roots in New Orleans and mixes with the aromas and tastes of Creole cooking. It echoes in the memories of Uncle Oscar, who insisted upon disciplined training, civilized behavior, and artful expression. It resounds through the decades. Playing in Uncle Oscar's band was far more demanding and strenuous than going to school. Music was a source of immediate connection to Mary, who had lived in an apartment over Preservation Hall in New Orleans, who had come to know several of the local jazz heroes, and shared his love of the sounds they produced. Music has always been a release from the harsh realities of political and social discord. Tony recalls the activism and radicalism of his days at the University of Wisconsin, the rage and grief after the killing of Martin Luther King, Jr. The demonstrations and marches, the blowing up of the physics building were made bearable because of the appearance of "my man Sonny Rollins," whose wailing saxophone sounds penetrated Tony's troubled soul.

I look over at the brooding face of Miles Davis filling the large poster across from Tony's desk and recognize that his image has been laced into our conversations. And I note the recent appearance of a Thelonious Monk poster that is leaning up against the wall waiting to be hung. "Straight no chaser" it says—words that I read as an admonition not to dilute the straight talk or compromise the bold vision. And now, in our final session, Tony is telling me about another source of musical nourishment, the classical guitar. It seems both continuous with the strong musical thread that has wound its way up from New Orleans and a departure from the jazz roots. Preservation Hall is a long way from Symphony Hall; the hot, juicy sounds of New Orleans jazz are a far cry from the subtle, spare baroque of Segovia's guitar. Music symbolizes the continuity and the discontinuity, the resonance and the dissonance of

Tony's life. Despite the different artistic and geographic origins, music is *home* in both places: New Orleans and Boston. In all the places in between—Memphis, Washington, D.C., and Madison, Wisconsin—it remained a soothing source.

I ask Tony to look over his life and identify the most creative moment or experience. His response is immediate. "I haven't lived it yet... I haven't done the most creative thing yet!" He is silent for a while and then chooses his words carefully. "When you asked me to bring in my vitae, I found myself studying it very hard." He is shaking his head in frustration. "The products listed on my C.V. all strike me as practice sessions. None of it feels final. None of it constitutes my final statement... I regard it as twenty years of preparation." I have heard this theme before, and it fits with the musical metaphor. Tony's frustration grows out of the need to produce "products" for his academic portfolio—products that prove his credentials as an academic researcher, but products that may not forward our understanding of the human experience. Tony's particular creativity, on the other hand, thrives when he has the chance to practice, to improvise, to make mistakes, to keep his work fluid and dynamic. If we regard research as practice, there is a better chance that we'll be open to collaborating with others; like an ensemble of jazz musicians working together, we'll strive together for harmony. And if we regard research as practice, then we are more likely to admit the weaknesses and imperfections in it and feel freer to pursue the truth. Tony recognizes the need for both the products and the practice. He knows he must collect the products for his professional portfolio and career advancement, but his own private agenda is to keep on practicing, to critically assess the work in progress.

For twenty years Tony has been preparing for his major creative work, which he describes as a study about "how large urban environments constrict development." At first he labels this "fantasy," then he says with decisiveness, "no, don't call it a fantasy, call it a *plan*." He is also searching for the right verb. "'Constrict' may not be right. It may be 'damage,' 'destroy,' 'violate,'... but the idea is that these big city environments are *suboptimal* to a child's development." He goes on to explain that most large cities have been designed for commerce, "not as places for people to grow up in." They have gotten bigger and bigger, "out of control," "totally unliveable," totally abusive of the human experience. "The mistake of civilization is to let the scale get too big." Tony's "plan" is to spend several years traveling around to a lot of cities—some that seem "out of control," and others that appear to be built to human scale. There are, of course, the cities, like Los Angeles and Mexico City, that are choking on their own pollution and overpopulation and "doing violence" to children's chances for successful growth. But there are also places, like Melbourne and Copenhagen, that seem to honor the human experience: the central part of the city is designed for commerce, but the surrounding neighborhoods are "well defined," "coherent," and "liveable."

Tony wants to study the variety of urban designs, asking the same central question across all of the settings: "What are the absolute necessities of context allowing a child to develop optimally?" His favorite analogy for this work is Charles Darwin's *Voyage of the Beagle*, a piece of science that he loves for its adventurousness, its disciplined observation, and its lucidity. His whole face shows his eagerness. "I want to learn about the landscapes, the history, the culture. I want to have good enough contacts in each place so I can work productively for three to six months—looking, observing, and telling stories about kids growing up." His plan is to focus his lens on young children, ages one to six years for three reasons: First, he regards these years as critical developmentally. ("What is happening in the first five years is in many ways irreversible in both a positive and a negative sense.") Second, since he will not be fluent in the language spoken in most of these countries, it makes sense to center his observations on nonverbal behaviors. He explains, "I am interested in how young children interact socially... how they cooperate and resolve conflict. To do this, I don't need to understand verbal, linguistic exchanges. I can learn a lot from gestures, eye contact, body language. Language, in fact, may just be another form of behavior." But the third reason Tony gives for wanting to study young children is perhaps what intrigues him the most:

"Young children are less biased and judgmental in their behavior than older children. There is such richness in their spontaneous play that provides a *window* into how they are experiencing the environment around them." The children's spontaneity not only allows us to document their social dialogues and relationships, it also, argues Tony, provides us with a way to examine the activities, priorities, and values of the society of which they are a part.

Tony claims that he has had this project in "the back of my mind" for at least twenty years, and that it has been the impetus behind much of his traveling around the world. "Mary has shared in a lot of this," says Tony about his partner, who has been an avid traveling companion with similar interests in culture and development. But with two "almost grown" daughters and with a lot of "practice sessions" under his belt, he feels almost ready to embark on this life's plan. He will be going to Stockholm for six weeks in the fall (and will return for six weeks in the spring) as a visiting fellow in child psychiatry at the Karolinska Institute. His plan is to make some initial observations and begin to develop the contacts and the methods that will shape this large piece of work. He also hopes to travel over to East Germany to look at how families and children are experiencing "the dismantling of the best developmental day care in the Communist countries." "Actually, I would like to study kids on both sides of the line, East versus West." His voice is full of excitement. In small ways, he is already at work on "the most creative piece of work" for which he has been "practicing" for almost a quarter century. He wants to make sure that he is "ready to do it," but he also feels some urgency. "I can almost see myself retiring from academic life and doing this for the next ten or fifteen or even twenty years," Tony says. "I don't want to wait too long!"

When I ask Tony to identify his most *successful* moment, his response is, once again, immediate and focused on his research. Without hesitation he cites the study he did on Martha's Vineyard. "I learned so much... Most of it got compressed into a lot of journal articles." In the midst of this "successful" venture, Tony experienced "something of a disappointment." In 1983, a reporter from the *New York Times* did a large piece on the Vineyard study that gave the research a sudden visibility. Tony, who had been working in privacy and seclusion on the island, immediately began to receive calls from numerous publishers who wanted him to write a book about his work. Doubleday made the best bid, and Tony signed a contract with them. For three months during the summer he labored hard to produce the book, but Doubleday was not satisfied with any of the drafts he produced. Despite the fact that Tony worked "very hard to stimulate the interest of the reader," he "wouldn't popularize it enough for them," and finally "the contract got canceled."

Tony seems to regret "the loss of all that time," but he doesn't seem to experience the canceled contract or the aborted effort as a career defeat. Perhaps he sees it as another practice effort; one that revealed the difficulties in translating his empirical discoveries into narrative language, the difficulties in moving from the laboratory to the public arena. He is still excited by a "clever idea" he tried in the book that ultimately "bombed." Tony admits, "At the time, I thought it was great... the publishers didn't like it at all. Now I think they were probably right." But he remains intrigued by the notion of providing the readers with "multiple data sources" on the family and then asking them to "match a child with a particular family." Based on the descriptions of the family, could the readers predict that child's temperament, behavior, and vulnerabilities? Actually, Tony was asking the reader to work with the central research question, "Is the child's personality a logical outgrowth of the family and environmental contexts from which he/she comes?"

I ask him to answer that question and he demurs. "It's a complicated answer... yes and no. Boys react to difficulties in the family and in the environment with much less complexity, giving a straightforward response... Boys are made vulnerable by family trauma. Girls, on the other hand, are much harder to figure out. They live in very stressful environments and can look amazingly good." In the Vineyard study, gender differences predominated, forcing Tony to consider the age-old question of whether these differences were the result of biological or environmental influences. "I've been pushed by my data to believe that biology is the most important," says Tony in a statement that he knows may not appear to be "politically correct." It is actually his next observation that is stunning to me. "I believe that boys and girls are more different when they are young than when they get older. One effect of socialization is to make girls and boys more alike... Socialization is designed to create more harmonious relationships between males and females; [to diminish the] differences that are more dramatic at the beginning of their lives." This strikes me as a statement that is counter to most views of gender differences. The common assumption is that differences between boys and girls are reinforced and exaggerated through acculturation: first through early training in gender roles and later through social bias and institutional tracking. Tony seems to be making a controversial assertion, but his face and voice reveal no irreverence.

Perhaps his counterintuitive statement stirs my next question about the creative impulses of men in their middle years. As I have listened to Tony's plans for his work in the next fifteen to twenty years of his life, I am struck by his generative energy. At fifty years old, he is still practicing, preparing, improvising, and planning for his major life's work. This seems to me so different from the midlife slump, the feelings of stasis and burnout that so many men in their middle years suffer. So I ask him whether he thinks of himself as different from his male colleagues in this regard. He is silent for a long time and then says, "Many men in their fifties turn toward jobs as big-shot administrators... but I don't think of that as particularly creative. I think of administration as status and stasis, not intellectual or moral growth." He does admit that a tiny proportion of administrators become "leaders," not just bureaucrats, and work to "transform institutions." But leaders are rare. He believes that most people who fill administrative roles are neither creative nor courageous. They get locked in their roles; they hide behind their masks and work hard to maintain the status quo.

Tony sees black men as particularly vulnerable. He cites the early lesson of his mentor, Chester Pierce, who warned his young black male residents to protect themselves from burnout. "Black men *do* burn out," says Tony. "Making it to fifty with energy, creativity, and long vision is rare, and it's hard." He takes a photograph out of his briefcase, a picture of Tony with three South African journalists—his good friends, his comrades, his "brothers in the struggle." "I call this photo 'grounding with my brothers,'" explains Tony with feeling, as if the image we are looking at is rare and precious. "At my level of operation—where we are professionally in the institutions within which we work—it is very difficult to shape a future with a group of people I'd call my brothers. I find myself in a group of *white* colleagues who share my work, training, and credentialing... I am very much alone in their midst." Being surrounded by white faces, hearing only white perspectives is not only isolating and lonely; it also gives you a distorted sense of your power and your authority. Your voice is amplified—much too loud—and you find yourself speaking for too many. Tony looks at the photograph with his South African friends and aches for the comfort, authenticity, *and* grounding of the all-black discourse. "I miss being a *minor* voice in a much larger sea that is harmonious... It is hard to put my point of view, my perspective on the table for discussion, for the refinement of ideas... You need a constituency to do that."

He recalls the magnificent feeling of being drawn into the black discourse in South Africa, "being readily embraced by my brothers." "We had deep and immediate connections through jazz... They know the work of Duke, Monk, Mingus, Armstrong... so that there was a musical union right away. But there was also this powerful political camaraderie... a harmonious way of expressing ourselves... a real sense of collective power." His eyes move away from the potent image of "grounding with my brothers," and he stares out the window and into the distance. His voice is almost a whisper: "The camaraderie is very difficult here. We are more diffuse in the structures we work in... Our self-defeating postures are upsetting and destructive... They mix with the institutional barriers." He shakes his head slowly.

I feel the echoes of earlier conversations and realize that we have come full circle. I remind Tony that this is where we began. During our first session together several months ago, Tony opened the conversation by pointing to his alliance with Derrick Bell. Tony had referred to that day's newspaper article showing Bell in angry protest, showing him all alone against a resistant institution. Tony, who has for years worked in the same institution but had never met Bell (a sign of "our diffusion"), had wanted to reach out to his brother in support. He had wanted to find "grounding with his brother" and feel "the musical union" he so desperately misses. Instead, in his office on the third floor of Harvard's School of Public Health, where Tony is a token tenured black professor, he is surrounded by the faces of Miles Davis, Thelonious Monk, and his South African brothers. I feel his penetrating loneliness. We've come full circle even though we've only just begun.

WORK AND JAZZ

Celebrating his fiftieth birthday, Tony Earls is reluctant to accept my praise for all he has accomplished. He feels as if he has barely gotten started, barely hit his stride. In terms of the traditional judgments applied to a career—a tenured professorship at Harvard, dozens of articles published in refereed journals, success in securing large grants—Tony admits that he has been successful. His portfolio is impressive and his career is mature. But measured by the more stringent standards that he applies to himself—the impact of his science in bettering the lives of people—his work is in its infancy. He is not yet satisfied and suspects that he never will be. He feels an urgency to pursue a more complex type of science: one that offers insights and direction to clinicians and policymakers.

This self-criticism is not self-deprecation. Tony is not putting himself down. This view of his work as unfinished and emerging inspires and energizes him. He presses forward, seeing the pieces in his portfolio as exercises, practice sessions, variations on earlier themes. He never views them as completed products; they are part of a process of discovery and improvisation. "I think like a jazz musician," he says. The creativity in his work is founded in the marrying of the discipline and ritual of an underlying structure with the freedom and risks of improvisation. The latter depends upon a mastery of the former.

Work is central to the development and identity of all the storytellers in this book. It consumes their time and their thinking. It captures their imagination and energy. It is a vehicle for their passion, a measure of their growth. For them, work is larger than career. "Career" is institutionally defined; it is judged by external standards, linked to status and position. "Work" is a more self-defined, dynamic notion that has less to do with station and more to do with commitment and contribution; less to do with product and more to do with process. Doing good work is more demanding than building an illustrious career, because one's work is judged by tougher, more complex standards. To these storytellers, good work must not only be inspiring to the individual; it must also have some impact on the world. Work must contribute not only to a person's development and growth, but also to transforming and improving society.

To fulfill such standards, Tony Earls must cross disciplinary and institutional boundaries. He makes judgments about the precision of his research but also evaluates its practicality and relevance. To document and explore societal problems—poverty, crime, trauma, violence—he must move back and forth between the academy and the real world, and he must work collaboratively with colleagues from other disciplines. This requires translation, negotiation, and bridge building. Again, jazz offers a model. Jazz musicians engage in improvisational conversation. Each instrument is important to the mix. Musicians must listen carefully to one another, take turns soloing, and find common ground. Each performance is different, a unique expression of the musicians' muse and mood; what they choose as context, structure, and theme; and how they respond to their audience. In Tony's work, he must also listen and collaborate, speak to various audiences, make emotional and intellectual connections, and create a conversation in several voices.

The need to cross boundaries, to use eclectic methods and speak to various audiences, is common to all those whose stories meet in this book. At the Harvard Law School, Charles Ogletree embraces the duality of his role as legal theorist and activist, as academic and public defender. He lives each of these roles in dynamic counterpoint. He could not tolerate the rarified life of an academic. His teaching has meaning only as it interacts with his activism. Likewise, his advocacy is constantly refined and informed by academic dialogue and collegial scrutiny.

When his old friend, who is counsel for the NAACP, called Charles in desperation ("These Negroes are about to support the nomination of Clarence Thomas. They're saying they can't publicly oppose the nomination because he's black—any black is better than no black at all"), Charles immediately responded to his friend's plea. In several days' time—"between all the other stuff"—he produced a legal document that analyzed the judicial opinions of Thomas and became the basis for the NAACP's statement of opposition to Thomas's nomination to the Supreme Court. Here Charles was in his element: helping an old buddy; responding quickly and strategically to a political crisis; using his academic resources, stature, and perspective to inform and influence public debate; acting as translator between the academy and the real world.

Although Charles moves across these boundaries several times a day, in a dizzying display of conceptual shifts, and although he appears to be making the transpositions with great facility, he admits to being in a state of chronic doubt about the legitimacy of his efforts. He is always asking whether this is the best use of his time, energy, and skills. Like Tony, Charles is able to distinguish between a comfortable and prestigious career and the challenging work that needs to be accomplished. He could easily feel satisfied with his visible and prominent career at *The* Law School, with his teaching, mentoring, and legal scholarship. But this role as legal academic is only a narrow piece of his work, which includes advocacy, activism, and witness in a variety of forums—lecture halls, courtrooms, schools, television programs, community meetings. In all of these settings Charles applies the same yardstick: "Am I participating fully in the struggle for justice? Am I being true to my homeboys?" He is constantly challenged by the disjuncture between the spheres he traverses; he is never at peace with the resolution. Living in these several worlds causes restlessness and yearning and occasional guilt. It requires constant calibration. But ultimately, Charles is forging a new kind of creative engagement that joins theory and practice, analysis and passion.

Charles's daughter's eleven-year-old eyes see the jazz musician in him—the combination of joyful rhythm, cool improvisation, and controlled rage. In "Blow, Jazzman, Blow" Rashida traces the fire and the cool to the generations of Ogletree men who wore hats and went fishing. The hat, which Charles's dad needed in order to make the frightening trip to his son's swearing-in at the Supreme Court, meant dignity and decorum for a simple man from rural California. His Harvard professor son still wears the hat that reminds him of his origins and inheritance, and the discipline and decorum that even privileged black men must wear for their own self-protection. As he plays his jazz blues in the courts, in public debates or congressional hearings, he remembers Charles Sr. and Big Daddy's pain and cool under their hats. His work—like jazz—expresses the dualities of rage and exultation, discipline and improvisation, dignity and expressiveness.

Toni Schiesler's first memory of her mother is hearing her sing on the radio with "some big jazz band in Chicago." "My first mother sensation was *auditory*." She recalls her mother's voice, strong and soothing, like a distant maternal caress. It still echoes as Toni struggles, in her mid-fifties, to discover the essence and power of her own voice. She, too, distinguishes between her career and her work. The former is related to her ambition to be "recognized and legitimized" by the church. Her battles with the bishop reflect her careerist impulses to gain status and authority in the church hierarchy, to climb the ecclesiastic ladder.

This career ascent is important, but nowhere near as meaningful to her as the spiritual "tapestry" she hopes to incorporate into her work. She wants to be recognized by the Episcopal hierarchy as a priest of the church, but she doesn't plan to wear her priestly collar and garments except for Sunday services. In her work, she doesn't want to separate herself—in her dress, behavior, or ritual—from the worshipers, to stand above them in patriarchal power. She feels "called" to the priesthood in order to create a spiritual "circle" that supports the "empowerment" and "relationships" among women, that helps them "discover their voice." Toni is already "practicing" this work with a small collection of staff women at her college. This spiritual collective is the most rewarding part of her work because she sees the changes in the women and she feels the growth in herself. In other parts of her career she is feeling "stuck," "bored," "unfulfilled," but in her work with this women's group she is feeling "creative." Toni is beginning to know that "this is what I was called to do."

In this "call," Toni discovers her mother's voice. Like Katie Cannon, she realizes that the work of her middle years requires a "reckoning with home"; for Toni this means a return to a childhood in which her mother blamed her for all that was wrong; a return to the knowledge of her mother's horrifying rape, which produced her unwelcome birth; and a return to the asylum but also the oppression of the convent, to the powerful relationships that saved her life but killed her spirit. But during this journey home, she discovers that her mother's voice was defiant, strong, and beautiful; she discovers her mother's exuberant and healing laughter. These are also part of her legacy, a legacy that is both barren and plentiful. Toni's journey home, then, and her mother's soulful song, fuel the creative improvisation involved in her emerging work as spiritual guide.

As Toni develops the eclectic liturgy for the women's group, she is pulling together threads from music, poetry, biblical readings, feminist literature, and meditation. She, too, must keep crossing disciplines. She is struggling against her temperamental inclination toward seeking closure and getting answers; she is trying to be open in her search for meaning and responsive to the relationships that are central to spiritual growth. In this she must work against the constraints of her scientific training that demand logic, rationality, and evidence. "I need to let go of the scientist in me," she says urgently. This is not easy, however. The belief in absolutes is deeply ingrained in her; indeed, it helped her survive while growing up.

It has now been twenty years since Toni left the convent, but time has not erased the legacy of submission, obedience, and piety. The convent had been a welcome asylum, a place that rescued her from poverty and dislocation. She had loved the quiet, the structure, the order, and the religiosity. She had found both family and home in the convent, and good mother images in her attachment to, and identification with, the nuns. Leaving was like a divorce— promising autonomy and freedom but threatening isolation and loss of status. Two decades later she relives the amazing sensation of eating when she wants and what she wants; of getting into her own car and traveling to a destination of her own choosing; of filling her closets with colorful, varied clothes. But she still struggles against the ancient silence as she tries to discover "her voice"; against the rigid hierarchies as she seeks to develop her own spirituality; against the dogma as she searches within herself for what she believes. As Toni ventures out into the world—away from institutional domination and personal inhibition—she feels herself journeying home. Her life is becoming a courageous improvisation as her calling brings her full circle back to her roots.

In dwelling on the "improvisation" in the work in each of these lives, it is important also to recognize the discipline from which it springs. Toni's early life was the most dramatically disciplined—from the early-morning devotions, to all of the liturgical rituals, to washing, starching, and ironing the pleats in her habit. Toni's religious discipline was enhanced by her choice of intellectual disciplines. In chemistry she searched for truths, evidence, authority. She was comforted by the certainty of answers, the replication of data. Her parallel pursuits—in religion and science—were motivated by her devotion to the safety and certainty of discipline. In deciding to break away from the convent, Toni was choosing to discard the rigidities, inhibitions, and masks of her cloistered life, but she was not choosing to discard the discipline. Even as she searches for ways to "open up other ways of knowing," even as she tries to resist the scientific impulses that limit her spiritual explorations, she still sees the value in the discipline—intellectual and emotional—and she knows that the discipline will enhance her creativity. After all, her ultimate fantasy of becoming a saint would require that she develop extraordinary self-discipline, the discipline that would allow her the freedom to communicate directly with God.

In her teaching, Katie Cannon can rely on the sureness of her craft. She has been practicing the discipline of teaching all her life—playing school with her siblings, mimicking her own teachers, taking courses in pedagogy, and being self-consciously critical about her communication of ideas. Over the years, her craft as a teacher has become more refined, more expressive, and involves more risk-taking. She begins her courses by challenging her students (refusing

to let them project pejorative black woman caricatures and explod-
ing their stereotypes of ministers) and risking their discomfort and
rage. While her teaching is demanding and carefully designed, it is
also innovative. Katie feels increasingly comfortable in challenging
"white male theology." Katie's version of black womanist theology
(actually southern, rural, working-class, black womanist theology)
can emerge only after she has become well versed in the traditions
and concepts of theological thought. She can then recognize, with
increasing clarity and force, the discrepancy between her academic
training and her commitments. Her innovation, therefore, emerges
out of the maturity of her craft, the mastery of her discipline, and a
conscious reckoning with her roots.

In the heat of courtroom battles, Charles Ogletree can feel the
imprint of his legal training in the way he conceives a case, structures his argument, and displays the evidence. The logic and structures of legal theory become the sturdy platform for his courtroom
improvisation. In the course he teaches on criminal defense,
Charles emphasizes both the "discipline" and the "richness," the
rigor and the innovation of effective courtroom practice. He tells
his third-year law students—who are, for the first time, experiencing
the messiness of practice in their internships—that their argument
must include three elements: theory, operations, and strategy. But
he spends most of his time on "theory," on defining the conceptual
framework that shapes the action. "What kind of theory do you
have," he asks, "when you put a witness on the stand? What is your
goal in pushing the theory?" Charles draws a detailed map on the
blackboard, a graphic representation of the conceptual plan. He
believes that it is critical that the students rehearse and internalize
this structure before they can become effective advocates for their
clients. Once they have learned the rules and rituals of the craft,
they can begin to express "artistry" in their strategy; they can begin
to recognize "the incredible amount of discretionary power lawyers
have." Only after the discipline matures are they able to see that
"the law is *not* a science... It is value laden, not pure, not objective."

For these storytellers, then, work is eclectic and interdisciplinary, requiring crossing boundaries, communicating with various

audiences, building multiple relationships. It must answer to standards of accountability and altruism. It is through his work that Charles remains connected to his roots and fills the debt he feels to his origins. It is through her work that Toni discovers the echoes of her mother's voice and nourishes spiritual development in her circle of women. It is through his work that Tony is able to pursue both his love for science and his need to fix things that are wrong in the world.

For each of these individuals, creativity lies in the dialectic between structure and improvisation. Jazz provides both inspiration and metaphor. "My roots are in New Orleans and the music there," says Tony with nostalgia. "I think of my speeches as 'performances'… jazz performances. They have a structure… but there is always opportunity for experimentation, revision, and improvisation."

CHERYLE WILLS

Sixth Sense

Beginnings

Cheryle Wills-Matthews walks into her office and glistens. Tall, in a royal blue jacket, white skirt, and flowing cape, pearl bauble earrings, and white three-inch spike heels, she dominates the room. Her brown hair, laced with silver, is pulled back tight from her face and rolled in a small bun. Her light-brown skin is smooth, unlined, and carefully painted: bright red lipstick on full lips, rose blush on high cheekbones, purple eye shadow above bright almond eyes, and heavily drawn brown eyebrows. Her face is in motion and animated when she talks and even when she listens. She carries herself with energy and grace, and as she talks she gestures dramatically. Her thin, elegant fingers are adorned with diamond and gold rings, and long, manicured red nails. Clearly used to turning heads, she moves aggressively and purposefully about the room. When she tells me later on that her favorite mentor always called her Duchess, I am not surprised.

This glamourous presentation contrasts with Cheryle's warm earthiness. As she leaves a telephone conversation in her office to come and greet me, her approach is direct, effusive. "You're just as *gorgeous* as I was told you were," she says, and then gives me a kiss on both cheeks. "Do you have a minute? It'll only take a minute. The black students are marching on Clark, thank goodness. I'll be off the phone shortly." She returns to her phone call with the president of Clark who is seeking counsel and solace from one of his favorite trustees.

Cheryle's office in the Boston Park Plaza Hotel is decidedly unglamourous. There are only two rooms. A cramped, windowless anteroom holds two large gray metal desks for a secretary and comptroller, computers, printers, fax machines—all business. There are no photographs or paintings, only an undistinguished picture calen-

dar that is rolling up around the edges. Cheryle's office is somewhat more spacious, with light coming in the large windows. There
is a large potted plant, a couch, a few chairs, and a big square desk.
But this space also has no personal character, no aesthetic touch. As
we walk out to lunch, Cheryle tells me that she "unfortunately"
shares this office with her husband (*"Not* a good idea," she says with
a smile) who is in the property management business. Although
he has other offices and only uses this one "once a month or so," it
is still "aggravating" having to share her space. She intends to look
for "new digs" soon.

We spend three and a half hours over lunch at Legal Seafood.
Cheryle has warned me that "this week I am on an eating binge—
serious, plentiful eating," and she lives up to her promise beginning with a glass of zinfandel, a heaping plate of garlic shrimp over
pasta, and a tall custard dessert. The conversation comes easily. Her
voice has hints of a southern Missouri drawl. I am fascinated by
her rapid-fire style. Her mind works fast, words tumble out, and
the ends of sentences get dropped. She is willing and generous in
responding to my questions, but she also has questions to ask me.
She seems to want to place me (my origins, my age, my interests,
my politics). There is a sisterly feel, a mutuality, an eagerness to
our exchange, which is laced with laughter. "You've made my day,"
she says at the end of our lunch. "No, you've been the high point
of my week!"

About a year ago, Cheryle moved to Boston, having spent all
of her "adult life" in Cleveland, Ohio. She had grown up in Bedford, Massachusetts ("one of two black families in the whole
town"), and in some ways, she was returning home. But her move
has not felt like a homecoming. It has been a difficult, wrenching
transition from "the small town" of Cleveland—where she had high
visibility, a big profile, and enormous clout, where "anything was
possible"—to Boston, which to her feels closed, arrogant, parochial,
and "boring." She has moved to Boston to live with her third husband, Roger Matthews, whom she married a year and a half ago.
Her two sons by her first marriage, Jae and Duane, twenty-nine
and twenty-four years old, live in Cleveland. So do her "precious"

grandchildren. Jae is married with two children, a boy who is five
and a two-year-old girl ("who is going to be a serious, strong
woman"). Besides children and grandchildren, scores of friends,
business associates, and political connections, Cheryle has also left
behind her second husband to whom she was married for twenty
years. He is from a large, powerful, light-skinned family in Cleveland; he continues to inhabit the palatial house in which they
raised her two boys along with his two children by a previous marriage. Cheryle seems to be only half joking when she says, "I had
to get out of town. Cleveland wasn't big enough for the two of us."
At forty-eight years old, this glamourous grandmother seems to
have lived several lives, which she speaks about with humor and
candor, almost as if they were chapters in someone else's story.

I sense that Cheryle is trying to get her bearings after this major
uprooting. She is working to find her place, to define her role, to
discover the ways she can contribute to the community. She is both
skeptical and open ("The jury is still out on whether I can survive
here"), both determined and impatient. She rails against the black
bourgeoisie of Boston that seems so wrapped up in their elite status
that they have distanced themselves from their "sisters and brothers in the community." She makes cynical jokes about the mayor,
who appears at fancy fund-raising parties in his golf shirt and khaki
pants. She is unforgiving in her judgment of Boston's parochialism. She says of Cleveland: "We may not do right, but we know
what's right." But despite these criticisms, she seems determined to
endure the "loneliness" and the "boredom" and get into the next
chapter of her life.

Cheryle's interest in my project may come partly from her wish
to stem the loneliness and reduce the boredom, but she may also see
it as a way to make productive use of this transition. She seems
ready to look back on her full, ambitious life. "You know, it seems
that great professional gains often come when there is personal
loss and pain." Later on, when I say that I think the participants in
this project need to be ready, even eager, for self-reflection and
introspection, for brave storytelling, Cheryle chimes in, "Oh, I'm
ready... This is the interlude before I commit suicide." We are

laughing together, but I think that this transition must feel treacherous. This "interlude" is pregnant with newness and opportunity, but it is also full of unknown dangers. Looking back on her life's journey, putting words and images to her story, Cheryle hopes to discover clues to her future.

At one moment she totally surprises me by saying, "When I grow up, I want to be like you, Sara." This strong, vibrant, mature woman who seems to have lived many lives talking about growing up! I am amazed, but I recognize that her feeling of "becoming" must be related to the big changes in her life—her new husband, her new home, her new city. The strangeness, the loneliness, are forcing her to adapt, to stretch, and to grow. Perhaps this project will make the change more conscious, more constructive, more creative. "I want to be productive with my life," Cheryle says emphatically. "I can't stand downtime."

We Cannot Allow Them to Live

Before I have a chance to give my name, the young black guard smiles at me, says that Ms. Wills-Matthews will be returning in a moment, and buzzes me in at the heavy glass doors. My eyes work to adjust to the change in light from the bright midmorning sun outside to the muted bronze light inside this cavernous lobby. I sit down on one of the long brown leather couches facing the door and gaze at the huge art—a massive abstract painting hanging on the gray wall, a six-foot wrought iron sculpture dominating the center of the lobby. I also watch the movement of people in and out, a parade of fast-moving, elite urban dwellers: lean white men in suits with slim attache cases, a tall muscular woman in a fancy jogging suit, an elderly couple dressed in sturdy walking gear, various delivery people with Federal Express packages, gourmet food, and architect's plans. Everyone is moving quickly, darting in and out of the door as the attentive guard nods, smiles, and buzzes them through.

After only a few minutes I see a statuesque figure strolling through the door and waving. Cheryle Wills-Matthews seems to bring bright sun into the lobby with her. Her appearance is even more arresting this time: she is wearing a blue-and-white-striped shorts suit, a deep red leotard top, and very high heels that accentuate her shapely long limbs and five-foot-nine-inch frame. Again, she has not been sparing with jewelry, and today her long, thick black hair is cascading down around her shoulders. As she hugs me warmly, I am bathed in her fragrant perfume. I can't help thinking, "This is a woman who loves her womanliness." "I just went to get some munchies for us," she says as she shows me the fresh bagels and croissants she is carrying. As we ride up thirty-five floors, Cheryle is chattering about her friends from Martha's Vineyard who have been calling her since 7:00 A.M. trying to invent "the party action"

413

for the long Memorial Day weekend. In addition to their city place, Cheryle and her husband, Roger, own a house on the Vineyard where they enjoy weekends and several weeks during the summer. Their social life on the island is active and playful, and networks of friends from their past lives gather there.

We walk along the gray carpeted hallway to the Wills-Matthews' apartment, and upon entering my eyes need to adjust again. There is sunlight pouring in the floor-to-ceiling windows overlooking the Charles River. The light ricochets off mirrored walls and shimmers on glass chandeliers. Two couches, cream-colored like the carpets, are piled high with shiny pillows in a rainbow of pastels, aqua, salmon, pink, gray. The same shades are repeated in the candelabra, side tables, chairs, and the table decorations. There is aqua material draped around the tops of the windows and mirrors, and around the bottoms of the small trees and large plants that are strategically placed in the room. While the place feels like Hollywood, it also feels warm and inviting—a reflection of Cheryle's theatrical yet welcoming nature. I walk straight to the windows and admire the view, which is spectacular on this clear day, and then turn to offer an approving comment on the whole scene. Cheryle gives a dismissive wave. "I neglect this place... We've been spending a lot of energy putting the Vineyard house together." In her tone I hear an implication that, by Cheryle's standards, "this little place" (actually a spacious three-bedroom apartment with three baths, a living room, dining area, and kitchen) is adequate, efficient, comfortable, but certainly not fancy. She has lived in fancier places and given fuller attention and resources to their decoration. "This is kind of thrown together," she says. "But it's fine for our needs... very convenient."

By the time Cheryle settles herself comfortably on one of the couches and stretches her long body across the pastel pillows, I feel totally at home. I sit cross-legged on the carpet, with my tape recorder placed on a large glass coffee table with gold trim. As I look up at this reclining light-brown-skinned woman with the perfectly painted face and the shiny long black hair, I see a queenly Cleopatra image—which is in stark contrast to the first sentences that come out of her mouth.

"They were standing there, their wrists and ankles in shackles, dressed in these orange prison uniforms... I have to force myself to watch. It is so deeply painful... I look at those shackles, and I feel the shackles around me, within me... the horrible humiliation, degradation, and confusion about why I'm treated differently." On this Memorial Day weekend she is still feeling the reverberations of a month ago—the Rodney King verdict and the chaos and violence that followed in Los Angeles. Her first reference is to the images she has seen on the morning CNN news program of the four black men who have been accused of beating the white truck driver.

Suddenly, I feel transported from this glorious sunny refuge to a dangerous place of collective black "degradation." Cheryle's language has changed from the chatter of social privilege on Martha's Vineyard to the political rhetoric of disappointment and rage. "People say it was senseless. That's wrong. It wasn't senseless. It was rage built up over time. The white truck driver represented 'the enemy'... It wasn't the individual that was the source of the anger... it was the decades of brutalization. It was a horrible travesty."

Cheryle does not try to bring order to her vehement comments. Since this is our first formal session, I have asked her to begin her "life journey" wherever she would like, and I have assured her that the story does not need to be orderly, systematic, or chronological. She can leap in anywhere she likes, jump around across time and place, be transported by imagery, metaphors, even fantasy. I will be responsible for finding the order in it, keeping track of the story, and reminding her of where we've traveled.

Cheryle is seething not only about the pointed assaults on "our black men" and the "terrible vulnerability" of black men in this society, she is underscoring not only the connections between the shackles on these four men in West Los Angeles and the shackles binding all black people—she is also criticizing the weak response from the black community. She is faulting us for not speaking out more clearly, more adamantly, more insistently. "I just can't believe that the National Bar Association hasn't made a public statement... We act so helpless... We should be doing so much more—initiating, demanding, compelling." She sighs heavily, "After watching the news story, I sent my little check in to help support the defense of these black men." There is resignation on her face as if she senses the inadequacy of her "little check" as a response to the "years of built-up rage" and "the societal assault on our black men."

After Cheryle's expressions of outrage, she circles around trying to find a place to begin. It is almost as if black folks who come together for serious conversation must begin with the Los Angeles events before we can move on. We must declare out loud our collective pain, our anger, our feelings of impotence. In the weeks following what Cheryle refers to as the "revolt" (*"not* riot"), this litany has become part of a ritualized greeting, a sign of solidarity and a cry of anguish. But once the litany is over, it is often hard to recapture the thread of an earlier conversation or to begin a new one. Against the backdrop of the fire and the violence, everything feels trivial or frivolous or less urgent. It is for these reasons that I think Cheryle's early comments sound scattered and aimless. She is—all at the same time—talking about the loneliness and estrangement of her high school years in Bedford, Massachusetts, her birth in Jefferson City, Missouri, her parents' long "partnership" of forty-nine years, the dilemmas of black identity and consciousness, the role of the church in the black community, her first year of college at Fisk, her radicalism as a Civil Rights activist in the late 1960s, and the homes her mother decorated. She leaps around, jumping generations and geography; I try to relax and follow the emotional thread, for I know it is premature to expect, or ask for, a coherent story. In my mind, however, I am beginning to sketch out a map of Cheryle's early life: her birth in Jefferson City, Missouri ("You know, young mothers always went home to their own mothers to give birth... so my mother went home to my maternal grandmother"), her young years living in Brooklyn ("when my father was a captain in the air force, stationed at Redwood City, New Jersey"), the move to Cambridge ("when my father was getting his Ph.D. in meteorology from M.I.T.—the first black to get a Ph.D. in meteorology"), from Cambridge to Bedford, Massachusetts ("where we were one of two black families in the whole town"), to a year of college at Fisk University in Nashville ("where I made lifelong friends and was all caught up in the Civil Rights movement").

The beginning of our session is also fragmented by telephone calls that Cheryle feels she needs to take. She is expecting an important call from one of her partners in Cleveland who has alerted her to some crisis involving taxes. "Wouldn't you know that this would be the day my business would be going crazy," she says with humor and cool. Each time the telephone rings she jumps up gracefully and glides over to the kitchen. While she awaits the critical phone call, she hears from a friend who wants to make plans for the weekend on the Vineyard (she promises to call her back later). She hears from her younger son, Duane, who needs two hundred dollars for a trip he will be taking to a friend's wedding. She hears from her husband who is already ensconced in their house on the Vineyard, wants to know her travel plans, and reminds her to anticipate terrible traffic. She hears twice from a bank in Cleveland where there has been some mixup over deposits. For four months, Cheryle has been trying to unravel the confusion with the bank and has only met with bureaucratic red tape and inefficiency. When the office from the bank calls today she is "totally frustrated," and her conversations are a mixture of disgust, determination, and demure politeness. She is unabashedly aggressive and forceful, then businesslike, then syrupy sweet. I sit in the living room hearing only Cheryle's side of the fracas, but I imagine that the bank bureaucrat at the other end must be wishing she had never tried to tangle with Cheryle. I am sure she is being outmaneuvered. Cheryle returns to her perch on the cream-colored couch shaking her head and smiling. She is not even recording this victory. "It's not even worth discussing."

Finally, the call she has been waiting for comes, and she is getting quick information from her longtime friend and colleague. Her tone is warm and playful even though they are discussing this financial crisis. She returns quickly with another "trivia story." "It seems that all of this nonsense is about thirteen hundred dollars! Can you believe it?"

Each time Cheryle hangs up the phone, it is hard for us to recapture the thread of her earlier thoughts, and we both experience some frustration. The interruptions mix with the tentative, scattered beginnings to produce a picture of a woman with many parts to her life, many past lives, and many agendas. I suspect, as well, that she is not a woman who has taken much time to reflect or deliberate on her life; that our work together may be welcome but strange and difficult for her; and that the telephone calls may be serving as a convenient distraction. Our work will require a shift in style and mode of operation. The telephone interruptions begin to feel like a transition, a bridge from the fast-paced action of the world in which Cheryle navigates every day to the deep, focused ruminations our work requires.

After the call from her Cleveland partner, the telephone stops ringing, and in a kind of unconscious synchrony Cheryle shifts her position on the couch, from lounging across the pillows to sitting tall and facing me intently. She begins her powerful and painful story by talking about her mother. "She was the last of the great homemakers... She was a wonderful cook, kept a marvelous house... In another day, she would have been a much-sought-after interior designer... We call her the 'Picasso of home design.'" Cheryle explains that her mother's renovations always corresponded with the style and architecture of the house in which they were living. When they lived in a Victorian house in Cambridge with high ceilings and hardwood floors, Cheryle's mother filled their home with antiques of the period. When they moved into a contemporary house in Bedford, she chose a "supermodern," avant-garde decor. Their home in Los Angeles offered her mother the opportunity to be theatrical and glamourous. "When my friends would come and visit us, they would say the place looked like pure Hollywood... It was fabulous!" Her mother's extraordinary energy produced surprising results. "My father and I need to get our rest, but my mother just keeps on going... We'd go to bed at night and we'd come downstairs the next morning, and she would have changed whole rooms! We'd find ourselves walking into a couch... Now, when I put down a piece of furniture it stays there forever... but with my mother it was overnight transformations."

The mother love spread to the plants, which were always a part of the home decor. Everything Cheryle's mother grew became "big and healthy and luscious... with shiny leaves." Cheryle leans back and laughs—"I'm just the opposite with plants… My kids used to say that even my artificial plants wilted!" I point to the large, thriving ficus tree standing in the sunlight by the window, neither artificial nor wilted. Cheryle dismisses my observation with a smile—"It's pretty new… in time I'll kill that one too." The differences in their success with plants seems to stand for the vivid contrasts between mother and daughter. Her mother—"the last of the great homemakers"—was a devoted wife and mother and gave her full attention to hearth and home. While Cheryle clearly cares about the attractiveness of her home, she is a woman out in the world. Home is a place to return to, after her jet-setting travel and her entrepreneurial pursuits. She has no time or patience for plants, no interest in rearranging furniture once it has found its proper place.

Cheryle is quick to point out that her mother's homemaker role was never considered subservient to, or less important than, her father's breadwinning responsibilities. "They were full partners. We all took her job as seriously as his… She also took some days off and went on vacations… She was lovely, attractive, and gracious… but powerful and determined." Her creativity and power—always recognized by her husband and children—were rarely expressed in the outside world. She was seen as her husband's demure and devoted wife. "My mother never had a job… she doesn't even have a Social Security number She uses my father's Social Security number with a "D" at the end." I ask what the "D" stands for. "'D' is for *dependent,*" says Cheryle.

The "D" word seems to hang in the air between us as I take in my breath in surprise, and we both fall silent. Cheryle sits there looking boldly independent—a breadwinner and a wife, an executive and a lady. (She says later on, "I don't want to be adored by my husband… I want to be respected.") The silence is broken by Cheryle's pensive comment, "If my mother knew what the 'D' meant, she'd get her own Social Security number immediately." The differences between mother and daughter are both dramatic and ephemeral.

The sunlight on Cheryle's face doesn't change, but I see a dark shadow descending as she tells me about the ultimate symbol of her mother's nurturance. "My brother was killed in a car accident in 1972, and mother still nurtures him and his spirit… It is a profound way of keeping him alive." "How does she do that?" I ask evenly, despite the fact that I am shocked and saddened by hearing of his death and disturbed by what I hear as a twenty-year vigil to "nurture him in death." "Well, she takes his picture and puts it up wherever she goes," responds Cheryle, "and she refused to move from Madison, Wisconsin, which is where he was originally buried, unless they would also move my brother's body." Cheryle's father, who had been teaching at the University of Wisconsin, Madison, had taken a faculty position at North Carolina State College. ("Both of my parents were southerners, so they hated the cold, frigid weather in Wisconsin… and wanted to move to a place where it was warmer.") Cheryle's mother couldn't bear to leave her son in Madison, but North Carolina did not "feel like home" to her. So she finally decided to have her precious boy buried at "home" in Jefferson City, Missouri. The body was moved from the cold northern soil of Wisconsin and reinterred in the family plot in Missouri, so her son's body could rest peacefully while she kept his spirit and his image alive.

The shadow has not lifted from Cheryle's face. Her eyes are filled with tears. I ask gently, "What is the story of your brother's death?" And then more softly, "Or don't you want to talk about it?" She says slowly, "It is a story we don't talk about in our family. It is too painful." But once she has named the pain, she moves on bravely. "His name was Charles Edward Anderson Jr., but we always called him 'Eddie.' He was an absolute genius by whatever measure you could choose to apply. He was a certified genius. You know, we were always a very close family… we always got a lot of love, and we always felt we got equal space and time… But even with all that equality and good feeling, everyone would have said that Eddie was the favorite… and no one had a problem with that." Eddie was a golden boy, an achiever, a star, a mensch.

Eddie, a few years younger than Cheryle, had followed his sister through the Bedford, Massachusetts, school system, then had gone off to Loomis, a traditional private boarding school for boys in Connecticut. Although he excelled academically at Loomis, he found the place lonely and stultifying. He was enormously relieved when his parents let him finish up his last year in a public school in Los Angeles. "I had never seen him happier," recalls Cheryle. "Eddie went to California and found his heaven." Within weeks of arriving for his senior year, Eddie had emerged as a leader, visible, likeable, and charismatic. "By year's end," says Cheryle proudly, "his classmates had voted for him as their graduation speaker."

Eddie chose to remain in California for college. At UCLA, he continued to be an achiever and a leader. "There was nothing he couldn't do... He loved jazz and classical music... He was a great dancer... He was the first black to be chosen as a YELL leader. It's like the head of the cheerleading squad, a huge and important role. He was even given a stipend. He pledged my father's fraternity and became a Kappa. To call him well-rounded would be an anticlimactic way of expressing the range of his interests." Cheryle's voice is full of enthusiasm and admiration for her younger brother.

In addition to the other achievements of his undergraduate years, Eddie became politically active outside of the university. "Like our maternal grandfather, he was an extraordinary politician. His political intuitions were amazing," says Cheryle. "I'm like that as well." Eddie used his political acumen in support of the Black Panthers, who were prominent and visible during the late '60s, particularly in southern California. Eddie grew his hair long and sported a "gorgeous Afro." He covered his tall, lean brown frame in dashikis and committed himself to "the movement." I ask whether Eddie actually joined the Panthers, and Cheryle responds carefully, "I think he was a Panther... He felt keenly about their work. But *my parents* would say most decidedly that he wasn't." Later on Cheryle tells me that even in the height of his "radicalism," Eddie was always careful not to offend his parents' more traditional values. "He would never have jeopardized the dignity of our family by telling us things about his political life that we might not want to hear." When he came home to visit his folks, he would always take off his "offensive" political regalia. Cheryle remembers him coming home looking "amazingly clean" and opening up his shirt with a big smile. "Look Mom, I have nice clean color-coordi-

nated underwear on today." Everyone smiled knowing he was honoring his mother's "difficulty with his militancy" by dressing, at least
for his short visit, in the way she would have wanted him to.

Eddie, who was "violently opposed to the Vietnam War,"
became the youngest delegate to the Democratic National Convention in Chicago. "Looking all-powerful and all-black" in his colorful dashikis and big crown of hair, he appeared in newspapers across
the country. "When he burned his delegate card inside the convention hall, that was a signal for the demonstrations to begin in
the streets." Cheryle felt a combination of anxiety and admiration
as she witnessed her brother's commitment to the struggle. She
shared his goals but sometimes questioned his means. During her
freshman year at Fisk University in Nashville, Tennessee, she had
been deeply involved in the Civil Rights struggle, and had engaged
in nonviolent protest. She followed the teachings of Martin Luther
King Jr. and believed in the philosophy and strategies of nonviolence. But the Panther protest—"in language and action"—was
"violent," and Cheryle questioned the efficacy of their brand of militancy and worried about her brother's safety.

After graduating from college, Eddie continued to be active in
leftist politics. But his aggressive radicalism seemed to be replaced
by a period of "introspection" and "melancholy" as he tried to figure
out how he was going to use his life productively. During this "quiet
period" Eddie kept a journal, a practice he had begun years before,
but now he was "religious" about writing his entries every day. In
these pages he ruminated about politics, philosophy, career choices,
family life, and love. He raged against racism, oppression, and the
Vietnam War. He reflected critically on his years of political activism.
He "came to a slow resolution that he would become a lawyer."

During the summer of 1971, when Eddie was twenty-six years
old, he took a long journey to visit his relatives and extended family in Cleveland, New York, Madison, and Jefferson City. He made
Cheryle's place in Cleveland his home base, but he seemed determined to touch base with the older generations and soak up all of
the bountiful family love. Cheryle had recently married her second husband, a man several years her senior whose aristocratic fam-

ily owned the largest and most prosperous funeral parlor in Cleveland called The House of Wills. They had moved into a magnificent home with her two boys, who were eight and three years old. She remembers the extraordinary impact Uncle Eddie had on her young children. "They just adored him. He spent a great deal of time with them... Even today they have clear memories of him—his vitality, his sensitivity—even though they were so young then." She also remembers that the wonderful, warm visit ended with an abrupt departure. Without any warning, Eddie came in one morning in September and announced he was leaving and heading back West. It was not only the sudden leaving that felt jarring to Cheryle; it was also the ominous tone in his voice and the mysterious message. Twenty years later, his sister's eyes cloud over with tears. "There was something about the good-bye that made me fearful... I can't really remember the words, except he said something like, 'Life is good'... but it was the *feeling* that made me think that this good-bye was *forever*." Eddie flew back to California, and Cheryle was left with a hard knot in her stomach. She ached with anxiety. "I remember being depressed for days... just crying and crying until I had no more tears."

A few months after Eddie left, on November fifth, Cheryle celebrated her first wedding anniversary at home in bed with the flu. "I was feeling miserable... We had a live-in housekeeper who shooed away the kids and left me alone... My husband was down at the funeral home, and I wanted to crawl into my own cubbyhole and be sick, completely alone." Feverish, Cheryle dozed in and out of a fitful sleep. When the telephone rang at her bedside, she picked it up and heard Eddie's voice. She remembers telling him she was sick and that this was "a crazy way to be celebrating" her first anniversary. And she remembers hearing his fragile voice apologizing because he wouldn't be able to be present at an upcoming family gathering. "He told me that he would like to go to Granny and Papa's sixtieth anniversary, but that he would probably not be able to make it... That was strange because the anniversary was several months away." As Eddie talked on for a while (the "feeling" in his voice still haunts Cheryle), she faded away into a deep sleep, and the phone dropped to the floor.

The next thing Cheryle knew she was awakened by the loud, sustained ringing of the doorbell. She wiped the sleep out of her eyes and struggled toward the front door. A man from the telephone company was standing there. The telephone had been off the hook for several hours, and finally the company had dispatched a messenger to deliver the news in person: Eddie had been in an auto accident and had been taken to the hospital. The words felt like knives, yet she stood there feeling unsurprised. Since Eddie had left in September, she had been filled with apprehension, a deep foreboding. She knew something terrible was on the horizon. Cheryle pushed the terror aside and whipped into action. After a few telephone calls she pieced together the beginning of a sketchy story, a story that is still unresolved.

Before she gives me the meager details, she wants me to know how treacherous it feels to reopen the old wounds. "This is too painful for my parents to talk about. In some ways, it is better to stop asking questions... better, and easier, to be at peace with it." I hear her wish to preserve the peace and offer her the chance to "leave it alone." But her words overtake mine. It is almost as if she is talking to herself as she turns over the jagged pieces of evidence. "He had been walking along the beach alone... He met a woman he hardly knew but had met before... a black woman, definitely not his type. They had left the beach together, heading off for Chinese food... and then a party... They were in her VW Bug; she was driving. The police report said that it had been raining, and her car skidded into the oncoming lane and swerved toward an L.A. bus coming in the opposite direction. The bus swerved too but couldn't avoid hitting the VW... the seat broke on the passenger side. My brother was stretched out, and the impact broke his back and neck." The violence of her story makes me cry out. Cheryle notices my presence and says again slowly, "I haven't spoken about this in a very long time."

Having obtained the initial police report, Cheryle called her mother and told her only that Eddie had been in a car accident and that he had been taken to the hospital. She did not tell her any more. Her mother wasted no time. "My mother caught the first thing smoking to L.A.... She is an incredibly strong woman... My mother goes out there all by herself. My father couldn't leave immediately. He had to wrap up some things at work. My sister, who has a nervous condition and lives at home, was in no shape to go..." (Although this is the first time I've heard about a sister, I keep silent.) "So my mother goes all alone... this woman who has never had a job... never even had a Social Security number... goes to L.A. and takes care of business."

When Cheryle's mother arrived in L.A., she went to the "community hospital in God knows where" and arranged to have her son transferred to the intensive care unit at the UCLA hospital. "She got in the back of the ambulance and rode with him." Eddie was completely paralyzed; he had tubes in his throat and braces on his head. They had shaved off his beautiful Afro, and his bald head made his eyes look much bigger. "He communicated with us only through his eyes," recalls Cheryle tearfully. "I arrived a few days after my mother, and Eddie and I had some amazing moments together... When I went in to see him alone, tears would come to his eyes. We'd weep silently together." But it was an encounter between father and son that Cheryle remembers as "the most tender." "You know, my father and brother had an affectionate relationship, but it was kind of macho-male... sort of tough... They had never hugged and kissed. I will never forget the day my father walked into the hospital room and gently bent over Eddie and kissed him... It was a beautiful connection."

The family kept the vigil. Every two hours they were permitted ten minutes of visiting time. "We'd go every morning at eight A.M. and stay until visiting hours were over at ten P.M. It was important for the family to be surrounding him and for the people in the hospital to know that he had family there." For eighteen days, Eddie stayed alive, lying stiff and still, sending messages with his eyes. Cheryle's mother knew that there was no chance that he would ever walk again, speak again, or even smile again, yet she desperately wanted him to live. Her determination was steadfast and fierce. "My mother had already called an architect to consult about adding rooms to her house so that they could accommodate him at

426 I've Known Rivers

home. She wanted him to live just like that." In the final days of his
life, his mother's love for him shimmered with pain and hope. In
this big broken man she could see her sweet little son. Cheryle
strokes her long black curls and remembers: "After they had shaved
his head, Eddie's hair began to grow back, just a little fuzz... There
was my mother's baby again. It was an incredible time. You know,
my mother had lived *uncomfortably* through Eddie's militancy, his
time with the Panthers. She had loved him, but she had never felt
comfortable about it... Now she was back with her baby boy... very
innocent, poignant." Eddie, the man, did not return until after he
died. "When they shaved his head at the hospital, they had been
smart enough to save his hair... his beautiful Afro. Friends of ours,
who owned the funeral home in L.A., put his hair back, and he
looked wonderful!"

As Cheryle continues, I sit speechless at her strange and troubling story.

After Eddie's death, after his body had been buried in a cemetery
close to his parents' home in Wisconsin, the family faced the mystery of his violent demise. Haunting questions hung around and
begged for answers. Cheryle and her father retraced the scene of
the accident and discovered half-truths and conundrums. First, they
went to see the woman's VW, which had supposedly been demol-
ished on the rainy night of the accident, and found that "it hardly
had a scratch." Then they went to talk to the people at the L.A.
Transit Authority about the bus involved in the accident and were
told that "it was not their bus, and no one could find the identity
of the vehicle." When they questioned the woman who had been
driving about her car, she said "she couldn't remember whose car she
was driving." Everywhere they turned, they discovered that the original story they had been told "didn't match the unfolding facts."

A long silence settles in the room and Cheryle whispers, "Very
strange, very mysterious... the whole thing is very troubling." She
casts around for other shreds of evidence, some half-answer. "You
know, my brother and I had a belief about the FBI that bordered on
paranoia..." Her voice drifts off. "My brother had four or five friends
with the same commitments and ideologies... the friends were both

black and white. One had to be committed to a mental institution, another mysteriously fell out of a window... Their lives ended in mysterious tragedy." I am working to piece together the puzzle. Is Cheryle saying that these leftist militants were killed by the FBI?

Then she is off on another tack. "You know, my brother was sitting up on the platform when Bobby Kennedy was killed... My mother and I were watching the television and heard a scream. We looked at each other and said, 'That's Eddie screaming.' It was *primal*, absolutely terrifying. My brother was never the same after that." Is Cheryle saying that the trauma of his hero's death pushed Eddie over the edge, that he had no wish to live after witnessing Bobby Kennedy's assassination? "A good friend of his told me later, several weeks after Eddie died, that he had gone to visit [Eddie] after he returned from Chicago, and he had heard these terrible, piercing screams coming out of his apartment... It was Eddie... the same kind of terrible screams we had heard on TV."

Cheryle leaps from talking about her brother's pain to considering the destruction of our country's heroes, the way we seem to need to kill the people who come bearing an honest, courageous message—people who come to us, as Cheryle puts it, "with a higher order of commitment and a deeper integrity." In one sentence she points to four victims—Malcolm X, Jack Kennedy, Bobby Kennedy, John Lennon. They were alike in the "*quality*" and "*intent*" of their message, a message that was too threatening to the powers that be. "Why is it," Cheryle asks, her voice blazing, "that Martin Luther King was killed when he moved from the Civil Rights struggle to speaking more broadly about economics, poverty, the Vietnam War?... When he really began to challenge the priorities and values of this country?" Cheryle puts Eddie in the company of these courageous citizens whose activism and resistance threatened the status quo, who lived by values that express "an absolute commitment to the American Dream." "We cannot allow them to live." Cheryle's voice is intense and her eyes are fiery. "As soon as they challenge the structure and power arrangements of society, we kill them."

In the midst of this angry statement about "the killing of our heroes," Cheryle remembers her brother's journal. Her flight from the large social mural to her personal story is swift. In talking about the "marvelous poetry" Eddie wrote in his journal, introspective and melancholy, she recalls lines composed for his longtime girl-friend: "If I live until the twenty-seventh hour, I will marry you...." "If I can survive until twenty-seven, I will survive." Cheryle draws in her breath as if reading the ominous words for the first time, and then explains, "His twenty-seventh birthday would have been on March 14, 1973,... and he was killed the end of November 1972... It's just unbearable to think about."

Cheryle's hands are waving in front of her face as if she is try-ing to push away the painful memories. She is reliving the mysteri-ous, haunting trauma. But the bits and pieces of evidence still do not add up; they raise more questions than they answer. She hears her brother's searing screams; she sees his shaved head growing baby fuzz; she remembers her mother catching "the first thing smoking out of Madison" to go and save her boy; she notices the first tender embrace between father and son as Eddie lay paralyzed in the hos-pital bed; she recalls her tears and sadness when Eddie abruptly left Cleveland and said good-bye forever. So many ancient images flood-ing her mind, so much anguish. Cheryle's eyes are red and swollen. The mask is off. "Shackles," she says bitterly. "These were his shack-les." With that metaphor we have come full circle. Her beautiful brother, the golden boy, is joined in Cheryle's mind with the four shackled black men, in their orange prison uniforms, who stood before the judge in the courtroom this morning accused of beating the white truck driver. The images all run together in Cheryle's head as she says softly, "The rage has been building for years."

Go Out and Be Somebody

Even Cheryle Wills-Matthews—a woman of enormous energy, a woman who "hates downtime"—admits that she was "totally exhausted" after our first session. All the way down to the Vineyard, on that Memorial Day weekend Friday, she felt a strange combination of deep weariness and exhilaration. Jammed in traffic and waiting for hours in the ferry line, she had plenty of time to reflect on the stories she had told me—old stories, surprising stories, "Things I have not thought about or talked about for years." She seems to have no regret or apprehension about having released these ancient tales, only amazement and appreciation for having had the chance to revisit them. "Very intense," she says with a broad smile. "Very deep... working with my heart and my head."

Today, when I arrive at Cheryle's house, she is ready and eager to resume. She greets me at the door and immediately tells me that she will be turning the telephone off so that we will not be interrupted. I find it impossible not to notice Cheryle's wonderful costumes; they are such bold declarations. This morning she is wearing an emerald green and black striped silk skirt and blouse trimmed, around the bodice and in a wide band at her waist, in black leather. Sheer black stockings and black patent leather shoes, again with three-inch heels, complete the picture.

Cheryle has been away for several days in Chicago fulfilling her duties as a board member of National United Way. The search committee, on which she sits, is reviewing applications for an executive director ("We've gotten 4,000 applications, 3,990 of them you could toss out immediately.") After the controversial departure of the former executive director, this search process has become highly politicized, and Cheryle is in "the thick of it." After returning from her Chicago meeting in the late afternoon, she raced out to a fundraiser for a political candidate whom she is backing. Before I arrived she has gone out "to do her domestic thing," and when I arrive she is in the midst of unpacking groceries. "You'd be so proud of me," Cheryle chirps. "I've gone shopping!" She holds up a jumbo package of blue toilet paper, "the bare essentials." A few minutes later she zooms down thirty-five floors to park her car, which has been waiting at the curb, and returns with a huge bunch of gladiolas. "Now they [the doormen] are convinced that I *live* here... They think 'She's bought flowers, she must call this home.'"

From one of the grocery bags Cheryle pulls out a couple of bottles of raspberry flavored soda, finds some fancy wine glasses, and pours us each a drink. We settle into our places in her pastel-colored living room. This time she kicks off her high heels, stretches her long legs under the coffee table, and sits with me on the soft rug. "I'm a floor sitter," she explains. With the tape recorder set up between us on the glass table, and both of us on the same level, facing each other, Cheryle is ready to work.

I remind her that last time she had wanted to begin this session by talking about her Civil Rights days in Nashville. In 1961 Cheryle was in her freshman year at Fisk University. At seventeen, she had chosen Fisk for "two great intellectual reasons." "First, and most important," she jokes, "my cousin was dating a woman who was a Delta at Fisk, and I thought she was great... And second, after Bedford, Massachusetts, I had a big desire to go to a black school." The second of Cheryle's reasons was "truly serious" and required that she challenge the advice and risk the disappointment of her high school guidance counselor. At Bedford High, she had been a top student and taken all of the honors courses. In her senior year, she had been awarded a National Merit Scholarship, and fancy colleges had tried to recruit her. "I heard from everywhere," recalls Cheryle. "This was the early sixties and all these elite white schools were trying to skim the cream off the top black students. Places like Radcliffe, Smith, Vassar were trying to recruit me, and they were offering big scholarships."

Cheryle's guidance counselor couldn't understand why this bright and cultured light-skinned girl from a good family would pass up the tremendous opportunity of attending a prestigious school with generous financial support and go instead to a "Negro college" ("This was a time when we were in that awkward moment between Negro and black... but we were no longer colored") that no one in Bedford had even heard about and where she would have to pay full freight. For weeks the college counselor tried to convince her to change her mind, but when Cheryle stubbornly and steadfastly resisted his appeals, he "backed off" and gave up on her. Her parents understood her desire to be in the midst of a black community, and they knew that if their daughter decided to do something, there was no way of convincing her otherwise. Fisk was the only school to which Cheryle applied.

At seventeen, Cheryle had already spent years "involved in Civil Rights." In high school she had taken part in demonstrations, marches, parades, and picketing. "As adolescents we used to go to Harvard Square—black and white kids—and picket Woolworths... People thought we were wonderful. In Massachusetts, it was considered a noble thing to do." As a star on the high school debate team, Cheryle often chose to debate issues of race, equality, and justice. "My *involvement* felt both exciting and effective." Her activism and commitment were rewarded by the NAACP, which gave her their National Youth Award. As Cheryle speaks about these early days of youthful activism, she is glowing with the memory of how deeply she "believed in the American Dream," how much idealism and energy fueled her Civil Rights work. "In those days we thought the world was really ours... I woke up every day and felt hope and promise. Now, at forty-eight, I am much more cynical... The parameters of all that promise and potential have become much more limited and finite."

Cheryle arrived at Fisk filled with energy, burning with optimism; eager to be part of a black social and intellectual community, and eager to join the southern Civil Rights movement. She found a student community mostly preoccupied with social life—pledging sororities, dating, parties. And she found a mostly moribund political scene in a resistant, racist southern city. "In 1961, the Civil Rights action in Nashville was far from high heat... On campus, it was dull to almost nothing." But there was a handful of students who shared Cheryle's ideological vision and activist inclinations, who were determined to move beyond the conservative inertia of the Fisk campus. Cheryle recalls several weekends of picketing restaurants in downtown Nashville that refused to serve blacks. The black students from Fisk would often be joined by a few white demonstrators from Vanderbilt.

One Saturday Cheryle remembers sitting in with Civil Rights leader John Lewis, who was then a seminary student at Fisk. She sees the scene vividly. "There was a mezzanine in this place where all the whites were sitting. We were downstairs sitting at the tables. I was wearing a hot pink jacket that I had purchased at the great Filene's Basement in Boston. Almost as soon as we arrived, the police came, followed by scores of detectives and the press. They were taking this thing very seriously." The press, sniffing for a story, spotted the gorgeous young woman in the hot pink jacket and began to take her picture. John Lewis, the most senior and experienced among the demonstrators, leaned over to Cheryle and said, "Be proud, hold your head up." Cheryle stretched to her full height and struck an "arrogant pose" that was recorded in the local papers and police files the next day.

Cheryle's eyes seem to scan the scene of thirty years ago as she remembers the odd presence of a "Scottish Caucasian man wearing a kilt" and sitting at one of the downstairs tables. He was curious about all the commotion and gravitated toward Cheryle, hoping for conversation and explanation. A reporter followed close behind. It turned out that the Scotsman was a scientist traveling to various research laboratories around the country. He had recently visited with colleagues in Woods Hole, Massachusetts, and had— "amazingly, incredibly"—met Dr. Anderson, Cheryle's father, at a scientific meeting there. "He asked a question none of us could answer," she recalls: "How could he have just been in Woods Hole conferring with this distinguished black scientist, and yet the man's daughter 'can't eat in the same restaurant with me in Nashville?'"

A few weeks later, Cheryle and some other student demonstrators were actually arrested as they sat in at a lunch counter. They were booked, fingerprinted, searched, and thrown in a jail cell. "We were seen as criminals and treated very roughly," remembers Cheryle. "In the jail they separated whites from blacks, but not men from women... We were in the cell with black males, hard-core criminals waiting to be sent to the state penitentiary... One was in there for murder." At their booking, some of the police recognized Cheryle from the photographs taken of her weeks before. They began to taunt her, threaten her, and single her out for abuse. One red-faced, meaty officer jabbed his finger in her face and spit out a warning: "We're going to take care of you... you light-skinned, uppity nigger... Look in my eye... you won't survive if you pull that Diane Nash stuff!" A few years earlier, Diane Nash, another Fisk student, had become something of a legend in Nashville. She was also a light-skinned, dramatically attractive woman who seemed fearless in the face of racist harassment. The police saw Diane's incarnation in Cheryle—the same glamour, the same northern assertiveness—and they were determined to squash her.

Cheryle remembers the mean threats of the prison guards and the veiled sexual innuendo. She remembers trembling with fear. "I felt such aloneness, such desperation, such a sense of betrayal." But the most vivid memory is of the "brothers" who shared the cell with her and the other students. These hard-core criminals became their protectors. "The brothers were wonderful... The guards would threaten us, and they would come to shield us. *They never yielded.* At one point, the guards opened all the windows to freeze us out and harass us... after a while I must have fallen asleep out of sheer exhaustion. When I awoke I felt a warmth... These brothers had taken off their flannel shirts and covered me up to ward off the cold." Cheryle's voice is full of emotion: "They were warriors to the very last. They protected their women."

When their bail had been paid and the Fisk students were preparing to leave, Cheryle found it hard to "abandon" the brothers. "Here they were, going to the penitentiary... and we were going back to Fisk to pledge sororities, get pinned, and party... But, amazingly enough, they showed no bitterness, only pride in us." Cheryle remembers going up to the brother who seemed to be "the strongest and wisest among them" and saying something "trite" like, "Is there anything I can do for you?" His penetrating eyes, his gentle voice, and his words will forever be imprinted in her heart. Cheryle's voice is a whisper as she feels his tenderness. "He said, 'Little sister, just go out and be somebody.'" It was an extraordinary moment for her, one that will resound in her forever. She felt "a big transformation. Suddenly I felt like a grown woman!" exclaims Cheryle. "Responsible to something larger than myself, accountable to our community." The brother was tenderly, protectively calling her "little sister," but his charge that she "be somebody" made her feel "womanly," gave her a sense of empowerment and responsibility. "Weekly, I think to myself, Would the person I've become be the woman they'd [the brothers in the prison cell] want me to be?"

Cheryle seems to have told this Civil Rights story in order to get to the final, haunting question that still echoes through her. In the poignant moment between "the strong brother" and Cheryle, in the gift of his words, in the generosity and warmth of his gesture she still finds comfort, admonition, and challenge. I hear several stories in one. First, it is a coming-of-age story. It tells of the dramatic transformation of a girl—a privileged, light-skinned black beauty from the North—into a woman: the loss of innocence, the gaining of responsibility and commitment.

Second, it is a tale of bonding, of black brother-sister connections. Cheryle calls the brothers "warriors" and is thankful for the way "they protected their women." She feels the heat of their flannel shirts guarding her against the cold like a warm sibling embrace. She recalls that they "never yielded." She will forever be grateful to them, indebted to all black brothers. But there is another dimension to her indebtedness, which has been imprinted by this event and many others: she will always know the special vulnerability of black men in our society. She will always be alert to the assaults to their manhood and their power; they endure "the worst assaults of all." Using Cheryle's own metaphor, "the shackles" are heaviest around the brothers. In her eyes "the strong brother" in the prison cell—whatever crime he committed—was a victim of the most virulent kind of racism inflicted on black males. She knows that the

cumulative assaults of this racism weakened her warrior and undermined his spirit. So Cheryle's indebtedness includes a lifetime commitment to protecting and soothing the brothers, to recognizing
their special vulnerability and offering balm.

The third story played out in this experience in the Nashville
jail is about standards, about what Cheryle uses as a measure of her
success. "Would the person I've become be the woman they'd want
me to be?" is the question she puts to herself. It is a rigorous standard. Has she been a good sister, a committed activist, a standard-
bearer for justice? Has she become "somebody"? Of all the possible
measures this "successful sister" could apply, the "strong brother's"
admonition is the most demanding and enduring of them all.

This tale of Cheryle's early political activism reminds her of a
childhood incident in Portsmouth, Virginia, one of those incidents
that makes her wince when she thinks about it. Cheryle was nine or
ten years old and traveling with her family on a vacation through
the South. In Portsmouth, her father stopped to ask directions of a
white policeman, and Cheryle was horrified to hear how the white
man addressed her father. "What do you want, boy?... Get out of
my face, nigger!" She couldn't believe what she was hearing. "Here
was a man who was no comparison to my father—didn't have my
father's education, his dignity, his intellect, or his income —talking to my father in this abusive way... Even as a kid I thought about
the injustice of it all. Now I know that there is no protection from
racism in this society... You can't be educated enough, kind
enough, committed enough, wealthy enough to escape it. There is
no protection... Any black person who claims they've not experienced racism, hasn't gone outside of their house!"

Although there is no real "protection from racism," when
Cheryle thinks of the shields that have warded off some of the worst
assaults, she pictures her family. She sees generations of strong black
people who "prized education" and who were "arrogant about being
black." "People in my family say, 'I am black, and I would never want
to be anything else,'" claims Cheryle. "We have a sense of our own
empowerment... a belief that you give back *and* forward to the black
community." This "arrogance" ("almost a reverse racism") has been

passed down through the generations, drawing the family close and shielding them from some of the societal assaults.

I ask Cheryle to describe some of these strong, arrogant fore-bears. She can draw full portraits of her maternal and paternal grandparents, all of whom she knew very well. She begins with her father's side of the family, with her paternal grandfather, a man with the "gorgeous name" of Squire Henderson Anderson. He was a beautiful man with strong Indian features. His ancestors had been a mixture of free coloreds and Indians from Tennessee and Mississippi who had intermarried. At some point, he and his brother Edward, a "dapper dude and heart-breaker," had migrated to Canada. His brother had stayed in Canada, but Squire had trav-eled South and settled in St. Louis. He married a "much younger woman" named Zetta Scott who came from a proud family also of black and Indian parentage.

Zetta's father was one of the highest ranking blacks in the labor unions, and her stepfather, who raised her, was an AME Zion minis-ter. Ella Scott, her mother, is a legendary figure in family lore. At five feet, Ella seemed tall because of her elegance and poise. She had high cheekbones, a reddish cast to her light brown skin, and her long, straight hair cascaded "down to her ankles." She was an imperious lady who, it is said, used to recline on her couch, issue directives to her family, and pronounce, "Whatever Lola wants Lola gets."

There is a romantic story about Squire and Zetta's courtship. When Zetta said she would marry him, Squire planned an elaborate wedding. He rented a horse-drawn carriage, hired a string orchestra, and took his new wife to a fully furnished home he had built. Cheryle laughs—"Squire did all of this elegant stuff, but he was also known as something of a penny-pincher... It was said that after fully furnishing their house for his wedding day, he never bought another stick of furniture."

Zetta had been to a white college in Fulton, Missouri, and prized education. Cheryle remembers many summers when she and her siblings used to visit Zetta in St. Louis. (Zetta, who lived to her mid-eighties, died ten years ago.) She would take her grandchil-dren to museums, to the opera, to anything that would expand their horizons and broaden their education. "She valued culture," says Cheryle, "not in the high-society, country club sense, but in the love of beauty and good things." Zetta had also inherited some of her mother Ella's sense of entitlement. "She was definitely in the Queen of the Nile category... She knew she was *fine*... There was a sense of superiority." I am reminded of my initial impression upon seeing Cheryle reclining on her cream-colored couch—of thinking of her as Cleopatra. Cheryle's reference to Zetta and Ella as Queens of the Nile seems just right. She definitely has inherited some of their grace, style, and "arrogance."

Zetta and Squire had seven children, one of whom drowned when he was very young. The surviving six—two boys and four girls—all went to college and became "productive people." Mary Anderson Beane, the oldest, taught school in Connecticut and served on the local school board. Elaine Anderson Guilas (after whom Cheryle *Elaine* is named) is a "gifted artist," runs a small gallery, and is a "true New Yorker." Charles Edward Anderson, Cheryle's father, would probably be considered the most successful, the most highly educated of this well-educated family. He is now in his "third or fourth retirement" and continues to do research at North Carolina State. He is working on a "revolutionary technique of advanced warning of storms," running his project on computers and satellites between Madison, Wisconsin (where he is a professor emeritus), and North Carolina. Evelyn Anderson Dire is a nurse who spent most of her career training nurses at Homer G. Philips, the black hospital in St. Louis. Earl Anderson, the second son, is a teacher in New York. The youngest, Jane Anderson Grandberry, the mother of five children, is the only sibling who is no longer living. "One of her children fell out of the window and died," says Cheryle. "From that time on Jane was not emotionally strong."

The maternal side of Cheryle's family lived in Jefferson City, Missouri, "a midwestern city with a very Southern flavor." Verna and Charles Eugene Robinson, always called "Granny and Papa," were married for sixty-two years and produced five offspring. When Cheryle mentions Granny her eyes cloud over with tears. "She was the closest, most special person in my entire life," she says forcefully.

"You know, with mothers and daughters the relationship may be close when they're older. But earlier on, there are usually tensions, sometimes even a competition between them. But my Granny I could say *anything* to... I could talk to her about sex, men, dreams, fears... *everything*." Most people saw Granny as a "kind, gracious, and sweet" woman, a simple, caring soul. But underneath this lovely facade there was depth and wisdom. Cheryle saw a special gift in these deeper layers. "Most people missed how extraordinarily profound and intelligent she was."

Not only did Verna and Charles's marriage endure for six decades, it was also a great romance. Cheryle admits that as a child, she probably "didn't notice anything more than their affection for one another." But as she grew into adulthood, she recognized the "strong, erotic, passionate love between them. They had a *smoldering* relationship... My grandfather had a way of saying 'Honey' to my granny that was so deeply loving. To this day, if a man calls me 'Honey' in that way, I swoon." Although Charles and Verna had five children, and Verna devoted great energy to raising them, she always saw her relationship to her husband as primary. "Granny felt she married Papa and *that was the essential bond*," recalls Cheryle. "Her life's work was ironing his shirts to perfection. Her joy was in pleasing her man."

Granny's "life lessons" included advice on loving a man. She dispensed this womanly wisdom forcefully and clearly. "Granny talked about the techniques and planning of love. She used to say a man needs to be held... If he gets comfortable enough to cry in your arms, he will be bound to you forever. Be a lady in public but a whore (actually she would not have used that word, but that is what she meant) in bed... work hard to satisfy his needs." The beds Granny prepared for sleeping and lovemaking were "sensuous pleasures." She would tell Cheryle, "Always keep a pretty bed, keep your sheets clean and fresh... and remember to powder the sheets." Granny felt the same way about the allure of a woman's garments. "She always ironed her slips because she said men liked to feel the texture of fabrics... They were not simply aroused by the naked body... after all, all women had the same anatomy. She wore the

finest, sheerest stockings so that Papa could feel the smoothness...
She'd be wearing a simple cotton housedress and these fancy slips
and stockings underneath... taking care of those details that would
arouse the man. Her skin was beautiful... She had gorgeous hands
with manicured nails." Cheryle recalls her granny's lessons with
enthusiasm. *"Those things were all love."*

Then she laughs, "Interestingly, Granny never had advice about
children." There were, however, hints of the ways in which the raising of five children—three boys and two girls—might have felt burdensome to Granny. Two months before she died, she spoke to
Cheryle about being a child playing the piano at home, the pleasure
and joy of making music. Then she said sadly, "But then I had the
children and never played it again." During that same visit she
spoke about her large and intense emotional life that had remained
hidden underneath a veneer that Cheryle describes as "Granny's
Mona Lisa image." On the eve of her death, she tried to explain the
feelings to her granddaughter. "I often have a sensation that I'm so
full, if I could only just cry... I need the release, to get the pressure
off... to lose myself in the emotion." Cheryle remembers feeling
identified with the depth of Granny's feeling, with the buildup of
highly charged emotions and the need to cry, *and* also with the
"Mona Lisa image" that maintains external serenity. "When I heard
Granny talk this way," says Cheryle, "I was struck by how often I
feel the same way."

It was in Granny's concern about her sons, "the boys," that
Cheryle heard most clearly her maternal apprehensions and disappointments. At eighty-five, as she anticipated her death, Granny
worried about who would look after "her boys," who were at that
point in their sixties and seventies. "Promise me you'll look after my
boys," she said to Cheryle. "These were her sons, who were *my
uncles,* who were full-grown men... She was entreating me to take
care of them." Even after her sons reached full maturity, Granny
worried about the special vulnerability of her boys, "the special
quality of black males who are still becoming, still getting it
together, still evolving." Cheryle smiles—"She didn't have the
slightest worry about whether her daughters would survive." She

thought of girls as constitutionally stronger and more resilient, and she believed that "black women were not as victimized by society."

Cheryle had felt that same impulse with the black prisoners with whom she shared the cell in Nashville thirty years ago. She experienced it as she watched the four shackled black men who were accused of beating the white truck driver in the recent revolts in Los Angeles. She always felt the need to protect her younger brother Eddie from the societal "assaults and degradation of the black male." And with her own two sons, now in their twenties, she feels a similar need. "I understood Granny's appeal to me about her boys," says Cheryle, "because I feel the same way about my sons."

I then venture to ask Cheryle, who is now in her third marriage, how she feels about the contrast between her marital experiences and her grandparents' long, devoted union. She looks surprised by my question, pauses briefly, and tells me about her grandmother's response to hearing about her first divorce. She had seemed undisturbed by the news. "Honey," she said, "in the old days, you didn't have the options you have today. In all relationships you have your good and your bad days. In my day, there was no way for a woman to support five children. But you have your own money, your own sense of self, and many more options..." "Granny always encouraged me to be selfish, to be independent." Cheryle smiles. "People would be *amazed* that this advice came from Granny."

Again, I pursue what I see as a potential contradiction. I ask, "Doesn't Granny's advice about how to love a man conflict with her idea of being independent, even selfish?" "No," responds Cheryle firmly. "Although they may at first *appear* to be contrary." Then she launches into a passionate statement about the coexistence of love and work, and the balancing of private and public domains in a woman's life. She begins, "If I could write myself as a woman... I would want to be described as someone who loved a man totally, who brought her *self* to the relationship. There is enormous joy in loving someone whom you are pleasing... This opens up opportunity... You are not in competition with anyone, only in competition with yourself." She speaks about the aggressiveness and ambition in her public life and says that for her to feel "whole," her public persona needs to be joined with her inner self. Her talk is slower as she searches for the words to describe her feeling. "Love is a very private thing, singularly yours, mysterious, the ultimate secret. My public life—work and politics—is where I am independent, strong, successful. The contrasts are at the center of my creativity... The contrasts are actually a powerful synthesis. When there is this synthesis, I think my best, work my best... I feel joy. You can also do extraordinary things in great pain, too... but I prefer the joy."

As I listen to Cheryle, I feel the legacy that she has inherited from Granny, the search for a "smoldering," "erotic" relationship, a union that is mysterious and very private. But I also feel an expanding womanly repertoire—the creation of more options, the building of self-sufficiency. When the two ways of being are in balance there is joy; when the work overtakes the love, there is pain despite the *appearance* of well-being and success. Cheryle admits that joy has been an elusive goal. "I'm still in search of what I saw in my grandparents." She claims that she is not necessarily searching for the long, enduring union Granny and Papa knew but for the balance between the private and public sides of life. "I have never been bound by the idea of 'this is forever.' I have found good love, good partners, good friends when I have had different needs... But we've all had traumatic experiences with people who have not been good receivers of our love. *There is art in accepting the gift of a person.*"

Cheryle's words seem to hang in the silence. Finally she says quietly, "My grandmother and my brother were my *safe harbors*... You know I've never found another man to be my safe harbor—a person who offers nonjudgmental love... a person who says, 'It's all right, you're at peace here.'"

Lonely on the Fast Track

"Our first schooling was at home," says Cheryle when I ask her to recall her first educational experience. Cheryle's mother was the primary teacher, and her brand of education was disciplined, intentional, and focused. "We had writing lessons, flash cards, required reading... We were reading fluently by the time we arrived in kindergarten." When Cheryle says "we" she is referring to herself and her brother Eddie, who was two years her junior; he was her "partner in learning" and absorbed their mother's teaching with the same enthusiasm as his older sister. Since Cheryle's sister was eight and a half years younger, she was "in a different sphere" and was never in the same school as her older siblings. Cheryle believes that her enthusiasm for learning, her thirst for knowledge came from her mother. It was not only the fact that her mother cared deeply about education and was a dedicated teacher; it was also that she was always at home, always there to answer questions, reinforce lessons, continue conversations. "She was always helping us seek things out... [helping us learn] the skills of questioning, observing, reading... building our curiosity and independence." There was time, endless time, for follow-up and reinforcement, for embroidering learning experiences into the everyday texture of life. Eddie or Cheryle would ask a question about something obscure, and they would all take a trip to the library to look it up. They would find a resource book, take it home and study it. "By the time we enrolled in kindergarten," claims Cheryle proudly, "we were very advanced. Our friends were always *amazed* at what we knew... We were always ahead of where our class was."

Cheryle did very well in the structured environment of school. "I loved playing school... all the daily routines." But she thinks that her intelligence did not "really shine" in the classroom. She feels most productive and creative as a learner when she is given scope to learn in her own idiosyncratic way. "My brother and I were *free spirits* with learning… We were the original Montessori kids. At home we were always given leeway in satisfying our own intellectual curiosity and creativity… and this made us somewhat uncomfortable in the school situation. I enjoy the openness, the expansiveness so much more." She remembers a class at UCLA in which she and her brother were both enrolled as undergraduates. She can't recall the substance of the course, only that it was a huge lecture with hundreds of students and several teaching fellows. One day the professor gave them an essay examination that baffled most of the class. He was asking questions that did not seem to be covered in the readings. Most of the students fumbled with answers that attempted to mask their ignorance. But Cheryle remembers Eddie sitting calmly across the lecture hall bent over his paper "writing on and on." A few days later when the professor returned with the exams, he chided the class on their generally lackluster performance and then announced that "one extraordinary class member—Eddie Anderson—set the curve." Eddie had not even tried to answer any of the professor's questions. He had made up one of his own; he had made it a question that related to the course material and revealed the depth of his knowledge; a question he could answer "fully and creatively." The professor applauded him for his initiative and his "thorough and masterful" response.

For the first three years of schooling, Cheryle attended Willard Elementary School, a public school in Cambridge, where she says, "I did very well… I rarely got under one hundred percent." She remembers school as "pleasant," "satisfying." She made good friends and liked her teachers. Each year she worked hard to establish then sustain her near-perfect record. In second grade, Cheryle broke her right arm just at the moment when the children were beginning to learn cursive writing. She worried that her injury would force her to "fall behind" the other children, so she quickly adapted a way of accommodating her injury. Even with her heavy cast, she could manage to print. So after printing a line of writing, she would go back and connect the letters, producing what looked almost like script. "That's still my style of writing," smiles Cheryle, and her style of responding to adversity. "It is my way of adapting... making sure that I don't lose ground."

Third grade was the "high point" of Cheryle's time at Willard. England's King George died, and Cheryle's teacher spent a lot of time talking to her students about the momentous event. She asked the children to write letters of condolence to Queen Elizabeth. Cheryle became completely caught up in the drama of the event. "I felt so identified with the new queen... I felt so much anguish for her in losing her father." Her letter expressed her grief and her heartfelt concern. The teacher was so moved by the young girl's letter that she sent it to the *Boston Globe*, where it was published. She also sent the exemplary letter to Buckingham Palace. Cheryle's voice still sounds amazed. "The Queen answered on her own morning stationery... in her own hand. It was thrilling, very exciting."

Cheryle believes that her achievement and involvement in school was "directly related" to her mother's vigilant advocacy. Every day her mother would walk the children to school, and she would be waiting at the front door when they were dismissed in the afternoon. She made it her business to know their teachers very well, and she wasn't shy about letting them know how special her children were. "The teachers responded to my mother's interest,". recalls Cheryle. "My mother's view was that I was a brilliant child, and the teachers were lucky to have me as their student." Soon the teachers began to share Mrs. Anderson's view, believing that they were fortunate to have a gem among their students who would excel and make them feel successful as teachers. "I don't think I was necessarily brighter than the other kids," Cheryle confesses, "but the expectations were so high... My mother was determined, dedicated, and people expected success."

By the time Cheryle was in fourth grade, the Andersons had moved to the suburbs, and the children were attending the Bedford Public Schools. In Bedford, the schools were embarking on a "new experimental system of teaching," and Cheryle was immediately assigned to the "fast track." Fourteen A students were put in the top level, and they remained together as a group through their twelfth-grade year. They thought of themselves as high achievers with great potential. They were aggressive in their pursuit of high grades and soaring test scores. "It was an extraordinary education," Cheryle says proudly. "It was a great distinction to be in this group. There were only two black families in all of Bedford, and I was the only black student in my grade... and I was known as a high achiever." She remembers *all* of her teachers as "very supportive." They saw her as bright, ambitious, and disciplined in her studies. In this sea of white faces, it was not hard for them to forget that this light-skinned achiever was black.

The "other black family had a pig farm, and their experience was very different," recalls Cheryle. Even though they had lived in Bedford much longer—for three generations—they were never accepted in the same way. "The kids called them niggers. The racism was explicit and overt." They were always made to feel like outsiders and second-class citizens. The Andersons experienced the opposite response from the white community. They were seen as the "exceptional Negroes"—sophisticated, well mannered. "Our family was viewed as a *model* family. They thought we fit in well," says Cheryle. "I know there was a class distinction there. It is *always* true that white folks manage to choose *one* acceptable black... and we were the ones they chose." Being the chosen ones, however, did not protect Cheryle and Eddie from "the loneliness and exclusion of subtle racism" even if it spared them the most virulent attacks of name-calling.

Despite these feelings, Cheryle was right in the center of school life, expressing her talents in many spheres. She thrived on the demanding schedule and the variety and threw herself into each activity with high energy and a determination to succeed. Of all the many activities in which she participated, Cheryle liked the debate club the best. Both she and Eddie won the state prizes in "debate, elocution, and extemporaneous speaking." They were known for their charisma, their style, and admired for how quickly they could respond on their feet. "Extemporaneous speaking takes incredible discipline, practice, and training," says Cheryle. "We liked it and became very good at it. We excelled at a time—developmentally—

when a lot of kids are feeling awkward and reticent... But early on in our family we learned not to fear awkwardness... We were taught how to present ourselves and our ideas publicly... that was socialized in our family." Cheryle lists the three ingredients of educational success that she had in abundance and that are born out by her experience in Bedford. "It is a combination of a good home environment, a well-designed curriculum, and extemporaneous speaking."

Cheryle's smooth rhetoric and public persona were important dimensions of her achievement. So was her test-taking acumen. All through school she was the kind of student who "tested very well" on standardized achievement tests. She enjoyed the routine of tests, rarely became anxious about them, and never "sweated them out." I ask her why she thinks the standardized tests were so easy for her, and her immediate response comes with a big laugh. "You know, I must be a superficial thinker, Sara." Then more seriously—"I am a quick decision maker... I do not labor all the shades of gray between black and white. On a true or false question, or multiple choice exam, I can soar." Cheryle's successful test-taking culminated in her receiving a "very high score on the National Merit exam" in her senior year. Her high score reflected her "extraordinary" schooling and her particular kind of intelligence that is "decisive" but "not subtle," that "doesn't labor over the shades of gray."

An award given to Cheryle *outside* of school stands as her proudest moment in her high school years. During her senior year she won the state's NAACP National Youth Award, which was presented to her by Roy Wilkins, one of her "greatest heroes." One of her teachers, she does not know which one, nominated her for the award that honored achievement, leadership, and community service. It seems very important to Cheryle that her nominator was a "white teacher" (of course, all the teachers in Bedford were white) who felt she "deserved the award on its merits." At a large breakfast, Cheryle was celebrated. She got up in front of "an audience that was ninety percent white," proudly received the award from Wilkins, the president of the national NAACP, and gave an eloquent acceptance speech. It all seemed "very right" and very much in keeping with family tradition. Her grandfather had been one of the early leaders of the NAACP in Jefferson City, Missouri, and the value of public service and civil rights had been passed down through the generations. As Cheryle shook her hero's hand at the awards breakfast, she felt she was carrying on her family's legacy.

The loneliness that Cheryle felt in high school was usually connected to her social life, not her academic experience. When "the kids began to date, to pair off," she could sense a "big difference" in the way they related. She does not remember her white classmates as unfriendly or unkind; she just remembers the beginning of a split, a separation that she had never experienced before. Cheryle returns to a theme that she has revisited many times. Her parents, particularly her mother, forbade interracial dating, so the white boys in Bedford were off-limits. Instead, her parents arranged for her to meet other "suburban blacks" from the surrounding towns and city kids from Boston. These meetings required elaborate arrangements, travel, and usually parental involvement. They had a forced, staged quality. Cheryle always felt awkward; she was the one who didn't know the latest dances, the one who "used the wrong language." Back in Bedford, the black princess increasingly experienced the distortions of tokenism. "I'm a different color. I do different things to my hair... The difference was seen as a negative, a weakness." She felt caught between two worlds at a time when she was "desperately longing to be accepted. I found myself in limbo—not belonging to the black or the white world... having two voices... neither of which was very adaptive, neither of which worked very well."

By the end of high school Cheryle wanted to escape this limbo. She wanted to go to a college where she would not feel awkward or torn or separated. She wanted to find a place where one voice—her own voice—would work. Despite the fact that she was being pursued by a number of elite white schools, Cheryle determined that she would go to a historically black college. When she applied to and was accepted by Fisk University in Nashville, Tennessee, she hoped that this would be a place where she would feel that she belonged.

"Fisk was *incredible*," she says, beaming. It was everything she had hoped for, and more. It was fun and serious, comfortable and challenging, black and excellent. "The teachers were extraordinary, intellectually gifted. They cared deeply about imparting values and building character... civility, good manners." She especially remembers the inspiration and challenge of two of her favorite teachers. Her French teacher, Dr. John Cotten (she pronounces his name with a dramatic French flare), was "tall, distinguished, Paul Robeson-like in character." He permitted "no foolishness" in his class, demanded impeccable manners, and made his late-adolescent students feel like full-grown ladies and gentlemen. "When I think of being in his presence, I think of the word 'lady,'" says Cheryle. "I felt grown, mature... He made us feel like black nobility." He insisted that all of his students "work hard and be successful," and he knew each of their diverse talents. Cheryle arrived in his course having had four years of high school French. Other students were total novices. On the first day of class, Monsieur Cotten addressed Cheryle, "Mademoiselle Anderson, you will stand and teach the class how to conjugate verbs." Cheryle rose up, with a knot inside her stomach but with a poised exterior, and taught her fellow students. Cheryle smiles at the memory of how, in time, each of the students responded to the expectations of this dignified and demanding professor.

Dr. Collins, Cheryle's English professor, was an "impeccable man," unbelievably perfect in his style and dress. "We always used to say that if a fly flew into the crease of his pants, it would cut the fly," laughs Cheryle. "You could see your reflection in his shiny shoes." Like Monsieur Cotten, Dr. Collins treated his students with respect and formality. "He called us 'Miss Anderson, Miss Smith, Mr. Jones'... After a little while, you stop being Cheryle, the majorette from Bedford High School, and you become a lady." The classroom civility was accompanied by an intellectual enthusiasm that was infectious. "It felt like he had a limitless source of knowledge... It made you want to absorb it all." Cheryle does not remember the substance of the knowledge she absorbed: what books were read, what essays were written, what questions were asked or what issues explored. But her memories of the rigor, the discipline, and the high expectations are vivid. And she has a "deep appreciation" for the linking of educational excellence and black culture. It felt so good, so thrilling, to be in a classroom full of black folks, all of whom were expected to achieve. "To be in a totally black environment was like dying and going to heaven!"

She feels so thankful for the Fisk experience, and so convinced about how it transformed her life that she says forcefully, "If I could dictate one thing for all black high school students, it would be to spend at least a year in a black college. In black colleges, students get to see black people as policymakers. At Fisk, we became the creators of school culture... we were in the *majority*. We thought differently about ourselves and our destinies... Our strong sense of self was tied to the intellectual process, creating an empowerment of the mind. And our intellect was tied to the spirit." Cheryle's voice is intense, her eyes moist.

More than thirty years later, Cheryle relives the memories of this "extraordinary education" with her schoolmates, many of whom have remained her very close friends. Although she was in Nashville for only a year, "I made deep, important, lasting friendships that I will have for all time," she exclaims. These friends have become her "bosom buddies," her "soul sisters," her business partners. They live all over the country in a lively network that can be activated whenever there is need for support, fellowship, advice, or resources. She contrasts these important relationships with the great distance she feels from the white friends she had in high school. "I've lost all contact," she says. "No telephone calls or correspondence... No one is to blame, just no communication."

After this description of her rich and exciting experience at Fisk, I am puzzled by how quickly Cheryle recounts the events surrounding her departure. "That summer, Spanky and I eloped." Spanky was an upperclassman at Fisk and they had gone together for most of Cheryle's freshman year. After their quick and secret marriage, the couple returned to Cheryle's home in southern California, where they faced the disappointment and outrage of her parents. Cheryle uncharacteristically understates the scene. "My mother and father were not overjoyed... but we loved the sunshine... we loved the Hollywood scene, so we stayed."

By the time Cheryle resumed her education at UCLA, she had been married for two years, had a young child, and was working to help support the new family. The large state university—with 35,000 students, 125 of whom were black—could not have been more different from the intimate black school in Nashville. "It was mass education," says Cheryle. "The GM of education... it was never the center of my life... I never felt intellectually challenged." Cheryle spent her energies balancing her various commitments and taking full advantage of the lively Hollywood scene. Spanky, who at first worked in endocrinology at a veterans' hospital in Los Angeles, quickly found his way into "showbiz." Hollywood's nightlife was infectious, and the young couple loved going out to clubs and discos. They would dance until dawn, "doing the peppermint twist," listening to great music, mixing it up with celebrities and would-be movie stars. "We would go and listen to Ike and Tina Turner. I would have sold my soul to be an Ikette!" It was an exhilarating time for twenty-one-year-old Cheryle, who had led a "pretty serious, pretty sheltered existence" before going out West. "It was a real eye-opener... The perfect balance to my life," she laughs. "I wouldn't have traded that era for anything!"

The House of Wills

When Cheryle speaks about "The Home," she is not referring to any of the three places she currently owns (the condominium in Boston, the house on Martha's Vineyard, or
the one in Cleveland); nor is she talking about any of the several
"wonderful houses" that her parents bought over the years; nor is
she thinking about the palatial residence in Cleveland where she
lived with her second husband and raised her children, and which
he still inhabits with his new wife. When Cheryle speaks about The
Home, she means the House of Wills, the funeral home owned by
her former husband's family—the place where she "grew up,"
"learned the business," and was immersed in black culture. Called
"Cleveland's most beloved institution," the House of Wills was
Cheryle's home away from home. It was the place where she spent
most of her waking hours, where she received her best training in
economics and politics; where she felt enmeshed in black life.
"Except for my one year at Fisk," says Cheryle, "this was my first
experience being around black people, poor black people. I was
constantly overwhelmed by their goodness, their faith, and their
hope in the face of overwhelming odds and ordeals."

The House of Wills (whose corporate name was J. W. Wills
Company) was founded by J. W. Wills in 1903. For two years Wills
had a partner in the funeral home, but by 1905 he had taken over
sole ownership and was beginning to give the business his unique
signature. Always called Senior, J. W. Wills became a "true black
millionaire of grand great style." He was an ardent student of history and an enthusiastic storyteller. Senior was ninety-three when
Cheryle arrived to work at the House of Wills. He was still elegant, shrewd, autocratic, and worldly. Seventy years his junior,
Cheryle brought her youth, energy, ambition, and glamour.

Together, they made an extraordinary pair. Cheryle listened intently to his tales, absorbing the lessons in history, culture, politics, and business. There is no one she has learned more from; there has been no more forceful and influential mentor than Senior.

In the 1890s, J. W. Wills had been the personal valet of a northern general's son who was enrolled in Antioch College in Yellow Springs, Ohio. Wills not only waited on his young white charge hand and foot; he was also required to accompany the boy to his college classes, to carry his books, organize his papers, and assure his comfort. Senior was very fair in color and "could pass for white." He was also "extremely bright and very ambitious." As he sat in on the college courses, he determined right away that he would not squander this wonderful educational opportunity. Alongside his less ambitious employer, the white-skin-colored boy quietly studied and learned the academic material. Despite his careful deference, the general noticed his extraordinary intelligence. "He was so proud of Senior's *mind,*" says Cheryle, "that he enrolled him in college at Antioch." His presence caused no shock waves because "no one knew he was black."

Graduating from Antioch in 1899, Senior headed for Cleveland, where he hoped eventually to study medicine at Case Western Reserve. Before applying to medical school, he had to earn a living and save money for his tuition. Senior became a streetcar conductor, "the first black trolley man" in Cleveland. He was not breaking the color bar, or challenging the policies and practices of segregation, because his employers thought they were hiring a white man. Cheryle is determined that I understand the subtlety of Senior's black identity. She explains: "You must know that Senior was extremely proud of, and clear about, being black... *He never passed.* In no way did he try to hide his racial identity... but he never corrected people when they thought he was white."

While he was working as a trolley conductor, he decided to enroll in a course in embalming at Case Western Reserve. His ambition continued to be medicine, but he was fascinated by the science and mystery of embalming. Early in the semester, the instructor displayed an "awful-looking dead body" and told the class to return the next day after the body had been injected with formaldehyde. The following day the students saw the amazing transformation: "The body that had formerly looked terrible now looked wonderful!"

The transformation fascinated Senior. He also knew a good business prospect when he saw it. "Senior recognized funeral homes as a great enterprise for the black community," exclaims Cheryle. "He knew that black people died and went to funeral homes... that it wouldn't require much capital outlay." But beyond the practical advantages, Senior completely understood the spiritual needs of black people. He recognized the African roots in the reverence and resources black people devoted to the funeral ritual. "Funerals are the closest link we have to our African roots... The embalming process grew out of an Egyptian cultural tradition. The funeral hymns speak about rivers winding through the fertile ground... The gods smiled on the rivers. The humming and moaning of our deep grief is like the African chants... and like our African ancestors, we believe that life on earth is a transition to a higher life. If you listen to the African tribal music, you hear the connections to the New Orleans jazz... to the funeral processions—the same phraseology, the same tempo, the same emotion."

Senior knew that next to buying a house and a car—neither of which were affordable to a large percentage of his clients—the "funeral was the biggest expense in life." But more important, he understood that for an oppressed people, for black folks who had meager opportunity to experience lives of dignity and beauty, the funeral provided the chance for a royal ritual. "Senior always said, 'Honey, funerals are not for the dead. They are for the living.' The honor, respect, and glory you gave to a person was shown in the funeral... Families were judged by the way they put their mother away." In contrast to the experiences of infantilization endured by so many blacks throughout their life—experiences that denied them their full humanity—the funeral was seen as an "explicit ritualized passage... a chance to finally come into manhood and womanhood."

Senior also understood the role funerals could play in joining the aspirations and realities of black people. After a life full of "dreams deferred" and broken promises, funerals offered people the chance to re-create their vision of what they wanted life to be. Cheryle describes a related dissonance in black lives: "For blacks, our expectations and our reality are vastly apart. White people only see the reality. So often they deny the expectation and the visions... Black people's attitudes toward their children's schooling is a good example of this contrast," claims Cheryle. "People think that because black parents endure their children's school failure they, in fact, find it acceptable. But that is not true. Their *reality* is failure, but their *expectations* are like those of *all* parents. They are desperate to have their children achieve and succeed." Senior understood this interior dichotomy that black folks negotiated daily: the vision of greatness and goodness that jars with the reality of impotence. He used to say, "Just because we don't have better, doesn't mean we don't *want* better." He knew why funerals had to be elaborate events designed to fulfill ancient and unrealized expectations. "Folks would say, 'Put all of Mama's rings on, dress her up fancy, press her hair right, make her beautiful,'" Cheryle smiles. "These were *very* important things... Finally Mama was getting what she deserved.

"Senior had an extraordinary need to do his own thing, and he truly revolutionized the funeral business," says Cheryle proudly. She admired his independence, his creativity, his savvy and wants to achieve these in her own future work. "In my own business experience I've been successful, but I've never had anything that was one hundred percent my own. *I'm festering for that now!*"

When the funeral home first opened its doors, the main branch was in a building located on East 25th Street, a neighborhood where "blacks replaced the Jews who replaced the Germans." By 1949, Senior had bought a magnificent building on East 55th Street in the heart of a thriving black business district. At the height of his business, the House of Wills was averaging twenty-five funerals per week; it was "the largest per volume funeral home in the country."

The "historic landmark" that Senior purchased had originally been a famous German beer garden. It was an immense structure housing a bowling alley, drinking halls, and restaurants. As the neighborhood "turned," the beer hall was purchased by a large syn-

agogue and turned into a Hebrew Day School. The United Negro
College Fund often held their meetings at the Day School, as did
other Civil Rights groups. Over time it became known as Cleveland's convening place for blacks and Jews. On Sundays, the syn-
agogue would rent out space to black churches. On Saturdays, you
could hear the haunting minor keys of the Jewish cantor singing the
Sabbath service, and on the following day, the spirited, rhythmic
beat of the black church choirs. Right next door to the Hebrew Day
School was Shiloh Baptist Church, a large and powerful institution in Cleveland's black community.

When Senior bought the building in 1949, he appreciated its historic legacy and envisioned its glorious potential. The external structure was strong and elegant, but the interior showed the signs of
deterioration of a building that had had so many lives. Using the
services of "a white internationally renowned architect," Senior gut-
ted the building and started from scratch. On the first floor, he
created an environment of "Egyptian decor, copied by funeral homes
all across the country." Cheryle's face brightens as she re-creates the
splendid interior. It had the largest funeral chapel in the country,
surrounded by an ornate balcony. The floors were covered in deep red
plush. "The piece de résistance was the domed ceiling, which was
covered with tiny lights made to look like a constellation of stars...
This was heaven, of course." Cheryle says forcefully, "*This was the
best, not the black best.*" It was the Music Room upstairs, however, that
seemed to hold a special magic for Cheryle. "It was amazingly beautiful with a twenty-foot ceiling, huge crystal chandeliers that were
always shimmering, gorgeous heavy drapes, and mirrored walls.... It
was designed to resemble the Palace at Versailles." On Sunday afternoons, elaborate teas would be staged in the Music Room. String
quartets would come to play Brahms and Beethoven, poets would
read their work, and vocalists would entertain with a repertoire rang-
ing from jazz to blues to opera. People would come to these elegant
events in their Sunday-go-to-meetin' best clothes. "Senior *never*
charged them," recalls Cheryle. "The teas and performances were
better than any downtown hotel where they couldn't go."

Senior thought of the House of Wills as more than a funeral

home, and so did everyone else in the city. When he coined the motto, "Cleveland's most beloved institution," he hoped to embrace the many ways in which the House of Wills lovingly and masterfully served the black community. It was the cultural center for art and performance, but it was also a place that dispensed social services. "People felt enormous comfort coming into the funeral home for all kinds of services—if they needed something notarized, if they couldn't understand an insurance form, if the city didn't pick up their trash, or if their electricity got turned off... they'd come to the House of Wills... and Senior better not hear that someone was being charged for these services." The funeral home was also a black institution that employed a large number of people. Cheryle laughs—"People used to say that you just had to stand around for a couple of days, looking ready and willing, and Senior would hire you. They always needed a driver or something... and if you did a good and responsible job, you could stay a long time and get paid well. Senior took care of his people."

In creating this grand, multifaceted institution, Senior was a pioneer, a maverick, an innovator. He was a businessman, politician, philanthropist, and purveyor of culture. He cared deeply about each role: making money, providing a first-rate service, building a healthy black community, and creating a beautiful empire. As a black entrepreneur and leader, he was also the critical link to the white power structure. Cheryle offers two glimpses of his unique status—sitting on the black-white boundaries. "You know, one black person will always be treated differently, and Senior was the person in Cleveland. The fact that Senior looked white meant that he had the benefit of hearing white conversation." He had special access to power and influence in Cleveland because of his color and his station and because white folks felt most comfortable dealing with the one person with whom they could feel at ease. Cheryle is shaking her head as she reflects on the echoes of Senior's experience that resonate in hers: the casualties and opportunities of tokenism; the special responsibilities of being the black chosen by the whites; the treacherous bridges that both connect you with and distance you from your own people. Cheryle watched Senior carefully, observed his style and his strategies, and learned lessons she has fully incorporated in her own life and work.

But when she thinks of the most important lessons, Cheryle returns again and again to Senior's teachings that merged business, culture, and aesthetics. She often seems to be repeating Senior's actual words, especially as he spoke about his business code.

"When we as blacks are in business, we must give *superior*, not inferior quality. It is very important that you get the best in death, even if you never had it in life... Here everyone gets the same service regardless of what they pay... People must be treated well, welcomed fully, and made to feel they are really somebody."

Cheryle explains the philosophy behind Senior's business practice. "No one understood better than Senior that black people are a very *cultured* people... Our sense of artistry and beauty, our sense of color, the way we aspire to the aesthetic—there is a direct linkage to our African roots.

"No one understood better than Senior how a black man who worked in the steel mill all his life would need to be suited up in the coffin—with his shiny shoes, dress shirt, nice silk tie—so Senior started having men's suits made (with opened backs)... and ladies' dresses in soft pastels that he had made to match the pastel casket linings. He bought brand-new Buicks so people would ride in style no matter who they were. Then he moved up to Cadillacs... Up until Senior started purchasing Cadillacs, General Motors was refusing to market to blacks... to do so would be to decrease their value... But Senior brought style to their industry."

For Cheryle, the House of Wills provided a window onto black culture. She could sit in her office on the first floor and witness black life in Cleveland. She had arrived in the small midwestern city from Los Angeles. (Cleveland was a place she had never imagined living. "I thought it was far too provincial.") "I was twenty-three years old and pregnant with my second son," she recalls. "I really came to divorce my first husband.... We had said we wanted to try to put together our marriage again. But I knew it wouldn't work." In California, the young mother had been working a couple of jobs—part-time modeling and working for an insurance company—and finishing up her undergraduate degree at UCLA. "I was used to working long hours and working hard." As part of her internship training at Occidental Life Insurance in Los Angeles, Cheryle had learned the procedures for processing Medicare claims. She brought those skills with her to Cleveland and decided to take a short-term summer job doing insurance claims at the House of Wills before teaching school in the fall. Senior had been desperate to find someone with Cheryle's talents. He hired her immediately, took her under his protective wing, and made her feel indispensable. When September rolled around, she was fully ensconced in, and committed to, the funeral home. As her first marriage predictably crumbled and her "home life fell apart," she carved a secure place in the House of Wills.

"In black funeral homes, cash comes basically through insurance," Cheryle explains. "Since I handled the insurance claims, my office was the first place people came to. Folks came asking me every question under the sun... and because they asked me the question, I had to find the answer. It was an amazing education." She remembers the parade of people who came through her office, illiterate, without Social Security numbers, even lacking the birth certificate that was required as documentation for getting a Social Security number. They would bring in their Bibles with family names carefully inscribed in the front—the only shred of evidence that they, in fact, existed. Cheryle would listen to their stories and trace their journeys as she helped them search for clues to their history. "Some man who was sixty-five years old would never have had a birthday. He wouldn't know when or where he was born... There was something very tragic about this," says Cheryle. With Cheryle's help, he would piece together the fragments of his life: "I lived on Mr. Tom's place when they had the great flood... or when so-and-so was president, I came to Master Fred's." When there was neither a birth certificate nor a Social Security number, Cheryle would go to the census data and find "so-and-so believed to be at this time twelve years old" or "so-and-so living on the plantation of..." Cheryle would collect the meager information, fill out the necessary forms, and follow the laborious bureaucratic procedures.

The process required perseverance, patience, and detective work on Cheryle's part. But when it was completed, she would have the undying gratitude and devotion of those whom she had served. "It didn't take a lot to fill out the forms, but it was like *gold* to them. I felt that I was there to do this task. It wasn't much. But they would say to me, 'You've given me my whole life.'"

Cheryle took enormous satisfaction in being able to provide this service, to restore these lost identities. "These were people who had to give themselves birthdays... That's why you see a lot of people born on January first or July fourth. Those were the days they chose. Literally, in America these people never existed. How does that make you feel?" She is horrified. "This was the sixties and seventies, but it still goes on today... It still doesn't seem important to America that all these folks are lost, unreported, unaccounted for... God knows how many blacks there are in the U.S." Her voice is hard and cynical. "You know, the census only becomes important when city money is tied into it... then suddenly the numbers become significant."

When Senior bought the grand building on 55th Street, he became part of "a prosperous and healthy black business strip" in Cleveland. Surrounding the House of Wills—between 55th and Woodland and 55th and Euclid—there were the offices of black lawyers, physicians, dentists, and accountants, a mix of small businesses, and the black-owned newspaper. In 1949, when Senior moved in and began renovations on the funeral home, this was a thriving and productive business community. "It was completely self-sufficient," claims Cheryle. "Their act was totally together... They were never dependent on public financing, never received loans from banks."

This successful black enclave was destroyed by the invasion of public housing. Ernie Bohen, a white developer and bureaucrat, was the first director of public housing in the United States, and Cleveland became his first project. "Strategically, he chose to tear down the prosperous black strip on Fifty-fifth Street and replace it with public housing." Cheryle's voice is rising in outrage. "He dispersed the whole community... replaced capitalism with socialism. You know, of course, the first public housing was never built with black people in mind. It was built for *white* soldiers returning from the war. For these white boys, it was a major step up the social ladder." Along with other black entrepreneurs, Senior tried unsuccessfully to fight off the "white socialist invasion." "He always felt it was a *deliberate* attempt to disperse the centralized black business strip," recalls Cheryle. When he died at ninety-eight years old, Senior went to his grave hating Ernie Bohen.

Cheryle remembers Senior's rantings about the systematic destruction of black capitalism, about how historically "white people have seized every opportunity to destroy" our communities when they are thriving and productive. She sees long shadows of this early destruction "of what once was working" in the decay and deterioration of our inner cities. The response to "the regression" in our communities should not be the invasion of social services. Cheryle gives an example: "After the burning of East Los Angeles, the black people Bush called on were all *social workers*—the Urban League, Dorothy Height, and others like that." Instead Bush should have gathered together black business people who know about building capital in our communities. Cheryle's voice is cynical. "Think about it, Sara. Slavery was the only time when we had full employment… We are a people who have been denied capital. We've always had the ability to work but not the ability to pay for work."

The image of Senior's "extraordinary establishment" that combined business, art, and social service, surrounded by a thriving black business community, makes the "regressed" inner cities appear grotesque by contrast. "This is not by our own hands that we've been so destroyed," says Cheryle angrily, "but it is by our determination, discipline, and resourcefulness that we will begin to move forward again." She searches for lessons from other times when black folks were more energized and hopeful. Her voice is filled with nostalgia about the 1960s. "When I came to Cleveland, *we were in our ascendancy.* Carl Stokes was mayor then. He was gorgeous, suave, sophisticated—what we called 'pressed.' He had an amazing aura. He'd come in the room, and mayhem would break out—yelling, screaming, stomping of feet." But the excitement and promise were not limited to the mayor's charismatic persona; Stokes symbolized a collective strength. "We were an empowered people… This was the only political life we knew. We knew our power, and *they* knew it... We saw Cleveland as our place in space!" Even after Stokes finished his second term in office and there followed a string of white mayors, "Blacks were still powerful in all divisions of the city." Cheryle recites the list of black leaders who were in place about five years ago; twenty years after Stokes's departure: "The president of the city council was black; the senior member of Congress was black; the head of public housing was black; the president of county commissioners was black; the head of community colleges was black; the president of the transit union was black... I was the president of the United Way... It goes on and on... and no one thought that was unusual!" Cheryle's voice is now ringing with pride. "The mayor was white, but the *power* was in *black* hands."

When Cheryle arrived in Cleveland she was captured by the vitality and the optimism of black politics and entrepreneurship. She got swept up in the momentum of change—"young, gifted, and black... and ready to make my mark." Cheryle does not discount "being at the right place at the right time." "When I came to Cleveland, I found myself under thirty, black, and female... In one shot, they could get all three. I am not being overly modest when I say that I was given the *opportunity* and I had the ability to perform... But others—who didn't have the same opportunity—were certainly just as talented. I get credit for seizing the opportunity, *not* being the best or the brightest." Cheryle underlines this point as she explains how she measures her own success. "You know, a lot of us have resumes that say he or she was the first black to do this or that. But we are *not* the first to have the ability. We're the first to have the opportunity. We must measure our success by whether we have created a process that will assure that there will be a second, a third, a fourth black in place when we leave... That is the judgment we must make. Have we paved the way for others?"

"This Is Your Destiny"

On Cheryle's second day of work at the House of Wills, Senior invited her up to his apartment for breakfast. The ninety-three-year-old businessman had a keen eye for talent, intelligence, ambition, and elegance—all of which he saw immediately in his brand-new employee. And the twenty-three-year-old woman was "captured by the black patriarch who was so extraordinarily successful." Right from the start, they were drawn to one another. "Senior just started calling me Duchess," recalls Cheryle, "and I always thought of him as my mentor." As they dined on a lovely linen tablecloth, sipping their orange juice from crystal goblets and eating their eggs and bacon on ornate china, Senior began to convey to Cheryle the values and vision that guided his business strategy. Cheryle listened intently. She heard his deep commitment to black community survival, his "genius" for developing a market, and his long experience with combining political and economic strategy. Senior was generous and discerning in passing on these hard-earned lessons, and Cheryle embraced them enthusiastically.

After breakfast they strolled into the majestic Music Room. Senior took Cheryle's hands and led her over to look at the two large paintings hanging on either side of the couch. Silently he pointed to each one and let Cheryle slowly absorb the contrasting images. One portrait showed a woman in her late twenties or early thirties who was dressed in a pale slinky dress. Leaning back against a couch, her long black hair cascading around her bare shoulders, the woman looked seductive, provocative, voluptuous. The other portrait was of a young bride, fully covered in her wedding dress, looking prim and proper, "innocent and virginal." Her hair was cropped short, and her dainty gloved hands held onto a bouquet of flowers. Senior directed his gaze to both paintings and whispered dramatically to Cheryle, "My dear, this is your *destiny*." Senior's declaration made "immediate sense" to Cheryle, who saw herself in both of these women. "I still am both of these people," claims Cheryle. "I'm the bride—innocent and tender, looking for protection and assurance... and I am the seductress—mature, sophisticated, and worldly." She continues, "These ingredients have always lived together in me. I have always been extraordinarily *female*... I'm still very much my daddy's *little girl*... and I'm also a very *self-sufficient* woman."

As she speaks, Cheryle is stretched out on her couch with her dark hair pulled back in a ponytail. A shimmering turquoise jumpsuit is stretched tightly over her long frame, the top covered by a loose turquoise, white, and lime green jacket. Her bare feet sport gold sandals. Today she is looking young, sexy, bold. Her "female" self-assuredness dominates, but I catch some of "Daddy's little girl" when she is describing the twenty-three-year-old woman sitting at Senior's breakfast table "sucking in his wisdom."

The two portraits hanging in the Music Room had the place of greatest prominence. "In size and positioning they seemed like family members," recalls Cheryle. The only other large paintings were of Silas Wills, Senior's father, who looked just like Ulysses Grant, and a large portrait of Senior. "Every time Senior would show his portrait to visitors, he would say mischievously, 'Put your eyes on the eyes of Senior, and his eyes will follow you across the room.'" Sure enough, Senior's piercing gaze would seem to trace his guests' every move. They would smile nervously at the eerie energy that flowed out of those dancing eyes. Senior's portrait and the portraits of the two women were painted by "a renowned African-American artist." Although no one knew for sure whether the "bride" and the "seductress" were the same woman or whether they were related to the artist, Senior claimed that they were two images of the painter's first wife who had abandoned him. When she left, he "vowed he would never marry another beautiful woman" and sold the pieces to Senior.

Several years after her introduction to the paintings, a local news team was doing a story on Cheryle. The camera crew arrived at the funeral home and searched for a place to shoot the interview. They decided on the Music Room when they saw the portrait of the seductress. "Please sit on the couch in front of your picture," they directed Cheryle. "That's not me," responded Cheryle even though she felt a deep resonance with the glamourous subject.

"I vacillate between these women," Cheryle says slowly. "Sometimes I am unsure and I need assurance. At other times, I want people to get out of my way." As she looks backward, Cheryle sees shifts that she calls passages. "When I was in my twenties, I was young and unclear. I needed lots of assurance. By the time I was in my thirties and early forties, I was building self-confidence and needed less support and guidance. But now as I approach fifty, I feel the need for assurance again." She admits to being very selective about those to whom she shows her "tender and soft part," and very disappointed if the chosen few do not respond to her expression of need. "The more I risk," says Cheryle, "the more I have the need for safe harbor." "What do you define as risk?" I ask. "I took a huge risk," she explains, "when I divorced my husband of twenty years and married for love… when I went from an environment where I was known and knew everyone and moved to this town where I knew no one. There was no sense of guarantee." Risk often brings excitement, but it is also accompanied by apprehension and loneliness. She yearns for the support of her grandmother and brother, her "safe harbors." "They always knew what I needed, and they knew this *without instruction*."

When Cheryle reflects on her inner resources that give her the courage to take risks, that allow her to feel more vulnerable as she approaches fifty than she did when she was in her thirties, she points to another side of her being. "I'm very *spiritual* about things," says this aggressive businesswoman who admits to "hating downtime." She anticipates my skepticism and offers an example: "When I was five years old, saying my prayers at night, I would always end by saying, 'I pray that I will one day be the captain of the majorettes'… and I didn't even own a baton… But I had very vivid pictures in my mind… And when I was in high school, I became captain of the majorettes… I saw it coming—pictures, images, premonitions." I am amazed by the image of leadership, poise, and glamour that five-year-old Cheryle drew in her mind's eye, and how the image seemed to serve as a source of ambition and determination. But Cheryle seems to be speaking of a special capacity within her that is more than purposefulness. She alternately calls herself "spiritual," "psychic," and "blessed."

Cheryle offers another example of the sixth sense that she possesses. In 1988 she came to Boston to give a speech, more than twenty years after her last visit to the Northeast. She had agreed to speak to the annual meeting of the YWCA, and as usual her assistant made all of the travel arrangements. "On that trip, everything that could [go wrong] went wrong. The plane left Cleveland four hours late, and when I arrived, I discovered I wasn't scheduled to speak for two days. My secretary had gotten confused on the dates." It made no sense to return to Cleveland, so Cheryle checked into a hotel and found herself in the very unusual position of having time on her hands. "There I was in the hotel, lying in bed in the middle of the day. Very strange for me. I began to get dizzy, so I got out of the bed and lay on the floor. This is also very unusual for me, because I am very germ conscious—especially in hotels—and I even avoid contact with bedspreads." As she was stretched out on the floor, images and messages began to float through her mind. "I began to get the sensation that there was someone I needed to find... I began to get the vision of green eyes... These eyes became a theme in my head." Cheryle picked up the Boston telephone book and began to search for the name of the person she was "compelled to find." For two solid days she was bent over the tiny print, perusing her way through the alphabet. She never discovered the name of the person, but not long after —in an equally mysterious saga— Cheryle ran into the person with the green eyes: a Boston man who appeared in Cleveland, a man whom she had not seen since her high school days, the man who would become her third husband.

Cheryle tells these tales intently, remembering small details, vivid imagery and feelings. In the stories she is "compelled," driven to do something or go somewhere. Her destination is fuzzy, the motivation is unclear, but she presses on. The longest odyssey she describes is the "incredible story" of meeting Roger Matthews. It is so long, so filled with details and detours that I keep losing the point. There is no way I could keep up with the many paths converging in her head. All I could record were fragments of this complicated saga.

"I had been out of the country for a few weeks, I can't remember where... But I was coming back to town specifically to attend the christening of Carl Stokes's daughter. I get back to the house—completely exhausted from my trip—and call down to the funeral home. One of the guys says, 'See you at the dinner tonight.' I had forgotten, or I had not known... I guess it had just slipped my mind, that my good friend Charlie was being honored at a dinner. I also remembered that a young girl that I had mentored over several years was getting married, and she and her mother very much wanted me to be there. So even though I was dead tired from my trip, I decided I'd do all these things—the wedding, the christening, and Charlie's dinner. It was Saturday and I went to the wedding and came home and changed my clothes for the reception... I came back home, washed up, changed again, and headed out for Charlie's dinner. I was real ambivalent about going to the dinner... I was just feeling so low in energy. It was pouring down rain. I stopped for a red light at the corner of East One hundred-fifth Street and Chester. But the brakes went out, and instead of stopping the car accelerated. Luckily, there was no accident, but I was very shaken up. At any other time, I think I would have just headed home. But something was pushing me forward. I drive my car—minus the brakes—from One hundred-fifth Street to Fifty-fifth Street where the funeral home is. It's late and there is only one elderly man down at The Home. He gives me the car they have available, but the window on the car is cracked and the rain is pouring in. Even though I'm not even sure I want to go to this dinner, I continue to drive. When I arrive, a guy greets me at the door, actually he's a convicted drug felon, but he's also real gorgeous and a wonderful person. He takes my hand and begins to lead me through the crowded room up to the speaker's table in the front. Lots of people are stopping me to say hello and tell me stuff. Since I've been out of town for a while, they're catching me up on the gossip. I pass a table with about ten women, most of them recent divorcees. One of them, who has been 'happily' married for thirty years has just left her husband, not because she was angry with him but because she just wanted to not be married anymore. It was a crushing blow for him."

I am listening to this tale unfold, patiently waiting for the story to focus on her "incredible" encounter with her future husband. As someone who relishes details, I am drawn into the dreamlike web she is weaving, but I am also beginning to feel frustrated by her giving me no clue about what is important and what is trivial.

"The liberated women want me to stop and chat and want me to introduce them to the handsome man I'm with. But I'm not about to have them meet my drug felon. When we finally arrive at the speaker's table, they are apologizing but tell us there are no more seats there, so they assign me to another table. Charlie, my friend who is being honored, is a national officer of the black Shriners, so there are all these guys dressed up in fezzes. The men are all in their tuxedos, and the women are wearing formals. I'm sitting there wishing I had done more with myself. I'm not shining. I'm not dressed sharp enough for this occasion... All of this is running through my mind. I have now made my appearance and I'm ready to leave. But the speaker turns out to be my good friend Lou Stokes [Carl's brother]. He's not only a close friend; I'm also the treasurer of his campaign. So I don't feel I can leave while he is speaking. In addition, the minister who is officiating is Charlie's, as well as mine, and I think it is rude to leave while he is doing his thing. Finally, the speeches are finished. Lou stops by my table to see if I want to walk out with him."

Now that Cheryle is about to leave the dinner without meeting Roger, I wonder again where this story is leading. In her rapid-fire talk, I worry that I might have missed some clues, so I ask her a couple of pointed questions. "Was Roger sitting at a table close by? How did you finally manage to run into him?" But Cheryle seems not to hear me as she presses on with her story.

"I get up and walk toward the elevator. As I'm pressing the elevator button, that group of liberated, formerly married women, who had spoken to me earlier when I came in with the drug felon, comes up behind me. They're exclaiming about all the good-looking men at the dinner. I tell my friend Jane, 'I can't believe you're out here scooping men. I'm a married woman, and I'm *certainly* not going to be scooping men.' But they keep teasing me and start talking about one man who is *really* fine. As I'm standing there, someone comes up to me and says that there is a policeman downstairs who wants to see me. It turns out that the policeman has come to tell me about the death of Jackie Presser, a man who was head of the AFL-CIO, a good citizen of Cleveland, a guy who has had cancer for years... But why did the policeman come to tell me this? All of this is going on—people moving in and out—but *my* goal is go by Sisters [a restaurant] and get some strawberry shortcake, some ribs, and go home and get in the bed. I'm hungry and tired. I'm still waiting at the elevator. The liberated ladies are still chattering. I go to turn toward the elevator door and turn right into a large body. I hear the women start laughing. This voice says to me, 'Are you Cheryle?' and I say, 'Wills,' and he says, 'Anderson.' Now, there are probably only two or three people in Cleveland who know my maiden name. I look up at this large body and see his name tag, 'Roger Matthews'... and as they say, the rest is history."

In telling this circuitous story, Cheryle wants to convey the power of the "sixth sense" she possesses that kept her moving toward Roger—through the rain, through her weariness, through the brakes going out in her car, through the liberated ladies' chatter, through the long dinner speeches. "In every other situation I would have just headed home and gone to bed. I was very ambivalent about going to Charlie's dinner. I kept questioning it, but I kept on moving toward that destination." She concludes her account with one final "crazy kind of thing." "You know, I go through wild hair changes all the time—I wear it wild and out, cut it short, wear it frizzy and straight, put it in a ponytail, pull it back in a bun... People who know me say they can tell how I'm feeling by how I'm wearing my hair that day. Well, that evening I wore my hair pulled back. It was a style my husband didn't like... But Roger said later that he wouldn't have recognized me if I hadn't had my hair pulled back, because that is the way I wore it in high school."

Cheryle extends her psychic capacities to the policy arena. She tells about strategies and plans that she "projected twenty years ago that are now happening." "In my nonprofit world, for example, I was always trying to convince policymakers that if we were going to get anything for poor black children, that we would have to make an appeal that included *all* children, that said that *all* children are in trouble. As long as we focused only on *black* kids, they'd never get the needed support. I said that when my children were babies. Only now it is finally happening."

Cheryle has also "talked for a very long time" about the distorting experience of tokenism, about how it feels to be black in a predominantly white elite environment. "I've been speaking about the aloneness of being black on some of these boards I sit on—of belonging but not belonging, of white people not seeming to listen and then stealing your ideas... of having to constantly worry about what the white folks can tolerate hearing. I've said these things way before these were things people were talking about." Cheryle is sitting on the edge of the couch, leaning forward intently. Suddenly her eyes are moist with tears. "People have said to me, 'Cheryle, you should write about these things'... But I don't feel ready to write. *If I ever write, I'll write truth, and the truth hurts.*" I shudder as I hear these words. For me, they carry pain, challenge, admonition, and responsibility. Cheryle has allowed me to write her story. She trusts me, but she sees the risk and anticipates the hurt that will come with disclosure. This project seems to be a first effort to face the truth, a first step in preparing herself for coming into her own at fifty.

"I've always thought it will be in my fifties that I will come into my own as to who and what I am," Cheryle says dramatically. "I've never used my full talents. I'm almost in escrow—I've developed lots of talents, had a lot of opportunities, been given a lot of exposure. Others judge these as accomplishments, but I see it as preparation." She speaks about the excitement and vulnerability of this transitional moment when she is "letting some things fade away"—ending her tour of duty with the United Way, selling her cable television business, getting rid of some of the radio stations she owns, redefining her business partnerships—and "making room for the next phase." "Up until now, every day was a new *crisis*. Now I have more time for reflection. You know, I've never ever talked about this psychic side of me... but I *know*, I *know* this [time in her life] is the start of something *big!*"

As Cheryle prepares herself to "come into her own" at fifty, as she reflects on the special capacities and responsibilities she has as a person who is "blessed," she is reminded of her friend Jesse Jackson, who is "not living up to his potential." She thinks that the spiritual side of Jackson has not been seriously mined or fully expressed by him. Her focus is on his appearance at the Democratic National Convention in New York, where he gave a rousing message that echoed his speeches of a decade ago. "He was standing there screaming, 'Up with hope! Down with dope!' and the audience was responding enthusiastically. But I could have throttled him. I was enraged with Jesse... He's giving the same old stuff. We need a new and challenging message. How can he talk about hope with Los Angeles burning?" Cheryle's rage at Jackson not only reflects a criticism of "his lack of discipline"; it also mirrors her own strong self-criticism.

Her criticism goes deeper. She is raging at Jesse and angry with herself for the lack of discipline but even more for the way she believes they have both squandered their special relationship to God, their spiritual capacity. Cheryle tells a long story about Jackson's recent trip to Cleveland to speak at the annual Men's Service at the city's largest black church, Olivette Institutional Baptist Church. The tale ends in a back room at the church, where Jackson is getting a haircut from a local barber before his appearance. He has invited "Sister Wills" to join him in private conversation along with another prominent citizen and vestry man of the church. At one point, Jackson asked them, "Where is Carl?" (Carl Stokes, the former mayor of Cleveland), and the vestry man had given an oblique, but negative response. (Cheryle explains, "Carl is a very powerful and attractive person. He is a gorgeous man with a keen intellect. A lot of people are threatened by his strength. They don't want him around because his big presence makes them feel small.") Jesse had heard the pejorative tone in the vestry man's comments and he warned, "I'd be careful about saying those things about Carl… People can try to diminish or weaken him, but Carl's battle is with God. Carl is God-blessed." Jackson's voice was soft and intense as he spoke about Stokes's godliness. Cheryle remembers a "big silence, a pregnant moment" before she whispered to Jackson, "So are you. You are God-blessed." "Yes, I am," said Jackson in a simple declaration that sounded like he was accepting the serious spiritual responsibility, not flaunting his talents. Cheryle's voice is passionate as she recalls this moment of witness. "I *do* believe that about Jesse, and I feel that way about myself. We are *blessed*… Carl, Jesse, and I."

Not only does "coming into her own" at fifty mean reckoning with the special challenges and responsibilities of being "blessed"; it also is represented in Cheryle's growing comfort with her upper-middle-class origins. I ask why she thinks that as soon as Senior laid eyes on her, he named her Duchess, and Cheryle immediately awards the credit to her mother. "The duchess in me is attributed to my mother, who is a grand and royal kind of a person." She knows that although Senior admired "the duchess" in her, all black folks do not regard it positively. "Some people think it's grand, sophisticated, and royal," says Cheryle. "Others think of it as snooty and snobbish. I have always been devastated by the latter image. There is nothing that hurts me more. *I've spent my whole life trying to refute this!*"

This view of inherited royalty inspires a discussion of social class differences among blacks. Cheryle now understands that "the duchess" in her reflects the experience of growing up middle-class in a white community and the cumulative experience of generational abundance. "In a middle-class white community blacks learn different ways of survival. The American racial concept sees blacks as inferior and whites as superior. But if you've been raised in a majority community, you know how untrue that is. You are not awed by whites. You have competed against white folks, and you've won." This early experience offers a close-up view of white folks' vulnerabilities and fallibilities. It also offers early lessons in socially acceptable behavior. "As a child, you learn that you are acceptable to the degree that you mimic their behavior… So that at almost fifty, black people are still saying, 'You have white girl ways'… and white people are saying—as if this is a compliment—'You don't seem like a black person to me.'" There are trade-offs. Having survived and excelled in the white world as a child growing up, you are not cowed or awed or amazed by white accomplishment and privilege. You know you can successfully compete with the best of them. But at the same time, your socialization distances you from black folks and gives you the mark of royalty that causes blacks to be suspicious or envious, and causes whites to feel more connected and comfortable. It is the discomfort and suspicion of blacks that Cheryle has been trying to refute all her life.

Now Cheryle has determined that she will make peace with who she is—with her roots, her history, her family lineage. "I no longer feel the need to apologize about my privilege," she says adamantly. "I've grown very comfortable with it." "From a black perspective, I come from royalty… We always had the nicest house, the nicest cars, the nicest clothes, the first TV in the neighborhood, the first automatic washer and dryer. On Western Avenue in Cambridge, where I spent my early childhood, the black men in the neighborhood revered my father. They never thought of themselves as his equal. They were proud of him, deferential to him. It took the sixties to question that sense of privilege and presumption. Back then it was assumed and honored."

Cheryle tells an extraordinary story of going to third grade at Willard Elementary School in Cambridge. Willard was mainly a white school generously sprinkled with black students from families who had managed to get their children transferred from the all-black Houghton School. Cheryle's mother, who felt entitled to "push the system" and maneuver on behalf of her children, had successfully petitioned to have her three children in the better white school. The Willard School, though superior to the Houghton School academically, was an old facility with wooden desks and chairs that gave the children splinters. Cheryle's third-grade teacher put a pillow in Cheryle's seat so that she would avoid getting splinters. "No other child had a pillow," says Cheryle straightforwardly. I am incredulous. "Why?" I ask. "I don't know," she responds. "I never asked why, and no one else did." Even in this classroom full of white children, the light-skinned black girl, who lived in the nicest house in her neighborhood, was awarded special privilege. This favoritism went unquestioned until it became a habit of presumption and entitlement. "I was treated like a princess," says the Duchess of her third-grade year.

Along with the privilege came a sense of heightened responsibility. Because Cheryle's family always had the best of everything, they also felt compelled to give the most. "We always had a sense of noblesse oblige," claims Cheryle. "We always helped others, clothed the poor, fed the starving." She quotes the Scripture, "'Those to whom much is given, much is expected'... That is my story, my *obligation!*" Then she laughs, slightly embarrassed. "We even had an intolerance to pretenders to the throne." It is a relief for Cheryle to be able to talk about all of this: to be able to admit to the royal heritage, to be able to feel comfortable with her upper-middle-class origins, *and* to own up to the special responsibilities of her privileged life. "Now that I'm *comfortable* about who I am, it will help me release my full potential." There is enthusiasm and eagerness written all over her face. "I have a sense of being up to the challenge,... It takes leadership and *I am a leader.*"

All You Can Do
Is Give Forward

It is a rainy, humid September day. The early morning feels dark and gray. I open my front door and see Cheryle Wills-Matthews unfold her tall body—first the high heels, then the long slender legs—and emerge from the yellow cab. She is dressed in bright red from head to toe, from her crimson beret to the red patent leather shoes with gold buckles. Along with a shiny red and purple shawl she carries a cellular telephone, from which she has called to make sure that she was heading to the right address. Her dazzling costume cuts through the morning grayness like a shaft of light. She kisses me on both cheeks as we murmur greetings that end in a long embrace. I have not seen Cheryle since June, and it has been a hard summer for her.

A couple of weeks earlier, when I called her on Martha's Vineyard to confirm our appointment, she told me that she was getting a divorce—a divorce from her third husband to whom she has been married for only two years; a divorce from the man for whom she left her beloved city of Cleveland, where her roots are deep and her networks vast; a divorce from the man who was her high school sweetheart; a divorce from the man with whom she hoped to build a new, adventurous life in a new city. I feel saddened but not shocked by her news. Saddened because of the anguish I know she must feel over the loss, the dislocation, and the "big risk" that soured so quickly; but also saddened because what for Cheryle felt like a bold act of love was not allowed to mature and flower.

I am not surprised, however, by the news of Cheryle's separation because over the months I have been feeling Cheryle's loneliness. At first I interpreted it as the isolation of a stranger. Of course, she would feel lonely, I thought, leaving all her family, friends, and work in Cleveland and moving to a brand-new town, facing the cool reception of an unfriendly city. Even someone as gregarious and attractive as Cheryle would feel moments of isolation. But over time, I had begun to sense a more profound loneliness. There was something deeper that she seemed to be battling against. Now she describes the battle in a single word "boredom." "When I think back over the two years, Sara," she says with tears misting her eyes, "it's not the pain and anguish, or giving up my life in Cleveland that is most memorable... it is the boredom, the emptiness."

I am surprised by the word she repeats several times. "Boredom" does not fit the image I have had of their coupled life, full of globe-trotting, entrepreneurial pursuits, social gatherings with friends, and extended family commitments. I search for clues in Cheryle's description of their recently celebrated second anniversary—"a dull, traumatic evening"—and in the contrast she once drew between her "passion" and Roger's "cool and control that drives me crazy." "I'm an Aries and Roger's a Gemini," Cheryle said by way of explanation.

Cheryle and Roger have been separated since midsummer, and the days and weeks have been tumultuous, involving nasty and pushy lawyers, restraining orders, police banging on doors, struggles over property—what Cheryle calls "the crazies." "The *ugliness* is so unnecessary... it is *not* me," says Cheryle who tells the story with surprising balance and compassion for the husband with whom she is embattled. She had hoped that the divorce would be straightforward after a short marriage with no shared children and relatively little shared property. She had hoped to emerge from this relationship "still friends." "It is a matter of *pride* with me," she claims, "that I *always* remain friendly with the men with whom I've had relationships... but it may be impossible to do that this time around... and that is sad." She has just returned from Cleveland, where she visited her "sons' great-grandmother" (her first husband's grandmother) who had undergone open-heart surgery. And she describes the respectful and civilized divorce with her second husband with whom she had been married for twenty years. "We came to a point where our lives were diverging. I had married him when I was twenty-seven, and he was a lot older. Two decades later he was ready to think about retirement homes in Florida (I hate the whole *state* of Florida)... and I was ready to take on the world. So we sat in the judge's chambers, his lawyer and mine, all of us friends from way back... and we worked it out... In *that* marriage, there was a lot of property to be settled, but it was done in a dignified way."

The second and third marital partings were different in another way. With the second she felt "sorrow and tears"; with the third she felt as if a "big heavy weight had been lifted" off her. "I remember weeping and weeping, deep grieving when I left the judge's chambers... This time I only feel relief... It reminds me of the time before my hysterectomy when I had had a year and a half of bleeding and constant anxiety about whether this was a malignancy or not... and I thought my life might be over..." Her voice trails off. The convergence of all her sadness leaves deep creases in her smooth face. "When the surgery was over and the doctor said there was no malignancy, I was so relieved... That is the way I feel now, just relief, no tears."

We sit at my kitchen table talking for more than an hour. The stories keep coming, unedited, scattered, full of feeling. I do not listen for the details or the specifics of her summer's tale, but I do hear the disappointment and the pain. It is clear that there is much more to tell, much more that needs to be expressed, but Cheryle looks at her watch and stops herself. "We'll have to get together one day for lunch to just talk girl talk," she says decisively as she draws the boundary between our work and sisterly conversation. I pick up Cheryle's cue, turn the tape recorder on, and remind her of where we traveled during our last session.

I suggest to her that we focus on her work—both her career and her political and community activism—and she dives right into the conversation appreciatively. We both seem eager to move away from the private arena. Cheryle lifts her body out of a slump, clears her eyes, sits up tall, and looks directly at me. "There are intertwining connections between my business and my volunteer work... They are both part of my service to the community... deeply connected to one another." Before she can begin to describe the character and scope of her work, she feels "compelled" to honor the roots of her commitment. "My determination *and* obligation to do these things comes from my family first. I grew up in an extraordinary family that encouraged us to be the best we can be... expected us to be achieving and talented. And I grew up receiving the gifts of neighbors, friends, and teachers whom you can never pay back. *All you can do is give forward.*"

Cheryle pauses for a moment while she searches for an example. By now, she knows that I will press her for a story that will elaborate her declarations. By now, she can hear the sound of her own rhetorical flourishes, which seem to ask for explanation. She smiles at me as she listens for my silent question, "Could you give me an example, Cheryle?" She finds the story in a television program she accidently watched the night before as she waited for the much publicized episode of *Murphy Brown*, the sitcom made famous because Vice President Quayle used it as an example in his assault on single mothers and broken families. The preceding program, starring Burt Reynolds and Ozzie Davis, was about the lingering longings of an ambivalent father-son relationship. After the death of his father, the character played by Reynolds clings to his father's memory by holding onto a building on which he can no longer afford to pay the mortgage. The building represents his father's legacy and love, a love the father was never able to express fully to his son when he was alive. Ozzie Davis, an old friend of his father's, tells Reynolds how much his father loved him, how much he used to brag about him, how proud he was of him despite his shyness about saying so openly. Davis advises the son, "Let the building go. That is not your father... the memorial to your father is *you* yourself." Cheryle replays the television drama almost as if she were there. "I am blessed with coming from *good* stock," she concludes. "I was always taught a sense of sharing. I memorialize my forebears by giving of myself."

Cheryle's voice is forceful as she makes a declaration that seems central to her personal and professional identity: "I believe in tithing at church, and *I believe in tithing in life*—not just money but time... not just bricks and mortar, but people and feelings." This disciplined act of "giving forward" is not only a gesture of generosity, it is also closely linked with her success as a businesswoman. It is both giving and getting, charity and productivity. "My business relationships come from my volunteer relationships... You make yourself *visible* through good works. The visibility carries over to business networks and prominence." Although there is strategy and calibration in joining these two ambitions—public service and business—Cheryle claims it does not work if the "good works" are not done out of authentic commitment. "It is only effective if it's *real*. People can tell when you are only in it for yourself, when it is pure self-interest."

Cheryle learned how to accomplish the "intertwining connections" from Senior. As she watched her ninety-three-year-old mentor, she saw his deep dual commitments. The House of Wills, "Cleveland's most beloved institution," was an exceedingly successful business *and* the most caring and responsive social service institution in the community. Senior was respected both for his business acumen *and* for his generosity and commitment to community building. Cheryle speaks proudly of this legacy. "Senior was the first president of the NAACP in Cleveland... He started the Urban League... He worked on behalf of the United Negro College Fund." But his efforts were not limited to building organizations. He also spent a lot of time encouraging individuals—prodding, challenging, supporting young people to develop their talents to the fullest. "Senior would always encourage some of the boys from the local high school who would come hang out around the funeral home. He'd speak to them about being men, and more than men, about being *gentlemen*—about manners, discipline, hard work, civility. He gave many of them jobs and paid them well... He cared about their futures and the future of the black community." Cheryle watched this ancient pioneer "giving forward" and observed the deft linkage between his "good works" and his lucrative business.

By the time Cheryle was twenty-seven years old, she was following in her mentor's footsteps, bringing her style, savvy, and intelligence and new energy to the cause. She joined the board of the Phillis Wheatley Association in 1972 and became the board's youngest president in 1975. One of Cleveland's most prominent social service agencies, the Phillis Wheatley Association was started by Jane Edna Hunter in 1903. Hunter, a nurse, who had migrated from the Deep South to Cleveland as "part of the great migration to industrial cities in the North," saw the need for protecting and training the "young colored women up from the South." With grit and determination she began to raise funds to build an organization that would do this. With a combination of assertiveness and deference, Hunter enlisted the support of J. W. Wills, who became her "colored president" for fund-raising, and of John D. Rockefeller, as Senior's white counterpart. With the help of these two powerful men Hunter built her home designed to protect young women from the harsh and dangerous realities of northern city life and teach them "manners, discipline, and poise." In addition, Hunter built a cafeteria and tearoom where "gentlemen could come and call on the young ladies." The men were required to wear shirts and ties and to follow strict rules of punctuality and decorum, or else "they would be ostracized from the tearoom *and* from the entire black community."

Hunter also had another goal: to prepare the young colored women to take jobs as maids in Cleveland's affluent households. Cheryle shakes her head when she talks about these young women being trained to become the servants of rich white people. But she also admits that her criticism is based on contemporary standards and perspectives. "It is very difficult now for me to accept this as a laudable goal, but if you consider the historical period, it was important for its time." Cheryle feels the same ambivalence when she thinks about the art and life of the heroine for whom the home was named. "Phillis Wheatley came to Boston as a slave, overcame the huge barriers of racism and prejudice to write poetry..." This first image of Wheatley—as courageous, strong, and talented—was the one Miss Hunter embraced when she named her association in Cleveland. But Cheryle is aware of a contrasting picture of Wheatley: "She was actually a very vain, self-centered person who wrote verbose, mediocre verse, but, again, we have to judge her (and her poetry) for its time."

By the time Cheryle joined the board of the Phillis Wheatley Association in 1972, it had become a large, multifaceted social service organization with a broad political and economic agenda. Its executive director was Mrs. Tommy Petty, whom Cheryle describes as another mentor. "She was kind of a big sister to me—a strong woman, amazingly competent, a trained professional highly regarded in the community. She was a CEO who ran the largest social service agency in town, and I watched her and learned a great deal." Although Cheryle had sat on a few small community boards before coming to Wheatley, she had never been a director of a large organization that was efficiently managed. At Wheatley she "learned the skills of boardsmanship." The board meetings would begin at noon. The directors would have lunch as they followed a strict agenda and would adjourn by 1:30 P.M. Cheryle became an avid student of organizational leadership. "Through this experience I learned the efficient use of time, the discipline of organizing your thoughts, the importance of a well-planned agenda, the economy of words, *Roberts Rules of Order,* how to negotiate airtime, the effectiveness of precise minutes, how to form common interests." She enjoyed watching and participating in "the board politic" and became increasingly adept at "making the best use of their time."

As she recites the "skills of boardsmanship," it is clear that Cheryle relishes the action, the strategy, and the politics. It is also clear that she has a particular genius for this kind of work. "Where did your talents and enthusiasm for this come from?" I ask. Without skipping a beat she says firmly, "My family. The skills I learned at my family's dinner table translated easily to the board room. We had certain rituals at dinner: We had to read the newspaper and come to the table prepared to talk about an article, what we learned and our opinion of it. We had to follow acceptable manners—no singing, no fidgeting. We had to learn how to be respectful in sharing our ideas—how to negotiate airtime, how to read your crowd, how to organize your thoughts and be precise, how to be an *active* listener, not just a quiet receiver of information." As Cheryle sat eating lunch at the board meetings at Wheatley—with other black and white city leaders—she could feel the echoes of her familial training at the dinner table.

Cheryle does not want to leave me with the impression that she finds pleasure or expression only within these highly structured organizational settings, however. She admits to "relishing the discipline and efficiency and insisting upon using her time productively," but she contrasts that with her own "inner need" for creative self-expression. "I think of myself as a *free spirit*," she says boldly. "I am more comfortable with my own assignment to myself. You know, I do a lot of speaking around the country, and I talk about things that have been burning in my heart and soul for weeks, sometimes years... These things I talk about in my speeches are often too intimate for me to share *intimately*—they are more easily shared with strangers in a pubic forum. By the time I get up and speak, it *appears* to be effortless, but that is because I've been working on it inside me for so long." Cheryle's eyes are searching my face. She is looking for some sign that I understand the contradictions that seem to be a part of her work and her person. She sees my puzzled look. Why is it easier to speak publicly about intimate things? What do you think of as intimate? And how do you trust an audience of strangers with those feelings that have been burning in your heart?

As I urge Cheryle to elaborate on her thoughts, I find myself wondering whether our work together bridges these polarities and embraces her contradictions. Here we are, intimate strangers talking about Cheryle's personal feelings and experiences. Perhaps she is using this opportunity to explore the boundaries between public and private dialogue. Even as she speaks openly, candidly, intimately, she knows that our encounters will become a public document. Does that make the intimate talk easier?

"Would you give me an example of the intimate thoughts that you would offer up in a speech?" I ask. "Sara, I *internalize* everything," Cheryle begins. "Last week I watched the news report about Marion Berry, who won his election for D.C. city councilor. He is standing up there afterward at a news conference, and part of me is saying, This is a slick con artist. I don't know him personally, but I'm feeling jaded in my judgments about the man... But another part of me is watching the young black men who are standing there listening to him. They are standing there with tears in their eyes. He's telling these young men, 'If you have the monkey on your back—drugs and alcohol—look at me. You can come back. If you have been incarcerated, look at me. You can come back.'" Cheryle is leaning across the table, her hand jabbing the air emphatically, her voice rising as though giving a speech to hundreds. "Berry was offering an effective, strong message to these men. This was the best thing I had heard in ten years. Some people say Berry is a dishonest crook… but in this case I say you have to forgo the messenger for the message… I can forgive the messenger because of the power and timeliness of his message."

The television newscast, the image of the "vulnerable" young black men with tears in their eyes, ignites the fires within Cheryle. She is speaking passionately about "the lost generations of kids who have never seen any adults in their life get up and go out to work." She is raging at "the totally ineffective" federal policing of drugs. "It is not surprising that these kids are on drugs. The system deliberately makes drugs available. We've managed to keep health and education out of the black community. We could certainly keep out drugs." Her voice rises to a shout as she condemns the way blacks are labeled as "the problem. In this society the drug problem is widespread. This is *not* a black male prerogative. This is an *American* problem. Somehow we don't hear about all of those CEOs of major companies who are drug addicts or those white suburban housewives who are bored out of their skulls and turn to drugs for relief." She is railing against the incarceration of "defenseless black males. Going to prison has become the Bar Mitzvah for young black males. Prison provides them with a kind of safety they've never known: a room, a bed, a meal… They leave prison and can't get a job."

As Cheryle rages, I hear personal anguish beneath the public outrage. As she sketches a mural of black male genocide, she is eloquent in her assaults on "the system," but I think the tears in her eyes are for her sons—black males who are vulnerable despite their legacy of privilege. Almost as soon as I think that thought, Cheryle mentions her older son. Her voice is bitter. "You know, my son had trouble with drugs… and it has been a long, hard struggle for him and his family. He had all the trappings of being middle-class but all the pressures of being a brother. Just think of the kids who are poor, who live in the projects. What chance do they have?"

Cheryle's question hangs in the air. She covers her eyes with her hands and a weariness suddenly consumes her body. She no longer looks defiant in her red costume; she looks helpless, like the sons whom she can't protect from the ravages of a "dangerous society." Finally she looks up and says, "In a few weeks I'll be speaking to the Urban League in Topeka, and I'm sure I'll talk about all this. It will be simmering within me... It's burning in my heart."

Boardsmanship

When I turn on the tape recorder and speak her name "Cheryle Wills-Matthews" into the microphone, she gently but firmly corrects me. "It's Cheryle Wills—the Wills-Matthews was never the real thing. My mother always used to say the names didn't sound good together." A few minutes later, she is sitting tall, looking mischievous and defiant. "For the first time in my life I'm a *single woman*—no husband, no prospects... It feels good." I say, "Well, I hope you will enjoy the adventures and liberation of being single." But I think to myself that this single status will probably be a short interlude for Cheryle. She has told me many times how much she "likes and loves" men, how important it is for her to be able to give and receive love. In order for her life to feel "balanced," she needs to feel the counterpoint of independence and dependence, aggressive autonomy and "safe harbor." She admits to never having achieved the balance, but she believes that it is possible and that she deserves it. She yearns to find a man "ready to receive my love."

Cheryle has just returned from a quick trip to Washington, D.C., where she attended the annual gathering of the Congressional Black Caucus, and where she experienced her new status as single woman. It is not that in the past her husbands have accompanied her on her work jaunts; mostly she has been "alone on the road." But the recent trip to D.C. "felt different." In the midst of old friends, colleagues, and associates, she was single and unencumbered, and news of her separation had traveled quickly through the grapevine. She could feel the changes in people's responses to her. They were solicitous: "Cheryle, are you sure you can make it back to the hotel safely?" They were curious: "So what are your plans? Are you going to stay in Boston?" They were concerned:

"How are you managing through all of this? Is there anything I can do?" They were nosy, digging for "the dirt": "Is there anyone special?... Well, you'll find someone soon." Their questions were in their eyes, in their tone of voice, in their gestures.

Cheryle gracefully assured them that she was fine, that she was enjoying her newfound freedom. She went to the festive banquet and caught a ride in the limousine with Magic Johnson, "a lovely man and a perfect gentleman." The two of them talked seriously about his experience as an advocate for AIDS research and his public declaration of his illness. "I thanked him for his courage and told him what a profound impact his message had had on my younger son." In the less than twenty-four hours that Cheryle was in D.C., there were other greetings and adventures with politicians and celebrities, most of them people she has worked and played with over the years. In her life the boundaries between work and play, and between politics and business, are not clearly drawn; each enlivens and shapes the other.

Underscoring a theme from our last conversation, Cheryle says, "The more you are involved in the community and the more people feel good about you, the more they will want to do business with you. There is a *power* of relatedness and connectedness of service between business and volunteer work... *It is all about relationships with people.*" When Cheryle first started her board career, it was rare to see a black director even in those organizations that served the black community. It was also unusual for women to be licensed funeral directors. In both of these roles, Cheryle gained high visibility. And in both of these roles folks in the community saw her as someone they could come to for counsel, advice, and resources. "They come to you with a need and you respond. There is always a business component." Cheryle had watched this equation work for Senior: "Senior was always clear about his involvement in the community. If there was a fire in the projects and four or five children from a poor family died, Senior felt it was his responsibility to do the burial and the service for free—and it was always *first-class*, with dignity and style. He would make no money on that. But people would remember that... and it would bring a kind of business and loyalty that advertising could never bring... People would *return* again, and they'd now be doing well enough to pay for the services. When you are *repeating* business, that's when you're doing well."

Cheryle tells the tale of her rapid ascendancy on the United Way board and her political strategizing on the board of the Cleveland Public Library as a way of showing the back and forth between community work and business, and as a way of describing how she functioned in combining the roles and crossing boundaries. After her first experience as a director on the Phillis Wheatley board, Cheryle joined the board of the Neighborhood Centers Association, an umbrella organization for several of the social service and community groups in Cleveland. One of her colleagues on the Neighborhood Centers board, a successful Jewish entrepreneur, became a colleague and yet another mentor to Cheryle. He was also president of the volunteers for the United Way of Cleveland, and he paved the way for her to join the United Way Leadership Class, "a group of thirty young people—three of whom were black—chosen for their leadership potential." After serving for a year with the young leadership group, Cheryle began to work with volunteers. A role as associate vice president of administration with the volunteers led to a seat on the board of Cleveland's United Way, one of the most powerful, effective, and influential of United Way's urban affiliates. After several years on the board, Cheryle became the chair— "the first black and the first woman" to hold this position. Within a few years, she was voted in as president of the statewide organization, again "the first black and the first woman" to achieve this status. Membership on the national board of the United Way followed, and there she became chair of the executive committee. And, finally, Cheryle became "the first black and the first woman" to chair the board of the International United Way.

Cheryle quickly recites this list of accomplishments without fanfare. She seems less interested in displaying her success than in underscoring the relationship between her volunteer activities and her business career. "In the not-for-profit world you meet influential people. When we were looking for financing for the cable company, it followed directly from the relationships I made at the United

Way." She also wants to mark the special significance of being a *black* member of these boards. "The fact that *I* was there on the board meant that the community began to support the organization. It built strength among black people, a kind of solidarity. And the fact that I was the black person *chosen* by the white people meant that I felt a special responsibility to my community."

The United Way board was not only a great source for business contacts; it was also a place where Cheryle met other black leaders whose commitment to "the cause" was deeply inspiring and challenging to her style and perspective. Minnie Player, one of her colleagues on the board, was the president of the Welfare Rights Organization. Cheryle watched with awe and admiration as this "powerful sister" labored tirelessly on behalf of her constituencies. "She had an incredible influence on my life... I loved the tenacity and resilience of this black woman spirit." Cheryle felt deeply identified with the rage that she saw in Minnie Player. They both hated injustice and oppression. She also felt joined in their "special sister power." But she also recognized the vast differences in their experiences and their often contrary styles of accomplishing common goals. From her background of privilege Cheryle admired this woman who had "lived in the projects and had been on welfare... whose English was not the best but whose message was golden... who could take so little and make it into so much." Cheryle, who came from "black royalty," saw the grandeur and self-confidence in Minnie. "She walked in royal glory... She was at peace and comfortable with herself." Most impressive to Cheryle was Minnie's view of black men: "Even though I never knew a man in her life, she had an absolute respect for black men. She recognized their helplessness, their vulnerability, the hopelessness of their lives."

In so many ways Cheryle "wanted to grow up to be like Minnie"; her power, her compassion, her tenacity, her resourcefulness, and her inner peace were qualities to which Cheryle aspired. But as all good mentors do, Minnie Player challenged Cheryle to be more generous and more courageous. Whenever she was trying to raise money for some community cause, she would call Cheryle and lean on her. She would chide, "To those to whom much is given… and so forth." Or in even more critical *and* loving tones she would admonish, "As good as you are, Cheryle, you could be so much better." Minnie's words often come back to haunt Cheryle these days when she feels she is not living up to her full potential. "I hear Minnie scolding me when I'm only half stepping."

When issues of financial management became the primary agenda, the tables were turned: then Cheryle became the teacher and Minnie the eager *and* resistant student. "When it came to anything having to do with actual managing and financial control, Minnie Player called on me. Her accounts never jibed with anything there was in the real world. She would use the money—from whatever source—for a family in crisis or for people who were starving or whose heat got turned off in the dead of winter." Minnie's chaotic and compassionate style of management often conflicted with the board's way of doing business. "The United Way brought a discipline and an efficiency to the nonprofit sector that often felt unfriendly to people representing grassroots organizations." Cheryle was sophisticated in the rituals of boardsmanship and appreciated the rigorous etiquette of *Roberts Rules of Order*. "I knew about the restraint, language, and timing that was required to be effective in that environment." But she also understood the impulse of some of the "community folk" who were impatient with the strict forms and imposed civility. "It is understandable why people who haven't been given voice have the need to talk, to vent… They need more time to express their feelings and emotions." For Cheryle, there was an "important education" both in Minnie's example *and* in the stark differences between the two of them. Minnie was one of those "precious" people in Cheryle's life who was both admiring and suspicious of Cheryle's privilege. Their powerful sisterhood was critical as well as loving.

Even though her work with United Way gave Cheryle a regional, national, and international prominence, it was her experience on the board of the Cleveland Public Library that seems to have been crucial to her as she learned to transfer the lessons of community activism to her business career. In 1972, she was nominated to the library board by Arnold Pickney, who had been a longtime associate. A black man and owner of an insurance company, he had served on the Wheatley and NAACP boards with Cheryle, and they had worked together on Carl Stokes's mayoral campaign. Pickney had himself twice run unsuccessfully for mayor and was president of Cleveland's school board. It was while he was serving in the latter capacity that he asked Cheryle to join the library board. The school board appointed the seven-member library board, and Cheryle was the first black woman to join the board in its one-hundred-seven-year history. There were other prominent black elders in Cleveland—including W.O. Walker, a city councilman and owner of the black newspaper, *Call and Post*; and Ruby McColloch, head of the Harvard Community Center—who strongly urged Cheryle's participation on the board.

At the same time that Cheryle was appointed to the board, Lee Holly Jr., a "young WASP businessman and the son of a prominent and successful attorney," also took a seat as a new member. Both young and ambitious but very different in style, the two new members were initially suspicious of one another. Cheryle laughs—"Lee and I originally did not get along very well. Instinctively, we didn't like each other." As a matter of fact, Lee and Cheryle had both been anointed in the United Way Leadership Class, where they deliberately kept their distance from one another, it was "a kind of unspoken antagonism." They joined the library board at a time of "great conflict and divisiveness"; the board was engaged in very public battles over affirmative action and minority hiring, and the opening and closing of neighborhood branches. The controversies were aired in the local newspapers and became part of the public dialogue about race and education, about educational opportunity and literacy.

The library board elections were fast approaching and everyone expected that Reverend Raymond, "a prestigious and grand white minister who had a magical way with words and amazing charisma," would become the next president. Cheryle "admired and liked" Raymond and expected that he would be elected president. But she also noticed that he made no effort to solicit her vote. "Traditionally, they had always given some office to the black on the board," recalls Cheryle matter-of-factly. "Raymond had in his mind that this new young black woman on the board would make a nice little secretary," but Cheryle was not particularly interested. She knew that being secretary was a meaningless, subservient role, and that there were only "three power sources—the president, the chairman of finance, and the chairman of personnel."

A few weeks before the election Cheryle was surprised to receive a call from Lee Holly, who said he wanted to meet with her. Cheryle was immediately skeptical. "I said he could come to my office. It felt very awkward, very distant. I sat behind my desk the whole time." Lee got right down to business. He announced to Cheryle that he wanted to be president of the library board. Despite the fact that his declaration was a "total shock" to Cheryle, she remained cool. Lee could read nothing on her face. "How many votes do you have?" Cheryle asked. "I have two," he responded. "I have two, too," Cheryle shot back. Now Lee's face managed to mask his surprise as the two novice politicians "cut a deal." (Cheryle figured she had the vote of the other black newly appointed to the board, who was "truly a real brother. I thought it was likely to be the two of us against the world!") "I want to be chair of the personnel committee," said Cheryle. "You got it," said Lee, and the meeting was over. "We had cut a deal. He left."

Cheryle was interested in being chair of personnel because she wanted to be right at the center of the debates on affirmative action. She knew that the library had an "obscene" record on minority hiring, and she knew that was the arena where she could make the most important contribution. On the day of the elections, Reverend Raymond came with his predictable slate, which included the nomination of himself for president and Cheryle for secretary. Lee countered with a "totally irreverent" slate. Behind the scenes he had organized "a coalition that no one would have ever guessed." With his two votes and Cheryle's two, Lee won with a 4–3 margin. Cheryle won her "little black girl" secretarial slot with a unanimous vote of 7–0 *and* the coveted chair of personnel, which, as promised, the new president bestowed upon her. *"That* was the job!" Cheryle beams as if she is still relishing the sweet taste of victory. It was not only a successful win; it was also a critical lesson in politics. "In this business, all you have to be able to do is count your votes. With a seven-member board, victory required four votes each time. It was as simple as that."

The coolness and early distrust between Lee and Cheryle melted as they became effective political collaborators and strategists, and as their relationship grew into a warm, mutually admiring friendship. Cheryle speaks proudly of their work on the board: "We accomplished lots collaboratively. We learned how to pick our battles, build our support, establish our priorities." They discovered that they shared values and goals. "We both felt the library should be a beacon of hope, an *alive* institution, a magnet for education." To that end, they worked to resurrect and rebuild the neighborhood branches: making them more accessible, increasing the library hours, and expanding the community services they offered. They provided bookmobiles to tour the neighborhoods and storytellers and dramatists who drew children and their parents into the previously unfriendly library branch buildings.

Working for the library was deeply satisfying for Cheryle. "My focus has always been on *literacy*. I grew up in a home with books, and I understand that reading offers the extraordinary gift of vicarious experiences." She felt this most especially with the poor kids in the community whose lives "were limited by birth," who needed to expand their horizons and dreams through books. Cheryle could also see the "heinous system" of racism in the ways in which people used the libraries. "You couldn't point to where it began or how it grew." In the neighborhood library close to the funeral home, for example, she used to see the children sticking little white paper slips into their books and leaving them behind in the library. For a long time she wondered why the children were not checking books out and what was the significance of the paper ritual. After talking with several neighborhood kids, she discovered that they didn't know that they could take the books home, and "no one had told them otherwise." This was not a matter of innocent miscommunication. There was something "purposeful in keeping the children ignorant" of the library loan policies.

But it was in the area of affirmative action that Lee and Cheryle devoted most of their collaborative energy. They worked hard to increase minority hiring. "The only way to go was up!" But the pool of trained blacks was so small that their efforts made little impact. So they raised the funds and initiated a program at Case Western Reserve that was designed to train minorities in library science. It attracted bright young people, many of whom went on to apprentice in Cleveland and then take positions at major libraries across the country. These initiatives required time, energy, and resources, and Lee and Cheryle combined their talents and their networks to produce change.

Several years before Cheryle had joined the library board, Cleveland had become the first school system to be issued a license for a public radio station. The station had been licensed for radio when the school system was in "great shape," but over the years the public schools had deteriorated and "were on the brink of going into receivership." "When it fell upon hard times," the schools could no longer afford to support the radio station. Lee "saw the opportunity" and suggested that they buy the radio license from the school board, but initially let the school system continue to operate it. Cheryle had never thought about owning a radio station and knew "nothing about the communications field." But by now she trusted Lee's business acumen. More importantly, she felt she "owed him the support on this one. He had done so much on my behalf, particularly in all of the struggles over affirmative action." By this time, Cheryle had resigned from the library board (in the middle of her second term) to become a member of the city planning commission. She wanted to avoid "the appearance of a conflict of interest," so she left the library board, where she felt "satisfied" with her contribution. Even though she and Lee were no longer on the library board together, they both remained devoted to volunteer work (Cheryle had gotten him to join the Wheatley board) and they continued to be business partners.

Cheryle spent a good deal of time studying the field of communications and learning as much as she could about the operation of public radio stations. She traveled around the country looking at other facilities, including a visit to the University of Wisconsin (where her father was then a professor), which owned two well-run radio franchises.

Lee and Cheryle formalized their partnership, and over the years their involvement in radio has turned out to be a profitable endeavor. The business has grown, flourished, and changed as they have entered new markets and taken advantage of opportunities. Currently they own FM and AM stations in Flint, Michigan, and in Seattle, Washington, which they are in the process of divesting so that they can purchase another group of stations. By now, Cheryle can talk knowledgeably about "the communications field" *and* the business; it is work that appeals to her business ambitions ("Financially we have been *very* successful") and her social commitments. ("As a community, we must have a way of sending messages... We must control our communications networks... There needs to be a vehicle that allows us to articulate our feelings, express our ideas, and vent our rage.")

"What does it mean to have a black woman in radio?" Cheryle asks with her own ready response in mind. Her answer combines her commitment to service and to capital. "It means, first of all, that I can support the NAACP, the United Negro College Fund, the Urban League... *It means I am you*. I am put there to be responsive to your needs." But she also believes that part of her "obligation" to the community is to become a successful capitalist. She claims somewhat defensively, "I'll *never* apologize for having lots of money. I'm a capitalist in a capitalist society. I hope I'll make much more money... for me and for other blacks."

Making money is critical for "building our community," and Cheryle believes that black people must be more sophisticated and ambitious in what goals we set for ourselves. "It is *not* about jobs. It is about owning and distributing resources. We must declare, 'It's our cake and we'll eat it.'" But this requires strategy, initiative, *and* responsibility. She challenges blacks "to pay our own way" and "not be beholden to anyone else." She is impatient with our always "begging" for help. "We need to *give* money for elections... We must give contributions of dollars in exchange for the promise of participation... We must *buy* opportunity and use our productive talents." Her voice has now risen in a great crescendo. She is spreading her arms wide in a big inclusive gesture. Her message is bold and her audience is all black people. This notion of black capitalism is at the heart of her work. She thinks that too many black folks are sentimental and unrealistic in their view that capitalism is contrary to community development and social change. She believes that capitalism is essential, that we must be strategic and aggressive in amassing resources and learn to use them wisely. Again she says, *"I will never apologize for making lots of money."* She shakes her finger in admonition—"But there is a litmus test... You must tithe your money, and you must tithe to black organizations."

The story of the beginning of Cheryle's involvement in cable television is much the same as that of her initiation into public radio. "Connections, relationships, and networks" that she made in the not-for-profit world became the basis for the ideas, trust, and resources she needed to build capital for new business. This time Cheryle hooked up with Ted Bonda, a man she lovingly calls her "business father. Next to my real father, he has provided the most guidance." White, Jewish, and wealthy, Bonda grew up a "poor kid in Cleveland" and always believed that education was the key to his success. Acting on that belief, he had become a member of Cleveland's school board and generously given his time and his considerable resources to supporting minority business. "His support was with *cash* and *actions*, not with words," says Cheryle forcefully. Through various community and business initiatives Cheryle and Ted became associates, then friends, then partners. He provided critical financial support for both the radio and the cable television projects. Cheryle describes their contributions to the partnership. "Ted had the deep pocket. He could go to the banks. Our third partner, Earl (a brother, who had gone to Fisk with me), and I had the political know-how. We understood people, the community, the politics. And with fifteen years in the funeral business, *I* knew business and understood finance. These were not foreign things to me." It was a lucrative and satisfying partnership. As chairman of the board, Cheryle emerged as the visible leader with the charismatic profile. As a chief investor in the company, she became a "capitalist. This is how you make progress. It is about maximizing talents."

Cheryle laughs at the "wonder of it all." "I knew nothing about communications—radio or television. I had never known anyone in the field," she confesses, striking a dramatic pose, "although *everyone* is always asking me whether I ever thought about becoming an actress." "I wonder, why would anyone even *think* of asking that question?" I ask, deadpan. "Probably because I'm so melodramatic. I see all the world as my stage."

Balancing Act

This is our final session, and we have saved the best for last. Over the months, we have moved—with increasing comfort—across the public/private boundaries and arrived at the most intimate place. When I suggest that we talk about Cheryle's "mothering," she beams. "My boys are truly the joy and essence of my life." Then she leaps into the story of Jae's birth. "As my son always loves to say, he was born on Sunset Boulevard in Hollywood." It was February of 1963 and Cheryle had just celebrated her nineteenth birthday ("I was a teenage mother"). After thirty-six hours of labor, her firstborn son came into the world weighing a strapping ten pounds. Cheryle laughs—"He was brash and bold." Then she purrs, "He was *perfectly* formed, an absolutely beautiful baby. It was truly miraculous when they held him up after his birth... a *perfect* baby." The obstetrician had warned Cheryle that she was carrying twins—one four and a half pounds, the other five pounds. "Instead there was only one. I've often told Jae he's been like two children." I ask whether she and her husband had planned to start a family when they were both so young and recently married, and Cheryle grins—"No, we hadn't planned it at all. But we were very excited when he came. Absolutely thrilled. But my mother wasn't excited about being a grandmother. At forty-one, she wasn't prepared for that elder status."

The new grandmother may not have wanted to be an "elder" when she was barely middle-aged, but she put herself in the center of her firstborn grandchild's new life. Cheryle had chosen to have her baby at a "lying-in hospital" where the newborns were supposed to sleep in the same room with their mothers. But Cheryle had lost so much blood during her excruciating labor that the doctors would not let the baby room with her. They told her that hospital policy would permit visits only from her husband. Cheryle needed to rest quietly and regain her strength. Cheryle's mother was outraged by the hospital policy that would not allow her to be by her daughter's side. She determined that if she could not move into Cheryle's hospital room, she would move mother and baby to her home as soon as it was safe to do so. Cheryle shakes her head recalling her mother's fierce determination, her "incredibly strong sense of nurturing." She says, "Even though we had fixed up the baby's room in our apartment beautifully, and worked hard on all the preparation, my mother moved mother, father, and baby to her home. It was instantaneous love. From that moment on, Jae was my *mother's* kid." No baby could have been more loved or more coddled. "Jae's father was incredible with the baby, fixing the formula, diapering… my mother was omnipresent… There were so many hands available to take care of this tiny child. We had bought him a crib, with a fancy canopy on it, made out of English cherry wood—covered with lace sheets, lovely quilts—and this *boy* underneath it all."

Cheryle admits that she had felt a "real nervousness" about becoming a mother. Would she know what the baby needed when he cried? Would he be safe through the night? "But all that fell away after the birth," she recalls. It all seemed to flow so naturally—the feeding, diapering, bathing—and besides, she was rarely responsible for doing it. The baby's grandmother did most of the primary caretaking and quickly developed a very deep and protective bond with Jae. When Cheryle regained her strength after Jae's birth, her mother coached her in maternal care but usually ended up taking over. Cheryle recalls being grateful for her mother's help and supervision. Unlike many new mothers, she did not resent the intrusiveness of the baby's grandmother. "I hardly noticed my nonparticipation," she says. "You see, I discovered I'm not a baby person —when they begin to talk and are potty trained, then it's love!"

Cheryle also remembers feeling "very young" as a "teenage mother." In fact, she herself was barely beyond enjoying the status of being a "much-loved child" in her extended family. "I was seen as the baby by the older aunts, and it was very strange to be having a baby of my own… The sense of nurturance didn't appear immedi-

ately." Cheryle was, understandably, somewhat reluctant to relinquish her role as the baby in the family and become the mother,
particularly when *her* mother was so eager to take on the nurturing
and care. "The close age difference between me and Jae meant that
he has always felt more like my *best friend* than my son," claims
Cheryle. It was not until her second child, Duane, arrived five years
later that she felt "the mother instincts" come alive in her. "Duane
was always very much my son."

Long after early childhood, both of the boys continued to be very
close to their maternal grandparents. At the end of each school year,
they would travel to Madison, Wisconsin (where their grandfather
had moved to take a faculty position at the University of Wisconsin),
and spend the entire summer vacation with their grandparents.
"They developed very close and intense bonds... They were always
surrounded by so much love." The circle of love extended beyond
the maternal grandparents. Through the boys' adolescence, the
great-grandmothers on both sides were still alive and relatively
involved in caring for them, and so were the great-great-aunts.
(Their paternal great-grandmother, who just survived open-heart
surgery, is still thriving.) Their father's family has also been "loving
and supportive. Even their step-father's family has been there for
the boys... and even their step-father's ex-wife." The boys have
always experienced the layers of love and consistent care, always
known they are "loved without limit. This has been very important
for them with all of my divorces and major transitions," says Cheryle.

The boys, now men in their middle and late twenties, have
given back in full measure. "They are generous almost to a fault,
very comforting to me... extraordinarily protective of me."
Cheryle's eyes mist over. "They've been so *consistent* in my life... It
is my boys and myself. *That is the constant.* Whatever I achieve and
have, *it is for them.*" Even though they are now adults and living
hundreds of miles away, Cheryle speaks to her sons every day. She
tells me about a message that Jae left on her answering machine yesterday. She had returned from a "brutalizing" day of work; everything had gone wrong and everyone was beating up on her. "I came
home beat, spent, depleted, and there was Jae's voice on my answer-

ing machine saying, 'Hi, Mom. Just checking to see how you are. I love you and I enjoy being your son.'"

Even though Cheryle was not a mother who enjoyed her children as babies, she did become actively involved when they became school-age. She was devoted to their education and determined to make her presence felt in their school lives. She was the "homeroom mother" for both boys all the way through the elementary school years—organizing field trips, throwing parties, running bake sales, planning programs, rallying parent support, and frequently visiting the classroom. "My boys always saw this as my *duty* whatever else I was doing in my life." She tells a couple of stories about her children's perspective on their mother's loyal activism and advocacy. When Duane was in second grade, his teacher asked him in disbelief, "Your mother is *amazing!* How does she manage to do all that she does?" Without skipping a beat, Duane responded, "Very poorly." Cheryle throws her head back and laughs. When Duane was in fourth grade, on Valentine's Day the teacher had the "terrible idea" of asking the children to vote on who was the best mother. Duane arrived home with a report on the Valentine's Day election. "Mom, you got all the votes except mine. I voted for Tike's mother."

Even though Cheryle's sons considered it her duty to be the classroom mother year after year, I am amazed by the commitment of time this must have represented, especially given the responsibilities of Cheryle's career and her other volunteer work. I pose the same question that Duane's second-grade teacher had asked. "How did you manage that?" She responds nonchalantly, "Well, it usually required time in the late morning or afternoon, and I put that in my schedule, blocked it off on my calendar." Her work at the school was part of a very active nonstop day, packed with appointments and meetings that usually lasted well into the night. In her role as classroom mother, she would make frequent appearances at school but rarely be at home when the children returned from school, or be there for dinner and bedtime.

Most of the time, Cheryle felt good about the way she organized her life. She needed to work in order to "provide" for her children, and she relished "being out there" making a contribution. She knew that she was not her mother, who "was always there at home every single day we came home from school," who got her greatest pleasure from "nurturing her children." Cheryle always knew that she did not have boundless maternal energy, and that she would be doing herself and her children a disservice if she pretended to be an "earth mother" type. From time to time, however, "when something would go wrong" with the kids, she would feel guilty for not being there in the way her mother had been *and* for not wanting to be there more.

Only one time does she remember a complaint from her older son, which came "half-heartedly" only a few years ago. Jae said casually, "It might have been nice to have you there when I came home from school... to make brownies for us." Maybe Jae was just testing out the idea, but Cheryle's response was immediate and vigorous. His question had touched a raw nerve. "'First of all,' I told him, 'with your sports and school activities, you never came home until five or six P.M. What good would it have done for me to be *waiting* there for you?... Second, you don't even like brownies... Third, Aunt Evelyn (their great-aunt on their father's side who was also our housekeeper) loved you completely. She would have killed for you... Forget the brownies, *every* night of the week Aunt Evelyn fixed wonderful full-course meals. She was a great cook. She would fix three different meats every night, mashed potatoes *and* macaroni... and assorted fresh-baked desserts.'" Cheryle's voice is charged, as if defending an important self-perception. She was not like her mother—always there for her children—but she was a "good enough" mother. "I don't think we did badly at all raising our children," she says quietly.

Cheryle's response to Jae concluded with a fourth point, one that stressed her role as "provider" and the trade-offs that come with privilege. She explained to her son that if he wanted to wear "Giorgio Armani slacks" in high school and "own a Buick Regal" at age sixteen, then he would have to live with his mother's frequent absences. "You can't have it both ways," she warned. "If you want all these gorgeous things, then I have to work."

Jae had inherited his mother's taste and the "sense of entitlement" that was passed down through the generations of royalty.

Cheryle smiles at the memory of how the family legacy of privilege occasionally backfired. "I remember going with Jae to some fancy clothier to buy him a jacket. The jacket needed alterations… The salesman, who was very supercilious and condescending, said, 'Well, you know that will be extra for the alterations.' And I spoke up in righteous indignation (a tone I got directly from my mother), 'Cost is not a factor. My son wants it altered'… then I got the bill and it was four hundred-plus dollars!"

Despite Jae's adult musing about what life would have been like if his mother had been more like his grandmother, he and his brother have always been proud of their mother's success and visibility. They admire her ambition and her commitments. Cheryle remembers one of the many times when folks in Cleveland were urging her to run for public office and rumors about her candidacy for mayor were circulating around town. A journalist from the Cleveland daily called to set up an interview with Cheryle's sons. She wanted to do a story on what the children of this ambitious businesswoman felt about their mother's life as a public figure and mayoral candidate. The reporter was pleased when the boys agreed to talk with her, Jae reluctantly and Duane enthusiastically. ("Duane had already anointed himself as my personal manager," laughs Cheryle. "Jae is a shy person, and he was not at all interested in being in the limelight.") But the reporter was surprised when Cheryle allowed her to meet alone with the boys. She came to interview them at the house, and they spent a couple of hours in candid conversation. The next day "this hard-nosed journalist" called Cheryle. "She told me that the boys said beautiful things about how much they loved me." This "comforting and reaffirming" story about her mothering reminds Cheryle of a funny exchange between her sons after she had definitely decided that she would not run for mayor. In the process of preparing to become Cheryle's personal manager, Duane had discovered that the mayor's salary was about fifty thousand dollars per year. He asked his big brother, "Do you think we could live on that?" to which Jae responded, "No, I don't think so." Cheryle laughs, "That was the last conversation I heard around our house about my running for mayor."

The boys attended school in Shaker Heights, an upper-crust Cleveland suburb, which was reputed to have "one of the best public schools in the country." Despite its elite image, Shaker Heights prided itself on being a "designed" community, a place where city planners had "worked at racial balance." For the first several years that Jae and Duane were in school, however, their experience was that of being one among a few privileged black families in an affluent white community. They felt like the token blacks in a sea of white faces. By the time the boys reached high school, "more and more blacks had arrived in Shaker Heights, and they were of a different caliber." As the numbers increased, blacks began to be seen as a "racial threat." Cheryle welcomed the influx of blacks, but she watched the apprehension and paranoia of whites increase as blacks came in larger numbers *and* from less privileged backgrounds. She knows that her wish for her boys to live among blacks was related to her all-white experience growing up in Bedford, Massachusetts. "I wanted my kids to be with blacks," says Cheryle adamantly, "to know a kind of balance I had never known growing up."

As the number of black students grew at the high school, Cheryle began to receive frequent calls from the teachers who worried that her boys were "associating with kids whom she wouldn't want them with." Cheryle always knew that this was code for "low-income black kids, or working-class black kids," but she would always inquire about what the teachers meant, then listen while they fumbled around, expressing their concern but trying not to reveal their prejudice. Both boys were drawn to the other black kids, and both of them struggled with shaping a comfortable and workable black identity. "It was a tough balancing act," sighs Cheryle. "My boys had a broad range of friends, but they had a particular sensitivity to those who were left out. Both boys drove when they were sixteen and had cars of their own... They were often working to overcome the barriers of being little rich kids—trying hard to be one of the guys... wanting so much to be *black*." Cheryle watched her sons trying to strike this balance. She identified with their desire to be embraced by their black peers. She even understood the guilt they felt in having so much more than their broth-

ers *and* their wish to "even things up by giving things away." But she
also worried about their vulnerability as they "tried to work out
having a foot in both worlds." She was afraid that their guilt might
potentially lead to self-destruction. "I often warned them that their
incredible generosity might be felt as patronizing by the kids who
had so much less."

This "balancing act" is by no means fully resolved in the lives
of Cheryle's sons. "They are still trying to work it out," she sighs.
Cheryle recognizes that she has faced some of the same struggles.
With her sons she has found herself reliving the unease associated
with her own coming of age as a black woman, her own treacherous dance between the black and white worlds. But she believes that
the issues are even more difficult for black men. "I have a theory
about young black males," she says. "They come into their own at
thirty years old. My boys are still in their twenties, so I'm hopeful."
She is crossing her fingers and grinning. But her face grows serious
as she works to find an explanation that is not pure rationalization.
She does not want to mask her concern for her young adult sons
who have not yet found their way. "My boys are having a good time,
and they know it. I think it is important to seize life in its moment—
to live fully, to experiment before you get into a carefully planned,
programmed climb to the top. So my boys are experiencing the
chaos, the unstructured life while they're in their twenties. But the
chaos makes me want to give them a circle of protection." She
includes her stepson, the son of her second husband whom she
"raised as a teenager" and "loves deeply," and who is also in the
process of "becoming." Like her sons, he is still finding his way. "All
three of them are somewhat in escrow... even though they might
not admit it," she says softly. After a long pause her voice is confident. "Time molds a person. All of them are coming into their own."

Jae is married and lives in Cleveland. He and his wife Esther
have two children—"Little Jae," whom Cheryle calls "my main
man"; and two-year-old Alexis, whom she describes as "the world's
most assertive woman." When little Jae was born five years ago,
Cheryle was in her early forties and "had no real sense of what it
meant to be a grandmother." She experiences a real difference

between the anxiety, patience, and hard work that went (and still go) into parenting and the pure pleasure of grandparenting. "I go to Cleveland and lavish all this love on these beautiful kids, then I walk out the door and say good-bye." But she still does not "really feel" like a grandmother. Little Jae and Alexis have always called her "Cheryle," as if they too don't see her as a family elder. Alexis parades around the room crowing, "Cheryle loves me." "They call *my* parents 'Grandma and Granddad' just like my sons do," and they go to stay with their great-grandparents each summer, just like Jae did when he was growing up. I ask Cheryle how she feels about her grandchildren calling her by her given name. "I like it," she exclaims. "It makes me feel *distinct* and *special.*"

A few moments later Cheryle is making a seemingly contrary statement. She is claiming her "ordinariness." She is saying boldly, "I'm a very *ordinary* person. I have been blessed with *extraordinary* friends, family, and circumstances... but I'm ordinary." She is quick to warn me that in claiming her ordinariness, she is not being "self-effacing" or self-demeaning. Her self-description reflects her wish to squash "the Superwoman" image that masks human frailties, "distances us from one another," and creates caricatures. More importantly, she wants others to know that they can be successful, that success is based less on extraordinary talent and more on "seizing the opportunity." "We—you and I, Sara—need to talk about the ordinariness of ourselves, rather than projecting perfection or superiority... We are ordinary citizens who have had great opportunity."

This declaration does not surprise me. I have heard Cheryle talk many times about the distinction between "ability" and "opportunity," and about how she has been blessed by having people in her life who have believed in her, mentored her, and promoted her. But I am surprised when she talks about the ordinary nature of her individual characteristics. I wonder, Is she being modest or disingenuous? Or does she really think of herself in these terms? "I've always felt I was of ordinary intelligence (I knew growing up that I was the least bright member of my family)... with ordinary skills. (I can do a *range* of things relatively well, but nothing in a superior way)... with ordinary looks (my features are nothing special)." This last claim—about her looks—is particularly hard for me to believe. I gaze upon this glamourous, regal woman. "Really?" I ask disbelieving. "Sara, I've never had an image of myself as being pretty or attractive. I really think my most striking feature is my height." She is five feet nine inches tall and her high heels make her almost six feet. Her carriage, proud and graceful, makes her appear even taller.

Cheryle sees the look of skepticism still lingering on my face. *She* may not see herself as pretty, but I think she must be aware that other people do. She must know her dramatic impact: the ripples of pleasure, appreciation, and envy that she leaves in her wake as she parades through a room. I ask her about the discrepancy between her self-perception and others' view of her. "In my family my mother did not allow us to say someone was pretty, or someone had good hair, or someone was light-skinned... She would say, 'Pretty is as pretty does.' We felt secure and loved, which made us feel pretty *inside*."

Her mother's insistence on a deeper beauty was mixed with the messages Cheryle received from the white suburban town in which she grew up. At Bedford High School, Cheryle was the "exception"— popular, respected, and envied by her white peers. As captain of the majorettes, president of the student council, and princess of the senior prom, she enjoyed positions of high status and visibility. Some of her prestige was based on her physical beauty. Cheryle's voice is bitter as she describes the way in which people tried to compliment her. "White folks would say, 'You are the prettiest colored girl I ever met.'" Or seeing her beauty, they would try to make her into someone more exotic, not just an ordinary colored girl. "It always offended me when people would ask me what race I am—because I think I'm so clearly black... I always thought that was so dumb of them." Cheryle is very exercised. Her mind is racing to try to reconcile the jumble of feelings that emerge as she tries to explain how she feels about her looks: being from a line of royal, decorous women who claim that prettiness is interior; growing up exotic among whites, admired for the part of her that is not black, yet claiming that she and her family feel "arrogant" about their blackness. The power of her emotions is clear, but the explanation feels confused, elusive.

Finally she tells a story. "When I was a senior in high school, there was a popular white boy—a real big man on campus—who wanted to date me. His family invited me over to their house for some gathering. Before the guests arrived, his mother admitted to me that she had told her friends that I was Hawaiian!... I was stunned by this... and disgusted. I told her, 'You don't understand, my parents don't allow me to date white boys.'... There she was, patronizing me for my blackness, wanting to make me Hawaiian... and there I was asserting my black arrogance." Her voice is a whisper—"I still have some unknown places in me related to these early experiences of dating... of exclusion from both worlds... the loneliness."

Cheryle shakes her head as if she is trying to chase away the old feelings. She realizes, for the first time, that her need for sustaining friendships ("where you can laugh and cry, share interests, be supportive, *be a sister*") comes from the early loneliness of being the exotic one. "All of us have experienced an extreme sense of loneliness... of not being in the club—the loneliness of tokenism... the loneliness of others' jealousy (that I regarded as a normal human frailty)... the loneliness of asserting ourselves. It is very lonely getting there." Her face brightens. "I think the bonding that we feel comes out of this loneliness. Sometimes it is too painful for us to articulate—we seek comfort without saying the words." The bonding is in the silent understanding.

∼

We let the silence surround us. Cheryle's last words seem like a fitting benediction, a wise reckoning with the casualties and opportunities of success, the losses and gains of ascendancy, the loneliness that nurtures deep bonds. I think back to our very first session, to Cheryle's shocking and painful story about Eddie's death, and I feel the profound loss and the power of his nourishing spirit. Cheryle's eyes lock with mine; her "sixth sense" is tuning in as she speaks Eddie's name out of the silence. She too is feeling like we have traveled a great distance and returned to the same place. She too is feeling the paradoxical sensation of Eddie's painful absence and his rich presence in her life.

Cheryle's voice is quiet, penetrating. "Since his death, I have my brother's strength in addition to my own—his intellect, his courage, his perceptivity... In my sleep, Eddie sometimes comes to talk to me, sometimes he gently admonishes me. He'll say to me, 'Slow down, sit down, calm down'... It is not so much that he has the answers, it just soothes me." She pauses, as if she is feeling Eddie's comfort and heeding his warnings, and then continues slowly. "I understand, of course, that in many ways this is me speaking to myself. This is *my* voice... But the feeling is one of never being alone when Eddie comes. I have the sense that my brother is out there somewhere, but still deeply communicative. This is all very *natural*... It's like having a best friend."

This feeling of brotherly companionship has made the transition to Boston less alienating. When we met almost a year ago, Cheryle was feeling "loneliness" and "boredom" in Boston. She was railing against the city's "deathly combination" of parochialism and elitism that makes newcomers feel isolated and unwelcome. She was skeptical about whether she would ever feel comfortable or useful in a community where the separation between the "black bourgeoisie" and "the brothers and sisters" were so starkly drawn. Cheryle had remarked, "The jury is still out on whether I can survive here."

Life in Boston has, in fact, been difficult. There has been the disappointing demise of her third marriage and the trauma of an ugly divorce. She has longed for the warmth and love of her family and old friends and has missed the familiarity and influence that she earned from living and working in Cleveland for twenty years. But over the months "Boston has come alive" for Cheryle. She no longer worries about being bored. She has painted a new landscape for herself—a mosaic of entrepreneurship and service. Her life is busy and full: mentoring young black professional women, creating a power base in local politics, raising money for regional chapters of civil rights and social service groups and acting as liaison to the national organizations; joining the boards of the city's cultural institutions (the Wang Center for the Performing Arts, the Huntington Theatre); speaking to high school students about "commitment," "educational excellence," about "seizing the oppor-

tunity" to do good works. Now Cheryle exclaims unabashedly, "I'm
excited about being in Boston. It is a challenge for us here."

Her voice is full of hope and determination as she describes a
recent membership meeting of Boston's Coalition of 100 Black
Women. "The person who is the membership chair asked me to
come and say a few words and to talk about what our committee was
doing in voter registration, volunteering with the elderly, tutoring
students in school, and so on. When I stood there and looked out at
one hundred sisters, I saw this sisterhood, and I saw how unique
each of us is... All of our emotions are so intense—the pain is
intense, the joy is intense, the passion... I think we have the range
of emotions and commitments that only we can understand. Even
though I'd never seen most of these people before in my life, I felt
I could touch them, know them... I could sense the anxiety and
frustration... the unmet expectations... the questioning of where
we want to go... the sense that we are survivors... *and* that we will
prevail. It was such an incredible, exciting experience... It was so
energizing to me!"

For this ritual farewell, I have found an antique bracelet from
North Africa, a wide carved silver band with amethyst stones, to
give to Cheryle. I searched for a piece that I hoped would appeal
to her sense of drama and her personal taste, even though I know
the bracelet is unlike any of the jewels I've seen her wear. Cheryle
reads my card and opens the box quickly, fighting back tears. A
smile spreads across her face. "This looks like *you*, Sister Sara... just
like you. I will cherish it." Her eyes look out into the crisp fall day,
to the trees turning gold, orange, and red. Her voice is almost a
whisper, "You know, Sara, in the *spiritual* sense, I feel so fortunate...
I'm blessed. Truly."

ORLANDO BAGWELL

Look Into My Eyes and See the Fire

Beginnings

 Orlando Bagwell arrives at my house on a golden midsummer morning and falls back into a chair on my deck with weary relief. He is recovering from two rugged weeks shooting his upcoming film on Malcolm X. Filming in New York City for fourteen straight days, he and his crew of six ("three on the production side and three on the technical side") have done sixteen interviews, the longest of which lasted six hours. Despite his weariness, he looks much younger than his forty-one years in his loose-fitting tan cotton slacks, his green, gold, and gray striped shirt open at the collar, with the sleeves rolled up. He is lean and muscular and moves with a smooth grace, like an athlete who is comfortable in his body. His black hair, cut in a short Afro, frames an oval face with strong, clear-cut features and intense, glowing eyes.

Still feeling the deep exhaustion that lingers after such demanding and consuming work, he reclines, loose and relaxed in the chair, seeming to need the rest. But his face looks eager; his eyes seem to show the apprehension and excitement of embarking on this project. I offer him something to drink, and he chooses a glass of cranberry juice. Then in a gesture that feels like family to me, he asks, "Do you have a muffin or a bagel or something? I'm feeling hungry." I offer to toast him a couple of thick slices of homemade bread with blackberry jam and orange marmalade, and he beams. Seated back at the table with the tape recorder between us, Orlando takes two bites of the toast and then forgets the rest on his plate as he leans into our work.

I think how strange it must be for him to be on the other side of the tape recorder. As a documentary filmmaker, he has spent most of his professional life interviewing others, putting them in the spotlight, pursuing their life stories. He knows the perspective of the inquirer and the intrusive lens of the camera. He knows the dangers of misinterpretation and the promise of authenticity. He has grown comfortable in his role as questioner, listener, recorder, and audience, but he also knows the extraordinary responsibilities of these roles. Now the tables are turned. As I begin to describe how I would like to proceed, and I offer gentle words of reassurance and support, he interrupts, "Wait a minute, wait a minute... what are we doing here?" Judging that the anticipation must be much more difficult than the real thing, I suggest we jump into the conversation and see where it takes us. I tell him that he is not to worry about chronology, that it will be my responsibility to piece together the narrative and give it order and shape. I also tell him that I am interested in the details, not the abstractions; that I welcome detours, embellishments, and reinterpretations. He nods knowingly. "Okay, let's begin."

The first time we met, about a month ago, Bagwell warned me that when he is in the midst of working on a film, he becomes "totally preoccupied" with it. He lives it, breathes it, is haunted by it. "You can ask me any question," he had said, "and I will talk about the film." Since I know what it feels like to be fully absorbed and carry around the scenes and characters in my head, I suggest that he start by talking about making the movie. He is now sitting on the edge of his seat, looking directly into my eyes. "It has been a very difficult and different experience," he says slowly. "I never attempted doing a biography before. This is a first." He pauses for a long time and says cautiously, respectfully, "I am *uncomfortable* talking about Malcolm X... You never really get to know a person unless you have the chance to be with him... Everything I know is from the stories other people tell me." His voice is heavy with the responsibility of interpreting Malcolm's life. "So I am *reluctant* to talk about him—I don't want to give the impression that I really know him."

His caution seems to lift as he describes his relationship to the material. "In doing biography I am drawing on guidance from my own life... I am constantly asking myself what I can draw on from my own life that will let me feel connected and identified." The filmmaker, he explains, must discover reflections in his own story that resonate with the life he is re-creating on-screen, and these reflections must be authentic. "I must identify my *honest* response," claims Orlando forcefully. "*Not* the response that I think I *should* give, but my honest, truthful response." I ask him for an example, and he offers one without hesitation: "Malcolm's family was much more *extreme* than mine, but there were definitely similarities. He grew up in a family that was determined not to be *typical* black people. They didn't even live among other black people... They were independent-minded people. They raised their own food, built their own home, taught their own kids... They had their own rules and regulations, which the family lived by... This was an incredible challenge for parents to do this in a small town in Michigan in the twenties and thirties."

Bagwell has been talking to Malcolm's surviving siblings, cousins, friends, and colleagues (many of whom are speaking publicly for the first time), and he feels identified with the "independent-minded" character of his subject's family. Orlando recalls his own family signature. "My parents were not anywhere near as demonstrative as Malcolm's, but they were determined that their kids would be what they thought they should be, and they had very strong ideas about what was right for us. This could be something as simple as how we were supposed to talk. My parents had rules about the use of language... I remember my buddies teasing me about talking all 'proper.'" Orlando is careful to remind me that as a child, he never recognized the distinctive socialization he was receiving. "As a child you just *live* the experience. It never dawns on you that it might be special or unusual... You don't even get it when other kids are teasing you about these family eccentricities." As the adult filmmaker, however, he discovered for the first time, or rediscovered, resonant developmental and familial themes while working on the Malcolm X documentary. The filmmaker is both camera and mirror as he develops the chronicle. "As a storyteller, you are always asking yourself what would *I* have done? How do *I* feel about this?" Fortunately for our interview, the insight that good biography requires autobiographical reflections leads us quickly and naturally into his family story. In just minutes he is no longer talking about filmmaking, he is reliving the details of his family's "unusual" odyssey.

By the time Orlando's parents were both twenty-two years old, they had three children. The oldest, Janesta Bernice Bagwell (named after her paternal grandmother), was born on July 8, 1949, when her parents were nineteen. Less than a year later, on June 11, 1950, Donald Wesley Bagwell Jr. arrived, followed almost twelve months later by Orlando Nathaniel Bagwell, on June 2, 1951. Orlando inherited his first name from his maternal grandfather and his middle name from his mother's brother. He throws back his head and laughs—"They were going to name me 'Orlando Fernando' (which was my father's father's name), but thankfully they decided against that. They knew I'd never make it through life with that name!" Three years later, the "younger ones" arrived. On February 6, 1954, Brian Dominic Bagwell ("The only one whose name I don't know the origins of") was born, followed two and a half years later by a second daughter, Doreen Gwynette Bagwell, born on July 7, 1957, and named for a friend, Miss Doreen, and a favorite cousin.

Orlando's father, Donald Wesley Bagwell Sr., lost his parents to tuberculosis when he was a small child. He and his brother "bounced around for a while" and were finally taken in by their uncle's family. As children, they lived a grueling life on the edge, having to work long hours to survive, having to learn to be self-sufficient in a treacherous world. Before completing high school, Donald Sr. "lied about his age" so he could join the armed forces, find stability, and earn a living. He met Barbara Valentine Jones when they were both students at Dunbar High School in Baltimore, Maryland. She was from a "more together family of two parents" who were "strict and protective" of their several children. Barbara Valentine finished high school and completed a year and a half at nearby Morgan State College before quitting to marry Donald. Orlando shakes his head at the "incredible weight" of this young couple's life. "By the time I was born, my father was an army sergeant in Korea, and my mother had her hands full with three little babies."

After all five children were born, Donald and Barbara decided to return to school. Since Donald had not completed high school, he had to take evening classes to build up the credits for his diploma while he worked during the day. Only then could he enter as a full-time day student at Morgan State. In the meantime, Barbara returned to college as a part-time student and worked to help support the family. With their large family and very meager resources, the Bagwells scraped by from day to day. "These were very tough times," recalls Orlando. "We had no money. There were days without oil when our house was freezing... There would be no food in the house... We would go to school with a hard-boiled egg for lunch, or sometimes no lunch at all." Again, he makes the distinction between the adult appraisal of his early experiences and living through those experiences as a child. "When you're a child, you don't know you're poor. It is just your reality."

But Orlando does recall a Christmas, when he was about eight, when even his child's eyes could see the fragility of their existence. That Christmas season both his parents were working in the post office at night and doing a variety of other seasonal jobs during the day. "I remember my father trying to get as many jobs as he possibly could. He was working round the clock." Bagwell squints his eyes as if he is trying to bring the visual memory into focus. "This is one of my strongest memories," he begins. "My father got a job delivering flowers. We had an old beat-up Plymouth that he was hauling the flowers in... I'll never forget my father coming in the house, real tired, real slow... and sitting down in the 'phone chair'—you know, one of those chairs they used to have in schools with the desk part attached to the arm. I remember him calling us kids downstairs, sitting us down, and telling us that we wouldn't have a nice Christmas this year... that there would be very few gifts, and we shouldn't plan on getting any toys (Christmas was the only time of year when we ever got toys). He explained to us that the car had broken down full of the flowers, that he had to pay for all the flowers that spoiled, and that there would be no money left over." Orlando's body is slumped over the table as if he is reliving his father's desperate disappointment. "I see my dad is starting to cry... It hurts us to see him hurting so bad. We try soothing him. We say, 'It's no big thing, Dad. Just don't cry!'" When Christmas day arrived, the children braced themselves. They needed to be stoic in order not to make their hardworking parents feel guilty. They couldn't stand to see their father's tears again. Orlando's face suddenly brightens at the memory. "Actually, it ended up being a good Christmas. Everything we got was great since we had expected nothing."

The hard struggles of survival were contrasted against, and mitigated by, a vitality and energy they all shared. "We were a *young house*. We grew up with our parents." The children watched their father go to school, work hard on his studies, make friends, and pledge a fraternity. ("He pledged Alpha. My mom became the fraternity queen.") They went with their parents to "watch the step dancers," cheer at football games, and attend college picnics and rallies. "On Sundays my parents would get us all dressed up and send us off to church. They'd stay home." He smiles and admits, "I now know that they did this so they could have a break from us. We'd come home and find the house full of my mother's and father's friends... These were college kids, most of them young and single... The music would be blaring, and they'd be dancing, jamming, doing the Madison... laughing, having a good time." His face is beaming as he proudly describes the abundance of fun and energy. "Our house was the place where people would come. Every Halloween it was our house where we'd party, our basement where we'd build the haunted house. You see, my parents *created* home... We grew up in that kind of intentional environment. It was their way of controlling the environment... not in a bad way, but in a protective way."

The Bagwell children were not only included in the lively, social life of their young parents; they were also very aware of the strenuous demands of their parents' academic life, so occasionally they were called on to offer their help. Orlando remembers his father's struggling to master his German course and his worries about not being able to pass the language requirement. Donald Sr. decided to appeal to the teacher's goodwill and sympathy by inviting her over to meet his wife and children. A big grin spreads over Orlando's face as he remembers how his father's plan worked like a charm. "Before she came, he teaches us all to say 'Good evening' in German, in unison, the perfect pronunciation. She comes for a good home-cooked meal. When she walks in the door, he calls us all down, has us stand in a group at the bottom of the stairs, and say it in chorus. What he's really saying to her—actually he's *begging*—'I've got five kids. I'm doing the best I can. Please don't flunk me!'" Now Orlando is laughing. "We kids put the big one on her… We're playing it full tilt, working for my dad."

Because Donald and Barbara were always extremely busy with going to school and earning a living, the children learned early how to take care of themselves and manage the household. Orlando recalls their extraordinary collaboration and self-sufficiency, an early maturity born out of the need and requirement that everyone pull his or her own weight. "Our house was a real *active* place," says Orlando. "Because there was so much going on, it had to be orderly. Like Malcolm's family, we all appreciated the importance of structure. My older sister was in charge, but we all took care of one another… It was very organized, very responsible, very strict. My parents insisted on that." The household chores were clearly delineated, and every two weeks the jobs were rotated. When Orlando arrived home from school, he was responsible for cleaning the bathrooms, straightening up his own room, getting his homework done, and washing the dishes every other evening. His sister Janesta was in charge of cleaning the dining room and the living room, and Donny had kitchen duty. "When the younger kids got to be old enough to work, it was a big relief, because then I only had to do dish duty every third day." The regimen was so strictly organized that it soon became habit, and the five children would work together like a well-oiled machine. They did not dare defy their parents' expectations and requirements, nor did they want to act irresponsibly in relation to one another.

Their collaborative training in household management also served them well in times of emergency. Orlando remembers when his younger brother Brian had a terrible fall and badly injured his head. "We all whipped into action immediately, taking care of business. Within minutes one of us had called the ambulance, one of us went off to get the neighbor, another notified my mother at work, and one of us stayed with Brian and cleaned and iced the cut. We became very competent, very organized, and very protective of one another." This early parenting of one another, these experiences of

collaboration and collective survival probably cemented the deep
sibling bonds that they continue to depend upon and enjoy today.
When Orlando speaks about his relationship to his brothers and
sisters, his voice is full of tenderness. "We are *real close*... sometimes
it scares me. It frightens me to think of any of us dying... If we can't
all go at once, I hope the boys die first... My sisters are like the book-
ends. I always feel that they have their arms around us." His eyes
have misted over with tears as he thinks about the "incredible love"
they have for one another, and how deeply entangled their lives
are. He leans forward and whispers, "Now I'm really going to get
weird on you... astrological. My sisters are both Cancers, born on
the seventh and eighth of July—" He stops abruptly and decides
against going down this astrological path. I urge him to continue.
I'm curious to know how he sees the stars that define their fate. But
he resists. "No, it's too far out, too weird." "Nothing is too weird," I
urge. "Nope, it's stupid," he says with finality. Even though I haven't
heard the "weird," otherworldly tale, I clearly sense the essence and
potency of his sibling relationships and the ways in which they are
forever "spiritually joined."

As the youngest child of the older kids, Orlando had a special
place on the sibling boundaries. "My older siblings were looked up
to by me, but *I* was the older brother for my younger sister and
brother. It was almost as if the older and younger kids experienced
two different families: The three of us born first grew up through
really hard times. But the younger two, especially my younger sister,
knew a different reality. She was born into a more middle-class life,
when we had more money."

As the youngest of the older kids and the older brother to the
younger kids, Orlando remembers mostly the complicated and difficult life managed by his parents. As a child he, of course, never fully
realized or appreciated the burdens they carried. As an adult, now
with his own two children, he looks at his parents' courage and
stamina with admiration. "I now realize how hard it was for my
parents to try to negotiate all the parts of their lives—five kids,
going to college, working several jobs." With their energy, organization, and discipline, they "mostly managed very well." They even

found a way, from time to time, to stop the grueling work and carve out space for play, for partying, for dancing, for conversation, for political activities. Their life was not grim. It was hard and spirited. "Our house was the place where people came," Orlando reminds me again even as he lists the overwhelming family agenda.

But the pace and the complexity would sometimes take their toll on Donald Sr. and Barbara, and the children would see it in their moments of weariness or impatience, in the severity of their discipline, in their tears of disappointment or frustration. Orlando's voice reveals the pain of seeing his parents' anguish. He finds it very difficult to tell the story of the time "when his father just disappeared." It was Donald Sr.'s senior year in college. Orlando was about nine, and he recalls it as "the first time I remember seeing my mother being frightened." The images are vivid even though the event is shrouded in mystery. "I never totally understood what happened," he says slowly. "I can remember people coming over to the house to comfort my mother... I could hear people talking about my father... You know, I was always the kid listening in on the grown-up conversation. They were telling stories about no-good men leaving their wife and kids. I remember being real scared but feeling angry at them for talking about my father that way... My father was like my hero at that point. He was everything that I wanted to be." Orlando wanted to protect his father from their harsh judgments, but at the same time he could feel his mother's pain and wanted to rage at his father for causing such grief: "I remember watching her sitting alone in the living room . . It was the first time I ever looked at my mother and she seemed old to me."

The days dragged by as they waited for their father's return, impatient and fearful. The anguish seemed to inhabit Barbara, creasing her face, stooping her body, and misting her eyes. Orlando has no idea how much time passed, "maybe four or six weeks, maybe more." One day, "as usual," his mother sent him to the store for something. "I was the kid that *did* stuff," he recalls. "I was the go-get-it kid... *As the third child, I had to show I was present.* They always called me 'Butch.' ...'Butch, go get it,' and I'd be on it. You didn't have to say it twice, I'd *run* to the store and *run* back... I would try to set records each time." His words are racing. "I was *proud* of being quick, fast, responsive… I was eager to please!"

On this particular day, on his way back from the store, Butch picked up the mail and found a letter addressed to his mother, with a picture drawn on the envelope. It was a stick figure drawing of a man running with speed lines drawn from his heels and the words "run postman run" scrawled underneath. Orlando took the letter to his mother and asked her why anyone would "scribble" all over the envelope. "She saw it and went crazy," recalls Orlando. "She immediately recognized it as my father's drawing, the signature he always put on letters." Barbara opened the letter very slowly and began to read it. Orlando saw the mixture of emotions on her face. "It is hard to define the feelings—relief, joy, anger—all changing very fast… It was not an easy letter for her. We wanted desperately to know what it said." Barbara never revealed the letter's contents to the children. She read it over and over and then put it away. But even without knowing the message, Orlando felt enormous relief that his "father had made the contact." "It was the best letter we ever got. He was back in a couple of weeks." Orlando hung on to the image that brought good news. "After seeing my father's symbol on the envelope, I started using it myself on all my letters."

The unanswered questions still linger within him. Why did his father leave? Where did he go? What was happening between them? What made him return? In this family that "talked a lot to one another," this story remained a mystery, clouded with fear and silence, and the determination to move beyond it. Orlando's voice is full of empathy. "I'm not clear about the reasons… Maybe he had failed something in school… maybe he thought he was messing up. But what does it mean to mess up when you're twenty-five years old with five kids, school, and jobs?… You feel life speeding by, you feel overwhelmed. It's all too much."

Brotherhood

When Orlando entered kindergarten, his mother and father were undergraduates at Morgan State, the historically black college in Baltimore. Anticipating their return to school and wanting to live in a safer neighborhood with better schools, the Bagwells moved from McCullough Street in the Druid Hill Park section of West Baltimore to Northeast Baltimore. It was considered a move up, from a solidly black and poor ghetto to a neighborhood where they were one of only two black families. Their new neighborhood, called Wilson Park, was largely Jewish and working-class when they moved in, but it was "changing fast." Within two years the white population had fled, and the area had become totally black. Just above the Wilson Park area, within a few city blocks, the complexion and social class of the community changed radically. This neighborhood bordering Johns Hopkins University was "upper-class, rich, and WASP."

On the border between this affluent district and Wilson Park sat the Guilford School, Orlando's first school, where he attended kindergarten and first grade. Each morning he and his older siblings would walk to school, moving in the direction of Johns Hopkins, which—in its prestigious academic isolation—seemed so distant from their everyday lives. Their parents would take a long walk in the opposite direction to Morgan State, where the boundaries between family and school were crossed with ease and familiarity.

Guilford was a predominantly white public school with a "very small" black population. Orlando remembers little about his early schooling there. Mostly it stands as a vague backdrop for his much more vivid Catholic school experience. By the time he reached the second grade, his mother had decided to forsake the public schools and move her children to Blessed Sacrament, a parochial school. Orlando is quick to tell me that Blessed Sacrament was "not much better" than Guilford, but that Barbara felt that Guilford was a "basically racist" environment, where the teachers began with the presumption that all black children were "marginal students." She was not so naive as to think that in Blessed Sacrament her children would be spared prejudicial treatment, but she did think that Catholic schools had a higher proportion of good teachers than the public system and that "as long as her children paid attention, they were bound to learn something." She also believed that because she and her husband would be paying tuition, they would feel entitled to exert more pressure on the school to do well by their children. But mostly, the move to Catholic school was an effort to find a more disciplined environment that would reflect the strict and structured environment Barbara and Donald insisted upon at home. Barbara talked this decision over with her sister, who also lived in the same neighborhood, and they both decided to move their children to Blessed Sacrament. The Bagwells' five children and their four cousins created a significant black presence in this working-class Irish school. "The nine of us represented ninety percent of the black population of the school," laughs Orlando. "So there we were going to integrate the Catholic school."

Except for the presence of his siblings and his cousins at the new school, Blessed Sacrament was a lonely place where Orlando always felt "outside the group." "I was the only black kid in the second grade," recalls Orlando. "I went through the whole year barely talking to anyone, fearful and uncomfortable." The awkward feeling was not just the discomfort of "a sea of white, unfriendly faces" surrounding him; it was also the strangeness of being taught by a nun. She was a powerful, overwhelming presence in her insistence on moral rectitude and religiosity, as well as discipline and learning. The Bagwells were Catholic, but they were not "religious Catholics," and the children had not been fully exposed to what Orlando calls the "culture of Catholicism." But at Blessed Sacrament, they got a quick and complete immersion in the dogma, the values, the rules, the habits, the punishments. And they practiced the elaborate church rituals. "We became more churchgoing at school. We participated in the whole scene—altar boy, choir, communion."

The Bagwell children felt that the "culture of Catholicism" was mixed with a heavy dose of paternalism, which sometimes made it difficult to disentangle subtle racism from genuine caring. "I remember when my little sister was in the first grade, the nuns would send home clothes that had been donated to the church," says Orlando with a grimace. "My mother would say, 'Don't take those clothes.'... It was humiliating... In general, the nuns thought of us as charity cases." Of course, this was hard for a six-year-old child to understand. The little girl knew the family desperately needed clothes, yet she also saw her mother's hard resistance to the handout. Maybe her young eyes even saw the nuns' disdain seeping through the gift giving. "My mother's refusal of the clothes was a matter of dignity," says Orlando, who remembers that one advantage of Catholic schools was that the school uniforms masked the differences among the students. "We liked the uniforms, and we kept them clean and pressed. It meant that we couldn't be discriminated against because of our clothes... It solved a major problem for us."

Much of the time it was not difficult to decipher the racism that was part of school life. "As soon as they saw we were black, most of the teachers assumed that we had limited potential," says Orlando. His seventh-grade teacher was particularly insensitive in displaying "her real racist stuff." Not only would she denigrate Orlando's efforts in the classroom; she would also use stereotypical images and humiliating caricatures when she talked about history or culture or politics. "She had us singing slave songs—'Old Black Joe' or 'Way Down upon the Swanee River'—or she'd be talking about darkies." Sometimes Orlando would ignore the teacher's stinging assaults and the mockery and laughter of his classmates. He would sit there in stony silence and feel the rage building inside. Other times—when he could no longer bear the pain—he would speak up and confront the teacher.

He could hear his mother's dual admonition as he tried to retaliate "respectfully." On the one hand, Barbara was forceful in challenging her children to get the best out of their schooling despite their teachers' prejudice. "My mother always told us that we should not concern ourselves with what the teachers thought about us. We should put forth the effort and we would learn." On the other hand, Barbara taught her children to be courageous in protecting themselves and standing up for what they believed. "My mother always taught us that people had to *demand* our respect. We were not supposed to be disrespectful to adults, but we were also expected to stand up for what was right." The Bagwell children heard both of Barbara's lessons loud and clear, but often they were forced to make choices about which inner voice they would follow. Neither alternative—to be silenced and excel despite the humiliation, or to be outspoken and get in trouble—seemed comfortable or productive.

Orlando moved through "cycles" of anger and volatility. He recalls one year at school, when he was twelve or thirteen, when he was "physically fighting every day." "I have ugly memories of getting spit in the face," he says sadly. But he admits that the fighting often provided release—even pleasure—and that he would sometimes initiate the confrontation. "I definitely provoked some of the stuff. Part of me enjoyed the racial tension—looked forward to the fighting—but the other part of me didn't like myself very much for allowing myself to become involved." What hurt more than the outbursts of violence was the chronic feeling of being "on the outside," excluded and distanced from "the center of things." He offers one measure of the extent of his exclusion at Blessed Sacrament: "I didn't have tight friendships in school... The kid who I thought of as my best friend lived in a big house in the Guilford area close to Johns Hopkins. In the whole time we were in school together, I went to visit him only once."

But it was not only the individual racism of the teachers and the harsh taunts of white classmates that were hurtful and oppressive; it was also the institutional racism embedded within "a segregated southern city." "It wasn't just the school—it was *Baltimore*," recalls Orlando. Each spring, the students at Blessed Sacrament were treated to a special day at Glen Oaks, a large amusement park in Baltimore. But since Glen Oaks was not desegregated at the time (it was desegregated in 1963), each year, when the school made its ritual visit to the park, the black children would not be able to go. "They'd send us someplace else for the day," says Orlando bitterly.

For years, Barbara and her sister challenged the school about this discriminatory policy, finally taking their case to the monsignor of the church. The mothers threatened, "Either everyone goes or no one goes." Finally, in 1961, they prevailed, and the amusement park trips were discontinued, only two years before the park became desegregated. Baltimore was a city where segregation reigned strong through the 1950s and into the early 1960s, when the more pernicious forms began to be dismantled. Orlando remembers, "We were living on the edge of the white community, but we couldn't go to the movie theater there except for one day a week, which was set aside for blacks... I remember my father picketing the theater and it opening up to us in 1961. And there was a very popular teenage dance show on television called the *Buddy Dean Show*. That was a segregated show. We watched it religiously. One day a month the dancers were black... all the other days it was a totally white show. Rather than desegregate the show, they took it off the air."

There was one teacher in Blessed Sacrament—a lay teacher who taught fourth grade—who seemed to resist successfully the discriminatory policies and practices of the school and the community. Her classroom became a welcome oasis for each one of the Bagwell children. "My sister had her first, and she excelled in her class. After that we all did well in her class. For each of us it was our best year." Orlando does not remember her as particularly creative as a teacher. It wasn't her innovative curriculum or dazzling pedagogy that made her so special; it was that she treated them as students. She did not assume they arrived in her classroom with deficits or "limited potential." "In her class, it was completely about *performance* and achievement. That was her focus... that was her sole expectation."

When I ask Orlando about his memories of "teaching and learning" in elementary school, his response is immediate. "We memorized *everything*—memorized the questions and the answers, memorized the spelling lists, memorized English grammar books from cover to cover, memorized the catechism from cover to cover, memorized the rules to everything, used the rules, wrote the rules... It was rote learning, pure and simple." In retrospect, Orlando recog-

nizes the lack of depth and creativity, and the "incredible monotony" of this approach to teaching and learning. He knows it was
effective in producing students who could parrot back the academic
and religious dogma, but he also knows that it never fully challenged the students' minds or allowed them to use their own initiative and explore their curiosity. But as a young student at Blessed
Sacrament, Orlando did pretty well with the rote learning. He
quickly learned the rules, expectations, and rituals. He always knew
what to anticipate and how to succeed. He was efficient in discerning the structure of "the game." "I'm a *gamer*. I get the rules real fast.
It did not take a great deal of effort to recite the stuff correctly once
I put my mind to it. That's always been easy for me."

In order to describe himself as a student, Orlando needs to compare his capacities and style to that of his siblings. So much of his
self-definition seems to be shaped by contrast with his brothers and
sisters, particularly the older ones. He looks at them as mentors, com-
petitors, collaborators, and loving nurturers. His deep knowledge of
them helps him to know himself. His response to my question about
his identity as "student," therefore, begins with a reference to his
sister Janesta, then his brother Donny, and finally circles back to
himself. "My sister was a very good student. She read a lot, worked
hard, had a very broad range intellectually. My older brother was
incredibly capable. He is probably the smartest of all of us in terms
of raw intelligence. He could get A's without studying. I was always
considered a marginal student. I studied when I wanted to. I didn't
take it as seriously as my sister and brother. I read very little."

This does not sound to me like a self-deprecating statement. In
comparing his mediocre achievements in school to his brother's
extraordinary intelligence and his sister's diligence and range, he
does not seem to be putting himself down. His heart was not in
memorization. He never gave his full energy to schoolwork. He
beams suddenly as he recalls how he stood out in relation to his
older siblings. Now there is pride in his voice. "I was the *hard
worker*. I was very task oriented." Most of this zealousness was
focused on tasks outside of school. "I'd come home from school
and move right into my chores—clean the bathroom, clean my

bedroom, do my homework. I'd do it *thoroughly*, completely, methodically. I'd clean the tub, then the toilet, then get behind the toilet, then mop the floor. The whole time I'd be thinking, when I get this done, I can go on outside… with my guys."

On occasion, Orlando would set his mind on achieving and "winning" in school. Then he would combine all his gamesmanship skills and all his task-oriented drive in a strategic effort to achieve. One such time was when he took the entrance examination for a Catholic high school that was offering a tuition scholarship to the student from each grammar school who had the highest score. Since the sixth grade the teachers had been preparing the students at Blessed Sacrament to take these competitive exams—drilling them with facts and figures, making them practice test-taking techniques, pushing them to give quick and accurate responses. Orlando took the preparation seriously and worked over the years to "overcome the obstacles" of testing. When he reached eighth grade and was submitting applications to secondary schools, his first choice was a Jesuit school known for its academic rigor, but his teachers warned him that he would "not be able to make it" at such a difficult school. He ended up applying to a "good" school run by the friars, Archbishop Curley High, where his brother Donny was a student. Curley, a boys' school, was the most competitive school to get into because it drew the most applicants.

When the exam results were returned, it turned out that Orlando had the second highest score in his school. The top scorer was offered another citywide scholarship, so the scholarship for Curley High went to Orlando. For "the gamer," for the "marginal student," this was a tremendously satisfying victory. "I'm excited, thrilled, really feeling proud of myself," chimes Orlando as if he can still taste the sweet success. "My parents are all smiling and proud of me." But the pleasure was short-lived. Within a few days an administrator from Blessed Sacrament called to notify the Bagwells that the high school had decided to award the scholarship to a "needier" student. Orlando's voice is incredulous. "All the time they've been treating us like charity cases and giving us these handouts that my mother has to refuse in order to maintain our family's dignity... Then they call and tell me that I don't deserve this thing I *earned*, this thing I *won*. They turn around and give the scholarship to some poor white kid."

Orlando's voice is flat and cynical. His words bite the air. He responds to my look of shock with a weary gesture. His shoulders slump forward, and his eyes lose their intensity. "Sure I felt ripped off... but I also felt this is just one more example of the racism, and I know it will not be the last one. You see, this is what white people don't understand about growing up black in America—the accumulation of these events, the expectation that there will always be more." I am not shocked by the tale, but it does sadden me. What causes me rage, however, is not the unfairness of this situation as much as the cynicism that it caused in the thirteen-year-old boy on that day the school "stole" his hard-won victory. *Orlando's* greatest sadness, however, seems to be centered on his *parent's* powerlessness to reverse the injustice. I ask urgently, "Didn't your folks come to your defense?" His voice is a whisper: "I don't know whether they challenged the school or not. They never told me what they did. They do not need for their children to see them being made impotent. But my mother did understand how hurt I was." Incidents like this one eroded Orlando's young spirit. Most of the racist assaults were not as dramatic—nor was the impact as deeply felt—but the cumulative experience built up the rage inside of him. "By this time, I greatly resented being in school."

The discipline and order in the classrooms at Blessed Sacrament erupted into threatening "jungle behavior" on the playground. The violent behavior during recess felt especially dangerous to Orlando and his kid brother because they couldn't count on having allies to protect them; they were doubly vulnerable. In class, the girls sat on one side of the room, the boys on the other. On the playground—a large fenced-in concrete lot—the gender segregation was maintained with "the girls just standing around talking" while "the boys got into the fight thing." Orlando describes the male scene: "It was all about turf. Everyone is protecting his own... everyone is playing it. It is a violent and dangerous world." The violence would often be channeled into games. In one game, called

North Against the South, boys would line up on either side of the playground, and at the signal they would charge at each other at top speed, shoving, pushing, kicking, banging each other down, pressing their bodies into the hard cement. The boys would return from recess scraped, bruised, and bleeding. "Why didn't the teachers intervene?" I ask. Orlando laughs—"They had enough sense not to risk life and limb trying to break this stuff up." For the Bagwell boys and their cousins, the playground held special dangers. Not only did they have to watch out for the *male* "turf thing"; they also knew that their blackness made them particularly vulnerable to attacks. "My brother and I were covering our backs all the time."

In contrast to the "dangerous world" of the school's playground and the tokenism and paternalism of the classroom, the neighborhood where the Bagwells lived felt warm and welcoming to Orlando. Sometimes he could hardly wait for the school day to finish so he could run home, get his chores and homework done, and go out into the streets to "hook up with" his buddies. This was his favorite part of the day. Most of the action took place at the recreation center at the public school where all the neighborhood kids went. ("There was some slight resentment against us because we didn't go to the public school. Some people thought we were stuck up, or they would make fun of the way we talked.") They had neighborhood sports teams in baseball, basketball, and football, "good competitive teams." "We were the city champions several times over," boasts Orlando. *"This was the brotherhood.* This was real camaraderie. We had gangs, but not bad gangs. Just groups of guys. And there was a sister gang. We'd have parties—darken the windows in the basement and turn on the low lights." With these boys whom he "hooked up with every single day," Orlando felt safe, challenged, adventurous, and cared for. There were about six of them who were "real tight and inseparable," but the group could swell to twelve or fourteen, "circles of friends across a range of ages."

I ask Orlando how he was perceived by the "boys in the brotherhood," and his response underscores the depth of their commitment to one another. His eyes narrow as he tries to describe what his buddies thought of him. He seems to be trying to see himself through their eyes. "I never thought of myself as the leader who stepped out. But they always knew I was there for them. When the chips were down, they knew I'd be there. In a crisis, I would often become the leader because I think fast... I'm quick and follow through. I will not panic. I won't abandon you." He pauses for a long time, seeming to relish the old memories of deep connection, and then comes up with a vivid example of the kind of leader he was. "I remember a conversation I had with a guy who I thought of as more or less our leader. He said something to me that surprised me at first. I was not one of the biggest or strongest guys. But he told me, 'You are the only one I wouldn't want to fight.' You see, he knew we'd be there 'til the end. He knew he'd have to kill me. The leader does not necessarily turn out to be the toughest guy. He turns out to be the *one who will not leave you.*"

With all this talk of "the brotherhood" and gangs—even good gangs—Orlando is eager to underscore the vitality of the neighborhood and the sense of community among the families in Wilson Park. "It was a very close black community. My parents were active in the neighborhood association. I remember going from house to house with my dad handing out leaflets for some community event. My mother was a teacher in the local public school, so all the kids knew her. We knew everybody... our house was where everyone gathered."

Against this backdrop of community spirit, the young teenage boys—of thirteen and fourteen—caused mischief but not damage. "We were not bad kids," Orlando explains. "We were just kids who were a bit bored, sort of waiting on the fringe. We'd get into trouble, little stupid stuff like shooting BB guns and breaking somebody's window or stealing all the cherries off of someone's tree." The brotherhood's mischief did not threaten the neighborhood or worry their parents. It was only when their mothers and fathers began to anticipate the future that they would feel some apprehension. At this point the pranks of thirteen-year-olds were relatively harmless. What was going to happen when the boys turned sixteen or seventeen? "There is trouble waiting for us," says Orlando ominously. "As a group we're getting bigger and bigger... We're beginning to increase our scope and rubbing up against other gangs of kids… As we're getting older, the ante is always going up. I'm responsible. I do my chores. I'm not looking for trouble, but I'm a street guy, and my parents are beginning to worry."

Orlando tells two stories about "the ante going up" in Wilson Park as he got older, stories about how harmless mischief was beginning to turn into a serious threat. Both incidents took place at the recreation center where he and his buddies gathered every afternoon. Orlando had gone to the center to play baseball, and he found a "bunch of older guys" who were already on the field but missing an umpire. When they saw him coming they yelled, "Hey Butch, you can umpire the game." Orlando resisted at first. "No one wants to umpire. That just means trouble. I think to myself I don't want to do this… But they're big guys and they *persuade* me." He stood behind home plate and did the best he could. The players challenged several of his calls, but the mood stayed pretty affable until the game became competitive. "My luck," smiles Orlando. "The game gets close, and one team wins by one run. Afterwards this big, scary guy comes up to me and gets all in my face. He yells, 'You gave them the game.' I'm laughing, thinking he's just joking. But he's serious… He takes both hands and pushes me in my chest. I lash out and swing as hard as I can… He's much bigger than me… And wouldn't you know, I hit him straight in the mouth." As Orlando is telling the story he is acting out the scene, making his face grimace, punching the air, bobbing and weaving, fading back. He looks like the fourteen-year-old Butch. "When I punch this big guy out, the whole crowd that has gathered around goes 'Oooh!' They can't believe I'm doing this. Luckily, my good buddy Magellan steps in and parts us. He pushes me back, talks in my ear, makes me calm down. He won't let me fight." Then the crowd dispersed, things cooled down, and everyone walked away. But Orlando knew that there was danger lurking around the corner. "Now I've got this guy out there looking to retaliate, ready to come after me… I'm thinking I need to get out of town."

The second incident at the recreation center felt even scarier because it involved Orlando's big sister, Janesta. Usually Janesta didn't go up to the rec center; she didn't feel welcome there. Because she didn't attend public school, the neighborhood girls "thought she was stuck up," and they could be nasty to her. ("You know, girls are much meaner than boys in that way.") Janesta's boyfriend, Ronald Cook, was a wonderful guy. "He was a golden kid—smart, handsome, a great athlete—and he was so in love with my sister. They were the great love of the neighborhood." When Janesta and Ronald arrived at the center, they ran into a tough girl named Ida, who was "sweet on" Ronald and who detested Janesta for her beauty and her good fortune in having Ronald. Ida began to stir up trouble with Janesta, teasing and taunting her and trying to provoke her into a fight. Ronald stepped in to defend her, and an angry crowd began to circle around the pair. Orlando, who was playing baseball in the field nearby, could hear some of the commotion but had no idea that Janesta was in the middle of it. "Suddenly, some guy comes running to get me, telling me my sister is in big trouble and I'd better come immediately." His voice is breathless, reliving the panic. "I race back and see this huge crowd. My sister is standing in the center with Ronald, and he has a bat in his hand. The crowd is yelling obscenities at them, and Ronald is threatening them with a bat. With all my speed I run home and tell my dad, 'They're going to kill your daughter.' He jumps in the car, speeds down to the rec center and drives the car straight into the crowd. My father is a fighter. You can see the fire in his eyes. He pushes everyone back with his fiery glare, grabs my sister and gets out of there."

Donald and Barbara could feel the danger coming on, particularly for their third child who loved the streets, and their older girl whose beauty and dignity brought her a certain kind of vulnerability. "This kind of thing scared the stuff out of my parents," exclaims Orlando. They could also see that as the lure of the streets was growing stronger for Butch, his life at school was growing increasingly antagonistic. At fourteen, Orlando was in his first year at Archbishop Curley High (his parents had managed to scrape together the tuition after the high school "stole" his scholarship), "trying to find a way to get thrown out. By this time I had a chip on my shoulder and I had a lot of mouth. I found myself in detention after school every day. For a while there, I had my parents believing I was on the track team. I was still doing okay as a student, still getting my work done, but I was constantly fighting with my teachers or with other kids." When in the winter of his ninth-grade year, his parents announced to him and his siblings that the family would be moving to New Hampshire, Orlando hated the idea of leaving his beloved brotherhood—the camaraderie and the street life—but he loved the idea of getting out of Curley High.

Isolation

After Donald Sr. graduated from Morgan State with a major in physics, he was employed as an engineer at Aberdeen, "a proving ground for the United States Army." He had been looking for other career opportunities that would be more challenging and more lucrative, that would offer the family the chance to "escape the city." Orlando remembers his father "almost taking a big job in Dallas" in 1963, but at the last minute deciding not to go because he couldn't face taking his family to the city where John F. Kennedy had just been murdered. "My parents were always talking about other places, other opportunities... always making plans." In 1964 a job opened up in Nashua, New Hampshire, at a high-tech defense plant called Saunders Association, and Donald Sr. seized the opportunity. With his background in defense systems, his wish to pursue a more promising career, and his determination to move his family out of Baltimore, this seemed to be a judicious choice. In December of 1964, Donald moved up to Nashua alone, and in June of 1965, when the children and Barbara had completed the school year, the family joined him there.

When Orlando talks about his father's career as an engineer, and his training in science, his voice is admiring. He says simply, "My father was real smart," and then he describes the complex ingredients of his character. "My father is a street guy—self-taught in terms of manners. He is street tough and very proper all at the same time." But the most important quality that made Donald Sr. a hero to his son was his father's commitment to passing on what he knew. "He was a wonderful teacher. He had the extraordinary *patience* of a teacher. He used to spend lots of time with us around homework... He taught me how to play baseball, do math, play every card game you could think of... We used to spend all day and all night playing chess. I'll never forget the day when I could finally *really* beat him... But he still continued to play with me. My mother was the schoolteacher, but my father was the teacher at home." I am amazed by this description of the young father—who was juggling a large family, school, and work—being able to find the time and energy to devote to teaching *one* child to play chess. Orlando explains that his father did not have a lot of time in his strenuous life, but he did have a way of "giving you his undivided attention... and sticking with you until you learned something." His voice is nostalgic as if he still feels bathed in his father's attention. "I remember him playing catch with me *all* day... just tossing the ball back and forth in the backyard."

Donald Sr.'s patience and focus were sparked by a surprising playfulness. Orlando's face lights up with the memory. "My father was *fun!* He would surprise you with something." The surprises were simple and unextravagant, but they always seemed to cut through the monotony of ordinary routine. He'd whisper to his youngsters conspiratorially, "Okay kids, we're not going to tell your mother, but we're not going to go to church today." They would sneak out, hop in the car, and go to visit a relative. Or he would take them on "a little adventure" to the cafeteria at Morgan State, and they would have lunch, or they'd go over to the campus and hang out with his fraternity brothers, listening to their raucous conversation or watching them practice their step dance.

Orlando's smile then fades as he realizes the tricks that memory can play, and as he faces the reality of his current relationship with his father, which feels distant and strained. He admits that we all reconstruct stories of our childhood, choosing to select or magnify those memories that are pleasant and reassuring. He thinks the image of his young father as "all patient and all fun" must be something of a distortion, and he suspects that the rosy nostalgia surrounding his father must have, to some extent, diminished his memory of his mother's good qualities. "My father was always seen as being more fun... so my mother became the heavy." Donald Sr. would provide the inspired, focused teaching and the spirited, playful adventures while Barbara orchestrated the household, demanding that the chil-

dren do their chores and follow the rules. Orlando sees echoes of
this gender pattern in his own household, which is one reason why
he finally recognizes the distortions in the old pictures of his parents. "I see this in my own life now with my kids. I've been on the
road, working endless hours, and I come home late at night with a
surprise ice-cream treat. We gather around the kitchen table and
have a wonderful conversation. Their mom, who's been home with
them the whole time, is making them clean their rooms."

The gender differences also mix with temperamental contrasts
that get interpreted differently at various points in one's life. Not
only did Orlando's child's eyes see his father as the adventurer and
his mother as the heavy, but also they saw his mother as the aggres-
sor and his father as the understanding peacemaker. "When they
had struggles, I always thought my mother was the explosive one
who was striking out, and my father was the calm one who was trying so hard." He corrects himself. "These were not struggles... My
parents had big fights... and I appreciated the fact that they never
fought privately. If they were going to fight, they were not going to
hide out and be secretive. They were going to fight in front of the
children." Orlando remembers the typical way the dramas unfolded.
"I'd see my mother strike out at my father, and my father turn away,
ignoring it and refusing to become involved." But sometimes his
father did not simply absorb the blow. One day Orlando flinched
when his father retaliated. "He was burning and he hit her, hard."
Both of them knew that the line had been crossed, that if their
rage had erupted in "physical abuse," they "needed some space.
They needed to live apart for a while."

Donald and Barbara sat the children down and explained their
decision to separate. The children were not surprised; they had witnessed the anger building between their parents. They had been
frightened by their father's uncharacteristic loss of control. But
even though the news was expected, it felt devastating. They all listened in stony silence until Orlando's voice cut through the air. "I,
who always have the big mouth, speak up and say, 'You guys always
tell us how we've got to reconcile and figure out a way to resolve our
differences. How come you can't figure out a way to do that your-

selves?'" He was pleading for all of them. "'Why do you got to split up? How about *us?*'... They didn't have a sufficient answer. The only thing they could say was, 'Ours is much more complicated.'"

Donald Sr. moved out for a while and went to live with a cousin. Orlando is telling this story not so much to draw a picture of the marital conflict as to make a point about the dynamic between his parents, the roles he saw each playing. "I always blamed it on my mom. I saw my mom pushing my dad out. My mother was assaulting my dad. Now I realize that it was much more complicated than that." Now he sees that his dad's "passivity" held a certain kind of arrogant power, and that his mother's aggression was a desperate attempt to get a response from her husband. As a grown man, Orlando has experienced this struggle between men and women, he recognizes that a relationship based on aggression and intimidation always holds the threat of violence. All at once he is talking about his father, himself, and his son, teaching and learning the essence of male power and dominance. As I listen to Orlando, I feel suddenly very *female*, "on the one side of the line," and realize I am only half getting his analysis. "The man always knows that he is physically much more powerful. The woman is screaming, raging, and the man is over there being quiet, brooding. In his silence he is saying, 'Don't cross that line, because if you do, this *beast* will lunge.'... It is very provocative. She is saying back to him, 'Don't tell me I can't jump over that line.' Boys begin to play this with our mothers before we're playing this with other women... At a certain point my brothers and I knew we could intimidate our mom with our physical power. And I see it in my own son. At fourteen, he is beginning to do that with my wife. He thinks he can take his mother, but he knows he can't take me... He can look into my eyes and see the fire."

This analysis of male power feels incongruent with the gentle, sensitive man who is sitting across the table from me. He claims to have inherited his father's fiery eyes, eyes that scream danger. But he has also developed the capacity to see the male-female dance, to distance himself far enough from the action to see the limitations and distortions of male dominance. He knows that the tales of his dad's playfulness *and* the stories of his raging fiery eyes are caricatures drawn in retrospect. "I've just held onto the good memories of my father. I've made it all far too simple."

Now, as an adult, Orlando rarely experiences the echoes of his childhood memories. There is pain in his face as he speaks about his current relationship with his father. "I see him differently now. He is a very private person, very closed and distant... This is probably related to his being orphaned as a child and having to protect himself from all life's dangers. Now our relationship is strained. It is hard to get his attention. He doesn't reach out to be in touch and doesn't talk about his feelings or want to hear about mine." Then Orlando makes a large abstract statement that he feels is related to his discussion of male power and male-female relationships, but it also seems to express a central dilemma in his own life: "Work has a way of consuming all your attention and energy. I see that in my father's life and my own... You begin to see home as a sanctuary, but you have nothing left to give when you get there. There is altogether too much emphasis put on work and production, to the compromise of family and community."

Orlando was fourteen when the Bagwells moved to Nashua, New Hampshire, an old, sleepy mill town with one main street that people called downtown. Saunders Association, the company where Donald Sr. was employed, was one of a few industries that had relocated to Nashua, transforming it from a lazy working-class village to a "boom town attracting suburban middle-class types." But for the "big-city kid" from Baltimore, Nashua seemed like a ghost town, remote and dead. Orlando recalls the family's first drive down the main street. "I'll never forget sitting in the backseat of our car taking in the scene. *'This is it!'* We couldn't believe it." For the first two months they lived in a motel while the contractors finished building their home, the first house being built in a new subdivision. "All these woods and no people around... The contrasts were huge! We were moving from a place where rats were crawling in the gutters to a place where deer were stealing leftover food from our garbage."

At first, the contrasts felt catastrophic, disorienting, impossible to get used to. "Those first few months we were up there in the woods all alone, my brothers and sisters and I spent all our nights cursing our parents. They'll never know the things we plotted up there in our rooms. We were all *raging*. We couldn't believe our parents would do this to us." Slowly they each became more or less acclimated to the rural white scene, but the effects of the move have been long lasting. Orlando puts it simply—once again he finds a point of deep resonance with the "isolation and aloneness" Malcolm X experienced in his life—"The move had the most profound effect on all of us—more than anything else in our lives."

Orlando remembers the first day of school in September, "the shock of getting on a school bus and seeing the sea of white faces." He felt so far away from his roots, from his people, from the brotherhood, and from the action. "I felt remote from the rest of the world… The geographical distance was not so great, but the psychological separation was vast." The first summer after his tenth-grade year, Orlando and Donny tried to break the isolation by going to work as dishwashers at a joint in Atlantic City. "We were still rooted in Baltimore in some important ways. This was our chance to reconnect." The first thing they did with their first week's pay was to go out and buy "leather jackets on layaway." Each week they would pay a little bit more on the jackets. By summer's end, they were able to return to small-town Nashua looking like big dudes from the city. Orlando smiles at the motivation and the affectation. "I tried to use my city slickness to get over in New Hampshire, but I'm *playing it*, not living it."

After his initial resistance to the parochialism and whiteness of New Hampshire, Orlando had grown increasingly comfortable—never totally comfortable—with his teenage life there. His adaptation to the loneliness included becoming a "confirmed integrationist." Being an integrationist required that he do all the work of assimilation; that he not be strikingly different from his peers (except in the visibly unavoidable distinction of color); and that he not make waves. "During this period I am not threatening to white people. It is only *me*, not a crowd of us." His white friends could sense his willingness to be one of them. Since there was only one of him, since he was a "nice guy," and since he was making every effort to fit in, Orlando grew to be accepted by, even popular with, his peers.

The distortions of tokenism demanded that he make a "critical distinction." "I am *not* their *mascot*, but I am *exotic* in that environment, and that exotica becomes part of my identity." He is giving words to a subtle complex of feelings, interior definitions of self. I listen and feel identified with the black adolescent trying to assert his dignity in a white world.

As Orlando lived the "critical distinction" he also struggled with balancing the pieces of his teenage life. "As an adolescent I was constantly negotiating what I needed to feel *whole*—at eighteen years old it was women, sports, and school." He was like all of his friends in that way. "I was *me* and I thought everyone could just be themselves. I'm not reading James Baldwin, Malcolm, or Richard Wright... I'm reading Ayn Rand... Maybe I had read Martin Luther King's *Stride Toward Freedom* by then."

By his senior year of high school there were new stirrings within him. He began to feel some of the costs and burdens of assimilation. He began to sense the claustrophobia of small-town New Hampshire and began to want to test out some of the dimensions of his blackness. "I was beginning to get edgy about it all. I was doing small things like wearing *black* socks when I ran track... or like feeling that the coach was not giving me adequate attention because I was black, and deciding to quit the team in protest." These were little demonstrations of increasing discomfort and alienation; he did not yet have a fully formed ideology, but the old yearnings for his beloved Baltimore were reemerging.

Dating white girls made him experience his blackness with full force. He remembers that most of the girls were "uninteresting"; a few of them were "genuine." But their parents—all of them—were "assholes who worried about my involvement with their daughters." Not only were the *girls'* parents apprehensive; Orlando's mother lived with the fear that her son would get one of the white girls pregnant. "I was dealing with my mother who is scared out of her mind... worried sick about my safety." I nod to show my understanding of the seductions and dangers of this volatile situation: the eager white girls, the raging and protective white parents, the frightened black mother, and the black boy seeking pleasure and adventure, and wanting to be part of the adolescent action.

Orlando leaps in to correct what he thinks might be my mis-perception. He has read my mind right. "You've got to know, Sara, I'm not sexually active with any of these girls. My mother is terri-fied, but I'm not doing anything. I'm not feeling comfortable enough in any of these relationships to be *doing* anything." His face is intense and serious as he struggles to define the "discomfort." "I have lots of conversations with my sister Janesta about sex and sex-uality—the beauty of it, the passion, the sweetness... how good it can make you feel... But I know that it can't be that way with these white New Hampshire girls. So I stay away from it."

His "timidity" is so different from the more spontaneous and open relationships he had known with girls in Baltimore. "I was much more restrained when I was seventeen and eighteen than I was in Baltimore at fourteen years old. In Baltimore I was really out there, much more comfortable and aggressive... I'm sure I waited much longer to be sexually active because I was living in New Hampshire than I would have if we had stayed in Baltimore." His face breaks out in a big grin. "But once I got into it, I enjoyed it... I made up for lost time!"

However difficult Orlando's experience was dating white girls, it was nowhere near as painful as the rejection his sister Janesta suf-fered. Even though the "asshole" parents expressed their ugly racism, their daughters wanted to be with Orlando and sought him out. "The white boys were much more cruel," recalls Orlando angrily. "I couldn't stand the way the white boys dealt with my sis-ter. I *know* that there were many who were very attracted to her. They *wanted* her. But they could never express it *publicly*. They wouldn't take her out... only talk about her in secret... as if she was some kind of *whore*." His words sting the air.

Actually, when Orlando relives the rage of his family's uproot-ing from Baltimore, it is *Janesta's* anguish Orlando feels most deeply. "My older sister was really beautiful... a dark-skinned beauty. In Baltimore she was very popular and had lots of boyfriends. But in New Hampshire she had *no* social life. We had to *find* her a date for the senior prom," Orlando says sadly. "It hurt me to see her in New Hampshire. I loved to see her glowing and joyous. But there she was, lonely and sad... It made her lose a sense of herself... made her forget how wonderful she was, how beautiful she was... Her measurement of those things changed. The standard was white and rejecting. When you spend so much time trying to become a part of something that has rejected you, you *lose* yourself... You begin to create yourself in *their* image... You've changed." His voice trails off. He seems to want to wipe away the corrosive experience and leave me with a beautiful image. "I saw my sister as a *queen*... I still do."

Eyes on the Prize

Orlando Bagwell has just returned from three weeks in the sun: a family visit to the Dominican Republic, a solo vacation in Puerto Rico, a film festival in St. Thomas. He is looking radiant and rested. His brown skin is several shades darker and redder; his body looks fit and lean. He reentered his frenetic world of work a few days ago, but he hasn't yet lost the serenity, the balm left over from his Caribbean holiday. He is eager to regale me with his "vacation stories" that he doesn't dare take to work. "The folks wouldn't be able to stand it," he laughs. Fresh from his daily morning run, he is wearing a yellow-orange Guatemalan shirt with faded jeans. He pulls out a banana and a blueberry yogurt from his bag, sips cranberry juice, and launches into tales of fun and adventure. He paints the scene of a gorgeous night in Puerto Rico with a full moon and gentle sea winds. He tells his friends that he would love to go for a swim in the ocean. They pile in the car, travel through narrow, winding back roads to a secluded beach where Orlando rips off his clothes and runs into the dark waters. "I just lay out there, paddling around, staring up at the moon... so quiet, so peaceful, so amazing." His voice softens to almost a whisper. "Sara, as I am gazing up at the moon, I'm experiencing a whole lot of sensations... I'm experiencing my own mortality... I'm feeling in touch with the forces of nature."

The other stories he tells are also full of adventure, beautiful landscapes, sumptuous food, and good friends. He speaks in the present tense as if he wants to preserve the immediacy of it all. As he relives the experiences, his eyes dance and his body moves. After some appreciative listening, I warn him that I've had enough. I can't stand to hear about another sunset or sunrise or green-blue sea or moonlit night or white sand beach. He throws his head back and laughs—"Okay, I'll stop," he says. "But I can't resist one more story. I'm on my way home. I take the small plane from St. Thomas to Puerto Rico and find that my plane out of San Juan has been canceled. I have to wait five hours for the next flight to Boston, and I think to myself, 'What if I just got on the plane and went back to St. Thomas... would anyone miss me?... Would I really miss anything?' This was not just a passing thought... I mean I *seriously* contemplated that possibility." He is still grinning at the mischief and abandon that his vacation allowed him to "seriously contemplate." "That's enough," I exclaim with mock seriousness.

Although I have pleaded with Orlando to stop telling his indulgent tales, I really love the sound of his exuberance. I know these few weeks have been a rare indulgence, and I know how hard he works. For these few hours we are sitting on my deck in the sun. But by evening Orlando will be taking a plane to Los Angeles, where he and his crew will be spending the weekend shooting more footage for the Malcolm X film. They will be working fourteen-hour days and spending long hours into the night preparing for the next day's shoot. Monday he will take the red-eye flight across the country, arriving back in Boston at 8:00 A.M., in time to make a morning meeting at his office. In the meanwhile, he is playing the scenes over in his mind, feeling the overwhelming weight of the hundreds of hours of unedited tape, and struggling to envision the structure and design of the whole piece. Counting the hours does not begin to capture the magnitude of the work or the energy it consumes. He is possessed. Most of the time, it is a welcome possession (he cares deeply about the work's message and artistry), but this absorption does take its toll.

I ask him to talk about how he "uses his vacations," to contrast the rhythms and experiences of vacations with those of his work. He is silent for a long time. (We have not met since early summer, and he seems to be trying to find a point of reentry into our conversation.) "Got to get my rhythm," he says after a lengthy meditation. "There are two kinds of vacations," begins Orlando. "The first kind is relatively brief... You take a few days off, you establish space from your normal routines... It's usually not enough time to escape the things that are taxing your brains. You end up thinking about your work... in a quieter, prettier place, with more solitude... but you're still in your work. But the second kind of vacation allows you to really get away, really escape the work. This three-week vacation that I took was like that... It was a real pause, a real separation, a real chance to reflect on where I am in my life."

Bagwell wants me to know that this "second kind of vacation" is rare in his life. It is only the second time that he has felt compelled to get away *and* been able to carve out the time, space, and resources to be able to do it. This summer he almost felt as if he "had no choice." His work was beginning to consume him, sap all of his energies, really string him out. "Things were totally out of balance." As the demands of his work grew in the last year and a half—the extensive travel for the Malcolm X film, the money raising and putting together of grant proposals to sustain the film company, the editing of the *Great Depression* series, the finishing of a dance film, the administration of the company—he realized he was losing touch with his family. "Working twelve- to fourteen-hour days at the office, I was missing my kids a lot... They were not on my schedule... and I had no space for myself." He began to feel the stress, the rising anxiety, the deep weariness. Although he already knew he needed a break, his internist's advice for a "real vacation" helped him "rationalize" the extended time away. So he planned a trip that responded to his need for family time, solitude, rest, and beauty. For the first week he joined his family in the Dominican Republic, which is where his wife Rosa's family lives, then he spent some days with old friends in Puerto Rico, and ended up in St. Thomas at a Black Film Festival, where he was serving on a jury.

The last time Orlando had an extended vacation was more than twelve years ago, but it was also in response to an urgent need to get space, evaluate where his life was going, and give more attention to his family. At that time, their son, Jaffar, was two and a half years old and Rosa was pregnant with their second child. Orlando and Rosa were having "marital problems"—struggling with the "tough realities" of family life, feeling "weighed down by big responsibilities and obligations." After a relatively short courtship—they

met in September and were married in July with Rosa already pregnant and "wearing a big dress"—they had approached the first
couple of years of marriage with "naivete" and enthusiasm. But the
coming of their second child seemed to be a difficult time of transition. "Two children seemed to be so much more than one. I very
much wanted to have another child, but my wife wanted to make
sure that I would be there for her. We both needed to consider what
we were going to do with our lives and whether we wanted to do
that together." The pregnancy was a source of tension and conflict, but there were other large questions looming on the horizon.
At the time, the Bagwells were living in Boston, and Orlando was
working at the Blackside film company doing "everything." "I was
being what we called a filmmaker," he smiles. "Shooting, producing,
editing, raising money, doing promotion… the works." He had
learned every dimension of the work and had "grown enormously,"
but he had reached a place where he needed more challenge and
more options, and he was "looking to make a career shift to L.A."

So the three Bagwells went off to the Dominican Republic for
six weeks with burning questions—"whether we'd have another
child and whether we'd move to California." "We were far away
from all that was," recalls Orlando. "We drove the island, visited
Rosa's aunt's house, talked a lot and made decisions." It was a time
of turmoil, conflict—"big fights, volatile words." He shakes his
head, remembering the shocking symbolism of Rosa's rage. "She
went out and got her hair straightened on me. I was horrified… I
screamed at her, 'What are you doing to me?'" It was also a time of
healing. The days were long and slow. "It was timeless time." The
hot sun, the gentle sea was soothing to their spirits, reducing the
tension between them. By the time they returned to Boston, they
had decided to recommit themselves to the hard work of marriage,
have the baby, and make the move. "We moved on Christmas Day
the following December. We sold all of our belongings (except for
a few paintings) and carried with us only what we could take on the
plane. I had no job lined up… It was a huge risk for all of us. The
following March our daughter Cira Janesta arrived. She was born at
home in L.A…. A midwife helped bring her into the world. It was

beautiful." Orlando's voice is breathless as he races through these big life events, the anguish and the joy. He does not seem to want to relive them again but rather to rush to their final resolution—a lovely baby girl and exciting new work.

As he looks back more than a decade to that "desperate trip," Orlando feels the special quality of his middle years. This summer's trip had none of the crisis and drama of twelve years ago, but it was demanding in a different way. Now he is not the young man trying to mend his marriage, build a family, and make a career move. He is a man in his early forties who feels the impulse to reflect on his life and its meanings. "It is a feeling of restlessness. Life has had a certain order, a certain rhythm, and I feel I want to *decide* what's next and make choices... even if I *choose* to continue doing exactly what I'm doing." There is optimism in his voice. Somehow the "restlessness" feels liberating. "There is a *yearning*... Is there something you want that you don't have?... To ask those questions brings a freedom."

A week after his family traveled to Santo Domingo, Orlando joined them there for a wonderful carefree vacation. They used the city as their base and made short trips to other parts of the island, traveling through the mountainous terrain to the sea. "We went to a fishing village close to Haiti, a magical spot where the mountain streams fall out of the mountains and into the ocean. There was nothing to do there... We'd hang out on the porch, rocking in our rocking chairs, or play cards, or take walks at night." Orlando wants me to know that he is not a workaholic, that "hanging out comes easy" to him. "You know, I'm not obsessed by my work. I'm not driven... Maybe the folks I work with would disagree." He admits, "I work hard, *very* hard. I am responsible, conscientious, and good at meeting deadlines... I know the importance of being organized and meeting schedules. But I do my work because it makes me feel *good*, not out of some feeling of guilt or proving myself." Then he smiles as he reveals the other part of himself that he clearly likes. "I am more happy hanging out than working... I could easily find life okay doing less... I enjoy myself *hard* and willingly too."

As Orlando describes the pleasure he gets in play, his beaming face looks boyish, and I am reminded of his childhood stories of coming home from school, racing to do his homework, rushing to do his chores, so he could go out into the streets and hang out with his bosom buddies. The work at school and at home was completed competently and efficiently (he prided himself on being a "gamer" and learning how to "get by"), but his focus was always on the reward at the end, the chance to "hang out with the boys." Orlando still relishes "the hanging out." He also enjoys his work and feels good when he is being productive and making a contribution. As an adult, he finds it is harder to carve out the time for adventure and play, but he is well aware of how much he needs it, how fully he lives it, and how important it is as a counterpoint to his strenuous work life.

On this vacation, the greatest pleasure was the chance to hang out with his children. At fourteen and eleven, they are wonderful traveling companions and great company. "I enjoy them the most," he says simply. It takes no time for them to find a comfortable rhythm together. Their comfort comes from all the time he used to spend at home when the children were younger. When Orlando was doing freelance work, he would go off on a shoot for several weeks and then be home for four to six weeks before he would take on another assignment. "These were great together times, spontaneous and easy," he recalls. "Hanging out with my kids comes *naturally*." But now it is even more enjoyable because there are "so many more ways of being together."

Orlando remembers an evening of sitting with his kids, rocking on the porch in the small fishing village. He had brought Toni Morrison's *Jazz* to read on the trip, and while they rocked on the porch, his son picked it up and started to read a passage from it. "He says, 'I don't get it. I'm lost,' and I tell him, 'You've got to read to Morrison's punctuation... Her writing is a train of thought. She's writing rhythm here... You've got to get the cadence... You've got to *sing* this book.' I take the book and begin to read out loud—it is this wonderful, passionate love story... My son sits there listening intently as I read it. After a while, he lights up and yells, 'I get it! I get it!'... There we are, screaming on the porch... We each take a turn... They can't wait to have their chance to read. All the other folks rocking on the porch don't speak English, but they listen to the cadence. They hear us screaming. They're sitting there rocking and smiling." As he spins out this story, Orlando's voice sings. He is smiling as he recalls the pleasure of Morrison's love song, Jaffar's enthusiasm and eagerness, the three of them screaming with laughter, and the quiet, smiling faces of the Spanish speakers. He will never forget this moment; neither will his children. His voice drops to a whisper—"When we were on vacation, there were times when we were doing something that I knew my kids would never forget... It was not so important *what* we were doing. It was about what was happening with us and between us."

Although Orlando can remember some moments of "togetherness" with his own dad when he was a child—like learning to play chess and playing catch for hours in the yard—he feels fortunate that his life has allowed him more time and intimacy with his children. "I have more opportunity for these kinds of interactions with my kids because I have not had to struggle so hard. I am more in control of my life than my dad was." Actually, when he thinks about the quality of communication and connection he enjoyed with his children in the Dominican Republic, his mother (not his father) comes to mind. "It is with my *mother* that I remember this feeling of her taking time out for me," says Orlando. "My mother took me to the movies... She took me to see *Dr. Zhivago* when I was about eleven. I thought it was a *great* film. Totally captivating."

It is the first time I have heard this filmmaker speak about a childhood experience of going to the movies, and I pounce on him. "Tell me more about that," I say enthusiastically. He wants to assure me that he "wasn't like Stephen Spielberg," or one of those "movie fanatics" whose childhood was consumed by the cinema. "Actually, I rarely went to the movies as a kid. I was not a lover of TV... I didn't go to the movies on dates when I was a teenager... I thought spending two hours in the dark was a waste of my time. I wanted to be out in the street playing." But even though he was not "freakish" about movies when he was growing up, he does admit to an early fascination. His first memories are of piling into the car and going to the drive-in with his parents and siblings. Often they would stay for the entire triple feature in order to get their money's worth. His brothers and sisters would often lose interest and fall asleep, and he would catch his parents nodding off. But Orlando would watch every minute of all three movies.

His mother noticed her middle boy's sustained attention and involvement and rewarded him with a trip to see *Dr. Zhivago*, just the two of them, "at my mom's initiation!" It was a memorable treat, much like one of the intimate parent-child events Orlando knows his children will never forget. The pleasure was marked as much by what was between them—mother and son—as by what was playing on the big screen. Orlando remembers another time when the family traveled to Atlantic City and spent the day enjoying the games, rides, and attractions up and down the Boardwalk. The Beatles movie *A Hard Day's Night* was playing, and Orlando went there first. "I spent my whole day in the movie theater watching *A Hard Day's Night* over and over and over again. I didn't go on any of the rides... didn't eat any food. They had to come and get me in the theater so they could go home... There was a special *energy* about the experience... I felt one with it."

When I push him to describe the feeling of oneness, this special energy he felt with the Beatles movie, Orlando looks at me blankly. I am amazed that he seems never to have examined his childhood fascination with film. I try again. "What do you think captured you?" He shrugs, repeats his observation that he was fascinated but not a fanatic, and then tells me of his first experience working with film when he was an adolescent. As a high school student, Orlando joined a volunteer service club called the Catholic Youth Organization. He and a friend collaborated on offering a leadership training workshop for new recruits to the organization. It was Orlando's idea to try to use films to "raise issues and motivate discussion." He chose two shorts—one about suburban life ("I think it was called *Sixteen in Webster Grove*") and the other about the inner city (called *Tenement*)—and tried to "play with creative ways of putting the stuff together—double images and other tricks." Even though he remembers enjoying the technical and artistic experience of "playing around with this stuff," he emphasizes the exciting connections between the images projected on the screen and the discussions they inspired. The double images of affluence and poverty, white and black, suburban and urban, provoked conversation and controversy among the high school students, a discourse that might not have been generated without the visual counterpoint.

Bagwell's description of the workshop is sparse. He doesn't dwell on the creative process of juxtaposing the images nor talk about the student exchange that followed. But, even in the brief glimpse, I see the seeds of his future work as a filmmaker. I see the motivation and impulse that shine through his recent documentaries. His films in *Eyes on the Prize*, a magnificent documentary series on the Civil Rights movement, offer a disturbing and inspiring historical chronicle. Through the film footage edited from news reports, speeches, marches, church services, and demonstrations the audience is drawn back into the sixties. We see the police turn their hoses and fierce dogs on the demonstrators; we hear Martin Luther King's splendid oratory; we witness the quiet courage of Rosa Parks; we glimpse the political strategy meetings of the Southern Christian Leadership Conference; we recognize the young, hopeful, angry faces of Jesse Jackson, Andrew Young, Harry Belafonte. We are enraged by the racism, the oppression, the stupidity, and the violence. We weep when we hear Fanny Lou Hamer's strong, defiant voice. As we watch Orlando Bagwell's film, we feel a "special energy"; we feel "at one" with our legacy.

We Controlled the Sidewalk

 When Orlando remembers his decision to attend Boston University he says, *"I came to Boston looking for my Baltimore again...* I chose B.U. because it was a city school. I wanted to escape the racial isolation of New Hampshire."

He no longer wanted to be the exotic stranger accepted because he made others around him feel comfortable. He yearned to be part of the black world again, one among many. "But I was in for a rude awakening!" he says with drama. He arrived on campus at the height of Black Power when relations between blacks and whites were strained and often hostile; when blacks were strident in their rhetoric; when the rage simmered just below the surface ready to erupt at the slightest provocation. "I went to college in 1969. The politics were loud and raw... Students were saying to me, 'Be specific about who you are.' The scrutiny was very tough, very critical... I was not necessarily okay... They wanted me to *demonstrate* my politics, and I wasn't sure what my politics were."

His first weeks on campus felt like trial by fire. Orlando had come expecting the embrace and comfort of the other black students. Instead he felt rejection at every turn. The first incident occurred because he was assigned a white roommate, a person whom he didn't know and hadn't chosen, "just someone the admissions office had matched me with." At the opening meeting of the Black Student Union, Orlando rose to speak after listening to several stinging presentations by some of the upperclassmen. Before he could say his piece, he was challenged by an angry voice from the back of the room. "How dare you even talk. You don't even know what you're talking about... You have a white roommate." Orlando stood there stunned. What did having a white roommate have to do with his right to speak or the veracity of his words? "They wanted me to throw this guy [the roommate] out! There I was, put in the position of defending a white guy who I didn't even know." Orlando had to withstand the further humiliation of the speaker exposing his ignorance about black literature. "He stood there and asked me whether I had read all the revolutionary stuff—*Soul on Ice*, *Autobiography of Malcolm X*, Nat Turner, Frantz Fanon... That's what *really* got to me. After that I spent the next several months reading *everything*. It was a lonely place to be. Everything was either black or white. You were either in or out."

Orlando remembers the day a high school friend of his from New Hampshire came down to visit him in Boston, "a girl, but *not* a girl-friend." They went out to get a bite to eat, and "two sisters," who were students at B.U., came up behind them and followed them down the street taunting their "brother" and "talking trash." "It was just horrible, totally humiliating and enraging." He also recalls the time he invited a black coed out on a date to see *Aquarius*. She accepted sweetly and enthusiastically, and then called the next day to say she couldn't go. "Her friends had told her that she would be selling out to go out with a guy who had sold out."

The rejection he experienced, from the very people he had yearned to be with, made Orlando feel isolated and miserable. "It was the most disastrous year of my life... the lowest time," he says grimly. There were two friends—both black women—who saw his misery and reached out to him. They dared to break rank with the other black students, and Orlando deeply appreciated their sisterhood. "The first was a down and hip, strong sister who said to me, 'You're cool, you're okay... You're trying to hang with a group that's wrong for you... Be patient, you'll find your way.'" The second was a young woman who was "feeling as out of it and as isolated" as Orlando was. She had come from a relatively privileged family, gone to a private school, and was struggling to find connections and make friends with her black peers. "The black kids could be vicious, and she found refuge with the white kids." But toward the end of the first semester, she and Orlando dis-covered their common dilemma and became fast friends.

These identity struggles consumed so much energy. In retro-spect, Orlando realizes that the black-white conflicts overlay the

554 I've Known Rivers

late adolescent coming of age. The "vicious" divisiveness among the black students was partly fueled by their need to discover who they were—as individuals, as men and women, as blacks, as students—and there were few models to follow. "We were groping with finding clarity about who we were and how to act it out," says Orlando thoughtfully. "This was new terrain for us. We were pioneering... We didn't have older black minds and mentors to help us figure out how to balance all of these identities... to help us figure out which way to go... *The university was our laboratory.*"

"All of this identity stuff" was fermenting in a complex and colorful political landscape. Black Power activities and antiwar demonstrations were at their climax. The campus was a cauldron of political and social unrest. The black students, particularly the black male students, channeled their young energy, suffering, and rage into angry protest and "posturing." The political activism of "the brothers" was often indistinguishable from "asserting our sense of manhood."

Orlando describes the early seventies as a time when universities were reaching out to attract black inner-city students. Most of these students were the first generation in their families to go to college, and too many of them were unprepared for the academic rigor and discipline of the university. Although the universities had sought them out, they were not prepared for their presence on campus. The administrators and faculty had not adequately thought through the ways in which university culture, pedagogy, and curriculum might be transformed by the black students. Bagwell remembers the university's "insensitivity" *and* "the brothers' alienation." "These were street brothers... inner-city kids... bright brothers with big energy and talent... but often the college didn't give them the right kind of support. We were caught up in what we considered Black Power... We were really acting out of a sense of *entitlement.*"

The brothers' sense of alienation was often masked by a cocky toughness. "We were too streetwise, too assertive, too bold, too loud... We ran it." The toughness would sometimes turn into threat and aggression. "We thought we could do anything we wanted. It was our world. We felt we could take anything we wanted and justified it by saying society didn't give us anything. 'Look at the rich kids with their fancy stereos. If we take their stereos, they can go out and buy another.' It was our way of asserting our *maleness*... very aggressive. We were saying, 'Get out of our way... Don't leave your door open because anything in your room will be mine.' The college campus was easy prey."

For the white students who were getting pushed around and ripped off, the brothers were a menacing force; the white students recoiled in suspicion and fear. There were some white liberal kids who felt identified with the black rage and joined in political alliance with the black kids. But many more whites felt as if they were under siege. This activism and "criminality" were merged in their white minds, reaffirming all the worst caricatures of black males. But even as the street brothers swaggered across the campus threatening the "normal order of things," they knew that their dominance was circumscribed. They knew that behind the powerful facade, they were impotent and vulnerable. Maybe some of them even recognized that their aggression was a cover for feelings of vulnerability and inadequacy. "You worked to capture some control of your world and your choices... But the territory we had to control was very *narrow*. We controlled the sidewalk. People stepped to the side when they saw us coming... We controlled the dormitory floor, the table in the cafeteria. This was *justice*... We were expressing something that in our own small way represented justice."

Although Orlando was not from the streets, he became increasingly identified with his street brothers. He had come to Boston University to find "his Baltimore," to experience again the action, excitement, and camaraderie of city life. He also came to college tired of the tokenism of New Hampshire and in search of a black community. He and many of the kids who had come from city schools did not share a common academic experience and background, however. "The college courses were not hard for me. I had been to Catholic schools in Baltimore and to a pretty good high school in New Hampshire, so I was ready for the academic stuff. I was a good student... But I could see that the guys were floundering. And they weren't getting the support." As he kept up decent, though not great, grades in his courses, Orlando was drawn to the black male scene. He joined in the protest, the aggression, the posturing. Along with his brothers he staked out black dominance over "narrow" territories. He shakes his head, "My experiences with these guys made me understand how precarious and dangerous it is to be a black man."

One afternoon in the spring of his sophomore year, Orlando was leaving the dormitory with a friend. Through the window they spotted a police car outside the building and immediately sensed that they were being watched. "They were waiting for us." For a few days Orlando had been borrowing his mother's car, and the two young men decided to move quickly past the police to the car parked nearby. "As we came out of the building we're watching them with eyes in the back of our heads. My friend has a broken arm that's in a cast. We get in the car. I'm driving, and he's in the passenger seat. The police come to the window and begin to hassle us. They ask to see my license and registration. I search around and give them what they want. Then they ask to see in my trunk. But I know my rights. I know the game... I don't let them in the trunk. They make us sit there for the longest time... then tell us to get out. As soon as I get out of the car, the police jump me, throw me up against the car. They also have my buddy with the bad arm pinned up against the car, and he's screaming. There are eight cops on us. They kick our butts, throw us in the paddy wagon, take us off to the station, and charge us with resisting arrest and assaulting a police officer." Orlando's voice is raging. A black Boston lawyer, Clarence Dilday, offered to take their case. Orlando and his friend were in the midst of pledging a black fraternity—Omega Psi Phi—and Dilday was a fraternity brother who offered his services gratis. News of their arrest spread rapidly, and the pledgees gathered outside the police station. "They stood in silence. It was a protest vigil." Dilday warned Orlando and his friend that this was a very "serious charge"; that it was their word against the word of eight police officers; and that their only hope was to locate a witness. The brothers were successful in finding someone who had seen the whole thing and was willing to testify. "It was settled," says Orlando bitterly, "when the police offered to drop charges if we promised not to countercharge."

The bitterness in his voice is mixed with tired resignation. He does not seem to be telling the story for shock value. It is not an unusual or surprising tale. The resignation in his voice comes from knowing how common was his experience. This was a time when it was not unusual to see young black men being hauled off to jail. Some were being rounded up for alleged criminal violations, others for participating in political demonstrations, and too many because they were only guilty of being black and male.

The aggression *and* the vulnerability took their toll. Orlando watched as many of his buddies began to self-destruct. The greatest tragedy was that of the "Puerto Rican brother" who was Orlando's roommate during his sophomore year. "He shouldn't have even been admitted to B.U.," says Orlando. "He was a junkie *before* he came to college... He was doing lots of drugs, burglary, and crime." Around the time that Orlando was harassed and hauled into jail by the police "for no reason," his "junkie roommate" was stealing stuff from stores every day and robbing other students to support his habit. He was involved in "real crimes, shootouts, serious arrests."

There was so much chaos and danger swirling around Orlando, so much distraction from "the academic stuff." He was watching his roommate "self-destruct" and often engaging in rescue missions to try to save him. He was witnessing the struggles and suffering of his friends who were unprepared for the academic demands of college. He was participating in the Black Power posturing, the anti-war demonstrations, and "acting out aggression." He was losing his grip. "Others might say, you're blowing your opportunity by intimidating and causing a fight... by pushing people around. You say yes, but we're *living* it. We're seeing it as *pure hell*. This feels alien, frightening... You walk into class and you are not on your territory. *They* decide what you should learn and how you should do it... You feel excluded from those decisions, rendered inadequate. I'm doing okay on that score—in the classroom—but some of my friends can't make it there... and it hurts me to see that. I'm captivated by some of the material. I'm studying, but I see them going down."

As Orlando recalls that time of "pure hell," he realizes that it was profound but short-lived. "The entitlement stuff was a brief moment in my life, but it provided a lot of clarity. I realized that I had to make a *choice*. That it was my responsibility to decide what things would no longer be a part of my life." He recognized, for example, that in order to save himself he would have to disentangle himself from some of "the casualties" surrounding him. "I had to let my roommate loose... This was one of my best buddies, but I had to be rid of him." His voice is almost a whisper. "And I had to be there when he left because I didn't want him taking my stuff. It was an awkward, painful moment."

Orlando needed to "get some space," needed to distance himself further from the "psychological damage," the turmoil, and "the shocking alienation" that consumed each day. He decided to leave school for a while, to take a leave of absence. "School was not working for me," he says simply. His parents were infuriated with his decision. They thought he was ruining his life, undoing all that they had worked so hard for. "They disowned me... They said if I was going to drop out, I'd have to make it on my own." But Orlando knew he had to go, *and* he knew he would return. This wasn't the end. This was the beginning of reclaiming himself, of rising from these ashes.

Making It Plain

A woman with whom Orlando was deeply in love was partly responsible for his getting himself back together. "Actually," he says, "it was the experience of *losing* a love that made me recognize I had to get my act together." He could feel their relationship slipping away. "I was losing myself... I was doing stupid stuff. And this woman was strong, clear. She was *doing* stuff." When she decided it was over, she didn't even have to speak the words. "I could see it in her eyes," recalls Orlando. "She was saying to herself, 'I like him. I like him very much. But this guy's a loser.'" Her eyes haunted him. He could feel her disappointment and her sadness. He knew she was right. This was a turning point for him; he had "to make something good happen."

The decision to study film was the light at the end of the tunnel. It is hard for Orlando to locate the origin of his interest in filmmaking. He never felt a burning desire. Rather it emerged as he tried to "find out what I had to say." "I had only had brief experiences with film as a kid. But they never made me feel that I wanted to do this as a career." Actually, when he left B.U. he had felt much more drawn to music. He had made good friends with some "older brothers" who were immersed in the world of jazz and had introduced him to the cool sounds of Miles and Coltrane. He spent most of his time listening to music. "I got into it deep. It had a tremendous influence on me. Every night we'd go down to the Jazz Workshop *watching* music. I felt there was nothing more satisfying than making music... I thought that brief moment jamming on stage, making those beautiful sounds, was fabulous, worth all the sacrifices of being on the road." Orlando is rhapsodic as he describes how the jazz captured him, how he loved losing himself in the rhythms. I am fascinated by his reference to *"watching* the music," and I wonder whether the visual scene was at least as powerful as the sound for him.

After a while, Orlando decided to try to make music himself. He had never studied music or played an instrument but he seized on the idea of becoming a musician. "I started playing the drums, percussion. I worked real hard at it and learned quickly. I got good enough to play in groups. People were amazed at how fast I learned the stuff. It was my first effort to find a creative field of expression… that might become a way of life."

He was casting around for other ways of expressing himself. "I wanted to say something… I didn't have any way to say it." One day he went out and bought a 35 mm camera. I ask, "What kind of camera? Did you buy a fancy camera?" He throws his head back, laughing—"I bought a *hot* camera! It was a camera, Sara. It worked." Like he had done with jazz, Orlando immersed himself in photography, learning everything he could, as fast as he could. Unlike his immersion in jazz, where he was tutored by his more sophisticated buddies, he learned everything about photography on his own. "Luckily I was by myself in this. I knew nothing about it, so I made my own way and taught myself *everything.*" Almost immediately he felt a special affinity for this work. "I found I could take pictures. I had an interest in people, and you could see it in my pictures. I was good at composition." Within a couple of months, Orlando had built a darkroom at the Harriet Tubman Settlement House, where he had begun teaching in the After School Program. He learned how to develop film, and began experimenting with creating graphics, images, posters, and slide shows. "Before I knew it, I was making money taking pictures," he smiles.

The speed of his talk matches the intensity with which Orlando pursued his new craft. He admits that he has a habit of "throwing himself into stuff," and offers a slight correction. "I told you before that I wasn't a driven person. But I am someone who *jams* everything into a very short period of time. When I say I'm not driven, I'm talking about all the things I know I'm *not* doing. I'm not talking about all the things I pack in." His success with his camera convinced Orlando that he should pursue serious study in film and that it was time to return to school. This time he would go to college with a mission. He applied to the B.U. film department and was accepted. "It was not easy. They only accepted fourteen students... But I had left school the year before in good standing. I had a good average when I took a leave of absence... and they could see I was coming back with a new commitment and big passion." He not only managed to get accepted, he also used his old contacts in the financial aid office to get a scholarship. Orlando lists the things that were "jammed" into the summer before he returned to college. "I got myself into the film department, found money, worked at the Tubman House, bought a camera, and taught myself to do photography."

The immersion continued after he entered school. Orlando continued to learn, to improvise, to expand his repertoire of tools and techniques. "I was totally in it. I looked forward to going to classes. I wanted to do as much work as possible. I was *captivated* by the material. I could see its meaning in my life. I began to create stage shows... do multimedia stuff... work with images." His first film, an untitled three-minute piece, captured the "ugliness" of drug addiction. "I shot my roommate getting off on drugs... It was one shot, but a powerful shot... a continuous series of close-ups put to the right music." "What did you title it?" I ask. "I don't know, some stupid title like 'Desperado,'" he says.

In his film classes, Orlando was the least trained and the least sophisticated. He had the energy and the intuition, but none of the experience of his classmates. "The other kids really knew film. They were doing very sophisticated stuff like planes landing and people falling off buildings. My understanding of the medium was very *crude*. I was like a *baby* speaking. They were like orators. I didn't know how to construct sentences in film yet, but I had some powerful words."

All the other film students were white. They were more technically experienced than Orlando, and he had a great deal to learn from them. But he also knew that their perspective and vision might contrast with many of the things he wanted to express, and that there were ways in which he wanted to resist their influence. In a class on aesthetics, for example, Orlando decided to do a project on drumming. He was exploring the aesthetics of rhythm and examining the search for personal expression through drumming. His classmates didn't get it. Many seemed closed to the ideas he was expressing. "I began to see myself educating *them* as I communicated my own personal aesthetics."

I ask Orlando whether in these explorations he was thinking of himself as an artist. He pauses. "No, I am not feeling like I'm an artist. I'm thinking I have to learn to *appreciate* art more. I didn't grow up going to galleries or to films... I knew something about music—jazz, rock 'n' roll, Motown—but I was not educated artistically. Art was not a major part of my life growing up." He felt he had so much to learn, and he was so determined to learn it quickly *and* deeply. He was aggressive in his pursuit of the new knowledge, hungry for the experience. "I had to educate myself... seek it out." He raced through the mandatory courses in the film department and pursued courses in the School of Fine Arts. None of his teachers encouraged his adventurous spirit. "I never got the feeling that they thought I had a lot of potential. I was not a great student. I got B's, some C's. They didn't think I'd become a filmmaker... so I struck out on my own... You know what you need and *you feed yourself*."

In his work at the Harriet Tubman Settlement House, however, Orlando felt nourished by the enthusiasm of the kids with whom he was working, and by the gratitude and support of the other teachers and community workers. Every day he would go to his job in Boston's South End, teach courses in photography, video, and film to black teenagers; and run the After School Program. It was demanding work, but he loved the teaching, and he loved working with the kids. They seemed to demand his maturity. "I knew I had to get myself together if I was going to be a model for those kids." In his teaching Orlando tried to help his students discover the connections between art and life. "We created skits about what the kids wanted to do. It all came from them... a video of someone robbing a house or hanging out in the park."

The After School Program was so successful in its efforts to involve inner-city kids in rich educational experiences that it drew lots of attention from the media. One day a crew from Channel 5 arrived to do a television news spot on the Harriet Tubman program. They visited the classes, interviewed the kids and teachers, and looked at the projects and exhibits. Orlando befriended the two brothers on the news team, a cameraman and a producer, told them of his interest in learning more about camera work, and asked them to call if they needed a volunteer to work with them. He was amazed when a couple of weeks later they called and asked him to join them, as assistant cameraman, on a jazz series they were doing. That first volunteer job led to many more as Orlando was initiated into the television/media world. "I enjoyed hanging out with these guys, and I learned an enormous amount," he says enthusiastically. "One day it turned into a pay job. They asked me to shoot a concert in New Haven as third cameraman. From time to time after that, I'd pick up paying jobs… I was becoming a real cameraman."

When Orlando graduated from B.U. in 1974, he reluctantly resigned from his Tubman House job, where he had been involved for two years, and headed out to California to visit his mother and "check out the scene." By this time his mother and father were separated. His mother had gone to California to work and do graduate study, and his father had remained in New Hampshire. "After we moved to New Hampshire," says Orlando tentatively, "their relationship was never really the same. They were just pretending, masking a lot of stuff… It was almost as if their hard life in Baltimore drew them together… But when we moved and life became easier and they had more resources, more time to think about their life together… they discovered the conflicts. It all began to fall apart." By the time Orlando started college, his mother had moved out of their Nashua house and was making plans to move across country, change careers, and study for a doctorate in clinical psychology. As Orlando briefly alludes to his parents' split, I wonder to myself whether the falling apart of their marriage might have contributed to Orlando's "losing" himself in college; whether the chaos and crises at school became unbearable because he could no longer count on the stability and nurturance of two parents at home. I also wonder whether Orlando's tales about the rage the Bagwell children felt about their "dislocation" to New Hampshire may have been enhanced by the

564   I've Known Rivers

deterioration they saw in their parents' relationship. Perhaps this was another reason to hate life in New Hampshire; the move "caused" the demise of their parents' marriage.

At the end of his summer in California, Orlando returned to Boston because he was "in love" with a woman, and because he hoped to be hired in the film department at WGBH. He had applied to WGBH but had heard nothing back from them. His woman was waiting, but there was no job in Boston, and there were no immediate prospects in the media field. When September rolled around, Orlando decided to substitute teach to earn some money while he searched for camera work. In the fall of 1975, the public schools in Boston were in crisis, pummeled by the controversies over desegregation and busing. Schools were dangerous places; battle lines were drawn; teachers were vulnerable to attack; parents screamed and wept with anger, and children were victimized by the adult warfare. Without fully realizing the heat of the flames that were burning all around him, Orlando accepted a substitute position teaching history and political science at South Boston High, the scene of the most volatile and fiery outbreaks. "I had done a minor in history at B.U.—I loved the material—but I looked like a high school kid myself," smiles Orlando before he stops abruptly. "But I *must* have told you about the South Boston incident." I tell him no. He sucks in a long breath and then dives into the action. The story is quintessential Bagwell: action packed, intense, dangerous, physical.

"I don't know that the city is providing chaperoned bus service for the teachers, so I take the public bus over to South Boston every day. I'm getting into my teaching. I'm liking it. I'm finding it engaging, challenging, stimulating. I'm enjoying my students. It's working... I'm reading this history stuff like mad trying to stay a day ahead of my students. One day I stay late after school in order to finish up some work. As always, I'm carrying an armful of books that I hope to read that evening for class the next day. South Boston High sits on the top of a hill. I'm walking down the hill, down Broadway to catch the bus to Andrew Station. I see an old woman coming toward me. As she comes closer I greet her, but she looks back at me frightened like I'm going to attack her. I'm confused, though, because she isn't really looking at me. She seems to be looking past me at something behind me. I glance around to see what she might be looking at and see this mob coming up behind me—a big bunch of white men and boys. They're getting real close, beginning to cir-cle around me... I manage to back up against the wall of a nearby building, and they begin to throw people in to fight with me... They lunge toward me, but it's clear that they don't really want to fight me. I'm in a low crouch stance trying to defend myself. As they throw people in to fight me, I'm dancing around, moving, darting, pushing them away with my arms outstretched. But one guy they throw in bounces off my hands, stumbles back, and slams into the wall. All hell breaks loose 'cause now I've hurt someone. They all come toward me, pull me off the wall. One guy kicks me hard in the center of my back and hurts me bad... They've got me down, kicking me, stomping on me, pulling at me. I can hear cars stop-ping on Broadway. I think they're stopping to help me out. But, no, they're coming into the circle and kicking me too. I think, *They're going to kill me!*... Just then a bus comes down Broadway, a city bus. The driver forces the bus into the crowd, and it moves some of the people back. He opens the door of the bus and yells at me, 'Grab on!' I reach out to try to grab the door. People are still hitting me, holding onto my legs... I manage to lock my hands around the door handle and hold on for dear life. My body drags behind, but some-how I manage to pull myself up onto the stairs of the bus."

The telephone in my kitchen rings and we both jump. Orlando has been totally absorbed in reliving this story. His body is tense, his eyes fiery, his face grimacing. Sweat rolls down the side of his face as if he has just been attacked from behind. I feel as though I was there with him in South Boston (a neighborhood I have never dared enter in my twenty years of living here). I've seen the face of the old woman, heard the jeering mob, felt the kick in my back and the blows to my body. The ring of the telephone startles us back to the present. We are safe. Orlando survived to tell the story. Relieved, we fall back in our chairs.

But there is more to the tale. "The FBI is there before I get home. Someone has already reported it to them. I'm living in

Dorchester on Intervale Street, and they're waiting there for me when I come dragging myself home. I'm feeling hurt, embarrassed, angry, confused. They want me to press charges, but I'm scared for my life. I resist. I don't want to risk being the target... But they manage to find a teacher from South Boston who witnessed the whole thing... who is able to identify one of the boys who was beating on me... so I go along with them. But I'm terrified all the time. I'm thinking, People are ready to kill you. *And they don't know anything about me*. I'm teaching their children. Probably some of them who jumped me are children I'm teaching, but I can't see their faces." He shakes his head, looks out the window and stares into the dark, gray day. He looks as if the old terror has consumed him again, and he ends the story with a hushed voice. "I go back to school. Everyone is talking about it. I'm threatened. I'm always paranoid, freaking out. I quit. I can't do it." He whispers, "The most disturbing part is knowing people will kill you for no reason."

After a pause, Orlando manages to put a good twist on this horrible incident in South Boston. "If I hadn't been attacked, if this had not happened, I probably would still be teaching today... I would not have become a filmmaker." Two weeks after he quit his teaching job, some people from WGBH—who had seen, and been impressed by an oral history slide show he had made about the Tubman House—called to ask him to be assistant cameraman on a film they were shooting on the Nation of Islam. He traveled to Chicago to shoot the film and returned to Boston, then a children's show at WGBH hired him to work second camera. "I learned filmmaking from the bottom up. WGBH had an excellent technical department. I would come home from the studio and work on my own projects."

One of the projects, on which he labored through the night, was a 16 mm film on a boy whom he had watched growing up at the Tubman House. The boy wanted to be a boxer, and the film showed his development as an athlete, his commitment to his goal, and his burning desire to become someone. Called *Boxer*, the film was really about "the kid coming of age." The seven-minute film was totally financed by Orlando. "I ran out of money, so I wasn't able to even make a print of it... I was so naive. At the time I thought the film had served its purpose. It had given me an opportunity to grow. I thought I didn't *have* to make a print... But now I recognize that the film was also a *statement*. It marked my own progression and development... It is also a story that someone *gave* me. It must be preserved... But I didn't know its full value then."

Even though Orlando was not able to make a print of *Boxer*, he did use it to make his next important career move. It was because of the favorable reviews of *Boxer* that in 1977 he won a grant from the American Film Institute and decided to make a film on Brother Blue, a street performer, dancer, and storyteller. With the grant from the AFI, he could stop freelancing and devote himself to working on his own project. He threw himself into the work, traveled with Brother Blue to several cities, filmed a seventy-six-hour storytelling marathon, did dozens of interviews. The work grew and grew. So did the number of things Orlando was balancing, "jamming into" his life. "I am working on the Brother Blue film. I'm deciding to go back to graduate school in broadcast journalism. I'm getting married. I'm having a child. I run out of money." He corrects the order. "Actually, Rosa and I are deciding to have a child, then getting married."

I struggle to catch up. "Oh," I ask, "Is Rosa the reason you returned from California?" "No," he says, his face breaking into a big grin. "I came back because I was in love with another woman. Then there was a woman in between whom I almost married. Then there was Rosa. I fell in love with Rosa big time... I was *totally* seduced... There was an immediate rapport... a clarity, a connection. You see, I'm not only intense, I'm impetuous—I met and married Rosa in five months." "You must love women," I say, stating the obvious. "I *love* women," he declares, then more thoughtfully he adds, "You see, I grew up loving my sisters. My sister Janesta is my best friend. As a kid she was everything I wanted to be. It is *amazing* to feel that way about your sister... Amazing and wonderful!"

Orlando never finished the Brother Blue film, but it was not because he ran out of money. "My vision was bigger than my understanding of the medium. I got lost in it." Money may not have been the real reason why the Brother Blue project was never completed, but by the end of his American Film Institute grant Orlando was completely broke. He was now married with a small baby. He had to find steadier work. An editing position opened up at WETA, the public television station in Washington, D.C. Orlando applied and was hired. He wanted to learn more about editing, and this was a good opportunity. For two years he labored in dark rooms, splicing and editing tape, and found it to be an unappealing and tedious "lifestyle." He needed more variety, more action, more interaction with people, and more light. "I found that I was not only working on films that I didn't like very much, but that I hated being stuck in rooms all day."

He was delighted to receive a call from Henry Hampton, at Blackside film company, asking him to shoot a small section of one of their films. "It came right on time" and opened up the door for much more work shooting, editing, directing, and producing at Hampton's film company. Blackside was a thriving, growing company, supported by big government contracts, and Orlando participated in making documentaries, dramatic films, public service announcements, and commercials. Every day he learned something new. Every day brought new challenges and problems to be solved.

After a couple of years, Orlando began to feel that he had mastered the fundamental tools of the craft; that he had taken full advantage of Blackside as a laboratory of learning; and that it was time to try out the commercial side of filmmaking. If he was going to expand his repertoire and develop a broader range of skills, he needed to go to Los Angeles to work. This was not an easy decision. He had enjoyed his eclectic experience at Blackside, believed in the values of the organization, and had learned so much. He knew that Los Angeles would be a much less friendly and supportive environment. Although he had some contacts and prospects there, he did not have a job. "It was a *big* professional risk, learning another kind of filmmaking, maneuvering in that tough town." In addition, the move to California would mean uprooting his family again. Rosa was pregnant with their second child; she and Orlando were feeling the fragility of their relationship and worrying about their family's future. In their six-week trip to the Dominican Republic, they struggled with defining the next bold steps in their lives: they would recommit themselves to the marriage, have their baby, and move to Los Angeles.

Los Angeles turned out to be a "real hustle." "I was freelancing all the time," says Orlando, "and I was hustling *with a family* with two tiny kids, living in a dinky apartment... going through the cattle calls... experiencing the racism in hiring—You know, it's all right to be an electrician, but if you're black in Hollywood, they don't see you as a director." But Orlando energetically pursued the openings, followed up leads, was aggressive in making contacts, and managed to find some interesting and challenging work. He hooked up with Topper Carew, whom he had worked with years before at WGBH in Boston. Carew started a company that was developing children's programming, musicals, and dramatic series, and Bagwell worked on several of his projects. Later on, he became the cameraman for the *Portrait of America* series. Even though there were some dry periods, one thing usually led to another. Just when he was beginning to feel discouraged about the meager work or despondent about feeding his family, something would break and he would be drawn into a new project. "It was another side of filmmaking... I was working with *dramatic* films. I would move up from electrician to cameraman... I got to work with named directors like Larry Elikman and Ivan Dixon... It was good work. Exciting work."

For years Orlando had yearned to own his own camera but had never been able to afford one. As his reputation as a cameraman grew, he became increasingly convinced that it would make a "huge difference" in the scope of his work and his choices. "A big *turning point* came when I bought my camera and rig," he says. It was a 16 mm camera that cost thirty thousand dollars. With the help of his mother he was able to secure a loan. "Actually, it was awful. It turned out to be a total rip-off, huge interest payments... But ultimately I was successful. I didn't lose my shirt."

He was now hitting his stride in L.A., shooting full-length films, making documentaries and dramatic series, getting enough work to keep his family fed, and enough "interesting work" to keep his spirit fed. He was surprised, one morning, to receive a call from Henry Hampton in Boston, and "stunned" by what Henry said. "I thought Henry might be calling to ask me to be a cameraman on something... But he was saying that he wanted me to be a director *and* producer on *Eyes on the Prize.*" When Orlando hung up the phone, he sat there very still. He was both intrigued by Henry's stunning offer and very apprehensive about it. He had deep respect for Henry and Blackside and was "captivated" by the ideas and energy behind the project. But he felt so far away from the rarified and serious world of historical documentaries. "I was at that time more or less brain-dead. I wasn't into critical thinking, not ready to engage in historical interpretation... I felt intimidated by the people I would be working with. I thought of the others as more intellectually prepared. I have good instincts, and I'm confident about them. But the headiness of this scared me."

But the more he thought about Henry's offer, the more he knew that he didn't want to pass up the opportunity. The challenge was not something that he could turn away from. Leaving his family for several months in L.A., Bagwell came to Boston to work on *Eyes.* It was total immersion. He shared an apartment with another filmmaker, in the same building as Blackside, and worked all the time, never far away from the work or his colleagues. He struggled with making the transition from L.A. to Boston. "The first four or five months were very hard," he says, shaking his head. "It was hard for me to *articulate* my vision. I felt a doubt in me and felt people doubting me." But things started to change when he actually began to make the film. When he moved from thinking and conceptualizing to filming and shaping the work, Orlando felt his strengths come forward. "When people saw me actually *constructing* the film—making the rough cut—people saw I really got it."

"The most difficult stage in film," claims Orlando, "is taking the raw materials and structuring them so they play as dramatic storytelling. It is so time intensive, and I'm not the most patient person." He is at this point in making the Malcolm X piece, and the moment feels treacherous yet full of possibility. He always feels confident as he goes out to shoot the footage or do the interviews. "I'm very good at gathering raw materials. I have a good conceptual mind. I can translate what is in my head onto the screen and make it work."

But once the raw material has been gathered, the work becomes daunting. His eyes are blazing as he talks about the challenge. "Filmmaking is like going into never-never land. This is a frightening, tortuous moment... You feel vulnerable." This fragile, scary moment comes with every film. But it has lessened as Orlando becomes more experienced. And he has become more patient. He begins to anticipate, even relish, the anxiety. "The more times you see your way through, the more comfortable you are in the *dark*. You begin to find this a journey you enjoy. It is full of problem solving. You are confronting each problem, large or small, and you are finding challenges in that."

I ask Orlando for an example of problem solving. He lets his head fall into the table in mock distress. As he's laboring on the Malcolm X film he is facing so many problems every day, every hour, how can I ask him to choose one? "How do you decide what to keep and what to get rid of—that's a *massive* decision... Or you find you have an element that is essential to the story, but you can't discover where it is... Or there is a difference of opinion about an important idea." In both *Eyes on the Prize* and the Malcolm X film (titled *Make It Plain*, after one of Malcolm's favorite refrains) Bagwell is both producer and director. As the director he emphasizes the importance of process—the constant dialogue, the often difficult debate, the sometimes fractious fighting. But he also makes a critical distinction: "Films are *collaborative* but *not* democratic enterprises... You want input, but decisions have to be made. You've got to move, make progress. Ultimately, it is the *director's* vision."

"How do you move from the collaborative process to the decision-making mode?" I ask. "Well, I get all this input from the coproducer, the associate producer, the researcher, the editor... We each talk about our likes and our dislikes, but no matter how passionately we feel, we all know that everything we want can't make it into the film. After a lot of debate, I close my door and make the next cut. Then we look at it again... more discussion and fighting... You try to stay open to suggestions, but you are always asking, How does this story maintain coherence, clarity, and focus? What fits? What's a distraction? Can I afford to take this turn away from the central theme?" Bagwell believes that this restraint, this commitment to focus, is particularly important in film because the "logic line is very narrow." Unlike writing a book, where he believes there is more time and more space to pursue detours away from the main story, "in film there is not much room to deviate. There is so much short-hand. You are always aware that you can't tell the whole thing. It would be too confusing, too complicated."

He offers an example of this need for restraint from his current work on *Make It Plain:* "There are two powerful pieces in this film. First, Malcolm and his ideas. This is the most fundamental. It's the whole reason we're making it. The second is the internal drama of his tragic ending. This is an incredibly gripping story. But you can lose Malcolm if you focus on his murder too much. Then, of course, there is the context—the personal context of his family, his roots, his experience and the historical, political context of a changing America... changing on a lot of difficult levels... These are all important, all compelling, but you have to keep your focus on Malcolm and his essence." I can't resist saying, "You've got to keep your 'eyes on the prize.'" "Yes," he responds without smiling.

Orlando looks as if he is feeling burdened by the heavy respon-sibility and tough challenges. A couple of hours earlier he walked in the door exclaiming about the beautiful, evocative interview tapes he had been screening the day before, the power of the mate-rial they had gathered for the Malcolm film. He also lamented the loss he felt in having to exclude some of the most "provocative and exciting stuff." But mostly he talked about the way the film was revealing new and difficult truths. "The tapes," he said, "are capti-vating, *dark*, disturbing, complex. In so many ways, his death speaks to the worst in us... We killed him." Now he is painfully aware of how hard it will be to speak the truth, and how hard it will be for the audience to hear and absorb it. He knows he will find himself in the middle of angry controversy. "We have such a need to rewrite our history... but I feel a responsibility to tell the truth as I see it... After all, people have given me their stories, trusted me to tell them... It is not so much the truth that they've offered, but some-thing more precious, their experience, their perspectives."

I listen, feeling totally identified with his searching, his anguish, and his determination to portray authentically the experience of those who have told him their stories. I too want to capture his experience, to live up to the trust he has bestowed on me. I feel that we are in a wall of mirrors; our reflections both distort and reveal. He seems to be reading my mind. "You can't be tentative in this work. You can't be awed by people. You must maintain your own clarity and stability. You must be honest, direct, up-front."

He lets out a long sigh then speaks about the hard-earned maturity that gives him the courage to "make it plain." "I'm glad I'm making this film now. Ten years ago I couldn't have done it. Now I'm much more comfortable with the tools, much more confident about who I am and what I believe... Before, the expectations and pressures would have consumed and paralyzed me. Now I have the maturity to better handle the material and the pressures. Now I like what I do more!"

Another Piece of
Your Heart Grows

It is a cold day in late November, the kind of day that forecasts winter. When Orlando Bagwell arrives at my door bundled up in a bright red parka, leather gloves, scarf, and baseball cap, I feel the seasons rushing by. This is our last session, and the summer day that warmed our first interview seems far away. I remember Orlando looking golden brown in the sun, in his cotton shirt and slacks. I remember sitting outside on our deck sipping fruit juice as we talked, surrounded by magenta and orange impatiens and red geraniums. Now we huddle in my kitchen gulping hot French Roast coffee. The several months of our work seem much longer, with more life passages than calendar seasons. We have covered so much ground. Orlando has brought the same kind of intensity and focus to our exchanges that he brings to the other things he cares about in his life, "jamming" in forty-one years of living.

Today he has brought along three family albums. Like most family albums, the early pictures are more plentiful than the later ones. There are pages and pages filled with Orlando and Rosa's wedding fifteen years ago; many photographs of Rosa's pregnancy (at six months, eight months, two weeks before, a week before, the day before); and dozens of beautiful shots of Jaffar's birth. But like most parents, this photographer-father has not been nearly so vigilant in recording the developmental changes of his children or the family rituals and events in recent years. There is one photograph taken last year of extended family and friends around the Thanksgiving table in the Bagwells' Brookline home; a few birthday party pictures; several photos of various gatherings of Rosa's family in Puerto Rico, the Dominican Republic, and New York and of the Bagwell clan in New Hampshire, Boston, and southern California. There is only one photograph from Orlando's childhood. It is a faded black-

and-white baby picture. He looks about eighteen months old and is sitting in a stroller and dressed up in a coat and hat. I stare at the tiny picture for a long time and finally decide that the intensity of his baby eyes feels familiar. I am not sure I would ever recognize the features forty years later, but I have convinced myself that I would know Orlando's direct and powerful eyes anywhere. As he walks me through the albums, Bagwell admits that his career as cameraman has not benefited his family picture taking. "If I'm standing behind the lens all day taking photographs, that is the last thing I want to do when I get home. By now I've resorted to using an instamatic."

None of the photographs surprises me. I am amazed at how the images of these people, which I have been carrying around in my head for months, match the pictures in the albums. As a young bride of twenty-five, Rosa is radiant. She is wearing a sleeveless white cotton dress, which hangs from thin straps over her small frame and barely swelling belly. She is five months pregnant. Her large Afro is beautifully decorated with baby's breath flowers that she has spray painted in a variety of colors and then stuck in all over her hair, creating a delicate crown. I look at a close-up of Rosa's brown face and quiet smile, surrounded by this halo of rainbow color, and can understand why Orlando fell in love with her. Both the bride and the groom look very young as they hold trays of elaborate food offerings and a large silver chalice; these are pieces of the wedding ceremony that they invented. They are surrounded by young men with large Afros and fancy dashikis and women dressed in a variety of costumes, from traditional silk dresses to African wraps. It all looks wonderfully homespun—mid-seventies quasi-political chic. I can almost hear the declarations of love and intimacy in the bold, black Pan-African celebration. I can feel the jazz beats of Coltrane and Miles. I can taste the rice and beans, the fried plantains, the big bowls of fruit.

Finally, I get to see Orlando's "precious" siblings in the "official" family photograph taken following the ceremony. Only his younger brother Brian is missing from the large and colorful group of grandparents, parents, and children. (Brian is the one taking the picture.)

Orlando's mother has come East from California, and his father has driven down from New Hampshire. Donald Sr. and Barbara stand side by side with the kind of ceremonial grace that estranged parents can sometimes manage at their children's weddings. And there is older sister Janesta (Orlando's "best friend") in a bright red-orange dress. Her face radiates the kind of luminous beauty that I had pictured in my mind. Rosa's father has flown up from Puerto Rico, and her godmother is standing in for Rosa's mother. I ask why Rosa's mother is not present and seem to touch a still tender place in Orlando. He shakes his head slowly, "She is a very religious person. She was against our getting married... She didn't know me... She was angry that Rosa was pregnant... She probably thought that I was taking advantage of her daughter."

Over the years, Rosa's mother has accepted the marriage and has grown to love her grandchildren with all her heart. But she still feels that she doesn't really know her son-in-law; a wariness and distance lingers between them. And this Thanksgiving, less than a week away, will be the first time the grandmothers will meet. Rosa's mother, who has been visiting family in New York, and Barbara, who will fly in from Los Angeles, will gather for a big feast around Rosa and Orlando's table. "Do you think they will get along well?" I ask, sensing Orlando's anxiety about the long-awaited meeting. "I don't know," he smiles. "They won't be able to talk to each other. Rosa's mother speaks only Spanish... and my mom only English... so we'll see how it all works out."

~

When Orlando met Rosa, he was twenty-six and she was twenty-five. Rosa, who is a black Dominican, had come to Boston from Puerto Rico hoping to do graduate study in social work and get a job to support herself while she was pursuing her studies. Her plan was to come north for a couple of years and return to the Dominican Republic to live and work. When they met, Orlando had just received the grant from the American Film Institute, had enrolled in graduate school at Boston University, was doing freelance work at WGBH, and was beginning to feel that his life had "focus and direction." Although his work life was full and productive, he could feel the urge building in him to start a family. "I was twenty-six," recalls Orlando, "and I believed that this was the age to do the family thing. You see, my parents had started their family at nineteen, so I felt old and wise compared to them... I thought they were young and foolish. I was worldly and mature."

Orlando was in the final stages of extracting himself from a serious relationship with another woman when he "accidentally" met Rosa at a friend's party. Still feeling shaken and vulnerable from his breakup with the other woman, the last thing Orlando wanted to do was begin another relationship. He went to the party reluctantly. "I was in a bad mood... I needed space and time to heal... I needed to clear myself... I certainly did not need the complications of another woman." He leans back and laughs—"But I managed to find a way to make it more complicated." For Orlando, it was not love at first sight, but he was immediately drawn to lovely Rosa. He experienced an unusual ease and familiarity with her. Even with their language differences, the communication was fluid. "She spoke very little English and I spoke very little Spanish, but we managed very well." Despite their apprehensions and reservations about being drawn into another serious relationship (Rosa had also recently ended a serious affair), Rosa and Orlando began to see a lot of each other. "Rosa and I got very tight very fast... It was comfortable and relaxing to be with one another... We were together a lot... day in day out. About the language differences, we were patient with one another... we had a lot going for us!" he says. His eyes light up. "Rosa is a strong, independent woman. I found her independent spirit very seductive... I had never met a woman who was so completely authentic, so *real*... There was no pretense about Rosa, no façade... I found her wonderfully available. I loved her clarity and found that very attractive."

After a couple of months of being together, Rosa discovered that she was pregnant. "We were diligent in practicing birth control," says Orlando. "But one day it didn't work." Suddenly they were forced to confront a serious decision: were they ready to become parents? "We were not talking about marriage at that point... we were trying to figure out whether we could commit ourselves to parenting." For two solid days they stayed inside their tiny apartment and talked nonstop. The conversation—in two languages—was raw, difficult, exciting. The world went on without them as they pressed toward understanding and resolution. In the midst of their marathon talk, they got a call from one of Orlando's good friends, a colleague at WGBH, who wanted to know why they had not yet arrived at his dinner party, a commitment they had made a couple of weeks earlier. They had completely forgotten about the party but decided that they would have to bow out. There was no way they could enjoy a social occasion with this heavy decision hanging over them. The next day they heard that their dinner party host ("a young Chinese guy, a wonderful cameraman, a real close friend") had been killed in a freak car accident. "It was a terrible loss," sighs Orlando. "I don't think that his death affected our decision, but we were very aware of his life being taken away." By the time they finished their long talk, they had decided to have the baby. It was a decision about which they both felt clear and comfortable. As they talked, Orlando discovered another dimension of their love. "I realized that I was with a woman who was willing to work through all of this with me. It felt very important that we could reach a conclusion *together*... We had tremendous focus. Until there was resolution, nothing else mattered." He recounts again the sequence of their decision making. "We decided we would have this baby... *then* we decided we'd get married... and we were right, very right in deciding to do both." Having decided to start a family, the young couple moved to a larger loft space and began their life together, "working, struggling, juggling, making it."

Rosa and Orlando could hardly wait for the baby to arrive. They decided to have natural childbirth so that they could both be involved in the baby's birth. They went to Lamaze classes, exercised a lot, and ate healthy foods. They chronicled the pregnancy with beautiful photographs of Rosa taken by Orlando. "We were together through it all," says Orlando about this exciting time of high anticipation. When their son Jaffar arrived, it was a transcendent experience. Orlando's voice is thick with emotion. "It was the best moment of my life!" He corrects himself. "Well, it was one of the two best moments of my life. You know, you think you know what it will be like... but there is no way to prepare for this thrill."

I cut into his rhapsody. "You mean you *enjoyed* going through natural childbirth?" I ask. He roars, "No, *having* the baby was terrible... You know, I was there through the whole thing. I sucked it up and tried to be cool, but it was real scary... Rosa was screaming at me, shrieking, crying out... saying wild stuff. I saw parts of her I'd never seen before... like seeing another piece of a person that you know you'll have to confront later on. But the *impact* of this child was the most wonderful, transforming experience I've ever had."

Orlando is quiet for a moment and his eyes fill with tears. "You know," he whispers, "as you are growing up you realize that you would put your life down for your parents... then you realize that you would do anything in the world for your brothers and sisters... But then you have a *child*, and suddenly it is not a matter of thought or consideration. There is no question about what you would do to protect this child." Orlando has both of his hands pressed to his heart. "It is like a whole other piece of your heart grows!"

After mother and baby were both sleeping soundly, Orlando left the hospital and headed home. Even though he had not slept at all the night before, he was filled with a kind of energy that would not let him rest. He found an old rocking chair, which they had bought weeks before, and began to strip the old paint off. He spent hours in feverish labor, scraping, sanding, and staining the chair until it was ready for the baby's room. "I can remember the sun coming up, the light hitting the walls... taking pictures of the baby's room... taking pictures of me in the mirror... trying to register the day... *trying to identify the whole new feeling in me.*" He stops and locks eyes with me. "There is not anything I love or care about more than my son and my daughter."

The extraordinary high of Jaffar's birth was followed by the "other new feelings of raising a child." Orlando had never felt so burdened by responsibility. "The profound realization is how dependent a child is... how much he needs you. Now you are responsible for his survival and protection... you must give your attention, devotion, time, and energy." The burdens are double-edged. "You suddenly feel trapped, confined, surrounded… This is especially true for mothers nursing the baby, but I recognized this as a father, too. There is a lovely side to all of this… moments of feeling so deeply connected." Orlando remembers the middle of the night when Jaffar always seemed to be in "his best spirits and most wide awake. I'd get him out of his crib, we'd laugh and play, then nap some… These were our private times, when we did our own kind of bonding."

Orlando's freelance work was a nice accompaniment to parenting. It was difficult for Rosa when he would go off for a few weeks on assignment, but it was always good to be able to return to full-time fathering when he was home between jobs. His time at home with Jaffar was intense, undiluted. His memories are of endless hours spent together. "When I went riding my bike, he'd be there with me… we had a wagon. We'd go everywhere, and I'd be pulling him behind me." Over the months, the young family managed to "pull it off," but Rosa and Orlando faced "rocky times." Despite Orlando's initial feelings of being "twenty-six, sophisticated, and wise," parenting made him feel raw and young. He was often overwhelmed by all that needed to be done, "stressed out" by the energy required to keep life reasonably balanced. His words come very slowly as he seems to weigh each one. "You know, child rearing is very difficult. It tends to draw you apart. I was not as mature as I had thought… and I was traveling a lot in my work. You are trying to provide for your family, be a good father, and be a lover and companion to your wife. These are not all the same. They require different kinds of energy and behavior… The last—lover and companion—can most easily be abandoned. The first two are *responsibilities*… the last is a *desire*, a want."

The "tough times" at home were magnified by the stress at work. After a couple of years of feeling energized by his work, Orlando had begun to feel "stymied" by the career options in Boston. "I began to see that Boston was not a place where I would be able to continue to grow and develop in my work." Rosa, who had been teaching school, also began to feel "unsatisfied" with her vocational choice. They could feel things unraveling. Their love for Jaffar was the pleasurable center of their growing despair. When Rosa became pregnant again, they were forced to "decide about our lives." Again, Orlando assures me that the second baby was unplanned. "Sara, we had been very diligent with birth control... we just failed." He smiles. "Our sex was always good no matter how tough our relationship was." But all of the indecision and anxiety disappeared when beautiful Cira Janesta arrived. Orlando looked at his tiny daughter and wept with relief and immense pleasure. For the second time, he could feel the sensation of his deepening love, his heart growing bigger. He also felt the heaviness of new responsibility.

Now Jaffar is fifteen years old, and Orlando figures he "will be with me for three more years." Like the double-edged emotion Orlando experienced when Jaffar was a baby, this time of adolescence has caused two reactions in Orlando. He sees his children leaving the nest and feels sad, a certain kind of abandonment. But he also knows that they must become "self-reliant and independent... they must make their own lives." And he can already taste the freedom that comes with their growing autonomy. "I will begin to live my life freely again," he smiles. "I don't yet know what that will mean to me... to me and Rosa... but I'm interested in investigating it." With the time flying by before his children will be gone, Orlando tries to savor their moments, however brief, together. "With my son, I am marginal. I catch small bits of his life. But I know there are bigger priorities in his everyday life that require his attention and devotion... But we remain good friends. He still thinks I'm cool. He's not embarrassed by me... and I *treasure* that."

His children's adolescence also offers Orlando another perspective. They keep him young and they bring him "a different worldview." When I ask for an example, Orlando struggles to find a specific instance of their contrasting perspective and then decides to describe differences in how they see, and interact with, the white world. Orlando believes that in his generation the territories held by whites and blacks were clearer and more circumscribed than they are for his children. When he was a child the boundaries between white and black provided a kind of protection and ownership for blacks. His voice is intense as he tries to get me to understand his childhood experience of racial identity. "We grew up believing that there was territory that we controlled... White people, of course, thought we were under their dominance, that they had all the power... But we had our own discussion going... we knew much more about them than they knew about us. When I was little, I would occasionally visit the home of white friends... They *never* came into my house... they never crossed into my territory. We owned our space. We shaped our conversation. This generation doesn't own it anymore... There has been a kind of popularization of black life. Before, white folks didn't even have the *vocabulary* to comment on our lives. Now they are all up in our space, in our talk." "What does this mean for your kids?" I ask. He pauses, thinking that he has already described the shifting reality. Then he begins slowly, thoughtfully, "My kids are no less aware than I was about their racial identity... but they are much less territorial about it. My kids' generation shows a much greater willingness to let the larger public into their world... and this openness informs how they will eventually organize society later on... At the same time, blacks are now much more recognized as part of the larger society... not necessarily *accepted* but *recognized.*"

Orlando uses an example to contrast his and his children's school experiences. When he was in school, in the Catholic grade school in Baltimore and in the public high school in New Hampshire, the references to black people in the curriculum were limited to pejorative caricatures. "We were the old black Joes, the heathen from Africa. But in my kids' classes they are talking about *us*... recognizing our experience as human beings... not ugly caricatures or stereotypes." His final sentences on the generational contrasts sound promising. "My kids are impatient about what they see as my rigidity... my black-white thing. They have a more dynamic, open view."

The discussion of generational contrasts leads easily into a question I have been wanting to ask, one that looks into the ways in which the socialization he received from his parents is echoed in his own parenting. He seems so attached to, and thoughtful about, both realms—his parents' and his children's, his family of orientation and his family of procreation. He speaks about his deep bonds with his siblings that continue unbroken from their childhood of powerful intimacy and solidarity. At the same time, he examines the new idioms and worldview of his own children. Both are important to him. The roots and the branches are vital to Orlando's identity and his growth. It is not surprising, then, that he has no trouble answering my question about the way his parenting is different from, and similar to, the parenting he received. He first points out the openness in both generations:

"My parents never made apologies, never hid from us, never tried to mask their strengths and weaknesses... There was no hypocrisy... Our house was *clear*, honest. I've tried to be that way with my own children... If I need space, if I'm not feeling well, if Rosa and I are having a problem... they know it. I want to say to them, 'Family is *this*—open, honest, unmasked, clear... You can always be yourself here. You can always express yourself truthfully.'"

This honesty, not always easy, was bolstered by love. "I always felt my parents *loved* me. They had their own way of showing that, letting me know—not through gifts (we rarely got gifts except at Christmas)—but through their actions... I don't remember hearing my father say, 'I love you,' but I always knew he did. I remember my mother giving kisses and hugs, being all affectionate and actually saying the words. With my own kids, I let them know I love them... all the time. I speak it... I act it."

When he comes to discussing the way each generation deals with anger, he emphasizes the differences. "Oftentimes my parents—with all of the stress and strain in their own lives—took it out on us. I work very hard at not letting that happen with my own kids. I let them know about my problems, but I try not to let them become the brunt of them. I never liked being struck as a kid. I hated being hit... It did something irreparable... It is a hurt you can't get past... It has something to do with losing respect for your parents... It erodes self-respect, as well. I'd *never* hit my kids."

Orlando pauses then tries to explain another difference between his upbringing and that of his children. "It may sound a little strange to say this, but I wanted my kids to be much more comfortable with their sexuality than we were. When they were young, I wanted them, for example, to be comfortable with their nudity and our nudity... I wanted them to know that we could have conversations about sexuality *anytime*... We can talk about it at dinner... It does not require a special conversation. My parents *never* talked to me about sexuality. It was always a clumsy, secretive topic."

One element of Orlando's childhood that has proven difficult to maintain is ritual events. "In my family growing up, there were more ritual events to look forward to, to bind us together... Like Sunday dinner at our house—the seven of us sitting around the dinner table for hours. My parents would always encourage debates and discussions. It was always lively, vigorous, fun. I always hoped it would last forever. Maintaining some of those old family rituals is difficult... In some ways the thread has gotten weaker." But he brightens as he recognizes the ways that he, Rosa, and the children have "invented new rituals." Each December, for example, they get together with a group of their close friends for a Kwanza celebration. "It is such a great occasion. All the kids love it... They stand up and give these wonderful speeches—real inspiring, real hopeful."

Some of the difficulty with sustaining ritual has to do with the complexity and subtlety of merging two cultures. It is hard enough when husband and wife each bring the traditions of their family of origin to the newly created family. But when the partners come from different cultural backgrounds, the complexity is magnified, a factor that Orlando and Rosa have only recently begun to appreciate fully. "When we got married," says Orlando, "I never recognized how difficult it would be to meld two cultures. I never understood the impact on the relationship." He seems to be searching for the right word. He says finally, "There is a certain *imbalance* there. You know, when Rosa came to Boston, she expected to stay two or three years... She's been here for fifteen years. She has, on purpose, never become an American citizen, and she misses her family. One of the reasons we moved back East is so it would be easier for Rosa to see her family. She goes back three or four times a year." He speaks about an obviously tender sign of "imbalance." "I've never really learned her language well." He traces the long arc of marital commitment and his voice grows even softer. "You don't want to feel indebted in a relationship... When do we reconcile the imbalance?... That is another one of those mysteries out there."

Both Orlando and Rosa are pleased with the ways that both of their children have begun to embrace both cultures; both children are completely fluent in Spanish and English. When they were vacationing in the Dominican Republic this past summer, Orlando and Rosa watched their children's growing understanding of, and identification with, their Dominican roots. The children were curious about their origins, eager to get to know Rosa's family better, comfortable with the cultural rhythms and idioms. They were making the translations with fluency and openness, and their parents were greatly heartened.

There are so many ways that Orlando sees the promise in his children's futures. It is not only that they are able to integrate their multicultural roots with finesse and versatility. It is not only that they have a more "dynamic and open" approach to black-white relationships or that they are at ease in walking across a larger social and cultural landscape. Their promise also lies outside themselves, in the way young African-Americans are regarded in our society today and in the echo of these more positive perceptions in the way they see themselves.

I have never heard Orlando's voice sound more exuberant or more certain. He is crowing. He is singing a song for his children. "There is nothing more *dynamic*, more *powerful*, more *exciting* than young, smart, attractive black people... *They* are the most exciting thing in America. When we're happening it's amazing, and our kids are happening... They are open-minded, loving, and compassionate. African-Americans have always had to confront issues with such complexity because of our relationship to this society... It means that we have taught our children this complexity, this versatility, this resourcefulness... They have the potential for having *beautiful* lives." This is such a sweet song, so pure, so clear in its hopefulness. We both let the uncommon clarity linger for as long as we dare. And then Orlando, though not wanting to spoil the lovely mood, offers two quick caveats. "Of course, you can never predict the emotional

side of things... but if they are spared the trauma, if they are fortunate like I was, their lives will be great." He shakes his head, "And,
of course, my son will have to live with the fact that he will inevitably be seen as a threatening black creature... He will be vulnerable
to the fears and prejudices and ignorance all around us."

As we talk, we realize that we have covered the trauma, the
pain, the vulnerability so many times before. It is part of our black
legacy, part of our litany. It must be remembered and retold, but it
need not consume us. We can live with both the pain and the
beauty, the rage and the hope. For us, they are inextricably joined.
Orlando can feel both. He can testify to both as he offers a final
upbeat chorus. "My kids will grow up to be the kind of African-
Americans that society will love to embrace!"

GIVING FORWARD

Cheryle Wills often refers to the obligation and responsibility that come with having lived a life of privilege. The nourishment of a loving family and good friends "are gifts you can never give back... all I can do is give forward... I memorialize my forebears by giving of myself." Cheryle's parents, the Andersons, who lived a comfortable and elegant existence, came from families who had been middle-class in the Negro community for generations. Her mother came from a long line of dignified women who carried their beauty and status like "royalty." They were proud of their blackness. As Cheryle puts it, "We are arrogant about being black." Not only did this black arrogance challenge white entitlement, it also signaled their deep identification with the black community, even when their education, status, and light skin gave them access to the white world. This lineage brought with it a sense of noblesse oblige. Because Cheryle's forebears had been blessed with a secure and plentiful life, they felt obliged to give much back to the community. Cheryle frequently paraphrases the Bible passage "to those to whom much has been given, much is expected" as she talks about her maternal great-uncle having started the first NAACP in Jefferson City, Missouri, and her parents always working to "feed the hungry and clothe the poor."

But it was a member of her second husband's family who served as Cheryle's most powerful symbol of "giving forward." Senior—the man who named Cheryle Duchess because of the royalty he saw in her—became her most influential mentor. Also coming from a very prominent light-skinned family in Cleveland, Senior ("who could have passed for white, but never did") stood on the boundary between the black and white worlds. He was "the one" black person chosen by the white folks—the one who had "access to white conversation," the one whom they respected and trusted. The white establishment would go to Senior when they needed something from the black community, or when they wanted to assuage their guilt, or when they needed someone to make the cultural translations or interpret the black political scene. As Katie Cannon would say, the whites in Cleveland made Senior an "honorary white person," a role he accepted only because he knew someone had to play it if the black community was going to survive. Senior's access to the white power brokers provided critical information and resources to the city's black folks.

A powerful leader, Senior built a funeral home into "Cleveland's most beloved institution." The House of Wills was a place of refuge for those journeyers from the Deep South who needed to establish their identities and plant new roots. It was the first place blacks would come for help when the city stopped picking up their garbage or their electricity got turned off. The building itself was an ornate architectural masterpiece that offered high tea, music, and culture free to people whom the downtown hotels refused to serve. It was a generous place of employment where, "if they hung around long enough," young men could find a job, get trained, and build a long career. And it was a thriving, innovative business that made the Wills family prosperous and powerful. Cheryle studied Senior's genius—the way he combined social service and entrepreneurship, the way he mixed high style with basic needs, the way he connected art and politics. His fluency in making the translations across racial lines and his dexterity in joining business and altruism became etched in Cheryle's mind and heart, and became central to the way she chose to live out her own version of noblesse oblige.

Even in the early months of working in the funeral home Cheryle experienced the opportunity to "give forward." Her office, on the first floor just as one came in the front door, was the first place people would arrive when they were seeking help. She remembers the parade of poor folks—many of them illiterate, many of them recent migrants from the rural South—who walked through the doors. Cheryle recalls their dignity and their hopefulness despite the despair and poverty that filled their lives. "This was the first time I'd actually known black folks, poor black folks, and I was amazed by their dignity and optimism." Many who came to her office would have no birth certificate, no Social Security number, no identity, and Cheryle would patiently help them patch together the meager remnants of their desolate history. Then she would fill out the appropriate forms and negotiate the bureaucratic mazes until their identities were legally assured. This was all done without fee ("Senior better not hear that any of us charged folks for these services"). The effort of completing the correct forms and making a few telephone calls for these people was more than paid for by "their undying gratitude." "They would say to me," recalls Cheryle, "'You've given me back my whole life.'" In that moment, the twenty-three-year-old Duchess felt the deepest satisfaction, the chance to balance the scales between her privilege and their needs, fulfilling some of the duties of her fortunate station.

Working at the House of Wills, Cheryle began to see the funeral home as a unique institution where service to the community could be embroidered into elegant rituals and cultural legacy. Senior had seen this potential as he built his business. He knew that for black folks, whose time on earth was so often filled with humiliation and struggle, the funeral might be their first moment of honor. Their unswerving faith in God's heavenly kingdom, as a place of final peace and liberation, gave them strength to battle earthly oppression. They could look forward to spreading their wings and "flying all over God's heaven." The funeral ritual marked a beautiful and dignified passage to the "other life," and Senior understood and respected its significance. For all of his clients, rich and poor, he offered an elegant send-off with silk-lined coffins, gleaming black Cadillacs, and elaborately prepared bodies. Families who had scrimped and saved for years would spend their hard-earned dollars for an extravagant funeral. "*Finally*, Mama was getting what she deserved."

Cheryle watched and learned the funeral business from Senior, seeing the ways Senior responded to the cultural, aesthetic, and psychic needs of black folks through this final rite of passage. This was part of the Wills family's way of giving forward. For black people who had been "shackled" and dehumanized all of their lives, the funeral celebration offered "full humanity" with style, respect, and beauty.

The funeral rituals also expressed a rich cultural legacy. Cheryle traces the African roots reflected in the metaphors, style, and music of funerals. "Funerals are the closest link we have to our African ancestry. The embalming process grew out of an Egyptian cultural tradition... The funeral hymns speak about the rivers winding through the fertile ground... The humming and moaning of our deep grief is like the African chants. If you listen to the African tribal music, you hear the connections to the New Orleans jazz funeral experience—the same phraseology, the same tempo, the same emotion." As their loved ones departed this earth, African-Americans could celebrate the African heritage that had survived brutal dislocation, enslavement, and oppression.

The early lessons learned from her own family, who felt the responsibilities of their privilege and gave generously to the less fortunate, combined with Senior's devoted mentoring, made a deep imprint on Cheryle. As a woman in her mid-twenties, new to the small midwestern city of Cleveland, she saw the chance to make a significant impact. "It was the late sixties... I was young, gifted, and black," she recalls. "I was at the right place at the right time." Cheryle had ambition, glamour, and youthful energy that sizzled in the climate of Cleveland's rising black power.

Using the House of Wills as her base, Cheryle moved out into the city and began to learn the ropes of public service, institution building, and political discourse by sitting on the boards of libraries, civic groups, and social service agencies. She found that, although she was new to this kind of work and had a great deal to learn, she had a special talent for the decorum and negotiations found in boardrooms, talents socialized in her childhood from when her family gathered around the dining room table each evening. She also found that she was adept at playing the role that Senior managed so gracefully, the role of translator and facilitator between the black and white communities. Not surprisingly, she, too, was "the one chosen" by the white power brokers. She, too, walked the treacherous boundary between identification with blacks and co-optation by whites.

Wills gave a great deal of her time, energy, and resources to community projects, and her efforts were heralded and deeply appreciated. But there was also an edge of skepticism expressed by some blacks who saw her privilege and pedigree and questioned the depth of her commitment, prodding her to do more. Even now the voices of some of her favorite "sisters and brothers in the struggle" echo through her and urge her to greater activism and advocacy. She hears the challenge from Minnie Player, her colleague on the United Way board scolding her for "half stepping," and begging her to give more fully. And she is haunted by an earlier admonition from the protective brother with whom she shared a jail cell during her Civil Rights days in Nashville, who urged her to "be somebody." He was pleading with her to be a good sister, and in doing so set a standard—of responsibility and accountability—by which Cheryle would measure her actions for the rest of her life. Now as she works at joining altruistic volunteer work with lucrative capitalism, she feels the loving and critical scrutiny of these powerful influences. Their voices challenge her to "tithe" a percentage of her entrepreneurial exploits, to be authentic in her service. In their eyes she feels herself "half stepping" and resolves to be more focused and more disciplined in her work.

Central to Cheryle's success is her talent for "seizing the opportunity." On several occasions, she tells me forcefully that "our generation was the first to have the opportunity, not the first to have the ability," and she claims that she is an "ordinary" person who has had "extraordinary" good fortune. She is also deeply suspicious of tokenism, being the one black and/or the one woman sitting at the board table. She refuses to see her seat at the table as a sign of singular achievement or even as evidence of progress. Instead she measures her success by the number of places she manages to open for the African-Americans who follow her. If she uses her talents wisely, she will create access for more "brothers and sisters," the complexion of the board room will change, and the institution may begin to shift its agenda and priorities.

Cheryle also feels heavy responsibilities growing out of her special personal endowment, her "sixth sense" that allows her to see into the future, anticipate danger, and make spiritual connections. Since the age of five, when she "knew" that one day she would be a drum majorette, Cheryle has harbored "premonitions of things to come." In this, she places herself in the company of two powerful men—Jesse Jackson and Carl Stokes ("We are God-blessed")—and believes that she must capitalize on these psychic capacities in giving forward to the community.

These psychic sensibilities are also linked to Cheryle's hopes for achieving "a powerful synthesis" in her life, a balance between her public and private lives. For Cheryle, success and achievement in the public sphere have come relatively easily. In the depth and vulnerability of intimate relationships she has always found a larger challenge. "My boys and myself... that is the constant," says Cheryle in describing a private life that has often been turbulent and fraught with pain. There is nothing that she wouldn't do for her sons; they are the impulse for her giving forward. But in being a "good enough" mother to her children, she has composed a life in which her style of mothering her sons contrasts in certain striking ways with the mothering she received. Like her mother, Cheryle was a vigilant advocate for her sons' education. When her children were in elementary school, she always took on the role of "classroom mom"—organizing class trips, running bake sales, and giving parties for the teachers. Like her mother, she knew that children thrived when parents and teachers shared values and were mutually supportive of one another's efforts. But unlike her mother—who gave all of her "boundless energy" to the care and nurturance of her family, who "didn't even have her own Social Security number," who was married to the same man for fifty years, and who was "the last of the great homemakers"—Cheryle was constantly working and rarely home when her boys returned from school. She usually returned home late in the evening after the boys were in bed, after a long day that included business meetings, political gatherings, social events, and her work at the House of Wills. Her sons, now grown, express pride in their mother's public commitments but tease Cheryle about the generational contrasts. They admire the "big healthy plants" that thrive in their grandmother's care and chide their mother for "killing even her artificial plants." In her giving forward, Cheryle knows that both her effectiveness and enjoyment will be enhanced when she can balance the private and public realms.

During the past year, Cheryle has felt an impatience stirring within her. She feels a readiness for change and growth. She is weary of "being in escrow," frustrated by her own lack of focus and discipline. Her friends and colleagues see all that she has accomplished and judge her to be a productive, talented, and ambitious person. But she knows that she could do so much more. If she put her mind to it, made full use of her spiritual insights, and became more determined in her focus, she could make a bigger contribution. Middle age marks a transitional moment, a time of self-scrutiny and preparation. "I expect to come into my own at fifty!" crows Cheryle.

In the years ahead, Cheryle wants to help create a kind of capitalism designed to support community development and social change. She believes that black business leaders must become much more strategic and entrepreneurial in raising capital and in developing and distributing resources. She is frustrated by the rhetoric of some who sulk about the community's impotence but do little to build initiative and self-sufficiency. She wants to seize the moment to build capital (both personal and collective) and to work toward new definitions of black power that include politics *and* money. This will require loyalty, leadership, and altruism, especially from those of us who are most privileged.

Cheryle's determined activism bridges her vocation and her volunteer work. Her strong rhetoric is matched by time and money. Her investments in radio franchises and cable television stations offer black communities more access to the airwaves, increasing the opportunities for expression, communication, and solidarity. "I am the voice of the NAACP, the Urban League," claims Cheryle. "I am you." Her tireless efforts on behalf of political candidates have increased their visibility and added to their coffers. Over the years she has been the treasurer for Carl Stokes's mayoral campaigns in

Cleveland, the strategist for Jesse Jackson's presidential bid, and more recently a key fundraiser for Carol Moseley-Braun of Illinois, the first black woman U.S. Senator. Cheryle sits on the national boards of the United Way, Big Brothers and Big Sisters, and several other social welfare organizations that are concerned with the education of children and the support of families. "I believe in tithing in life," she says adamantly. "You make yourself visible through good works."

~

Just as Cheryle, through her entrepreneurial pursuits, shapes a vision of a reconstructed and revitalized black community, so Orlando, through his documentary film work, shows us new angles on our collective past. Both are searching for ways to reenvision our place on the cultural and political landscape: Cheryle through the building of power and capital, and Orlando through the creation of powerful alternative images. Both believe not only in the black community's capacity but in our readiness to hear the truth. Orlando has chosen documentary films as a vehicle for uncovering the truths about our past. He knows the historical story is not pure, simple, or easy to see and hear. There is no single interpretation of the facts, no one truth. Unlike feature films, which are driven by the demands of the market and shaped around a single dramatic theme, documentaries allow him to tell a much more complicated, nuanced story. Orlando resists the "black and white" and searches for the shades of gray that stretch in between. Documentaries that challenge and inform are Orlando's medium for giving forward.

Even as a young child, Orlando searched for a way to make a difference. He says plainly, "I was the third child in my family... I had to show I was present." Early on, he felt the urge to make his mark, to make his presence felt. Orlando was the child who watched closely and listened carefully. "I was the kid who was always listening in on adult conversation," he recalls. His memories are rich in detail, both the visual experience *and* the feeling. He sees his father sitting in the corner in the "phone chair" (actually an old wooden school chair that had the writing desk attached to one arm), his body slumped in weariness, sadness, and embarrassment after the whole car full of flowers he was delivering for a florist at Christmas time was spoiled after the car broke down. He hears his dad's pained explanation of how that meant the children should not expect to receive any Christmas presents that year. He sees his father's tears and the children's efforts to comfort him. "Please, Dad, we'll be all right. Just don't cry!" In the same way, Orlando can still feel his mother's pain when his father one day suddenly disappeared. "It was the first time I saw my mother looking old." He can hear the neighbor's gossip in the front room. "They were telling stories about no-good colored men leaving their wife and kids." He can feel the pull between his wish to defend his father's honor and his need to offer his mother protection and solace.

When he bought his first "hot" camera more than a decade later, Orlando discovered his special talent for recording "human relationships." Almost immediately, he realized that he had an unusual capacity for discerning the subtle interactions, capturing the feelings and framing the scene. He saw things others missed. He learned very quickly—immersing himself in the medium; shooting hundreds of roles of film, spending endless hours in the darkroom; relishing the whole process as well as the product. Orlando's goal was not to make pretty pictures. From the beginning his filmmaking was linked to the recording of social processes and devoted to helping others tell their own stories. His first efforts in still photography, film, and video were quickly integrated into his work with kids at the community center where he worked in the South End of Boston. The youngsters became the subjects of his portraits, and he taught them how to produce their own work, to create their own documentaries about their lives in the city. Their work was rough and simple, but it gave them new powers, new opportunities to shape their reality and tell their versions of the truth. Orlando's early film about "the coming of age" of one of the boys from the community (which won him a grant from the American Film Institute) merged art and social commentary. Its power lay in its raw simplicity, its clear vision.

Orlando brought the same passion to filmmaking as he did to his quick immersion in photography. When he started film school at Boston University, his first short, on the drug addiction of his roommate, was moving but crude and undisciplined. Compared to his classmates' "oratory," his footage was "baby talk"—potent words but no sentences or paragraphs. He worked hard, but sometimes he found that his vision was too ambitious for the craft he had developed. Now, as a mature filmmaker with twenty years of experience, he has full command of the medium. From this firm base, he can now explore more risky material and can tolerate—even enjoy—the dark moments of uncertainty and vulnerability that are a vital part of the creative process. As he labors on the Malcolm X film *Make It Plain* he speaks about the journey through "never-never land," moving from the "raw material to dramatic storytelling." It is a tortuous, intense moment, the moment of greatest "creative challenge."

As I listen to Orlando speak about his vision and his films, I can't help thinking that his reconstruction of black history, his retelling of a more authentic story, is not just a general way of giving forward; it is a gift he is creating for his own children. While they are for a broad public, his works are also deeply personal offerings. Over and over again he tells me that his children are the most important thing in his life, that when they were born it was "like another piece grew on my heart." His devotion to his children's future strengthens his determination to tell probing and truthful stories about the world they inhabit. Orlando vividly recalls the pejorative "colored" caricatures from his school days at Blessed Sacrament in Baltimore. He remembers the teacher who led his class in singing "Old Black Joe" and spoke unself-consciously about "darkies." He can still feel the jeers and laughter of his white classmates. Orlando sees changes and improvements in the experiences his son and daughter are having in school. Some of their teachers use materials and methods that challenge old stereotypes and provide richer and more complex interpretations of history. He reports that his children are "impatient" with his "black-white thing." They are "well aware of the racism" that still poisons our society, but they have a more fluid view of racial identity and social reality.

As his children grow more sophisticated, Orlando's work

matures as well; his family and his craft are both growing. His two newest works, still on the drawing board, cover a broader historic landscape than his earlier films. The first, on the Great Depression, and the second, on the War on Poverty, are not explicitly focused on black figures or black lives. The films frame a larger reality, one that includes the special victimization of blacks during the depression era and the critical roles blacks played in the struggle for justice and equality. But the films neither aggrandize nor diminish the African-American place in the overall historical journey. Orlando's search for authenticity, for a valid rendering of a painful past, is his way of giving forward. As a perceptive young child, he saw both his parents' joy and their anguish, and now in his films he neither exaggerates the historic achievements nor masks the pain. In *Make It Plain*, for example, he documents Malcolm's heroism but also his vulnerability; his generosity but also his narcissism. Secure in his craft and mature in his judgment, he finds the courage to tell complex truths.

~

Like Orlando and Cheryle, all of these storytellers feel the responsibilities of their present privilege. Their gratitude to ancestors and their obligation to their children are felt by each one of them no matter how modest or abundant their parents' resources. Cheryle, whose family owned lavish homes with swimming pools, and Charles, whose family worked as migrant laborers from dawn to dusk and were often forced to be on welfare, both feel compelled to use their special capacities to give forward.

The generational contrasts can be bittersweet. Katie Cannon recalls her feelings upon receiving a graduate student fellowship from the Union Theological Seminary in New York, which amounted to much more than her sister's full-time teacher's salary in North Carolina that year, and more than both of her parents ever dreamed of making annually. How could she call home and complain that she was depressed and lonely when she had so much more than they had, when they thought she was "sitting on top of the world?" Toni Schiesler looks at her elaborate wardrobe and comfortable home and recalls the three homemade blouses that had to last the school year at St. Frances, and the night she and her mother had to spend in the train station in Philadelphia. Charles Ogletree goes out for an elegant dinner with his wife and friends and remembers that his mother was never able to treat her children to a meal in a restaurant. "Well, maybe on some special occasion we would go to some greasy spoon... maybe once a year." Or he contrasts the experience of his children, who have known black professionals—lawyers, doctors, professors, entrepreneurs—all of their lives, and his own upbringing, during which he didn't even know that black professionals "existed."

Each day there are vivid reminders of the generational contrasts that shape the ways that these storytellers construct their lives. Their lives may not have required the same kind of courage and forbearance as their ancestors who survived more lethal forms of discrimination and oppression and who were denied access to the white institutions in which their children are now employed. But their work is shaped by a resourcefulness and especially by a resistance that would have been familiar to their elders. For example, in Tony Earls's hybrid scholarship that merges science and social activism, he resists the disciplinary divisions and underscores the connections that can be drawn between the academy and the real world. Toni Schiesler has spent much of her life in quiet, determined resistance. Liberating herself from the doctrine, inhibitions, and hierarchy of the convent, she is currently negotiating the power pyramid of the Episcopal Church. In the process she has had to fight against her own needs for approval and security—needs that grew from the poverty and traumas she experienced as a young girl. Toni focuses her current work on helping other women "discover their voice," their identity and their power. In the circle of trust she creates among the women, she and they experience the connections between resistance and growth, resistance and creativity.

Charles Ogletree is steadfast in his challenges to the status quo. His tactics may have become more strategic and subtle, his rhetoric may have mellowed, and he now mostly wears suits rather than dashikis. But he has not lost any of the passion and commitment that made him a student leader at Stanford and at Harvard Law

School. At forty, he continues to fight for justice, but now his efforts are more visible and have wider scope and impact. His standard for giving forward, however, remains the same: "Is this the best way to repay my debt to the home folks?"

Like Cheryle Wills, Katie Cannon was blessed with powerful mentors. She remembers the noble black women teaching in the segregated schools in Kannapolis who were the most respected figures in town. They "insisted that *everyone* learn... and so we *all* did." They knew how to make the crucial connections with their students' families. And there was a passion in their work that extended beyond the walls of their classrooms. "They were determined to save the race," recalls Katie. These women live on in Katie's teaching, in the demands she makes on her students, and in the commitment she brings to the classroom and beyond.

Katie's Grandma Rosa offers a poignant but instructive model of giving forward. Grandma Rosa joined her spiritual life with her political activism. Katie watched her grandmother's gritty courage, the dignity that often masked the pain. Later on, Katie came to see the personal costs that were the result of Rosa's smooth exterior and gracious decorum. "She turned the rage inside her," says Katie. "Ultimately, it made her sick and killed her." As Katie carries on Grandma Rosa's legacy and honors her work, she wants to hold fast to her elder's courage and convictions. But she is determined not to "take the rage inside." For Katie, giving forward means holding fast to the "ancestral wisdom" and resisting those elements of the lineage that she finds unproductive or damaging. It means "recognizing the evil and searching for the good."

At this point in the lives of the six storytellers, there is a strong impulse to find meaningful ways to give forward. No longer so driven by ambition, they have become more interested in the quality of their commitments. Their lives are less focused on what they will acquire and more shaped by what they will leave behind. They have developed an impressive body of work, refined skills, discernment, and self-confidence. They have learned what they do best and how to use their gifts wisely and productively. At fifty, Tony Earls is ready to embark on his most ambitious work, the "performance" for which he has been rehearsing for over two and a half decades. Anticipating her fiftieth birthday, Cheryle is ready to stop "half stepping" and use her wealth, her talents, and her "God-blessed" sixth sense to give to her children and her community. Orlando is now capable of the "oratory" that eluded him in his younger years and that will make possible work that joins art and social criticism. For Katie, giving forward requires reaching back, making the difficult "translations" between her "nurturant" and "sustaining" communities. "Katie's Canon" is enriched by the courage, wit, and perceptivity nourished in the Cannon clan. For all of us, giving forward means journeying home.

Where the Rivers Join

Taking the Time to Feel

As we listen to these six life stories, we hear many currents passing through many generations. Each is like a river, carrying the ancestral wisdom, soothing and cooling old wounds, and nourishing a younger generation's thirst. These six travelers have dared to explore all the currents, all the uncertainties, knowing that in order to capture the full gifts of storytelling they will have to relive pain and risk exposure. They knew from the start that this would not be a sweet sentimental journey. It would be a rocky adventure, with its own momentum, sometimes smooth, sometimes through white water and into whirlpools.

In this final chapter, I hope to trace the common currents running through these lives and also to reflect on the actual experience of telling, and listening to, life stories. In each of the sections that follow—on storytelling itself, on the effect of relationship in the process, on race—I explore themes common to all these lives. These currents are not discrete, of course. They blend into one another. The way these protagonists, for instance, envision and compose their lives affects the way they reconstruct their stories; their map of the barriers and bridges defined by their racial identity affects the style in which they confront the personal and cultural contradictions they experience.

Throughout these narratives I am struck by the way that the central ingredients of identity are dynamic, changing. The process of growth includes the reinterpretation of core sources of identity. Throughout a life, a person may perceive and experience race or social class or gender or family or home in myriad ways. For these six people, for example, it is not only that the labels put on their race have shifted with changes in the ideological rhetoric of different historical periods—from colored to Negro to black to Afro-American to African-American. It is also that their perception of their own racial identity has also undergone transformation, reflecting personal developmental changes, changing political and cultural contexts and affiliations, and emerging reconnections with family origins. I would say that each of these storytellers has grown "blacker" as they have matured, stronger and less ambivalent in their identity as African-Americans. They have also experienced with greater force the rage that is the cumulative result of both explicit racial assaults and more hidden traumas of the oppression, exclusion, and humiliation associated with race. The storytelling reveals this profound pain and rage, and it draws the connection between reckoning with rage and opening the path to liberation and love.

Racial identity is, therefore, complex and changing, never settled. For these storytellers, there is the chance to redefine it, to explore the role of racial identity in their everyday experience, to see it as providing both connection and barrier, to examine the visibility and distortions that come with tokenism. When Katie Cannon "scrapes the white off my eyeballs," she takes the opportunity to reenvision her blackness, to see the world anew without the white filter that inhibits her clear sight. This is just one among many reinterpretations in which she has been engaged throughout her life. Like race, other sources of identity are redefined and reconstructed over a lifetime. The work these storytellers have done reveals the evolution of these self-images.

The reshaping of these core sources of identity seems to be a critical developmental task for people in their middle years. The forties and fifties can be a generative and challenging life period— a time of self-critical reflection and greater risk taking; a time of meditation and analysis; a time to become wise, not just smart. Each of these storytellers found our work to be a timely opportunity to explore loss and gain, continuity and discontinuity in their lives. Poised between generations, they experience with force the world they inherited (and what they fashioned from it) and the world they have created for their children.

Just as important as the realization of marked generational contrasts is the desire these storytellers have voiced to pause and take stock. After years of achievement and vigorous ascent, the middle years are a time of reflection and remapping. Each of these people can look back on their accumulated accomplishments and see an impressive body of work, a portfolio of life exhibits, a retrospective. But this evidence of achievement can look different when there is a chance to "take the time to feel." For those who are used to the high velocity of ambitious pursuit, the pause feels risky and difficult. It forces them to ask questions, to revise their standards and goals, and to search for more meaningful ways to spend the next decades of their lives.

Tony Earls, for instance, feels that his "real creative work is just beginning." The scholarship and research that have distinguished his professional career are "practice sessions." At forty-one, Orlando Bagwell finally feels ready to document the extraordinary life and work of Malcolm X. After twenty years of making films, his craft is developed, his self-confidence is sure. He is now ready to withstand ideological controversy, to chronicle the depth and complexity of Malcolm's mission. When Cheryle Wills chides herself for "half stepping" through her thirties and forties (despite the evidence of many achievements), she is preparing herself to use her full talents in her fifties. She sees her middle years as a time for making deeper commitments. For all of these storytellers, then, the middle years are a time of reenvisioning the future. With their hard-won maturity and wisdom, they are becoming more focused and judicious about how they will use their energies. The work on this book both draws from and contributes to yearnings that arise in us all in the middle of life.

Telling Life Stories

The storytellers in this book are working within a powerful cultural tradition. The African-American legacy of story-telling infuses these narratives and serves as a source of deep resonance between us. Our cultural and historical roots have been given expression and meaning through stories. The slave narratives, for example, were elaborate tales of survival and cunning, but they can also be read as vehicles for individual empowerment, community building, and cultural transmission. In telling the story, the narrator defined his/her full humanity. A strong and persistent African-American tradition links the process of narrative to discovering and attaining identity. A more ancient source of story-telling flows from the African continent, where stories were often embedded in tribal ritual, filled with entertainment, adventure, moral lessons, and cultural wisdom. I think of the storytellers in this volume as modern day griots, perceptive and courageous narrators of personal and cultural experience. They are working in an idiom steeped with tradition and cultural legitimacy, and, therefore, supportive of their personal revelations.

Each of these six individuals experiences storytelling as a creative process. They feel their present lives being fueled by the reconstruction of their past. Rather than trying to banish old ghosts, or escape their ancient haunts (an often typical impulse in those seeking status and advancement), these journeyers are continually strengthened by returning to the source.

Storytelling can be creative in several ways. For some, story-telling becomes a creative force (creative with a small "c") in negotiating daily life, making choices, and composing experience. But I also hear in these stories ways in which artistic expression and creativity (creativity with a large "C") fuels their work, nourishes the spirit, offers perspective, and releases rage. For Orlando Bagwell, in particular, storytelling is his life's work; it merges art and history, celebration and critique. Not only do his documentary films offer a complex reinterpretation of history, they are also works of art. His blend of imagery and commentary creates a powerful vehicle for social transformation.

Miles Davis and Thelonious Monk on Tony Earls's office wall keep alive the music in his scientific musings. These black jazz artists—"my main men"—keep Earls company in a work world dominated by rationality, empiricism, and whiteness. The Monk poster, "Straight up, no chaser," warns Earls of the dangers of compromise and distraction. He must hold fast to his own kind of scientific inquiry—one that seeks to inform and shape social policy—if he is to use his full creativity. Monk and Davis urge Earls to continue to improvise and experiment in his scientific work, to push the boundaries of knowledge just as they pushed the musical canons. When Earls describes his work in jazz metaphors, he seems to be honoring their lessons. Through music he feels a "grounding with my black brothers."

Each morning before Katie Cannon "hits the ground working," she carves out a moment for "centering" and reflection, a space for spiritual awakening. She plugs in earphones and grooves on the undiluted soul sounds of Sweet Honey in the Rock. The voices of these "powerful black sisters" give Katie a few moments of peace, and if she is lucky, linger with her as she battles her way through the day. The outrageous irreverence, rage, and lyricism of Sweet Honey in the Rock support her efforts to "claim my place in the discourse."

All these storytellers are confident and clear speakers, and they love language. For each, language is the primary mode to express feeling and thought, to organize and shape their realities. Charles Ogletree's language is organized, crisp, and lucid. He assigns specific, defined meanings to his words and uses them with precision. Without hyperbole, his style is one of deft restraint. Katie Cannon, on the other hand, uses expansive, dramatic language laced with metaphor. Her speech offers opportunities for different and multiple interpretations. Her pace is rapid-fire, urgent. The words tumble out of her mouth, sometimes getting tangled up in a slight speech impediment. She speaks with great passion, dramatizing contrasts, exaggerating, and relishing the irreverence of her imagery. Toni Schiesler, a chemist by training and a nun by early experience, uses a language that is neutral and correct, conforming to the rules of empiricism and moral rectitude. It feels measured and precise in comparison to Katie's and reportorial in contrast to Charles's.

Orlando Bagwell's language is spare and descriptive. Not surprisingly for a filmmaker, he speaks visually. He is vigilant in his observations of detail, and his stories are always told in the present tense. Orlando captures your attention and lures you into the center of the action. You are right there, in his head, behind his eyes, seeing the scene. As he relives the drama, his body moves—crouching down low as he tries to deflect the assaults of the gang of white men who jumped him in South Boston during the busing crisis; leaning back, arms outstretched, and eyes closed as he describes the soothing calm of floating in the blue-green ocean off the coast of Puerto Rico.

All of these narrators are comfortable with and respectful of the power of language as a vehicle for shaping and controlling their lives. This comfort contrasts with the unease of other prospective participants in this project for whom telling stories in words either felt cumbersome or risked undue exposure. For example, two prominent and successful visual artists—a sculptor and a printmaker who were both drawn to this project but ultimately declined to participate—seemed to fear the literal precision of language. The sculptor, who declared himself a "very private person," worried that this project would leave him "too exposed." He preferred to let his "art speak for itself." He was most comfortable speaking through his sculptures, not revealing the person behind the work. He had spent years resisting the art critics' and reporters' questions about his life, his views, his values, and his politics. He always refused to interpret his sculptures to an audience and claimed to "hate" attending his openings, where he was forced to mix with his audience and respond to their queries. He would much rather stay in his studio producing his art, avoiding public scrutiny. The printmaker, whose work is more abstract and inviting of varied interpretations, also spoke passionately about his reluctance to become a "personage" whose celebrity might become larger than his work. Although he expressed some ambivalence on this point (enjoying the long-awaited acclaim and admiration but resisting the intrusiveness and scrutiny), having to reveal his life in words made him feel naked and vulnerable.

Interestingly, both of these artists are extremely articulate. They do not fit the stereotype of an artist who is sophisticated with images but crude with language. The printmaker is an especially gifted storyteller. So I do not take the two artists' reluctance as an expression of their lack of facility with "the word." But I suspect that in some way they fear the incisiveness and specificity of language. The visual images they create allow for much more diffusion and interpretation. I also suspect that these artists may be afraid that too much talk, too much inquiry may steal away the magic and mystery of their work. In the creative act there is a passion that is irrational and inchoate. It emerges organically, mysteriously. In describing it in words, in tracing the connections between the work and the artist, an artist may risk distorting the creative process. In refusing to expose their life stories, these artists may have been trying to protect not only their privacy but their creativity.

The protagonists in this book have just the opposite reaction; they see storytelling as a creative medium. It helps them trace the connections between past and present and allows them to shape a new future of their own design. When, for example, Toni Schiesler admits to large gaps in her story—not being able to remember anything that happened in her life before age seven or eight—she recognizes that the years without remembered stories limit her ability to give shape to her present life. She yearns to recapture these early tales, somehow to break the barriers of silence, so that she can "move on with my life." She knows intuitively that recovering the early stories is central to her giving shape to new ones. The reconstruction of childhood traumas is important to the creation of adult dramas.

We hear a similar impulse in Cheryle Wills's decision to join this project. She had recently moved to Boston from Cleveland, having given up her connections, her roots, her power, her visibility in the midwestern city for a place that feels cold, unwelcoming, and pretentious. She is feeling adventurous as she faces an unknown future in Boston, but she is also feeling apprehensive and lonely. Almost immediately she embraces the idea of the project as a way to counteract the loneliness and find personal connection. It becomes her way of looking backward into the future. If she can relive her early journey, she may discover clues about how she could most productively fashion this new existence. If she can speak about those events and experiences that have been silenced in family lore, she might be able to reconstruct a fuller, richer life story that admits the pain and reckons with the rage. Cheryle wastes no time. In our first session, she explodes the silence and moves directly into the vortex of her deepest anguish. She tells the story of the brutal death of her precious brother, Eddie, and she asks the haunting and horrible questions that remain unresolved on the twenty-year anniversary of his death.

With each of these storytellers, however, there are silences that must be respected, moments when the conversation stops, when the storytellers resist, when their faces close down or they look away. These are the places I dare not tread, the points beyond which—by silent mutual agreement—I must not go. Charles Ogletree's brief, flat description of his sister Barbara's murder does not permit my entry. There is anguish underneath his lawyer-like public rendition, and I know it would be cruel to pursue it. Toni Schiesler hints at the abuse (possibly sexual abuse) of her stepfather. "He was the meanest man I ever knew... I often fantasized about picking up a knife and stabbing him." "What did he do to you?" I ask quietly. "I don't remember... but he always made me come home every day directly from school... my mother wasn't around." Her voice trails off. Her eyes fill with tears. We let the silence sit there.

When Orlando Bagwell talks about his great love for his siblings, his voice is thick with emotion. He envisions his sisters, the youngest and oldest, as having "their arms around" the three brothers in the middle. Their embrace is comforting and protective. His siblings are his confidants, his allies, his best friends. "I sometimes wish we would all die at the same time," he admits. The survivors could hardly bear to live with the grief of losing any of the other precious ones. "Now," he says theatrically, "I'm going to get mystical on you." Suddenly his voice stops. "No, I'm not going to mess with that." This time I try to push through the silence. I plead with him to continue. "No, Sara," he says adamantly. "Why?" I ask one last time. "Because it is stupid," he responds with embarrassment.

For each storyteller there are these moments of silence and resistance. Each time I must decide whether to risk opening a wound. There are also other dimensions of their life experiences that all of the storytellers are deliberately reluctant to address. These are not the traumatic places that cause silence. They are places where storytellers fear public exposure. All of them, for example, are understandably hesitant to explore in depth their intimate relationships with children and partners. They and I know that there is risk that these ongoing relationships might be distorted by probing inquiry. Cheryle Wills, for example, feels protective of her two grown sons who she expects "will come into their own at thirty," but who are still "evolving," still "half stepping." The depth of her love for them shines through. "They have been the only constant in my life," and her pain is vivid as she denounces society's abuse and violence against "our young black brothers," an abuse that even her privileged sons have not been able to escape. But the stories of their lives—their work, relationships, ambitions, failures—are only hinted at, never fully developed.

Katie Cannon, who has no children, worries that her version of her life experiences might not be the story her family wants told. She does not want to cause her family humiliation. She knows the active grapevine that winds its way through the small southern town of Kannapolis, and she knows the damage it can cause. Katie is particularly concerned about her mother, who has been bruised and confused by earlier writings by and about her daughter, and who has had to absorb all the "rage" of her home folks who did not like the way they were portrayed. Her mother asks in disbelief, "Katie, did you forget that the tape recorder was on?" "You see," says Katie, "my mom will take all the heat" from the relative whom everyone knows—but no one will admit—is an alcoholic, or from the light-skinned aunt who has always rejected and demeaned the Cannon children because of their dark skin. "I'll be safe way up here in Cambridge, but my mom will hear about it from everyone."

I understand and honor the storyteller's judgment about who and what needs to be protected from scrutiny and exposure. Very occasionally, I even choose to edit out those parts of stories that would seem potentially damaging or hurtful even though they have been offered freely and spontaneously. These moments of silence and reluctance, however, are important to the story. Their presence means that some large or significant issues may be masked or underemphasized. I suspect, for example, that the four storytellers who are parents must think and speak about their offspring much more openly and with much greater passion to their trusted friends. Their narratives probably do not reflect the intensity of love, the anguish and confusion, or the details of their parenting. Likewise, I suspect that disappointment and conflicts with partners are filtered out of the detailed descriptions. It is safer to explore ancestral roots than it is to reveal ongoing intimacies. The distance of the past may make the narrator feel freer, the stories clearer and more penetrating. The closeness of the present may cause inhibition and ambivalence in the storyteller.

So even when these journeyers and their navigator share a view that storytelling is central to the creative construction of life, even when the journeyers choose to risk the treacherous currents, we both know that the stories they tell will not be a factual representation of history or experience. Our search is not for a rendering of objective truth or replicable evidence, but for the reconstruction and reinterpretation of experience, which can include perspective taking, projection, distortion, and fantasy. Part of what makes it possible for people to keep pushing forward is the selection of what gets remembered and revealed, the smoothing over of rough edges, the denial of pain, the making of coherence out of chaos, the humor that masks the trauma. In reconstructing life stories there are always things left unsaid, secrets untold or repressed, skeletons kept closeted. There is in good storytelling, then, the critical element of restraint and the discipline of disclosure. Even in the most textured stories, mysteries will always remain. There is a paradox in this work. The more we hear life's resonances, the more we recognize the silences. The more we reveal the life portraits, the more we appreciate the empty spaces on the canvas.

Out of both the stories and the silences I began to hear each narrator's central preoccupation. I recognize an insistent theme, a driving current that flows through his or her life story. There may be a variety of ways in which this central preoccupation gets expressed, yet it offers coherence, purpose, and definition to the journey. Part of my challenge is to begin to identify this central preoccupation, to document the ways in which it is expressed, to try to understand its origins and meaning, to interpret its symbols and metaphors, to find ways of displaying it. This central preoccupation, once revealed and traced, is a generative dimension of human experience. It is not like a worn-out story or a broken record. Quite the opposite. It is a source of growth in work and identity.

In my conversations with Katie Cannon, for example, it became clear, almost immediately, that teaching was her raison d'être. "Teaching," she exclaimed boldly, "is the fruit of my labor." Ever since she was a young child, Katie wanted to be a teacher. She played school with her siblings, relished being the teacher's pet and surrogate, and saw teaching as precious, respectable, loving work. Now a preacher, writer, researcher, and professor, Katie still sees teaching as the central dimension in all her work. She puts it at the top of her list of professional priorities; she works harder on issues of pedagogy and curriculum than she does on anything else; she is most happy when her teaching blends theater, inspiration, provocation, and intellectual challenge; and she believes that teaching is her primary vehicle for social criticism and activism. Throughout our weeks of intense conversation, teaching became the anchor to her professional identity, the mediating theme between her childhood origins and her greatly contrasting adult experiences. Uncovering it as her life litany allowed Katie to see it revealed in its many guises throughout her development. It also allowed her to see its shaping influence in the way she told and interpreted her story.

At the center of Charles Ogletree's life and work is the drive to correct injustices, to push toward equality for all. His definition of his own personal success includes, is dependent upon, the empowerment of his peers. He will not feel successful until the guys he grew up with back in Merced, California, are given the opportunity to fulfill themselves. As a professor at the Harvard Law School, he measures his achievements by those of the friends and family he has left behind. He sees the faces of his close friends back home who are strung out on drugs, unemployed, or incarcerated. Not a day goes by that he doesn't feel pain for his old friend Eugene Allen, whom everyone regarded as "the most promising" member of his old group but who, through catastrophic bad luck and an unjust and prejudicial legal system, has been incarcerated in San Quentin for more than twenty years. All of Charles's professional efforts, legal strategizing, and friendly support have not helped in winning Gene's freedom. There is a part of Charles that will be imprisoned as long as his friend is in jail. His ten years as a public defender in Washington, D.C., where he vigorously and vigilantly defended the rights of those who could not afford to hire an expert attorney, were an extension of his fight for Eugene and his other friends back home.

At Harvard, Charles tries hard to seduce many of his corporate-leaning students to consider doing criminal defense law. He laces his lectures with ethical principles and moral dilemmas, and he teaches about justice, not merely legal structure and strategy. He feels most happy when he is moving back and forth between the academy and the real world; between thinking critically and analytically about the law and doing it; between engaging in debate with his mostly white colleagues and fighting for the rights of the indigent who are disproportionately black and brown.

Closely linked to the discovery and rehearsal of these life litanies is the importance of memory in these people's lives. All of these narrators have vivid sensory memories that allow them to recall sight, sound, touch, smell, and feel. Tony Earls's memories of his beloved New Orleans are evocative and visceral. He can smell the Cajun catfish, hear the haunting, languid jazz of the funeral parades, feel the excitement and drama of Mardi Gras, see the sights on his daily bicycle trip from school to Uncle Oscar's band practice. He can close his eyes and take the sentimental journey back home. The yearning for all the old southern sensations—the food, the music, the warm embrace of family—offers him emotional sustenance in the midst of his northern existence.

When Charles Ogletree tells about sitting for long hours beside his grandfather at the edge of the river fishing, he is able to remember Big Daddy's posture, his silence, the way he held the fishing pole, the way he waited, the three layers of clothes he wore in the ninety-degree heat, the bait he used, the kind of fish he caught, and the way he as a youngster *felt* in his grandfather's company. He can link these memories with the lessons he learned about patience, waiting, discipline, and silence. Katie Cannon's memory is spectacular in its detail: she remembers the year, make, and color of a car; the words of a love song in a movie she saw twenty years ago; the lines from the first speech she ever gave. But more impressive than the specific details is her memory for the interior life she was experiencing when something happened—what she was saying to herself as the event occurred, the sweat she was feeling pouring down her back; the rage that swelled up inside of her. Katie's story of pulling the knife on her teacher is not only a compelling piece of storytelling; it is also powerful in its display of sensory memory.

In some ways, the important role memory plays in moving people forward in life (and up and out) might, at first, appear counterintuitive. That is, many believe that to move up the ladder of success and achievement, they must forget the past, repress it, relinquish it. They think that the ghosts of the past will inhibit their smooth progress forward. They worry that if they return to old memories, they may be swallowed up by them. So they avoid recalling them and deflect recollections when they make an unwelcome appearance in their reveries. But the storytellers in this volume have just the opposite view. They see old memories as a chance to reckon with the past and integrate past and present. This integration is one of the reasons for the extraordinary resilience of each person's character. The more they can remember, the more they can draw the connections between memories and new experiences, the more centered they will be in their developing adult lives. Charles Ogletree, for example, frequently returns to the memory of making rice pudding with his grandmother in the kitchen. As he recalls the language of her instruction, the sound of the spoon beating up against the thick ingredients, the smells that filled the house while the pudding was baking, the gait of his grandmother as she limped around the kitchen after her stroke, Charles unearths the valuable lessons and values that his early life of poverty has provided him.

Cheryle Wills also feels the imprint of her grandmother's teachings, particularly her instructions on sexuality and male-female relationships. Her grandmother, a woman of decorum and dignity, with a "Mona Lisa image," had fires burning inside. She taught her granddaughter about the passion, romance, and strategy of love— how to iron the sheets and powder the bed in readiness for love-making; how to select stockings and slips whose texture would entice a man into wanting to caress you; how to make a man feel safe enough to cry in your arms. These early messages have powerful echoes in the shaping of Cheryle's mature female identity. Cheryle holds fast to her commitment to femininity even as she aggressively pursues her ascent in the male world of entrepreneurship and profit. She knows that "real joy" will continue to be elusive if the public, careerist side of her is not balanced by the intimacy of family and the nourishment of a man's love.

But it is not only bringing up positive memories that helps construct present experience; reckoning with the pain of memory is also important. When Toni Schiesler recalls the humiliation of being the only girl in her parochial boarding school who could not afford to have seven white blouses—a clean one to put underneath the blue jumper uniform—she weeps for the first time in our interviews. As she remembers her meager wardrobe and reckons with the deep humiliation of the legacy of poverty it represents, Toni understands why she needs to fill four of the five huge closets in her house with her lavish wardrobe. She now owns scores of blouses, lots of white blouses and blouses in every other color of the rainbow. So memory allows life to be integrated, allows each of these people to become whole.

Storytelling and memory allow people to return home, but home is seen very differently by each of them. It is re-created by their stories. For Charles Ogletree, tiny, provincial Merced, California, is the center of gravity for his worldly, peripatetic life. The progress of his career depends upon a deep grounding, on the collective survival of his home folks. The journey home for Katie Cannon is a brave act of "translation" and reconciliation. With lingering ambivalence, she confronts the echoes of painful childhood experiences, the terrors of her "Jim Crow rage," and the casting of herself as "prodigal daughter," so that she will be able to accept the gifts of her heritage.

Baltimore is home for Orlando Bagwell. Although he left there when he was fourteen and never returned, it is the place where he feels most deeply connected. Like Tony Earls's move from New Orleans to Memphis, Orlando's transplanting in New Hampshire never took root. Orlando always resented being torn away from big-city life, from the familiarity and vitality of his black neighborhood, from the brotherhood of friends with whom he hung out. When he arrived in New Hampshire, he hung onto his big-city affectations—sporting his black leather jacket—for as long as he dared. After a while, he began to adapt to the white rural scene, and eventually he became a "confirmed integrationist" as a means of tolerating his experience of extreme tokenism. But he always yearned for Baltimore, always fantasized about returning home. And when it came time to choose a college, he chose Boston University because it was located right in the middle of the city. "I went to Boston looking for my Baltimore," he says with lingering nostalgia.

Living in many lovely residences as a child growing up—in Brooklyn; Cambridge and Bedford, Massachusetts; and Los Angeles—Cheryle Wills remembers the way her mother made each place beautiful with her designer's touch. She spent most of her growing up years in their suburban house in Bedford, which her mother decorated in a chic modern style. But the isolation of being Bedford's model black family made Cheryle always feel like a stranger in the community and made her decide to escape to Fisk University in Nashville, Tennessee, where she hoped to find the solace and comfort of black soul mates. When Cheryle speaks of home, she is referring to Cleveland, the place she migrated to in her early twenties.

But she is not speaking of the lavish house she inhabited with her children and her second husband. Home is the House of Wills, the funeral home where she was nourished, mentored, and educated; the first place where she actually felt part of the black community, as servant and leader.

Without any home that she can remember from her early childhood, Toni Schiesler recalls a nomadic existence of poverty and dislocation. The only home she can describe was Aunt Rose's house, a place "crowded with things," where she was taken after being rescued from the streets of New Haven. It is a fleeting and incomplete picture. She does not know whether she was there for hours, days, or weeks, only that Aunt Rose gave her a bath and cleaned her up. Years later, Toni found her real home in the convent, a place of stability, order, and ritual; a place where she found "good mothers" who offered guidance, encouragement, and mentoring. She was deeply attached to the convent, to its heavy authority of rules and relationships, to its deep bonds of connection and constraint. Leaving the order after twenty years was "like a divorce" from "a whole family, not just a husband."

If one is to understand their journeys, it is important to document the storytellers' connections to, and definitions of, home. Home is not simply a place. It is defined less by a geographic map than by the emotional terrain, the depth of the attachment. Even if the attachments are ambivalent (as they remain with Katie and Kannapolis) or severed (as they are with Toni and the convent) or yearned for (as they are with Orlando and Baltimore) or idealized (as they are with Cheryle and the House of Wills), they are penetrating and unshakable. Home is the reference point. And yet, home is not a static or fixed reality. It is an evolving, dynamic memory, constantly being reinterpreted by ongoing storytelling in the present.

Storytelling, then, is central to the way these six people make sense of, and give shape to, their lives. It helps them make the "translations" between past and present, trace their losses and gains, and rehearse preoccupations that have given purpose and direction to their journeys. Storytelling requires fluidity and facility with language, a tolerance for silence as well as a comfort with words as a creative medium for expressing (and composing) feeling and thought. The narratives are enhanced by memories that capture sight, sound, smell, and touch, along with ideas and emotions. Finally, storytelling reveals life's journey through a dynamic rein-terpretation of home, a chance to reconcile roots and destinations.

Vulnerability and Trust

These storytellers do not travel alone. I am with them; we are on this journey together. Their life stories emerge out of our constantly evolving relationship. The subtext here is the narrative of a relationship that is the vehicle through which the life story is remembered and expressed. Rather than being *"interviewed"* these six people are *"collaborators"* or *"cocreators"* of their life stories. The message and meaning of the stories come from the interaction, our duet, the convergence of our experience. I am both audience and mirror, witness and provocateur, inquirer and scribe. Sometimes I am also the storyteller. To achieve the intimacy and trust that will inspire the confidences of my collaborators, I must be willing to share my own experience.

The relationship I developed with each person is strikingly different, reflecting our individual temperaments, our combined chemistry, and also the context of our encounters. By context, I refer to a variety of political, social, and family events occurring at the time, the day's tempo and schedule, the season of the year, and the settings in which we met. On the most basic level, I asked each person to choose the place where he or she felt most comfortable meeting, the time of day, and the rhythm and frequency of our conversations. With Charles Ogletree, our weekly hour-long meetings took place in his office at the Harvard Law School; our concentration was always threatened by the pressing agendas of his multifaceted work life. Tony Earls also chose to meet in his office at the School of Public Health, a much quieter, more rarified research setting where telephone calls and colleagues were not permitted to intrude upon our two-hour biweekly sessions. Katie Cannon chose to come to my office, where she would always arrive early with notes on dreams, revelations, insights, or events that had consumed her thoughts since our last meeting. Orlando Bagwell, whose offices are only a few blocks from where I live, would come to my home for his morning sessions. In the warmth of spring and summer, we sat on my deck amid the jungle of plants and flowers. In winter, we were at my kitchen table, sipping coffee and eating muffins.

Toni Schiesler's study—"a room of my own"—was the peaceful and orderly place where we sat for several hours talking together, meeting for an intense two days at a time, morning and afternoon. Her study was the place that held the most history: photographs from her convent days, old and precious books, a collection of purple treasures, prayer books and Bibles, her guitar. Here she could interrupt her talk and find her favorite poem, retrieve a letter from her files, or play her favorite chant on the portable CD player. When I met with Cheryle Wills, we would gaze out of her condominium window on the thirty-fourth floor at the Charles River winding through the Boston landscape. She would begin stretched out on the long off-white couch, surrounded by a mound of pastel pillows. As her story gained in intensity and feeling, she would shift positions, sit up tall, and look directly into my eyes. I sat across from her on the floor, with the tape recorder and my notes perched on the glass coffee table. We sipped our seltzer water from wine glasses.

In each of these safe settings, it was also important that the sessions have a consistent rhythm and ritual. I was always careful to stay within the time frame we had established, recognizing how demanding and exhausting these encounters were even when the storytellers claimed they were not tired, or when they resisted closure. Before settling down with the tape recorder, we seized the opportunity for vigorous "catching up." We chatted and laughed, and they told me about recent developments at work, shared family news, or discussed ideas, dilemmas, or frustrations that were preoccupying them. Major news events—the Gulf War, the Rodney King verdict, the Clarence Thomas–Anita Hill hearings—were often points of departure, coloring our moods and shaping the discourse.

Despite the growing currents of familiarity and friendship, the sessions were always disciplined and focused. While we often crossed public-private boundaries, we kept the purpose of our encounters in mind. Central to this work, as a matter of fact, was the discovery of connections between personal realms of experience and the larger public conversations on race, class, gender, and culture. The dialogue was not always comfortable; the territory felt unfamiliar; the rules were uncertain; the ground shifted. All of us felt exposed and vulnerable, but we also uncovered layers of insight, sources of strength and support. Part of the success of each of these relationships lay in the storytellers' ability to tolerate the risk as well as the promise: the risk of exposure and the promise of revelation; the fear of vulnerability and the appeal of openness.

The courage of these individuals is underscored by the apprehension and ambivalence expressed by others who, after serious and thoughtful consideration, chose not to tell their stories. For the first time in my two decades of doing research I experienced being turned down by people whom I tried hard (and gently) to persuade to participate. At first I was surprised and dismayed, then puzzled and intrigued. Now I understand and appreciate the many reasons that a person might decline my invitation. The excavation involved in re-creating a life story is an extraordinarily intrusive process—time consuming, absorbing, demanding. I asked participants to tell a very long, detailed, and personal story; a story they probably had never told anyone with the same kind of focus, intensity, and continuity. In comparing our interviews to her years of experience in Jungian therapy, for example, Katie Cannon claimed that our work was more "dense," "demanding," "exposing." "With you, Sara," said Katie, "there is nowhere to hide." As she said these words, she put her fists up in front of her face, jabbing the air, darting and ducking, playing Muhammad Ali with a mischievous grin on her face.

The first person I approached to participate in this project, a gifted composer, was deeply apprehensive about there being "nowhere to hide" in this work. Giving my invitation long and careful consideration, he felt tortured by the conflicts within him, caught between his eagerness to explore important and complicated life issues, to say yes to me, and his apprehension about losing privacy. He did not want public exposure for himself and his family. Nor did he want to "air the dirty laundry" of the black middle-class community that he thinks has been mercilessly maligned and mis-understood by journalists, writers, and researchers. He did not want to relinquish the anonymity that he believes is so important for his art. He purposely "hides out" and doesn't "explain" his work so as to let listeners evolve their own interpretations.

I also sensed in this man another kind of reluctance that seemed to derive from "the guilt" he experiences as a privileged and suc-cessful African-American; a guilt that when exposed, could unnerve him and destroy his forward momentum; a guilt that could separate him from his community. He worried that if he partici-pated in the project, this guilt might be stirred up and magnified. He might end up feeling bad about his privilege. It might bring back the era of the late sixties and early seventies when "you didn't dare admit you were middle class... you did everything you could to deflect that question."

This composer's decision not to participate in the research—as well as the tortured deliberations of others who ultimately declined to be involved—was disappointing but instructive. Over time, I began to think of the early stages of these encounters as part of an elaborate courtship. It required the attention, the nuance, the sen-sitivity, and the candor of a good courtship. It required time and space, room for approach and avoidance. It was a ritual dance of greeting, trusting, knowing. Surviving the courtship was the first major hurdle in cocreating a life story.

The storytellers in this volume, who chose to risk exposure and guilt, are extraordinary people. There is no way to construe them as average. There is no way one could hope to generalize, in the sta-tistical sense, from this select group. They must be seen as special in their capacities for expression, reflection, and introspection; unusual in their willingness to uncover wounds and expose their vulnerabilities. Each is intrigued and energized by the process of self-examination. Each is at a point in the middle years when he or she wants to look backward as a way of anticipating the future. All six have developed enough self-confidence to be willing to acknowledge pain and release rage; enough ego to celebrate growth and accomplishments; enough humility to recognize how much more needs to be accomplished. Seeing themselves as storytellers, they believe that others might benefit from hearing about their journeys, not as tales of heroism or stardom, but as complicated stories of loss and gain, trauma and survival, sorrow and joy, rage and creativity. As we listen, we hear both extraordinary experiences and universal human themes.

My role as these stories take shape is both participant and mirror. I am constantly thrust back upon my own life experiences. Something painful hits a raw nerve in me or a raucous family tale touches my funny bone. We laugh and weep together. I underscore and interpret their ideas, reflect back their feelings, see my image in their eyes. But the reflections mirror more than particular events. I also resonate with many of the larger cultural and developmental themes played out in their stories. I, too, know the ugly distortions of tokenism, the guilt and challenges of privilege. I, too, have resisted the traditional canons in my own work and have felt a growing strength and maturity of voice in my writing and teaching. I, too, want to use my middle years to revisit the source, to journey home and give forward to my children.

As I explore these storytellers' lives, I use my own responses not only to mirror their experiences but also to help me identify and pursue the differences between us. As inquirer, I do not mask the differences in gender, class, family background, or temperament. I emphasize the contrasts and pursue the misunderstandings. My questions are probing and risk impertinence as I delve below the surface. I can picture Katie Cannon leaning toward me with a piercing gaze, searching my face. Her eyes seem to say, "How can I make you understand—the daughter of a father who was a professor of sociology like you, with whom you shared books, language, and ideas—how it feels not to be able to write to my father who is illiterate… even though my love for my father is as deep as yours?" I try to understand what this chasm of experience and education between father and daughter means to Katie. I try to explore not just her yearning but also her reluctance to reach out to him. Her three-line letter to her father, a tiny document, feels like an astonishing breakthrough to both of us.

My relationship with each storyteller was different, but they were all marked by a particular kind of fluidity. I was made aware of this quality by one of those who ultimately chose not to participate in the project. For almost a year, I talked with this man, a renowned printmaker, about joining me in this work, and he expressed both intrigue and apprehension. The elaborate courtship included several long telephone calls, an exchange of letters and cards, and a visit with my two children to his studio/home in the country. Describing himself as "intensely private, very cautious and reticent," he worried about the invasion of his time and space, and the potential distortion of his life story. He had been "burned badly," he said, by journalists, art critics, and curators who took his words out of context and indulged in a kind of pseudopsychological snooping into his life. He needed time, "lots of time," to consider my invitation, to see whether I was trustworthy, to test our chemistry and comfort with one another.

On a Sunday afternoon in the late summer, my children and I drove several hours to visit this man and his family in their home, a massive building that houses his huge studio and their living space; the boundaries between rooms are either wide open or easily permeable, one space flowing into the other. My daughter, Tolani, who was ten at the time, had danced and pranced her way from one room to the other and pronounced it to be a house filled with "liquid space." The printmaker loved her characterization of this mostly doorless place that he had designed himself.

Months later, when I returned from my first actual session with this artist, I was struck by how Tolani's view of "liquid space" not only described the physical environment; it also seemed to characterize the quality of our encounter, the dynamics of the relationship. From the beginning, it had felt difficult for me to mark the boundaries with this man, to define the line between inquiry and friendship, to make the distinction between social and work encounters. It all felt fluid and continuous. With the lack of clear boundaries I felt the promise of depth and intimacy, and the potential for vulnerability and overexposure... for both of us. Tolani's expression seemed perfect. This liquidity eased the flow of conversation, loosening rusty spots, allowing a free and open exchange. But the situation also felt dangerous, volatile. The free-flowing setting and our apparently intimate, intense, intellectual, and familial relationship seemed both promising and treacherous.

The fluidity also characterized this artist's shifting engagement in, and response to, our dialogue. As we sat down at the round work table in his study, he seemed weary, but relaxed. He looked as if he felt confident about how to manage himself in these situations, as though he had had lots of practice and experience. When I gently warned him about the extraordinary demands of this kind of work ("I have found that people are exhausted, worn out by this process... It kind of sneaks up on you... so I don't want to overtax you," I said), he looked unconcerned, almost cocky. "Oh, I've been doing a lot of this lately, lots of interviews... so I'm used to it." Despite my admonitions, he expected that it would feel like the many professional encounters he had experienced recently, like the interviews with art critics, curators, and collectors of his work. I made one more explicit try at making the distinction between my brand of human archeology that tries to excavate beneath the surface and the investigations by critics who seek to capture the aesthetic meaning of his work, or journalists who decide he is one of the best printmakers working today and treat him like a sudden celebrity. "I am not interested in your celebrity or in focusing explicitly on your art... except as these phenomena and experiences reflect or shape your life," I explained.

As the storyteller anticipated, the first part of our long session felt easy, enjoyable, much like the adulation, appreciation, and distant respect of the celebrity encounters he had begun to master. Many of the stories seemed practiced, not canned, but certainly rehearsed. "This feels comfortable, fine," he commented. Later on, when he had begun to talk about his parents and his early childhood, he offered an observation and a distinction. "This is really interesting, captivating, but it is *not* like therapy... I've been in therapy and this is different. You're asking me for my story, but I'm not having to deal with painful or difficult interior stuff like in therapy." This distinction came on the heels of his expressing a concern about "not wanting to edit himself... wanting to be forthright and honest." He did not want the fluency and clarity of his narrative to be compromised by editing, but he admitted to some hidden, painful realms.

I heard the conflict stirring within him—the wish to experience the insights and discoveries of this demanding process and the urge to protect himself and his family from an invasion of their privacy. He seemed to be consciously choosing the former—to be open, revelatory, trusting—but there was an evident undertow revealed in his long pauses, furrowed brow, and husky, sometimes inaudible voice. This was not as easy as he had thought. Another hour passed and the artist was shaking his head and declaring, as if there were no contradiction with his earlier statement, "This *is* like therapy." He was talking about things he "hadn't thought about for years." He was discovering connections between his early childhood obsessions and his adult preoccupations. This felt exhilarating and hazardous to both of us, and as I sat with him, I could hear the shifts in his perception of the deepening process. I experienced anew the liquid space we were swimming in, our changing relationship. He was interviewee, raconteur, dramatist, self-critic. He was adult and child, father and son. I was interviewer, fan, connoisseur, therapist.

The printmaker's decision not to continue the work on this project—after we had invested so much time and emotion—was excruciating for both of us. It left him feeling relieved, sad, guilty, apologetic (as he put it, "cowardly and lacking in courage... knowing I am probably passing up a major opportunity... a critical life experience"), and it left me feeling wounded and deeply disappointed. For the first time, I fully recognized my rawness and my vulnerability in this relationship. The dynamics of this work, after all, require that we both go deep, both excavate the layers of human experience and relive life journeys. It is a collaborative, negotiated experience, requiring mutual trust. When there is a rupture in the relationship, I also feel the loss; I experience abandonment.

The printmaker's tortured exit, and his courage in articulating the reasons, helped me understand that those who choose to "go the distance" in this work combine a developmental readiness, a temperamental openness, and an ability to tolerate this "liquid space." That is, they are the kind of people who relish and appreciate the value of introspection. They view the middle years as a generative time, a time to acknowledge loss and pain, to allow for growth, and they are confident enough to risk an intimate encounter involving shifting roles and outcomes.

Even though our encounters were sometimes marked by resistance, frustration, and inhibition, the six storytellers in this volume all seemed comfortable with our fluid, ever-changing relationships. Together we moved from the intense, revelatory probings that characterize therapy, to the visceral detail and candor that spark good storytelling, to the analytic mode of intellectual discourse. It was in these shifts of role and perspective; in the weaving together of recollection, interpretation, and catharsis; in the weeping and the laughter that the stories gained authenticity. The printmaker, though he lived in the liquid space, was uncomfortable about the unclear boundaries between narrative and therapy, and apprehensive about the uncertain direction of our sessions.

With each of the storytellers, our relationship evolved differently. There are, in fact, two intertwined stories: one that chronicles the life journey, the other that traces our relationship. This is more evident with some than with others. For example, with Katie Cannon, our relationship is always prominent. We laugh, hug, exclaim, cry together. The exchanges are charged, exuberant, sisterly. All this reflects Katie's passionate temperament, the extremes of her joy and her pain. But it also reflects our chemistry with one another and the fact that Katie's revelations grow out of, in fact require, that powerful chemistry. Her openness and vulnerability derive from our mutual identification and reciprocity, the way we see ourselves mirrored in each other's eyes. Even in our first encounter I feel comfortable making mischief, being playful. We talk about the details, the rhythms, the texture of our lives—a wide-open womanly encounter. Part of the story, then, is the tale of our encounters—the growth of the sisterhood, the deepening trust. Her story—with all its drama and passion—is born out of this relationship.

Even when a relationship is not as boldly expressed as with Katie, it remains central to the storytelling of all the collaborators.

In Tony Earls's story, for example, the greetings and departures that frame each of our sessions are not remarkable. But my responses to his experiences and insights, my identification with his perspectives, my challenges to his ambivalence, my sorrow at his pain, my laughter at his humor—all help the story along. These responses are embedded in our exchanges, but the momentum and structure of his narrative is shaped more by chronology than by our growing relationship. As Tony grows more comfortable with the process and more trusting of me, however, the stories become more detailed and subtle. In all of these six narratives, we witness the way that the human encounter shapes the telling of life stories. In each the relationship is the medium through which the story gets told. Each relationship expresses a particular chemistry; each is growing, changing, improvisational.

Beyond the individual contrasts between these relationships there is, I believe, a contrast in expressiveness between the women and the men in this volume. My encounters with Toni and Cheryle, like those with Katie, were sisterly, intimate, charged. There was great range and variety in their expression of emotion, and they expressed their feelings vividly and openly. The women seemed more practiced at this kind of dialogue—more comfortable with intimacy, more eager for the intensity of feeling than were the men. There was also a difference in the life terrain the women chose to travel. Their journeys were most often interior, focused on family and intimate relationships, on the connections between sexuality and power, work and love, achievement and loneliness. And they seemed to travel to these deep and dark places urgently, immediately.

In our first session, for example, Toni Schiesler began her story with the most awful fact of her life. "I was the product of a rape." More than a year later, she ended her tale with the painful revelation voiced by her mother just before she died: "I've blamed you for everything." Throughout her odyssey, Toni courageously revisited her feelings of terror as the daughter of a volatile mother, her rage at the men who abused her mother, her desperate need for nourishment and approval from the nuns in the convent. In reclaiming the roots of her pain, in her relentless search for identity,

Toni discovered her own resilience and the connections between her strength and her vulnerability. Cheryle Wills showed the same daring in her determination to face the loneliness and sadness that have consumed her since her brother's tragic death twenty years ago. In telling this story, she broke the family silence, confronted the mystery and terror, and traced the reverberations in her continued "search for safe harbor." In each of these womanly encounters, there was a raw, penetrating force.

Like the women in this book, the men were bold in revisiting painful experiences and expressing their feelings. Tony Earls's encounters with Blair T. Hunt, for example, were a harsh challenge to his self-esteem, an assault on his image of himself as a "smart kid," a drama of multiple abuses. However, there is a difference in the men's use of language. Orlando Bagwell tells a concise, spare tale about being transplanted from Baltimore and dropped into the alien, white New Hampshire scene. He conveys with restraint the rage he felt toward his parents; toward the sea of white faces staring at him as he boarded the school bus the first day; toward the way his sister's beauty went unappreciated by the white boys who secretly wanted her "like she was some kind of whore." These cruel events are recounted starkly, without repetition or embellishment. When Tony recalls Blair T. Hunt's devastating lie about the scores he received on his achievement test, he ends the tale, "That was the most damaging experience of my life." Charles Ogletree conveys the haunting anguish of his friend's twenty-year incarceration in one sentence: "A day does not go by when I don't think of Gene."

Not only does there seem to be more restraint in the men's language, their discourse also tends to remain more focused on the public sphere rather than on the realm of family intimacy. Charles Ogletree, for example, uses Gene's story as motivation for his deep commitment to fighting inequalities and injustice in society. Gene's incarceration stands as a powerful daily yardstick against which Charles measures the vigilance and legitimacy of his commitments. Orlando Bagwell's most powerful stories of racial identity and emerging manhood are told against the backdrop of the Black

Power movement. The political-historical landscape of the early 1970s in Boston is vividly drawn, and Orlando envisions his life in reference to it. This focus of the male storytellers contrasts with the women who begin inside their families (going as far back as Katie's mother's denial of her existence by refusing to scream out during her birth) and whose engagement with the public realm remains connected with these potent early experiences.

While in many ways, these six storytellers defy any typical male-female stereotypes, both exploring an interior landscape of feeling and thought, both journeying across private and public terrain, their voices do differ. The women begin with the highly charged intimacy of ancient family relationships and speak passionately about the values and behaviors that give shape to their adult commitments. The men, on the other hand, speak about profound experiences with more modulation. Charles's precise articulation of his rationale in fighting injustice or Tony's spare description of hearing about the death of Martin Luther King when he emerged from the soundproof chambers of the science laboratory feels measured and economical when contrasted with the exuberant talk of the women.

In underscoring the contrasts and convergences between the genders, it is important to note that all of the several people who decided not to participate in this project were men. This makes me suspect that the three men who agreed to take this journey were unusual in their readiness to participate and in their introspective and expressive capacities. Perhaps they are atypical men, exceptional in their openness and reflective inclinations, in their willingness to trust their intimate stories to me.

However, I also think that storytelling may serve to blur the gender lines. After all, storytelling reaches beneath the public persona, the protective attitude. It asks the same of men and women. Storytelling removes the masks and misinterpretations of stereotype and generalizations.

The relationship between storyteller and listener-inquirer is itself a journey. In turn, it shapes the life story. Each relationship is individual, idiosyncratic, defined by a particular chemistry. Each relationship evolves and changes. As I travel the distance with each person, our voices change timbre and decibels, our roles shift, our interactions gain in depth and intensity. These relationships were colored by contrasts in gender, contrasts in style and focus. But the storytelling relationship creates an opportunity for blurring gender lines, for supporting the journey—of both men and women—from abstraction to authenticity.

Rage and Love: On Race

In one of our early sessions, Katie Cannon worried that the truth of her "real life" might be too "raw" for me to tolerate. She does not want to assault me with her rage, with traumas that are "too painful to name." Katie reminds me of the distinction Maya Angelou makes between fiction, which is more palatable and bearable in its expression of pain, and nonfiction, which speaks about real lives and is sometimes "too hard to hear." I assure her that I am strong enough to hear the truth. I recognize and accept the rage in her. I feel it mirrored in me. But I am also sure that it will not overcome either of us. Katie's laughter and raucous humor defuse the intensity; her colorful, explosive language offers catharsis. Through storytelling she identifies the sources of her rage, making it subject to analysis, resistance, and critique, turning the rage outward. A lifetime of awareness, exacting observation, reflecting, as well as therapy has made Katie an expert at identifying trauma, naming the pain, and expressing the anger.

On several occasions she refers to "my Jim Crow rage," a diffuse, chronic, deep anger. This rage of many parts reflects myriad abuses and traumas: of growing up in a county where the KKK still rides; where blacks couldn't go to the library, the movies, or the swimming pool; where grueling work in the mills was the only livelihood; where she had to "clean up the dog shit" for the rich family whom Aunt Pearl worked for and held together. The "curse of blackness" was just below the surface of every encounter with white folks in Kannapolis.

Katie's tale of a five-year-old Donnary Butler captures the full treachery and tragedy of racism. "Some white boys called him into the lake... He couldn't swim. They knew it and they let him drown... They thought it was fun. Nobody did a thing because black people knew that nothing would be done."

634   I've Known Rivers

Katie uses Donnary's story in her teaching and mentoring of black students. It conveys the awareness, preparedness, skepticism, and "healthy paranoia" that blacks need to develop in order to survive. "Don't ever let anyone call you into the lake in water deeper than you can swim," she admonishes. "If you do, you'll be like Donnary and they'll just laugh at you as you fight for your life." She ends with an even more painful truth. Even young black children can't afford "the privilege of naivete." "Even at five, black children have to know good from evil... Even at five, Donnary should have known better."

It was not only the white abuses and insults that fired Katie's "Jim Crow rage." It was also the prejudice within the black community, the self-hatred that reflected an identification with the oppressor, a kind of ugly mimicry. It was, after all, also the bigotry of blacks—light-skinned blacks—that made Katie feel ugly ("black, ugly, puny with big bulging eyes and a big head"), that made her believe that her laboratory partner in college chemistry was smarter just because she was lighter. It was black self-hatred that denied Katie the starring role of the angel in the second-grade Christmas pageant, made her lose the part to a less talented, light-skinned girl "who had long thick hair, gray eyes, and a soft voice." Even before she spent weeks diligently rehearsing every line in the play, Katie knew the part belonged to Jackie Young. To make her "blackness less of a handicap" Katie devoted herself to her school work and became an excellent student, admired and respected by her teachers and peers. In Kannapolis, she couldn't be beautiful, but she could be brainy.

Even though the self-hatred fractured the black community's sense of wholeness and beauty and caused Katie to feel the double edge of the "black curse," she also discovered that the collective rage of blacks could draw the community together. Katie's ninth-grade classmates laughed when John F. Kennedy was murdered; when even his whiteness and wealth, even the best emergency medical treatment in Dallas couldn't save him from the deadly bullet. There was cynicism in their laughter, and a burning adolescent anger at the injustices that were already distorting and limiting their young lives.

"We knew we were not first-class citizens... Our lives were worth nothing to these white people. We were already working on critiquing society. We knew the country was evil and violent."

Five years later, the death of Martin Luther King Jr. shook the tiny campus of Barber-Scotia. Stunned and grieving, the five hundred students wept and wailed. Their pain turned into a fierce fury that their professors had to defuse so that they wouldn't do something "suicidal" like march on the town of Concord, North Carolina. But the ancient rage—echoing generations of black oppression and expressed in weeping, testifying, shouting, moaning, and music—got channeled into new resolve, new insights, new commitments. "The assassination of King gave us *voice.*"

There are two important lessons in Katie's story of "collective rage." The first speaks to a kind of perspective taking, a stance, an awareness that every black person must learn for survival—a "jungle posture." It is not a hostile position. It is a self-protective watchfulness from which creativity can grow. The eyes, trained to be discerning, can recognize both danger and beauty in the human scene. For Katie, this jungle posture is part of "the ancestral wisdom," passed on from one generation to the next. This "epistemological privilege of the oppressed" is a powerful piece of our legacy. In such a posture "You are in touch with the ancestors... You tap that wisdom, mine it, pass it on," give it forward.

The second lesson involves "naming the pain." Even when blacks receive the ancestral wisdom and learn the jungle posture, they will still face the wounds of racism. There will be murders. Our heroes will fall. In response to these traumatic events, large and small, we must identify the pain, speak about it, and decide how, when, and if we want to act on it. We must not repress it, dismiss it, or turn it inside. "Naming the pain" is part of channeling the rage "out" and into productive energy. It allows for expression and catharsis, for the beginnings of critical analysis and action.

With middle age Katie can see changes in her jungle stance. It is less shaped by the raw rage of her youth. Now as she "takes the time to feel," her watchfulness incorporates patience and even a tender understanding. She recalls her "ultrablack period" in college and graduate school when she wanted the "immediate eradication of racism." Now she realizes that her young fury threatened to consume her ("it was death dealing") and that she needed to find a more creative way to confront the rage, that she needed a shift of perspective so that she would not always feel disappointed and hurt. Nikki Giovanni's poem, "Like a Ripple on a Pond," reflects Katie's new posture and vision—one that doesn't deny the rage, but one that sees love as part of the ancestral wisdom, and as essential for self-preservation and creativity. Like the small ripples that spread from a pebble hitting the water, Katie's hopes are focused on changing the values of one student in each class she teaches. "If *one* person will make a lifetime commitment to be a doer of justice, that's all I ask for."

Toni Schiesler has no memory of the day when Martin Luther King Jr. was murdered. There were no reverberations of the tragic event inside the walls of the all-black convent. She does, however, vividly recall traveling to Washington, D.C., to see the funeral procession of John F. Kennedy (a tribute to the first Roman Catholic president) and weeping at the sight of "tiny John-John" placing a rose on his father's coffin. For Katie Cannon, Kennedy's death was "comic," a cynical turn of fate, a chance to show that blacks and whites are equal in death. For Toni, the president's murder was a "great tragedy" to which she had a deeply personal response.

Besides having no memory of King's death, Toni was shielded from much that happened on the social and political landscape during the twenty years of her cloistered life. She managed to escape much of the racism, rhetoric, and rage that engulfed the lives of blacks in the "real world." Even today, there is evidence of this missing chapter in her responses to racism and in her African-American identity. She sometimes sounds naive and awkward in her emerging recognition of the virulent and subtle forms of racism that she encounters—as if she is learning how to read a complicated cultural text, as if she has no idea of where the minefields are located. At a meeting with her fellow administrators at Cabrini College, Toni catches her image in the large mirror behind the table and sees her blackness for the first time. She suddenly recognizes her tokenism, her loneliness in this all-white world. As she works toward her ordination in the Episcopal priesthood, she confronts the bishop who keeps putting obstacles in her path. In a letter that courageously challenges his decisions, Toni purposely omits the word "black" from her self-description because she does not want to offend him.

Now in her mid-fifties, Toni is trying to develop a voice that will allow her to use her full creative powers. On the road to becoming the loving "saint" of her fantasies, she realizes that she must do the worldly work as well. She is beginning to let go of deeply socialized inhibitions so she can "name the pain," express the rage, and challenge institutional injustices.

Even though the cloistered life shielded Toni from some of the racial warfare in the real world, it did not protect her from the color castes within the convent. Within the Oblate community, the hierarchies of color were rigorously drawn and rarely challenged. Light-skinned nuns (many with Creole origins in New Orleans) dominated the elite positions, and dark-skinned sisters had to be extraordinarily talented to counteract their assumed low status. Even though their hair was always cropped and their heads covered, everyone knew who was blessed with "good hair" and who was cursed with thick "nappy hair." Toni found the locks of Sister Boniface's silky hair in her prayer book, the ultimate assurance of her beautiful mentor's loveliness. Now in her middle years, Toni shows off her white crown of hair. She is learning to appreciate her own beauty and express her rage. She is on her way to identifying the gifts she has inherited from her impoverished past. Learning to love her mother—"who blamed me for everything"—is part of learning to love her self, her black woman self.

In her "black arrogance," Cheryle Wills is self-protective and watchful. From her forebears Cheryle inherited a stance and style that challenges white entitlement, that sees blackness as a source of "privilege." In the corporate and philanthropic worlds she inhabits, Cheryle recognizes the racism in her token status on boards of directors, in the ways she is often excluded from critical backstage scheming, in the shock of her white male colleagues who can't believe that she has learned to play their game with subtle finesse. Even though bigotry is often more veiled in these elite circles, and even though Cheryle tends to be awarded the mantle of "honorary white person," she is conscious of subtle racist assaults. Over time they can erode her spirit. Using her "sixth sense" Cheryle sees more than she wants to see. She says flatly, "Any black person who claims that there is no racism hasn't walked outside their house."

As a young child, Cheryle watched her father withstand the abuse of a southern redneck cop ("who didn't even have half the intelligence or education that my father did"). She felt the injury and she noticed that her father's dignity would not allow him to reveal the hurt or permit the emasculation. Because of that occurrence and many others, Cheryle has been sensitized to the special "vulnerability of our black brothers," who are victimized by a society whose white primal fears will not allow black men their manhood. She thinks of her uncles—then in their sixties and seventies—whom her grandmother on her deathbed asked Cheryle to "look after"; of her brother Eddie whose death still remains a mystery; of her sons whose privilege has not protected them from the blanket abuse of black males. Cheryle's rage is both intimate and public. Throughout our conversations she returns to the haunting image of the "shackles" that enslave us. She looks at the shackles on the wrists and ankles of the black men in Los Angeles and claims that "none of us will be free of them" as long as one of us is unjustly victimized.

Cheryle's many-sided activism is the channel for her rage. Her love for her sons—for future generations of black children—fuels her volunteer and philanthropic work. As she "comes into her own at fifty," she plans to become increasingly involved in building a politically strong, economically viable black community that will buffer our children from the traumas of racism. She works to get more of us around the board tables so that the values and missions of institutions might become more inclusive. She labors tirelessly on behalf of black political candidates at the local, state, and national levels. She is a mentor to young black women who want to become entrepreneurs and executives, and gives inspirational and challenging speeches to high school students about building self-confidence, ambition, discipline, and responsibility to the community. Her radio and television stations give black communities more access to the airwaves, more opportunities for communication with one another, and more practice in expressing our views.

Tony Earls also felt the sting and horror of Rodney King's beating and the Los Angeles "revolt" that followed in its wake. His first response was not one of a scientist offering his analytic scrutiny, but the response of a black man diminished by "a profound feeling of vulnerability and hurt." He took it personally. "It made me wonder about my survivorship as an American... I realized once again that I'm not an American. I'm a black man." The day after the King verdict, rage—usually hidden well below his calm and gentle exterior—"exploded through his skull." Tony's equanimity was shattered ("I lost my bearings") and the world, which he usually sees in subtle shades, was suddenly drawn in black and white. For the first time, Tony, the resolute pacifist, was pushed to consider the "honor" and "necessity" of violence in the face of the "hopeless" and "obscene" social conditions in which people are forced to live. "I really want to know who my enemies are." This epidemiologist, who studies criminality and violence, says reluctantly, "Retaliation may be our last possible way to express our humanity."

Although Tony hates to feel this rage, he admits, "It is *in* me all along." The profundity of his rage is not so much a response to singular, dramatic events of racial violence, like the Rodney King beating, as it is a reaction to the accumulation of chronic and subtle "microaggressions" that he encounters every day. A white male colleague is threatened by Tony's success and visibility and refers to his journal article as "flaky." Harvard administrators offer bureaucratic remedies rather than consider the moral dimensions of institutional racism. A white woman student startles as she gets on the elevator and sees Tony's black figure in front of her. This "day-to-day negative stuff" feels like a "chronic scratching away at the surface" of Tony's soul. From Chester Pierce, one of Tony's mentors during his psychiatric residency, he learned to protect himself. "You mustn't let yourself get burned out," Pierce said, taking off the dark glasses that acted as a symbolic shield from some of the racist insinuations. These are words Tony will never forget as he tries to develop his own gentle version of jungle posture.

Tony channels his rage into work, questioning traditional structures and habits of scholarship. Through both science and activism, clinical work and policy analysis, he searches for the optimal environments for child growth and explores the cultural, temperamental, and economic roots of violence. His efforts to merge research and action began long ago when he moved from the neurophysiology laboratory at the University of Wisconsin to frontline emergency medicine in Harlem. Pure science appealed to his intellectual curiosity and discipline, but clinical work responded to an imperative raging within him. "After Martin's assassination I wanted to be in the streets, not in the lab." Tony believes in the "transformative powers" of science and "the emotional and intellectual connections" that enable him to transform his rage into informed action.

When Tony Earls was saving the lives of drug babies at Metropolitan Hospital, Charles Ogletree was embracing the Black Power struggle at Stanford University. In dashikis, black leather jackets, or army combat gear, Charles filled his days and nights with "movement" work. He tutored black children from the poorest schools in East Palo Alto. He pressed the university to hire more African-American faculty, worked to recruit more black students, and urged a more inclusive academic curriculum. He lended support for Angela Davis's trial and went to visit his buddy Eugene in San Quentin. He felt supported by a group of spirited "brothers and sisters," inspired by their "collective rage" and "organic analysis." Charles's political work on campus kept him connected to his roots in Merced, where Charles saw the "faces of his homeboys."

When Charles first arrived at Harvard Law School, he hated the coldness, the sterility, and the abstractions of the academic experience. Harvard seemed so remote from the volatile school "busing" controversy that was dividing Boston and victimizing innocent children. Disheartened and frustrated, he often felt tempted to leave. But even at Harvard, Charles found love, support, and "grounding" among black brothers. The Black Plague—a black law school students' "rough touch" football team—offered much more than a workout. "There was a strong sense of kinship... It was a source of identity... an inner circle of strength... important male bonding."

Alone, each of the brothers felt isolated and vulnerable; together they felt invincible.

Even now—having returned to Harvard as a professor hoping to reinterpret the academic mission—Charles knows the dangers of becoming too comfortable or too confident. He feels a restlessness, a constant questioning of purpose. He maintains his ties with legal activists, offers pro bono counsel on controversial and difficult legal cases, speaks at public forums about the social, ethical, and political dimensions of the law, and urges students to use the legal system to fight injustice. Charles's rage burns like a steady flame behind his cool demeanor. The rage burns for Gene in San Quentin, for the casualties, pain, and poverty of his home folks in Merced, for all the people who are dealt with unfairly in a legal system that claims to be just. The rage inspires creative action in all his roles: legal academic, public defender, and jazz lover.

Orlando Bagwell also hated leaving his homeboys behind when his family followed his father's work from Baltimore to New Hampshire. The "bonds of brotherhood" had been a source of comfort, protection, and camaraderie—a stark contrast to the violent male warfare and vulnerability on the playground at the School of the Blessed Sacrament; so different from his feelings of isolation and humiliation when his Catholic school teachers would begin with the assumption that he was incapable of learning just because he was black. In New Hampshire, he says, "I was always watching my back."

This combat position came in handy ten years later when he was attacked by a gang of men and boys in South Boston during the busing crisis. Wiped out at the end of a long day, he let down his guard for a minute. He barely escaped with his life. He has never completely escaped the feeling of vulnerability and rage inflicted by this senseless act of violence. "The most disturbing part is knowing people will kill you for no reason."

Like Katie Cannon, whose writings and teaching question the canons of white male theology, Orlando challenges traditional views and interpretations of history. In his films he reconstructs our historical chronicle, searching for a more authentic representation. He examines the roots of our "collective rage." Like Katie,

he believes that the authenticity of his work will come out of reckoning with his own history, his own fears and rage. "As a storyteller,
you are always asking yourself 'What would I have done? How
would *I* feel about this?'" Through this lens of personal analysis,
he creates a public document. Naming his own pain allows him to
chronicle cultural anguish.

For the sake of his children—for all of our children—Orlando
hopes that the truths he tells will help destroy the black and white
caricatures that support racism. Learning from his children, who are
impatient with his "black-white thing," he portrays a complex and
dynamic view of the social and political landscape in his films—
one that will not mask our pain or romanticize our achievements,
but one that will challenge us to tell the truth.

~

All of these storytellers will not be defeated by the abuses of racism
that echo through their ancestry, their family histories, and their
daily lives. Though they bear the scars of racist assaults and can
vividly recall moments of humiliation and terror, they refuse to be
bowed; they refuse to be passive. They have no time for lament.
Instead they have developed a protective "combat stance," a way
of guarding against the erosion of their self-confidence and the
wounding of their spirit. Each one has also discovered ways of
responding creatively to injustice, to the dual realities of African
and American, of roots and destinations, of blackness and whiteness, of poverty and privilege, of loss and liberation.

For the six people in this book, the world is full of constant contradictions. Each is adept at making the difficult "translations."
Storytelling and memory help in shuttling back and forth, and each
has a central preoccupation that gives his or her journey a consistent purpose. But the contradictions *never* disappear, nor do these
storytellers try to obscure or mask them. They work to discover
and incorporate contradictions, to live with them and use them as
a source of creative power.

Charles Ogletree, for example, has learned to embrace the discomfort of living on the periphery of Harvard while refusing to

become part of it. He has learned to embrace the contradictions between his passionate advocacy and the constraints of legal scholarship. He has learned to incorporate the contradiction between the peripatetic life of public service and his need to return to the slow provincialism of his hometown. His daughter Rashida's poem about him captures the polarity of his character—the turbulence and the calm, the chaos and the order.

Katie Cannon not only lives the contradictions; she purposefully emphasizes them in her life and her teaching. As she "tries to begin to tell the truth" about her adult life to the folks back home in North Carolina, she strives to make peace with the contrary pieces of her life. She knows, however, that the peace will be precarious and that she will always be vulnerable to shifting allegiances. Teaching is one of the ways in which Katie has coped with these inevitable contradictions. Her classes are intentionally provocative. She stirs up rage among her students; she challenges their assumptions; she threatens the values that have given shape to their lives; she insists that they take risks and experience the disharmony and vulnerability that she lives with every day. By exaggerating the dichotomies, by critiquing the prevailing theological canons, the students can begin to feel identified with the "twoness" of Cannon's existence and even recognize its creative and generative potential. "I name the dualisms... I help to make the dichotomies real."

Forty years ago, in his magnificent book, *Souls of Black Folks*, W. E. B. Du Bois described the gifts and burdens of "second sight" that our dualisms allow us.

> The Negro is a sort of seventh son, born with a veil, and gifted with second-sight in this American world,—a world which yields him no true self-consciousness, but only lets him see himself through the revelation of the other world. It is a peculiar sensation, this double-consciousness, this sense of always looking at one's self through the eyes of others, of measuring one's soul by the tape of a world that looks on in amused contempt and pity. One ever feels his two-ness,—an American, a Negro; two souls, two

thoughts, two unreconciled strivings; two warring ideals in one dark body, whose dogged strength alone keeps it from being torn asunder.

The history of the American Negro is the history of this strife,—this longing to attain self-conscious manhood, to merge his double self into a better and truer self. In this merging he wishes neither of the older selves to be lost. He would not Africanize America, for America has too much to teach the world and Africa. He would not bleach his Negro soul in a flood of white Americanism, for he knows that Negro blood has a message for the world. He simply wishes to make it possible for a man to be both a Negro and an American, without being cursed and spit upon by his fellows, without having the doors of Opportunity closed roughly in his face.

The six storytellers in this book have made courageous and imperfect attempts to create a convergence, to express their "truer selves" in their work and in their lives. They have recognized and embraced the contradictions. Each has learned the power of double consciousness—the special insights that derive from it, the generative discomfort and restlessness it causes, the interdisciplinary explorations it demands, the improvisation and resourcefulness it engenders, and the creativity that grows out of loss. Four decades after *Souls of Black Folks* they refuse to be the victims of white folks' "amused contempt and pity." They have reversed the lens and adjusted its focus. They know that their lives and accomplishments depend upon resisting the measurement of their "souls by others' tapes" and upon their ability to transcend "warring ideals" by composing a new and daring journey. Only then will the Brown River smile.

Index

FOR THE BEST IN PAPERBACKS, LOOK FOR THE

In every corner of the world, on every subject under the sun, Penguin represents quality and variety—the very best in publishing today.

For complete information about books available from Penguin—including Puffins, Penguin Classics, and Arkana—and how to order them, write to us at the appropriate address below. Please note that for copyright reasons the selection of books varies from country to country.

In the United Kingdom: Please write to *Dept. JC, Penguin Books Ltd, FREEPOST, West Drayton, Middlesex UB7 0BR.*

If you have any difficulty in obtaining a title, please send your order with the correct money, plus ten percent for postage and packaging, to *P.O. Box No. 11, West Drayton, Middlesex UB7 0BR*

In the United States: Please write to *Consumer Sales, Penguin USA, P.O. Box 999, Dept. 17109, Bergenfield, New Jersey 07621-0120.* VISA and MasterCard holders call 1-800-253-6476 to order all Penguin titles

In Canada: Please write to *Penguin Books Canada Ltd, 10 Alcorn Avenue, Suite 300, Toronto, Ontario M4V 3B2*

In Australia: Please write to *Penguin Books Australia Ltd, P.O. Box 257, Ringwood, Victoria 3134*

In New Zealand: Please write to *Penguin Books (NZ) Ltd, Private Bag 102902, North Shore Mail Centre, Auckland 10*

In India: Please write to *Penguin Books India Pvt Ltd, 706 Eros Apartments, 56 Nehru Place, New Delhi 110 019*

In the Netherlands: Please write to *Penguin Books Netherlands bv, Postbus 3507, NL-1001 AH Amsterdam*

In Germany: Please write to *Penguin Books Deutschland GmbH, Metzlerstrasse 26, 60594 Frankfurt am Main*

In Spain: Please write to *Penguin Books S. A., Bravo Murillo 19, 1° B, 28015 Madrid*

In Italy: Please write to *Penguin Italia s.r.l., Via Felice Casati 20, I-20124 Milano*

In France: Please write to *Penguin France S. A., 17 rue Lejeune, F–31000 Toulouse*

In Japan: Please write to *Penguin Books Japan, Ishikiribashi Building, 2–5–4, Suido, Bunkyo-ku, Tokyo 112*

In Greece: Please write to *Penguin Hellas Ltd, Dimocritou 3, GR–106 71 Athens*

In South Africa: Please write to *Longman Penguin Southern Africa (Pty) Ltd, Private Bag X08, Bertsham 2013*